Robert L. Vann of the PITTSBURGH COURIER

Underwood & Underwood, Washington, D.C.

ROBERT L. VANN
of
Pittsburgh Courier
AMERICA'S BEST WEEKLY

Politics and Black Journalism

ANDREW BUNI

• University of Pittsburgh Press •

Copyright © 1974, University of Pittsburgh Press
All rights reserved
Media Directions Inc., London
Manufactured in the United States of America

Library of Congress Cataloging in Publication Data

Buni, Andrew.
    Robert L. Vann of the Pittsburgh Courier.

    Includes bibliographical references.
    1. Vann, Robert L., 1887-1940. I. Title.
PN4874.V35B8   070.5′092′4 [B]   73-7700
ISBN 0-8229-3274-1

For Kelly

Contents

Illustrations • ix
Preface • xi

1. North Carolina and Virginia • 3
2. North Toward Home • 21
3. Birth of the *Courier* • 42
4. The *Courier* as a Social Force • 55
5. Politics and Patriotism: 1917–1919 • 87
6. Vann as Entrepreneur: The 1920s • 113
7. The Primacy of the *Courier* • 133
8. Time to Turn Lincoln's Picture to the Wall • 174
9. Washington: Confidence and Disillusionment • 203
10. The *Courier* Hits the Jackpot • 222
11. Schism and Decline: 1936–1938 • 264
12. Twilight: 1938–1940 • 299
    Epilogue • 325

Notes • 328
Bibliographic Note on Unpublished Sources • 399
Index • 401

Illustrations

Robert L. Vann • frontispiece
The Grady Askew house • 5
Vann at law school • 39
Vann as a young attorney • 46
Vann and Walter White • 58
"Bar the Door" • 64
"Making Hay While the Sun Shines" • 101
Vann at the *Courier* • 136
The *Pittsburgh Courier* Publishing Company • 171
Testimonial at the Pythian Temple • 201
Vann in Hollywood • 220
Vann at Schenley Park • 250
"Oakmont" • 263
Political Flyer, 1938 • 281
Vann leaving the White House • 284
Vann, Hamilton Fish, and Percival L. Prattis • 305

Preface

WHEN ROBERT VANN died in October 1940, his death merited only passing notice in national publications, if indeed it was noted at all. For white America, Robert Lee Vann had never really existed. The man who built the *Pittsburgh Courier* into the nation's leading black weekly, with a circulation of a quarter million and an influence that touched every black community in the country, was not even mentioned in a 1937 work partly devoted to the press in Pittsburgh, published when Vann and the *Courier* were at the height of their power. Nor did the *Dictionary of American Biography* supplement of 1940 include Robert Vann. Even his own city of Pittsburgh, where he lived for thirty-seven years and became a force in the legal, political, and journalistic spheres, gave him the most perfunctory recognition, and it is rare to find Vann's name anywhere in writings about Pittsburgh during the period when he lived there.

I have written this book partly to tell the story of one person who, although almost entirely neglected by historians, played a significant role in one segment of American history. Vann was a leader in twentieth-century black journalism. Along with men like Robert Abbott of Chicago and William Monroe Trotter of Boston, Robert Vann helped make the press a potent force in the black community, with the power to speak to and for his race. The *Pittsburgh Courier* became a vigorous advocate of social change among that city's blacks, as well as a conveyor of news. On a national scale, Vann's newspaper spearheaded the crusade for racial equality in America's armed forces during the 1930s and was an important spokesman for the race in many crucial political contests. Robert.Vann played a vital role in bringing blacks into the Democratic party in 1932. Blacks had been almost exclusively Republican since their enfranchisement in 1865, and Vann's newsmaking conversion to the Democrats powerfully influenced blacks, contributed to changing the composition of the Democratic party, and thus, in the long run, affected the course of political events.

Robert Vann was an unusual man, full of grit and determination to succeed despite seemingly insuperable obstacles. Vann became a historical influence, a shaper of events. But his chronicle is also important insofar as Vann was acted upon, affected by the times in which he lived, and this is the other reason for this work. Robert Vann was motivated by ideas held by most blacks in the early twentieth century, and he was part of the pattern of social, economic, and political flux of the period.

Like thousands of other blacks, the sons and grandsons of freedmen, Robert Vann came up out of the South at the turn of the century, attracted to Pittsburgh by its booming industry and promise of economic fulfillment. These blacks believed in the American dream that enough hard work could make a man successful. They found Pittsburgh a city in the midst of an enormous industrial boom, but also teeming with the social woes which accompanied rapid industrialization. World War I came, and more blacks streamed into the city. Ghettos were created, and dissatisfaction increased as the race saw its men dying in its country's cause while those at home continued to face discrimination. Tensions mounted, and 1919 found blacks rioting while government officials cried "Communist influence" and blamed the black press. Then the economic bubble burst in 1929, and blacks were hard hit by the Depression. Pittsburgh changed from a boom town to a city of bread lines, and black hopes withered. FDR was elected in 1932, and blacks anticipated being included in the New Deal he promised for the "forgotten man." Some of the New Deal promises encompassed blacks; others were miserably disappointing. In the mid-thirties blacks began to fight white invaders in Ethiopia, and Joe Louis appeared in the United States, a bright light in an otherwise glum world. Then as world war loomed once again, blacks determined to find in the armed forces the equality they were denied elsewhere. By 1940 the race was becoming more militant.

Robert Vann was affected deeply by some of these events, only peripherally by others; but all of them touched his life as a black man in some way, and so his story is important as part of the larger whole, a small pattern in the social fabric of black America.

Close examination of his career left me with a complex attitude toward Robert Vann. One has to admire his success as a black entrepreneur, which was in a sense his major achievement; he succeeded through his capacity to work long and diligently and his ability to keep his eye shrewdly on the main chance, which is a quality well regarded by the majority of Americans. And Vann accomplished many things for his race through his newspaper and his personal political voice. Vocal and strong-willed, he helped obtain some positive changes for the blacks for whom he spoke. Yet I must admit a certain ambivalence which arose during the period when I researched and wrote this work, an ambivalence created by Vann's protean quality. No powerfully motivating ideology sustained him with consistency. As his life went on his ideas altered to meet the exigencies of the moment. And while such adaptability is found in most leaders in the political sphere, I did not find it entirely admirable in Vann's case, perhaps because I perceived how Vann could have been even more effective had he acted differently. He was not a man of vision gone awry, for whom the means overwhelmed the goals; it is doubtful Vann had any great visions. He was a racial accommodationist, a man who worked toward limited ends within the realities of the time. Nor was Vann evil in any way. He did no ultimate harm in his reversals of stance, except to himself. What troubled me was a sense of lost potential. A man of his drive, capability, and, eventually, power, could have done much more. It may be inevitable that the treatment of any person is colored by the reactions of his biographer to the details of the subject's life. Nonetheless I have, I hope, presented Robert Vann in as fair a light as possible.

This biography is confined for the most part to the public man. While I have tried to examine his motives in many of the instances where his actions seem perplexing, this is in no way a psychoanalytical biography. Such a work would not have been possible, for Robert Vann never kept a journal of any sort and was very secretive about his personal life. He wrote a brief autobiographical sketch in 1938 and was compiling his papers in preparation for a full-length autobiography, but he died before beginning this work. The many letters Vann wrote to his wife over the thirty years of their marriage, which she carefully saved and which would have provided invaluable insights into the personal man, were destroyed by his foster daughter, Mabel Page Johnson, "to preserve privacy" when Mrs. Vann died in 1967, just as I was beginning my research.

This book is not an extensive account of the black community in

Pittsburgh, although the community has been described as thoroughly as possible at the points when it represented Robert Vann's major involvement. This subject requires its own thorough study, such as that currently being prepared by Professor Rollo Turner, Chairman of the Department of Black Studies at the University of Pittsburgh. Moreover, as Vann and his newspaper became better known and functioned in the national scene, the city of Pittsburgh and its black community became less pivotal to his life, so close description of it after the 1920s becomes much less relevant.

I am most deeply indebted to Mrs. R. L. Vann, who had faith in me and allowed me to use the papers her husband had kept in hopes of writing his own autobiography. In addition to providing me with interviews and valuable papers, Mr. and Mrs. Percival L. Prattis were gracious enough to allow me to use their home, and Mrs. Mabel V. Johnson, who was very close to the Vanns, was of great aid in supplying material on Mrs. Vann and their household.

Professor August Meier, of Kent State University, read the entire manuscript, bringing to it not only a scrupulous eye, but his vast knowledge on the subject of black history. Three of my colleagues at Boston College also read all or part of the manuscript. Professors Thomas H. O'Connor and Allen Wakstein made valuable suggestions for which I am truly grateful. Professor R. Alan Lawson's criticism made for a tightening and better structuring of the entire work.

Henry George LaBrie III, Charles Warren Fellow at Harvard University, while undertaking research of his own on Vann, unselfishly allowed me to use his findings. Included among his sources were taped interviews with eighty-three black publishers, collected over the past two years on a grant from the Ford Foundation. He also meticulously read all chapters in this work dealing with the journalistic phase of Vann's life and made helpful suggestions.

Professor Bruce Stave, of the University of Connecticut, read the sections which deal with political affairs and made useful suggestions stemming from his knowledge of the political situation in Pittsburgh during the 1930s. Professor Eugene Levy, of Carnegie-Mellon University, supplied assistance on the James Weldon Johnson imbroglio, graciously allowing me to use his own manuscript material.

Professor Rollo Turner, head of the Department of Black Studies at the University of Pittsburgh, provided me with information regarding the recent discovery of manuscripts at the Pennsylvania State Library at Harrisburg which deal with the history of blacks in Pittsburgh. Frank Zabrosky, Curator of the Hillman Library of the University of Pittsburgh, searched diligently for materials on Pittsburgh politics from 1906 to 1925.

The NAACP was most helpful in allowing me to use its papers at the Library of Congress. Roy Wilkins, Executive Secretary of the organization, gave me valuable information on the armed services struggle during 1938 and 1940. John Sengstacke, the owner of the *Courier*, kindly permitted the use of material from the newspaper.

Jervis Anderson, biographer of A. Philip Randolph, offered assistance during several telephone interviews regarding Vann's involvement with Randolph during the Pullman porters conflict. I am also indebted to A. Philip Randolph himself for allowing me to interview him on the many subjects with which he was intimately connected. Others who were gracious enough to allow interviews on areas of Vann's life included: George S. Schuyler, Chester Washington, Jr., William G. Nunn, Sr., Mrs. Emma Guffey Miller, Walter C. Rainey, Ernest Rice McKinney, James A. Farley, Hamilton Fish, Robert C. Weaver, Judge Raymond Pace Alexander, J. Austin Norris, Arthur Calhoun, Grady Askew, Mrs. C. S. Yeates, and F. Roy Johnson.

A number of libraries allowed me to make extensive use of their holdings, and their librarians were of great assistance. I appreciate what was gained from Mary Washington College, Fredericksburg, Virginia; Mrs. Katherine Jaffe, reference librarian, Bapst Library, Boston College; the Hillman Library, University of Pittsburgh; the Pennsylvania Division, Carnegie Library, Pittsburgh; the Pennsylvania State Library, Harrisburg; the Library of Congress, Washington, D. C.; the University of Pennsylvania Library, Philadelphia; the Philadelphia Free Library, Philadelphia; Chowan College Library, Murfreesboro, North Carolina; the Franklin Delano Roosevelt Library, Hyde Park, New York; the Schomburg Collection, 135th Street Branch, New York Public Library; the Beinecke Rare Book and Manuscript Library, Yale University; the Chicago Historical Society Library; Morgan State College, Baltimore; Virginia Union University Library, Richmond, Virginia; Washington and Jefferson College Library, Washington, Pennsylvania; Herbert Hoover Presidential Library, West Branch, Iowa; and the Ohio Historical Society, Columbus.

Finally, many thanks to Frederick Hetzel, Director of the University of Pittsburgh Press, for his patience and to Mrs. Beth Luey, Assistant Editor, for her tremendously hard work. To my own editor, Judith Bryant Wittenberg, goes my heartfelt appreciation for her tireless work of turning my very rough drafts into something readable. Without her assistance, this work would never have been completed.

Robert L. Vann of the PITTSBURGH COURIER

· 1 ·

North Carolina and Virginia

ROBERT LEE VANN was born on August 27, 1879, "somewhere on Old Dr. Mitchell's Farm" in Ahoskie, a small town in rural Hertford County, North Carolina.[1] Like the rest of northeastern North Carolina, Hertford County was then predominantly agrarian, and more than 50 percent of its people were black.[2] The broad, level fields of the coastal plain were deep with rich black soil, and tobacco and peanuts flourished, nurtured by the abundant rainfall and mild climate. Most blacks, the majority of whom had been slaves on local plantations, earned their living from these crops, either as small landowners or as tenants or workers on the larger farms owned by whites.[3] Growing tobacco and peanuts required little skill and no costly agricultural implements and could provide employment for all members of the family. A few blacks also worked in the county's two principal industries, lumbering and fishing.

Vann's mother, Lucy Peoples, worked on the Mitchell farm as cook for the family. She was the daughter of Fletcher Peoples and Martilla Holloman, ex-slaves who had remained in Hertford County after the Civil War and opened a general store in the crossroads community of Ahoskie. The store provided only a meager living for the Peoples family, so in her teens Lucy began to work as a domestic on nearby farms. Her first job was as cook to the Albert Vann family, and Lucy, following the custom of earlier slave times, took the last name of her first employer and bestowed it upon her son, though not upon herself. She remained Lucy Peoples until she married a few years later.[4] The name Vann, Lucy hoped, would give young Robert a certain status and respectability, for it belonged to several prominent white families in Hertford County. According to Vann, Lucy chose the names "Robert Lee" in honor of his great-grandfather, not the Confederate general.⁵

Robert Vann's paternal heritage is uncertain; it is likely that he was illegitimate. An earlier biographer suggests that Vann's father was Joseph Hall, a black fieldhand who lived with Lucy Peoples on the large Mitchell farm for the first few years of Vann's life. However, verification of his mother's relationship with Joseph Hall is almost impossible because there is no certificate of marriage or birth in the Hertford County registry of records. Vann's father may even have been a local white man. Vann himself never mentioned his father and when asked who his forebears were replied simply, "I came of a family named Peoples, and my mother gave me the name of her grandfather, who died before the war of 1860. I don't even know his name or where he was born, but my family, the Peoples, still live in North Carolina."⁶

When Robert was still very young Joseph Hall deserted the family, and Lucy Peoples, left to bring up her son alone,⁷ was forced to continue working as a cook. Despite its long hours, the position of cook was desirable for blacks of the time; it was considered much more acceptable than field labor. Lucy was favored for employment as cook because the hierarchy of skin color was much in effect, and she was light-skinned and attractive.

Before Robert was very old they moved to the Slaughter farm. "My earliest recollection," said Vann later, "is that of living on the old Slaughter farm, owned by Joseph Slaughter and located near Pitch Landing. This was on the old Ahoskie to Harrellsville road by way of the Big Swamp."⁸ About the time of Robert's sixth birthday his mother took a job for three dollars a month with the John O. Askew family in nearby Harrellsville. There Lucy and Robert lived in a kitchen cabin set apart from the main house, sleeping on beds near the stove. The thirteen years he spent in and around kitchens gave Robert Vann a lifelong aversion to cooking odors; in later years he refused to eat in a kitchen under any circumstances, and if he smelled kitchen odors in other rooms he opened windows.

The years he spent at the Askew farm filled Vann with the vision of a gracious and serene way of life. His hope of attaining such a life motivated him toward personal success, and he eventually attempted to re-create it for himself on an estate near Pittsburgh. Surrounded by deep lawns, the Askew home was a great white ante-bellum mansion set amid large oaks and elms, plantings of roses, and pink and white magnolias, with sweeping wide verandas on the first and second floors. The house had been built early in the century by Abner Harrell, the founder of Harrellsville and great-grandfather of John O. Askew, Lucy Vann's employer.[9] Askew was one of the most prominent men in Hertford County. He owned several farms and a mercantile business and was president of the Bank of Harrellsville.[10] On the Askew place young Robert played with the three Askew children, sharing their toys and riding their horses. John Askew regularly took Vann riding with him to make the rounds of his large property; Robert acted as gate-opener and cheerful companion. They were comfortable years for Robert Vann and would acquire an increasingly rosy aureole as time pushed them further into memory. At the end of his life he reminisced, "There I was surrounded with the luxury and aristocracy of the South. The large farm, any number of farmhands, an overseer, beautiful lawns, stately trees, labyrinth upon labyrinth of flowers and shrubbery surrounded me as if I, myself, were an heir to wealth. During those years, my life as it has been lived for this past half

The Grady Askew house, Harrellsville, N.C., as it looks today.
F. Roy Johnson, Murfreesboro, N.C.

century took definite form. I knew the best people of Harrellsville, played in their yards and with their children."[11]

Lucy Peoples, like many women alone, was determined that her son be raised correctly, with proper doses of discipline and religion. As Vann said later, wryly, "She wore to shreds many a cedar twig in her efforts to refute the tradition that a woman could not rear a child with any degree of success.... Whenever I broke her established code of behavior for me, she gave me a sound thrashing and thanked anyone else who performed the function for her."[12] Lucy saw to it also that Robert "got" religion by immersion, and he was baptized into the New Ahoskie Baptist Church in the waters of the Wiccacon River at age thirteen.

Lucy was aided in her child rearing by another resolute woman, her employer's wife, Mary Askew. "It was she who shaped my early education," said Vann, and along with his mother, Mrs. Askew strove to mold a good "character" in the boy. "It cost me all I have ever had in energy, patience and courage to maintain the standard they set for me when I was a boy," he admitted later.[13]

From an early age Robert Vann had the agreeable, elegant good looks that would facilitate his later acceptance in a world of business and politics as yet unprepared to embrace the most African of blacks. Vann's light color and an appearance deemed pleasant by Caucasian standards opened many doors that would have otherwise remained closed to a black man. He had inherited sleek black hair, coppery skin, and a strong straight nose from his half-white maternal grandfather. These were combined with his slim build and limpid deep-set eyes to give him a Middle-Eastern or Indian look. On at least two future occasions, acquaintances suggested the idea of "passing" to Vann. In each case he refused, preferring to affirm his blackness.

Vann's physical appearance, as well as the fact that his mother was a valued servant in a respected white home, made for a childhood of relaxed race relations. In an autobiographical sketch Vann wrote for the *Hertford County Herald* many years later, he had special praise for the whites he had known as a boy. Of the Williams, Wooten, Scull, Cullen, Sharp, Harrell, Sessom, and Yates families, Vann wrote, "Living among these white people, whose names I have mentioned, was a privilege, and in later years proved a great inspiration."[14]

However, Vann parted from his white playmates each day, beginning at age six, to walk the separate path to the Springfield Colored School. There he crowded into the one-room unpainted schoolhouse with sixty other black children ranging in age from six to fourteen. For just four months each winter, from December to March, he studied, sitting on a backless bench near the wood stove. The school term was short because the North Carolina state legislature failed to provide funds for additional time for blacks, and most of the children were needed in other seasons as fieldhands.[15] Although the education he received at the colored school was rudimentary, Vann proved an apt pupil and entered eagerly into the classroom competition. Learning quickly, he even managed to teach his unlettered mother to read and write.[16]

By age twelve, he had acquired a basic working knowledge of the "three R's," so venerated at the time, and was graduated from the Springfield Colored School. At that 1892 commencement exercise, Robert recited the first of many poems he was to compose for significant occasions:

> All can marry whom they like
> I know an easier life
> A lawyer need not soil his hands
> But live by others strife.[17]

It proved prophetic.

Robert Vann's hopes to go on to secondary school that fall were thwarted by his mother's marriage to John Simon, a local dirt farmer. Lucy yearned for a place of her own and Simon badly needed a wife to care for his five motherless children. The day Lucy and Robert moved to Simon's shack in the area called Red Hill marked the beginning of the unhappiest period of Vann's life.

Red Hill was only about a mile from the Askew farm, but for Robert it was a universe away. He spent the next few years either toiling on the farm at Red Hill or being hired out by his stepfather as a cook, seine fisher, or tobacco picker. The work at Red Hill was unremitting and seemed even grimmer when contrasted with the tranquil years Vann had spent on the Askew grounds. As he later recalled, "My mother's husband took me down to a swampy plot, filled with malaria, snakes and wild animals, and taught me to set steel traps for coons, opossums, and rabbits; how to kill snakes, and the greatest of all, how to plow an ox right near a creek at eleven o'clock on a hot July day. . . . I learned to split rails, dig ditches, hoe cotton and corn, cure tobacco in the barns, and everything else that a plow boy of a poor Negro farmer would have to know. . . . My stepfather thought that I was big enough to work but he never knew how the first ten years of my life constantly rebelled against the six years of torment I encountered under his jurisdiction."[18] For Robert the change from casual house servant to hard-working fieldhand was especially difficult because he was painfully aware that his status had depreciated greatly. As the stepson of a poor dirt farmer he was far less highly regarded in the limited society of Hertford County than he had been as the son of a favored servant in one of the region's largest houses. In addition, he was now forced to share his mother's attention with five stepbrothers and stepsisters. Vann nursed a growing animosity toward John Simon and would remember him always bitterly as "the world's most worthless man."[19]

On those infrequent occasions when there was no work to be done at the Red Hill farm, young Robert was hired out locally, a common practice among poor farming families. He usually picked and cured tobacco on nearby farms, but once he was sent with fourteen other men to a Virginia lumber camp near Portsmouth to cook for the working hands, a chore which he must have disliked intensely.

In the spring Robert was often dispatched to catch herring on the Chowan River. Enormous schools of these fish migrated annually up from the Atlantic Ocean, through Albemarle Sound and into the Chowan and its main tributaries, where they spawned before returning to the sea.[20] At times as many as 100,000 were caught in a single haul. The herring provided a valuable source of income for the fishermen of Hertford County, who exported a good deal of the catch. The rest was sold to local farm families, who either preserved it in brine or dried it to last through the year.[21] For six dollars a month, all of which went to his stepfather, Robert drove a team of horses around a windlass on the beach, hauling in one end of a vast seine containing the netted fish. The job was monotonous, but it did introduce Vann to an early mentor, "Captain" David Askew, one of the black overseers. A down-to-earth man who "could read the number of feet in a log without ever applying a rule," Askew entertained and possibly edified the boy with his "wise sayings and crude philosophy" as they worked together repairing nets.[22] Without a father figure he liked and admired, young Vann was happy to work beside a man like Askew.

These years of hard physical labor, though unpleasant for Vann, taught him perseverance, endowed him with the stamina to conquer several serious illnesses, and provided him with endless material for those "hard-work-as-the-key-to-success" speeches with which all self-made men come equipped.[23]

Just as Vann's chances for further schooling began to seem hopelessly remote, he had a bit of good luck. In the summer of 1895 he was hired as janitor and part-time clerk at the Harrellsville Post Office by A. C. Boothe, one of the few black postmasters in the country at that time. Vann "could never understand the political gymnastics [Boothe] performed in order to become postmaster, but I suppose Henry Clay Sharp had something to do with it because he was the only [white] Republican around Harrellsville."[24] As the weeks passed and Boothe grew confident in Vann's ability, he occasionally let him run the post office alone. Inscribed on Vann's memory was one such time when he accidentally locked the stamps in the safe at the close of a workday, leaving none for the following day's business. Not knowing the combination to the safe and unwilling to summon the absent postmaster, Vann arose the next morning long before dawn and rode a bicycle loaned by a white friend eight heat-drenched miles to Colerain, borrowed stamps from the post office there, "and was back in Harrellsville, wringing wet with sweat, in time to open the post office on time."[25] The incident would ever after prod Vann to "carefulness and [close] attention to business," but the thing that bothered him most was not the long ride but the fact that he had had to borrow the bicycle.[26] Vann was ashamed that he was too poor to have a bicycle of his own.

By the end of that summer Vann had managed to save sixteen dollars and was determined to continue his education.[27] To Vann, as to many other young blacks, education seemed the only way out of a highly unpromising situation, and John Simon gave his grudging approval to the boy's idea. The nearby Ahoskie Colored School exemplified all that was inadequate about black secondary education in the South. Open only for a two-month term, it was ill equipped and staffed with poorly trained and poorly paid instructors. Of all the black teachers in the state, fifteen males and five females held certificates to teach first grade; eight males and ten females, certificates for the second grade; and one male and three females, third-grade certificates. The average school term was 14.0 weeks for blacks and 15.66 for whites. The average monthly salary for white male teachers was $31.50, while for blacks it was $23.46.[28] The North Carolina State Superintendent of Public Instruction summarized the official white position which kept such schools so pitiful when he said that "education spoils the colored men as laborers, to their own damage, and the damage of the white people, who own almost all of the lands. . . . the colored people must not lose sight of the fact that manual labor . . . will be their lot to a larger degree than white people, because of the peculiar conditions and circumstances that surround them."[29] Even after the educational reform that took place under Governor Charles B. Aycock in 1901, the policy remained distinctly "separate and unequal," with limited improvement for blacks.[30]

Consequently, Robert Vann chose the private, Baptist-run Waters Training School in Winton, the Hertford County seat. Waters Training School, which was glowingly advertised by its headmaster, Calvin S. Brown, as having a "splendid curriculum and a faculty of seven teachers . . . excellent accommodations for boarding students," consisted of three modest two-story frame buildings, which housed both dormitories and classrooms, on Winton's main street. The tuition was five dollars a month for boarding students and four dollars for those who went home on weekends.[31] When students were slow to pay their tuition fees, Headmaster Brown turned for financial help to the Baptist Church or to Northern philanthropists. The school term lasted from October through May.

At the end of the nineteenth century, most educated blacks in the South were either ministers or teachers, and Waters's headmaster represented both professions. Born a slave in Salisbury, North Carolina, in 1859, Brown received his early schooling and teacher's certificate at the Freedmen's Aid Society School there in 1878. He subsequently graduated from Shaw University in Raleigh with both bachelor's and Doctor of Divinity degrees. He became a Baptist minister in Hertford County, then president of the Baptist Convention of North Carolina. In 1885 Brown founded Waters Training School and was its principal until his death fifty-two years later. Like many other privately run institutions, Waters was a one-man operation; Brown poured his earnings and those of his wife back into the school to help meet operating expenses.[32] Waters was more than a school to Calvin Brown; it was a cause, the embodiment of his lifelong effort to upgrade the quality of education for blacks. For those who attended Brown's school it represented salvation from the mediocrity of the public schools open to them.[33]

With the sixteen dollars he had earned at the Harrellsville Post Office, Robert Vann was able to enroll for four months' schooling at Waters Training School, saving a dollar a month by walking the eleven miles back to the Simon farm at Red Hill each weekend. His funds were depleted by the end of January, so he left school and spent the spring in the tobacco fields and on the fishing beaches. He worked in the post office again that summer and saved sixteen more dollars. Vann returned to Waters Training School the following fall, intending to stay until midyear, when his money would again run out.

But the long walks home each Friday soon ended. One winter weekend a heavy snow fell, and Vann set out to return to school. He collapsed upon his arrival, wet, exhausted, and ill. Headmaster Brown was sufficiently impressed by the boy's grit and motivation that he arranged for Vann to stay at Waters through weekends and during the full school year, and got him a job filling students' oil lamps and chopping firewood.[34] Except for summer vacations, Vann lived at Waters during the rest of his years there. While at Waters, Vann met Mattie Chavis of Winton. The two fell in love, and after a period of courtship they became engaged when Vann gave Mattie a tiny diamond ring he had purchased with a few carefully saved dollars.[35]

In 1898, when Vann was nineteen, he made his first trip north, to work as a hotel waiter in Boston for the summer. He went in part because a group of his fellow students, including his friend James Rooks, was going, and in part because the young sister born to his mother and John Simon in 1891 had died of malaria in May. Vann was determined to spend no more summers at the swampy Red Hill farm. His mother, who had never been more than fifty miles from Red Hill in her life, vigorously opposed the idea and only after persistent arguments did she consent to his going. Vann borrowed some money from Charles H. Smith, a white former employee of the Askews whom he regarded as his "father confessor,"[36] and started the long train trip northward in a segregated car. It was a courageous undertaking for a boy who had seen a train for the first time just a few years earlier and "did not know the sun rose and set anywhere else except in Harrellsville."[37] As a colleague put it many years later, "[Vann] never got far enough out of the woods to even see a train until he was nine years old."[38]

When he reached Boston, Robert went to live with his aunt, Mrs. Mary Odum, and found a job waiting on tables at the opulent Copley Square Hotel. In his off-hours, Vann worked diligently at odd jobs, including that of shoeshine boy. He was exhilarated both by the relative racial freedom of Boston and by the money he earned, with which he repaid his debt to Charles Smith, bought gifts for his mother, paid all his tuition at Waters for the forthcoming year, and outfitted himself with a pinstripe suit, raglan raincoat, tan shoes, and a derby.

By the time Vann returned to Winton in October, nearly all traces of the Red Hill farm boy were gone. Wearing the new clothes he had chosen in emulation of the wealthy patrons at the Boston hotel, with his sleek hair combed back and parted in the middle, Vann cut a dashing figure in his rural surroundings.[39] This began Vann's lifelong attention to careful grooming; he became meticulous about his clothing and appearance, dressing conservatively but well and being always fastidiously neat.

Robert Vann graduated from Waters Training School in 1901 as the class valedictorian. He had developed his oratory skills and public aplomb by speaking at biweekly prayer meetings, debating at the Lyceum on Friday nights, and competing in spelling matches, so he delivered his valedictory address, "Launched But Not Anchored," with a good deal of confidence.

Mixing his metaphors with youthful assurance, he proclaimed:

> The voyage of life is great and for its accomplishment the demands are great. In order to prepare for any contingencies, the pilot must plot his course with care for so many wrecks along the way of life today are occasioned solely on the account of deficient preparations. He who builds or ventures upon an infirm foundation is but a failure. Never would Abraham Lincoln have risen from his humble cot to the presidency had he not first chosen the position and, after choosing this lofty height, he strove with earnest and persistent efforts, ever keeping in view that executive mansion which marked his course from boyhood to the day of his greatest attainment. Once having found what he was best suited for, the individual should pursue aggressively his goal. Opportunity would then almost inevitably come his way. To every individual there comes as much as once in a life an opportunity which, seized at its flow, leads on to fortune; omitted, all his life is left a spectacle of failure and disgrace, and he together with his once glittering talent soon sinks into oblivion and despair.[40]

The speech not only reveals the tenacious pursuit of personal goals and the desire for self-realization which would mark Vann's life. It also typifies much that was prevalent in black thought at the beginning of the twentieth century—the idea that education and hard work would elevate oneself and one's race; the belief in fixing one's eye on a star and striving toward it; and the evocation of Abraham Lincoln as a paradigm of rags-to-riches success. It was the American economic myth, the bourgeois ideology, popularized during that era by the writings of Horatio Alger and propounded by black leaders of the time like Frederick Douglass and, of course, Booker T. Washington.[41]

In his valedictory, Vann also said that opportunity must be "seized at its flow." He did just that over the years, standing ready to profit by whatever might occur, and gradually progressed to the point where he seemed to have no long-range view, so engrossed was he in seizing opportunities. Vann's idealism became engulfed by opportunism; all visions of "lofty heights" vanished as he preoccupied himself with chances offered by the moment. This eventually had a devastating effect on his political career. While he never sank "into oblivion and despair," his tendency to act without regard for ultimate consequences kept him from attaining the meaningful hold on power he wished for. People came to distrust him.

Despite his years at Waters Training School, Vann still felt unprepared for college, and educational opportunities in the Winton area were limited. To complete his high school education in a satisfactory way, Vann entered Wayland Academy, the preparatory school of Virginia Union University in Richmond, in the fall of 1901. He chose Virginia Union University at the urging of Calvin Brown; it was, like Waters, a Baptist-affiliated school. By 1902 Vann had received an Academy degree and entered the university as a college student.[42]

Like many other black schools in the South, Virginia Union had been founded during Reconstruction through philanthropic efforts, in this case by the American Baptist Home Missionary Society.[43] The college was concerned primarily with training ministers; its avowed purpose was "to train leaders to teach, to preach and to guide and help men and women in the Negro race."[44] W. E. B. DuBois, then a professor at Atlanta University, ranked it as a "First Grade Colored College," just behind Howard, Fisk, Atlanta, Wiley, and Leland Universities. The academic program was solid, with courses in ancient and modern languages, mathematics, English, sociology, history, and philosophy.[45]

Vann did not attend Virginia Union with the ministry in mind. Already a practical young man, he was uninterested in religion despite his staunch Baptist upbringing, and he regarded most black ministers as semiliterate zealots given to emotional excesses. In later years, through his *Courier* editorials, Vann would criticize clergymen who regarded the saving of men's eternal souls as more important than providing for their corporeal beings on this earth.

14 • Robert L. Vann of the PITTSBURGH COURIER

By his own admission, Vann was not of serious academic bent; he was already too intoxicated by the heady brew of public acclaim. At Virginia Union his Greek and geometry studies languished while he attended to those duties befitting a campus luminary. He orated, debated,[46] and supervised campus political campaigns. He contributed prose and poetry to the *University Journal*, and the January 1903 edition featured his poem "Freedom," which celebrated the fiftieth anniversary of the Emancipation Proclamation:

> O days of blood! When human hearts
> Forgot the kindredness they bore,
> When Man for man became a slave
> When man for wealth alone did crave;
> Thou are dead to live no more.
>
> Dead, dead to all but history's pages,
> Thy bitter foes have passed us by;
> No more thy lash, thy stake we dread;
> No more thy clouds hang o'er our head
> But live we now 'neath brighter sky.
>
> Free, free as the air which princes breathe
> Free as the birds in the winged flights
> Columbia's land we claim as ours;
> We eat her fruits, enjoy her flowers,
> Fight for her flag, maintain her rights.[47]

In more capricious moments Vann gained a reputation as the school practical joker. He once turned the school milk cows loose in an onion patch with obvious results, and another time filled the school bell with water, giving the bell ringer an unexpected shower. The school administration was possibly relieved, Vann said, when in 1903 he "was given a diploma and politely asked to leave."[48]

While at Virginia Union, Robert Vann, like many another young person whose world view is in a germinal state, was susceptible to philosophical shaping by a strong model. Such a force in Vann's life was Dr. Joshua Simpson, his Greek teacher. While Vann never mastered the intricacies of Simpson's subject, he formed a friendship with the older man and carried away a strong respect for Simpson's Spartan, rigorous philosophy of living. One day in class Professor Simpson sent Vann to the blackboard to diagram a sentence. When Vann had finished, Simpson looked it over and then drew an X through the entire outline. When Vann challenged him, saying that there was only one small mistake, Simpson countered with, "Mr. Vann, a thing is either all right or all wrong," and drew another large X over the sentence.[49] Vann never forgot this incident or Dr. Simpson, and they may have had a fundamental effect on his character. As his life went on, Vann exacted much from himself physically, living simply for the most part, and often judged himself and others with harsh severity.

At Virginia Union, Vann formed friendships which lasted throughout his life with two young men who would also become prominent black leaders. The two subsequently developed quite different ideologies. One held views much like Vann's; the other, J. Max Barber of Philadelphia, was far from Vann on the ideological spectrum, a fact that makes the durability of their friendship interesting, if not a bit puzzling. Barber, editor of the *University Journal*, later became editor of the noted magazine *The Voice of the Negro*, which flourished from 1903 to 1907, and was a "radical" Niagarite and spokesman for an anti–Booker T. Washington faction.[50] Vann and Barber had both read serialized accounts of *Up from Slavery* in *Outlook* magazine and frequently argued over the merits of Booker T. Washington. Vann was mostly in sympathy with Washington's views, while the more militant Barber disagreed with much in his work. In 1902 Vann was instrumental in getting Barber to run for a precedent-breaking second term as president of the Virginia Union Literary Society and masterminded his victory. Despite the divergence of their racial philosophies, Barber remained close to Vann and admired him. "Vann was bold, frank, ingenious, a gentleman and a friend and delivered on all promises," he later said.[51]

Vann's other good friend was Eugene Kinckle Jones, who was like Vann a racial moderate. He eventually became executive secretary of the National Urban League and held a federal position in Washington in the Department of Commerce while Vann was there during the first administration of Franklin D. Roosevelt. Vann spent a good deal of time during his Virginia Union years at the James Street brick home of Jones's parents, both of whom were college professors—Mr. Jones at Virginia Union and Mrs. Jones at Hartshorne College, the women's branch of the university. Jones taught Bible, homiletics, and church polity, while his wife taught music. As a regular guest at socials held by the Joneses, along with girls from Hartshorne, Vann mixed with the elite of old Richmond's black society, learned to dance, and acquired further social polish.[52]

As Robert Vann's sojourn at Virginia Union University was ending, many forces were at work in the black world outside the college walls. These forces, weighed and considered by a realistic young black like Vann, made the decision to go north almost inevitable. One can only conjecture as to the exact cause of Vann's move, but the conditions of the period as they would have been viewed by a clear-eyed and resolute black like Vann must have contributed enormously to his decision to leave his native region. He wanted more for himself than could be found there.

The position of the black man in the South was deteriorating rapidly. Southern state legislatures were enacting wholesale disfranchisement of blacks; segregationist Jim Crow laws for public facilities were instituted on a wide scale; racist demagogues like Ben Tillman of South Carolina and James K. Vardaman of Mississippi were in the ascendant; and lynchings occurred almost daily.

In 1898 the North Carolina Democrats had mounted a white supremacist campaign which defeated the shaky Fusionist alliance of Republicans, blacks, and Populists. To judge from writings by white Democrats of the period, the drive to end what they viewed as Republican "Negro domination" in North Carolina was like a crusade in its intensity. The Republicans were denounced as having perpetrated the Union invasion of the Tar Heel State and, in Vann's home county, as having burned the county seat, Winton, to the ground in 1862. Further, during Reconstruction, to quote one vehement Democrat, "the South was overrun with carpetbaggers and corrupt politicians, when the ignorant Southern Negro was promised '40 acres and a mule'—during those years Harrellsville suffered and sacrificed with the rest of the South."[53] Even after the Democrats made their way to power in the state, party members complained constantly that the eastern counties, with their large black populations, were Republican strongholds.

In 1898 the Fusionists, who had controlled the state for three years, were accused by Democrats of having duped honest farmers into joining with blacks. The Democrats said the Fusionists had effected the repeal of "nearly every law that has been enacted by a Democratic legislature which had not been repealed in 1898, and enacted most offensive laws to the white people of the State. They flooded the State and eastern counties with Negro officers. In their madness they abolished almost all non-constitutional offices, and created others and filled them from their ranks." It was the duty of the white people, wrote Benjamin Winborne, an ardent Democrat from Murfreesboro and chairman of the party in Hertford County for many years, to "rise up in their mighty indignation and proclaim in a voice that thunders throughout the State, that their patience is exhausted, and that this is a white man's State, and white man's government, that they will no longer submit to the indignities and insults and misrule of the unworthy leaders, whose ambition for power and spoil has no limit, but that they will drive from power the haters of Anglo-Saxon blood and forever consign them to graves of dishonor and shame."[54]

In that vicious 1898 campaign the Democrats resorted to wholesale intimidation to keep blacks from voting. In Winton, for example, "the voting was done through the front window of the Registrar of Deeds office. Until late in the afternoon the Populists kept a long line of Negroes voting at this window. The people of the town [Democratic opposition] became so incensed at this procedure that they threatened to shoot the leader; after that the line melted away."[55]

A few days after the Democratic victory, which gave the party a large majority in both houses of the North Carolina legislature, there was a terrible race riot in Wilmington.[56] The riot, which claimed many dead and injured, was triggered in part by the blacks' resentment at having been chased from the polls by gun-wielding white Democrats. According to historian Helen G. Edmonds, "the Wilmington race riot had dire repercussions on the city, the state and the South. Most of the influential Negroes of Wilmington sold or gave away their personal holdings, packed bag and baggage, and moved to other parts of the state or out of the state. This migration left an apathetic Negro citizenry, fearful and resentful of the whites. So many of these Negro employees refused to return to their former white employers that the Democratic legislature in 1899 enacted a vagrancy statute for Wilmington, a coercive measure to force Negroes into white employment."[57] Few blacks dared to exercise the right to vote "after the racial whirlwind of 1898 had blown the ballot from their hands."[58]

In 1900 the Democrats elected Charles B. Aycock as governor and amended the state Constitution in such a way that blacks were essentially disfranchised. How effective the Democrats were in keeping blacks from the polls can be seen by looking at election results. In 1896 Vann's home county, Hertford, which was half black, had given 1,436 votes to the Republican gubernatorial candidate and 879 to the Democrat. By the 1900 election the proportions were reversed, with 1,368 for the Democratic gubernatorial candidate and just 429 for the Republican.[59] In the 1900 contest, few blacks dared to vote in the Winton area. "The Democrats were determined to control the situation. The hotel lobby [voting place] was well supplied with guns and many were carried personally by men in the crowd. The guns must have had a soothing effect. The election passed off quietly, the Democratic ticket went in and political upheaval was over in Hertford County."[60] The blacks, who always voted Republican, were clearly disfranchised.[61] What is more, the badly crippled Republican party in the state, in hopes of revitalizing itself, was attempting to change its former image of "the party of the nigger" to that of a "lily-white" party. Politics were in a sorry state for the blacks. The few who could still vote had no party to which they could give allegiance.[62] If Robert Vann had political aspirations, success in the South was out of the question in 1903.

A second condition that probably helped bring about Vann's decision to leave the South was that by 1903 black leaders in Richmond, where Vann was at school, and elsewhere were speaking out on the intolerable conditions; Vann and his fellow black students could not help but hear. John T. Mitchell, the crusading and influential editor of the *Richmond Planet,* had been campaigning in his newspaper against black disfranchisement since the 1901 Virginia Constitutional Convention proposed such measures and, in 1903, against that year's law segregating Richmond's streetcars. Mitchell was joined in this crusade by three professors from Virginia Union, the best-known of them being J. R. L. Diggs.[63] Vann was a member of the college debating team and usually delivered the announcements of forthcoming debates to the *Planet* offices for insertion in the newspaper; he had to be aware of, and influenced by, Mitchell's struggle against disfranchisement and Jim Crowism.

Further, Vann had recently finished reading Booker T. Washington's autobiography, *Up from Slavery.* The book had a pronounced influence on him, helping to crystallize ideas he already held. Washington placed great emphasis on racial pride, the gospel of work, and above all economic self-help. But while Washington believed blacks could live amicably in the South once the white man saw them making progress and realized they were an integral part of the region's economy, Vann departed from this view. Vann espoused the concept of hard work and economic racial uplift, but he wanted more than that. He found the racial abuses in Richmond intolerable, and he must have realized that he wanted greater social and political opportunity than he could ever hope to find in his native region.[64]

He was an ambitious young man, who had in his 1901 valedictory speech at Waters invoked Abraham Lincoln as hero because he "strove with earnest and persistent efforts" and "pursue[d] aggressively his goal." It was obvious that Vann intended to do the same, and the South was far from an ideal place in which to do it.

As an educated black in the South of that era, Vann would have a choice of occupation limited virtually to teaching or the ministry. In North Carolina in 1890 more than 95 percent of black professionals belonged to these two vocations.[65] In the South, Vann could look forward only to a subjugated status of "social isolation, occupational immobility, and the rigid enforcement of interracial etiquette" in "the private world of color and a limited world of work."[66] No matter what friendly whites in North Carolina may have thought of Vann as an individual, he was just another black man to the closed southern society.

Migration north undoubtedly seemed the only possibility for Robert Vann. Like many other blacks, he later recalled having felt "a great discontent, a great restlessness, a great determination somehow to escape."[67] While the first generation of freedmen had been relatively content with their lot, happy just to be free from the shackles of slavery, the second generation, which W. E. B. DuBois called "the southern free man's sons and daughters,"[68] found life in the South oppressive and saw little hope for improvement for their race. Their ambitions were too great for them to settle for a drudgery-filled life close to the soil and under the white man's thumb. Their hopeful eyes saw the North as the land of deliverance, and they began to migrate in large numbers. Hertford County lost many of its talented young blacks, including C. E. Askew, who became the pastor of a large church in Detroit; Hobson Reynolds, later grand director of the Elks (Black Division) and a representative in the Pennsylvania legislature; E. F. Askew, who entered the General Assembly of New Jersey; and George White, Jr., whose father, last of the black congressmen from North Carolina, told Robert Vann in 1902 he should go north if he wished to "get ahead."[69]

Vann applied to the Western University of Pennsylvania at Pittsburgh. He chose this city because of its relative proximity, and the university because it offered an occasional scholarship to worthy blacks in need of aid. He won one of these, an Avery Scholarship worth $100. Vann went to see Mattie Chavis, the young woman to whom he had become engaged the previous year. He ended their engagement reluctantly, telling her, "I'm going North. There will be no wedding plans," but he let her keep the tiny diamond ring he had given her.[70] Vann then paid a visit to his mother in the shack at Red Hill and began the long railway trip to Pittsburgh. Robert Vann would return to Hertford County a few more times, but in spirit he left the South forever that hot summer day when the train pulled out of the station at Cofield.

· 2 ·

North Toward Home

As Vann's train neared Pittsburgh, signs of the city's furious industrial growth were visible from the window of his railroad car. The booming steel industry had filled the hillsides above the Allegheny and Monongahela Rivers with fiery coke ovens, multiton Bessemer converters, and huge open-hearth furnaces which glowed day and night. Smoke filled the valleys; gray slag heaps dotted the horizon.

To most new arrivals in Pittsburgh, this sight represented progress and prosperity, the fulfillment of the American economic dream. "Pittsburgh is the apotheosis of American civilization," said one fervent partisan of the time. "Today it stands on the threshold of a future [infinitely] great."[1] The prospects seemed unlimited for a man willing to work hard.

The discovery of a vast wealth of vital raw materials such as iron, oil, and bituminous coal in the area around Pittsburgh had rapidly transformed the one-time trading post into a major industrial center. When coke began to be used as the main fuel for iron smelting, Pittsburgh became dominant in iron and steel production because of the huge bituminous coal fields and enormous deposits of iron ore nearby. By 1900, just twenty-five years after Andrew Carnegie first opened his steelworks and Henry Clay Frick started his coke business, the Pittsburgh district supplied half the nation's open-hearth steel and more than half its coke.[2] Companies were springing up everywhere in the district. George Westinghouse began to manufacture heavy electrical machinery, and his company soon was one of the most important producers in the nation. Other heavy industries developed in the region, including the Aluminum Company of America and the Gulf Oil Company, largest independent oil company in the world, dominated by the Mellon family. The Armstrong Cork

Company, founded by a former shipping clerk, was turning out thousands of corks, tons of corkboard, and hundreds of yards of linoleum each day. The Pittsburgh Plate Glass Company, begun in 1881 in a small factory in Creighton, expanded rapidly after the discovery of a new method of annealing plate glass in 1900. Though food seems an unlikely addition to this grimy list, the growth of the H. J. Heinz Company at the same time made the city one of the country's largest food-packing centers. In 1900, nearly 66 million tons of goods were transported in and out of the Pittsburgh region; that figure would more than double by 1910.[3] Pittsburgh was also an important banking center; by 1906 it ranked second in the United States in banking capital and surplus. In 1906 there were 179 bank and trust companies in the Pittsburgh district.[4]

These growing businesses required an enormous labor force to stoke their furnaces, carry their hods, and load their railroad cars. In 1900 the Carnegie Steel Company alone employed twenty-five thousand men in the Pittsburgh area. Because of fierce competition and intense opposition by management to labor unionization, industry called for an unskilled work force that would ask little in the way of pay or working conditions; fifteen thousand immigrants from all over Europe flooded into Pittsburgh each year to meet this demand. They came primarily from Eastern Europe and included Lithuanians, Poles, Croatians, Bohemians, Hungarians, Russians, Jews, Serbians, Slovaks, Ruthenians, Italians, and Greeks.[5] The population of Pittsburgh more than doubled between 1880 and 1900.[6] When Pittsburgh annexed Allegheny City in 1907, it became the sixth most populous city in the country. This fact was a great source of pride to the citizenry.

Blacks had been living in the Pittsburgh area since before 1800. A 1788 Pennsylvania law had abolished slavery in the state, and by 1800 there were a small number of blacks in Pittsburgh, most of whom worked at menial labor.[7] In 1810 sixty-seven free blacks and an undetermined number of runaway slaves lived in the city.[8] After 1820 migration to the city of free blacks and runaway slaves from the neighboring states of Virginia and Maryland increased.[9] Public sentiment, led by whites like Charles Avery, was strongly antislavery, and Pittsburgh served as an important way station on the Underground Railroad for fugitive slaves en route to sanctuary in Canada. Also deeply involved with the Underground Railroad was Martin Delany, who rose to prominence as a black leader during this period;

in 1843 he began to publish *Mystery*, an abolitionist black weekly of limited circulation but broad influence.[10]

With the passage and enforcement of the Fugitive Slave Act of 1850 many apprehensive blacks fled to Canada, reducing Pittsburgh's black population from 3,431 to 2,725.[11] But at that same time a large proportion of those remaining began to settle in the area around Wylie Avenue of the Hill District, and the area became known as "Little Hayti."[12] Previously, that region had been home to prosperous Scottish, Irish, and German merchants, who were followed by poor Jewish migrants and subsequently even poorer Italians. The black population of Pittsburgh nearly doubled between 1870 and 1880 and doubled again each of the following two decades, as blacks came to seek work in the roaring mills.[13]

Most of these new black settlers came to Pennsylvania because it was close to the Mason-Dixon line, and they came from the upper southern states; Maryland, Virginia, Kentucky, Tennessee, and North Carolina provided about one-third of the influx from 1895 through 1904.[14] Because of its closeness to the upper southern states, Pennsylvania had the largest number of blacks of any northern state. In 1900 Pittsburgh ranked high as a northern city in terms of its black population; only Philadelphia, New York, Chicago, and Brooklyn had more.[15] A majority of these blacks were single males. Over 70 percent of the 17,040 blacks in Pittsburgh were between the ages of eighteen and forty[16] when they came to find jobs in the rapidly expanding industries.[17] As of 1900, an additional 3,315 blacks lived in Allegheny, which was a separate city before its 1907 annexation.[18]

During the years Vann lived in North Carolina and Virginia there was strong northward movement from those states. Pittsburgh labor agents sought workers in cities like Richmond, using local men to recruit them. One regularly saw advertisements like "Colored Southern Help Furnished, Wm. Martin and Company, Richmond, Va."[19] From 1894 to 1904 approximately 30 percent of Pittsburgh's blacks had come originally from Virginia. Vann was undoubtedly aware of this emigration of blacks from the state and may have been influenced by it.[20]

The newly arrived blacks continued to settle mainly in the Hill District, in the Eighth and Thirteenth Wards (in 1905 these wards were redrawn as the Third and Fifth) around Wylie, Bedford, and Centre Avenues. The Hill District was a rough rectangle defined naturally by topography, with one of the short sides near the base of Pittsburgh's downtown area (the "Golden Triangle") and the other short side at the top of Herron Hill near the Pennsylvania Railroad tracks. It was bounded on the north by Bigelow Boulevard, which ran below a high cliff, on the south by Fifth Avenue, a main traffic artery and the low extremity of the hill, on the west by Tunnel Street, and on the east by Herron Avenue to Centre Avenue. Less than half the population of the Hill District was black, and some blacks lived in every city ward in 1900. The Seventh, Eighth, Eleventh, Thirteenth, Nineteenth, Twentieth, and Twenty-first housed at least a thousand each.[21] Blacks were thus not yet totally confined to a ghetto. They generally occupied a row of three to seven houses on a block where the rest of the houses were occupied by whites, mainly Jews and Italians.[22] In the Hill District the common bond of the residents, white and black, was poverty. As the whites became more prosperous they moved out. It gradually became common practice among white real estate and renting agents to shun Hill District house listings, and as the first decade of the twentieth century progressed, "Hill District" became synonymous with "black."[23] Even the Jewish people, who did "not seem to object to living near to them, sometimes in the same house," began moving farther out on Herron Hill and away from the district, to areas like Squirrel Hill.[24]

When Robert Vann arrived in Pittsburgh, despite a certain amount of recruitment of blacks for factory work, blacks were mainly employed in domestic or personal service: 58 percent of the men and 90 percent of the women were servants of some sort, maids, laundresses, coachmen, or janitors. A few blacks had "better" jobs as waiters or railway porters, and while some worked as elevator operators and shipping clerks in department stores, none were clerks waiting on customers.[25] One occupation monopolized by blacks was that of teamster, which required physical strength and little skill. More than half of the nine thousand teamsters who hauled sand wagons for municipal work on the streets were black.[26] For the few skilled black workmen—the stone masons, carpenters, and plasterers—employment was plentiful but nonunion; these black craftsmen worked longer hours for less money than their unionized white counterparts. Few blacks belonged to unions, although one small all-black union, the National Association of Afro-American Steam and Gas Engineers and Skilled Workers, was formed in June 1903.[27]

Despite the expansion of bituminous coal mining and steel manufacturing, blacks were employed only sparingly in both industries.

They were used primarily as strikebreaking "scabs," and they lost their jobs as soon as the strikes had ended.[28] Blacks believed they were justified in aiding management during strikes not only because they needed work of any sort, but because they were so discriminated against by the unions. For example, although the United Mine Workers theoretically accepted black members and even had a clause in its constitution fining any member $100 for refusing to work with a black, just 183 of the 3,350 employees in union mines were blacks.[29] Blacks were first employed as strikebreakers in the coal mines in 1880 and 1882. They were hired more extensively in 1892, after the formation of the United Mine Workers, when Henry Clay Frick brought black miners in from West Virginia, Virginia, Kentucky, Tennessee, and Alabama to break a strike at his Coal and Coke Company. Few blacks were permanently employed in the coal industry. By 1908, of an estimated twenty thousand workers in the mines, only 5 percent were black, and even in 1920 there were still fewer than three thousand black miners in all of Pennsylvania.[30]

Similarly, just a handful of blacks worked in the steel industry. The Black Diamond Mill on Thirtieth Street was one of the first plants to import black puddlers from Richmond, Virginia, to break a strike. Also in the 1870s blacks worked during a strike in the Moorhead Mill in Sharpsburg. Even more were employed during the notorious 1892 strikes at the Carnegie Mills in Homestead and at the Clark Mills.[31]

Unskilled labor at the turn of the century was so plentiful, mainly due to the large East European immigration, that blacks were not needed or wanted in the coal or steel industries. Immigrant labor still willingly accepted the low wages, twelve-hour workdays, seven-day weeks, the physical and nervous strain caused by speedup tactics used by foremen, and the spying of management in attempts to thwart unionism.[32] In 1907, of the seventy to eighty thousand steelworkers in Allegheny County, blacks were estimated to comprise only about 1 percent.[33] Even when unions were formed, blacks were not readily accepted. Though the Amalgamated Association of Iron, Steel and Tin Workers had been formed in 1876 and a few blacks were allowed to join, not until 1908 did the union formally vote to include them. But by that time the union was weak, and blacks still found themselves discriminated against by whites who refused to work with them in skilled positions.[34]

Some Pittsburgh blacks formed their own businesses; in the early years of the decade 1900–10, there were eighty-five black-run enterprises ranging from poolrooms to print shops which employed over five hundred people.[35] A very few blacks were quite successful, making a go of it without capital or any sort of business training. One black contractor employed 135 men regularly; another used 100 to 200 for asphalt paving and 30 for hauling. There was a prosperous catering business, Spriggs and Writt, and a successful wig maker. One exceptional black organized the Diamond Coke and Coal Company, which had 1,000 men on its employment roster. And by 1907 the city payroll included 127 blacks.[36] Only 1 percent of the city's black population was professional; in 1900 there were but 146 dentists, engineers, lawyers, physicians, and clergymen, the latter forming the largest group.[37]

A variety of religious and social institutions served the black community. Most dominant were the churches, which played a prominent role in black social and spiritual life. There were thirty to thirty-five Baptist churches, ten Methodist, and one each of Presbyterian, Episcopalian, Congregational, and Roman Catholic denominations.[38] Social clubs for blacks were numerous—about twenty-five for women alone and half-a-dozen for men, including Loendi, Elks, Masons, Odd Fellows, Knights of Pythias, and True Reformers. By 1900, blacks were building their own social welfare institutions in Pittsburgh. The Home for Aged and Infirm Colored Women, with twenty-one rooms, was erected that year at a cost of $42,500. There was also a Working Girls' Home that housed about fifteen to twenty girls per year and a Colored Orphans' Home in Allegheny.[39]

Thus, when Robert Vann came to live in Pittsburgh, he found a good-sized black community, flourishing despite its employment limitations as part of one of the nation's most rapidly growing cities. Of course, there was a dark side to this picture of industrial progress. As Lincoln Steffens put it so vividly, "[Pittsburgh] looked like hell, literally. Arriving of an evening I walked out aimlessly into the smoky gloom of its deep-dug streets and somehow got across a bridge up on a hill that overlooked the city with its fiery furnaces and the two rivers that pinched it in. The blast furnaces opened periodically and threw their volcanic light upon the cloud of mist and smoke above the town and gilded the silver rivers, which were high and threatening floods."[40] What had once been a dramatic and beautiful environment had been completely desecrated by burgeoning industry. All the land along the rivers was in use by commercial enterprises, most of which spewed smoke and dirt from their chimneys; the once-green hillsides rising steeply from the rivers were now filled with gray and grimy hovels.

While the humming machines of Pittsburgh turned out goods at a production rate never before equaled in history, the human aspects of life in the city went almost entirely neglected for the average worker. People were overworked to a degree that today seems superhuman; some men in the steel mills and railway switchyards labored twelve- or fourteen-hour shifts as many as seven days a week. Children as young as ten years old worked right along with their parents during long, arduous hours at the machines. Most of the wealth created by the booming mills of Pittsburgh went into the pockets of a few men. In the first years of this century, while the average laborer earned as little as $1.50 a day, thus bringing home only $400 or $500 in a year, Andrew Carnegie earned $23 million, which went untaxed.

Hazardous working conditions existed in the mills. Accidents were commonplace and compensation nonexistent.[41] One year 526 men were killed in work accidents. And the worker of 1900 had no recourse to unions to redress his grievances. The industries suppressed unionism, resorting to force when they deemed it necessary, as they had in the defeat of the striking Homestead steelworkers by violence and murder in 1892.

The average worker went home to an unpainted frame house crowded onto a steep hillside. Smoke begrimed the exterior; inside the rooms were small, poorly ventilated, and usually overcrowded. Indoor plumbing was rare.[42] The "Painter's Row" on the South Side of Pittsburgh, which belonged to the wealthy and powerful United States Steel Corporation, housed five hundred people in "back-to-back houses with no through ventilation, cellar kitchens, dark, unsanitary, ill-ventilated, overcrowded sleeping rooms, no drinking water supply on the premises and a dearth of sanitary accommodations that was shameful."[43] The hillsides were filled with coal-mining communities so defiled by pollution that not a blade of grass could survive, and garbage filled the gutters and gulleys. Disease was rampant. The Pittsburgh death rate from typhoid fever was the highest in the nation. Typhoid, along with respiratory diseases such as tuberculosis, bronchitis, and pneumonia, claimed nearly two thousand victims each year, and the infant mortality rate was extremely high.[44]

Living conditions for Pittsburgh's blacks were as poor as those for the white laborer and in many cases poorer. Most worked at menial, unskilled tasks, and very few could be called even "middle class" in any sense of the term. Blacks lived for the most part in totally inadequate housing. The homes in the Hill District had begun to deteriorate by 1885, when the Jews moved into the area. They had been built as one- or two-family residences, but the impoverished Jews could not afford the luxury of owning single homes, so they rented them and took in roomers to help pay the rent. The houses rapidly became overcrowded tenements.[45] By the time blacks inhabited the area extensively, the houses were even more crowded and rundown. Helen A. Tucker, a former teacher at Hampton Institute who surveyed Pittsburgh blacks in 1908, was appalled at what she found. "I think I never saw such wretched conditions," wrote Miss Tucker. "In some alleys there were stables next to the houses and while the odor was bad at any time, after a rain the stench from these and from the dirt in the streets was almost unendurable." She described the interiors of black homes as being in poor repair, with broken plumbing, torn wallpaper, and falling plaster, while the white landlords did nothing. She went on, "The houses I visited in Park Row were so dark that it was necessary to use a lamp even in midday."[46]

The black children growing up in these homes did poorly in school. An 1872 law required district school directors to set up separate facilities for blacks where twenty or more could be accommodated. This law was rescinded in 1881, but the separate and unequal pattern of schooling persisted. Schools blacks attended were inferior; the major one was in the damp, dark cellar of the AME Church on Wylie Avenue, and all were neglected and poorly staffed by comparison with white schools. Black children's attendance at school was irregular, and the inadequate nourishment they received at home made them inattentive. Most took two years longer than white students to finish the primary grades, and few went to high school. In 1906, only 40 of the 2,300 students in secondary schools in Pittsburgh were black, and a tiny number of these graduated.[47] There was an industrial school for blacks, the Avery College Trade School, established by the same white philanthropist who gave money for the scholarship Robert Vann held at Western University of Pennsylvania, but it did not live up to expectations. At least two-thirds of its student body had dropped out by the end of every year.[48]

Crime was common among the black populace. Black men without work or hope of finding it turned for income to bootlegging or selling cocaine. The women, for whom the only legitimate employment available was as household drudge, usually in distant prosperous neighborhoods, often became prostitutes instead. Many of the young blacks, to whom schools offered little and their overcrowded homes even less, spent their days in the poolrooms or saloons, with obvious consequences. There was not a single municipal playground in the Hill District where young people could congregate and exercise. One of the major forms of weekend entertainment in the area was watching the police raid speakeasies and brothels and carry off the malefactors in Black Marias.[49] Some children earned money by guarding the horse-drawn carriages of men who were patronizing the bawdyhouses. In 1906, of 1,124 cases before the Juvenile Court, 168 or 14.9 percent involved black children, although the city was only 3.5 percent black. Black adults constituted 14 percent of incarcerations, four times their proportion of the population. Cocaine was a serious problem; the warden of the Allegheny City jail said it was the single greatest cause of crime by black men and women.[50]

Whatever its faults, the city of Pittsburgh possessed a vitality and promise that Robert Vann must have felt as he stepped off the train in Union Station that day in 1903. It was quintessentially American in that period of rapid industrial development, alive with activity, a vast hodgepodge of penniless immigrants in search of a better life. The Irish had come, then the Italians, followed by people from all over Eastern Europe, bringing their hopes, languages, family possessions, and diverse religions, all to be added by turns to the boiling American cauldron. Many of these new Pittsburghers were frustrated and bitter, but many others were making their way, full of visions of progress and riches. Despite the pervasive dirt and smoke, the city's energy was almost palpable. Many of its residents felt a definite pride in the "Smoky City," and its champions vaunted, "A smoky Pittsburgh is a healthy Pittsburgh."

After he arrived in Pittsburgh, Robert Vann found a temporary room with a minister whose name a friend had given him. The following day he went to register at the Western University of Pennsylvania and have his Avery Scholarship verified. He also took an examination, the results of which qualified him to enter as a sophomore in the class of 1906.

The Western University of Pennsylvania was, like its city, expanding rapidly, and the growth of the two was closely related. The university reflected the city in many ways, placing great emphasis on technical, utilitarian education that would be useful in a highly industrialized region. By the turn of the century, engineering and science courses attracted the majority of students, and only small numbers were registered in the College of Literature and Arts.[51] Little attention was paid the liberal arts by either students or administration. As Samuel Black McCormick, who became chancellor in 1904, put it, "The University . . . aspires not to become a Harvard, a Princeton, or a Yale . . . but it aspires to become such a university as will understand the needs of its people [in its city] . . . it aspires to satisfy these needs."[52]

McCormick was also fond of saying, "The city itself cannot be big without a big university,"[53] and when talk began of Pittsburgh's annexing Allegheny City, he campaigned for "a greater University for a greater Pittsburgh."[54] The school that had begun as the tiny Pittsburgh Academy in 1787 when the city was a hamlet had by 1903 nearly one thousand students studying at locations scattered throughout Pittsburgh and Allegheny City in the Schools of Literature and Arts, Medicine, Law, Dental Surgery, Engineering, and Pharmacy, and the Observatory.[55] The university had begun to expand markedly in the decade preceding Robert Vann's arrival, paralleling the industrial growth of the city. In 1891–92, the Medical College was founded and a Department of Electrical Engineering added to the university; 1895 saw the establishment of the Schools of Law and Mines and Mining Engineering, the latter set up with a state appropriation of $50,000; in 1896 the Schools of Pharmacy and Dental Surgery were affiliated, and the university admitted women for the first time.

The year Vann enrolled at the Western University of Pennsylvania saw the inauguration of several projects to carry forward the school's expansion more extensively. In 1903 a serious campaign to raise endowment funds began, a "betterment committee" was formed to acquire a central site, and the Carnegie Technical Schools were built as a secondary system designed to feed greater numbers of science-oriented young men into further study at the university. When McCormick became chancellor the following year, he was successful in raising both interest in and funds for the university's growth, and the school obtained a forty-three-acre site known as Schenley Farms in Oakland where all the departments would be brought together on one campus. In 1908, the first cornerstone was laid, significantly enough, for the School of Mines. That same year the school's name was changed to the University of Pittsburgh, another step in the close spiritual alliance of town and gown.[56] Thus centralized and consolidated, the university continued to grow. By 1916, it would have more than four thousand students.

There were very few black faces on the various campuses of the university when Robert Vann arrived in 1903. There were in fact very few blacks in any institutions of higher education in Pennsylvania. A handful of blacks attended the University of Pennsylvania, Allegheny College at Meadville, Temple University, Dickinson College at Carlisle, and Jefferson College at Washington, but only a token number were at each school. There were a few institutions expressly for blacks—the Institute for Colored Youth in Chester County (now known as Cheyney College), Lincoln University at Oxford, the Avery College Trade School in Pittsburgh, Berean Manual Training and Industrial School in Philadelphia, and Downington Industrial School in Paoli.[57] Even Lincoln University, a high-grade liberal arts institution, offered manual training to equip the students for a trade, or else a "higher Christian Education" that trained blacks for the ministry or teaching in church-affiliated schools.[58] A black student like Robert Vann in search of a liberal college education was an anomaly.

Vann was such a rarity that when he enrolled the registrar, noting his light color, straight hair, and slim nose, suggested that he register as an Indian instead of a black to ease the years ahead. Vann refused, insisting he be classified as black.[59] It was an act of affirmation at a time when conditions were so difficult for blacks that the temptation to disappear over the color line must have been great. This was the second time Vann had resisted that temptation. In 1901, when he was at Virginia Union, his close friend Jim Rooks decided to cross the color line and urged Vann to come with him. "You look like a born Indian," he told Vann, "and Indians have more chances." "But they are on reservations, we are not," Vann retorted and declined to go with Rooks. Rooks later vanished into the white world and never again communicated with his friend, though Vann heard a rumor that he had become a dentist in Detroit.[60]

The fall of 1903 passed pleasantly for Robert Vann. He located more permanent lodgings with Mr. and Mrs. T. Mason Moore on Sandusky Street in Allegheny City, across the river from Pittsburgh. Vann rented a good-sized second-floor room overlooking the quiet, cobblestone street and began a close relationship with his friendly landlords. Mr. Moore was a genial, garrulous Civil War veteran and a prominent member of his church, where he functioned variously as Sunday school teacher, organist, church trustee, and choir director.

An employee of the Pittsburgh Academy, Moore was well liked and known for his many kindnesses. The quiet and dignified Mrs. Moore reminded Vann of his mother. The Moores were "OPs," or "Old Pittsburghers," members of the local black elite comprised of early settlers who were prosperous enough to support a middle-class life style. One observer called them "a little black aristocracy." This group was centered in Allegheny City and looked with slight disfavor on the "outlander" blacks moving in across the river around Wylie Avenue.[61] They were resentful because the influx of the rawer Southern blacks led to a loss of status for all blacks, including the "OPs," in the eyes of whites. The "OPs" believed the black immigrants were uncouth, set bad examples, overcrowded the areas where they settled, brought in totally unskilled labor, and forced the black community inward upon itself.[62]

The Moores introduced Vann to the genteel social life of local middle-class blacks, including the Pulpresses, Hances, Taliaferros, and Stewarts. Though not religious in the spiritual sense, Vann attended services and Sunday night socials at the Brown Chapel of the African Methodist Episcopal Church (one of the two most prominent black churches in the city, the other being the Bethel AME Church), where he once delivered a speech on education. Vann also joined literary gatherings at the newly formed Loendi Club in Pittsburgh. Loendi, named after a lake in Africa, was quickly becoming *the* club of local blacks, a place where one could dine and play billiards with other "gentlemen." His attendance there shows that Vann was quickly accepted as a candidate for the black social elite.[63] On a superficial level, Vann made friends easily, being good-natured and an able raconteur. It was more difficult to know him intimately, and he remained an enigma even to most of those close to him throughout his life. Vann's underlying seriousness and ambition pierced the cheerful surface from time to time, impressing people that he was a young man from whom more would be heard.

As always, Vann needed work to keep himself fed and clothed. Shortly after classes started, he found a job waiting on tables at a boarding house for whites on Stockton Avenue, facing Allegheny's South Park. There he served two meals a day to the twenty boarders and received his own food in exchange.[64]

That winter a note came from his stepfather that Vann's mother was seriously ill. He hastily packed a bag and spent some of his precious dollars on a railway ticket. The train trip to Cofield was long and arduous, and when he finally reached the farm at Red Hill, Vann was exhausted as well as worried. It was obvious that Lucy Peoples Simon was critically ill. After several days at her bedside, longer than he had intended to stay, Robert had to return to Pittsburgh. He did so with the gravest misgivings, fearful that he might not see her again.

Even before he got off the train in Pittsburgh, Vann felt ill and realized he had returned with an unwelcome souvenir of his trip to Red Hill, either pneumonia or a recurrence of malaria. His illness was predictable, given the strenuous schedule which allowed him little time for proper eating and sleeping, and caused him to suffer from chronic exhaustion; the stress of his mother's illness was probably the precipitating factor. By the time Vann reached the Moore's doorstep he was feverish and shivering badly. Once inside the house, he collapsed. Vann remained in bed, ill and often delirious, until the beginning of spring, 1904.[65] When he finally left his sickbed, thin and weak, he found a letter from a neighbor saying that Lucy Simon had died two weeks before.

It was a terrible blow to the young man. He had cared for his mother a great deal and was now utterly alone. He had no siblings; his father had never reappeared; and Vann would never be reconciled with his stepfather. His legacy was just the gold watch his mother had given him for graduation from Waters Training School and a determination to succeed. Not until years later would he even be able to afford a simple gray granite stone for Lucy's grave among the pine trees and honeysuckle on the property at Red Hill. This stone, which Vann placed on his mother's grave in 1934, read, "Lucy Vann, died 1904, erected by her son Robert L. Vann."[66] In death he gave her the name Vann, which she had never used, as if to achieve some final respectability for them both.

After the long spring of grieving and convalesence, Vann was badly in need of a change. He went to Bar Harbor, Maine, for the summer to wait on tables at one of the resorts. In the clear Maine air his spirits revived and his health returned in full. While he was there, Booker T. Washington came to speak at a fund-raising event for Tuskegee Institute. Vann passed around programs and collection plates and presumably was inspired by hearing the Tuskegeean's recollections that he had also once been a waiter at just such a resort in Saratoga, New York.[67] Vann also made friends at Bar Harbor with Walter Buchanan of Georgia, who years later gave Vann badly needed financial help for his magazine, *The Competitor.*

In the fall Vann was feeling so hale that when he returned to the university, he tried out for the football team.[68] This attempt was surely based more on his enthusiasm for the sport than on any realistic appraisal of his physical prowess, for he was only 5'8" tall and weighed about 140 pounds. Not unexpectedly, the coach pronounced him too small or, as Vann told a friend, " 'too light' for the team, which probably meant 'too dark.' "[69] The football team apparently did not suffer from Vann's absence. They rolled up a 10-0-0 record that fall. Unwilling to be completely thwarted, Vann found another way to appear on the football field those Saturday afternoons: he hastily learned to play the bass drum and joined the school marching band.[70] Vann was ever after an ardent spectator at almost any kind of athletic event.

By his senior year it was apparent that, as at Virginia Union, Robert Vann would be remembered more for his extracurricular activities than for his scholarly achievements. Once again the appeal of the limelight lured him from his desk. He became proficient in debating, oratory, and newspaper writing. In the spring of 1906 he was a member of the winning team in the annual Tri-State Debating League competition,[71] and he captured second prize in the Senior Oratorical Contest for his speech, "The Heavy Belgian Hand—Wrath That Makes for Praise," which denounced Belgian imperialism in the Congo.[72] The award amounted to twenty dollars; when Vann opened the prize envelope, he wryly recalled later, he found a receipt for the money in partial payment for the tuition he owed.

For two years he was a regular contributor to *The Courant, A Journal of the Student Body of Western University of Pennsylvania,* and in his senior year, Vann was selected as its editor-in-chief, the first black in the school's history to be so honored. One of the students on the journal's executive board objected to Vann's election, saying it would cause a furor on the board of trustees of the university and in the city. A white classmate of Vann's, Arthur Calhoun, retorted that most of the board of trustees "would not care in the least and that most of the people of Pittsburgh did not even know there was a University in their midst."[73] The others concurred, and Vann ran *The Courant,* a journal of short stories, humor, sports news, and gossip, all year without incident. Calhoun recalled this as one of the few instances he was aware of during Vann's undergraduate years in which Vann's race became an issue.

In February 1906, during his last year as an undergraduate, Robert Vann made his first sally into the fray of party politics. When he had first arrived in Pittsburgh three years before he had registered to vote as soon as he fulfilled the residency requirement. In the South, of course, that right had been denied him. For three years he voted and followed the political news, and by 1906 he decided to get personally involved.

It was a tumultuous year in local politics. William Magee, nephew and political heir of the powerful Christopher Lyman Magee, and William Flinn were the current rulers of the local Republican party. For years, the Magee-Flinn coalition had run the party with an iron hand in the best tradition of bossism. Pittsburgh had been a Republican overlordship since 1865, and the local Democrats were few in number and very weak. But in 1906 a group of rebellious Republicans led by Thomas S. Bigelow, an arch rival of the Magee-Flinn faction, defected and joined with the Democrats to put up a reform candidate for mayor, George W. Guthrie.

Vann, a loyal Republican, worked hard for the Magee-Flinn candidate, A. M. Jenkinson. He attended party meetings, marched in torchlight parades, and went to the political rallies held around roaring street bonfires in the neighborhoods. On election day Vann worked at the polls. The election results surprised everyone. Guthrie narrowly defeated Jenkinson 32,404 to 30,163, and the Republicans were temporarily ousted from their stronghold in Pittsburgh.

Vann was as fascinated by the byzantine workings of Pittsburgh party politics as he had been by campus electioneering. In college he was primarily an onlooker. Now, entertaining the idea of settling in Pittsburgh, where Republicans were dominant and the number of blacks was increasing each day, Vann realized a black Republican like himself might have a future on the political scene, though he did not become seriously involved in politics until some years later.

At his graduation in 1906, Robert Vann recited the class poem he had written. As in his valedictory address at Waters years before, he evoked the image of life as a sea voyage fraught with obstacles which must be met and overcome for the voyage to have any worth. Success in the face of adversity proved one's mettle:

> "The world can never know," said the Muse with a sigh,
> Whether life will be stormy or whether clear sky,
> One thing is promised, some storm will arise.

> That's just what you want; there's offered no prize
> For the ship that can cross when there is no blast.
> Build her bow strong, her starboard and mast,
> The stern and the keel and the rigging the same;
> Only storm-tossed vessels are worthy of name.[74]

Vann had already weathered a good many storms. Despite his age, almost twenty-seven, his poverty, and his blackness, he had managed to earn a bachelor's degree. That was an extraordinary feat, for between 1823 and 1909, only 693 blacks graduated from white colleges in America.[75] An average of just one black every two years graduated from the Western University of Pennsylvania from 1890 to 1909.[76]

Vann was intrigued by journalism as a result of his year as editor of *The Courant* and the time he had spent around the *Richmond Planet*, where he first encountered the "smell of printer's ink."[77] Urged on by his friend Max Barber from Virginia Union, who was now in Chicago working for *The Voice of the Negro*, Vann wanted to go on to the Pulitzer School of Journalism in New York. "But somebody said something about money and I retired with the idea in the back of my head," he told H. L. Mencken years later.[78] He chose instead to stay in Pittsburgh at the School of Law and thus became the only black in the school at the time and the first ever to take both the undergraduate and law courses at the university.

Vann helped finance his law education in a way that demonstrated both his capacity for a rigorous routine and his ingenious ability to use available opportunities. The law school classes met from three to six in the afternoon in the old Pittsburgh Academy building at Ross and Diamond Streets in downtown Pittsburgh. As soon as classes were over, Vann would rush out of the building and hurry the several blocks to Union Station. There he boarded the Pittsburgh and Lake Erie Railroad evening train to Connellsville, donning a waiter's jacket to serve dinner in the dining car. When the train reached Connellsville Vann stayed for the night and did his studying there. In the morning he again boarded the dining car and served breakfast into Pittsburgh, reaching the law school in plenty of time for his classes.[79]

Vann aroused the interest of his fellow students and law professors alike, not only because of his blackness but also because of the novelty of his job as a dining car porter and his amazing capacity for hard work. His teachers began to take a proprietary interest in the diligent young man. Elder Marshall, who instructed him in Blackstone, contracts, and domestic relations, said that "the professors were delighted that he had the necessary ambition to study law and become a lawyer, rather than continue in the dining car service."⁸⁰ The law school transcripts indicate that Vann was a shade below average in class standing, perhaps in the third quartile. Considering his background and burdensome work schedule, however, that record was quite an achievement. For example, in his senior year he took eight courses per semester. According to one source, even if each class had not been demanding, just switching academically from one subject to another had to be complex and burdensome.⁸¹

During his second year in law school Vann made use of the rudimentary political connections he had formed during the mayoralty election. A friend, M. T. Velar, an "Old Pittsburgher" who was president of the Allegheny Colored Protective League, used his influence with the dispensers of Republican patronage to secure a clerkship for Vann in the mercantile appraiser's office.⁸² This made him one of just a handful of blacks on the city payroll in a white-collar job.⁸³ He happily relinquished his demanding waiter's job on the Pittsburgh and Lake Erie Railroad for the amenities of an office position.

When his last year of law school began in the fall of 1908, Robert Vann was still a bachelor, and an eligible one, his down-home romance with Mattie Chavis having long since ended. Slim, well-dressed, handsome, and on the threshold of a promising career, he was undoubtedly a welcome sight at any respectable young black woman's door. In October, Vann was introduced to Jesse Ellen Matthews at a dance on Pittsburgh's South Side. Jesse Matthews was nineteen at the time, shy, pretty, and light-skinned. She had been born in a suburb of Gettysburg, the youngest of five children of Mary Jane and William H. Matthews.⁸⁴ Her father was a Civil War veteran who had run away from home in 1864 at the age of thirteen and enlisted in the Union Army. In 1869 he had married Mary Jane Crampton; Jesse, their last child, was born in 1889.

Her parents both died when she was very young, and Jesse was shuttled back and forth from uncle to uncle, none of whom treated her very kindly, while her court-appointed guardian misspent the Matthews children's only legacy, their father's Civil War pension. Jesse finally went to live with her oldest brother, Louis, in Harrisburg, and attended high school there, graduating in 1904 with a five-dollar gold piece for the highest scholastic average of all blacks in the Harrisburg high school system. After graduation, Jesse taught in a private black kindergarten in Harrisburg for a while and then worked in a restaurant in Gettysburg. Just a month before she met Vann, Jesse had come to Pittsburgh to live with Mrs. Louisa Washington, a sister of her Uncle Joseph's wife. Shortly after she and Vann met, he suggested that Jesse live at the home of Mr. and Mrs. William Page, to see how a genuinely warm family lived. Jesse had been shunted from one place to another for too long. While living with the Pages, Jesse developed a great affection for young Mabel Page, their daughter, and after the death of Mabel's parents, Jesse looked after her as though Mabel were her own daughter. In fact, Mabel lived at the Vann home for some time.

Vann pursued Jesse Matthews with characteristic persistence, in the proper, middle-class context of parlor conversations and evening walks. Their common experiences immediately formed a bond between them, and they talked of their similarly impoverished and periodically difficult childhoods, their wrenching lack of close family, and their wish to achieve, which had motivated Jesse to scholastic excellence in high school and was now impelling Robert through law school. Within a short time Vann told Jesse, in his straightforward manner, "My intentions are serious. If you are not, let me know. I don't want to waste your time and I have no time to waste."[85] Jesse was taken aback by the abruptness and businesslike quality of the proposal, but she recovered quickly. They soon agreed they would plan to marry early in 1910, after Vann presumably would have passed his bar examination.

In the spring of 1909, Vann did a rather surprising thing, considering his own scrupulous refusal to "pass" on various occasions. Jesse was having difficulty finding a job other than menial domestic work. She was also extremely light-skinned and looked even more Caucasian than Vann. So he sought out a man named Einstein "who owed him a favor" and asked him for work "for a friend." Einstein wrote a note to the proprietor of a local department store, Solomon and Bibrow, recommending that "the friend" be hired as a salesclerk. At the bottom of the recommendation, however, he wrote something in Hebrew. Vann, not sure that Einstein was sincere in his promise, erased that part of the letter before he gave it to Jesse to present to the prospective employer. Jesse took the note in and got the job, passing as white. But she was miserable while working there, plagued by guilt and fearful she would be found out. She worried and lost weight. Before much time had passed they both agreed she should quit the job. Jesse did so immediately, with a great sense of relief.[86]

Vann finished his law school courses in June 1909 and began preparing for his bar examinations. He was determined to pass. He sent Jesse off to Gettysburg so he would not be distracted, telling her bluntly, "Courting and studying do not mix." Vann then spent from July until December studying for the examination during all his spare time, while he worked each day in the mercantile appraiser's office.

Robert L. Vann, Western University of Pennsylvania Law School, class of 1910.

All Vann's close attention to his law books proved valuable; on December 18, 1909, he sent Jesse a two-word telegram: "Passed O.K." He subsequently graduated with the class of 1909.[87]

Vann immediately rented a small office in a building whose owner was willing to have black tenants, bought some secondhand furniture on credit, and prepared to receive his first clients. The office was at 433 Fifth Avenue, on a major, predominantly white, business thoroughfare. Optimistic about the future, Robert and Jesse set their wedding date for February 16, 1910. That evening, shortly before the scheduled ceremony, a client in search of legal advice during a night hearing appeared unexpectedly. Vann was in a dilemma, for clients were still very scarce, and he had barely a penny to his name. "Shall I let the case go or make the fee and pay the preacher?" he asked Jesse. She agreed it was worth postponing the wedding for a day, and Vann rushed back to his office. The following evening they were married without interference at the home of their close friends, Mr. and Mrs. William Page.[88]

Vann was one of just five black attorneys in Pittsburgh, a city with more than twenty-five thousand blacks in 1910. A black named Vashon from a prominent "Old Pittsburgh" family had applied to practice law in the city in the 1880s but was denied a license, so he went on to Washington, D.C. In 1891 two blacks were admitted to the local bar, William M. Randolph and J. Welfred Holmes. By 1910 they had been joined by William H. Stanton, "Captain" Frank R. Stewart, and George White, Jr. The ratio of just one black attorney for approximately every five thousand blacks remained constant for some years; in 1920 there were eight serving the legal needs of thirty-eight thousand people.[89]

Vann found clients very slow in coming, because the average black who migrated from the South to Pittsburgh remembered the great handicap lawyers of his race suffered there, because of discriminatory courts and inequitable law and custom. He therefore thought twice before hiring a black attorney. Further, black lawyers were less apt to have adequate schooling or the law library needed for researching intricate cases. Most blacks could barely afford a lawyer's fee, and if they had to pay a sizable amount of hard-earned money, they preferred to have a white attorney who, because of the inherent advantage of color, stood a better chance of winning their cases than a fellow black. The black lawyer almost inevitably encountered prejudice on the part of white judges and juries, even in the North.[90]

Robert Vann had early decided to be a criminal lawyer. He particularly enjoyed that part of his law studies and spent the requisite clerking time as a law student in the office of William H. Stanton, a black attorney on Fifth Avenue who specialized in various types of criminal law, particularly murder cases.[91] Vann once remarked to his friend Arthur Calhoun sardonically, "I might as well go into criminal law, since all of my people are criminals."[92] He believed that the average black person, poor and discriminated against both *de facto* and *de jure*, would have recourse to the law or have need of a lawyer only in a serious criminal case. Because he would be operating solely within the confines of the black community, Vann felt it was hopeless and unprofitable to work in any other branch of the law but the one where blacks were apt to seek out legal advice.

But Robert Vann's actual practice of criminal law fell far short of his expectations. He had a few major cases and was proud of his career record at murder trials, but almost none of the men Vann defended was accused of first-degree murder, for most blacks accused of so grave a crime sought out white attorneys. Except for a few second-degree murder and manslaughter cases, Vann had to content himself with mundane, uncontroversial legal problems involving property claims, deeds, and wills—cases which were not likely to come before a white judge and jury and for which he earned small fees.[93] Because of this, like most black attorneys,[94] Vann would soon seek out ways to supplement his income, turning to the newspaper business and politics.[95]

· 3 ·

Birth of the COURIER

ONE DAY early in March 1910, while patches of grimy snow still covered the less-traveled streets of the city, Robert Vann found a group of acquaintances on the doorstep of his law office. They had come to ask him to draw up incorporation papers for a new weekly newspaper, the *Pittsburgh Courier*. Vann was pleased to see them, not only as an addition to his still meager roster of clients, but because he had been interested in the project ever since its first abortive beginnings in 1907.

The *Courier*, which Vann referred to jocularly as a "two-page sheet initiated by a Negro in a pickle factory,"[1] had been the brainchild of Edwin Nathaniel Harleston, a big, broad-shouldered man with graying hair who worked as a guard at the H. J. Heinz food-packing plant. Harleston's job was ideally suited to his avocation, poetry, for it provided him with long, solitary hours in which to refine his ideas and polish his phrases. Harleston had a volume of his poems privately published as *A Toiler's Life*, and in 1907 he decided to put out a weekly newspaper. Harleston was "editor, reporter, treasurer, business manager and a complete newspaper company all in one."[2] At first the paper functioned mostly as a literary sheet, an outlet for Harleston's personal writings. He generally printed about ten copies at his own expense and sold them himself for five cents a copy; only rarely did he sell them all.[3]

Late in 1909, Harleston decided to make his venture more businesslike and began to look for financial backers. Harleston knew Vann from social encounters in Allegheny City, where they had discovered their mutual interest in poetry, and he probably approached him at this time. Vann would undoubtedly have been interested in investing, but he had a wife and office rent and no assurance that he would be able to afford either. So Harleston went to two fellow employees at H. J. Heinz, Edward Penman and Hepburn Carter. Penman and Carter had no money to put up, but they agreed to help run the business side of the paper, along with Scott Wood, Jr., and Harvey Tanner. Harleston had to provide the financial backing from his own savings. The name *Courier* was chosen for the newspaper, probably because of Harleston's admiration for his hometown newspaper, the *Charleston* (S.C.) *News and Courier*.[4]

Penman and Carter arranged to have the first issue of the *Courier* printed in Philadelphia, and Harleston prepared the copy at his home. The first run of five hundred copies reached Pittsburgh on Saturday, January 15, 1910. The *Courier* consisted of four pages, two of which were "boilerplate," syndicated material supplied in plate form, undoubtedly "borrowed" without payment to the original contributors. The other two pages were devoted to articles of local interest. Despite a heavy snowfall that day, the partners managed to sell most of their copies by hawking them door to door in stores, barbershops, and saloons throughout the Hill District. The *Courier* was launched.[5]

The next twelve issues of the *Courier* appeared on time each Saturday, often with articles or poems written by Robert L. Vann at Harleston's urging,[6] and each week a few more copies were sold. By March, however, Harleston's savings began to run out, even though the printing contract had been given to the Union News Company in Pittsburgh in an effort to save money on transportation. More funds were needed badly.

Harleston, undoubtedly with Vann's help, found four new backers for his struggling paper. The group that gathered in Vann's office that dreary March day included Samuel Rosemond, who worked in the Pittsburgh Post Office; William N. Page, a secretary to an officer of the Carnegie Steel Corporation and the man at whose home Vann had been married; Cumberland Posey, Sr., a master of transportation for the Diamond Coke and Coal Company who worked aboard ships on the Monongahela River that he himself built and owned; and William N. Hance, a well-to-do man who owned a good deal of property on the South Side.[7] Since it was obvious to the original *Courier* personnel that they would never have any money to put into the enterprise and that funds were what the fledgling newspaper needed most, Penman, Wood, Tanner, and Carter withdrew. Rosemond, Page, Posey, and Hance each agreed to make a modest investment and became the new officers of the *Courier*.

The paper was formally incorporated on May 10, 1910, with Vann acting as its counsel. He had been chosen as the paper's lawyer because he was Harleston's friend and, since he was the most recent addition to Pittsburgh's tiny corps of black lawyers, his services came the most cheaply. Since the *Courier* officers had no extra cash to pay Vann, he was given ten shares of stock valued at five dollars each in lieu of a fee.[8]

In the few months following, Vann devoted little time to his role as corporation counsel; the paper had small need of his services. Billed as "Pittsburgh's Only Colored Newspaper," the *Courier* continued to appear each Saturday, now in an eight-page format, with miscellaneous news about blacks in Pittsburgh and in black areas within thirty miles of the city. Members of the staff began to mail free copies to friends in other parts of the country, and the *Courier* advertised itself as a newspaper with a national circulation—a deception, but an enterprising one. Fewer than three thousand copies of the *Courier* were actually sold each week, mostly by staff members who peddled the papers on the streets and in various places of business.[9] Before long the masthead stated, "This Paper Is Read By 10,000 Colored People Weekly," which was, as it turns out, a fairly accurate assessment, since every person who purchased a copy subsequently passed it on to three or four others to read gratis.[10]

The *Courier*'s problem of too-slowly mounting sales was common to all black newspapers of that era. Though hundreds of black newspapers were started in the United States between 1880 and 1914, most of them were short-lived, one-man projects.[11] Unable to compete with the white dailies, they procured little advertising and had few regular subscribers. There was a high rate of illiteracy among potential black readers, and many who could read were too poor to spend money on an inessential item like a newspaper. Many middle-class blacks considered black newspapers too amateurish to deserve their attention. As one journalist of the time said, "There was a class of Negroes who were proud to say that they never read a Negro newspaper. They thought such newspapers were beneath them, that they were too intelligent and classy to be caught with such a publication around their house. . . . They used to think they could show their intelligence by *not* reading Negro newspapers."[12] And in fact the papers were not very good, usually consisting of four pages of old news cut from other publications.

The first decade of the 1900s was particularly difficult, even for established black weeklies. William Monroe Trotter was trying to keep his *Boston Guardian* alive; Robert Abbott was hand-peddling his *Chicago Defender;* James H. Anderson's *Amsterdam News* in New York was doing poorly; and in Philadelphia and Baltimore the *Tribune* and *Afro-American* were in trouble while their owners tried to update them. Even T. Thomas Fortune's influential *New York Age* was always in serious financial straits.[13]

Pennsylvania's first black weekly had been started in 1838 by William Whipper, a wealthy Philadelphia black who had previously formed a literary society for the purpose of educating blacks and developing antislavery sentiment.[14] By 1908 there had been at least fifty such journalistic attempts in the state, most of which rapidly went under because of inadequate financing. One of Pittsburgh's first weeklies was *Mystery*, edited by Martin Delany in 1843, and there had been a dozen since then, including the Baptist *Pioneer* and the weekly *Progressive Afro-American,* but none lasted even five years.[15] Black daily papers fared even worse than the weeklies; the *Philadelphia Tribune*, which had been publishing since 1884, tried to publish daily in 1907 and quickly returned to its previous format as a weekly. A similar attempt by the *Chicago Defender* in 1905 met the same fate. When Edwin Harleston began his first paper in 1907, there were twelve black weekly newspapers in the state, most of them in Philadelphia. Although there were at least two hundred thousand blacks in Pennsylvania by then, with an illiteracy rate lower than that of blacks in the rest of the nation, the black newspapers had a combined circulation of under twenty-five thousand. These papers concentrated mostly on church, secret society, and social news, paying little attention to business and politics. Polemics were almost nonexistent.[16]

Pittsburgh's black community, which numbered twenty-five thousand by 1910, had a real need for its own newspaper.[17] Of the six white newspapers, only the *Pittsburgh Press* had ever carried any black news regularly, and its Jim-Crowed "Afro-American News" column was discontinued in 1914.[18] When news of blacks did find its way into the Pittsburgh newspapers, it consisted mainly of sensational criminal cases or other lurid details of black life.[19]

But the fledgling *Courier* was having serious intramural problems in addition to feebly growing sales. Edwin Harleston, the editor, was battling with the board of directors. When the paper had been incorporated in May, Harleston felt that as the paper's founder he should have been given most of the stock. But his money was gone by that time, and the other directors insisted that all who received stock would have to pay for it in some way, with cash or work. Thus, Harleston had no equity in the paper and resented the fact bitterly. Also, Harleston was an idealist who viewed his editorial role romantically; he was bound to clash with the profit-minded businessmen on the board, and he did, all through that summer. Vann tried to mediate, but it was hopeless. In the fall, Edwin Harleston quit in anger and disappointment, leaving the *Courier* without an editor.[20]

The remaining partners decided to offer the editorship to Robert Vann, who was then the treasurer. He seemed a logical choice for many reasons. They all knew of Vann's editorship of *The Courant*

Robert L. Vann as a young attorney, about 1910.

at the Western University of Pennsylvania, and he had been contributing regularly to the *Courier* since its inception. And because of his college degree and his position as a lawyer, Vann was so exceptional in the eyes of the black community that he was a highly desirable figure to have at the head of a newspaper.

Vann accepted the offer, undoubtedly motivated more by his passion for journalism than by his pursuit of prosperity; though the editorship would consume a good deal of Vann's time it paid him very little. With so little money in the *Courier* treasury for salaries, Vann received just $100 a year, and even that was in *Courier* stock.[21] Nonetheless Vann plunged with gusto into his new role as editor, treasurer, and legal counsel for the *Courier*. He held these positions until his death some thirty years later.

Although being editor of the *Courier* paid very little, it indirectly contributed to Vann's growing law practice. His successful trial cases were covered on the front page of the *Courier*. As his legal prowess became known to the black community, more of them turned to the dapper young lawyer. The judges became familiar with his name and began to appoint Vann as defense counsel in murder cases, which gave Vann further publicity.

The process by which Vann's legal career was aggrandized through the *Courier* began with the case of a black man, Thomas Cass, alias Cash. While in jail in New York, Cash allegedly told a fellow prisoner he had killed a white Pennsylvania miner fourteen years earlier in an argument over a crap game. In 1911, Cash was brought to Pittsburgh with much fanfare to stand trial for murder, and Vann was chosen to defend him. Vann built a defense around the fact that the man being tried had been working in Virginia at the time of the murder. Vann was convincing; and despite the efforts of the two prosecuting district attorneys, the jury was out only eight minutes before acquitting Cash. "ATTORNEY VANN TRIUMPHS AND T. CASH IS FREE," trumpeted the headline of a front-page *Courier* article which devoted as much linage to Vann as to his client:

> Once more the Negro Attorney demonstrated his ability at the local bar. Attorney Robt. L. Vann, who was appointed by the court to defend the famous Tom Cash, more than triumphed over the two district attorneys who handled the case for the Commonwealth.
> The plea made to the jury was styled as one of the most eloquent ever delivered in the local courts.

> The jury remained out but eight minutes, when they returned with a verdict of "not guilty." When the verdict was announced the spectators in the court actually "yelled out" as evidence of the wonderful triumph.
>
> When the confusion was cleared, the defendant was taken out upon the shoulders of his friends, who had been brought by Attorney Vann from as far as Morrison, Va. The loyalty of his friends was remarkable. Seldom have Negroes been seen to rally to the aid of their own as they did in the Cash case. Attorney Vann says it is evidence of an increasing harmony among the race.
>
> As soon as the prisoner was discharged by the court he was taken out and provided with an overcoat, purchased by his attorney, and furnished comfortable quarters at one of the local hotels.
>
> On the following day Attorney Vann took his client to the train and bade him farewell.[22]

Within a month after the Cash trial, the court appointed Vann to defend another black charged with murder. This time it was Marion White, charged with stabbing his common-law wife. Vann tried to persuade the court that the stabbing was accidental and pleaded for leniency, and his client was sentenced to just eight years. Such cases were occasionally reported in the white press as well as on the *Courier*'s front page, and with each acquittal or light sentence, Vann's reputation as a shrewd lawyer and fluent racial defender grew.

Many of Vann's successes were possible because the average white judge did not regard a crime committed by a black against a black as particularly serious and thus was apt to let the defendant in such a case off with a relatively light sentence. Other successes of Vann's, however, were directly attributable to his prowess as an attorney. He was poised, articulate, and above all able at trial. His basic asset was his legal competence, but his immaculate grooming contributed to the good impression he made on the court: Vann once remarked to his wife, "I dress each day so that if I meet the President of the United States I will not be embarrassed."[23]

The *Courier*'s coverage of Robert Vann extended beyond his legal pursuits. The paper reported all of his public activities and thus enhanced his prominence in the black community. As Vann began to accept speaking engagements, the paper announced them beforehand, usually in the "Local News" section, and later reported the speeches in detail. Readers were informed that Vann addressed the

Colored Chauffeurs of the East End on the opportunities for blacks as chauffeurs when they met to promote their trade and organize their ranks;[24] that Vann defined "What Progressivism Means to the Negro" for the Bethel AME Church's Sunday afternoon gathering in Greensburg, Pennsylvania;[25] and that Vann was to deliver the Emancipation Proclamation Celebration Speech at East Liverpool, Ohio, on January 1, 1913.[26] Vann also acted as chairman of a $30,000 fund-raising drive to build a new YMCA branch on Centre Avenue and presided over a mass meeting at the Lyceum Theater for that purpose.[27]

The *Courier* continued to struggle. The staff of four, in addition to Vann, included a secretary, a reporter, a sports editor, and an errand boy who doubled as proofreader and mailing clerk.[28] The *Courier* office consisted of a spare room above Jackson's Funeral Parlor at 1212 Wylie Avenue, "mainly because it was obtained at low cost and most important, it was in the center of Pittsburgh's black belt."[29] The staff managed to put a paper together each week in an office furnished with one typewriter, a secondhand desk, and two hard chairs.

White newsstands refused to carry the *Courier*, so the paper continued to suffer from inadequate distribution. *Courier* agents tended to be migratory and erratic, usually indigent high school students or intensely race-conscious elderly black men.[30] To inform its readers of outlets where copies of the *Courier* could be located, the paper was forced to announce in the "Local News" section that, for example, "the *Courier* can be purchased from Miss Ethel Rice, daughter of A. B. Rice, 5211 Broad Avenue, East End,"[31] or "the *Courier* is now on sale at the Liberty Pharmacy, East End City. News items left there before Wednesday noon of each week will be telephoned into the main office for the current issue."[32] It was a makeshift method of distributing and gathering news.

Finances were always a critical problem. The cost of printing the *Courier* amounted to a staggering one-third of all expenses, so the paper needed capital desperately. But the stock sold poorly, and advertising was not forthcoming in any significant quantity. The *Courier* policy on advertising was as follows: "News, interesting to the public, will be furnished free if void of advertising matter. Local advertisements, one cent per word. . . . High class advertisements accepted at reasonable rates upon application." Unfortunately for the *Courier*'s solvency, most of the advertisements it received were of the local variety, at a penny a word, and rarely exceeded fifty words. The advertisers were usually from the Hill District around Wylie Avenue—merchants, druggists, funeral parlors, realty companies, express movers, and tailors. A sampling from one issue showed such local entrepreneurs plying their wares as D. Robert Lewis, Real Estate and Insurance, 1317 Wylie Avenue; A. G. Boykin, Express Moving and Hauling, 2709 Wylie Avenue; Thompson's Grocery Store, 2635 Wylie Avenue; Ward's Billiard Parlor, corner of Wylie and Logan; John M. Potter, Apothecary, 2639 Wylie Avenue; and Jackson Funeral Director, 1209 Wylie Avenue.[33] A careful count of the advertising wordage shows that the *Courier*'s revenue from this important source was a paltry $14.75 per week.

The "high class advertising" the *Courier* sought was larger advertisements embellished with illustrations or photographs, for which the newspaper could charge a higher rate, rather than "high class" as reflected in the elegance or deluxe quality of the goods advertised. Though the *Courier* received an occasional advertisement for a place like the Hotel Ridley in Atlantic City, New Jersey, its "high class advertising" consisted for the most part of pitches for mail-order goods like "The Original Poro Hair Grower," "Herolin, Pomade Hair Dressing," "St. Joseph's Liver Regulator," "Odell's Warrior, Kills Bed Bugs, Moths and Roaches," or "Knoxit Prophylactic, The Handy Prophylactic Kit for Men."[34] There were also advertisements for good-luck charms, clairvoyants, and religious articles. The lack of buying power of the black community was clearly reflected in advertisements for such inexpensive goods. The *Courier* could not attract large advertisements for products like automobiles, for the manufacturers were aware that few blacks could purchase such a luxury item. Though Vann once editorially warned the Overland Automobile Company that its refusal to advertise in his weekly would alienate blacks as potential auto purchasers, Vann's warning was based on hope, not reality; as late as 1925, only 14 of 156 black households surveyed in the Hill District owned automobiles.[35] Occasionally, Vann's newspaper was fortunate enough to receive full-page advertisements from local department stores, such as Bennie Nelson's Department Store on Fifth Avenue, which sold low-cost goods and catered to the black community; Newberg's Department Store on Market Street, when it wished to publicize its dollar sale; or Pickering's Store on Tenth and Penn Streets, announcing its storewide furniture clearance ("Nobody Cares About the Money! Your Credit's Good!"); but these wind-

Birth of the COURIER • 51

falls were rare. Vann used the editorial page to try to increase the number of advertisements. He admonished his readers that "there are quite a few stores on the Hill conducted by Jews and others whose patronage is largely made up from colored people. Patronize only those advertisers who patronize us, and you will not only help this paper but the Race. Think over this."[36]

In an attempt to increase revenue through added circulation, the *Courier* conducted subscription contests. "Attention! Attention! Attention! Ten Dollars in Gold," ran one 1911 enticement. The winner would be the agent who brought in the greatest number of new subscriptions.[37] In a more intensified effort in 1913, the *Courier*'s board of directors offered a new car to the person who obtained the largest number of new subscriptions. They obviously hoped for a substantial increase in *Courier* circulation through the competition. The happy winner was Mrs. Daisy Lampkin, an energetic woman who had become a prominent member of Pittsburgh's black society through her activities as a clubwoman.[38] She came to claim her new car, but the *Courier* had no funds with which to purchase it. To appease Mrs. Lampkin, the board gave her a check for half the subscription money she had raised. The check bounced. Mrs. Lampkin's pleasure turned to exasperation. Finally, Vann offered to pay her, partly in cash from his own pocket and partly in *Courier* stock. She accepted and in later years became a *Courier* vice-president and one of the paper's major stockholders.[39]

The *Courier* had other serious problems in addition to finances. Because the newspaper was not affiliated with any major news-gathering agency, the news it received from other cities via part-time or free-lance correspondents was either late, secondhand, inaccurate, or incomplete. These part-time reporters, who had full-time jobs elsewhere and mailed their news to the *Courier*, needed constant reminders of deadlines. Vann had to put into the newspaper such adjurations as "news from all Ohio correspondents must reach this office no later than Tuesday of each week."[40] The *Courier*'s difficulty was common to all black newspapers of the era. Existing news agencies were run by whites for whites and were relatively expensive; not only could the black papers not afford their services, but they could not really have made use of the agencies' news coverage, which either ignored news pertaining to blacks or wrote it up from a white, and therefore biased, perspective. There was a National Negro Press Association, an affiliate of the National Negro Business League, but it was weak and did not really function as a news-gathering agency. John N. Murphy, president of the NNPA, took the *Courier* to task for ignoring its efforts, saying, "In Pittsburgh, two weeks ago, was held an important conference at which representatives were present from all parts of the United States. The local Colored newspaper not only did not send out a bit of news but took its own news almost bodily from the daily press, and that it did publish was mixed up so no credit could be given the papers by the people most interested."[41]

Despite Murphy's criticism of the *Courier*, Vann was well aware that a news service for black publications was badly needed. He recommended some form of cooperative syndication among the black newspapers to rectify the lateness and occasional inaccuracy of the news they received, and devoted an editorial to the subject. "We are informed of an incident this week, and the next issue of the same informant changes this report and corrects some portion of the report. With syndication, 'yea' will be 'yea' and 'nay' will be 'nay' simultaneously in Texas, Boston, New York, Chicago, and Pittsburgh; and there will be no confusion over facts, nor will explanations which so often embarrass be any other than a part of our expenses."[42] Such syndication would also curb the practice whereby one weekly "borrowed" news from another, without the latter's consent or any form of payment. The formation of the Associated Negro Press in 1919 by Claude Barnett of the *Chicago Defender* was a significant step in the right direction, though it had difficulty getting underway. The *Courier* began using its services in November 1925. By 1926, only 87 of the 112 newspapers listed by the ANP were active participants; the remainder were in arrears or inactive. There were but eight regular correspondents in major urban areas, and though the ANP had an agreement with its members to send their own news to the Chicago central office for redistribution, only a few cooperated toward the common good.[43]

In an effort to solve these problems, many black newspapers turned to sensationalism, following the example of Robert Abbott's *Chicago Defender*, with its red-ink headlines in the manner of William Randolph Hearst. Vann eschewed this course in the *Courier*'s early years. He was idealistic about the purposes of his young newspaper, and his middle-class moralistic conscience disliked stories of interracial sex affairs or sordid crimes which catered to the morbid side of the readers' imaginations. Vann was somewhat naive at this time and did not realize, as he later would, that working-class readers wanted sensational news. Stories of Baptist conventions were fine, but there was nothing like a sex crime to arouse readers' interest. The *Courier* was almost totally free of such reportage then. Only rarely would a story creep in like "ATTEMPTS SUICIDE AFTER A QUARREL: Because she and a friend had a quarrel, Mrs. Sadie Johnson, colored, aged 28 years, of 1328 N. Bedford Avenue, made two attempts to end her life by drinking laudanum at her home Monday. Both attempts were unsuccessful."[44]

Despite the *Courier*'s constant struggles and rather amateurish format, it was apparent by 1914 that the newspaper was going to make a go of it. That year the *Courier* moved to more spacious offices at 518 Fourth Avenue. At the same time, Vann and the board of directors hired a new staff member, Ira F. Lewis. Vann had met Lewis in 1912. They immediately discovered they had much in common, from the same home state of North Carolina and the same job of waiting on tables, to similar drives and ambitions.

Ira Lewis had been born in Lexington, North Carolina, on August 25, 1883. He was the son of Adelaide Thomas Lewis; nothing is known of his father. His mother died shortly after he was born, and he lived in Charlotte with his grandparents until 1901. After high school, he went to Biddle University in Charlotte (later named Johnson S. Smith University) for one year. In 1901 Lewis migrated north to Washington and later went to Pittsburgh. There, before joining the *Courier* staff, Lewis worked as a waiter in the restaurant of McCreery's Department Store and took secretarial courses in the evening. Shortly after he met Lewis, Vann hired him for his law office, to do part-time work transcribing testimony.

In June 1914 Ira Lewis applied for a job at the *Courier;* his part-time stenographic work in Vann's law office did not pay him enough that he could be self-supporting. During his interview, the board of directors agreed to hire Lewis and told him, "We'll pay you $3 a week and 25 percent commission on all ads you bring in for the newspaper." "Well, I've already started to work," Lewis replied, laying down a sheet of paper. "There's my first ad and I've got the payment for it in my pocket."[45] The fact that Ira Lewis had sold his first *Courier* ad before even having been hired by the newspaper proved prophetic. Though he was hired to write sports news, his forte turned out to be selling. He secured advertising and nearly doubled circulation within a year after he started to work. Vann later made Lewis business manager of the *Courier* and turned that phase of the paper over to him entirely. Ira Lewis proved himself indispensable to the paper and also became Vann's consultant on personal dealings. Lewis acted as Vann's and the *Courier*'s business manager for the rest of Robert Vann's life.[46]

The business relationship which developed between Vann and Ira Lewis was surprising, for the men were so different. In contrast to the easygoing, cheerful manner of the bon vivant Lewis, Vann was somber and almost Victorian in his ways. He rarely drank, smoked only an occasional cigar, and often issued puritanical judgments on personal behavior. They differed even in physical appearance; Vann was slim, Lewis short and pudgy. While Vann was conservative in his personal life, entertaining quietly and sensibly, Lewis was expansive and colorful. In later years he bought a large mansion from a local bootlegger; on its elegant grounds Lewis, to the amused amazement of his friends, raised chickens in his spare time, distributing fresh eggs liberally among the *Courier* staff. Lewis also was well known for his large and noisy parties, for which he often boasted of spending three hundred dollars on liquor alone. Lewis often astonished listeners with his ability to recall scores and names of players in sports events played years before, to quote entire paragraphs from old *Courier* stories, to name every person involved in obscure political campaigns, and to recite accounts payable, to the penny, from memory.[47]

In a sense, Lewis humanized Vann's impact at the newspaper. While Vann was apt to move quickly about the office issuing curt orders and moving on abruptly with no wasted motion, Lewis followed leisurely after him, casually discussing Vann's directives with the employees.[48] Few people dared to contest Robert Vann's pronouncements, but Ira Lewis was one of them, and he did so in a way which rarely irritated Vann. Moreover, Vann was a good judge of ability, and he thoroughly respected Lewis's business acuity. The fine job Lewis did of running the *Courier*'s finances cemented the friendship and removed a large burden from Vann's mind.

Robert Vann closed the year of 1914 at the *Courier* with a Christmas editorial in which he noted that the *Courier* had now been published for five years, "having weathered the storm without the loss of a single issue," and rededicated the newspaper "to the cause of the Negro and all that pertains to his interests. We propose to continue our fight for the general advancement of the Negro . . . to abolish every vestige of Jim Crowism in Pittsburgh. . . . Let us leave no stone unturned which will lead [us] toward advancement."

·4·

The COURIER as a Social Force

IN THE EARLY DECADES of the twentieth century blacks in Pittsburgh, as elsewhere, had three groups through which they could attempt to effect improvement for their race: the church, racial organizations such as the NAACP and the Urban League, and the black press. A brief look at Pittsburgh's churches and racial organizations between 1910 and 1920 makes the need for Robert Vann's *Courier* as an additional force for social change apparent and indicates why it so quickly became one of the black community's most important spokesmen.

The church had enormous potential as an instrument of social reform. It was the strongest and wealthiest black institution, and its influence extended into every area of black life. Throughout the country black clerics were pivotal figures in politics, education, social welfare activities, fraternal organizations, and even business enterprises.[1] In Pittsburgh there were perhaps as many as fifty churches in operation by 1910,[2] and in each church the minister had, or attempted to have, the undivided attention of his congregation every Sunday, as well as access to its pocketbooks. The minister was generally regarded as a leader, and even outside the pulpit his voice was closely attended. However, the clergy often made little use of their opportunities to appraise the needs of the black community and initiate change. W. E. B. DuBois said that the average black clergyman was "a shrewd manager . . . a good talker, a pleasant companion, but neither learned nor spiritual, nor a reformer."[3] And a local critic of the time noted that "the rank and file of the forty or fifty Negro ministers in Pittsburgh have not a very high order of equipment or ethics."[4]

There was, of course, a reason for the churches' frequent failure to apprehend and act upon the extrareligious needs of their black followers above and beyond the inadequacy of individual clergymen. Most of the ministers, deacons, and other religious officials in Pittsburgh had recently migrated from the South, where any form of racial agitation was absolutely, if tacitly, forbidden. The southern white community at best had never tolerated outspoken blacks, and, at worst, fearsome night riders visited those, even ministers, who dared stray beyond the carefully defined boundaries of their daily duties.

The idea of the ministry as an activist, agitative body would not come until much later in the century. Around 1900, church efforts for social change were pretty much limited to involvement in education and development of welfare institutions, particularly orphanages and homes for the aged. August Meier has pointed out that the Presbyterian and Congregational churches did the most elaborate benevolent work,[5] and Pittsburgh had but one small church representing each of these denominations. In general Pittsburgh's black clergymen confined themselves to revivals, parish socials, open air services, and debating societies. When the new Bethel AME Church was built on Wylie Avenue at enormous cost, one onlooker angrily recorded the pastor's plans for the coming year: "First to pay the debt on the church, second to have a revival to fill it up. Not a word was said of the great need for active social work at its very doors."[6] Robert Vann early recognized this inadequacy on the part of the Pittsburgh churches. A regular worshiper at the Brown Chapel AME Church in Allegheny City and occasional speaker at the Chapel's Sunday evening socials, Vann often chastised local black churchmen for not getting out among their congregations and working with them for better schools, parks, hospitals, and other badly needed reforms. Vann believed that social change was "far more important than spirituals."[7]

The churches could have had a much more meaningful social influence in Pittsburgh, but they made only the merest token efforts in that direction. As a result, many blacks became disaffected and began to turn away from the church. The younger and better educated blacks in particular started to look elsewhere for answers to the rampant problems in their community.[8] This search for a more effective voice led throughout the nation to the sprouting of racial organizations like the NAACP and the Urban League, but these were slow to take root in the black community of Pittsburgh until the 1920s. Their influence in Pittsburgh and other cities was greatly advanced by the black press, which has been called "the vanguard of the NAACP" and the "focal point" and "independent center" of the civil rights movement.[9]

At the beginning of 1915 three organizations made serious recruiting efforts among local blacks. The biracial NAACP sent its chairman, Dr. Joel Spingarn, to speak in Pittsburgh about "The New Abolitionists" in an effort to attract new members.[10] More than three thousand people came to hear Dr. Spingarn speak and gave him a warm reception. One of the local branch's organizers reported happily, "In the afternoon we [he and Spingarn] were both in the AME Church on Wylie Avenue, and the place was packed even to the danger point. The enthusiasm was tremendous, and lasting good will surely came from that wonderful meeting. Doctor Spingarn won every heart by his masterly plea. In the evening, he addressed another audience in a smaller church, but the attendance was so large by 7:45 it was impossible to enter the building."[11] The Pittsburgh branch of the NAACP had just been established, and hopes were high that many prominent citizens, white as well as black, would come forward to provide the much-needed leadership for reform. On paper, the membership figures were encouraging, with 285 members added almost at once. The Pittsburgh secretary, Samuel Morsell, telegraphed this fact enthusiastically to the national office and said drives were underway for an anti-lynch bill, suppression of the movie *Birth of a Nation*, and the hiring of black teachers in the city.[12]

Very few of the new members had joined the NAACP to work actively. Blacks, who comprised the vast majority of the membership, did not significantly aid the organization with either time or money. Vann chided whites for not supporting the NAACP, but was doubly harsh on blacks in his editorial "THE PENALTY OF UNCONCERN: The race collectively is at fault. For many years there has been a tendency to lapse from the close contact which is essential to amicable conditions for the improvement of all the people in a community. Afro-Americans have by their silence and inertia gradually yet nonetheless surely become separated from their white neighbors. . . . And yet, they have evidenced a dissatisfaction when not accorded the advantages, the rights and privileges to which they assumed as citizens they were entitled."[13] Over the years, local officers of the NAACP wrote many discouraged letters to the national headquarters, full of phrases like those from Ernest Rice McKinney, executive secretary of the Pittsburgh branch, to Mary White Ovington: "The people seem to have

Vann with Walter White at the 1921 meeting of the NAACP, Pittsburgh.

lost faith in the local Branch. It has been very hard to revive interest. ... We can not function properly and effectively unless we get some influential white people on the board,"[14] or from its new president, Reverend J. C. Austin: "This organization comes into my hands just about as Christ found Lazarus after the fourth day of his death, not only dead but buried."[15] Finally, the Pittsburgh office was notified "Your branch ... is weaker than any other unit we have in a city of the same size."[16] Not until Homer Brown and Daisy Lampkin reorganized the Pittsburgh branch in the mid-1920s did the NAACP become effective there.

Shortly after Joel Spingarn visited Pittsburgh for the NAACP, William Monroe Trotter of the *Boston Guardian* came to the city on behalf of his National Equal Rights League. Unlike the NAACP, which stressed biracial cooperation, the NERL was exclusively black and put its emphasis on self-help for the race by the race.[17] But Trotter received an even poorer response from the black community than had the NAACP.

Finally, in the same month as Trotter's visit, the Pittsburgh branch of the Urban League, then called the Pittsburgh Council of Social Services Among Negroes, was formed, with Robert Vann as one of its twenty charter members. This organization was an outgrowth of a group founded by Charles Zahneiser, a local clergyman; Samuel Morsell, executive secretary of the Centre Avenue YMCA; and Dr. Charles Cooper, former director of Kingsley House, whose purpose was to improve social conditions in the Hill District. The organization, chartered at the beginning of 1915, had laudable aims, but it was hampered by a lack of finances and functioned mostly as a limited charitable organization.[18] Its only major achievement was to commission the well-known report by Abraham Epstein on the black immigrants in the Hill District.[19] The Pittsburgh Council of Social Services Among Negroes finally became a branch of the Urban League on January 15, 1918, three years after it began, because its members agreed that a more extensive organization was needed to meet the demands of the growing numbers of black immigrants. Robert Vann became a member of the executive committee of the new Urban League branch and handled its publicity.[20] The Urban League began an ambitious program of services. Its Travelers Aid Program provided a representative to meet newly arrived black migrants from the South at Union Station, a room registry to help them find housing, an employment bureau and placement service, a home-and-school visitor to aid black students, and a program to help juvenile delinquents. The Urban League initiated among blacks a week-long Health Education Campaign, which became one of its most important annual functions.[21] But this organization, too, had serious problems. It could not garner adequate financial support for its programs—despite extensive efforts on its behalf by its president, Walter May, a wealthy Pittsburgh druggist who also contributed generously from his own funds, nor could it arouse sufficient enthusiasm in the black community.[22]

Pittsburgh political and fraternal groups augmented somewhat the reform activities of the national racial organizations. The city had several black political groups by 1910, including the Allegheny County Colored Protective League, the Young Men's Civic Club, the Northside Progressive Club, and the Sixth Ward Colored Protective League, but most of these were short-lived and limited their efforts in scope to local politics and in time to the few months preceding an election. The half-dozen men's fraternal organizations stressed ritual and socializing and paid little attention to racial uplift.[23] Pittsburgh had at least twenty-five women's groups, many of which were more attentive to charitable activities and racial self-improvement than the male organizations, but their effectiveness was lessened by two factors. First, each served a small segment of the women in the local black community, so any action by one group was fragmentary and restricted in scope. Second, the average respectable black woman who belonged to these organizations was conservative and reticent, so the groups were unlikely to be strident or militant enough to offer any sort of unified protest.

Part of the reason these racial organizations did not do well in Pittsburgh was that they appealed primarily to the educated black middle class and upper-middle class, which were small. Pittsburgh was "a muscle town" filled with poor working blacks who were too busy "hustling to stay alive," as one observer put it,[24] to pay much attention to causes. The middle-class orientation of groups like the NAACP and the Urban League was a basic weakness that separated the bulk of the black population from its leadership. Another reason was that it was difficult for people to find out about the organizations' activities, since they were given no attention in the white press. The result was that blacks were denied any effective racial organization.[25] Pittsburgh blacks, newly arrived from the South, mainly unskilled and uneducated, needed a strong local voice to give them a sense of community, the will to upgrade the condition of their lives, and information about available opportunities. The black churches either did little or closed their eyes entirely; the national racial groups were unable to arouse the proper response in Pittsburgh blacks; the local organizations were limited in their goals and effectiveness. A vacuum in leadership existed, and Robert Vann's *Courier* stepped in and began its serious crusade for social change in the black community.

Vann spoke from the *Courier* pages in the early years with the spirit of a hopeful reformer. Although he never approached the missionary zeal of William Monroe Trotter or Robert Abbott, Vann was very earnest about his efforts in behalf of black people. It was the one period in his life when Vann was devoted to and consistent in a serious, long-range reform effort based on an ideal vision of how things should be. Even when he was unsuccessful in bringing about change, Vann's attempts and his constant addressing of blacks as a unified group imparted a sense of community which was in itself beneficial. The *Courier* crusade touched on all the facets of black life which needed improving: housing, health, education, job opportunities, political awareness, crime, and less crucial but perennially frustrating, social Jim Crowism and misrepresentation in the white press.

The inadequacy of housing for blacks was dramatic. "The lack of proper housing conditions in Pittsburgh makes it unbearable for the Negro wage earner to live here," wrote Vann. "He is now being attacked by disease of nearly epidemic prevalence as a result of the neglected housing conditions. Ninety-eight per cent of the houses occupied by Negro laborers are unsanitary. The houses are crowded; the rooms have four and five beds in them and the beds are in many cases doing double turn."[26] These "germ-laden tenements" were breeding grounds for misery and disease.[27]

The housing problem centered around the Hill District, an area comprising the Third and Fifth Wards. By 1910, nearly half of the city's twenty-five thousand blacks lived in the Hill District. After 1910, while the population of this district remained steady at about forty-five thousand, the percentage of blacks more than doubled, from 22.6 percent to 53.5 percent.[28] The houses of the Hill District were already old and substandard when blacks began to settle there, having previously been inhabited by other groups of immigrants—Eastern European mill-workers, Italians, and Jews. Dilapidated houses stood close together on narrow, often steep, garbage-littered streets. Inside, wallpaper was torn, plaster hung from naked lath, broken windows went unrepaired, and low-ceilinged, damp rooms had insufficient light. More commonly than not the toilets were outside privies, and the drinking water came from outdoors; the lack of sanitation was nearly total, and refuse accumulated in the streets and yards.

When the heavy migration from the South into Pittsburgh began in about 1915, more and more blacks crowded into the already overpopulated Hill District.[29] The housing shortage became acute. Blacks were living in every conceivable sort of place—attics, cellars, storerooms, even abandoned box cars. By 1917, a surveyor found workmen living four to a room. There was a constant shifting of roomers, and often men slept during the day in beds vacated by day workers. Fewer than four percent of blacks owned their own homes in the Hill; the rest paid a disproportionate amount of their wages as rent to white landlords. Frequently the rents were so high that the black tenants were forced to take boarders into their apartments to help defray their costs, thus further increasing the overcrowding. Because of the nature of the migration and the transience of the lodgers, the Hill District gained notoriety as an area infested with bootleg places, bawdy houses, crime, shootings, knifings, and brawls.[30]

As the number of blacks moving into Pittsburgh increased during the Great Northern Migration of 1915–20, the white community attempted to confine them to certain areas. The black population of Pittsburgh increased by an amazing 47.2 percent from 1910 to 1920, while the white population increased only 8.3 percent. The huge influx of black faces frightened the white community, which, in some instances, banded together to keep blacks from moving into many areas of the city, as they had previously done, albeit in limited numbers. The blacks lost what housing mobility they had had and were forced into segregated communities; a black ghetto was developing in Pittsburgh.

Robert Vann's own housing difficulties mirrored the problems besetting many blacks who tried to move out of the Hill District ghetto into more desirable residential areas like the East End, Homewood, East Liberty, Beltzhoover, and South Pittsburgh. In March 1911, after Vann had been married little more than a year, he and Jesse decided to move out of Vann's second-floor bachelor room on Sandusky Street on the North Side. They came across a roomy frame house for rent on Homewood's Monticello Street, a quiet avenue of pleasant houses and tidy lawns. At that time, Monticello Street was home to only one other black family, the Howard Rickmonds, and they were virtually white in appearance.[31] When Vann asked to rent the house at 7337, the owner said, "I won't rent to colored, but I'll sell." It was capricious reasoning, but Vann impulsively seized the chance to become a homeowner. He borrowed $500 for the down payment from a friend and moved in. The Vanns' initial furnishings were meager—a floor lamp in the living room, a table and chairs in the dining room, and a bed and dresser in the bedroom.[32] It might be expected that the neighbors, upon discovering that the new residents were not only black but seemingly of marginal means, would rise up in protest. But aside from one brief, halfhearted meeting called by certain white families on the block, the Vanns met with no racial incidents and lived on the street in relative tranquility for six years. However, things changed dramatically by 1917, when Vann bought the house next door to his own and rented it to another black family. Though Vann had proved his respectability and his financial solvency to his neighbors during the six years he had lived on Monticello Street, the white neighborhood was far less ready to accept another black than it had been in 1911. When Vann's tenant moved in, the "Battle of Monticello Street" began. Irate white neighbors distributed handbills which demanded the ouster of black residents from the street and held meetings. Vann attended one of the meetings, and when the talk centered on the "undesirables" moving into the neighborhood, Vann asked the audience who these "undesirables" were. No replies were forthcoming. But white neighborhood talk focused on the topic for months.[33] Whites began moving out of the area in panic, and within ten years, Vann's block on Monticello Street was almost solidly black.[34]

In the pages of the *Courier*, Robert Vann did more than just rail against the disastrous housing conditions encountered by blacks. He proposed that blacks form their own building and loan association and real estate development concern. This was one example of the theme of "black capitalism" which Vann stressed throughout his life.[35] Vann believed that black financing and management of building programs would make better and cheaper housing available. As he had said earlier, "Our right to acquire and dispose of property may be considered the salvation of our present [low] standing and our security against further oppression in the future."[36] However appealing Vann's idea, it was impractical at the time, for blacks simply did not have surplus capital to invest in such costly schemes. As late as 1925, there was still no black building and loan association in Pittsburgh.[37]

Clearly linked with the issue of inferior housing was the problem of inadequate medical facilities. The overcrowded and substandard places in which most blacks lived were breeding grounds for disease. Sickness and death visited the black community at a much greater rate than the white populace. In 1910 the black death rate was 23.4

"Bar the Door," by Wilburt Holloway, the Pittsburgh Courier, *1924.*

per thousand, while that of the whites was 17.7. By 1917, when hordes of black immigrants were crowding into Pittsburgh, the black rate of death had soared to 31.3 per thousand while the white rate dropped to 17.5.[38] Tuberculosis, influenza, whooping cough, scarlet fever, and venereal disease all plagued the black community. Yet despite their desperate need for adequate medical attention, blacks received negligible care. Vann revealed that, with the exception of the Passavant Hospital on Reed Street in the Hill District, Pittsburgh's twenty-eight hospitals rarely admitted black patients. They usually told the ailing black man that the hospital was filled and that he would be notified if a bed became vacant, which, of course, it rarely did. On those infrequent occasions when a black patient was admitted, he was segregated and given poor service.[39] And not one of the black doctors practicing in Pittsburgh was allowed to admit his black patients to the white hospitals. As a result, blacks frequently had recourse to patent medicines, home remedies, and quack practitioners, with the consequences reflected in the high death rate.

Another aspect of the problem was the lack of black physicians. The only medical school in Pittsburgh, the University of Pittsburgh, almost never admitted a black student. The university maintained that it refused black students only because they lacked the necessary qualifications, but the real reason may have been that the Pittsburgh hospitals did not wish to have blacks as interns after they had finished their medical studies. With no local hospital available for internships, the University of Pittsburgh felt it futile to admit black students.[40] Whatever the causes, there was a constant paucity of black physicians to treat the diseases taking such a toll of the race, as Vann pointed out in the *Courier*. "Let the training of the [black] physicians proceed," he urged.[41]

As early as February 12, 1915, Robert Vann issued a call in his newspaper for an Afro-American Hospital to serve the black community, saying it would be "of immeasurable value." Again on March 26, he asked for blacks to help form a hospital association. "There is absolute necessity for [a hospital]," he affirmed. By March 1916, definite plans were underway for a hospital to be named Livingstone, in honor of the explorer, in which black doctors could treat their black patients and young black girls could be trained as nurses in a three-year program. The proposed hospital would cost $50,000 to build, have 150 beds, and be located in the East End. In his role as attorney, Vann drew up the charter for the hospital, and it was granted by the Court of Common Pleas. The Livingstone Memorial Hospital Association was formed with C. H. Trusty as president, J. W. Brown as treasurer, and Charles J. Powell as secretary.[42] Vann spoke at a large fund-raising rally for Livingstone Hospital in December 1916 at the Lyceum Theater, in which he pleaded for contributions and roundly criticized the city of Pittsburgh for not seeing to it that there were better health facilities for blacks. "It is a disgrace," said Vann. "Refusal of existing hospitals to admit colored patients makes it necessary for the colored race to build its own institution. If we knock at the door of any of the hospitals here, the answer is invariably the same, when we announce it is a colored patient."[43]

Persistent discrimination also forced the black communities of other cities to create segregated institutions to provide the health care they needed so desperately. Black leaders wished for an end to segregation, but they saw that blacks had to build their own health care facilities if they were to have any at all. In Philadelphia the blacks built Mercy Hospital and Douglass Memorial Hospital; in Chicago they helped organize Provident Hospital, which initially had a biracial staff but within ten years became virtually all black; and in Washington they built Freedmen's Hospital.[44] As Robert Vann perceived it, the very real and pressing need blacks had for their own hospital far outweighed the disadvantages of perpetuating segregation by building a facility exclusively for blacks. So he began to fight for Livingstone Hospital, in person and in the pages of the *Courier*. But the project was doomed, though Vann urged the blacks to remember that "Rome was not built in a day."[45] There was some peculation, and the money that had been so painfully amassed for the proposed hospital vanished. Later, there again seemed to be hope, when the Livingstone Memorial Hospital Association was given an old building in the Hill District by the Federation of Jewish Philanthropies,[46] but still the hospital never materialized. Vann continued his interest in a black hospital for Pittsburgh to the end of his life, but none was ever built. As late as 1937, Vann was writing to the governor of Pennsylvania, urging him to back a legislative measure for the erection of such a hospital. But this 1937 bill was defeated because it was considered "class legislation" favoring blacks.[47]

Vann used the *Courier* to ask for changes to improve other aspects of the health problems facing blacks. He called for black health officers in Pittsburgh "who are in sympathy with [our] life and methods of living,"[48] and strongly pleaded for "effective corrective [health] measures" in the nearly all-black, poverty-stricken Hill District.[49] Vann even went so far as to recommend "agitation" by the black community to have the unsanitary conditions eliminated.

Many blacks migrating to Pittsburgh from the South from 1910 to 1920 found educational possibilities somewhat better than in their home states. But here, too, inequities existed. There was already much *de facto* segregation in the Hill District; as the black population became more concentrated, the schools became nearly all black. Second, too few blacks completed their education through high school. Because many of the students were ill prepared by the inadequate school systems of the South, their white teachers in Pittsburgh considered them backward. With such low expectations on the part of their teachers, it is hardly surprising that few blacks were motivated to continue in school. And last, though there were more than four thousand black students in the Pittsburgh school system by 1915, there was not a single black teacher.[50]

These three facts bothered Robert Vann a good deal, as he believed in education as a means to racial uplift, and he mentioned them often on the *Courier*'s editorial page. He advised high school students to "complete the course selected. Make the best out of yourself there is to be had in your line."[51] Later he said, "What we need is more education of every kind."[52] He exhorted parents to be sure that all their children who should be in school were there. "Enlist in an active endeavor to provide for the education of the children . . . NOW."[53]

Vann was outspoken on specific cases. He publicly chastised a white teacher in the Lincoln School on Frankstown Avenue for using the term "nigger" and telling her class that it was an acceptable abbreviation of "Negro." "Ignorance is better than such teaching," Vann argued.[54] When a young black woman made known her hope of being a teacher in Pittsburgh, he devoted two long editorials to the topic. "The Negro population must to a man stand behind this young woman. . . . The *Courier* admonishes every man and woman to demand that this right be extended."[55] In April, Vann noted the "precarious condition of our school facilities . . . we need MIXED SCHOOLS AND MIXED TEACHERS."[56] Vann had once given a long speech on the need for young blacks to have black teachers to identify with:

> It is very necessary that [the black child's] teacher have sympathy, patience, interest and love. The teacher that can best meet these requirements is the Negro, because

> his sympathy, patience, interest and love for his race are qualities innate and natural and do not have to be acquired. [The Negro teacher] knows the peculiarities of his students, their nature; understands their modes of expression, their temper; can read their emotions far better than anyone else. With him these peculiar traits are no problem for his special study, he has them in common with his pupils, and he can sympathize or censure with perfect consistency. Being naturally interested, he will discern the child's tendencies in their earliest stages and provide remedies accordingly.[57]

After the young black woman in question had graduated from the Cheyney Training School for Teachers fifteenth in a class of ninety, Vann warned, "People of Pittsburgh, be it to your lasting shame if you fail to rally zealously . . . to this representative of your race."[58] Unhappily for Vann and the young woman, she was not hired. Despite the fact that qualified blacks with teacher's certificates were graduating yearly from local schools like Cheyney and the Henry Clay Frick Training School, Pittsburgh did not get its first black teacher until twenty-three years later; the perennial excuse made by the Board of Education was that the "time was not ripe."[59]

Going hand in hand with educational problems were employment difficulties for Pittsburgh blacks. The poorly educated black had trouble finding decent work, and even those who were educated found few worthy jobs of any sort open to them. Most occupations open to blacks were menial and unskilled. Menial black labor was recruited in white dailies by such advertisements as this one, which ran for a local department store: "Require a number of mature COLORED WOMEN for cleaning in various parts of the building."[60] The *Courier* also advertised openings for blacks, almost all of which were for unskilled or at best semiskilled labor.

Blacks had great trouble entering the building trades in Pittsburgh. They made up only 3.5 percent of that work force in 1910 and even in 1920 constituted a meager 4.1 percent. This situation existed not only because blacks did not have the skills to enter the building trades, but also because blacks were discouraged from, or outrightly denied membership in, most of the skilled unions which commanded better wages. These included the Plasterers' Union, the Carpenters' Union, the Painters', Brick Layers', and Plumbers'. The only exception was the relatively weak Hod Carriers', Building and Common Laborers' Union, in which 75 percent of the four to five thousand members were black. White union members refused to work with blacks, and union officials did not encourage integration, often administering stiff examinations to black applicants that few men of either race could have passed.[61]

As noted earlier, despite the expansion of coal mining and steel manufacturing, blacks found little work in either field, save as strike breakers. Blacks were desperate for work and could not afford to worry about the need for unionization, but of course their work as strikebreakers further increased the white union members' antagonism toward blacks and hardened their resolution not to have them as members of their organizations.

Robert Vann editorialized constantly on the subject of black employment. On one occasion he wrote of how self-defeating it was for the black to play the role of the scab. In a 1916 editorial, for example, he praised a group of black engineers from Pittsburgh for refusing to go to Youngstown, Ohio, to break a strike, commenting that blacks needed to join the existing unions, or, even better, to "organize themselves into a substantial union of their own . . . and thus get control of their own labor. We now stand divided, disorganized."[62] Vann said that it was time for the black man to take his proper place in Pittsburgh's major industries. "The colored man has shown his ability in many places about the furnaces." He must henceforth be "a persistent seeker after his share of American labor."[63] He urged companies like United States Steel to give blacks, who were as deserving as foreign laborers, a chance in the mills.[64] When United States Steel sent down South for more than a hundred experienced black steelworkers for its Homewood plant, Vann wrote, "This shows that the Negro, if he makes good, can find employment. . . . The Steel Corporation intimates that it prefers Negro workmen if they can be relied upon." He urged the race to make good use of such an opportunity. "Really, brother, in this day of keen competition, if you expect to succeed, do well that which you find to do and above all cultivate the habits of reliability."[65] However, despite all Vann's exhortations, until the production demands of World War I the steel and coal industries made little use of Pittsburgh's black labor supply.

Vann also campaigned against the unfair hiring and firing practices of white employers in other fields, such as the restaurant business, where blacks had in the past comprised the majority of waiters but were rapidly being displaced by whites. In one such instance, forty black waiters were dismissed from service at the Rittenhouse Hotel, whose proprietor had previously employed more blacks than any other hotel in Pittsburgh. They had allegedly been released because one of them had been caught trying to steal from a cash register; all their places were to be filled by whites. Vann lamented that "the incident is another illustration of how all Negroes are burdened with the crimes of the few. The conduct of the one waiter served as sufficient cause for the removal of all, thus forcing the many to suffer for the conduct of the few."[66]

Vann tried editorially to correct those whites who denigrated the working ability of blacks. When a white baker published an advertisement in *The Homewood Booster* saying that "Nicholas Bakery is owned and operated by Americans exclusively—no cheap foreign or Negro labor employed in the making of our . . . products," Vann replied angrily in the *Courier*. First he reminded the bakery owner that his father had founded his business in a black neighborhood on the corner of Pasture Alley and Fulton Street and prospered from the purchases of his black customers before moving the business to Homewood. Vann urged a complete boycott. "There are a few Negroes in Homewood . . . let everyone of them eat no bread at all if they cannot find another baker. This same coward was fed by Negro patronage from his cradle up; his father before him lived right out of the hands of the Negroes of Pittsburgh. Such a man is a menace to the Negroes of this city, and the sooner we starve him to death the better."[67]

On occasion, a breakthrough occurred and a white business yielded to the *Courier*'s pleas for employment of blacks en masse. In December 1916 Kaufmann's, the city's oldest department store, was having difficulty with its white delivery van drivers, who were organizing a union, and decided to use black drivers during a test period. The management of the store reportedly contacted Vann who, with the help of Ira Lewis, formed and directed a group of seventy-six black drivers.[68] Vann wrote jubilantly, "The entire service, including mechanics, helpers, greasers, oilers, shifters, gasoline men, vulcanizers, chauffeurs and delivery men was turned over to our men with the hope that we can take hold of this new opportunity and make good or die in the effort."[69]

Vann's enthusiasm was inconsistent with his earlier public statements, for Kaufmann's was employing the black drivers as strike-

The COURIER as a Social Force • 71

breakers, a practice Vann had deplored earlier in the year. Vann could be vehemently principled and decry the use of black scabs in an Ohio city; when presented at home with the very concrete opportunity of gainful employment for seventy-six Pittsburgh blacks, Vann was willing to forgo all abstract stances and see his people seize their chance. In fact, Vann's attitude toward unions over the years was very much a matter of personal, business, or racial expediency.

The *Courier* praised Kaufmann's for taking such a bold step and advised its black readers to patronize the store which "gives our people a chance to earn our bread."[70] But the experiment was not a success. The former white drivers were hostile, and when the customers were informed by the union of the practice and their fears were aroused, they became unhappy to see a black face at the wheel of a delivery truck. And many of the blacks, chosen hastily by Vann and Lewis, untrained and thrust suddenly into positions of some responsibility, made mistakes. In June 1917, Kaufmann's announced that the black drivers "were found wanting" and dismissed the lot of them. Vann was very disappointed and criticized the store for having unrealistically high expectations of the novice drivers. "We had never been in the delivery business before. . . . The whole responsibility was shifted upon our boys, with little or no cooperation on the part of the other white employees, and they rendered our men no assistance. . . . We were called upon to furnish 76 men who were perfect delivery men. The percentage was too high; we could not do it."[71] The *Courier* also charged that Kaufmann's had capitulated to pressure from its white customers. "We are told that the store was deluged with letters 'from a customer' stating that 'my account will be discontinued' if the delivery service is not changed."[72] Once again, Vann suggested a boycott. "Let us . . . spend with the store that gives our kind employment," he proposed. "Our money has a greater influence than we have, and we must husband our influences."[73]

Vann was hopeful that World War I would improve the blacks' employment status. In 1915, before America's entry into the war, he envisioned great numbers of the European immigrants in Pittsburgh returning to their homelands to take up arms, thus opening up many jobs to local blacks.[74] And after the United States joined the fighting in 1917, the great northward migration of blacks began. Vann was positive that the migration "placed the race in the limelight . . . placed [the black man] on an equal industrial footing with other peoples."[75] To some degree, Vann's hopes for increased black employment were realized. Shortly before the United States entered the war, with production already beginning to increase, the Westinghouse Electric Company hired 400 blacks for their Pittsburgh plants. However, many of the new black employees, unused to decent wages and regular work, behaved erratically, vanishing after payday to spend their new riches or not "sticking to their job" as the work ethic demanded. Vann grew worried that the race would lose this golden opportunity to become regular employees of a large, expanding corporation and devoted many an editorial to the subject. In exasperation he wrote, "The man who expects to work three weeks and loaf one, just because his salary is larger than he ever earned before, is paving the way for his own dismissal. He is lowering the standard of labor and destroying the confidence of the employer in our men. . . . If our boys ever expect to take part in the onward march of the country and to be respected for their skills and usefulness, they must learn that the steady man, the constant man, has a better chance to become efficient, and thus gain promotion, than the man who works until payday and loafs until his wages are spent."[76]

As the war went on, blacks found decent employment more available. They were needed because of industrial expansion, to replace workers who had gone to war, and because immigration had slowed since 1914. The black labor force in Pittsburgh jumped from 9,940 in 1910 to over 18,000 in 1920. The *Chicago Defender* urged southern blacks to take advantage of employment opportunities in the North, and Pennsylvania railroads and industries sent out labor agents to recruit black workers. Agents from the Pennsylvania and Erie Railroads or the Carnegie Steel Mills enticed blacks to leave their $1.25-a-day jobs in Birmingham, Alabama, Hattiesburg, Mississippi, or Americus, Georgia, for the promise of a $2.85 daily wage in Pittsburgh's industries. Despite efforts by southern states to curb this emigration, it was estimated that between 1916 and 1918, 84,000 blacks migrated to Pennsylvania, 18,500 of whom settled in Pittsburgh. Most of these workers were unskilled or semiskilled but managed to get decent jobs in heavy industry. In 1910, just 507 black men worked on blast furnaces and rolling mills; by 1920 there were 4,350. In manufacturing and the mechanical trades the number increased from 2,859 to 7,971. Carnegie Steel, which employed 1,500 blacks prior to 1916, had 4,000 in 1918; Jones and Laughlin increased its black labor force from 400 to 1,500 during the same period; and Westinghouse climbed from 25 to 900. In 1910 only 28.8 percent of the black laboring force was in industry, but in 1920 it was up to 52 percent.[77]

Vann exhorted these newly employed blacks to look to the future when wartime prosperity would be over. He wrote an editorial entitled, "YOUR LAST PAY, WHERE IS IT?" in which he predicted that after the war ended and the white soldiers returned to reclaim their old jobs, blacks would once again find employment scarce. Therefore it behooved black wage earners, "who live by the sweat of your brow," to "lay aside something before the sweat goes dry."[78] Such exhortations to the race to be careful and frugal were fairly common in the black press of the time; Vann's editorial provides a typical example of this Dutch-uncle attitude. On more than one occasion, when admonishing fellow blacks to save their earnings, Vann urged them to emulate the Jewish people; they, too, had suffered as a minority group, but had worked hard, banded together, and marshaled their savings until they were a powerful financial force in America.[79]

All the obstacles Pittsburgh blacks faced in finding decent housing, jobs, and other essentials of the good life led to frustration, defeatism, and often crime. Crime had long been part of life in black neighborhoods, but it worsened after 1910. During the Great Migration of 1915–17, when blacks poured into Pittsburgh, crowding into the already-jammed Hill District, tensions increased and many found their outlet in petty crime, which went up a dramatic 200 percent.[80] The huge rise in the crime rate at this particular time came about partly because of the quality of the black migrants entering Pittsburgh. Unscrupulous labor agents who were paid by the head for their southern recruits did not bother to screen their applicants much, if at all. And they often promised the rural youths high wages, good housing, and easy working conditions. When the migrants arrived and found the terrible conditions which prevailed and, because of lax control of licensing in the Hill District, "a saloon in almost every door on Wylie Avenue,"[81] it was not surprising that the Hill became known as "the bad Hill." There were "no less than half a dozen cutting and shooting affrays in which two citizens lost their lives and several others wounded," all within a fortnight.[82] It was so easy to purchase firearms, knives, and razors in the many pawnshops and secondhand stores that it was small wonder that there were many arrests on charges of felonious assault, carrying concealed weapons, and armed robbery. The black migrants, who had little faith in "white man's justice" and felt they had to protect themselves as they had had to in the South, considered weaponry their equalizer.[83]

The Pittsburgh police did little to improve the situation. Vann editorially charged them with neglecting their duty and being "conspicuous by their absence . . . on the darker streets and around the darker places." The police tolerated many iniquities, as long as they were perpetrated by black against black, as in the case of gambling parlors or houses of prostitution. When they did act, it was invariably in a rash and indiscriminate manner, with little consideration for innocent bystanders. In one case, a police action was begun on orders from the police superintendent to stop a wave of pickpocketing in a downtown, white area. The police were to "clean up the town." The outcome was, wrote Vann, that the policeman "arrests every [black] man, boy and woman he can see on the beat, takes them all to the police station and calls them the 'criminals' the boss had ordered him to 'clean up.' . . . He arrests everybody: working men, churchgoers, heads of families, night laborers; all until he has 'cleaned up.'"[84] Vann was cynical about such periodic cleanups. One time he wrote, "The police raids on the Hill have begun. There must be a political campaign somewhere in the distance."[85] In another instance, after two daring holdups of businessmen in stores downtown, night detectives led raids into the Hill District. The night squad rounded up forty-two blacks "of suspicious character" loitering on the streets or in poolrooms and put them into the Centre Avenue jail overnight for questioning. The night before that, twenty-two blacks had been arrested and fined ten dollars each.[86]

In one such case, Robert Vann became directly involved as a lawyer. On the evening of November 27, 1916, Israel Saffir, a Jewish merchant in the Hill District, was murdered in a holdup attempt, allegedly by two blacks. The following day the police reacted angrily and began rounding up all black men they saw on the street corners and arresting them for vagrancy. By the time the police had finished making "a general charge upon every colored man in sight," two hundred blacks had been picked up. An unsympathetic magistrate sentenced at least eighty of them to the workhouse for up to sixty days. The black community became aroused immediately, and a mass protest meeting was held in the Ebenezer Baptist Church on Wylie Avenue. A fund was collected to pay for the services of Robert Vann and two other black attorneys, J. Welfred Holmes and Frank R. Stewart.[87] The three lawyers spent Thanksgiving Day in the workhouse talking to the imprisoned men, then petitioned the court for blanket writs of habeas corpus, while Vann publicly rebuked the police and the sentencing magistrate. "A vagrant," said Vann in a speech to a church group, "must be a man with no visible means of support. These men possessed money and pay checks showing they were employed by various companies."[88] In the *Courier,* Vann condemned the indiscriminate wholesale arrests "as a vicious thrust at the entire race as there is no [other] class of citizens in this community which is made victims of such infamous treatment."[89] Finally, after multiple court appearances by Vann and his older colleagues, most of the prisoners were released. The injustice was corrected, and Vann had proved himself to be both able in court and a convincing spokesman for black rights.

Vann believed the police attitude toward black wrongdoers would be greatly improved and such miscarriages of justice avoided if there were more black police officers. He pointed out in the *Courier* that "white officers, when they start to look for a Negro suspect, are not too careful whom they pick up. In a way, all Negroes look alike to them."[90]

The *Courier* crusades sparked by Robert Vann often extended beyond efforts to improve the tangible essentials of daily living like housing and employment into less tangible, but psychologically vital, facets of black life which had to be improved for the blacks of Pittsburgh to achieve a feeling of worth and racial pride and a sense of community. Thus Vann attempted to end misrepresentation of blacks in the white press, to stress black achievement in all areas, to communicate local news for the purpose of creating bonds among black citizens, and to overcome social discrimination.

One of Vann's missions in the *Courier* was to combat the distortions in the white press's portrayal of black people, whether deliberate or not. The white press in Pittsburgh did not take black news coverage very seriously, as one aspiring young woman journalist found out when she tried to get a job setting up an "Afro-American [News] Department to have the same general style as any of the other departments. . . . I trudged from one newspaper office to the other, only to be looked at in cold blooded astonishment at my request or to have it rated as a huge joke."[91] What little news there was about blacks in Pittsburgh's white dailies was invariably bad. Vann particularly blamed the *Pittsburgh Press* for inciting racial unrest through biased writing which stereotyped blacks as criminals and undesirables.[92] One of the more flagrant examples of such distortion Vann found in the *Pittsburgh Press* during January 1918. The *Press*'s version of a robbery in nearby Washington, Pennsylvania, was that fifteen blacks robbed two white men and then brutally raped their white female companions. After being molested, according to the *Press*, the women ran to telephone for the police. This sort of coverage, as Vann recognized, was not only inaccurate, but dangerously inflammatory. He rebutted the *Press*'s report in the next issue of the *Courier*, charging that it would have been impossible for two women each to have been raped by fifteen men and then immediately give competent evidence against their assailants. "Any person of any intelligence will recognize this condition as a PHYSICAL IMPOSSIBILITY," wrote Vann. He went on to cite the coverage of the incident in two other white newspapers as proof of how exaggerated the *Press*'s version was. The *Washington* (Pa.) *Reporter* told simply of two men being robbed and their female companions going for help, and the *Washington Daily News*, while mentioning the alleged rape, added that police officers were skeptical about the report.[93]

Another such distortion occurred in an incident involving Booker T. Washington, in March 1911. Washington, looking for the apartment of a friend in New York one Sunday, was examining the numbers on an apartment house door when the building's janitor burst out of the house and beat Washington with a stick and his fists.[94] The *Pittsburgh Chronicle Telegraph,* owned by Senator George T. Oliver, labeled Booker T. Washington a "voyeur," saying he had been peeping through the door of the building in question. Vann was outraged. The *Courier*'s front-page headline announced "BOOKER T. WASHINGTON ASSAULTED. *Race Insulted: Senator Oliver's Paper Yellow."* The accompanying article described the incident and added, "Nor does the insult stop with the incident. We as a race have been held up before the world in a most shameful light by the public press generally, whose editors at once resorted to yellow journalism as a means of revenue. Without an investigation, without even the courtesy due the man, without any regard for the truth, but with the zealousness and agility of a serpent bent upon the very life of his prey, these unscrupulous writers . . . sought to cast a universal slur upon a struggling race. . . . The *Chronicle Telegraph,* owned and controlled by our United States Senator, resorted to unusually large headlines that bespoke the 'yellow' as no other paper in the city. . . . We expect better than this from a paper whose boss enjoys the franchise of 30,000 Negroes."[95]

What little coverage blacks received in the white press of Pittsburgh, even if not inaccurate, stressed crime almost exclusively. Typical articles in Pittsburgh newspapers of the time included: "THIEVES WORK IN DAYLIGHT," about a home in Squirrel Hill that was robbed while a witness on the front porch noticed "a Negro in front of the house acting suspiciously."[96] "WOUNDS FATAL TO NEGRO," as William Jefferson dies, killed during an argument over a fifteen-cent wager.[97] "NEGROES QUARREL OVER WOMAN," and two blacks sustain bullet wounds.[98] Or "ARGUMENT ENDS IN STABBING, *Accused Negro Captured After Exciting Chase,*"[99] and "X-RAY REVEALS RING IN NEGRO'S STOMACH: *Alleged To Be Stolen.*"[100] Such representation of only the more sordid or sensational aspects of black life by the white press perpetuated the stereotype of the "bad" black man and increased the fears and dislike of white society, further polarizing the races.

Even when the distortions in the white press were minor, Vann felt they were damaging. When the great heavyweight prizefighter Jack Johnson was called "the black" or "smoke" in the *Pittsburgh Press* and "Big Cinder" in the *Chronicle Telegraph*, Vann replied with an editorial accusing the two papers of bad sportsmanship. "If these sports writers entertain any doubt as to the identity of the Negro fighters they might insert their photographs, then their readers could get a more exact conception of the fighter in question. Aside from the unsportsmanlike spirit of these articles a decided disposition is shown to go to extremes in the art of 'picture painting.' " And he went on to needle a bit: "We suggest that the gentlemen spend more time developing a real fighter who can lick some of these Negro pugilists, and in this way they may be able to entertain our readers more to their gratification."[101]

The white press also committed the sin of omission, failing to report major events taking place in the black community. When, for example, the Knights of Pythias held their annual convention in Pittsburgh in 1911, only the *Courier* reported the event. "The six daily papers treated the Negroes with silent contempt, notwithstanding the public meetings and the grand parade which extended over seven city squares. These same papers never overlook an opportunity to publish in glowing and attractive headlines any and all reports concerning the Negro, if these reports carry with them any scandal or even alleged scandal. . . . We do not complain that we are ignored by the dailies; but we do complain of the gross ignorance of the many Negroes who spend their money to read such a biased press. . . . Until we unite the forces about us and thereby command not only attention, but recognition as a people, we may expect a repetition of this silent contempt with added emphasis."[102] Another even more important black event held in Pittsburgh the following month was also virtually ignored by the local white press. The National Baptist Convention, the leading black religious organization in America, met on September 12–19, 1911. For many weeks in advance, the *Courier* had heralded the convention as "The Biggest Affair That Was Ever Held in the City of Pittsburgh," and designated itself as the "Official Paper for the National Baptist Convention."[103] A crowd of twenty thousand was expected, with Booker T. Washington as the keynote speaker. Robert Vann was also to speak, on "The Kingdom and the Press." Although at the last minute Washington was unable to appear, W. E. B. DuBois delivered a "stirring address" to blacks to "For God's Sake, Fight" for their civil rights.[104] And yet the press in Pittsburgh, aside from the *Courier*, gave the Baptist Convention barely a line of coverage.

Thus the urge for recognition needed satisfaction it did not receive in the white press. For that reason, Vann pledged his *Courier* to the policy that "racial achievements shall be heralded far and wide, that others, perhaps too easily despaired, may take heart for renewed effort." He promised that "racial fitness and merit shall be set forth that we may know even in the time of stress there is a hand poised to act in our behalf."[105] The emphasis on black achievement was another important function of the *Courier;* it was a means to create and maintain within blacks a feeling of pride and dignity, a sense of race consciousness they could get from few other sources. The *Courier* paid homage to members of the race from all areas of accomplishment, often with front-page prominence. There was a lengthy biographical sketch of Frederick Douglass entitled "GREAT STATESMAN'S INTERESTING CAREER, *Frederick Douglass Rose From Obscurity to Fame, From Slaveboy to Statesman.*"[106] The *Courier* gave extensive coverage to Samuel Coleridge-Taylor at his death, as "the most important of Negro composers."[107] The achievements of Dr. Daniel Williams, one of the black founders of the Provident Hospital in Chicago, were described at length.[108] On another occasion the first black to be appointed an army major, Charles Young, was written about.[109]

The *Courier* noted the feats of black pioneers in various fields whose accomplishments paralleled those of contemporary white heroes. There was "THE FIRST NEGRO AVIATOR," Wesley Peters,[110] and the

"FOREMOST NEGRO EXPLORER," Matthew Henson, who was in the Peary expedition and was actually the first man to reach the North Pole.[111] The newspaper reported how blacks had proved themselves throughout history in its coverage of the findings of the Negro Society for Historic Research in Yonkers, New York, with a "list of twenty eminent colored men . . . who have won their spurs as authors, scientists, philosophers, statesmen and warriors [that refutes] the charge made by some persons that the colored race is incapable of higher culture."[112]

In the early years from 1910 to 1920, the *Courier* did not have a regular sports section, but even the limited coverage of black athletes was laudatory. The most prominent black athletes of the time were the boxers, for the nation excluded blacks from virtually all organized athletic teams. In prizefighting, which Robert Vann followed ardently and used in later years to skyrocket his *Courier* to national prominence, blacks had no peers. The *Courier* noted this fact in a long article:

PRIZEFIGHTERS ALL DREAD THE BLACK QUARTET
Johnson, Langford, Jeannette and McVey Have Cornered the Game

> . . . a quartet of men whose physical prowess has placed them in the lead of all others in their profession without regard to race or creed. They are Jack Johnson, Sam Langford, Joe Jeannette, and Sam McVey. These four men are the leading characters in the heavyweight division of pugilism. Jack Johnson, the acknowledged heavyweight champion pugilist of the world, is the center of attraction at the present time in view of the fact that he is matched to fight Jim Flynn some time in July. . . .
>
> Jack Johnson was the first of his class among the colored fighters to appear upon the scene after the passing of Peter Jackson. . . . His physical strength, coupled with his knowledge, experience and skill, makes all aspirants for the heavyweight championship title stand in fear of him. . . . If he continues to use good common sense he will long be the world's champion, the pride of his race in this particular and the idol of sporting men the world over.[113]

Pittsburgh was a city of avid sports fans, with its pennant-contender baseball team, the Pirates, led by the immortal Honus "The Flying Dutchman" Wagner, and the Pittsburgh Panthers football team with an impressive record under Glenn H. "Pop" Warner. But blacks, while generally admitted to commercial athletic exhibitions as spectators, were excluded as participants. If they played at all, it was on segregated teams, such as the baseball nines sponsored by the Homestead Plant of the Carnegie Steel Company. But whatever news there was of local black athletes, the *Courier* reported it enthusiastically. It predicted "the fur will fly September 21 when the Clay Giants and the Homestead Grays come together for the Colored [Baseball] Championship of Western Pennsylvania."[114] When the Pittsburgh Monticello A. A. team defeated the visiting Howard University basketball team 24–19, the *Courier* carried the headline, "PITTSBURGH SHOOTERS ARE NEW WORLD'S CHAMPION COLORED BASKETBALL PLAYERS."[115] This close coverage of black achievements in the world of sports, as well as in medicine, politics, and science, helped to increase racial pride.

The third important role played by the *Courier* in attempting to improve the less tangible aspects of black life in Pittsburgh was thorough dispensing of local information to the black community. This indirectly created ethnic bonds and gave blacks a sense of cohesion in the face of the multiplicity of a large city. The lengthy "Local News" section of the *Courier* was virtually an encyclopedia of middle-class black events in Pittsburgh, and in the early years it was one of the most important parts of the newspaper. There a black could read news of the Arnett Literary Society of the Euclid Avenue AME Church, the Hesperia Social Club, the Frogs Social Club, Young Men's Civic Club, or the prestigious Loendi Club. The latter, for example, featured Assistant Attorney General of the United States William H. Lewis and Judge H. Terrell of the Washington, D.C., Municipal Court as speakers for the Grant Birthday Celebration,[116] held a symposium led by William D. Grimes, attorney and former assistant city solicitor, who spoke on "The Spirit of Pittsburgh,"[117] and conducted billiard contests, which were very popular and in which Robert Vann took a strong personal interest.[118] One read that the Charity Club would meet at the home of Mrs. R. L. Vann on Monticello Street on July 3, 1911. There was news of who had gone on vacation, married, or had parties, and announcements of coming events from sports to church gatherings. There was news of the Pittsburgh black upper crust, the William H. Stantons, the S. P. Marshalls, the R. E. Byrds, the Louis Allens, and the A. L. Andersons. Church news received much coverage, especially that from the Brown Chapel, the John Wesley AMEZ, the Warren ME, the AME Zion Church, Bethel AME, and Euclid Avenue AME. Secret societies like the Malta Commandary, Odd Fellows, Knights of Pythias, International Order of St. Luke, Grand Lodge of Masons, and Iron City Council also received their share of coverage. One could also read black news from surrounding communities filed by part-time reporters from Homewood, Homestead, New Castle, Tyrone, Uniontown, Greensburg, Leetsdale, Philipsburg, Pittstown, Washington, Monongahela City, Beaver Falls, Altoona, and Sharon, as well as from East Liverpool, Youngstown, Cadiz, Lisbon, and Dayton, in Ohio, and Huntington, Wheeling, and Morgantown, in West Virginia.

The *Courier* furnished news for recently arrived immigrants from the South of happenings in their home states, to help ease their transition to life in Pittsburgh. The "News from Back Home" section had articles like "WORK OF WATERS NORMAL SCHOOL . . . ITS INFLUENCE IN WINTON [N.C.]"[119] and "FARMERS CONFERENCE BENEFICIAL, *North Carolina Negroes Listened To Many Able Addresses At Convention*"[120] and "EIGHT HUNDRED NORTH CAROLINA MASONS MEET."[121]

The last major area in which Vann carried on his crusade in the *Courier* during the years from 1910 to 1920 was social discrimination. In his efforts to end the pervasive discrimination practiced against blacks, Vann was joined by other northern black weeklies, with militant names like *The Defender, Advocate, Protest, Whip, Guardian,* and *Broad Ax.*[122] Vann campaigned almost as strongly in this area as he had in housing or employment, though it was, of course, less crucial to the daily life of most Pittsburgh blacks. This may have been because it touched Vann's own life where none of the other inequities could. Unlike most other blacks, he had an education, money for decent health care, challenging and well-paid work, and a pleasant home. One would prefer to believe that it was because it seemed to Vann the one area where real improvement was imminently possible for the Pittsburgh blacks, and, moreover, the area in which he and the *Courier* could have the most specific impact.

After the Supreme Court had declared the Federal Civil Rights Act of 1875 unconstitutional in 1883, many state legislatures outside the South adopted statutes modeled on the 1875 act. The Pennsylvania law of 1887 forbade discrimination for reasons of race in places of public accommodation like restaurants, hotels, railroads, street railways, omnibus lines, theaters, concert halls, or other places of entertainment. However, the ensuing failure to enforce the state legislation indicated that Pennsylvanians were content to have the law on the statute books as long as it was not applied.[123] Blacks who entered white restaurants in Pittsburgh often found salt in their coffee, pepper in their milk, and overcharges of up to 500 percent on their bills.[124] Nickelodeons made a practice of charging blacks double price for inferior seats, even boldly displaying signs on the theater doors advertising their double price policy. Downtown theaters along Fifth Avenue either refused to admit blacks or, in the case of the Harris theaters, segregated them in "the peanut gallery." Other theaters like the Nixon, the "World's Perfect Playhouse," and the Harry Davis Company, a local theater enterprise running the nightly Hippodrome performances at Forbes Field, also forced black patrons into the galleries or certain sections of the stands. The *Courier* advised its readers that it was better to "stay away and keep our money than to be subjected to such contemptible treatment."[125] When blacks in East Liberty complained against discrimination in the nickelodeons there, Vann replied tartly in the *Courier:*

> The very fact that the discrimination continues shows that the Negro is still an ardent patron of those places where every possible means is resorted to in the effort to convince the Negro that he is not wanted. It seems to be our own failing to force ourselves into places where we are not wanted, and pay the price for the privilege. While there are many instances where we have to fight for our rights in public places, and in all such instances, we may fight to the finish; but certainly the nickelodeons are not such places. We can well afford to remain away from them for all the moral uplift they afford; and certainly we have need of the money. If we are being discriminated against, and object to it, then stay away.[126]

In department stores, Vann noted in the *Courier*, whites like immigrant Italians, Greeks, or Jews were served quickly, while "the Negro meets the most embarrassment, regardless of the amount he seeks to spend. . . . He stands and waits. . . . with money in hand, but little or no attention is paid him. The clerks see him—and then forget his presence. He is the last man to get attention, and often his patronage is practically imposed upon indifferent attendants."[127] Vann suggested that, for the moment, "this condition [could] be stopped" by blacks' boycotting the stores. Hotels either excluded blacks outright or embarrassed them so severely that they were discouraged from ever returning. For example, when Mrs. Daisy Lampkin, one of Pittsburgh's prominent black women, went to the Penn Hotel to see a friend, she was forced to use the freight elevator.[128] As a result, when black leaders came to visit Pittsburgh, they either had to patronize an all-black hotel, usually Bailey's, or stay in private homes; this latter course was followed by A. Philip Randolph and W. E. B. DuBois, who stayed upon occasion at Robert Vann's house.[129]

To end these social indignities, Vann felt, more was required than halfhearted boycotts of public establishments. The state needed a strong equal rights bill so that offenders could be prosecuted and fined. There had been one attempt to introduce such a bill in March 1911, when Representative Harry Bass, a black man from Philadelphia, brought his amendment before the state legislature, but it had failed.[130] Then early in 1915, Vann began to mention hopefully another such attempt in the *Courier*. To be introduced by State Representative A. C. Stein from Vann's First Legislative District in Pittsburgh, the Stein bill was to come before the House in March.[131] The bill had the strong backing of black organizations, including the Pittsburgh, Philadelphia, and Harrisburg branches of the NAACP. In March, Vann announced happily in the *Courier* that Stein had brought his bill before the House. The bill demanded that "equal accommodations and equal rights be given all men by proprietors of public conveyances, hotels, public places of amusement," and so forth, or they would be liable to "fines and imprisonment." Every black, said Vann, "has his share of work to perform in securing the passage of the Bill. Let us begin now to organize . . . to make our future secure against the abuses we have suffered in the past."[132] On April 2, he recalled the defeat of the Bass bill of 1911 and said "we [blacks] must work without ceasing," and told of his plans to go to Harrisburg for the final vote on April 14 to exert what influence he could.

By April 9, one could feel Vann's tense involvement with the fate of the Stein bill. He asked other "local [white] editors to devote a little space to the . . . Bill," and called for every black church to take up an offering and send a member to Harrisburg to work for the bill. "Stein needs men on the floor of the House," he pleaded, and the church "owes the public a service . . . not confined to soul saving especially, but to COMMUNITY SAVING."[133]

Vann made several trips to Harrisburg. On April 14, before the House vote on the Stein bill, he presented a pledge signed by eighty-three legislators in support of the measure. He also exerted pressure by claiming the support of U. S. Senator Boies Penrose. The Stein bill passed the House 138 to 36, Vann announced triumphantly in the *Courier* of April 16.[134] The bill was then sent to the Judiciary Special Committee of the Senate, where Vann felt it was in "safe hands." "We must keep watch on proceedings and if our presence is found to be needed in Harrisburg," he vowed, "we must go at whatever sacrifice."[135]

The Stein bill passed the Senate 34 to 11, but Governor Martin G. Brumbaugh vetoed it on June 15, 1915.[136] The governor argued that the 1915 act was not necessary because "the act of May 19, 1887 (P.L. 130) is substantially the same as this, with a more severe penalty for its violation. Pennsylvania would be remiss if she did not secure equal rights to all her citizens. She has not been remiss." Brumbaugh noted secondarily that the bill was vetoed because it had been "greatly modified" from its original form as presented to the legislature.[137] Vann felt that the measure failed in part because it did not have the support of the white press. Only the *Dispatch* and the *Leader* had made any editorial reference to the Stein bill, and the *Harrisburg Patriot* coverage was limited to a single, four-line note on the day the bill came before the House.[138] The bill's modifications came about because of the indifference of white Republican legislators who felt secure in their hold on the black electorate and thus were less than passionate in their support of the bill, allowing it to be amended drastically.

Exhausted physically and emotionally from his long fight for the Stein bill, Robert Vann developed complications from a cold he had caught in Harrisburg and became quite ill. He did not fully recuperate until late in May, more than a month later. Vann mentioned the fate of the bill only sparingly in his editorials for some months, almost as if he could not bring himself to discuss it. But it obviously made him bitter. In July, writing on local politics, he sounded cynical for the first time. He referred to the empty promises made to blacks in the past and said, "The Negro need not heed the promises this year."[139]

Vann finally brought up the topic of the bill in September, before the Republican primaries. He told all blacks to register without fail. "Remember the defeat of the Equal Rights Bill. Vote . . . WITH THE INTEREST OF THE RACE ALWAYS BEFORE YOU."[140] A few days before the primaries, he wrote bitterly, "The Negro has but little from which to choose. The recent episode at Harrisburg is fresh in [our] minds . . . we can not readily forget how useless were promises and pledges."[141] By December, he regained enough objectivity to say that, despite the defeat of the Stein bill, the work on its behalf helped to solidify the black community, and "in union there is strength."[142]

Two years later the subject of an equal rights bill came up again, but Vann was skeptical. He only commented briefly that it was to be brought before the Pennsylvania House again. "Its fate . . . is problematical," he concluded tersely.[143] Two weeks later he commented cynically, "We do not hesitate to state that this . . . Bill is introduced for no other purpose than to flood the legislature with Civil Rights measures so as to create a fight against all such measures. We are aware of the tactics of the Pennsylvania politicians. . . . We learned much about the gentlemen two years ago."[144] The bill was tabled on June 20, 1917.[145]

Equal rights bills were introduced again and again in Pennsylvania. Vann worked vigorously but fruitlessly for those of 1921 and 1923, both introduced by black legislator J. C. Asbury of Philadelphia.[146] In 1921 he told the House Judiciary Committee, "I share the embarrassment of some members of the House in having to come before you so often for a civil rights bill. Your embarrassment arises from the fact that you have not aroused yourselves to inform yourselves about our Negro fellow-citizens nor allowed yourselves to be aroused." He gave the committee moral reasons why they should support the bill and then warned them that blacks were becoming politically disaffected by the constant defeats. "We have reached the point where it is becoming more and more advisable to break away from the different factions in Pennsylvania politics because the Negro is not given any consideration whatsoever."[147] But the bill was tabled by the Judiciary Committee. It was a lesson to Robert Vann in the realities of politics. As long as blacks had no significance in the electoral columns, they would receive no consideration from white legislators, who were rarely motivated by moral dictates. It would require political power, which as yet the blacks did not have to any degree, for them to obtain meaningful social reforms through legislation. After making vain attempts for over a decade, Vann finally abandoned the fight for new equal rights legislation and worked for a more stringent application of the 1887 state law.

During these years of the *Courier*'s campaign for social change in Pittsburgh, there were few notable successes and Vann must have been discouraged often. Nonetheless, the *Courier* did become an important spokesman for the black community of Pittsburgh, and its crusades continued even after it became more national in its outlook. With its frequent clarion calls for racial cohesion, Vann's *Courier* gave blacks a sense of themselves as a body with common interests and implicit power. As he said at the end of 1917, "Activity in community life is a necessity. . . . That which we achieve by our own efforts is enjoyed with so much greater freedom," and gave a year-end call for group action. "Right here in Pittsburgh is the place for racial exertion."[148]

· 5 ·

Politics and Patriotism: 1917-1919

As PART OF his *Courier* campaign to improve the black man's lot in Pittsburgh, Robert Vann editorially advocated black political unity. He felt that unification of the local black vote could provide a force for social change, and he constantly tried to goad the race into political awareness. In 1912 he ran the following on the front page for several weeks in succession:

> No one will probably realize the value of his vote until he is called upon for it, no one may hope to cast a vote who willfully neglects to register, so long will we be ignored politically, for the very plain reason, we are of no value. It is utter folly to boast of a Negro population of 16,000 when we have only about 9,000 voters. What we need is to register every Negro in the city and county and then when we are approached for our ballot, we, like the Hebrews, may ask, what shall we receive for our support. Numbers count for naught in politics; it is the votes, nothing less. Get registered now.[1]

Vann compared his readers unfavorably with other ethnic minorities in the city from a political standpoint, hoping to rouse them to action. He noted editorially that in the fall registration drive of 1912 more than seven hundred Italians had received their naturalization papers and had qualified to vote in the November presidential election. "This activity on the part of the Italians makes very conspicuous the political lethargy of the Negro, who is relieved of the necessity of securing naturalization papers, and has only to register and vote." Yet blacks constantly complained that Italians had been given preference for jobs when they were not even American citizens. To this Vann replied, "In the face of such activity on the part of the foreigner we are driven to conclude that the preference given is warranted. The Negro might as well learn that actual and not alleged worth is what counts in the present age."[2]

The *Courier* editor was dismayed that many blacks put so little value on their ballots that they sold them to the highest bidder. During the 1911 Pittsburgh and Allegheny County elections he addressed himself to this problem:

> Regardless of motive, principle or anything relating to the real issues involved, the Negroes are "looking for the money," to use the expression so common to political parlance . . . As soon as it was known that certain candidates were putting money into the hands of their lieutenants, the free-for-all scramble began. The result is that the Negroes are as badly divided as are the various factions.
>
> The condition reflects sadly upon the colored man. It but argues that he does not place any value upon his ballot further than what it will bring in the money market. He uses his ballot for purely mercenary purposes. For this the white man who buys him gives him no credit, and at the same time loses all confidence in him, for he fears that the market may be "bulled" by the opposing faction and the Negro voter resell his franchise.
>
> It goes without saying that if the Negroes were as closely organized as are the Jews, Italians, and other races, they would be sought by every faction, and not with money either, but with their full quota of political recognition. We are throwing our rights to the winds, brethren.[3]

Vann constantly reiterated the need for blacks to organize into a strong political force. "The only possible way for the Negro to obtain anything in the political field is by organization. So long as we stand divided the white man cares not how we vote so evenly distributed will be our strength," he said. "But if we can effect an organization—and we mean a real, live popular organization—we will become a factor in the politics of Pennsylvania and the Union, and always help to dictate the affairs of our county and city."[4]

Vann's idea was sound, for it is of course political organization that has eventually given other minorities an audible voice in the American political process, beginning at the level of city government. But Vann's concept was unrealistic in Pittsburgh, where blacks were neither ready to be organized and unified politically, nor of sufficient numbers to be reckoned with until World War I.

In 1917 Robert Vann changed the nature of the dicta issued from his editorial rostrum. Since large-scale general changes were not feasible, Vann turned his full attention to a local political contest. He became heavily involved in the Pittsburgh mayoral election that year, more than he had been in previous contests, both as a private individual and as *Courier* editor. The results altered the course of Vann's career. He secured a political plum after the election, which was the start of his twenty-three-year sojourn in the political spotlight. The gains for Vann were considerable; he gradually acquired prestige, power, and eventually a post in Washington. But there were some losses. As Vann gained personal recognition and began the process of political self-aggrandizement, he left behind his idealism and something of his decency. Protective of his newly acquired honors, he increasingly steered a course between obstacles to his career, which caused him to change party allegiance on two separate and dramatic occasions, removing all consistency and authority from his public comments. Vann followed this pattern of expedient reversal not only in his personal political career, but in his newspaper. As the *Courier* increased in renown and circulation, and as it grew from a local to a nationally known weekly, Vann looked more and more for issues that would further augment circulation. In so doing, he occasionally changed the paper's editorial position so drastically that the *Courier* lost any sense of philosophical continuity as well as concern for and effectiveness among local blacks.

The 1917 Pittsburgh mayoral election is of interest not only because it marked the real commencement of Robert Vann's political career, but because Vann's relation to that election demonstrates much that was characteristic of Pittsburgh politics at the time. From the time Vann had first dabbled in mayoral politics in 1906, he had logically supported William Magee's machine-controlled faction of the local Republican party. Vann's allegiances were typical for a Pittsburgh black; they were the product of the remarkably monopartisan nature of politics in Pennsylvania and Pittsburgh during the fifty years prior to 1917, of the workings of the machine in Pittsburgh, and of the black's relationship to these political phenomena. Once these factors are examined, it is clear why Robert Vann was a Republican, loyal to machine candidates, and a moderate rather than a reformer—a fact which initially seems surprising in the face of the crusade for social change he had carried on in the *Courier*.

In Pennsylvania, the Republicans had been fully in control since 1865 when Simon Cameron, briefly Lincoln's secretary of war, became the state party leader. After Cameron died in 1877, the mantle of leadership passed to Matthew S. Quay, who consolidated his forces, made the state machine more efficient, and held control until his death in 1904. Senator Boies Penrose then took control of the Pennsylvania Republican party and was still very much in charge in 1917. Under Penrose's rule, not only was no Democratic senator or governor elected in Pennsylvania, but the state legislature was overwhelmingly Republican and the congressional delegation predominantly so.[5] The Democrats were powerless, their party structure was weak, and at most they were able to elect a few candidates to the state legislature and some local offices. They were usually restricted to holding offices allotted by law to the minority, as in Philadelphia and Pittsburgh, where a statute required that the minority party have at least one seat on the county board of commissioners.[6]

The political situation in Pittsburgh almost exactly mirrored that of the state, with an Irish Republican dynasty handing the power down through successive generations of political bosses, and only rare disruptions in the flow of control. Republican control of Pittsburgh began in 1863, two years before Simon Cameron began to run the state organization, when Squire Tommy Steele founded what was to become the Smoky City's Republican machine. Steele succeeded in passing the reins to his nephew, Christopher Lyman Magee, who came to power in the 1870s.[7] Magee formed an alliance with William Flinn, an ambitious young contractor, and created a highly effective machine which ran the city for many years.[8] Christopher Lyman Magee reportedly studied the workings of other city machines to discover their strengths and weaknesses before expanding the one he inherited from Tommy Steele.[9]

Magee and Flinn, both able if voracious businessmen, made their mounting political power interdependent with their businesses, and so amassed large fortunes while holding various local offices and controlling most others. For example, Magee's Duquesne Traction Company easily obtained franchises and controlled the building and running of the city's railways, while the construction firm of Booth and Flinn held a monopoly on the municipality's public works.[10] During their years in power, Magee and Flinn controlled the city and county governments almost completely. In 1887, the state legislature wrote a new charter for Pittsburgh which placed much of the power of the city council in the hands of the Departments of Public Works, Public Safety, and Public Charity, all of which were headed by Magee-Flinn henchmen. Magee also controlled the county, through the Allegheny County Republican Executive Committee, from which he managed most offices and patronage. The county remained a stronghold even on the rare occasions when the city wavered in allegiance, and even that wavering ceased when Flinn became chairman of Pittsburgh's Republican Executive Committee.[11]

Democratic opposition was minimal. Its organization was known derisively as "The Steps Crowd," because the few members met on the steps of a building on Liberty Avenue. Magee, in effect, gained control over the Democrats, too, by helping to elect tractable Democrats, who could thereafter be expected to do his bidding. How effective he was in this respect was seen near the end of his life, when Magee wished to be a state senator, and both parties forthwith united to nominate him unanimously.[12]

The machine's control of Pittsburgh was so complete that there were few challenges to its power. It had the support not only of the political hacks, but tacitly of the city's businessmen, powerful industrialists, and bankers, who raised no objection to the Magee-Flinn rule as long as it did not interfere with their private concerns.

However, one challenge came in 1896, when a Democrat named George Wilkins Guthrie, a lawyer and son of a former mayor, ran for mayor and almost succeeded in unseating the machine candidate.[13] After Guthrie's defeat, the Citizens Municipal League, a reform group, charged that he had been cheated of his rightful victory by dishonest election officials who counted the ballots incorrectly, but their outcry came to naught. In the 1898 city council elections, the Citizens Municipal League again claimed election fraud when its candidate, Councilman George Stengel, an antimachine man, lost by three votes. The League charged that over two hundred blacks had been bribed and brought in to vote for Stengel's opponent at least once.[14]

George Guthrie was undiscouraged by his 1896 defeat and made another bid for the mayoralty in 1906. In that election, more factors were working in his favor. Christopher Magee had died in 1901, and confusion followed his death. Matthew Quay, head of the state

Republican organization, who had agreed not to interfere with Pittsburgh politics while Magee was alive, stepped in and temporarily seized power in the city. Quay's revolt against the Magee-Flinn machine, to which he had once belonged, led to the support of Guthrie in 1906 by an unlikely amalgam of Quay's followers, reformers like the Citizens Municipal League, and regular Democrats. Guthrie managed to defeat A. M. Jenkinson, the machine candidate for whom Robert Vann campaigned while still a college student, and became the only Democratic mayor of Pittsburgh until 1933. Though victorious, the Guthrie forces raised the issue of possible fraud by Jenkinson's partisans, charging that Jenkinson "and his cronies in the pilgrimage to the saloons and clubs have been making a strong play for the colored vote," and that blacks had been brought into Pittsburgh to vote illegally.[15] Vann personally salvaged something from Jenkinson's defeat—his first political appointment. As a reward for his vote-getting efforts in black neighborhoods, he was given a clerkship in the office of the mercantile appraiser. Vann was a member of the Allegheny County Colored Protective League, a black political organization, and its head, M. T. Velar, used his influence to help him get the position.[16] Vann was one of the few blacks on the city payroll, and most of the others were laborers, messengers, janitors, firemen, letter carriers, and postal clerks.[17]

In 1909, William A. Magee again consolidated the Republican power that threatened to slip away after his uncle Christopher's death and was elected mayor. Magee then set off a new rush of city building, with the lion's share of the contracts going once more to the firm of Booth and Flinn.[18] Graft, held in abeyance under Guthrie, began to flourish once again, with city council members bribed to vote away valuable franchises. Once more, the reformers objected vociferously. The Voters Civic League, organized by A. Lee Weil and other prominent Pittsburghers, brought the corruption to light in 1912 and presented their damaging evidence against Magee's administration to a grand jury.[19] As a result, over one hundred persons, including councilmen, businessmen, bankers, and the heads of the Departments of Public Works, Safety, and Health, were indicted, and a number received jail sentences.[20]

Nonetheless, Robert Vann and most other Pittsburgh blacks remained loyal to Magee's group. For one thing, Magee and his cohorts gave a certain number of patronage jobs to blacks. In 1911, Mayor Magee "broke all precedents and appointed a Negro to a position of rank" when he named William Randolph Grimes an assistant city solicitor. It was the highest position a black had ever held in Pittsburgh's city administration.[21] Further, Magee's ally, William Flinn, employed blacks as laborers in his contracting business, for example, in the job of removing the Hump (a three-block-long hill in Pittsburgh's Triangle District between Diamond and Sixth) which was levelled beginning in 1912 to make the central area more usable.[22] Vann editorialized, "Nor should a man of this type be forgotten in a day. It is by and through such men as Mr. Flinn that the Negro must get his little portion of the world's goods; and it is an ingratitude of the deepest kind to turn upon the ladder by which you ascend and curse it."[23] And Vann pointed out in a later editorial, "Nor has the Negro any complaint to make regarding the treatment he has received in the hands of the Mayor. The *Courier* has no hesitancy in saying that the Negro has a friend in Mayor Magee."[24] Thus the Magee machine offered employment, unskilled though it was, to some of its black constituents, providing a vital economic opportunity guaranteed to make the recipients loyal ever after to the givers. The loyalty of Pittsburgh blacks to Magee was not unlike the relation of white ethnic groups to big-city machines. For those at the lowest end of the economic scale, the small benefits provided by the organizations insured continued support.

It was also unlikely that the blacks would turn to a reform group because the reformers were often contemptuous of blacks and so were frequently more distasteful to them than the obviously corrupt machine politicians. The Voters Civic League, "an organization of white men," as the *Courier* called it, which was exposing the Magee administration, also took an exaggerated view of vice among blacks and seemed bent on ending that too. The blacks were understandably resentful of distortions in the League's statistics. Vann wrote angrily in an editorial:

> The zealous officers of the League have charged, among other things, that colored men can be seen day and night leading young white girls and white women to houses of shame. . . . We are at a loss to know why these gentlemen did not charge the whole truth as it is . . . for certainly these same gentlemen must know that there are more colored girls and women led to the houses of shame every day by white men, than there are white women by colored men in a whole year. There are houses of shame in this city where

colored women are maintained by the patronage of white men, and them only. Any such work as the League professes to do must be directed to conditions among all of the people or it is a shame and a failure.[25]

Vann took a dim view of other reform groups like the Morals Efficiency Commission for their conception of blacks as brutes, keepers of white women, proponents of vice, gambling, and physical violence. Why, wondered Vann, weren't other ethnic minorities similarly regarded? "The Greeks have 'open house' on Wylie Avenue every day of the week. It is a common thing to see card-playing in almost every Greek establishment on the Sabbath Day. . . . If the Negro of Pittsburgh should attempt a card table display on the Sabbath Day such as is common among the Greeks of Wylie Avenue, we need not say what would have happened ere this writing. The work house would be crying for additional room in which to house the victims."[26]

W. E. B. DuBois observed the black's relationship to the machine at the beginning of the century in Philadelphia and recorded it in a 1905 article. To most blacks, "politics" was synonymous with "machine," and their loyalty to it was economic—a product of either direct or indirect bribery. Direct bribery was the buying of black votes; indirect bribery was the distribution of patronage jobs to blacks. "Probably in no other way could these people get employment that would give them half their present incomes. Their jobs are 'in politics' and their holders must and do support the machine. Moreover, such civic pride as the Negro has is expended on these representatives of his race in public life and they support the party that puts these men in office."[27] In this manner the machine cemented and perpetuated its hold over blacks. And DuBois noted, as did Vann a few years later, how little appeal political reform movements had for black voters. First of all, the reformers were not promising jobs for blacks. "Thus the Negroes have always been suspicious that the reform movements tended not to their betterment but to their elimination from political life and consequently from the best chance of earning a living." To further lessen their appeal, "the attitude of some of the reformers and their contempt for Negroes has not improved this race opinion,"[28] as Vann noticed in the two Pittsburgh reform movements of 1912.

For these reasons, a rising Pittsburgh black like Robert Vann would almost inevitably be a Republican and, on the whole, loyal to the local machine. The reformers offered little, and the Republican organization had been solidly entrenched in the state and the city since the Civil War. Then there was, of course, the strong emotional appeal the Republican party still had for most blacks as the party of Lincoln and emancipation. Blacks had been voting the ticket since they won their freedom from slavery, and the majority would continue to do so for nearly two more decades. Like the reformers, the Democrats offered little to blacks and, moreover, represented oppression by southern whites. The Democratic party was anathema to the average black. As Vann put it in 1912, when writing about the national contest between Woodrow Wilson, William Howard Taft, and Theodore Roosevelt (running as a Progressive), "Anything [for president] but a Democrat."[29] And in a lighter mood he wrote, "Can any Negro imagine himself doing anything under a Wilson administration except manipulating a mop, or juggling a cuspidor? Aunt Hannah from Georgia to bake the corn cake and Uncle Epps from Virginia to care for the fox hounds will about constitute the Black Cabinet.... Brethren, black Democrats will not be in style this fall."[30] Vann's prophecy turned out to be correct when, after Woodrow Wilson's election, segregation was effected for black office workers in the Treasury Department and postmaster general's office. In 1912, it was unthinkable to Robert Vann that he would ever join the Democratic party.

In the Pittsburgh mayoral contest of 1913, Vann remained loyal to the Magee machine and supported its candidate, Stephen G. Porter. Since 1910, Vann had been secretary of the Allegheny County Colored Protective League, a black voters' organization; though blacks numbered but 7,719 of Pittsburgh's registered voters in 1910, there was always the chance they could influence the vote in a close election. In the 1913 contest, Vann worked through James Malone, city councilman and longtime party boss of the heavily black Fifth Ward, to try and gain black votes for Magee's mayoral candidate.[31] But Porter was narrowly defeated by Joseph Armstrong, a member of the opposition faction within the party. By 1917, William A. Magee was ready to run for mayor again. That year he was opposed by Edward Vose Babcock, a fellow Republican and member of the same faction that had supported Joseph Armstrong's successful mayoral bid in 1913. Babcock, a wealthy, socially prominent lumberman, had entered Pittsburgh politics in 1911. As a result of the scandals within the Magee administration, Governor John K. Tener had appointed an interim city council in June 1911. Babcock was one of his choices. In the regularly scheduled November election which followed, Babcock ran in his own right and led the ticket. He served on the council until 1913.[32]

In the 1917 mayoralty race there were two Republican factions, one headed by Magee and the other by United States Senator George T. Oliver and Max Leslie, chairman of the Ninth Ward. (It was charged, however, that the Mellon family was its real head, controlling from behind the scenes.) In the black wards, particularly the Fifth, John Elmore, an Irish politician and owner of a saloon and theater in the Hill District, was Magee's spokesman. The blacks who remained loyal to Magee were led by Robert Logan, a black real estate agent. James Malone, another Irish politician, sought the black vote for Babcock. Malone's political longevity was due in part to his own machine's strength in the Fifth Ward, based on small favors and minor positions he had awarded to blacks. Because of Malone's control over the vote in the Fifth, whichever GOP faction sought his support had to come to him with political promises. On the basis of this strength, Malone remained a force in city politics until 1929. When Vann deserted the Magee group in 1917 he worked through Malone.[33]

Robert Vann made a critical decision to defect from the Magee group. Two important factors prompted this change. The first was that the corruption which had surrounded the Magee name like a cloud since 1870 had by 1917 become a choking miasma.[34] The corruption itself probably did not trouble Robert Vann much: it was a perennial part of the Magee image that had long been known and tolerated by the public and the business community. Vann had readily supported him in other elections over the years. But since 1912 the outcry against Magee had been so constant that it began to look as though he had little chance of winning. Vann, clear-eyed opportunist that he was, realized the time was ripe to break away from the machine; Edward Vose Babcock looked like a certain winner. Babcock was not a reformer by any means, but his name was untainted, and that seemed to be what Pittsburghers were going to want in 1917. At the very beginning of the year, Vann editorialized in a general way about "OUR NEXT MAYOR," referring to the "unfortunate corruption-breeding process of politics" and asking that the next mayor be "intelligent, upright and worthy . . . free from political entanglements."[35] Though Vann mentioned no name, that description certainly did not fit Magee.

The second factor which led to Vann's decision to defect from the machine was that Babcock promised him an appointive political office in return for his support and that of the black community.[36] This is significant because it shows that by 1917 Vann and the blacks had some political bargaining strength and could perhaps provide the balance of power in a close intraparty struggle. Though black voters had numbered only 7,719 in 1910, the Great Northern Migration during the war years increased their numbers to approximately 25,000.[37] The number of blacks of voting age had increased from 5.6 percent of the total number of voters to 7.2 percent since 1910. This is by no means a large rise, but it does show that the blacks were becoming worthy of political consideration. As the *Courier* editor, Robert Vann was one of the most visible members of this growing black community and wielded considerable influence through his weekly editorials. The offer of a political job to Vann was a painless way of winning his support and potentially that of 25,000 black voters. A position on the city payroll for Vann thus became a quid pro quo from Babcock in return for weekly portions of praise in the *Courier*.

Vann also supported Babcock because he advertised in the *Courier* and Magee did not. To the *Courier* editor it made sound business sense "that the man who favors another with his business stands a better chance to receive a favor than the man who refuses to patronize another's business."[38]

As the year wore on and Vann made public his commitment to E. V. Babcock, his battle with the Magee forces became heated. After Vann began influencing his fellow blacks to switch to Babcock, Magee followers prepared a circular for distribution in the predominantly black Fifth Ward, saying that it was an easy matter to buy black votes and E. V. Babcock was buying them. Vann struck back, charging in front of a large meeting at the Watt Street School that a Magee worker had "sought to buy his vote" and influence for the tidy sum of $1,000.[39]

The primary, listed as nonpartisan but in truth Republican, took place in September. Babcock ran first with 31,138 votes; Magee was next with 25,926; and Dr. J. P. Kerr, president of the City Council, polled 16,679.[40] With such a small majority for Babcock, Vann's apparent role as the balance of power in the run-off election was greatly strengthened. The November run-off would be between Republicans Babcock and Magee; there was no Democratic candidate for mayor.

As the final election neared, charges and countercharges proliferated. In reading newspaper accounts of the time, one is struck by the amount of hyperbole in which the candidates indulged. Babcock denounced the Magee "mud and slime campaign" and accused the Magee-dominated city council of being solely responsible for a current vice and crime wave. Still smarting from his loss in the September primary, Magee charged Babcock with being the "Gang candidate" dominated by the Penrose-Leslie-Armstrong forces and having employed "the most unscrupulous, cold-blooded and foul tactics ever brought out by men who make a practice of debauching elections," including the use of thugs to intimidate Magee voters, police "turned Cossack" to drive away Magee poll watchers, and floaters to move from place to place voting over and over for Babcock.[41]

One issue that particularly raised Robert Vann's ire during the campaign was the front-page article in the Magee-supporting *Pittsburgh Dispatch* belittling black servicemen from Pennsylvania at Camp Lee, Virginia, who worked at manual labor and lived in segregated barracks, despite the fact that many were college graduates. The article referred derogatorily to the black soldiers as little more than "crapshooters."[42] Vann saw this as an "un-American attack upon the race,"[43] for he was especially proud of the black soldiers who could rise above the terrible irony of being "lynched in time of peace . . . and shot down for [their] country in time of war."[44] Vann continued to protest against the disparaging remarks made by the Magee press and against the treatment blacks were getting at Camp Lee. Vann wrote angrily in the preelection issue of the *Courier*, "Does it not appear strange that every paper supporting Mr. Babcock gave our boys front-page articles, praising the valor of the colored men in arms, while the Magee organ, evidently biased, prejudiced and wicked, devoted two columns to libellous statements about the Negroes who left our city [for Army camp]?"[45]

Not yet sure of his candidate's final victory, Vann worked hard and long writing pro-Babcock pieces for his newspaper and foraging for votes in the black neighborhoods. The *Courier* issue of November 1, five days before the election, featured an enormous editorial, "BABCOCK FOR MAYOR." Vann pronounced that "the backers of Magee have repulsive records . . . as against an administration of immorality, financial extravagance and political machinery built for the favored few, as against little men . . . foul words and un-American principles. The *Courier* advises the election of Mr. Babcock and the assurance of a wise . . . clean administration, with all men recognized, all races, all creeds and conditions protected."[46] One notices that Vann at no point in his campaigning for Babcock spoke about what the candidate would do for the black man if elected; he spoke in more innocuous generalities, because at that time, while white candidates wanted the black vote, they were not ready to make specific promises to obtain it.

At this point in his career Robert Vann would undoubtedly be classified as a minor accommodationist politician. He worked within the white power structure, delivering the black vote or at least taking the credit and the emoluments—in this case a promised political appointment of less than major importance.[47] One observer called such jobs "the political leavings of the whites."[48] And yet it would have been futile in that year for Vann to attempt to work outside the white-dominated system as a politico; there was not a sufficient black power base.

The day before the election Vann and Ira Lewis, who was very interested in seeing the candidate for sheriff on Babcock's ticket, William S. Haddock, elected, stayed up most of the night preparing a special Babcock-Haddock issue of the *Courier*. Vann hired special trucks and had the copies distributed throughout the city's black wards.[49]

Vann's efforts paid off: Babcock defeated Magee, 40,604 to 36,174. He carried the mostly black wards by a margin of 1,326 to 1,267 in the Third and 1,944 to 1,821 in the Fifth, while losing by a margin of 1,398 to Magee's 1,924 in the Thirteenth. Magee threatened to demand an investigation into what he alleged was voter fraud leading to his defeat, but he never carried out his threat.[50]

Vann was given credit for swinging a sizable amount of the black vote to Babcock, a not inconsiderable feat when one remembers how loyal blacks normally were to machine candidates. Babcock rewarded him with an appointment as fourth assistant city solicitor at a starting salary of $2,650 per year.[51] Vann was elated. It was the highest position a black had ever received in the municipal bureaucracy. It meant great personal prestige for Vann, particularly since nearly all of the seven hundred blacks who held city, county, state, or federal jobs in Pittsburgh were messengers, telephone operators, laborers, policemen, or firemen.[52] A newspaper item announcing Vann's appointment described the *Courier* editor as "a natural orator, an indefatigable student and a close observer . . . [who] has been both in print and on the hustings a fearless and tireless exponent of Republican principles and an advocate for the rights of his people."[53] Vann's colleague Ira Lewis was given a clerkship in the office of the newly elected Sheriff Haddock, in gratitude for the work he had done.

The Pittsburgh City Council, which had to confirm Vann's appointment, was still dominated by members loyal to William Magee. Thus it managed to delay Vann's confirmation until March 1918, after Mayor Babcock had been in office for over two months.[54] Once his appointment was finally approved, Vann celebrated by buying himself a new Lincoln sedan, even though he did not yet know how to drive. When the frugal Mrs. Vann asked him if it was wise to take on such a large financial obligation, he replied, "All my boyhood I wanted a bicycle in vain. I'm taking no chances on wanting a car and not having one."[55] It was soon clear that his enthusiasm exceeded his driving ability, for within a month the Lincoln collided with another car in Altoona, and Vann suffered a fractured rib. It was the first of a whole series of collisions, for he never became a skillful driver.

Vann delved into his new job as assistant city solicitor eagerly. The city solicitor, Stephen Stone, who had not known Vann before, was immediately impressed by him. "He was very anxious to work, was very anxious to learn and to know and to understand everything that went on in the office of the City Solicitor. What appealed to me was his desire to improve his opportunity and make the best of it. This he did to a surprising extent."[56] Vann was initially given routine damage and claim suits to try, cases almost exclusively involving black people.[57] But within a few months he had demonstrated his ability and capacity for hard work and acquired more responsibility. Soon he was trying appeal cases from the police department as well as jury cases before the County Court, in which he acted as assistant corporation counsel for the city in all matters to do with property. Vann was justifiably proud of his record in this area. "I tried these cases for four years before juries, chiefly all white—certainly the judges were all white and the witnesses were all white—and was not reversed a single time. I was taken to the [State] Supreme Court only once and won the case before that tribunal, making a perfect score for my years as an attorney for the City of Pittsburgh." [58] Vann was also appointed as public defender for a number of indigent blacks accused of murder and began to compile an impressive record of acquittals and lightened sentences.[59]

Vann's appointment as assistant city solicitor coincided with America's participation in World War I. He devoted a good deal of space in the *Courier* to the black man and the war. Vann's patriotic sentiments are best described as conventional or middle-of-the-road, and he felt that World War I offered a chance for blacks once again to prove their loyalty as Americans. Only occasionally did Vann reveal a perception of the enormous irony surrounding the black man's lot in this country—at last freed from slavery, blacks were daily subjected to the grossest forms of economic, social, and political discrimination

"Making Hay While the Sun Shines," by Wilburt Holloway, the Pittsburgh Courier, *1924.*

and even lynched, yet they were asked to give their lives for America.

In 1914 Vann opposed the War Department's suspension of black enlistment and asked that the black man be allowed to serve "in the Army of his country whose soil he has enriched."[60] Two years later he wrote of his dismay when President Wilson allowed blacks to enlist in the Eighteenth Regiment in Mexico, because the black volunteers could serve only as waiters, barbers, and cooks, and were not permitted to fight.[61] When America entered the war, Vann said it was time for a black regiment in the Pennsylvania National Guard. He argued that if New York could have black regiments, and Massachusetts, Maryland, and Ohio use black battalions, then why not Pennsylvania, which had the largest black population of any northern state? As things stood then, Vann wrote, a black wishing to enlist either had to offer himself individually to a white Pennsylvania regiment or leave the state to join a black regiment like the New York Fifteenth.[62]

Like most black weeklies, the *Courier* patriotically backed America's entry into the war, hoping that "the war to end all wars" would somehow improve the lot of the nation's blacks, once they had shown themselves as fighting men like any others. Vann saw the black soldiers who left Pittsburgh on October 21, 1917, as having "the same kind of blood as made lasting victory on Boston Commons, at Fort Donaldson, Vicksburg, El Caney, San Juan." The soldiers are determined, said Vann, "TO A MAN . . . that the trust imposed [in them] shall not be betrayed."[63] "When this war shall have ceased THE NEGRO WILL HAVE ASSUMED HIS RIGHTFUL PLACE IN THE OPINIONS OF AMERICANS." He could then "ASSERT HIMSELF AS A MAN—not as a black man—AS A MAN."[64] After the war had ended, Vann made the astonishing statement that it had been of too short duration for the blacks to prove themselves fully:

> . . . the colored man of this country could have, and we think would have profited a great deal more had the war continued another two or five years. . . . Had . . . the enemy bled white the American forces to the same extent it did the French; had there been a larger percentage of the "flower of America" cut down on the field, and corresponding larger opportunity thereby offered the black soldiers of the world to fill the vacancies, a higher and nobler sense of appreciation for our sacrifices would have been obtained after the Armistice.[65]

At thirty-eight, Vann was too old for military service, but he worked vigorously on the home front. He participated in Liberty Loan drives, Red Cross campaigns, and YMCA rallies and publicized them in the *Courier*. The blacks of Pittsburgh responded enthusiastically to these efforts, subscribing to more than a million dollars in a single Liberty Loan drive headed by local black leaders. This effort impressed the white community, which had been skeptical of the blacks' ability to handle the drive alone.[66]

Vann's vocal and unceasing love of country had some interesting consequences for himself and for the *Courier*. First of all, he became Mayor Babcock's official emissary to the local black community for all wartime and postwar public functions. On New Year's Day 1919, for example, Vann presented an American flag to the Negro Emancipation Proclamation Committee and saw it raised ceremoniously at the Carron Street Baptist Church.[67] Vann was named to a "special" committee of the Mayor's Welcoming Committee, which greeted all incoming Pittsburgh servicemen.[68] (Why he was not on the official committee is a matter for speculation; probably some whites opposed his appointment.) And in March 1919, Vann supervised the parade for the returning black 351st Field Artillery Regiment, which had distinguished itself in Europe by helping "to drive the Hun across the Rhine."[69] Vann had crowds of enthusiastic blacks at Union Station at 8:30 A.M. to meet the regiment, which then marched proudly up Wylie Avenue and through a good portion of the Hill District. Mayor Babcock delivered a formal welcome on the steps of City Hall. The festive day ended with a huge ball held at the Duquesne Garden.[70] With each appearance at such functions, Vann became increasingly recognized by whites as the most prominent member of the local black community. Among Pittsburgh blacks, Vann's position as leader and spokesman solidified. He was gaining a firm base of prestige and local fame.

Vann also played a national role during the war. Emmett J. Scott, special assistant to Secretary of War Newton Baker, named Vann to a "Committee of One Hundred," a group of black spokesmen formed to report on conditions encountered by blacks in the armed services and in the nation generally.[71] As a member of the Committee of One Hundred, Vann helped form a black National Publicity Bureau to publicize black wartime achievements; he fought for a black war correspondent to be allowed at the front to report on black military deeds and was successful in getting Ralph Tyler sent over. When the *Pittsburgh Post-Gazette* objected to Tyler's appointment as "an unwise courtesy" because "there should be no color line in war news," Vann replied that he was in accord about the color line, but asked when the last time was that the *Post-Gazette* had published any account of black soldiers' deeds.[72]

Vann also petitioned Emmett Scott to intercede with President Wilson for an anti-lynch bill in behalf of the southern blacks who, though either fighting in the armed services or toiling patriotically at home, were still being lynched with alarming regularity. Sixty-eight blacks were lynched in 1918. Vann made specific reference to a barbarous lynching in Georgia in May, in which one of the victims killed in connection with a murder was an expectant mother.[73] Both Scott and Robert R. Moton, president of Tuskegee Institute, forwarded letters of protest to Wilson pleading with the president to speak out publicly against the crime because a "strong word definitely from you on this lynching proposition will have more effect just now than any other one thing." Wilson's brief reply to Moton was forwarded to Vann. While the president said he was "seeking an opportunity to do what you suggest," nothing substantial was done during the remainder of the Wilson administration to end lynching.[74]

Robert Vann revealed a middle-ground conventionality in his patriotic activities, and he showed the same tendency to eschew any deviation into radical or militant statement during the events of the summer of 1919, when more than twenty race riots took place and the country seemed about to dissolve into utter chaos and pervasive racial violence. Such widespread racial troubles had been threatening for two full years. In July 1917, closely following a similar incident in Memphis, there was a race riot in East St. Louis which made national headlines. It had been the most serious racial outbreak in the twentieth century, taking the lives of thirty-nine blacks and nine whites. Vann reacted strongly on the editorial page of the *Courier*. He attributed the riot to "the malicious labor unions that objected to Negroes making bread and butter," expressed his "wrath and disgust," and condemned " 'The Hellish South,' " adding that "the [white] South is overcome with the spirit of Hell and there seems to be no redemption for the people who inhabit that part of our great country."[75] Four weeks later he urged Pittsburgh blacks to attend a mass meeting at the Lyceum Theater and register a protest to the administration in Washington so that "the East St. Louis incident shall not pass without action on the part of this government."⁷⁶ Vann's views were moderate, however. He advocated orderly, lawful protest, and when 125 men were indicted in connection with the riots he asked reasonably that any innocent black "defenders of their own lives and property . . . be promptly released."⁷⁷ When a report of the incident exonerated local authorities, Vann's comment was angry but not incendiary: "The report does little or nothing toward curing the evils already committed, to say nothing of preventing a repetition of the curse which stands as a lasting shame to the country."⁷⁸ In that same month there were also racial disturbances in Chester, Pennsylvania.⁷⁹

Just afterward came the infamous Houston riot of August 23, 1917. A group of one hundred black soldiers of the Twenty-fourth Infantry from nearby Camp Logan responded to a series of provocations from the white citizenry of Houston and an altercation with white police by taking up their weapons and rioting through the city. The following morning the casualties numbered eighteen dead, of whom seventeen were white Houstonians. Nineteen others were wounded.⁸⁰ Thirteen of the alleged perpetrators were hanged and the rest imprisoned in the federal penitentiary at Leavenworth. Despite the tremendous severity of the punishment visited on the black soldiers, Vann's reactions in the *Courier* were temperate. He wrote in defense of the hangings, "The lesson from it stands out with significance. The honor of the Army must be upheld. Mutiny and murder are crimes that merit death upon conviction. Soldiers who participate in lawlessness must take the consequences." On the other hand, he went on, "the oppression and abuse [black soldiers] have suffered in every southern town to which they have been assigned borders on the unbearable. Those crackers heap every possible insult on our boys, and then hasten to have them arrested, if they resent the insult. We are human, and we ought to be treated as such. Uncle Sam ought to see to it that we are. To be hanged is a dear price to pay for the life of an abusive cracker, and it would be the greater measure of Democracy, if Uncle Sam could make this country safe for his soldier boys who have to serve near southern towns."⁸¹

Two years later, in the summer of 1919, the monumental upheavals began with the Chicago race riot of July 27, which was set off by the stoning of a black youth who had accidentally strayed into a portion of Lake Michigan designated for whites only. In the blood-soaked days which followed, as blacks again suffered at the hands of white attacks, twenty-three blacks and fifteen whites were killed in Chicago, and hundreds more seriously injured.[82] Soon after, riots were touched off in other cities throughout the United States, from Longview, Texas, to Washington, D.C., from Omaha to Indianapolis to Knoxville to Phillips County, Arkansas.[83] Vann's reaction to the Chicago riot was moderate: "We had just as well view the situation sanely." He did blame the Chicago whites for the riot and referred to the deep-rooted racial conflict not altogether coherently as "man against man in the deadly grip of the clutches of the animus of his very soul." But he devoted the main portion of the editorial to a lament for the city of Chicago. "Riots breathe losses . . . economic, political and social. Chicago is no more the city is [sic] was, nor will it ever be, until the participants in the recent riots shall have gone to judgment. The Negro has lost a wonderful city . . . such is the reward of riots, regardless of the cause."[84] In the light of the enormity of what happened, this comment is surprisingly mild for a black editor.

The roots of the trouble were many and deep-seated. The great black migration northward which began in 1915 greatly increased racial tensions in the cities. Housing was overcrowded, and whites were becoming alarmed by the floods of blacks who poured into their cities. Whites also feared increased competition for the skilled and semiskilled trades they had always dominated. Moreover, black hopes for equality in all sectors of life had been raised by the war. By proving themselves in the eyes of white society as ready to fight and die for their country, they reasoned, they would then finally be rewarded with the rights denied them for so long. When their lives continued full of the same old inequities and discrimination after the war, they were disappointed and bitter. In many blacks the bitterness turned to anger and hostility. It took only a small spark to touch off the conflagration.

But many of the government officials investigating events after the riot-torn summer saw it differently. They ignored the deeper causes of the upheavals and turned their attention to the black press, whose inflammatory handling of the happenings, they felt, incited further rioting. Attorney General A. Mitchell Palmer and the Department of Justice began an investigation of black newspapers, with the results published in November 1919 as "Radicalism and Sedition Among Negroes as Reflected in Their Publications."[85] The Palmer report said, in essence, that the black press must assume much of the responsibility for the summer riots and that their constant protests against disfranchisement and lynching were incendiary. The spectre of Bolshevism was raised, and black newspapers were accused of being dominated by Communists. Such publications as A. Philip Randolph and Chandler Owen's *The Messenger*, the NAACP's *The Crisis* edited by W. E. B. DuBois, and the *Chicago Defender* owned by Robert Abbott were singled out as radical and seditious. Within two months after the Palmer report appeared, two bills were introduced in Congress. The Sterling bill (S 3317) and the Graham sedition bill (HR 11430) would have given the Justice Department the right to deny postal privileges to all books, magazines, newspapers, and communications of any sort which appealed to racial prejudice with the intention of bringing about rioting and violence.[86] The fear was evidently not as pervasive as the bills' sponsors thought, for neither bill passed.[87] However, close on the heels of the federal actions came the Lusk Committee Report of the New York State legislature, which dealt in part with radicalism in the New York City black press. The forty-four-page report intimated that the Communists had influenced, if not completely radicalized, many of the black newspapers and journals in New York, particularly *The Crisis*.[88]

Robert Vann and his *Pittsburgh Courier* escaped government scrutiny and criticism. This was partly due to the fact that the *Courier* was still a local paper of limited circulation and influence. It was due also to the orthodox patriotic feelings that Vann voiced all through the war and afterward. He felt the black man's loyalty to America was unquestionable, regardless of what unfairness he suffered. "The Negro is essentially and vitally American. He attaches no hyphen to his name and knows no love save that for the land of his father's father."[89] Vann saw the black man as a more loyal American than those he called the "hyphenates," the immigrants who had arrived in America much more recently than the blacks. He voiced this sentiment many times in his editorials for the years 1915 through 1919. A major reason for his opposition to immigrants, particularly Italians, was that in Pittsburgh they were being favored over blacks in the labor force. Vann also firmly approved of restrictive quotas on immigrants. Writing in behalf of the National Origins Act, which passed in 1924, Vann said:

> The prevailing thought in the minds of those responsible for the measure seems to be to get rid of the hyphenated citizen, or rather resident, in this country. . . .
> It is more than interesting to note how many applications are made in this country for citizenship papers

> for no other purpose than to use the papers as a protection while the holder desires to remain in this country and earn money. . . . He earns all the American money he wants, and at his own sweet convenience, he leaves for his native fireside, and forgets America until more money is needed.
>
> The immigration measure now before the American people will reduce this half-hearted attitude to a minimum. The law proposes to take away the opportunity to enter this country, except to the stipulated quota. This arrangement will reduce the number of half and half citizens whose names and lives are hyphenated to suit their own convenience.[90]

Moreover, Vann was nothing if not an ardent anti-Communist. When Emma Goldman and 249 other "anarchists" were deported to Russia, Vann wrote, "The departure of these troublemakers marks a glorious beginning."[91] Later he wrote about Victor Berger, Socialist congressman-elect from Wisconsin who had been found guilty of violating the Espionage Act, that "the proper thing to do, and the sooner the better, is to deport Berger. Deport every man of his type and convictions, if it necessitates deporting the whole of Wisconsin. Democracy demands it."[92]

On other issues, Vann was middle-of-the-road and temperate at this time. He viewed the race riots as futile and damaging to all elements of American society. "There was never a riot that did not set back the community it visited. There will never be a riot that does any community any good. There is always a loss. There is an economic loss that can not be retrieved. There is a loss of National Morals. There is a loss of National Progress, and then, there is a loss of fellow feeling that can not be replaced except by years and years of earnest labor and patience. The loss is always the reward."[93]

When Vann did protest about mistreatment, he did so not with thunder and passion but with irony. His irony was often bitter, but seldom inflammatory. After the Palmer Report was published in November 1919, Vann wrote sadly that "the only conclusion therefore is: as long as the Negro submits to lynchings, burnings and oppressions—and says nothing, he is a loyal American citizen. But when he decides that lynchings and burnings shall cease even at the cost of some human bloodshed in America, then he is a Bolshevist."[94]

Robert Vann's mild xenophobia and the antiradical sentiments he shared with many Americans were much in evidence in the *Courier*

Politics and Patriotism: 1917–1919 • 109

during the steel strike which began in September 1919 and dragged on until January 1920. The strike occurred because the American Federation of Labor (AFL) wanted recognition by the steel industry and reduction of the twelve-hour workday. While much of the leftist press and black publications like *The Messenger* and the *Chicago Defender* backed the striking union, other journalists like Robert Vann, along with most businessmen and middle-class Americans in general, viewed it as an issue of "Americanism" versus "radicalism," with Samuel Gompers, his AFL, and its "foreign" followers (particularly the Eastern European steel workers) the villains. Right after the strike began, Vann wrote in an editorial that "In almost every large steel center the foreigners led the way out. The American laborer remained on the job, and the mills were kept going.... Americans are for America first. And conspicuous among those who are for America first were the black Americans who never left their posts."[95] The blacks failed to support the steel strike, despite the strong urging of William Z. Foster, who represented the National Committee for Organizing Iron and Steel Workers in the AFL. When the strike began, blacks numbered between 15 and 20 percent of the workers in the large plants and between 35 and 40 percent in the smaller plants. But of a total of twenty-five thousand strikers, only twelve were black.[96] Others came willingly to work as scabs. Blacks said they stayed at work because although the AFL did not discriminate against them in its constitution, most of the AFL locals refused to accept black membership applications.[97]

Two weeks after the strike began, Vann voiced his disapproval of Samuel Gompers and intimated that Gompers had Communist sympathies:

> Mr. Gompers is credited as an American Citizen....Yet as head of the labor organization he sits before the House Committee and states that he would not advise his men to obey an anti-strike law which had been declared constitutional by the Supreme Court of his country....
>
> Shall we conclude that Mr. Gompers is the agent of some foreign organization bent upon controlling American industries through organized labor?[98]

In 1919 Vann tended to be wary of unions, not only because of their radical connotations, but because of the negative experience blacks had had with organized labor. Few unions offered membership or encouragement to blacks. Thus most blacks, including both workers and those of bourgeois outlook, were strongly anti-union. Booker T. Washington provides an excellent example of the middle-class black viewpoint which Vann shared. Washington revealed in his autobiography severe skepticism about the value of the labor movement, saying a strike "usually occurred whenever the men got two or three months ahead in their savings. During the strike, of course, they spent all that they had saved," and were worse off when the strike was over.[99] Washington, in turn, had been much influenced by the writings of Tileston T. Bryce in the *Southern Workman*, the magazine of Hampton Institute. Bryce believed labor unions were conspiracies to defy the laws of economics and try to get something for nothing.[100] Bryce felt that God intended man to work and if a man wished to work eighteen hours a day, that was no labor union's business,[101] and that "strikes generally cost more than they come to, even if they are apparently successful."[102] To the bourgeois black, then, unions were objectionable because strikes ran contrary to the work ethic and upset the economic balance, whereas the black worker disliked unions because they offered him no place on their rosters, and strikebreaking was a means of gainful employment.

In the next issue of the *Courier*, three weeks after the steel strike had started, Vann asserted that blacks were showing themselves to be loyal, one-hundred-percent Americans by staying on the job at steel mills throughout the country, while the "hyphenates" were attempting to paralyze the economy:

> America and her institutions are first in the hearts of the Negro. . . . The black man is playing a very important part in the present steel strike. . . . He is preventing a general paralysis of production in many sections of this country. . . .
>
> At the present rate of departure of foreigners to their native lands, the Negro may yet take his proper place in our American industries. When he does, and when America learns to appreciate him as a factor, disturbances such as face our country now will be almost impossible.[103]

Robert Vann continued his anti-union editorial stance through at least two more strikes. In mid-April 1920, in the midst of a railroad strike, Vann chided the workers for what he perceived as their lack of common sense:

> [A railroad man] ought to know that when he strikes and stops the railroads he is thereby running up the prices of the very foods he must buy for his own family . . . Strikes get him nowhere, but . . . they do retard the people and make living harder.
> Whether strikes improve labor is a serious question. When raises are granted, prices at once advance to cover the raise and the striker is none the gainer.[104]

Vann saw this strike in the same way he did the Chicago riots, as a question of simple economic loss, of dollars and cents on some kind of balance sheet. He failed to deal editorially with the larger issues of human dignity, of the rights of the downtrodden, whether they be laborers or blacks or both. It is difficult to know whether this *reductio ad pecuniam* marks a new trend in Vann's thought, away from what seemed to be his crusading passions of earlier years, or whether this vision had been there all along and had only become more pronounced. One can only speculate, but evidence seems to point to the latter. Vann's outlook was solidly bourgeois, and he had a great fondness for economic success stories. As time went on, he forced onto a variety of issues the question of economic gain or loss.

In May 1920, for example, when the Pittsburgh street-railway employees threatened to strike, Vann avoided the topics of whether a pay raise was needed or deserved, the workers' current situation, working hours, living conditions, etc., and wrote, "We are asked too much by these men when they expect us to pay additional fare to afford them a raise, and then lose a substantial sum in business losses while the dispute over wages is being settled."[105]

And again, during the coal strike of 1922, Vann voiced no support for the miners, seeing it as merely an issue of economic inconvenience for the middle-class public:

> It matters little whether the strike is settled favorably to the operators or the miners, the people will have to bear the inconveniences and pay the expense in the last analysis.
> Our industries must have [coal] if the wheels are to be kept moving . . . the men who would work, and

want to work, will be out of employment because there is no coal.

...the government will have to take a hand. The people must have the fuel.[106]

Four years later, when A. Philip Randolph started his Brotherhood of Sleeping Car Porters, Robert Vann suddenly became pro-union, but only when that stand promised the possibility of enormous circulation gains for the *Courier*, and he as abruptly reverted to an anti-union stand when circulation leveled off, in a dramatic and controversial incident.

· 6 ·

Vann as Entrepreneur: the 1920s

DURING THE EARLY 1920s, Robert Vann turned to the pursuit of financial success coupled with further fame. He involved himself in several business ventures which verged on the reckless, especially when one considers what a moderate sort of man he was. Vann seems to have been touched by the exuberant optimism which affected the entire country during those years; belief in the American Dream of individual opportunity and economic progress and prosperity was never stronger than in the 1920s. The myth that success was possible for anyone willing to try animated America, even black America. It was a time for business endeavors and for risk-taking, both of which were very much present in Robert Vann's undertakings in that decade. He introduced a magazine for which there was no market. He doubled the price of his newspaper when indications seemed against it. He became involved in new business enterprises which ranged from impractical to unsound. He was also deeply involved in local politics and ran for public office twice when blacks had little chance of being elected. And he defended a sensational murder case that was predestined to loss. The last two ventures, while outside the sphere of commerce, are relevant not only because they were contemporaneous with Vann's forays into business, but because they involved the same sort of hopeful risk-taking as the commercial efforts.

Yet even Vann's many defeats only served to consolidate his preeminence further, either because the mood of the time was to admire brave lost causes, or because Vann was too shrewd to get involved in endeavors from which nothing could be salvaged. One must give special weight to the latter possibility. By 1920 Robert Vann was already forty-one years old. He had been seriously ill several times; his health at best was precarious. Because of the late start Vann thought he had made professionally, he was constantly haunted by a sense that time was running out for him. He worked almost obsessively; employees remember him often working far into the evening without stopping for dinner. It is difficult to believe that he would have poured his energy into undertakings altogether futile and unrewarding. He must have foreseen that possible reversals would not be final, but would merely be prologues to greater attainments for himself or his newspaper.

The American Dream was very much a part of the black man's mental baggage at this time, and Robert Vann's business philosophy exemplifies it. The Dream involved freedom, equality, and liberty for all in the political and social sense, but it also had a strong economic cast. Economic advancement was considered a step toward achieving the "good life," and the pursuit of happiness included a vision of economic opportunity and equality. Robert Vann and much of his generation of blacks believed in this Dream. Raised in freedom, they were nurtured on the American myth of the worth and possibility of individual success.[1]

Vann had always had great enthusiasm for black business success stories, and from the early days of the *Courier* he gave them front-page space. Typical items he published were:

ROBERT R. CHURCH
MILLIONAIRE OF MEMPHIS IS DEAD

Deceased was 74 Years Old
Owned Large Amount of Valuable Real Estate

HAD $6,000 MONTHLY INCOME

The singular circumstances of a Negro, born a slave, rising from cabin boy on a Mississippi river steamboat to the mastery of a fortune estimated at a million dollars made him a conspicuous character....

Conservative estimates are that he left between 200 and 300 houses in various parts of Memphis.... He owned a subdivision of 135 acres on the Raleigh car line east of Memphis and was founder and first president of the Solvent Savings Bank and Trust Company, the first Negro financial institution in the city.[2]

E. W. GREEN IS ONE OF MISSISSIPPI'S RICHEST MEN

He Owns 1000 Acres of Land Eight Head of Stock and Employs 70 Persons[3]

FACTS AND FIGURES SHOW ADVANCEMENT

Great Progress of Colored People in Business— Outlook is Bright and Inspiring[4]

One of Vann's favorite success stories was that of James C. Thomas, a New York undertaker, who rose "FROM PORTER TO BUSINESSMAN." "Mr. Thomas was born in Harrisburg, Texas, and went at an early age to Galveston, Texas, where he received his common school education and spent his early manhood years. As a young man he was always anxious to make his mark and began his rise in the world by working as porter and waiter on the steamboats," the story went on. "Twenty years ago he took up residence in New York and found work in the hotels for some time. For eleven years he worked as a steward in a fashionable club of New York and by strict economy saved enough money to enter business. It was then that he began his business which is today valued at $24,000. A member of the National Negro Business League, he remarked that 'I owe my success to honest dealing and being prompt. I am fond of my business and believe that the only way to make a success is to be honest and square and prompt.' "[5]

The homilies quoted by Mr. Thomas were very much in line with Vann's own philosophy, which was that of most any self-made businessman, to work hard and be frugal. The masthead he chose for the *Courier* iterated the qualities Vann prized: "Work, Integrity, Tact, Temperance, Prudence, Courage, Faith." Vann's outlook was like the black self-help philosophy of Booker T. Washington, who had formed the National Negro Business League. Because Vann was generally in sympathy with Washington's economic credo, the *Courier* gave excellent coverage to the black leader's movements. It reported the twelfth annual meeting of the Negro Business League in Little Rock, Arkansas,[6] or outlined "Tuskegee Teaching Methods,"[7] or told of the international conference to be held at Tuskegee Institute in April

1912 with "all the important missionary societies in the United States and many societies in foreign nations in attendance to begin a program to aid needy Africans."[8] The *Courier* proudly announced that "BOOKER T. WASHINGTON IS GUEST OF ROSENWALD, *Addresses Many Meetings in Chicago and Thousands are Turned Away*":

> Dr. Booker T. Washington left here for the east, after having spent a week in Chicago as the guest of Julius Rosenwald, the philanthropist and trustee of Tuskegee Institute. Dr. Washington delivered more than 15 addresses during the week. The educator spoke under the auspices of the Chicago Sunday Evening Club and fully 8,000 persons tried to crowd into the auditorium, thousands being turned away. The Tuskegeean spoke at Sinai Temple, the largest Jewish house of worship in Chicago. Then again hundreds were unable to secure admission, so great was the rush to hear Dr. Washington.[9]

Vann agreed with Washington on many points regarding black business, including the need for solidarity, self-help, and economic chauvinism.[10]

In later years, Vann spoke before the National Negro Business League several times. Once in the twenties, giving his view that racial pride could often be measured by the yardstick of financial achievement, Vann stressed the dignity a black could achieve through personal accomplishment: "Negro business [is] the bulwark of our racial progress."[11] And another time, speaking before the same organization, Vann emphasized the need for self-help, a theme Washington often used. Blacks must aid themselves, said the *Courier* editor. They had labored too long for the white man, and while this subservient condition continued, they would subsist on the outer fringes of American life. Creating black-run businesses was the answer, as he saw it. He advised blacks to "concentrate your earnings, and make capital. Hire yourselves, produce for yourselves, and sell something for yourselves. Let's stop going to the white man with nothing and ask them to loan us something. We must establish in industry. You will then have a different philosophy in life."[12] American blacks, insisted Vann, earned and spent two billion dollars a year, and black businesses should share in and profit from that wealth. It was up to black businessmen to educate their people and show them that investment in black business was safe and profitable.[13]

Vann as Entrepreneur: the 1920s • 117

It seems somehow symbolic that the car Robert Vann purchased once he had acquired some money was a Cadillac, the apotheosis of what a believer in the American Dream might wish for as transportation. Sleek and long and shiny, the Cadillac bespoke success and achievement. Vann paid $3,570 cash for his first one, which he bought in 1926.[14] Much of the joy was taken out of Vann's car purchase, however, because the Pittsburgh dealer refused to sell him one, fearing his white customers might begin calling the Cadillac "a nigger car."[15] Robert Vann had to buy the success symbol he coveted from a dealer in Altoona.

As a portent of the years that lay immediately ahead, Robert Vann began the very first month of the twenties with an adventurous journalistic project—the monthly *The Competitor: the National Magazine*. Vann was editor and treasurer, Ira F. Lewis was secretary, and Elliot C. Alexander was president. It was a large-scale venture; Vann was making a bid for nationwide readership. The authors listed in the table of contents formed a roll call of most of the prominent blacks of the day. There was James Weldon Johnson, author and NAACP official; R. R. Moton, who had become head of Tuskegee Institute after Booker T. Washington's death; Emmett J. Scott, secretary-treasurer of Howard University; and Archibald Grimke, former minister to Santo Domingo. Vann also called on his old friends for articles. Pieces appeared by Eugene Kinckle Jones, his friend from Virginia Union University and now executive secretary of the Urban League, and Dr. Calvin Brown, the headmaster of Waters Training School in North Carolina.

The Competitor was ambitious in both format and scope. Printed on glossy stock and containing a generous number of photographs, the issues ran up to ninety pages. A wide array of subjects of contemporary interest to blacks was treated. The magazine contained articles about Frederick Douglass, the recent race riots, "The Negro and Labor," "The Discharged Soldier and War Risk Insurance," and "Radicalism and the Negro." There was special emphasis on success stories of blacks in the business world in articles like "How C. H. James Rose from a Pack Peddler to Head of a Quarter-Million Dollar Business"; "A Live Bank in a Live City," about the prosperity of the black-run Tidewater Bank and Trust in Norfolk, Virginia; and "Why Work?", the report of a persevering hod carrier who became a bank president after ten years of hard work.[16] There were also short stories, poetry, and articles on sports, theater, cooking, fashion, farming, and the world of business. Hardly any aspect of black life was neglected.[17]

Yet *The Competitor* did not do well, for a number of reasons. Vann had chosen the most eminent blacks of the day as contributors, but they failed to generate sufficient excitement to create a large market for the magazine. The Harlem Literary Renaissance, with all the talent it uncovered and enthusiasm it aroused, was still in the offing; in that respect, Vann's magazine appeared on the scene a few years too early.

A second factor was the price, which aroused automatic sales resistance. *The Competitor* cost twenty cents, or two to four times as much as a newspaper, and the black populace was not accustomed to buying the more expensive periodicals. Further, *The Competitor* needed lucrative advertising to pay the costs of printing, paper, and distribution, but Vann and his staff were unable to obtain that advertising. White businesses were not interested in advertising in a black periodical, and black concerns preferred to use local newspapers, rather than a national magazine.[18]

Finally, a journalist of the time who analyzed the problems of the few black magazines that appeared during the early 1920s (such as *The Colored American Review* and *The Crusader*, edited by Cyril V. Briggs in New York; *The Negro Farmer*, a southern publication; and *The Favorite*, edited by Fenton Johnson, Willis N. Huggins's *The Upreach Magazine*, and Anthony Overton's *Half-Century*, all published in Chicago) said that magazines had much more difficulty being accepted by blacks at that time than did newspapers, for magazines appeal mostly to the highly literate and cultured; there were not large numbers of such blacks in 1920.[19] Moreover, according to one source, though "*The Competitor* was perhaps the closest approximation to general [white] magazine standards, with attractive features and stories . . . one possible explanation for its failure was that it so closely paralleled the character of the magazines for the general public that it succumbed to a competition not so acutely felt by the [three or four] Negro magazines with special racial appeal."[20] Only a magazine like the NAACP's *The Crisis*, edited by W. E. B. DuBois, which had a circulation of approximately 100,000 in 1919,[21] or *The Messenger* of Chandler Owen and A. Philip Randolph, with a militant racial stance, flourished at that time.

Vann tried desperately to make a success of *The Competitor*. When his capital began to be exhausted, he wrote to Walter S. Buchanan, an associate editor of the magazine with whom Vann had worked during college summers in Maine, and asked for financial assistance. Buchanan obliged, but his funds were too small to do much good in the face of mounting printing costs. After eighteen debt-ridden months, *The Competitor* expired. A little good came from its demise, however. Vann sagely gave all the former *Competitor* agents copies of his *Pittsburgh Courier* to sell, thus making good use of already-established contacts, and since these agents were stationed around the country, Vann began to build up the nationwide circulation of the *Courier*.[22]

A few months after starting *The Competitor*, Vann raised the *Courier*'s price to ten cents. The decision had been difficult, though Ira Lewis had been urging it on the stockholders for some time. He believed such a drastic action was necessary if the *Courier* was to become a success; otherwise, he predicted, the paper would remain in the doldrums and eventually fold. Lewis felt that if they enlarged the newspaper to ten pages, built up the features, and added photographs at the same time they raised the price, the public would regard it as reasonable. Also, if they increased the number of newspapers printed each week, production costs would decrease proportionately, and they might be able to sell more copies. At any rate, a price increase seemed unavoidable. Like most black papers, the *Courier* made almost all its money from circulation sales, and it was running on a precariously slim margin. It had finished 1919 with a bank balance of just $102.20, total dividends for the year amounted to a paltry $100.50, and printing costs were about to go up significantly.[23]

The price increase was hazardous, and most of the stockholders felt it was a poor move since "there was not a cooperative spirit among the leading editors of Negro weekly papers" for the increase.[24] However, Vann corresponded extensively with Robert Abbott of the *Chicago Defender* on the subject and sent Ira Lewis to see him. Finally Abbott was persuaded that it would be a sensible move in view of the higher price of printing stock and the increased cost of labor, and he agreed to raise the *Defender*'s price. That decision was critical to Vann, for the *Defender* was the leading black weekly of the time; where it led, others would eventually follow.[25]

All was ready; the first copies of the *Courier* at the new ten-cent price rolled off the presses on July 28. Vann and the staff held their breath. At first the news was all bad; the circulation dropped dramatically, from twelve thousand to eight thousand.[26] Pittsburgh's other black weekly, the *Pittsburgh American*, established the previous year, drained off many *Courier* readers, for its owners, R. F. Douglass and William P. Young, had staunchly refused to increase the *American*'s price.[27] But little by little the black community accepted the change, for the *Courier* was better than before and offered much more variety at ten cents than it had at five cents. As the year went on, circulation gradually returned to nearly its previous level. The risky decision seemed to have paid off.

In 1925, undaunted by his failure with *The Competitor* and by the alarming months when his raising of the *Courier* price seemed a grave mistake, Robert Vann became involved with perhaps the rashest business ventures of his entire career. It was the first time his confidence in his abilities carried him into the realm of total impracticality. Prompted perhaps by the intense interest in Africa which Marcus Garvey had aroused, Vann and some friends tried a series of schemes for investing in the Gold Coast region of West Africa. Their undertakings included exporting manganese mined around the city of Sekondi, exporting animal hides, and growing cocoa and rubber. Vann wrote to William Cathcart Arthur, a friend in the executive office of the B. F. Goodrich Rubber Company, trying to interest him in one of the propositions. "We control 2,000 square miles of Gold Coast acreage granted to us by the African chiefs themselves . . . suitable for growing para rubber (heavy variety). Your company might be interested. . . . You have but to notify me and I will bring you a gentleman direct from the Gold Coast."[28] But Arthur was leery of the scheme and informed Vann that his company intended to continue its longstanding policy of not owning plantations and of leaving "the risks in that field to others."[29]

Vann's idea of importing leopard, goat, sheep, and bush cat skins from Africa was equally unsuccessful. When the skins finally arrived in the United States after a long delay, they were so cut up, marked, and worm-eaten that Vann was unable to recover any of his investment.[30] Little is known about the fate of the manganese mining project except that it failed. Robert Vann lost several thousand dollars in all these schemes, a not inconsiderable sum in that era. His naive optimism—or abundant faith in his business acumen—led him into water too deep to navigate successfully.

Also in 1925, Vann embarked on another unsuccessful enterprise, though this one had more of a chance for success than the African attempts. He tried to start a bank funded and run by blacks. Vann was but one of many blacks who was convinced he could make a bank prosper; the busiest period in black banking was 1900 to 1928, when twenty-eight commercial and savings banks were started.[31] For many years Vann had argued that the reason there were so few black homeowners was that white-owned banks were unwilling to provide mortgage loans. "We are deprived of good homes because we have not the means, and often when we secure a home we lose it for the same reason." When white-owned banks did loan funds to blacks, they were usually "unscrupulous agents who make handsome profits out of the ignorance and poverty of our people."[32] Vann himself had been unable to get a loan in 1911 for the purchase of his house on Monticello Street and had had to borrow the $500 he needed from a friend. Aside from a few fraternal and beneficial societies, there was only one small loan company that offered funds to blacks buying homes.

Nor were business loans available to blacks. In 1921, Ira Lewis had asked indignantly that the *Courier* close its meager savings account of $283.85 at the Potter Title and Trust Company because the bank would not honor a *Courier* loan request.[33] Then in January 1923, when the *Courier* board of directors needed $500 to send a staff member on a circulation drive in New Jersey and Ohio, no bank would loan the funds. Instead, the board members themselves had to take the note on ninety days promise of payment at 6 percent, with Vann subscribing to $100 of it.[34] These incidents illustrate the inability of black enterprises or individuals, even those of apparent solvency, to get financial backing. White banks and lending associations simply considered them bad risks.

There was already one black-run bank in Pittsburgh, the Steel City Bank headed by Reverend J. C. Austin, the flamboyant and forceful pastor of the Ebenezer Baptist Church. The Steel City Bank had opened in November 1919 and seemed to be prospering. When the bank cashed a $5,789.30 check "on the spot" for the 1924 Elks' convention, the *Courier* remarked that with financial solvency like that in evidence, black citizens had little to worry about regarding black-run banks in the Smoky City.[35] By 1925 Vann felt the time was ripe to open another such enterprise in the growing black community. He enlisted the aid of the Reverend Austin in framing his plans and told prospective backers it would be an "Honest to God" bank,[36] alluding, no doubt, to the holy influence of the minister with whom he proposed to be associated. But the prospective investors had their extra monies tied up in the Steel City Bank and were unable to give Vann anything. Moreover, Vann proposed to capitalize the bank at the unrealistically high figure of $500,000, or three to five times as much as that of similar institutions.[37] Vann had no luck; the bank died before it ever became a reality.

As an interesting postscript to Vann's banking endeavor, just four months later, the apparently healthy Steel City Bank folded suddenly. Its failure was caused by an excess of frozen assets—the bank had made extensive loans on real estate which had exhausted its monetary reserves, but it had been unable to dispose of those loans to raise additional cash. There was also a question of incompetence in the management. Though more than five million dollars had passed through its coffers in six years, the Steel City Bank went under.[38] Vann may have been luckier than he realized when his own bank failed to materialize. Black banks in general had difficulty at that time. They needed solvent savers and investors, and unfortunately "the [black] clientele constitutes a thrifty group, but an impoverished one." With limited deposits from savers, therefore, it was difficult to raise capital to loan to prospective black enterprises. The black man was caught in a vicious circle: "On the one hand, he needed banks to help establish successful businesses, and on the other he lacked the successful businesses upon which to base a banking industry."[39]

Vann only made one other extrajournalistic business attempt during his lifetime. In August 1928 he became regional sales manager of Philipot, Goff and Company, a New York brokerage firm. The *Courier* reported he would spend Wednesday through Saturday in New York City each week working primarily on black investment opportunities.[40] This endeavor undoubtedly was brought to a halt by the great stock market crash the following year.

Despite Vann's financial vicissitudes, by mid-decade, he felt he had become an important enough figure in the Pittsburgh business world to apply for admission to the Chamber of Commerce. That organization, of a power and influence unequaled in any other American city, was then planning a "Forward Movement" program for Pittsburgh, and Vann thought the time was ripe for him to be admitted. He wrote a letter to the Chamber of Commerce stressing his background in the legal profession and journalism and said his membership would greatly "aid in the struggle for economic improvement" within the Pittsburgh black community.[41] It refused his application; he was, after all, a black.[42]

Vann had two other interesting failures during this period, both in 1921. The first was local politics, when he ran unsuccessfully for elective office, and the second was the law courts, where Vann lost the biggest and last substantial case of his legal career.

His one futile attempt to be a successful political candidate was preceded by two setbacks in local politics. The first was at the city level. The majority of the Pittsburgh City Council had remained loyal to William Magee's faction of the Republican party and opposed to the current mayor, E. V. Babcock, who had appointed Vann to his job as assistant city solicitor. During 1921 the hostile councilmen made some drastic reductions in Mayor Babcock's budget; one of the items eliminated was Robert Vann's job, at which he was then earning $4,200. Vann not only lost his city job, but when William Magee won the Republican primary nomination for mayor in September, Vann lost his influence in city politics, for Magee would not forgive Vann's outspoken opposition in the 1917 election.

And Vann had another failure in June 1921, this time on the state level. As state chairman of the black GOP, Vann wanted to organize the blacks of Pennsylvania into an effective statewide group and invited all interested blacks to Harrisburg on June 8:

> In order more perfectly and completely to form and establish a statewide organization among our people for the better promotion of our civic and political interests throughout the Commonwealth, a call is hereby issued to every loyal and interested race man and woman of the state to meet in session assembled at Harrisburg, at high noon on June 8, 1921, when and where a constitution and suitable by-laws will be adopted, and the purpose and scope of the organization determined by the people. Every district in the state is requested to send representation.[43]

But there is no indication that anything concrete resulted from the meeting or even that many blacks attended.

Almost as if the adversity made him more determined, Robert Vann decided to run for public office in the September Republican primary, for judge of the Allegheny County Court of Common Pleas. It was his first bid for an elective position, but his hopes for victory were not entirely unfounded. Vann's reputation as an attorney of uncommon shrewdness had grown consistently over the years, and the increase in the black population brought about by the great wartime migration, along with the coming of women's suffrage, had vastly increased the number of Vann's potential supporters. Pittsburgh's black population, according to the 1920 census, now numbered 37,688, a rise of 47.1 percent since 1910, while the white population had increased just 8.3 percent, to 550,301. In Allegheny County the number of blacks had skyrocketed 62.2 percent to 53,517, while the white population increased just 13.1 percent.[44]

Vann announced his candidacy for the judgeship in the *Courier* and said it was "the maiden effort of the race to elect men on the county ticket" and proved "the Negro has decided that his own political salvation is his political independence."[45] Vann showed admirable restraint in not editorializing on his own virtues and qualifications for the post, saving that for a speech reported elsewhere in the newspaper: "I submit my record as a private citizen to the city of Pittsburgh as an American, a Republican and my record as a practicing attorney," he said, and with justifiable pride told of his successful handling of 16 murder cases, 176 divorces, 578 criminal cases, 376 civil proceedings, 110 appeals from summary conviction, 94 habeas corpus actions, and 5 corporation cases. Vann failed to mention race during his campaign, nor did he promise judicial reforms for the black community. He remained silent on these subjects to gain the white support he needed badly.

Vann's tactic was to "single-shot," or to campaign just for a vote for himself rather than for a party ticket; in that way he could obtain votes from blacks who would not support anyone else on the ticket. This was a common practice among black office-seekers of the time. He wrote a confidential letter to this effect to the secretary of the Fifth Ward Citizens Protective Organization. "I believe with the united support of my people, I can win. I need the help of every Negro man and woman, and I desire very much to have the support of every race member. I am writing this letter to ask your organization for its support, whether as a body, or through the individual effort of its members. I am a candidate for one place only. I am interested in no other candidate. I have no interest in factional candidates for any office. I am in the middle of the road for the one office, that of County Court Judge."[46]

Vann campaigned hard in the late summer and early fall. With Ira Lewis handling the publicity, Vann stumped through Allegheny County. He concentrated on the newly enfranchised female voters, for whom he must have had special appeal, with his elegant good looks and courtly manner, and managed to win the support of several organized women's groups with the help of Mrs. Daisy Lampkin, a well-known clubwoman who was later on the *Courier* board of directors. When the votes were counted on September 20, Vann had received 21,000. It was a decent showing in the light of the number of black voters in the county, but far from enough to win: the victor tallied 101,000, and even the fifth-place candidate garnered 55,000.[47]

Vann's defeat, and the defeat of other black candidates, was attributable to the fact that the blacks of Pittsburgh still did not enjoy political power as a group and were usually unable to elect a black candidate. Though the black population had greatly increased, its numbers were dispersed through several wards in addition to the heavily black Third and Fifth, so that it was difficult to unite them. Many blacks remained nonvoters. As newly arrived migrants from the South, where they had been disfranchised, they had a lifelong habit of ignoring politics; they regarded voting as white man's business. It was difficult to shake this group out of its political apathy and interest them in a specific contest. Various black political organizations had been formed for this purpose since 1910 (the Colored Protective League of Allegheny County, of which Vann was an officer, the Fifth Ward Progressive Club, and the Colored Political Club of Herron Hill among them), but most such groups were undermanned, usually formed to promote the interests of a small group of individuals, and of short duration (usually the length of a political campaign), because they received insufficient support from the wider black community.[48] As a result, very few blacks were elected to public office in Pittsburgh in the years 1910 to 1934.

One of those elected was William H. Thompson, a Hill District grocer who won the position of school director in the Fifth Ward in 1911.[49] The most noted was Robert H. Logan, who was elected to the Board of Aldermen from the predominantly black Fifth Ward in 1919. The *Courier* credited his winning the highest elective office ever held by a black man in Pittsburgh to the solid bloc effort of black voters in the ward.[50] However, when Logan was not reelected, Vann blamed the defeat on the apathetic blacks who had absented themselves from the polls.[51] When Thomas Dennis and the well-known black attorney Captain Frank Stewart ran for the state legislature in the First District (comprised of the First, Third, and Fifth Wards) in the May 1918 primary, they were unable to get the support of the Republican party regulars, who were afraid of harming white candidates' chances by putting a black on the ticket. With approximately eight thousand voters in the district, three thousand of whom were black, there should have been enough of a turnout to get at least one of the blacks a place on the ticket. But both suffered crashing defeats. Stewart, though a recognized community leader, did not get even half of the known black vote, and Dennis polled less. Not surprisingly, Ernest Rice McKinney, editor of the *Pittsburgh American*, sarcastically summarized the black man's attempts for office as follows: "Pittsburgh tries, feebly, every two years, to land a colored man in Harrisburg, but fails dismally. One candidate [Frank Stewart] has run four times from a district thickly settled with Negroes, but the *Jews and the Irish always win.*"[52]

Vann blamed the defeat of black candidates not only on voter apathy, but also on the fact that blacks who did vote failed, out of jealousy, to get behind one black candidate in a solid bloc vote.[53] Black candidates could not rally enough community support, and until they could convince the party machine of their ability to do this, they would not receive the backing of the regulars. The GOP still feared that white candidates' chances might suffer with black names on the slate. Since most blacks were safely in the Republican column, the GOP saw little need to sponsor black candidates and thus add to the party's financial burdens. And blacks like Vann were still political amateurs, with little knowledge of vote control and of how to play from strength in making demands of their party.[54]

Robert Vann fared better than previous black candidates in his 1921 bid for office, partly because the *Courier* gave him wider influence and because he "single-shotted." However, in the same election in which Vann was defeated, his by now bitter foe William Magee soundly trounced his Democratic opponent, William McNair, 72,186 to 32,448. With Magee as mayor, Vann had no hope of appointive office in Pittsburgh for the next four years.

Vann later summed up his feelings about politics in a tone of amused exasperation: "This thing called politics is the most frigid, pig-ironed, heartless, unconscionable business ever known to man. Let not your heart be troubled, dear readers, nor be ye enraged or disappointed; it was ever thus."[55] Disillusioned after his first defeat at the polls, Vann stayed away from personal involvement in politics for the next few years, except in his role as *Courier* editor. He sensed that blacks could have more political influence in Pittsburgh but realized that for the moment they were seriously hampered by their relatively small numbers and lack of unity. At that time blacks' rare opportunities for effectiveness came only when the ranks of white politicians were divided. "[Only in a split election are] the small fry needed to make a decisive victory. . . . It pays [blacks] to have division among the bosses."[56]

Throughout most of the 1920s the Republican party organization in Pittsburgh was relatively cohesive, and this prevented any significant breakthroughs by black politicians. James Malone, white boss of the Fifth Ward, where most blacks lived, was also president of the City Council, and his power rivaled that of the mayor. He brooked no challenge by would-be black candidates. Malone's power increased after 1925, when Charles Kline defeated incumbent William Magee in the mayoral contest, because Kline began to build his own political machine by catering to Malone and the other ward bosses.[57] Malone was able that year to engineer the defeat of black alderman Robert Logan of the Fifth Ward, who had been in office for six years, by using another black, Earl Sams, to split the black vote in the primary, so that Malone's man, Martin Griffin, a white, could win.[58] Because of conflicts between Vann and Logan dating back to 1917, Vann supported Sams's candidacy before the primary, but he soon recognized Malone's ploy and urged Sams to withdraw.[59] Sams refused, the black vote was divided, and Griffin won.[60] Vann viewed the outcome as a real defeat for blacks. The *Courier* headline read, "RACE LOSES POWER IN FIFTH WARD."[61] When Logan ran on an independent ticket in the November election Vann toyed with the idea of supporting him, but he realized that Logan had no chance and stayed with the machine ticket. The preelection issue of the *Courier* carried a picture of the Republican organization's candidates and an article supporting them.[62] The dilemma was intensely frustrating for Vann; blacks were politically impotent whether they supported the machine or rebelled against it. The machine exploited them, but they had little hope for success as independent candidates.

Despite the near futility of political aspirations for blacks in Pittsburgh, in 1927 Vann ran again for public office. He announced his candidacy for judge of the Court of Common Pleas of Allegheny County, the same post for which he had run in 1921. Vann's effort was not supported by the local machine, so he did poorly, finishing last in a field of twenty candidates in the September primary, with 22,855 votes.[63] Blacks were at the nadir of their effectiveness in Pittsburgh that year, gaining only one office, the lowly one of constable.

Though defeated again, Vann retained his assertiveness about the need for black officials. "It is better to elect a Negro generally speaking than ANY white man . . . [far] better to have a Negro speaking in [the race's] behalf than any white man."[64] The *Courier* editor knew blacks were still migrating northward in sizable numbers and believed they could thus gain political power: in Pittsburgh alone the black population increased 50 percent during the twenties.[65] And by the end of 1927 local blacks were finally beginning an earnest effort for political unity. They formed the Third Ward Voters' League, headed by Walter C. Rainey, which soon claimed a membership of at least five thousand registered black voters. The Voters' League recognized that they at last clearly outnumbered whites in the ward and set out "to get what was rightfully theirs" by way of patronage jobs and elected positions.[66]

Blacks' potential for local power appeared to increase even further by 1929, when their bitterest foe, ward boss James Malone, was defeated by incumbent Charles Kline in the mayoral primary. Malone's arrogant control of his political territory angered Vann and many Pittsburgh blacks, for Malone denied support to black candidates and used all his power to keep blacks in line politically. He had the temerity to tell a large group of blacks at an Emancipation Day celebration in 1929 that they would advance much faster politically by following white leadership than their own "educated leaders."[67] Vann was furious. "Some Negroes had the nerve to hail him as 'our next Mayor' in a travesty of ignorance. . . . Can you imagine an audience of Negroes *applauding* . . . a mere ward boss whose expression showed him to be at heart a Negro hater?"[68]

Despite his intense dislike of James Malone, Vann was reluctant to endorse Kline, who had done little for blacks during his term in office. Vann had difficulty procuring from Kline even so small a concession as time for blacks on the public golf course and sent him a sarcastic letter on the topic. "Yes sir, Negroes are actually trying to learn to play golf on the green. I mean American golf. They are already well-versed in African golf. I hope you will see that the proper party makes arrangements for some morning."[69] The official reply was barely palliative. "We will insofar as possible give [your people] the right on Friday morning for each week."[70] Vann found Malone totally unacceptable, however, and by primary time had decided to support Kline. The preprimary *Courier* headline ran "KLINE SETS NEW VALUE ON BLACK VOTE" when Kline joined Vann to greet Oscar DePriest at a large rally.⁷¹ Kline handily defeated Malone in the primary and went on to be reelected in November. Soon after Kline bested Malone on another front, when he managed to depose the longtime boss as head of the Fifth Ward Republicans and installed his own man. Vann was delighted. "The striking defeat of James Malone marked the end of his iron heel and anti-Negro leadership tactics in the Fifth Ward."⁷² Moreover, Kline finally showed some concern for black demands; he promised more black detectives in the police force, offered more city jobs for blacks in general, and guaranteed that a newly built municipal swimming pool would be integrated.⁷³

Yet even while blacks were gaining some recognition from Mayor Kline, there was internal turmoil among them. According to Walter C. Rainey, head of the Third Ward Voters' League, his organization had agreed to support Kline, who would reciprocate after his victory with patronage. But Kline reneged on his agreement with the League. Gus Greenlee, the Hill District numbers king and bootlegger, went to Kline behind the backs of League officials and told the mayor that he need not worry about the League. Greenlee assured Kline that if he allowed him to maintain control of the rackets and bootlegging in black Pittsburgh then he would see that blacks "stayed in line" behind the mayor. When Rainey protested to the mayor, insisting that the Third Ward Voters' League was the ward's political spokesman, Kline did not believe him and stuck with Greenlee. Undoubtedly Kline's reasoning was that in the past, blacks had been unsuccessful in building a strong political base, and this League, like so many of those of past years, would die aborning. It was smart politics, therefore, to go along with a person like Greenlee who had been around a long time and had been effective in the past.⁷⁴

By the end of the twenties, then, blacks began to see slight improvement in matters of local politics, though Vann himself, discouraged by his two defeats at the polls, never again ran for office in Pittsburgh.⁷⁵ Besides, throughout the twenties Vann was occupied intensely with his legal practice and his newspaper.

Immediately after losing the 1921 election, Vann became involved in the most sensational murder case of his legal career. The murder had taken place nearly a year before, on December 16, 1920, when Mrs. Anna Kirker, a white woman from Buttermilk Hollow in nearby Mifflin Township, was found slain in her home. The scene indicated that the killing had been done in the course of a robbery. The only clues were some footprints in the snow outside the house, which matched those of Mrs. Kirker's husband. For some reason known only to the police, Kirker was never arrested, though he was known to have quarreled with his wife the night before the murder, and he left hurriedly for California. The public demanded a solution to the case. In February 1921 Joe Thomas, a burly black bootlegger, was wounded in a gun battle with police during an attempted robbery. He was taken into custody and hospitalized. The police reportedly found a watch belonging to Mrs. Kirker and an overcoat of her husband's among Thomas's effects. He immediately became the prime murder suspect the public had been clamoring for, and a heavy guard was placed around Thomas's hospital room. But Thomas managed to escape from the hospital by jumping from a second-story window.

Joe Thomas eluded recapture for nearly six months, until he was identified in a Baltimore police station and returned to Pittsburgh by train. When the train pulled into the station, a large crowd of angry whites was on hand to greet Thomas. Whether by coincidence or not, the crowd included Mayor E. V. Babcock, who delivered a "welcoming speech" to Thomas in which he assured the gathering that Thomas would be found guilty. Babcock's words further inflamed public opinion, in which the murder of a white woman by a black man was already cause for outrage. Babcock subsequently described his speech as no more than "some remarks relative to his return. . . . I was glad to see Thomas returned here that the law might take its course and the man be tried for the crime he was charged with . . . as a public official, I was interested in the capture."[76] An official said Babcock's address was made in a moment of spontaneous exuberance, but Vann scornfully called it "asinine exuberance."[77]

Thomas's trial began at the end of November 1921 and continued into December. Vann was merely an interested observer at the outset, since Thomas had engaged as his defense attorney George H. White, Jr., son of a former black congressman from North Carolina. White, for some curious reason, entered no defense on Thomas's behalf, while the prosecutor presented the case as "one of the most brutal in Allegheny County's history."[78] Thomas had no hope for a favorable verdict. The jury quickly found him guilty, and Judge Stephen Stone, who had been the city solicitor when Vann was an assistant, sentenced Thomas to die in the electric chair.

Thirty-one black churches, lodges, and other organizations immediately raised money and hired Robert Vann to appeal the sentence and try to have it commuted to life imprisonment. There was almost no chance of Thomas's being released, regardless of Vann's findings, for there was no greater crime in those days than the murder of a white woman by a black man. Vann prepared a weighty and convincing petition for commutation of Thomas's sentence and presented it to the State Pardons Board at Harrisburg. In it he charged that the pretrial newspaper accounts prejudiced the case and that there should have been a change of venue; that Mayor Babcock's "welcoming speech" was inflammatory and detrimental; that injustice had been done the prisoner when his counsel failed to present a defense; that the evidence incriminating Thomas had been planted; that Thomas in fact had an alibi for the night of the murder; and that the facts pointed to the murdered woman's husband as the strongest suspect.

To no avail. The Board of Pardons denied Vann's petition for the last time on November 22, 1922. Thomas was sentenced to die on December 11. The Reverend Clarence D. Allen, pastor of the Bethesda Presbyterian Church and the only black man with Thomas during his last hours, reported on the execution for the *Courier*, which the newspaper ran on the front page under a gigantic headline, " 'I DIE AN INNOCENT MAN' SAYS JOE THOMAS." Reverend Allen relayed every horrifying detail of the electrocution to the reading public, which purchased every last copy of the *Courier* almost the instant the paper reached the newsstands.

> The door of Joe's cell was opened and out he stepped. He was surrounded by almost a dozen overseers [guards]. One of them stooped down and ripped the outside seam of the left leg of his trousers up to and a little above the knee, exposing the bare limb, and the clean white underwear; he wore the usual prison garb. The shirt was opened and laid back from his throat and chest, and we were ready to march to the "Chair."
> At eleven minutes past seven o'clock the electricity was turned on, instantly the body of Joe Thomas stiffened and jumped against the straps that held him in the chair. Three times the contact was made and before the current was finally shut, the flesh on the side of his leg was burnt and smoking.[79]

Although Robert Vann lost the case, he unquestionably benefited from his role in it. As Thomas's attorney for the appeal, Vann received extensive coverage in the white press for the first time. Also, Vann had done a thorough job in Thomas's behalf; even beyond Pittsburgh, blacks began to regard him as one of the major black attorneys in the country. In this case, Vann's concern was a curious admixture of righteous indignation against the wrongs inflicted on one of his people and the shrewd intent to make his newspaper profitable and widely read. The *Courier*'s relentless coverage of the sensational case had increased its circulation by many thousands.

As the *Courier*'s editor, Vann was pleased by these figures, although troubled by the yellow journalism used in reporting the case. Earlier in the year he had told the staff "he was opposed in principle to sensationalism," though he did recognize that "the weekly sales of the *Courier* could be greatly increased by the publication of more sensational and morbid stories."[80] "I do not mean," explained Vann, "that we should by any means surrender our high standards and ideals by making the paper entirely yellow, but that more, or rather some, yellow matter should be printed each week." Ira Lewis then made several suggestions favoring such methods and pointed out that "the public is really anxious for real live news, with a slight tinge of scandal."[81] Nonetheless, Vann must have been disturbed to see himself first as a lawyer defending a man's right to live, then as an editor watching his newspaper make money from the fact that the man died. It was one of the few occasions when Vann's multiple careers conflicted with each other so overtly.

The wide range of Robert Vann's pursuits during the early twenties, though hopelessly futile and often reckless, produced some positive results. Vann sowed his wild oats, and by the end of 1925 he was ready to settle down and turn his full attention to building the *Courier* into a nationally eminent publication. Politics would always play a part in his life, but the *Courier* would occupy most of Vann's time and interest during the next five years.

· 7 ·

The Primacy of the COURIER

IN THE MID-1920s, Vann saw Tuskegee Institute for the first time, when he was invited to be one of the guest speakers at the institute's Founder's Day ceremonies. Tuskegee was the creation of Booker T. Washington, whom Vann greatly admired and staunchly defended. He was tremendously impressed by it as an institution and as a spiritual accomplishment. After his visit, Vann commented, "Many of us theorize, froth at the mouth and talk. Dr. Washington demonstrated. We can appreciate now why Dr. Washington never took the time to reply to the mad froth of those who tried to use him as a means to 'climb into notice.' The man was busy with his demonstration. The froth is still froth, nothing more, while Tuskegee towers as a mountain to the capabilities of the black man. There we see the crude, raw material taken into the great plant and, after processes of refinement are applied, the finished product is given to the world."[1] This visit undoubtedly renewed Vann's determination to make the *Courier* an institution of comparable importance, and from 1925 to 1929 he devoted nearly all his time to his newspaper. He eliminated his business interests outside the paper and poured his extra funds into the purchase of *Courier* stock until in 1926 he became the majority stockholder. He turned over the bulk of his legal practice to a young partner, Wilbur C. Douglass, a recent graduate of the University of Pittsburgh. And except for his political activity, especially during the 1928 presidential campaign, Vann occupied himself almost exclusively with the *Courier* for over four years.

The paper benefited greatly from his undivided attention. The crucial components of the *Courier*'s new soundness were national advertising, a more professional staff, its own printing plant, and a national circulation increased by stories, features, and editorials that aroused intense widespread interest.

Vann's bid for national advertising had begun at the end of 1920, when he hired the William B. Ziff Company to secure national advertising accounts for the *Courier*. Ziff was a white man who had succeeded in obtaining national accounts for nearly all the major black weeklies of the era, including the *Amsterdam News*, the *Baltimore Afro-American*, the *Chicago Defender*, and the *St. Louis Argus*.[2] Ziff charged a very high commission—between 35 and 50 percent of the fees paid by the advertisers—but he guaranteed payment to the newspapers and thus eliminated collection problems. Moreover, Ziff brought much new advertising for national products to the *Courier*, increasing the newspaper's income and giving it a less parochial look. By the middle of the 1920s the *Courier* was occasionally carrying advertisements for companies like Gulf Oil, Lever Brothers, Colgate-Palmolive-Peet, Pillsbury Mills, and Vaseline.[3] Even with these advertising revenues, the *Courier* and other black weeklies dealing with Ziff still depended upon circulation for about 80 percent of their revenue.[4]

Vann could have tapped the supply of potential national advertisers even further had he agreed to submit the definite proof of circulation figures that would have been obtained by joining the Audit Bureau of Circulation. Ziff implored him to do so, saying, "The future of the race field exists only upon the possibility of proving to the general advertiser that here is a large group of people well worth merchandising to and ably represented by a number of capable newspapers. These newspapers must be proven to the advertiser to represent the bone and sinew of the Colored man."[5] But Vann refused to submit to the audit, partly because he resented the idea that an outside agency like the ABC was needed to confirm the worth of his newspaper for potential advertisers and partly because he may have feared to admit that the circulation was not as high as he tended to claim. This attitude was prevalent among black editors in the 1920s; as of 1922, only 4 of 217 black newspapers listed in Ayer and Sons' *Newspaper Directory* made sworn statements of circulation. However, blacks had other reasons for not submitting to an ABC audit. Many newspaper owners simply could not afford the expense of a yearly audit. Further, since so few white businesses advertised in their weeklies anyway, blacks generally did not feel confident that an ABC audit would improve their lot no matter how high their circulation rose.[6] At any rate, even without the audit, about 25 percent of the *Courier*'s advertising by the middle and late 1920s was for national products.

Vann felt the *Courier* deserved even more national advertising and once wrote an angry letter to the head of the Firestone Rubber Company giving his reasons for refusing to publish news of that company's activities in Africa and censuring him for not advertising in black newspapers. Vann complained that while the *Courier* might thus be "spreading this very healthy propaganda" for Firestone, the newspaper had not received any of Firestone's advertising, and went on to claim that his newspaper circulated in every state in the union and in Liberia, the Gold Coast, the West Indies, the Philippines, Europe, Alaska, and South America. "It might surprise you," he wrote, "to know that there are close to 400,000 Negroes driving automobiles and they might use Firestone Tires if they could see one of your advertisements appearing in a Negro journal. . . . Money is money regardless of the color of the skin of the man who spends it."[7] That same day Vann returned a Firestone publicity release to the agency that had sent it, N. W. Ayer and Sons of Philadelphia, with the irate comment, "It seems to us that this is nothing less than a bold imposition, to send a whole page of propaganda out to Negro newspapers expecting them to use it when you don't spend a 5¢ piece with Negro newspapers advertising any single one of the great commodities you have the honor to handle."[8]

The second important aspect of Robert Vann's improvement of the *Courier* during these years was the additions he made to the staff. Vann was able to hire a number of capable men and women drawn from the growing ranks of black newspapermen. In the postwar period, due to an increase in the circulation and power of the black press along with a new sense of pride in all things black, journalism was beginning to attract spirited, talented young blacks who wished to become full-time newsmen. They were not trained graduates of journalism schools by any means, and only a few had attended college, but they were eager and able.[9] Previously, employment by a black newspaper was not considered as good and steady a profession as, say, school teaching, which gave one security and status in the community. P. L. Prattis, then with the Negro Associated Press, recalled once having to convince a woman that her husband would not become a tramp if he took a job as a newspaperman.[10] Only after World War I did an occasional aspiring black newsman go to journalism school; and then they were so few that not until 1929 was one elected to Sigma Delta Chi, the honorary journalism fraternity.[11]

Vann made his most significant addition to the staff in 1925, when he hired George Schuyler to write a "Views and Reviews" column for the editorial page. Schuyler, who since 1921 had been working for A. Philip Randolph and Chandler Owen's socialist publication, *The Messenger*, was a native of Syracuse, New York.[12] He had come to journalism almost by chance, after eight years in the Army and brief stints as a longshoreman and hod carrier. Schuyler met Randolph and Owens when he became interested in socialism and eventually went to work for their magazine, writing a popular monthly column entitled "Shafts and Darts; A Page of Calumny and Satire," as well as book reviews and a series on "Business and Industry." When Vann offered him a job at the *Courier* for the minute salary of three dollars a week, Schuyler replied that he was not insulted, but delighted to accept.[13]

The low rate of pay tendered to Schuyler, though it seems incredible,

Vann at his desk at the Pittsburgh Courier *in the mid-1930s.*

was by no means unusual. Vann himself, writing the entire editorial page of five or six different pieces each week, as well as supervising the running of the newspaper, earned less than two dollars a week for his labors until 1922, when his pay was raised to the munificent sum of nearly seven dollars a week. Ira Lewis, the *Courier*'s business manager and perhaps the most vital employee besides Vann, had to hold down an outside job because the paper could not pay him a living wage. He continued the clerkship in the sheriff's office to which he was appointed in 1917, because it paid him $115 a month.[14] In fact, most black journalists of the time were able to support themselves only by working for more than one newspaper, as Schuyler did (he continued his column for *The Messenger* after coming to the *Courier*), or by having some form of additional employment, such as a job in a store or factory. W. Rollo Wilson, for example, was a pharmacist during the hours when he was not writing his excellent sports features for the *Courier*. There was hardly a single full-time professional black journalist working solely for one publication; the newspapers simply could not afford such a luxury. For example, when Vann was seeking a society columnist to cover New York City, he knew he would have to use someone already doing similar work for another paper. He wrote George Schuyler, "Can you get Miss Thelma Berlack of the *Amsterdam News* to do for us society news each week under any name she assumes for the purpose? We say 'assumed name' because we do not want to embarrass her with her present employers. Since she covers Harlem for her own work, it will be easy to send it to us."[15]

Despite his role as columnist for two publications, George Schuyler contributed immeasurably to the *Courier*. His "Views and Reviews" column soon aroused a great deal of comment and controversy; before long, people were calling Schuyler the black H. L. Mencken. Each week readers turned eagerly to his column, anxious to see what outrageous thing Schuyler might have to say. Late in 1925, Vann sent Schuyler off on a nine-month tour of the South to write a series of on-the-road observations, to build up the *Courier*'s circulation and hire distribution agents in the area. Schuyler visited every city or town with more than five thousand blacks in Kentucky, Tennessee, Arkansas, Texas, Oklahoma, Louisiana, Mississippi, Alabama, Florida, North and South Carolina, Georgia, and Virginia. Out of the trip came a series on "Aframerica Today," socioeconomic studies of the more than two hundred cities and towns in the South heavily populated by blacks. Schuyler described their racial situations, the prominent black citizens, businesses, schools, and churches, often with the biting satiric touch for which he was becoming known to *Courier* readers. "For the year 1925, the great state of Florida wins the pennant in the Lynching League of America. There are eight lynchings to the credit (or discredit) of the great commonwealth of real-estate boosters, while closely following it is magnificent Texas with a paltry seven. Then there are our old friend Mississippi with four; South Carolina with three; Arkansas with two; and Georgia, Kansas, New Mexico, Tennessee with one each. . . . The total is 29."[16] When Schuyler visited Louisville, he described it as "gray, drab, dull, and dirty [but] awakening from its long sleep imposed by that enervating force; Southern tradition. . . . The great war disturbed its slumber."[17] He coined epithets for all the southern cities. Helena, Arkansas, was "Red, Hot and Tough"; Martinsburgh, West Virginia, "Poor but Presumably Honest." In Okmulgee, Oklahoma, it was "Ku Klux Klan Uber Alles."[18]

By the end of Schuyler's southern tour in mid-1926, Vann estimated happily that his articles, combined with his circulation drives, had increased the *Courier* circulation by at least ten thousand.[19] That figure represents an increment of about 25 percent for the newspaper; a considerable single-handed feat for a new staff member. Just three years previously the *Courier*'s board of directors had been very pleased when a reporter's circulation campaign in eastern Pennsylvania increased circulation by less than nine hundred.[20]

Shortly after Schuyler returned from the South, Vann made him a member of the newspaper's editorial staff, and he soon became the main editorializer. This promotion, too, had excellent results for the *Courier*. Journalists who evaluated the black press during this era had high praise for the *Courier*'s newly trenchant editorials and Schuyler's feature column, "Views and Reviews," both of which they felt had contributed dramatically to the paper's improvement.[21]

Schuyler attacked hair straighteners and black clergymen with equal vigor.[22] He criticized black fraternal organizations for being insensitive to the needs of the black masses, saying it was depressing to see "unsanitary, congested shacks . . . bursting with Negroes when a block or so away stands a large office building erected by a fraternal society."[23] He ridiculed one segment of the Harlem Renaissance as "Negro Art Hokum."[24] He referred to the ill-fated Marcus Garvey, then in a possibly bigamous state, as "America's Greatest Comedian" and berated his tendency to accumulate "wives and ships freely. The ships disappeared but the wives stayed with him."[25] Schuyler regularly assailed the black church for ignoring the social problems confronting the race. Whenever a new church went up, he commented on the inappropriateness of the sizable investment required, as in the case of the $600,000 St. Marks Church in New York. "Think of Negroes investing that much in a church when the majority of them are so pressed for funds that they have to take in roomers, hold rent parties and laboriously follow the 'numbers' and the horses! Think of the washerwomen, scrubwomen, laundry workers, ham fryers and others who raked and scraped to pay tribute to wealthy white contractors and merchants."[26] Schuyler was fond of repeating, "Any Negro community that can afford a church should have a clinic."[27]

As might be expected, Schuyler's caustic tongue brought a good deal of protest mail to Vann's desk. One irate letter writer, angry over the manner in which Schuyler maligned Marcus Garvey, wrote, "When a writer for an outstanding publication such as the *Pittsburgh Courier* elects to publish arguments void of truth and foundation, his misconceptions are capable of doing much harm to the reader's intelligence and understanding."[28] Another critic of Schuyler, U. S. Poston, felt that Schuyler's soul needed attention. In a *Courier* piece headlined "POSTON NAMES PREACHER TO CONVERT SCHUYLER," Poston said he knew a minister in Detroit, the Reverend R. L. Bradby, who could win Schuyler back from his godlessness. He charged that the writings of Schuyler, Mencken, and Sinclair Lewis had done much to corrode the power of religion, especially among youths who had lived the academic life, traveled, and seen social problems. "It is this question-asking Christian who will not dismiss such men as Schuyler, Mencken and Lewis as lightly as others would like." Poston recalled that he himself had been a freethinker until Reverend Bradby had returned him to the fold and added that he was certain the good reverend would be as effective with the unbelieving Schuyler.[29] Not only did Schuyler incur the wrath of godly men; he was also attacked by the irreligious. When he opposed the Communist handling of the Scottsboro case in the early 1930s, he was castigated by the *Daily Worker* and another Communist sheet, *The Negro Liberator*. A group of Communists wrote a letter to the *Courier* denouncing Schuyler: "We hold the *Courier* jointly responsible with Schuyler for all the disruptive and slanderous attacks which have appeared in his column, upon the militant struggles of the Negro workers. We demand the immediate dismissal of George Schuyler from the staff of the *Courier*.

We demand an end to the provocations against the Scottsboro–[Angelo] Herndon defense and other militant struggles."[30]

But Vann made no effort to dull Schuyler's barbs. He agreed with much of Schuyler's criticisms and liked the outspoken writer. The two in fact had much in common. Both were blunt, often vituperative, and both regarded themselves as realists who did not expect too much from the human race. Vann admired the younger man and realized he was a most valuable addition to the *Courier* staff. For the most part, Vann gave Schuyler a free hand with the editorials and rarely interfered with comments or directives. Schuyler remembered, "Once in a while a letter would come from one of them [Vann or Ira Lewis] suggesting treatment of a certain subject; but there were not over a half-dozen of them. I instinctively knew where and how to tread, and there was never a reprimand for having overstepped the bounds."[31]

Many other young feature writers joined the *Courier* staff about the same time George Schuyler did; Vann was making an all-out effort to expand the range and appeal of his newspaper. Wilburt Holloway, a native of Indiana, was in his twenties when he began doing the illustrations for Schuyler's "Aframerica" series in *The Messenger* and his incisive political cartoons for the *Courier*'s editorial page. Before Holloway was hired, most of the political cartoons had been borrowed from white dailies. Holloway also brought humor to the paper with his comic strip, "Sunny Boy Sam."

Floyd J. Calvin, who as a young man migrated from Washington, Arkansas, to New York City and attended school there briefly until he found he had some writing talent, had for a time worked for the *New York Age* and *The Messenger* before coming to the *Courier*.[32] Calvin was just twenty-three when he became special features editor of the *Courier* in 1926. The following year he went to New York to manage the *Courier* branch office there and began weekly radio broadcasts of the "*Pittsburgh Courier* Hour" on station WGBC in New York, which the *Courier* boasted marked "the first time in the history of Negro journalism that a Negro newspaper has brought its own program to the radio world." The black weekly called it a "fitting celebration to the one hundredth anniversary of the Negro press. . . . Although John B. Russwurm must have viewed the future of his profession a century ago as doubtful and uncertain, if he could witness today the centennial of his effort being celebrated with its first 'Radio Hour' he would probably feel that his labors were not in vain."[33]

Sylvester Russell began an entertainment section from Chicago which covered radio, movies, vaudeville, theater, and recordings. Society news was covered in Pittsburgh by Julia Bumbrey Jones, a graduate of Wilberforce University, in her well-received social column "Talk O' the Town." H. L. Mencken, a *Courier* subscriber, once remarked to George Schuyler that Jones wrote the best column of its kind in American journalism.[34] Through her close coverage and promotion of Frog Week, a seven-day festival which took place in Pittsburgh each August, Mrs. Jones was responsible for its elevation into a major social event that drew prominent blacks from around the country. On a national scale, society news came not only from the larger cities, as in "New York Society" by Mrs. H. Binga Dismond, "From the Woman's Point of View" by Alice Dunbar Nelson, or "Jersey City Notes," by See Bee Jay, but from as far away as Keokuk, Iowa, Humboldt, Texas, and Premier, West Virginia.

John C. Clark was hired in 1926 to do a series on Pittsburgh local life and politics which he called "Wylie Avenue." It wryly depicted the pool halls, gambling houses, bootleggers, bookmakers, and policy kings of the Hill District. Typical was the column which read, "An Avenue patron observing the race horse fans perusing the 'Race Form' remarked: 'If these fellows had studied their school books as they study ways to lose their money, the race would have been rewarded with many a good lawyer. Preach it, brother, preach it.' "[35] In another column he noted, "Colored police are noticeably absent from the Avenue. Possibly the Safety Director believes white officers can take care of disturbances that occur in places owned by Negroes where the patronage is white—exclusively."[36] When Clark did not write his column, the Hill District was covered by Blanch Taylor Dickinson's "Smoky City's Streets" and Chester Washington's "Deep Wylie." No matter which reporter wrote it, the column was widely read and extremely popular.

The *Courier* also began special features, such as the series by writer-historian Joel A. Rogers.[37] Self-educated, Rogers, author of several books and a column in *The Messenger,* was sent to Europe and Africa by Vann at the beginning of 1927 to do a series of articles based on his observations, which ran under headlines like "ETHIOPIA AND EGYPT MADE NORDIC CIVILIZATION POSSIBLE" and "ROMAN IDEAS OF LIFE CAME FROM ETHIOPIA."[38] There were also serialized novels by prominent and lesser writers, ranging from Blanche Taylor Dickinson's *Nellie Marie From Tennessee,* a melodramatic love story about "A Waif with a Soul," to a serialization of Walter White's *The Fire and the Flint,* which ran from February 6, 1926, through the remainder of the year. White also wrote "The Spotlight," a weekly book review column with comment on news articles, theatricals, "or on any human and interesting subject." Most of White's column covered works written by blacks like *The New Negro,* edited by Alain Locke; *Why We Behave Like Human Beings,* by George A. Dorsey; Octavius Roy Cohen's collection of black stories; *Color,* by Countee Cullen; *The Weary Blues,* by Langston Hughes; and *Blues: An Anthology,* by W. C. Handy. But White also wrote on whites such as Carl Sandburg, Sinclair Lewis, and Carl Van Vechten, the leading white patron of black artists and writers. He notified Sinclair Lewis of this: "I am sending you enclosed a clipping which gives my measured opinion of the magnificence of your refusal of the Pulitzer Prize. I do this column every week for the *Pittsburgh Courier* which has a nation-wide circulation."[39] White wrote to many prominent whites and publishing houses announcing he was working for the *Courier.* "Through this medium I will be able to reach by the newspaper a great many people who would not ordinarily be reached by the newspapers and magazines which carry book reviews."[40] Anxious to involve the *Courier* in the Harlem Renaissance, White said to Ira Lewis, "Mr. Carl Van Vechten of New York City asks that you send him a sample copy of the *Courier* and let him know what the subscription rate is. He was nice enough to say that he wanted to subscribe so as to read my column."[41] In asking for review copies of books from Doubleday, Page and Company, White touted the *Courier* as having a circulation of 90,000 and within a few short months he wrote a theater owner, Otto Kahn, that the figure had increased to 104,000;[42] White had an exaggerated view of the size of his audience.

Vann himself began to do a front-page column in 1927. "The Business Camera," changed in March 1927 to simply "The Camera," dealt with business, economics, industry, and politics. It was an innovative venture for as yet few other black weeklies allotted specific sections to business and finance. The column was full of reports of local business activity not unlike those appearing in white dailies. There was also thrifty advice like "Don't borrow money to spend; it is a sin. Borrow money to invest; it is good sense."[43] Vann stressed even more the need for blacks to form their own businesses and for the community to support them. He complained when blacks did not patronize local black-run drugstores, but went instead to the cut-rate white stores: "Get together druggists, and pool your buying power, and then, buying more, and buying cheaper, you can sell to us more cheaply than now, and we can buy more because we can get more for our money. This is the way to meet competition, and at the same time make more money. Try it."[44] Vann held up the example of the Jewish clothing merchants:

> The early Jewish merchants who came to this country made the instant discovery that the one thing above all else about which the American people are crazy is dress. The country is simply clothes crazy, and the Jewish merchants know it. What have they done? Go to New York and seek out the leading merchants. They are Jews. Look in Chicago for your largest stores and they are controlled by Jews. The Gentiles get vexed a little at the prices and bargains but the Jews control the stores. . . .
> The Jew knows the American people are crazy about clothes. He knows the clothes will sell as long as the people have a dollar in cash or a dollar in credit. Mr. Negro, what is it that your people are crazy to buy? Find out and get into the business of furnishing the thing. Time will build you a wonderful business.[45]

Sports news was rapidly becoming one of the *Courier*'s strongest features, consuming as much as four pages in any given week. Whether it was a local victory by the *Courier* Five basketball team over the Brushton Civics or a thirty-five-game winning streak by the powerful Homestead Grays baseball nine, the *Courier* had excellent reportage by W. Rollo Wilson, Chester "Ches" Washington, Cum Posey, Jr., and William G. Nunn, Sr. When in 1926 the *Pittsburgh American* became defunct, the *Courier* picked up W. Rollo Wilson. His "Sports Shots" was a popular feature of Vann's paper. The *Courier* claimed that Wilson, also a deputy athletic director in Pennsylvania, had covered more major sports events than any other black sports writer. His coverage of the football season, particularly the annual Thanksgiving gridiron rivalries, was especially well received. The game between Lincoln and Howard was the highlight of the football season for blacks and also an important pageant for black society. As Eugene Gordon, who surveyed the black press in 1926, wrote:

> If the white folk of the country read the Negro newspapers they would know that Harvard and Yale do

not settle annually the football supremacy of collegiate America. There is another classic, played on alternate Thanksgiving days at Howard University in Washington and Lincoln University in Philadelphia. All the larger Negro newspapers treat this event precisely as the dailies of the East treat the game between Harvard and Yale. Hundreds of photographs are made by staff photographers, and since the game is important in the social calendar, "society" reporters mingle with the scribes from the sporting departments. The city at which the game is played becomes temporarily the social capital of Aframerica. No other event draws together so many of the educated and wealthy folk.[46]

Soon Rollo Wilson was praised as the best of the black sports writers, because not only did he know sports, "but he can write of them. Most of the others know the subject but cannot write."[47]

Chester Washington, a native of Pittsburgh, had worked at the *Courier* as a high school student. When he was sixteen, Vann encouraged him to enter Virginia Union University. After graduation, he joined the *Courier* sports department and began a column called "Ches Says" of commentary on the local and national sporting scene. His selection of a college All-American team for football was a noteworthy yearly feature that started in 1926. Washington traveled to every major black football conference, as many as ten thousand miles each fall, reporting on gridiron contests and checking out the players in preparation for the selection of candidates. His "gridiron greats" were chosen from such schools as Wilberforce, Tuskegee, Fisk, Virginia State College, Wiley, Bluefield, Howard, and Lincoln. And in announcing his selections, he was given to dramatics:

SUPERMEN ON COURIER ALL-STAR TEAMS

Southeast Gets Five Representatives on Mighty First Eleven

COURIER'S Fourth All-American Teams Product of Long Tours and Much Research

Challenging the brilliancy of even the sun itself, five sparkling stars of Gridironia have upheld the athletic glory of the sunshine-polluted far South by winning for Dixie five places on the *Pittsburgh Courier*'s fourth All-American eleven.[48]

The Primacy of the COURIER • 145

As Ches Washington covered the gridiron, Wendell Smith reported from the baseball diamond. Long a crusader for integrated baseball in the major leagues, Smith gave the black baseball players their due in the pages of the *Courier*. When he reported the 1927 World Series, it was not the one between the New York Yankees and the hometown Pittsburgh Pirates, but between two black teams, the American Giants and the Atlantic City Bacharacks. Babe Ruth hit a record sixty home runs for the New York Yankees that year, but the feat went unmentioned in the *Courier*, which had its own heroes. William Nunn, who as a young man of nineteen had left a "secure" job in the Pittsburgh Post Office to join the *Courier* staff in 1919, also covered baseball in his columns "Diamond Dope" and "WGN Sports Broadcasts Talks."[49]

Instead of rooting for the Pirates, Pittsburgh blacks cheered for their own Homestead Grays, managed by the colorful Cumberland "Cum" Posey, who also wrote a column, "Sportive Realm," for the *Courier*. Usually in early October, after the regular baseball season, the Grays played against an all-star team of major-league baseball players and invariably beat them. Led by the brilliant fireballing of "Smoky" Joe Williams, ace pitcher for the Grays, they proved to any onlookers how much the black players would have added to the major leagues, had they been allowed to play there. The *Courier* reported enthusiastically in 1927, "GRAYS SHOW GREATEST INFIELD IN COLORED BASEBALL,"[50] and in 1928 "GRAYS END SEASON: BEAT STARS, *Homesteaders Win Five out of Eight Games From Big Leaguers*."[51]

At this same time the *Courier*'s front page was much enlivened by the addition of photographs. This was mostly the idea of Ira Lewis, who had pushed especially hard for front-page pictures of beauty queens. But the pictures were not at all suggestive, just of pretty girls, some of whom were in school or in the black "social set," like the girls of the Delta Gamma Theta Sorority of Chicago or the May Queen from the Clark Memorial Baptist Church of Homestead.

Also, the *Courier* began to receive more national news from outside sources. It joined the Associated Negro Press in November 1925 and was using the services of Louis Lautier, a Washington-based correspondent. Lautier supplied the *Courier*, along with the *Baltimore Afro-American* and the *Chicago Defender*, with news from the nation's capital.

Sensationalism, which had played little part in the *Courier*'s reportage until the early 1920s, increased as the newspaper became more national in character, as an obvious means to increase circulation. The

Courier's front page generally had two or three large headlines; invariably the major ones dealt with murder, crime, or interracial love affairs:

THREE SLAYERS DIE IN CHAIR: TRIPLE EXECUTION STAGED IN DEATH ROW AT ROCKVIEW PRISON[52]

HUSBAND ENDS LOVE TRIANGLE BY TURNING SMOKING GUN ON SELF[53]

NINETEEN-YEAR-OLD GIRL KILLS YOUTH[54]

COLORED GIRL AND WHITE LOVER ARE KILLED IN SOUTH[55]

Despite this, however, one person who examined black weeklies reported that the *Courier* had slightly less sensational news than the *Baltimore Afro-American* and only about half of that of the *Chicago Defender*.[56]

The increased and more professional staff Vann hired for the *Courier* improved the quality of the newspaper greatly. By the end of 1928 the *Courier* had been declared America's best black weekly and first in editorial standing by Eugene Gordon, a *Boston Post* reporter who made a close study of the black press throughout that year. Gordon based his appraisal on the improved staff, the editorials, special features, sports coverage, cartoons, and national news. He described the sixteen-page weekly as original in theme, racial yet rational and not approaching the red-ink style of the *Chicago Defender*, and invariably successful in accomplishing its purpose. The *Courier*'s emphasis had shifted strongly from local affairs to national issues. In fact, one of the paper's few weaknesses was its increasing neglect of local news.[57] By the end of the decade, H. L. Mencken called the *Courier* the "best colored newspaper published."[58]

With the weekly responsibility of writing editorials gradually being taken off his hands by George Schuyler, Vann was free to embroil himself in several "national issues"—highly controversial conflicts of the time. These conflicts, featured in the pages of the *Courier*, helped to increase further the circulation and hence the stability of the newspaper. The two most important of these were Vann's attack on James

Weldon Johnson and W. E. B. DuBois, and his involvement in A. Philip Randolph's efforts to organize the Brotherhood of Sleeping Car Porters.

In challenging James Weldon Johnson and W. E. B. DuBois, Vann and the *Courier* were flinging stones at two Goliaths of black America. Johnson was a poet, a pivotal figure in the Harlem Renaissance, a former editor of the *New York Age*, a diplomat, and executive secretary of the NAACP. In 1925 he received the Spingarn Medal, awarded each year to the American black who had made the highest achievement in any field of elevated or honorable human endeavor. And W. E. B. DuBois was a brilliant writer and educator, well known as the editor of *The Crisis*. Exactly why Vann chose to attack them remains unknown. He may well have seen the issue as genuine. Also it was certain to cause a great sensation and a large increase in the circulation of the *Courier*. Vann had never before shown any real muckraking instinct, so it is possible that he undertook the siege in part to build up sales of his newspaper.

Before 1926, Vann had enjoyed good relations with Johnson and the NAACP. In 1924, Vann had been an enthusiastic participant in the NAACP's attempt to get the seventy remaining black soldiers who had allegedly been involved in the 1917 Houston riot released from Leavenworth Prison, visiting President Coolidge as one of a group of ten prominent blacks headed by James Weldon Johnson to present a petition with 124,000 signatures. The group in President Coolidge's office included most of the august blacks of the day: James Weldon Johnson of the NAACP, William Monroe Trotter of the *Boston Guardian*, A. Philip Randolph of *The Messenger*, Robert Abbott of the *Chicago Defender*, Carl Murphy of the *Baltimore Afro-American*, S. S. Booker of Alpha Phi Alpha, Reverend L. K. Williams of the National Baptist Convention, Nathan D. Brascher of the Associated Negro Press, Archibald H. Grimke, former minister to Santo Domingo and Spingarn Medal winner, Mrs. Daisy Lampkin of the National Association of Colored Women, J. E. Mitchell of the *St. Louis Argus* and the Negro Press of America, Channing H. Tobias of the YMCA, and Bishop J. S. Caldwell of the AMEZ Church. Johnson presented the petition to President Coolidge,[59] and the soldiers had their sentences lightened.[60]

But Vann called for a full pardon, not just commutation. In a May 3 editorial he wrote adamantly that "the petition asked the President to pardon these men, NOT COMMUTE their sentences. We are for pardon and the President of the United States may just as well be informed that the Negroes of this country are as decided about this petition as he is about the Teapot Dome Scandal. We want the men PARDONED, Mr. President."[61] Vann's militant stance is puzzling in the light of his 1917 defense of the thirteen hangings: "Mutiny and murder are crimes that merit death upon conviction. Soldiers who participate in lawlessness must take the consequences."[62] Time and reflection may have caused him to alter his view of the incident radically, or he may have been influenced either by pressure from Johnson or simply by the honor of being asked to participate in the presentation of the petition. Though Vann, Johnson, and the NAACP had hoped for a broader and more rapid pardon, they were not entirely displeased with their limited victory. Appreciative of Vann's efforts in the matter, Johnson wrote him a warm letter of appreciation in May. "The results are gratifying. . . . We are proud indeed that in this great cause in which you so whole-heartedly joined, giving to the world the greatest demonstration of unqualified cooperation on the part of the colored people that such results were secured. . . . For your own great share in this victory, we extend our most sincere thanks."[63]

The *Courier* had also reported favorably at first on the NAACP's handling of the case of Ossian Sweet, a black man charged with murder. One approving editorial ran in part: "The local branch of the National Association for the Advancement of Colored People began to hold mass meetings and secure funds to fight the case. The national office of the Association was soon brought into the case and because of the great principle of human liberty involved, made it a national issue. No delay was caused in securing immediately the best legal talent to defend the case. And it was not long before the New York office of the NAACP had announced that it had retained through Mr. Arthur Spingarn the best lawyers in America, Mr. Darrow and Arthur Garfield Hayes of New York, well known constitutional lawyer for the American Civil Liberties Union."[64]

But this amity was forgotten by Vann in 1926. The battle began on October 9, when a large, front-page copyrighted article entitled "NAACP 'SLUSH FUND' AIRED" appeared in the *Courier*. The article attacked Johnson in his role as director of the Garland Fund for allocating funds strictly to Johnson's favorite projects rather than to what would be most beneficial to the race as a whole. The Garland Fund had been set up by Charles Garland of Massachusetts, who bequeathed

The Primacy of the COURIER • 149

$900,000 in his will with the stipulation that it be used for liberal, radical, and otherwise unpopular causes that could get no assistance from other sources, and that the funds be used with great rapidity. As the only black director of the Garland Fund, Johnson had great influence on decisions as to which black causes would receive assistance, and Vann and the *Courier* charged that he had misused that influence.

First, the October 9 *Courier* article charged that DuBois, an officer of the NAACP and close friend of Johnson, had been awarded the relatively exorbitant sum of $5,000 by the Garland Fund just "for study of Negro education in South Carolina;" a study not only of great cost, but, it said, of questionable worth. Second, said the article angrily, the NAACP had received "the lion's share of the money given [by the Garland Fund] to Negroes," nearly $35,000. Some of this was used, according to the *Courier*, for salaries of NAACP officers and for rent on "expensive and palatial offices on Fifth Avenue," while the Brotherhood of Sleeping Car Porters (then being championed by Vann and the *Courier*), currently in the throes of organizational problems and fighting the Pullman Company, received only $11,200.

Next, the *Courier* recalled that the Fund had given $26,552.80 to the defense of Ossian Sweet: "The 'Sweet' fund bids fair to become the biggest scandal of the new year." Sweet, a black physician in Detroit, was charged with murder in 1925. He had purchased a home in a white neighborhood, and when an angry mob of whites gathered around the house to shout imprecations and throw stones, a white man was killed by a bullet fired by someone in Sweet's house. Sweet, his brother, and a group of friends who had been with them in the house at the time were brought to trial. The NAACP took up the defense, employing Clarence Darrow and Arthur Garfield Hayes, and all of the defendants were acquitted after two trials that received a great deal of publicity. The *Courier* had no quarrel with the NAACP's victory, but was incensed by Floyd Calvin's allegation that of the $26,552.80 given by the Garland Fund, only $5,000 went to the defense attorneys, while the rest "is now being banked by the NAACP," a fact which had not been made public. "We want to lay the facts bare, and let the Negro Public decide whether it is contributing to the preservation of its liberties and principles or to the upkeep of a few Fifth Avenue barons who might otherwise find such fat salaries somewhat difficult to draw." (The Garland Fund contributed only one-third of the funds, one dollar for each two given by the public.) "Indications point to the fact that the NAACP and its officials are answering the roll-call to a money-made 'slush fund' party; held under the auspices of the General Public. What has been done with the money raised by the public has not been reported to the public. How much money has been raised has not been reported and with emphasis placed on the amount given the organization by the Garland Fund, the officers should 'come clean.' "65

Even before the *Courier*'s accusations of October 9, Vann had strongly disagreed with Johnson about white novelist Carl Van Vechten's *Nigger Heaven*. Van Vechten was a leading white patron of black artists and writers during the Harlem Renaissance of the 1920s, and Johnson was both his close friend and one of the leading black figures in that same movement. Vann felt, as did others of the black bourgeoisie,66 that such literary activities were a waste of time, that the title of Van Vechten's novel was a malignant insult to blacks, and that Johnson was somehow betraying his race by his kind words for the work. Initially, Vann even refused an advertisement for *Nigger Heaven*, a gesture whose significance is increased by the *Courier*'s desperation for advertising revenue of any sort. Walter White pleaded with Vann by telegram to retract his refusal, stressing that

> I HAVE READ THE NOVEL AND IT IS A MAGNIFICENT PICTURE WITH AMAZING SYMPATHY AND UNDERSTANDING OF THE NEGRO'S POINT OF VIEW. THE TITLE WHICH I ASSUME IS CAUSE OF *COURIER*'S REFUSAL OF ADVERTISING IS AN IRONIC ONE AS WILL BE SEEN UPON READING BOOK. MAY I URGE RECONSIDERATION OF REFUSAL, ... ESPECIALLY IN VIEW OF FACT THAT ANOTHER COLORED NEWSPAPER WHICH HAD REFUSED ADVERTISING HAD RECONSIDERED UPON READING MY ARTICLE ON JUNE 19 REGARDING MR. VAN VECHTEN.67

After White's intervention, Vann did reconsider and later accepted the advertisement,68 but he retained his bad feelings toward Johnson.

Johnson ignored Vann's attack on his literary sensibilities but was quick to strike back at the *Courier*'s allegations about the NAACP's use of monies given it by the Garland Fund. In private, Johnson labeled the accusations "absurd, baseless, and malicious." He went on to charge that Vann had long opposed the NAACP and was especially hostile to DuBois. Vann, he acidly noted, was a Republican "henchman" and "petty office seeker."69 Johnson issued a long and angry press release a few days after Vann's newspaper made its charges. Johnson began by saying that Vann's "investigation" of the Garland Fund's relations with the NAACP consisted of nothing more than "a representative of Mr. Vann [phoning] the NAACP for information and [being] courteously referred to the Garland Fund headquarters where figures were freely given in good faith."[70] He went on, "As to undue influence exerted by myself, even if I had wanted to 'loot' the Garland Fund, as Mr. Vann implies, I was the only Negro on the Board of Directors and I should hardly have been able to induce the other members to abet me in my villainy. . . . There are so many absurd statements in Mr. Vann's tissue of lies that I cannot even discuss them all." As to Vann's outcry against the amount of money donated by the Garland Fund to the NAACP, Johnson explained:

> When the Negroes of this country were appalled at the crisis confronting the Sweet family and their friends, the Garland Fund, realizing that this was one of the crucial cases involving the protection of minority rights, stepped in with an initial offer of $5,000 outright and in addition offered one dollar for every two dollars raised by the NAACP for the Legal Defense Fund. The total amount thus given for Legal Defense by the Garland Fund was determined by colored people themselves and their white friends, who raised money to meet the Garland Fund's offer.... [The NAACP] explicitly announced that in undertaking a Legal Defense Fund it had in mind not alone the Sweet defense but other cases involving the rights of the Negro.... Mr. Vann is guilty of deliberate misstatement.

Johnson asserted that all expenses of both Sweet trials had been scrupulously examined by a firm of public accountants and would be published in the annual report of the NAACP. "Not one penny of the Garland Fund or the moneys contributed to the Legal Defense Fund . . . has ever gone or will go to the individual profit of any member of the Board of Directors or of the staff of the NAACP." Finally, Johnson defended the $5,000 given DuBois for his study of Negro education as not for the study of a single state, but for "study of Negro public school education throughout the South." Further, "any reasonable person knows that $5,000 is an entirely inadequate sum for such a stupendous task."

Johnson concluded his press release with a biting barrage of criticism of Vann himself:

There remains a word for the man who will so lower himself as to make the type of malicious, underhanded and false attack published in the *Pittsburgh Courier*. Can such a man, who attacks the one organization effectively defending the civil and constitutional rights of the Negro in America, who spreads untruth about it, can such a man have the good of the Negro at heart? Can the poisonous gossip-monger and falsifier who perverts his public position as editor to spread lies, pretending to have derived them as facts in an "investigation," make any justifiable claim to be acting for the "public good"? I leave the answer to this question to all fair minded people, white and colored, who know what the NAACP has accomplished in fifteen years . . .

Mr. Vann states that the Negro of America needs such an organization as the NAACP. At the one organization which is actually meeting this need, he has struck. He has struck unfairly, untruthfully, meanly. He has written a more poisonous attack than has emanated from any white Southerner in the entire history of the NAACP. I think the colored people of America have a little account to settle with Mr. Robert L. Vann, Editor of the *Pittsburgh Courier*. They should examine the motives for his attack upon the NAACP and other organizations as well as the Garland Fund. It is Mr. Vann, in view of his proved lying, and not the NAACP, who stands on trial before the bar of public opinion. He stands accused of the greatest offenses of which a public man can be charged with, of offenses violating the commonest standards of honor, decency and regard for his race and his fellow citizens.[71]

According to Johnson's biographer, Eugene Levy, "Johnson never denied that he used his influence within the Garland Fund, and, for that matter, with other groups and individuals, to garner money for the NAACP and for other black groups. He considered fundraising, after all, as part of his job. What did anger him was the *Courier*'s implication that he was raising money for his personal benefit, an implication that phrases like 'slush fund' left in the reader's mind."[72]

Next Johnson came to Pittsburgh on October 19 and gave several speeches before gatherings of blacks in which he attempted to vindicate his actions as a director of the Garland Fund. At one point, Johnson lost his temper completely and called Vann a "liar" and a "scoundrel." But Vann remained calm after Johnson's tirades and produced a photocopy of a Garland report from the year before which stated that the allocation to DuBois was in fact for studies in South Carolina alone. With Johnson and the NAACP seemingly on the defensive, the *Courier* continued its attack, commenting on Johnson's behavior. "The night was Johnson's 'Day in Court.' He came, he 'cussed,' and he went. And still what about the figures?" This story and others ran under needling headlines like "JAMES WELDON JOHNSON AIRILY

SLUSHES OVER SLUSH FUND" and "HE SINGS 'EM—BUT HE DOESN'T DENY 'EM FIGURES."[73]

When the conflict between Vann and Johnson seemed to many blacks to have degenerated to an unacceptably low level of abusiveness, a self-appointed intermediary stepped in. Kelly Miller, professor of mathematics and sociology at Howard University, political columnist in the *Norfolk Journal and Guide,* and a racial moderate, played arbiter and attempted to smooth over the ruffled feathers. Miller's role came naturally; he had long been a seeker after racial unity and in February 1924 had founded the "Sanhedrin," a movement which attempted to coalesce all black organizations into a common effort.[74] Excerpts from Miller's summary and conciliatory editorial follow:

> We were all regretfully amazed several weeks ago to find that the *Pittsburgh Courier,* through its leading columnist, had issued a broadside against the National Association for the Advancement of Colored People. This broadside did not indulge so much in accusations or harsh criticism as in insinuating queries. It purported to give facts and figures as to income and expenditures, with the evident purpose of directing public attention to the . . . organization, in a frame of mind not wholly friendly. . . . James Weldon Johnson was called to task, not only for his stewardship in N.A.A.C.P. matters, but for his relations to the Garland fund as well. Mr. Johnson enjoys the singular honor of having been chosen as chairman of the board of trustees, of which he is the only colored member.
> . . . The *Courier* questions Johnson's sense of proportion and impartiality. It complains that he engineered the larger allotments to the movements with which he was most intimately related, to the neglect of others equally worthy.
> If it be conceded that Mr. Johnson acted as alleged, he was but exercising his own judgment and discretion as a trustee. . . . If Mr. Johnson preferred his circle of intimate interests above all the rest, he was but acting manly, in about the same way that the *Pittsburgh Courier* would have acted if placed in a similar situation.
> The N.A.A.C.P. forthwith issued a release vindicating Mr. Johnson and the integrity of the organization. This vindication was hotly supplemented by Mr. Johnson in several addresses in the city of Pittsburgh. It was like bearding the lion in his den. Unfortunately . . . he lost his temper and thus put himself at a serious

disadvantage as a controversialist. He indulged frequently in ugly names and uncomplimentary epithets. . . . Mr. Johnson weakened his case and his cause by his ill humor.

No one who knows Mr. Vann would believe that he would tell a deliberate lie to discredit a worthy movement, any more than he would believe a like charge against James Weldon Johnson. I know both of these men, and regard them as men of equal integrity. One or both of them has been led into misstatement of facts and misjudgment of motives. Both of them ought to be ashamed of themselves to make such an unseemly scene before the public.

Mr. Vann has shown his superiority in that he has kept his temper. The . . . difference between them hinges on a single issue of fact. Did Mr. Johnson use his good offices as trustee of the Garland Fund to award Dr. DuBois five thousand dollars to investigate Negro education in South Carolina or in the South? Mr. Vann said that the grant was limited to South Carolina. Mr. Johnson replies that this is a lie, the grant covered the whole South . . . But Mr. Vann comes back with journalistic shrewdness and gives the public a photographic copy of the reports of the Garland Fund, where it is specifically stated that on March 25, 1925, a grant of five thousand dollars was awarded to W. E. B. DuBois to study Negro education in South Carolina. . . . What is a photographic copy against a man's integrity of character built up during a lifetime of uprightness of thought and conduct?

Is it not more than likely that the board may have intended one thing and the secretary recorded another? The misunderstanding of a word on the part of the scribe might easily account for the difference.

The right-minded public will let the incident pass into regretful memory that these two outstanding examples of the Negro intelligentsia should have set such a sorry example to the proletariat whom they engage to lead.[75]

Unfortunately, as the Sanhedrin had failed, so too did Miller's conciliatory efforts in the Garland affair. A long editorial in the *Atlanta Independent* of November 18 sarcastically chided Miller for his intervention and accused him of being blind to the moral questions raised by Vann. The *Independent* felt Vann had made some telling points:

> Dr. Kelly Miller, one of the ablest logicians of the race, stepped into the middle of the controversy . . . and said both Bob and Jim were right, that neither were wrong . . . the Doctor in his effort to make both of these disputants speak the truth, has inadvertently neglected the moral side of the question at issue. . . . Mr. Vann alleges that Mr. Johnson violated the trust imposed in him, when he appropriated a part of the fund to interests that he was directly and indirectly interested in personally, and called on Mr. Johnson for an accounting of his stewardship. Mr. Johnson, instead of replying to Mr. Vann in kind, denounced him as a liar and a common scold; and thus the issue is joined. As the issue is joined, Dr. Miller steps into the breach and says, "If Johnson did use his official position to give his friend Dr. W. E. B. DuBois $5,000 for the study of Negro education in South Carolina, and gave to other concerns that he was personally interested in $25,000, more or less, as Mr. Vann alleges, since Mr. Vann would have done the same thing, had he been similarly situated, Mr. Johnson did no wrong; and Bob did not lie when he insinuated that Jim Johnson had misused a Trust Fund to his own personal advantage. . . . But, after all, the joke is really on Doctor Miller. Overlooking the fact that both cannot be right, he takes the position that two wrongs make a right—a new and strange philosophy under our code of morals. . . . It is not a question with us whether Bob or Jim won the argument. We are concerned only about the truth and morality of Mr. Johnson's conduct as a trustee and as supported by our good friend, Doctor Miller. The public is not interested in which of the two disputants is the best lawyer, but whether Mr. Johnson violated the trust imposed in him as a public servant.

Soon after this article appeared and Miller's meliorist efforts had come to naught, James Weldon Johnson retired from the battle and W. E. B. DuBois took up the cudgel in his stead. In his yearly report in *The Crisis* DuBois listed the black man's "Assets and Liabilities." At the top of the "Assets" list, DuBois placed "Sweet Trials" and "Defense Fund," and at the bottom of the list of liabilities, below even "31 Lynchings" and " 'Anglo-Saxon' Virginia" was simply "Vann."[76] The *Courier* quickly retorted:

> Like the monarchs of olden time, [DuBois] can do no wrong and is always right. . . . The Pope of Fifth Avenue is omniscient. Those who dare to criticize him are summarily punished.
>
> Of course the inclusion of the editor of the *Pittsburgh Courier* among the liabilities of the Negro race is due to the inquiries made by this paper concerning some of the activities of the National Association for the Advancement of some few Colored People; and the learned doctor's investigation of Negro schools in South Carolina, SOMETIMES KNOWN AS THE ENTIRE SOUTH. Evidently these mild inquiries tremendously exercised the sage of 69 Fifth Avenue. He snorts!
>
> The army of readers of the *Pittsburgh Courier* will merely smile when they hear of the characterization of Mr. Vann as a Race "Liability". . . . About 20 times more of them read the *Pittsburgh Courier* than read Dr. DuBois. They know that the *Pittsburgh Courier* is ever on the fighting line for the great masses of Negroes in this country.
>
> The strictures of Dr. DuBois and his ilk are of no consequence whatever. . . . If DuBois is a sample of the Highly Educated Negro, there is little wonder that his following of twenty years ago can now be numbered on the fingers of the one hand. The old boy is dead on his feet and doesn't know it.[77]

In addition to Vann's charges about DuBois's misuse of money from the Garland Fund, there was a basic animosity between the two men, not unlike that between Vann and Johnson. DuBois, the Harvard-educated intellectual, thought of Vann as little more than a hard-headed bourgeois businessman from the Smoky City, while Vann, pragmatic and conservative in his outlook, regarded the scholarly DuBois as pompous, aloof from most of his fellow blacks, and impractical. Their differences in personality and outlook made some sort of conflict inevitable.

These contrasting approaches are illustrated by an incident in 1919, when Vann disagreed, albeit rather mildly, with some of DuBois's public utterances in an article in *The Crisis*. Early that year DuBois made a trip to France in behalf of the NAACP to "gather the historical data concerning Negro troops and to call a Pan-African Congress."[78] While in France DuBois was astounded by his discovery of a number of gross injustices that had been perpetrated against black American troops in Europe during the World War. Some of these findings he revealed in the May 1919 issue of *The Crisis*. Further, DuBois attacked both Robert R. Moton, head of Tuskegee Institute, and Emmett J. Scott, special assistant to Secretary of War Newton Baker, who were also in France at the time, for not having commented on the deplorable conditions. DuBois charged that Moton, instead of investigating and reporting the plight of black soldiers, made meaningless guided tours and speeches in the company of his white superiors. Of Scott, DuBois asked three pointed questions: Did you know the treatment which black troops were receiving in France? If you did NOT know, why did you not find out? If you DID know, what did you do about it? The intimation was that Scott knew of the conditions and did nothing.[79]

After reading DuBois's article, Vann wrote a long editorial defending Moton and Scott against what he saw as too intense an attack. Vann did praise DuBois for the "splendid results of the Pan-African Congress" and for uncovering truths about the way black troops had been treated, but he reminded DuBois that the latter had advantages that Moton and Scott lacked, to wit, that DuBois spoke French and was a free agent "at liberty to 'nose' around to whatever extent the courteous French allowed him."[80] By contrast, Vann pointed out, Moton and Scott went to France as representatives of the American government and were limited by their official positions. It was further possible, said Vann, that Scott and Moton uncovered data which had been turned over to the War Department instead of released publicly. Added Vann, "No one knows better than Dr. DuBois with what difficulty Mr. Scott has labored since he has been in the War Department." The *Courier* editor wrote in conclusion that DuBois was too intent on indicting the two men for what they "DID NOT DO" while in France, and should have been more concerned in discovering what they had done. "We are interested in what Dr. DuBois DID DO while in France; and not interested in what someone DID NOT DO while in France. We believe it is not difficult to sense the difference." Emmett Scott warmly thanked Vann for coming to his aid. "I must not fail to fell [sic] you how much I valued and appreciated the splendid support the *Courier* has given me during the recent 'brush' with the editor of the *Crisis*."[81]

One sees in this incident DuBois's tough-minded militancy and angry addressing of philosophical issues contrasted with Vann's pragmatic awareness of limiting realities, his ability to accommodate, and his quest for the middle ground. By early 1926, the outspoken DuBois had assailed Vann directly with his lacerating tongue, commenting that the *Courier* had developed "mental and physical dyspepsia" since President Coolidge failed to award Vann a political appointment after his election in 1924.[82] Vann was still smarting from that attack and thus very ready to do battle by the time the Garland Fund issue presented itself.

Soon others, most notably Walter White, then assistant executive secretary of the NAACP, were also drawn into the Garland controversy. White wrote Vann that he could not continue the column he had been writing for the *Courier* because of Vann's October 9 attack on his organization.[83] Vann replied to White's letter:

> In spite of the intelligence the general public accredits to the members of the NAACP, I have yet to find a single one of them who can separate personality from organization work. Judging from your letter, any criticism of your organization is accepted by you as a criticism of yourself. In all other activities with which I have any acquaintance, the organization effort and the effort of the individual are things apart, but with you gentlemen the NAACP and your personalities are evidently your whole existence....
>
> My personal regard for you remains the same, and I want to assure you that my attitude toward your organization will continue to be based upon available facts and information tending to disclose the deportment of your organization toward the public. I hold nothing against your associates, except perhaps the personal references they have made to the writer and the personal attacks, and I attribute this to the fact that they are unable to separate me from my newspaper any more than you seem to be able to separate yourself from the National Association for the Advancement of Colored People.[84]

White, who had called Vann's attack on Johnson "venomous and vicious,"[85] wrote a lengthy letter to Vann defending his organization. He stressed that in his nine years of service with the NAACP he had never heard of mismanagement of funds. As to separating the personality of individuals from the organization, White remarked:

> The *Courier*'s attack upon the integrity of the NAACP could not in any sense be construed other than as an attack upon the integrity and honesty of its officials. When the Association of which I am an integral part is accused directly or by implication of dishonesty, that accusation naturally is affixed to those who are responsible for the conducting of its affairs. To fail to take the *Courier*'s criticism of the honesty of the Association as being also an attack upon my own personal honesty

would be to convict myself either of being a mere figurehead in the organization ignorant of its affairs and with no power whatever with regard to its management or to permit to go unchallenged the charge of mismanagement and dishonesty. . . .

Neither the NAACP nor any of its officers possess anything more than their good name. Slanderous attacks upon those reputations, whatever may be the motive, must be answered in the most vigorous and uncompromising terms.[86]

Vann seemed to have aroused the entire officialdom of the NAACP. Their anger rained down upon his head in long defensive letters. At Johnson's request, Joel Spingarn, the organization's white treasurer, took Vann to task. Spingarn issued a public statement in which he began by listing the offices he had held in the NAACP and insisting that he was in a position to state frankly and precisely the organization's business methods. He said he had thoroughly examined an auditor's report and could find no evidence of misuse of funds, assuring the public that neither Johnson, DuBois, White, nor any other salaried executive had ever signed a single check.[87] "In view of these facts I think I may say that no Association organized to perform a public service has ever been conducted on a more business-like basis or on a plane of higher integrity or disinterestedness. I resent any imputations that may be cast on the good faith and honesty of the salaried officers of the Association who under the supervision of a distinguished Board of Directors have devoted their lives to the service of their race and their country."[88]

Nearly every member of the black press entered the dispute. Though there were weeklies such as the *Tuscon* (Ariz.) *Times,* which called "INVESTIGATE THE NAACP,"[89] and others like the *Chicago Whip, Detroit Owl,* and *Cleveland Gazette* that joined the *Courier* attack, most black journals either remained neutral or sided with the NAACP. The black reporter Ernest Rice McKinney prepared a syndicated article for the Preston News Service in which he used Joel Spingarn's line of defense, that the white officers of the NAACP like Spingarn and Mary White Ovington were above reproach and therefore the *Courier*'s accusations must be baseless.[90] McKinney's reasoning seems sophistic, but a number of newspapers used it. Other papers, such as the *Charleston* (S.C.) *Messenger,* took another tack; its headline said, "LET'S HAVE THE PROOF," and the copy asked Vann to substantiate his charges against Johnson.[91] The *Philadelphia Tribune* averred that if the NAACP "did nothing for the next ten years every Negro should support it for the splendid manner in which it effected the acquittal of Ossian Sweet."[92] The *Chicago Bee,* the *Baltimore Afro-American,* and the *Richmond Planet* also defended the association.[93] Others, begging the question of whether the charges were true, asked for a quick settlement because the dispute was giving blacks a bad image in the eyes of the white world. The editors felt the race had at best a tentative hold on unity and could ill afford any sort of disharmony. One said, "The whites are thousands of years ahead of us. They can afford taking all the time they please exercising their wits and enjoying contests with each other. But the Negroes cannot really be natural. We cannot afford knocking and kicking against our prominent race leaders and builders unless some fundamental principle is at stake. Let us lay off. We have not enough to think out and still have some left like our white brothers and sisters."[94]

James Weldon Johnson apparently had no trouble defending himself to the Garland people; he was reelected president of the fund on May 6, 1927. But the controversy dragged on for three years before any sort of truce was reached. Johnson's biographer offers the opinion that the dispute abated because Vann had undergone a tremendous amount of criticism and "perhaps sensing he had put himself on the end of a limb, . . . the best mode of retreat was silence," while Johnson, though continuing to be irritated by Vann's attack, turned to more pressing matters like the *Nixon* v. *Herndon* "white primary" case in 1927.[95]

The matter was finally resolved in late 1929 when Vann, DuBois, and Johnson wrote brief public letters which were published in the *Courier* and *The Crisis* under the heading, "NAACP—*Courier* 'BURY THE HATCHET.' "[96] Vann apologized, "I regret very much the appearance of the article in the *Pittsburgh Courier* on October 9, 1926. I do not believe the accusations and if I had seen the article before it appeared it never would have been published." DuBois replied to Vann's apology matter of factly: "I have read the above statement of Mr. Vann and I accept it in the spirit in which it is given and the incident is hereby forgotten." Johnson's comment, equally brief and to the point, was, "I have read Mr. Vann's statement. I accept his word, and therefore withdraw what I said about him personally in my address at Pittsburgh, October 19, 1926. I regret the whole incident as unfortunate and am happy to see it closed."[97] Within ten years, DuBois had become a regular contributor to the *Courier,* and Vann claimed he and DuBois were good friends. "Why, I put up most of the money for DuBois to make that trip he took to the Orient, and I would do it again."⁹⁸

Not all the rancor was forgotten, however. Robert Vann never forgave Johnson for having called him a "liar" and a "scoundrel," and when Johnson died in 1938, Vann refused to go to the funeral. Asked by Walter White if he would attend, Vann replied, "You know, Walter, I must be frank about this. . . . Jim and I were not friends when he died, and had not been friends for some time. I have never forgiven him for the way he treated me over my difference with the N.A.A.C.P. . . . And so I say about his funeral the same thing I said about Huey Long's funeral—'I shall not be present, but I am glad it happened.' "⁹⁹

Vann's anger at Johnson was protracted also because, after his attack on the NAACP, Johnson took steps to have Vann put out of Sigma Pi Phi, popularly termed "the Boule," a black Greek letter society for college graduates which had a good deal of social cachet, and to which they both belonged.¹⁰⁰ Johnson was an officer, an "archon" of Beta chapter in New York City. Vann told Walter White that Johnson "made charges against me and then failed to show up when those charges were to be heard on the floor of the Boule, and as a result of this I was cleared of those charges. He was never man enough to face me with them on the floor of the Convention. . . . The Boule advised Jim Johnson that he could present his charges at a second convention following the filing of the original charges. This Jim declined to do, and so the Convention, having received an account of the matter a second time without Jim's appearance on the floor, dropped the whole matter and I was cleared. I have never forgiven Jim for this, and I have always considered it a low-down, dirty trick."¹⁰¹ Johnson's biographer accurately concludes that Johnson's actions in the Boule contributed to Vann's 1929 withdrawal of his 1926 charges against the NAACP official. "I'd say Johnson was angry enough to shaft Vann in such a way, but I have no evidence that he did so. Something, however, caused Vann to retract his charges, and I doubt if it was out of the goodness of his heart."¹⁰²

Perhaps the most significant and controversial issue in which Robert Vann and the *Courier* became embroiled was A. Philip Randolph's efforts to organize the Brotherhood of Sleeping Car Porters. Randolph and Chandler Owen had edited the socialist publication, *The Messenger*, since its founding in 1917. In the summer of 1925, he focused his attention fully on the grievances of the Pullman porters. Virtually all the Pullman porters were black, and their treatment by the Pullman Company was far inferior to that given the white conductors. The porters started at the miserly wage of $67 a month and so were utterly dependent upon tips from white passengers to augment their pay. They had heavy expenses in their jobs which they had to meet out of their wages, including the cost of uniforms for the first ten years of service, shoe polish for patrons, and meals during runs. Moreover, the porters worked 400 long hours a month, while the other train employees, including conductors, put in only 240 hours. These are only the grossest of the inequities suffered by the porters; there was a lengthy list of others.

Randolph began a series of articles in *The Messenger* in July and August 1925 discussing the porters' working conditions and urging them to organize themselves into an effective union. At a meeting in Harlem on August 25, the Brotherhood of Sleeping Car Porters and Maids was formally set in operation, with Randolph as head of the union with the title of "general organizer." The union asked for a wage of $150 a month, so that the degrading practice of tipping could be ended, and an end to "doubling," or having to leave on another trip right after arriving from one.[103]

The fledgling union immediately met resistance from a number of sources. The Pullman Company refused to have anything to do with the Brotherhood and tried to thwart it by forming its own company union, called the Porter's Employee Representation Plan. Some of the porters themselves, whose jobs were among the best blacks could get and who had the middle-class prejudices of white-collar workers and upper-class servants, had been swayed by Pullman propaganda in which the company pictured itself as a benefactor of the race. Randolph was opposed by black politicians like Perry Howard of Mississippi, a Republican national committeeman, who intimated that Communists and radicals were behind Randolph's organizing efforts (it was rumored that Howard, then a special assistant to the attorney general specializing in railroad cases was in the pay of the Pullman Company), and Melville Chisum of Chicago, who tried to appeal to blacks' basic opposition to labor unions of any sort. Black churches and organizations like the YMCA and the Urban League and, not least of all, the black press, many of whose outlooks were middle-class and staunchly anti-labor, also opposed the Brotherhood.[104] Important papers like the *Chicago Defender*, the *St. Louis Argus*, and the *Chicago Whip* were extremely hostile. Chicago was the city with the most black porters and was crucial to the success of the Brotherhood's organization plans. There, the *Whip*, which became the major union opponent, felt compelled to attack the porters because 55 percent of the *Whip*'s stock had been sold to Daniel J. Schuyler, attorney for the Pullman Company.[105] However, Chandler Owen of *The Messenger* charged that the *Whip* was involved instead in "shakedown activities," mostly for advertisements for the black weekly.[106] The *Defender* feared that blacks would no longer be hired as porters if they formed a union. Further, Abbott's weekly charged that the union had created a black monopoly which could only have an adverse effect, widening the division between the races.[107] Other newspapers and periodicals were neutral, but verging on the negative. *The Crisis*, though favoring the porters, did not take a strong stand in its support.

The *Courier* was far and away the strongest supporter of the Brotherhood. Vann early recognized that "the *Pittsburgh Courier* must fight the battle of the porters almost alone. In fact, the other colored papers seem to be afraid of the Pullman Company or too willing to accept its money . . . something is evidently wrong when a so-called independent newspaper is afraid to fight the battle for common humanity."[108] Vann gave nearly unlimited space to the porters' grievances and was militant in his advocacy of the cause. The *Courier* ran weekly headlines like "PORTERS DISGUSTED AT WAGE CONFERENCE"[109] and "A. PHILIP RANDOLPH TAKES PACIFIC COAST BY STORM"[110] and stories about "THE PULLMAN PEONS."[111]

Robert Vann knew the heated dispute between the Brotherhood and the Pullman Company was bound to arouse reader interest and hence circulation. Vann also saw the Brotherhood as a vast, untapped reservoir of potential subscribers to his *Courier*. "There are 10,000 Pullman porters and I am perfectly willing to fight their battle and allow them plenty of space each week to be heard, but I think they ought to be willing to give me a little financial support. I want the *Courier* to go into the home of every porter."[112]

Moreover, Vann and Randolph liked each other personally, Randolph having considerably moderated his radical outlook since 1921, when his *Messenger* had attacked Vann as a conservative Pennsylvania politico who was only seeking patronage and not looking after the general welfare of the black people. Randolph had called the *Courier* "the journalistic spokesman of the petty black bourgeoisie" that year.[113] And in a scathing article about black Republican leaders who were pressing President Harding for jobs, published in the July 1921 *Messenger*, Randolph wrote, "For the last two decades the same old political hogs have been at the trough." He then listed leaders like William

H. Lewis and Perry Howard who "have had their day and done nothing. A group of lesser local Republican lights is equally vicious and useless." Among them was, "in Pittsburgh, Robert Vann."

> All are simply after jobs, patronage and pork. They seldom take any part in civic interests. They have no independent opinion. They are constant defenders of the present state of things.
> ... This old crowd is standing between the Negroes and progress. They are the satellites of the old crowd of whites.
> ... When this old crowd of me-too-boss, hat-in-hand politicians has passed from the scene of action, the Negro will be ready for new political alignments, conceived in intelligence and perpetuated in the public interest.[114]

But by 1925, Vann and Randolph had reached some sort of entente and discovered they had a grudging admiration of each other, despite their differing ideologies.[115]

For nearly three years, Vann staunchly supported Randolph and the Brotherhood in his newspaper, and Randolph responded by plugging the *Courier*. Randolph would make a request to Vann like "Kindly write strong editorial against discharges of Porters by Company because of supposed connection with union. This will help us greatly."[116] The editorial appeared, and the following month Randolph sent this letter to all *Messenger* agents:

> At this time we want to call the attention of all our agents to the support given to the cause we advocate by THE PITTSBURGH COURIER. This great Negro weekly is, we consider, the most progressive, enlightened and militant of all race newspapers. It devotes more space to the cause of the working class Negro than all of the other Negro newspapers combined. Moreover, it has a large certified national circulation and is sold in more different communities than any other Negro newspaper. We think you will find it an excellent seller and if you are not already handling it, we urgently REQUEST YOU TO DO SO.[117]

Vann ran a regular column on "Brotherhood Progress: What Happened in the Union Sectors Last Week," with reports like "Organizer Des Varney calls Pittsburgh the 'hard boiled district'. The men have been so terrorized by the czaristic company that they are often scared to converse with the union organizer on the street."[118] When Randolph came to Pittsburgh to speak, he received extensive and laudatory coverage in the *Courier.* "RANDOLPH RECEIVES OVATION AT LOENDI," ran the front-page headline of February 19, 1927. When Randolph returned in May, the *Courier* ran advance advertisements like "HEAR A. PHILIP RANDOLPH—the Most Outstanding Orator of the Present Day on The World of Black and White Workers." Vann and the Committee of Fifty sponsored Randolph's visit, and Vann wrote him beforehand, "The idea has already gone over big and the committee is elated."[119] When Randolph arrived, Vann met him at the train and put him up at his house on Monticello Street. After the speech at the Watt Street Auditorium, the *Courier* gave a full and favorable report.

The porters helped *Courier* circulation not only by subscribing themselves, but also by hand-carrying bundles of the newspaper into black neighborhoods of cities in the Middle West, South and West where it had not been sold before. The Brotherhood thus aided significantly the *Courier*'s expansion into a national market. Vann hoped ultimately to supplant the *Chicago Defender,* then the nation's leading black weekly, as the number-one newspaper. Since the *Defender* was anti-Brotherhood, the *Courier* managed to win away many readers who were sympathetic to the union's efforts.[120]

During 1926 and 1927 membership in the Brotherhood rose, and there seemed some basis for optimism, but no settlement was reached. By 1928 there still had been no negotiations between Pullman and the Brotherhood. The Pullman Company absolutely refused to deal with the union. That year the Brotherhood threatened to strike, in hopes that the newly formed Labor Mediation Board would settle the dispute and force the Pullman Company to recognize the union. When no action was taken by the board and a hearing before the Interstate Commerce Commission likewise brought no results, Randolph's bluff was called, and he felt he should go ahead with the strike as planned. But William Green, president of the AFL (which had been giving the porters "moral support"), advised against it. The union was just not strong enough yet to take on Pullman. What they needed was a campaign to win over elements of the general public who still did not favor unionization. The Brotherhood reluctantly agreed to postpone the strike, which was a way of calling it off in the face of overwhelming odds. The Pullman Company recognized the Brotherhood's weakness and began to levy fines on union members and threaten other union sympathizers.[121]

In 1928, as matters reached an impasse, trouble began between Vann and Randolph. In January, Vann, contrary to his earlier policy of publishing everything sent him by the Brotherhood, refused to carry a story on the Chicago Labor Conference. He told Randolph, "I think you ought to practice a little silence until the [Interstate Commerce] Commission hands down its ruling" and added in a discouraged tone, "I hate to carry columns and columns of useless propaganda."[122] In March they had a meeting in which Vann said he thought he might be able to bring about a settlement with Pullman by having Randolph alone meet secretly with executives of the company and make some sort of compromise agreement. Randolph refused, because he did not like the idea of a secret meeting and felt all the other Brotherhood officers should be involved.[123] Vann was disgruntled and told Randolph so on April 7:

> Where you and I differ on the whole situation is on the question of your own personal position in the whole picture. . . .
> The company is at the place where it is known to be ready to deal with anybody but A. Philip Randolph. This is embarrassing but it is nevertheless a known fact. I have tried to impress it upon you without the embarrassing features but I am quite satisfied that you are thoroughly convinced that if the Pullman Company is ever to deal with the porters they are going to do it through you or not at all. I am just as convinced as long as you are in the picture you will never get anywhere with these porters. . . .
> [The porters] are standing at the Red Sea under your leadership with no possible convenience in sight to get them across. The Pullman Company will not divide the waters so long as you stand as the Moses. This is an embarrassing fact for you personally and I appreciate it in the extreme.

Vann told Randolph that his socialist past was the main impediment to success with the Pullman Company:

> Your history speaks for itself and the beginning of the *Messenger* with you and Owen still lives in the minds of the people who are determined not to accept any proposition from any socialistic group regardless of what they represent or how hard they fight. I am dealing with facts while you prefer to deal with the theory taught in your school. The best proof in the world that you cannot win is the fact that you have repeatedly lost. A man of your calibre, high character and splendid attainments is too useful to be crushed because you cannot see that your history is the strongest militating force against your efforts to succeed.[124]

The Primacy of the COURIER • 167

Two days later Vann told a correspondent about this letter, saying that "the *Courier* is convinced that the porters will never get anywhere as long as Mr. Randolph and the socialistic crowd he is associated with there in New York are at the head of this movement."[125]

Then on April 14 Vann made public one of the most abrupt turnabouts of his career and issued a front-page, open letter to the Pullman Porters and Maids in the *Courier*, demanding Randolph's resignation as the head of the union:

> The *Courier* does not want any thanks or special credit from anybody for the stand it has taken in behalf of the porters and maids. . . . We are still for the porters and maids and we want them to know it. . . . For almost two years the company has refused to have anything to do with the porters. . . . There must be a reason for this attitude. . . . Mr. Randolph has been told that the company objects to dealing with him and their reason is based on the history of Mr. Randolph in this country as a socialist and a radical . . . It must be remembered that Mr. Randolph and Mr. Owens are the men who several years ago started the most radical and socialist magazine ever issued by Negroes in this country, *The Messenger*.
>
> Mr. Randolph has been informed that the company will not deal with him because of his history as a socialist and his identification with the socialistic school. . . . The Pullman Porters ought not to suffer because Mr. Randolph years ago decided to be a socialist. . . . He is now at the place where he can go no farther and it is time the porters realized it and worked out some other way to get some of the things they want.

Randolph replied to Vann in a release from his headquarters, later run as a *Messenger* article, "RANDOLPH REPLIES TO VANN." As to Vann's charge that the Pullman Company would not negotiate with the Porters while they were led by Randolph, Randolph replied, "*The Pullman Company is not going to deal with the porters and maids led by Randolph, or anybody else, until it is compelled to deal with them.* Anyone with the slightest knowledge of American labor history knows this. This is nothing strange. . . . This procedure is adopted by all employers when their employees seek to organize." In answer to Vann's statement that he and others had told Randolph that the company objected to dealing with him because of his history as a socialist, Randolph said, "*In the first place nobody has ever made this statement to me except*

Mr. Vann. What friends he has in mind I don't know." As for Vann's charge that American capital has always refused to deal with socialists, Randolph retorted:

> Of course this is not true, but granting that it is, did he know this when he began supporting the Brotherhood two years ago? If so, why didn't he, in the interest of the porters and maids, expose this dangerous nightmare then? *Why did he support the Brotherhood for two years led by a Socialist, when, as he now says, American capital has refused to deal with such organizations?*
> There is a certain colored gentleman in the woodpile somewhere and the Brotherhood will smoke him out before this fight is over. Now Mr. Vann admits that he knew that I was a Socialist two years ago. . . . *Obviously, either Mr. Vann must plead guilty to having misled the porters for two years into believing that they could win, even when led by a Socialist and a radical, or that this* ELEVENTH *hour discovery that the Pullman Company would not deal with the porters under my leadership is not a discovery. . . . His own statement indicts himself as being guilty of either bad judgment or insincerity, either one of which renders him untrustworthy.*
> He says further that it is known on good authority that the Pullman Company will deal with the porters and maids if I step aside. What GOOD AUTHORITY is this? I have seen no evidence of any such alleged good authority. . . . *Assuming that the Company has told Vann that it will deal with the porters if I resign, what reason have we for believing that the Company would keep its word? What is there to compel it to do so? Absolutely nothing.*
> Furthermore, Mr. Vann says that the porters are licked. Then *why would the Company deal with them under anybody's leadership if they are licked?* The Pullman Company is not dumb enough to spend hundreds of thousands of dollars over two or more years trying to beat the Brotherhood of Sleeping Car Porters and then turn around and recognize and sign an agreement with it if it had succeeded in beating the Brotherhood which it started out to do.[126]

Vann next countered with a very angry front-page article, "RANDOLPH'S RAVINGS NO ANSWER TO OPEN LETTER OF *COURIER:* If anyone ever suggests a change in Randolph's methods or program, such persons are accused in the vilest language of being in the pay of the company. The whole world is in the pay of the Pullman Company, except one man, and that man is Randolph. He is the ONLY SIMON PURE man in all the world. All the others are 'crooks,' 'bribe-takers,' 'Niggers-in-the-woodpile,' and enemies of the Porters."[127]

Randolph adamantly refused to resign, and the *Courier* moved into the camp of Brotherhood critics.

This perplexing reversal remains a mystery. Vann had known all along that Randolph was a socialist, for Randolph had been extremely outspoken in this regard for many years and his magazine declared itself an organ of socialism. Of course, Vann had always been a strong believer in the capitalist system and opposed to unions, but the grievances of the porters were legitimate and Vann expressed belief in the cause for at least the first two years of the Brotherhood's efforts. Vann may have changed course and asked for Randolph's resignation out of sheer frustration at the impasse between the company and the union since Pullman refused to deal with a socialist; Randolph believed "this was true in part."[128]

There was also the slight possibility that Vann believed that Randolph did not have the Brotherhood interests at heart. He wrote in a letter that "I was laboring under the impression that Randolph was interested in the Pullman porters and maids. It was a shock to me to learn that he is not interested in the porters and maids but is a self-appointed labor leader with a socialistic backing, endeavoring to drive a wedge between Negro labor in this country and American capital. . . . His own history in this country makes him impossible as a labor leader not only in the eyes of American capital, but in the eyes of American labor."[129] But this letter still does not explain why Vann waited so long to make clear his worries about the harm Randolph's socialism might do the porters' cause.

Perhaps Vann saw the hopelessness of the cause and wished to dissociate himself from a losing battle. And one must entertain the strong probability that circulation gains for the *Courier* were at the heart of Vann's reversal. He had watched the circulation of the *Courier* increase as he intensively backed the Brotherhood. Then, when the union reached a stalemate in its attempted negotiations, the sales of the *Courier* became static; as reader interest declined, so may have Vann's desire to support the cause. One observer felt that "Vann got all the mileage he could out of the porters for the paper, then he dropped the issue."[130] According to one of the Brotherhood officials at that time, Vann was also angered because once Robert Abbott's *Defender* switched sides and allied with the porters' cause, Randolph began allotting weekly news items to Abbott. Vann believed that the *Courier* should have had exclusive coverage, while Randolph viewed the union struggle as bigger than a *Courier-Defender* contest and welcomed Abbott as a much-needed ally.[131] Further, *The Messenger* had suffered financial setbacks and was about to go out of business in 1928 when Vann made his reversal; Vann may have seen his reciprocal support agreement with Randolph coming to an end. Even Randolph admitted that Vann's reasoning may have been closely connected with *Courier* circulation. "You never really knew what Vann wanted to get out of you," he said.[132] Bennie Smith, second international vice-president of the Brotherhood, who was working with the Pittsburgh branch at the time, considered Vann completely untrustworthy. He considered Vann a black capitalist and believed that though Vann admired Randolph personally, he was not committed to the Brotherhood cause.[133]

Still another motive for Vann's change of heart is alluded to in a recently published biography of Randolph. There is no way to substantiate the allegation, but it was "a general kind of history that gets around" among Brotherhood officials that Vann may have been actually "paid off" by the Pullman Company to drop his support of the Brotherhood. Randolph's biographer implies that Vann asked Randolph, "Would you resign from the Brotherhood if the Pullman Company agreed to recognize the union and sign an agreement with it?" as a secret emissary of the Pullman Company and that Randolph himself described Vann as "the dark person in the woodpile."[134] If indeed there is truth in the allegation, then the money Vann would have received might have been used to complete construction of the *Courier*'s printing plant the following year.

Judging from the correspondence between Randolph and Milton P. Webster, first vice-president of the Brotherhood, money may not have been the payoff. Rather, Vann was attempting to wrest negotiating control away from Randolph for himself. There was little doubt in Webster's mind that Vann had the prearranged backing of the Pullman Company. According to Webster, Vann was attempting to build his name nationally, in order to provide himself with "a mighty nice gravy train" to ride into political prominence "in the spring as a sponsor of [Frank O.] LOWDEN" [of Illinois] for the Republican presidential nomination.[135] More than one person characterized Vann as an opportunistic loner who "wanted to be the greatest Negro in America."[136] Perhaps Vann believed that the Brotherhood issue was a step in that direction. Whatever the reasons for Vann's turnabout may have been, it dealt a serious blow to Randolph's efforts on behalf of the porters.[137]

After Vann turned his back on the Brotherhood, he became engrossed in an enormous project, building the *Courier*'s own printing plant. As early as 1926, a printing plant had begun to seem to Robert Vann not only a possibility but a necessity. It was within the realm of possibility now that the *Courier* was on a solid footing; the circulation was at nearly 55,000.[138] The staff was competent and nearly complete, and the paper was of increasing national importance, In fact, both a city and a national edition of the *Courier* were being published, and Vann had opened branch offices of the newspaper in Philadelphia and New York City.[139] The branch offices sent social and theatrical news and other features from the cities, but they were not as successful as Vann would have liked. The *Courier* could not build up a following sufficient to compete with the local black publications in each city. By 1927, Vann closed both offices, but he retained his agents in New York and Philadelphia and continued to publish the *Courier* national edition.[140] The building of a plant seemed necessary because as the circulation grew, so did the costs of having the *Courier* printed by an outside company. By 1925 the *Courier* was paying $25,000 a year for printing costs to the Herbick and Held Company, situated on Pittsburgh's North Side. (Untroubled by ideology, Herbick and Held printed, in addition to the *Courier* and Pittsburgh's other black weekly, the *American*, the official Ku Klux Klan organ, the *Keystone*

The Pittsburgh Courier *Publishing Company, including the new printing plant, about 1930.*

American.)[141] Vann estimated the cost of building a plant at about $35,000, a gross underestimate as it turned out, and reasoned simply, "It takes just a little common arithmetic to see that within two years we could have our own concern, employing many of our own people, and making the profits that now go to white printers."[142]

A plant and press committee had been set up in 1920 which mostly just conferred occasionally until 1926 when, at Vann's urging, full-time efforts got underway to make the new plant a reality. The paper increased its capitalization from $50,000 to $75,000 by selling more stock to raise funds for the proposed building.[143] Ira Lewis went out personally to peddle shares of *Courier* stock to his friends and associates. Meanwhile, Vann wrote to influential blacks like R. R. Moton, head of Tuskegee Institute, in the hope that they would become shareholders.[144] Despite Vann's and Lewis's efforts, the stock sold slowly. So Vann dug deep into his own pocket and bought as much of the new stock issue as he could afford. By the end of 1926, he had become the *Courier*'s major stockholder.

Vann and Lewis also held a contest with prizes of a Marmon Straight Eight car, a Dodge Senior Six, a trip to California, and a baby grand piano, raising an additional $7,000.[145] Then Vann began to search for lenders. One person who helpfully loaned the *Courier* much of her savings was Mrs. Daisy Lampkin, who had won the *Courier* subscription contest back in 1913 in which she received no prize. Every possible means was used to gain new capital. Lewis even resorted to withholding payment to the printer, Herbick and Held, to help the cause. Vann was furious when he found out, as he disliked debt of any sort.[146]

The fund raising was still far short of its goal when a white philanthropist providentially appeared on the scene. Vann had for some time known Michael L. Benedum, the wealthy head of Benedum-Trees Oil Company, who was an independent Pittsburgh oil operator specializing in the development of new properties.[147] Benedum, known as "the Wildcatter," had contributed to many black causes, from shoes for needy children in the Hill District, to equipment for the black YMCA, to cash for the Urban League. Exactly how much money Benedum loaned Vann for his printing plant is not known, but it must have been a substantial sum, for Benedum was ever after referred to around the *Courier* as the "great white father."[148] According to one contemporary source, the money Vann received was not a loan and was never repaid. Rather, Benedum gave Vann the money to build up the *Courier* nationally so that in the future Vann would use it to influence black voters toward Benedum's political choices.[149] Benedum also allegedly gave more than financial support. When Vann encountered a zoning problem because the lot on which he proposed to build (at 2628 Centre Avenue) was in a residential district, Benedum intervened with the Board of Adjusters and used his influence to gain approval for the site.[150]

Construction of the *Courier* plant began in 1928, after Vann gave up his involvement with the Brotherhood cause. It was completed late in 1929, at a total cost of $104,000—vastly more than Vann's original estimate.[151] But it was, relatively speaking, a splendid place, full of modern if secondhand equipment. There were three typesetting machines, a slug casting machine, one Ludlow ad setting machine, and complete stereotyping equipment. At a time when most black newspapers were coming out of small side-street shops with limited and inadequate equipment,[152] Vann was doubly proud of his twenty-four-page Hoe Simplex Straightline Press that could turn out an astonishing fifteen thousand newspapers an hour.[153]

Vann wrote to a friend on December 9, "Tomorrow we begin work on our own new press in our own new home. . . . I am tired and worn out, but very happy."[154] The first copies of the "Dedication Edition" of the *Courier* rolled off the presses on December 14, 1929. The paper now had enormous potential to meet any circulation increases, no matter how large, and the staff morale was rejuvenated by its new quarters.

It seemed a propitious time to expand, for the prospective *Courier* audience had increased greatly. Further migration of blacks northward, mainly in 1927, when great numbers came to the area to break strikes in the coal industry, had swelled the number of blacks in Pittsburgh to 54,983. The city now had the nation's fifth largest black population.[155] Blacks were also flocking to other large cities like Philadelphia, New York, and Chicago, where Robert Vann would attempt to reach them with a national edition of the *Courier*.

The timing was disastrous in an economic sense, however, for the Great Crash had occurred just over a month before, and the paper would have many years of devastating financial struggle ahead. But such things were temporarily pushed out of mind as Vann and the rest of the *Courier* staff proudly surveyed their new surroundings and the stacks of freshly printed newspapers waiting to be loaded into the new trucks for distribution.

· 8 ·

Time to Turn Lincoln's Picture to the Wall

ALONG WITH HIS INTENSIVE EFFORTS to expand the *Pittsburgh Courier,* Robert Vann pursued an interest in national politics which had been increasing since 1920, when he became involved in his first presidential nominating convention. Vann had been a member of the Republican party since 1903, but in 1932 he defected to the Democrats. He was not the first black leader to do so, nor was he the last, but his defection drew nationwide attention and was influential in turning a large black vote to Franklin D. Roosevelt.

His political *volte-face* had been presaged by his treatment at the hands of the Republicans after the presidential campaigns of 1920, 1924, and 1928, and then in the 1930 Pennsylvania gubernatorial race. By 1932 his patience with the party that, as far as he and most other blacks were concerned, promised little and gave next to nothing had been exhausted.

Vann's disillusion with the Republican party mounted due to post-election personal disappointments and the failures of each administration to deal with racial questions satisfactorily. In June 1920 Vann went to the Republican National Convention in Chicago as an alternate delegate and watched Warren Gamaliel Harding win the presidential nomination on the fifth ballot. It was Vann's first participation in a national convention, and he was undoubtedly enthralled. While Vann was in Chicago, he met many influential Republican figures, some of whom would later play roles in his political life. By the time the convention was over, Vann had managed to be named to the publicity committee in the New York office of the Division of Colored Voters.[1]

Early in the year Vann had been disenchanted enough with the inadequacies of Republican racial policies to write, "To be denied by any enemy is not half so bitter as to be deceived by a friend."[2] But the convention renewed his partisan enthusiasm, and he returned to Pittsburgh ready to campaign vigorously for Harding. After Governor James M. Cox of Ohio received the Democratic nomination, Vann immediately rose to the attack. Cox's acceptance speech should have been called an "Exceptance Speech," Vann wrote in the *Courier* on August 20. "Mr. Cox excepted the Negro in everything he discussed, even the great war." During the fall, Vann campaigned vigorously for Harding as well as Republican candidates for Congress in Pennsylvania, Maryland, and Ohio, the home state of both presidential candidates, generally addressing black audiences in churches, lodge halls, and school auditoriums.

Harding was victorious on November 2 by seven million votes, and Vann prepared himself for a possible federal appointment. When the rumor spread that a race relations commission might be established, Vann wrote to Henry Lincoln Johnson, a national committeeman from Washington whom he had met at the convention, and asked him to speak to President Harding on his behalf about being named a member. When Vann heard nothing further on the topic of the commission, he applied for the position of recorder of deeds for the Pittsburgh district. That appointment, too, failed to materialize.

By the following year, Vann was thoroughly disillusioned with the new president and his lack of efforts in behalf of blacks. Harding's campaign slogan had been "Back to Normalcy," and it appeared that "normalcy" included the same old lack of consideration for the black man's lot. In July, Vann reported that "President Harding will not make any appointments of Negroes whose appointments require the confirmation of the Senate" and accused the Republicans of "making a bid for the Solid South by appeasing the whites."[3] He later suggested that, if Harding was so apprehensive about southern white opposition to black appointees, why not offer blacks positions in Santo Domingo or Haiti? "[Harding] can make appointments there without friction [and by so doing] he can [also] take care of lawyers and other Negro leaders who can control sentiment through the Negro press."[4]

Near the end of July 1921 a group from the NAACP visited President Harding to discuss his failure to appoint blacks to positions of federal responsibility. Harding conceded that he might consider appointing a few northern blacks, but he refused to do anything for blacks in the South, fearing he might stir up white hostility.[5] At the final tally, Harding's record in this area was dismal. He made only three major federal appointments of blacks: Arthur G. Froe as recorder of deeds for Washington, D.C., Reverend Solomon P. Hood as minister to Liberia, and Charles W. Anderson as collector of internal revenue for New York City.[6]

There seems to be little doubt that Harding was pressured by the "lily-white" faction of the party, but he also lacked the sense of moral urgency or strong political necessity required to deal with racial issues.[7] Harding even went so far as to say that "There is a fundamental, eternal, inescapable difference between the Negro and the white man."[8] Also, while he initially backed the Dyer anti-lynch bill after it passed the House, when it reached the Senate and a southern bloc threatened to filibuster, Harding dropped his support for the measure; it was killed without ever coming to a vote in the Senate. President Harding was also extremely hesitant to condemn the Ku Klux Klan, which in the Pittsburgh-Carnegie area boasted seventeen thousand members. Pennsylvania as a whole had an estimated enrollment of one hundred fifty thousand, led only by Indiana, Ohio, and Texas.[9] Harding also made a poor showing in a wrangle over the staffing of blacks at the Tuskegee Veterans Hospital.[10] By August, Robert Vann had given up all hope of a federal job and wrote bitterly in an editorial, "It seems the Negro will be sacrificed [by the Republicans]."[11]

President Harding died on August 2, 1923, and Vann hoped that his death would mark the end of the "humiliations visited upon the loyal black voter" by the Republicans.[12] Had Harding lived and sought reelection, the *Courier* might have bolted and gone Democratic out of sheer exasperation, despite the realization that the Democrats would have offered little to Vann. But Vann was more enthusiastic about Harding's successor, Calvin Coolidge. Even before the 1924 Republican nominating convention, he declared that the *Courier* would support Coolidge, claiming it was the first black weekly to do so.[13] Vann went to the convention as an alternate delegate-at-large. At the convention Vann and Alderman Louis Anderson of Chicago introduced a resolution which read:

> We advocate the enforcement of the Fourteenth Amendment to the Constitution of the United States through appropriate legislation, which will determine the number of citizens of the United States whose right

to vote is denied, or in any way abridged by the several states of the United States. We favor the reduction of representatives in Congress from states where the right to vote is denied to any citizen of the United States or in any way abridged (except for participation in rebellion or other crime) in the proportion which the number of such citizens shall bear to the whole number of citizens 21 years of age of such state.[14]

The resolution did not pass.

After Coolidge was nominated, Vann entered the presidential campaign wholeheartedly and was promoted to vice chairman of the Eastern Division of Colored Voters. Since World War I, black vote totals had increased dramatically in northern states, and a close election could mean that the balance of power was held by the approximately one hundred twenty-five thousand registered black voters in New York and the two hundred fifty thousand to three hundred thousand in Illinois and Indiana. Vann's position, therefore, was more than a courtesy title, as the national Republican party may have feared that blacks would desert the Coolidge ticket and support either John W. Davis, the Democratic candidate, or the Progressive Party of Robert La Follette. As he had in 1920, Vann moved around the eastern states speaking for Republican candidates and coordinating publicity for the black press. He also used the *Courier* extensively for Republican coverage and saw to it that during the campaign more than sixteen thousand special copies of the newspaper were distributed in West Virginia, Maryland, Delaware, and New Jersey.[15]

The *Chicago Defender* ran Vann's photograph as one of the black "Political Leaders Who Are Working for a Republican Victory," and the paper described him as a "member of the strategy board of some 30 nationally prominent Republicans who work with Chairman [William M.] Butler."[16]

But even if the black press considered Vann and other black leaders crucial to Coolidge's campaign, the Republicans had apparently taken the black vote for granted once again and were making no effort to court it.[17] Nor were the Republicans particularly attentive to black party regulars; Robert Vann had a great deal of difficulty obtaining even basic equipment for his Harlem headquarters. As the opening neared, the office was still ill equipped. Vann was forced to write to the director of the Republican National Committee to get such fundamental items as a telephone, two desks, fifty folding camp chairs, an American flag, and even some stamps.[18]

When Coolidge was elected in November, Vann felt that he had made a significant contribution that should be acknowledged with an appointive federal office. He set his sights on the position of registrar of the treasury, a post which in previous years had generally gone to a southern black. Vann's sponsor, Henry Lincoln Johnson of Georgia, a member of the Republican National Committee and dispenser of federal patronage jobs to blacks, felt that it was an opportune year for a northern black to be appointed, now that such large numbers of blacks in the North were supporting the Republicans.[19] But President Coolidge passed over the opportunity to name Vann to the post. One factor working against Vann was that he was not from Philadelphia, where most of the state's black population lived. Coolidge did appoint one Philadelphia black, E. Washington Rhodes, editor of the *Philadelphia Tribune*, to the position of assistant district attorney of Pennsylvania and undoubtedly bypassed Vann because the vote he represented in Pittsburgh was far less crucial to the party than that in Philadelphia.[20] It appeared that yet another Republican president was going to ignore most blacks who had been loyal to the party of Lincoln; President Coolidge paid scant attention to racial issues during his entire term of office.

By 1928 Vann was seriously considering leaving the Republican party. He had been less than pleased by his failure to receive a federal appointment from Presidents Harding and Coolidge after campaigning arduously for them and disappointed by the lack of effort by both presidents for the black people in general. When it appeared that the presidential campaign of 1928 would pit Governor Alfred E. Smith of New York against Herbert Hoover, Coolidge's secretary of commerce, Vann contemplated a move into the Smith camp. He was attracted to Smith who, as a Roman Catholic, was also a member of an often-maligned minority. Moreover, Smith vigorously opposed the Ku Klux Klan, a fact which the *Courier* had applauded early that year in an editorial, "AL SMITH 'SITS ON' KLUXERS,"[21] and noted again shortly after Smith's nomination in a headline which read "KLAN LINED UP AGAINST SMITH."[22] So immediately after Smith was nominated in June, Vann contacted the Democratic National Committee in New York about a possible role in the presidential campaign. Implicit in that assistance would be, of course, some form of political reward for Vann. Julian D. Rainey, a lawyer and prominent black Democrat Vann knew, arranged for a meeting in July between Vann and James A. Farley, chairman of the New York State Democratic Committee.[23]

At that meeting, Vann told Farley of his willingness to campaign for the Democrats, provided he receive the proper postelection "appreciation" in the form of some appointive office. The Democratic leadership pondered the matter for over a month, and Farley regretfully wrote to Vann on August 22 that the Democratic grandees were not interested in having him join their campaign on the terms he had offered, adding, "I must confess to you that I am somewhat disappointed that your proposition was not accepted by the people in charge of Headquarters."[24]

The Democrats' notable lack of enthusiasm for Vann's offer may well have stemmed from their feeling that, as in the past, there was no hope of winning the vote of Pittsburgh blacks, who had long been entrenched in their obeisance to the Republican overlords of Pennsylvania politics.[25] Further, there may have been strong opposition from southern Democrats to the idea of recruiting black voters into the party at that time. A black Democratic leader referred to the party's discouraging attitude toward black would-be adherents in that election when he remarked to FDR the following year that it was the unsatisfactory "approach of the National Democratic Party to the colored voter ·that makes it hard for him to leave the Republican party."[26] Despite the pallor of the Democratic welcome, a surprising number of black newspapers, longtime ardent GOP backers, changed their political allegiance during the presidential campaign of 1928, undoubtedly for the same reasons Vann had considered going Democratic. Most notable were the *Norfolk Journal and Guide*, *Atlanta Independent*, *Boston Guardian*, *Chicago Defender*, and the *Baltimore Afro-American*.[27]

Vann remained a potential Smith supporter until early September. The *Courier* announced in a front-page headline on August 25, "SMITH FOR PRESIDENT CAMPAIGN LAUNCHED," reporting "It is no secret that Lily White Republicans and Democratic bolters in the South have formed an alliance with the hope of carrying Dixie for Hoover by completely eliminating the Negro." And on September 1 the *Courier* ran a headline, "SMITH-FOR-PRESIDENT CLUBS FLOOD EAST."

But Robert Vann was not ready to change parties unless assured of a warm reception. So he reluctantly climbed aboard the Hoover bandwagon on September 8, with a *Courier* editorial in which his support seemed based solely on the fact he felt Hoover would win, rather than on any enthusiasm for the man: "Hoover and Curtis will be elected without a shadow of a doubt. These blacks who want to wander off for some new experiences will have four years to find their way back to civilization and safety. We predict and promise that there will be more room in the Republican party for those who remain with it, after November 6." He became chairman of the publicity department of the Colored Division of the Republican party, supervising the advertising and press releases for the nation's black newspapers and attempting to maintain party loyalty among black editors.[28]

In an October speech Vann denied that blacks were deserting the GOP in any significant number. He cited the *Courier*, the *New York Age*, and the *Amsterdam News* as examples of leading weeklies still loyal to the Republicans. He attacked Al Smith as having capitulated to the southern white supremacist branch of the Democratic party with "its Heflins, its Pat Harrisons, its Cole Bleases, its Carraways and its Hoke Smiths"—racists hated and feared by blacks in the South. Whereas in June the *Courier* had described the Democratic presidential nominating convention at Houston with headlines like "TOLERANCE 'IN THE SADDLE' AT HOUSTON" and "PREJUDICE AND FACTIONS FADE," by October, Vann charged that the most depressing example of the Democratic attitude toward blacks had been the Houston convention. There party officials had used chicken wire to screen off a small space in the rear of the convention hall and literally penned up the fifty black observers. Vann warned, "The Democrats fenced in a few Negroes at Houston, *but they fenced out the remaining ten million.*"[29] And Vann wrote the following week, "We admire Negro Democrats for their courage in attempting to defend the Democratic party and to plead its cause. They have no easy job to convince intelligent Negro audiences that they should vote for Senator Robinson of Arkansas [Democratic vice-presidential nominee and a white supremacist; the prospect of his succeeding to the presidency frightened blacks] and all the horde of hungry Democratic politicians who will descend upon Washington if Governor Smith is elected."[30]

Vann's campaigning that fall was more anti-Democratic than pro-Republican, for the party offered little to arouse black enthusiasm. In fact, many believed that Herbert Hoover and the Republican National Committee were attempting to by-pass the black-and-tan state organizations in the South and instead to convert many white southerners by a policy of "lily-whitism." At the Republican presidential nominating convention, some white delegations had been seated instead of the traditional black-and-tan ones. Many prominent southern

Republican black leaders were threatened with being ousted from their leadership positions.[31] In July, Perry Howard was indicted on a charge of selling federal patronage jobs to the highest bidders and suspended as a special assistant attorney general in the Department of Justice. That same month Benjamin Davis, also a Republican National Committeeman, was charged with the same crime of misuse of patronage, selling postmasterships, though he was quickly exonerated by the postmaster general.[32] The next week, the *Courier* reported an attempt to oust black leader Robert Church of Tennessee on trumped-up charges.[33] The *Courier* called all this "The Great Lily-White Conspiracy": "The white Republicans in several of the southern states, notably Georgia, Mississippi and Louisiana, have for years planned and conspired to get rid of Negro leadership in their respective states. Methods, no matter how dubious, have been used to discredit the Negro bosses and break down their authority."[34] Hoover's attractiveness to blacks was lessened still further by his advocacy of prohibition, which blacks generally opposed, and a previous record which did not commend itself to the race.

Hoover could not be defeated. The national prosperity which the country credited to the Republicans swept him into office. He defeated Smith by nearly 6.5 million votes—21,430,743 to 15,016,443. His southern strategy was evidently effective, for he carried the previously Democratic states of Florida, Texas, North Carolina, and Virginia. In Pennsylvania the Republicans were still all-powerful, and Hoover won handily by over a million. Hoover also won in the predominantly black wards of cities like Pittsburgh, where he had been greatly aided by Vann's efforts, and Philadelphia,[35] although more voters (including blacks) in Pennsylvania had voted Democratic than ever before.[36]

In his postelection column Vann wrote, "The best the American people can hope for is a sound, sane and constructive administration. Mr. Hoover can be depended upon to give just that kind of an administration."[37]

Surely Robert Vann would at last get his federal appointment. Stories began to appear in the press that Vann was being seriously considered for a post as an assistant attorney general, a position so high that it had been held by only one other black, William H. Lewis, and that was back in William Howard Taft's administration. Oscar DePriest, newly elected black Republican congressman from Chicago's predominantly black First District, wrote confidentially to Vann, "You are being favorably considered for one of the appointments in the

Department of Justice. . . . If you have extra pressure to bring to bear, do it at once."[38]

But despite the "extra pressure" applied on his behalf by such notables as Senator David A. Reed of Pennsylvania and R. R. Moton, president of Tuskegee Institute, Vann did not receive the appointment as assistant attorney general. To worsen the blow, a lesser position, as a federal deputy attorney general for Pennsylvania, was also denied him.[39] According to Judge Raymond Pace Alexander, then a promising young black Republican who had graduated from Harvard Law School in 1923,[40] Vann went to Washington with William Lewis after Hoover's victory to plead for the appointment of a black man as special assistant attorney general. Vann wanted the position, but Lewis, a former assistant attorney general, spoke instead on behalf of Alexander. Neither Vann nor Alexander got the job, Hoover's reason ostensibly being that he already had two Pennsylvanians in his cabinet—Andrew Mellon as secretary of the treasury, and James J. Davis in the Department of Labor.[41] There were several other possible reasons for Hoover's action. First, he had defeated Smith so totally in Pennsylvania that the safely Republican black vote was not considered an important contributing factor to his victory. Second, Hoover undoubtedly did not wish to alienate his newly-won southern supporters by appointing a black to a position of prominence. Third, there was speculation that Hoover himself was a racist, opposed to appointing blacks to federal positions.[42] Also, it had been apparent that until September Vann had been uncommitted to Hoover and was leaning toward Al Smith. The *Courier* did not come out for the Republicans until virtually the last minute. Some sources have also suggested that Vann was being punished by the Republican bosses for allegedly having accepted money from the Democrats favorable to Al Smith early in the presidential campaign while he was still nominally a Republican.[43] Last, the *Courier* intimated that Andrew Mellon had a hand in Vann's not being appointed. One columnist charged, "The Mellons just won't give employment to a Negro."[44] Judge James A. Cobb of Washington told Harry Webber that while Hoover was in favor of Vann's being appointed, Mellon was not. Webber said further, "Pittsburgh well knew that Mellon did not particularly care for Negroes."[45]

About the only thing Vann was offered by Hoover was an appointment in October 1929 to a commission to supervise plans for the erection of a national memorial building in Washington, D.C., as

Time to Turn Lincoln's Picture to the Wall • 183

a tribute to the black contribution to America. Congress had passed legislation for such a building on March 4, 1929.[46] Vann promptly refused the position, writing in his front-page "Camera" column in the *Courier:*

> We are very sorry, but we do not subscribe to the National Memorial. Our reason; the act of Congress creating the memorial provides that Negroes or the general public must raise $500,000 before the government hands over one penny. As soon as "the general public" (Negroes in this case) raises one-half million, the government will give, donate, or spend, the sum of FIFTY THOUSAND dollars for the memorial.
> Well, we have never thought of building a memorial to ourselves for services rendered someone else. The Negroes who are responsible for the act of Congress creating our memorial will have to pardon our lack of interest. We simply cannot see this thing, try as we may. We have published the full text of the act of Congress in this issue of the *Pittsburgh Courier*. Read it, and then read it again, and then read it once more. If the whole thing is not the prettiest joke Congress ever perpetrated, we sign off definitely on the subject of memorials to Negroes. What Price Retribution![47]

For Vann and many other blacks, the one bright spot in the contest of 1928 was the election of Oscar DePriest as congressman from Chicago's First District; he was the first black elected to Congress since 1901. The *Courier* announced the triumph in a postelection front-page article and pondered its implications in an editorial, "THE ICE IS BROKEN," which viewed the victory as a happy portent for blacks and urged them to organize their forces in other cities before the next congressional contests. "A precedent has been set. Let us take advantage of it."[48] As if to keep the example constantly before the eyes of Pittsburgh blacks, the *Courier* chronicled DePriest's every move. The saga began with "DEPRIEST TAKES OATH MONDAY" and went on with virtually weekly coverage through his seating, the casting of his first vote, his visit to President Hoover, his naming of blacks to West Point and Annapolis, the furor caused by the appointments, and the myriad details of "A DAY WITH OSCAR DEPRIEST."[49] When DePriest made his maiden speech in Congress, it merited a long front-page article. The *Courier* described the address as "an impassioned plea for the improvement of conditions among the black people of America as well as those of Haiti," and noted proudly that DePriest "walked slowly with dignity . . . spoke fluently" and was interrupted by "two outbursts of applause," and went on to record the speech in its entirety.[50] It was obvious from the *Courier*'s close and extensive coverage of DePriest how much the blacks wanted and needed a political hero of and for the race. Political victories for blacks were still few and far between.

As bitterly disappointed as he was with the aftermath of the 1928 election, Vann remained Republican for one more campaign, the Pennsylvania gubernatorial race of 1930. He was a rebellious sort of Republican, however, for he backed an antimachine reform candidate, Gifford Pinchot. Pinchot, a former forester and conservationist, governor of Pennsylvania from 1923 to 1927, was running as an antimachine rebel, as he had in 1922. Prior to 1930, Vann had been doggedly loyal to the "organization" Republican candidates in the state. For example, in the 1926 United States senatorial contest, he backed William Scott Vare, Republican boss of Philadelphia, when he defeated Pinchot and incumbent George Wharton Pepper in an acrimonious primary. Vann wrote then, "In the East the Negro must thank Congressman Vare for what recognition he now enjoys."[51] But in 1929 Vare was denied his Senate seat after a three-year committee investigation into charges brought by Gifford Pinchot and others that Vare had been guilty of corrupt electioneering and excessive campaign expenditures.[52]

When Vare decided to sponsor a candidate to oppose Pinchot in the 1930 Republican gubernatorial primary, Vann joined the Pinchot forces. William Vare's man was Francis Shunk Brown, a respected Philadelphia lawyer who had once been the state's attorney general. Vann had little to gain from the Vare organization, which was Philadelphia-centered and gave all political plums destined for blacks to residents of that city.[53] So Vann declared the *Courier* pro-Pinchot, and in an editorial the paper praised Pinchot for being free of the influence of bosses like Vare. "If [Pinchot] is elected governor—everyone will know who the governor is."[54] Vann also realized Vare had been badly tarnished by the three-year investigation that cost him his Senate seat and was, as well, a very sick man. Vann felt the progressive Pinchot would do something positive for blacks. A *Courier* editorial said, "The colored population of Pennsylvania can get more protection out of the Governor than it can of any other officer of the state. . . . Gifford Pinchot would be the governor in the fullest sense of the word—Governor for all the people—yes, even the colored people."⁵⁵

The primary campaign was intense, and Pinchot's May victory was very narrow; according to Vann, the black vote may well have provided the balance of power for Pinchot. He won with 633,000 votes; Brown was close behind with 613,000, while a third candidate, Thomas W. Phillips, managed 281,000 votes for his antiprohibition stand. Pinchot had lost Philadelphia, Vare's territory, completely, with only 55,000 votes to Brown's 245,000 and Phillips's 116,000, but he carried all the other sixty-six counties.⁵⁶ For the November 4 general election Pinchot's Democratic opponent was to be John M. Hemphill.

Vann pitched heartily into Pinchot's fall campaign. On two occasions, Vann arranged for Congressman Oscar DePriest, himself running for reelection, to come to Pennsylvania. The first time was in Pittsburgh on September 3. Speaking at the Rodman Street Baptist Church before a black audience of about five hundred, the legislator urged blacks to "stay in the Republican party and clean house from the inside." When DePriest, a "wet," was asked how he could be for a gubernatorial candidate who favored prohibition, he replied that Pinchot had been fair to blacks in his previous administration and he "deprecated the 'wet' Democratic appeal for votes."⁵⁷

The second of Vann's major efforts was to help organize a large, black-supported rally at the Royal Theater in Philadelphia in October. Vann was to be one of the main speakers, along with DePriest. Vann ran into some trouble gaining the support of black Philadelphia leaders, who were resentful of Vann as an outsider organizing a rally in their city. Finally he had to appeal to Pinchot's headquarters "to have you suggest to Mr. Ed Henry [a police magistrate] and to Mr. Rhodes [the influential editor of the black weekly, the *Philadelphia Tribune*] that the success of the meeting on October 19th can be assured if they will take hold and do what they can to put it over."⁵⁸ There was also some rivalry between Vann and E. Washington Rhodes as editors of newspapers which both wished to expand their black readership in the state; they were competing for some of the same audience.⁵⁹ But about a month before the October 19 rally, Vann had written to S. Davis Wilson, deputy city controller for Philadelphia, assuring him that he was not attempting to take over leadership of the city's politics from acknowledged leaders like Henry and Rhodes.⁶⁰ Vann needed all the cooperation he could get in Philadelphia in his efforts for Pinchot, because while leaders like Henry and Rhodes stayed loyal to the Republican candidate, "regulars" like John A. Asbury and others had bolted and gone over to the Democratic candidate, undoubtedly with the tacit consent of Boss Vare.

Vann finally got the help he needed in organizing the rally, and it came off successfully. More than a thousand blacks crowded into the Royal Theater to hear DePriest and Vann, while another thousand milled around outside. According to the *Philadelphia Tribune*, the gathering was so large that "it was necessary for a detail of police to be on hand while all vehicular traffic with the exception of trolleys was rerouted. Amplifiers on the outside made it possible for those who could not wend their way inside to hear while standing in the street."[61]

Vann also used his front-page column to chide William Vare for not getting his forces behind the party candidate. "It is the fight of the people for the Governor they nominated, and Mr. Vare ought to be a 'regular Republican' and support Mr. Pinchot. His friends might rally to him better in 1932 if he shows the right attitude now."[62] Vann explained that he opposed Vare because he represented the Republican "organization," and "the colored population of the state has received nothing from organization state politics to brag about and feel that their only way out is through an independent executive."[63] By November 1, the *Courier* was predicting "PINCHOT VICTORY CERTAIN."

Vann's efforts came to naught in Philadelphia, where Pinchot lost all forty-eight wards, but were hugely successful in Pittsburgh: Pinchot carried every single ward.[64] He won the governorship by just 50,000 votes of 2,079,000 cast, so narrow a margin that Vann could claim the black vote as providing the balance of power. The *Courier* reported, "Negroes are rejoicing everywhere over the election results."[65]

Once again Robert Vann held out his political cup to the victor, and once again he was given small change; Pinchot sent him a little note of appreciation for his assistance in the campaign.[66] Not until many months later did he make any official gesture of gratitude to Vann, and then it was of almost no significance—he named Vann to represent Pennsylvania at the fiftieth anniversary celebration of Tuskegee Institute.[67] To judge from Vann's postelection correspondence with Pinchot, the governor earlier had agreed to some political concessions for Vann after the victory. Vann reminded Pinchot, "You will recall certain commitments that were made when you, Judge [Edward] Henry and myself had that little conference in the

Yale Club, New York City, about a year ago. I have tried sincerely to abide by your suggestions and wait your pleasure in matters political, and I am still standing by my guns." Apparently Vann received nothing, and Judge Henry was in charge of black patronage, as Vann angrily requested Pinchot to "be good enough to release me from commitments made to you at the Yale Club as far as Judge Henry is concerned so that any appointments you make will not impose upon me the necessity of any explanation to the colored citizens of Pennsylvania."[68]

Vann was finished with the Republicans after that campaign of 1930. He had suffered a surfeit of personal disappointments at their hands in the past and could foresee little improvement for himself in the future, either on a state or a national level. He had few hopes for statewide recognition because as a spokesman for Pittsburgh's 55,000 blacks he would always be overshadowed by men like Judge Edward W. Henry, who spoke for Philadelphia's 210,000 blacks. On the national scene, Vann had been slighted by three Republican presidents for whom he had worked diligently, and the ascendant Republican policy of "lily-whitism" seemed to preclude any major acknowledgement of black leaders like himself.

Vann warned of his impending disaffection in a letter he wrote late in 1930 to a Republican party official who had asked for 250 free copies of a *Courier* edition containing an article about the GOP. Speaking for himself as well as for the newspaper, he replied sarcastically that he was tired of giving things away and gaining nothing in return:

> We feel this way because we have a lingering memory of the celebrated year of 1928 when the editor of THE COURIER gave nine weeks' service to Mr. Hoover's campaign for nothing but room and board and railway fare, and at the same time THE PITTSBURGH COURIER gave to the use of the Republican Party and we didn't receive enough money to pay the linotype men, much less pay any of our overhead, buy any of our paper or pay any of our portage. We didn't even get a letter of thanks.[69]

The setting for Robert Vann's dramatic departure from the Republican party had been nearly completed by the political events of 1928 to 1930. It remained only for the next two years, the nadir of the Depression, to add the finishing touches, to give Vann the final shove out into the spotlight where he would deliver the speech that rocked the nation's black community.

The Depression, which was affecting nearly everyone in the country in some way, was particularly cruel to Pittsburgh. As a major center of heavy industry, the city felt the economic blows keenly. In 1929, United States Steel Corporation stock had sold as high as 262; by 1932 it had bottomed out at 22. The steel mills were operating at only one-tenth of their capacity, and workers' wages were cut as much as 60 percent. Other factories in the region cut back their production sharply. In April 1930, more than 20,000 Pittsburghers were out of work and 5,900 laid off. Nine months later the figure had climbed to almost 60,000 unemployed and over 19,000 laid off. The blacks of Pittsburgh were hit hardest. By 1933, 43.4 percent of Pittsburgh's blacks would be on the relief rolls, compared with 15.7 percent of whites, more than in any of fourteen other cities with black populations of 50,000 or more. The unemployed were reduced to purchasing apples for two cents apiece and selling them for a nickel on street corners. Men lived in squalid packing boxes on the outskirts of the city; when the police burned them out, a shantytown sprang up in the city's Strip District. A Catholic priest, Father James R. Cox, was named its honorary mayor and presided over his impoverished flock, ultimately leading a "march of the jobless" on Washington, D.C.[70]

The Pittsburgh City Council had voted emergency appropriations, and the Mellons and other wealthy local men had donated hundreds of thousands of dollars to the welfare fund. The *Courier* joined with leading black citizens in battling poverty in the Hill District. One of the paper's most intensive efforts began at the end of 1930, when the Depression was still relatively young. The paper announced, "*Courier* LEADS IN MOVE. *Local Organizations to Unite in Gigantic Effort to Relieve Situation of Unemployed.* Appalling Conditions Among Race Citizens Unearthed by *Courier* Management—Every Organization, Citizen, and Institution Asked to Cooperate."[71] Within two weeks, the *Courier* had enlisted the backing of the city council, the mayor, and the district attorney for its "Neediest Family Drive." "GENEROUS RESPONSE EXPECTED" ran the *Courier* headline. "Mayor Kline Pleased with Plan to Help 100 Neediest Families—Workers Volunteer to Investigate and Report Situations and Conditions."[72] By the following week Vann had gotten his own staff to contribute. "*Courier* Gang Does Its Bit for Needy. Employees Give Day's Pay as Their Contribution to the *Courier*'s 'Neediest Family Drive.' "[73] At Christmas, even the local black underworld joined the *Courier*'s drive: "Well Known

Hill Citizens Stage Christmas Feed. Woogie Harris, Bill Snyder and Gus Greenlee [local businessmen, policy kings, and bootleggers] Will Give 1,500 Dinners to Poor, Needy and Unemployed Christmas Day from 6:00 A.M. Until 8:00 P.M."[74] But these token gestures did little to alleviate the people's plight. Pittsburgh's boisterous optimism had been replaced by hopelessness and despair.

Nor were things much better in the rest of the state.[75] More than 1.25 million people were unemployed in Pennsylvania, and the Republican-dominated legislature was mired in quibbling and inaction. Little effective action was taken until a special legislative session was convened in November 1931. Presented with the overwhelming evidence of need documented by Governor Pinchot's Planning Committee on Employment Relief (the Baker Committee), the legislature in a stormy session passed the First Talbot Act, appropriating $10 million "to the Department of Welfare for payment to political subdivisions charged by law with the care of the poor. . . ." Instead of acting favorably on the measure, Pinchot attacked it in a public statement as having been "conceived in politics and born in hatred," emphasizing that giving "state aid to public subdivisions without state supervision is a most unhealthy precedent." He refused to sign the bill on the grounds that it might be unconstitutional, but he did not veto it either. If the Talbot Act were held constitutional in the courts, the governor believed it would offer "some relief to the unemployed and save the Commonwealth from the disgrace of refusing to help her people. I cannot destroy that chance."[76] The first Talbot Act became law on December 28, 1931, without Pinchot's signature. The Act went into effect in April 1932, and unemployment relief was administered by Poor Boards without state supervision. It met with only limited success; Pinchot charged that much of the $10 million had been wasted or spent for political purposes.

The Talbot Act had barely gone into effect when it was realized that the $10 million would not meet the state's unemployment crisis for very long. Pinchot reminded the legislature that Pennsylvania had 1,150,000 unemployed and that at least $60 million would be required for relief within a year. As a result, a special legislative session was called for July 1932. The Woodward Act was adopted, establishing a State Emergency Relief Board to plan unemployment relief programs from the expenditure of Reconstruction Finance Corporation funds by the governor. The second Talbot Act was also passed, appropriating $12 million to the State Emergency Relief Board for direct relief and work relief. However, the legislation was not implemented until September 1, 1932, and despite the efforts made, the "lack of adequate advance planning was one of the most serious handicaps of the organization during the initial months of its existence."[77]

Party unity had been ruptured by the 1930 election, for it pitted a reform governor against a machine-controlled Senate. To make matters worse, the strongest of the state bosses, Joseph Grundy, William Vare, and the Mellons could not agree among themselves on most points.[78] Governor Pinchot, though nominally a Republican, was not supporting Hoover and was even showing signs of going over to the Democrats before FDR got the presidential nomination that year. William Vare was not backing Hoover with all his strength, since he was still angry over Hoover's lack of support in his battle to take his Senate seat. Joseph Grundy, former chief collector of campaign funds, was leaving the task of filling the campaign war chest to others. The internal party struggle was crushing the GOP, and the days of the "almost impregnable state Republican organization" seemed gone forever.[79] The Republican fortress that had dominated Pennsylvania politics for nearly seventy years was crumbling.

With the nation in such a sorry economic state under its Republican president, with formerly solid Republican Pennsylvania in such poor political condition, and with his own personal political history a series of humiliations at the hands of the Republicans, Robert Vann was more than ready for a change of party.

Two men were instrumental in bringing about Vann's final conversion to the Democratic party.[80] The first was Michael L. Benedum, the "great white father" who had helped finance the new *Courier* printing plant in 1929. Benedum, a native of West Virginia, had earned a vast fortune from his shrewd wildcatting for oil in Texas, Louisiana, and South America; he is generally credited with having discovered more oil than almost any man in history. A lifelong Democrat, Benedum had supported the conservative John W. Davis as presidential nominee in 1924, describing him as the ablest man who had run for president on any ticket in his time. Benedum nursed a bitter dislike of the Republican party because under three successive GOP administrations he had been prosecuted for income tax delinquency in the astounding amount of $79 million. (Benedum won the highly complex case after nearly eighteen years of litigation.) In 1932, Benedum contributed generously to the Roosevelt war chest because he believed FDR to be conservative and began to ponder on whom he could win over to the Democrats—specifically what he could do about the 181,000 registered black voters of Pennsylvania, who were mostly still Republican.[81] One source reports that Benedum was advised by his black valet-butler, Joseph Howard Gould, who had organized the Pittsburgh Butlers' Association, to see Robert Vann. Benedum contacted Vann and reportedly asked him, "What had the Negro ever gotten by voting the Republican ticket?" To which Vann answered, "Nothing."[82] Benedum then told Vann that he admired the blacks' loyalty to the Republican party, but he did not feel they owed any further debt to the GOP for what Lincoln had done seventy years before. By 1932, he said, the blacks "had already paid this debt many times over and with plenty of interest."[83]

Vann needed no further convincing. Shortly after this meeting, at Benedum's urging Vann contacted the man who completed his political reformation. Perhaps because he was as yet unwilling to admit his defection publicly, Vann had Eva DeBoe Jones, an itinerant black beautician, tell Mrs. Emma Guffey Miller during a manicure that Robert Vann wished to speak to her brother, Joseph Guffey.[84] Guffey was leader of the embryonic Democratic organization in Pennsylvania and one of the strategists for Roosevelt's presidential campaign. He was born in Westmoreland County, Pennsylvania, in 1875 to a Scotch-Irish family whose ancestors crossed over the Alleghenies into the region in 1750.[85] Two of his uncles, "Colonel" James Guffey and Wesley Guffey, moved to Pittsburgh and speculated in oil, accumulating rich properties which became the foundation for the Mellon Gulf Oil Company. His father was part owner of a natural gas company and sheriff of Greensburg. All the Guffeys were in Democratic state politics, but in such a strongly Republican state, the possibility for advancement was slight.

During two years at Princeton, Joe was a member of the undergraduate Democratic Club, where he met Professor Woodrow Wilson, with whom he was greatly impressed. When Grover Cleveland was elected president in 1892, Guffey's uncle, a loyal Democrat, got Joe a supervisory position in the Pittsburgh Post Office. The young man later worked as the Pittsburgh secretary to President Cleveland's newly formed Civil Service Commission, then became a general manager of a utilities holding combine and a speculator in oil leases. Active in Democratic politics over the years, in 1916 Guffey was named chairman of the State Democratic Committee, and in 1920 Democratic national committeeman from Pennsylvania.

The 1920s went badly for Guffey. When Harding was elected, the Democrats lost what power they had in Pennsylvania. Then in 1922 Guffey was indicted for misappropriation of federal funds and illegal tax avoidance of nearly $1.8 million in his corporate businesses, though these charges were later dropped. Guffey backed Al Smith in 1928, but Smith's defeat revealed anew the paucity of Democrats in Pennsylvania: in 1929 only 5,200 of Pittsburgh's 175,000 registered voters were listed as Democrats. Little had changed since the time in 1912 when Guffey gave an assistant $2,500 to pay poll watchers, and the assistant returned with $1,500, unable to find enough Democrats to hire with the money. But by 1932 the Depression had changed things, and it appeared that a Democrat might win the presidency. Guffey chose to back Franklin Delano Roosevelt, then governor of New York, and worked feverishly for FDR at the 1932 nominating convention. He managed to produce fifty-five votes from Pennsylvania for Roosevelt, more than any other state gave him, and FDR was deeply indebted to Guffey.[86]

Guffey's sister, Mrs. Miller, told Guffey about Robert Vann's wish to confer with him, but Guffey was reluctant. He felt that much campaign money would be needed to win over the black vote, and the Pennsylvania Democrats had little enough of that. But Mrs. Miller persisted, and Guffey finally met with Vann. At their rendezvous, Vann surprised Guffey; the years of smoldering resentment Vann had harbored toward the Republicans burst into an ardent denunciation of the party. Vann convinced Guffey that he could personally help the Democrats capture the state's black votes.[87] It was a potent promise, for Pennsylvania had 275,754 blacks of voting age, more than any other northern state at that time. As Joseph Alsop and Robert Kintner, political analysts who saw Guffey as an opportunist, described it, "Joe's horizon, always elastic, suddenly broadened; at the end of a bright vista he saw millions of Negro voters, Republicans no longer, Democrats all."[88]

Guffey acted quickly. He went to James A. Farley and Louis McHenry Howe and persuaded them to establish an effective black division of the Democratic party.[89] If Farley and Howe were reluctant to go along with Guffey, they had good reason. For despite the fact that the GOP gave blacks little recognition on the state, county, or local level, and nominated almost none for elective office, it was estimated that in 1932 there were not ten thousand black Democrats

Time to Turn Lincoln's Picture to the Wall • 193

in Pittsburgh.[90] There had been a Negro division of the party in the 1924 and 1928 presidential elections, but it did very little. Now, in 1932, the Colored Advisory Committee to the National Democratic Committee was established;[91] it was planned that it would be a truly effective organization. Robert Vann was named one of the "Big Four" to head the Colored Advisory Committee, along with attorney Julian Rainey of Boston, Dr. William J. Thompkins, editor of the *Kansas City* (Mo.) *American*, and Dr. Joseph L. Johnson, former minister to Liberia and chairman of the board of trustees of Wilberforce University.[92]

Vann went to work with a vengeance. He journeyed to Philadelphia and persuaded two prominent blacks of that city to campaign for Roosevelt: they were his old friend J. Max Barber, former Niagarite and then publisher of the new *Philadelphia Independent*, and Samuel Brown.[93] That was no mean feat, for Philadelphia had been firmly in the hands of the Vare Republican machine, and nearly every black in that city was loyal to it. Getting Barber and Brown into the Roosevelt camp was also important because Philadelphia had 146,234 blacks of voting age; only New York and Chicago had more.[94] Vann formed the Allied Roosevelt Clubs of Pennsylvania, of which he became Pittsburgh director, while Barber and Brown headed the Philadelphia branch.[95]

Vann's first public appearance on the Democratic rostrum was scheduled for September 11, 1932. He was to deliver a speech at the St. James Literary Forum of Cleveland. Vann knew it was an important speech, for he would not only have to justify his political turnabout, but do it in such a way that other blacks would emulate him. He had found that most potential black Democratic voters were under forty, and he had searched long and hard for phrases to catch their attention. The following is an excerpt from the result, the crucial "Patriot and the Partisan" speech which he delivered on a warm September evening and which catapulted him to national prominence:

> So long as the Republican party could use the photograph of Abraham Lincoln to entice Negroes to vote a Republican ticket they condescended to accord Negroes some degree of political recognition. But when the Republican party had built itself to the point of security, it no longer invited Negro support. . . . Instead of encouraging Negro support, the Republican party, for the past twelve years, has discouraged Negro support. . . . The Republican party under Harding absolutely deserted us. The Republican party under Mr. Coolidge was a lifeless, voiceless

thing. The Republican party under Mr. Hoover has been the saddest failure known to political history. . . .

The only true gauge by which to judge an individual or a party or a government is not by what is proclaimed or promised, but by what is done. . . . In those years, the early years, when Negroes held the highest offices, the literacy of the Negro was only ten percent. Today, when the literacy of the Negro in this country is eighty-four percent, that same Republican party not only declares the Negro unfit to hold office, but organizes Lily-Whitism as an excuse and justification for keeping Negroes out of office. . . .

It is a mistaken idea that the Negro must wait until the party selects him. *The only true political philosophy dictates that the Negro must select his party and not wait to be selected. . . . I see millions of Negroes turning the picture of Lincoln to the wall.* This year I see Negroes voting a Democratic ticket. . . . I, for one, shall join the ranks of this new army of fearless, courageous, patriotic Negroes who know the difference between blind partisanism and patriotism.[96]

The long speech contrasted patriotism with partisanism and then reviewed the history of the Republican party from its beginning through Reconstruction and up to the present, and the ways in which it used and misused the black man. Vann listed several "sins" committed by the Republicans in recent years against blacks, from the mistreatment of black Gold Star Mothers in 1930 to Hoover's attempt to name Judge John J. Parker, a southern conservative, to the Supreme Court. But the phrase which captured the imagination of thousands of people and became a catch phrase of the Democratic campaign directed at blacks was, "I see millions of Negroes turning the picture of Lincoln to the wall." The picture of Lincoln was as common a fixture in the average black household as a kitchen table. Lincoln the savior: tens of thousands of freed slaves had revered him as second only to God. Their children revered him. He was the symbol of freedom, of hope, and finally of Republicanism. Turning his picture to the wall was the final renunciation.

In the weeks that followed, Vann's rousing speech was printed by many other black weeklies and reproduced as a widely distributed booklet. Right up until election day, Vann traversed the Northeast delivering variations of the speech, always stressing the betrayal of blacks by the Republican party.[97]

On October 8 Vann again lashed out at his former political party in a way which attracted a great deal of attention. Vann wrote a biting editorial in the *Courier* entitled "AND THERE STOOD THE ONE

HUNDRED." It was prompted by a visit of one hundred old-line black Republicans to the White House for an audience with President Hoover. The meeting had probably been called by Hoover at the recommendation of GOP leaders panic-stricken over the possible mass desertion of blacks to the Democrats.[98] The *Courier* editorial characterized the group (led by Roscoe Conkling Simmons of Chicago, Emmett J. Scott of Howard University, J. Finley Wilson, the grand ruler of the Elks [Black Division], Dr. L. K. Williams, chairman of the National Baptist Convention, and John R. Hawkins, a prominent Philadelphia Methodist leader) as subservient and groveling, pleading with President Hoover, "Give us your photograph and tell us Lincoln still lives and we will do the rest." They asked the president to have his picture taken with them, something he had reportedly refused to do previously. The president then pontificated, "You can be assured that our party will not abandon or depart from its traditional duty of the Republicans."[99] To all of this the *Courier* replied, "God save us from 'traditional duty'!" The day would surely go down in history as "the Black Saturday of the Century," being "the saddest spectacle Negroes ever witnessed in the history of this country." The editorial was capped by a cartoon by Wilburt Holloway, depicting Hoover in top hat, smiling as he looked down at the One Hundred from a window in the White House saying, "I love to hear the darkies sing."[100] The ridicule Vann heaped on those black Republicans still foolish enough to remain loyal was perhaps cruel, but effective.

Vann used his paper intensively throughout the presidential campaign that fall, reporting all membership gains by the Roosevelt Clubs and printing long lists of individuals and organizations supporting the Democrats. The *Courier* gave full play to all Vann's efforts in behalf of Roosevelt, like the fifteen-minute demonstration he led for FDR when he appeared at Pittsburgh's Forbes Field before a crowd of thirty-five thousand.[101]

When the *Courier* was not praising FDR, it was condemning Hoover. The president was criticized not only for his inability to end the Depression, but for allowing racial discrimination in government relief efforts. The *Courier* reported that, despite protests by Walter White of the NAACP to the secretary of the interior, as of October 1932 only thirty blacks were part of a four-thousand-man work force employed on the construction of the Boulder Dam, and the administration took no action to rectify the situation.[102] The *Courier* charged the administration with the misuse of $2 billion appropriated to the

Reconstruction Finance Corporation; none of the funds were allocated to blacks. Blacks also failed to receive any of the $2.7 billion awarded to the Home Loan Bank to relieve home owners' mortgages.[103] And when Hoover ordered the "Bonus Army" dispersed from the banks of the Potomac River, there had been many "Brown Buddies" among that group; the *Courier* publicized the removal with a photograph of a policeman hauling away a black veteran.[104]

The Hoover administration was also condemned for its treatment of black Gold Star Mothers, whose sons had died in Europe in World War I. The women had been invited in 1930 to visit the graves of their sons at government expense; however, the government announced that the boat to Europe would be segregated. The *Courier* cried outrage, "GOLD STAR MOTHERS WILL BE JIM-CROWED!" and denounced the action in an editorial entitled "THE LAST STRAW."[105] Despite appeals by the NAACP, the press, and various black organizations, the War Department refused to alter its position and ignored the charges of Jim Crowism. Said Vann's *Courier*, those black women who took the voyage were segregated "like so much cargo," while the white mothers "wined and dined on floating palaces."[106] When the women sailed from New York, the *Courier* gave it a large headline on page one: "GOLD STAR MOTHERS BITTER, *374 Declined United States Jim Crow, Only 56 Sail on Freighter.*"[107] The following week, the paper ran another angry front-page article, " 'SEGREGATION BEST THING FOR BLACK GOLD STAR MOTHERS,' WAR DEPARTMENT OFFICIAL SAYS . . . *Evident that War Department Has Definitely Committed Itself to a Policy of Discrimination and Segregation of Negroes.*"[108] After the mothers arrived in Paris, the *Courier* featured a sarcastic editorial, "CHICKEN AND WATERMELON."

> What struck our attention most was the fact that the White Americans who arranged the receptions for the Negro Gold Star Mothers had to go out of their way to procure fried chicken and watermelon for their enjoyment. . . . What more natural than to have chicken and watermelon on hand for Negro "Mammies"? . . . We congratulate the government on its solicitude for the comfort of the black mothers. We only wish it showed as much solicitude for their relatives in this country.[109]

The *Courier* also attacked Hoover for his attempt to place Judge John J. Parker of North Carolina on the Supreme Court in 1930.

When running as a Republican for governor of North Carolina in 1920, Judge Parker had given a speech in which he said, "The Negro as a class does not desire to enter politics. . . . We recognize the fact that he has not reached that stage in his development where he can share the burdens and responsibilities of government. The participation of the Negro in politics is a source of evil and danger to both races."[110] The NAACP had filed a protest with the Senate Judiciary Committee, and the *Courier* editorialized at length.[111] The NAACP then mounted a campaign of publicity and pressure in conjunction with the AFL, which opposed Parker for having favored the "yellow dog" contract. This resulted in the defeat of Parker's nomination. The *Courier* reported the fact in huge type.[112]

Finally, the *Courier* looked at Hoover's past career as a mining engineer and expounded the theory that Hoover suffered from Negrophobia as a result of "his life in China, Australia, and Africa, in the role of slave driver and slave trader. . . . He got that way by long experience in exploiting the lowly of the earth and sweating gold from their half-starved carcasses."[113]

The election results were gratifying to Vann. In the western end of Pennsylvania, where his influence was strongest, blacks voted solidly for Roosevelt. Allegheny County, which included Pittsburgh, had never voted Democratic before, but came out for FDR 189,000 to 152,000, with an estimated 35,000 black votes going to the Democrats for the first time.[114] According to Vann, the blacks provided the balance of power. Pittsburgh's Third Ward (40.1 percent black), previously 80 percent Republican, gave FDR 1,579 votes to Hoover's 858. In the Fifth Ward (53.5 percent black), estimated before the election to be 88 percent Republican, Roosevelt was narrowly beaten, 2,614 to 2,375,[115] but Hoover's 1928 plurality there had dwindled from 60 percent to just over 50 percent, and the *Courier* estimated that 53 percent of the blacks voted for FDR. Exhilarated by the local victory, the *Courier* announced that nationally, 2 million black votes had provided the balance of power for the Democrats in fourteen states.[116]

However, a closer look at the election returns indicates that the newspaper was indulging in some enthusiastic overstatement. Vote tallies in the black wards of cities like Detroit, Cleveland, Chicago, and Cincinnati reveal that most blacks remained faithful to the Republican party. In those wards of Philadelphia that contained a majority of black voters, FDR received only 30.2 percent of the vote,[117] the most important reason being that William Vare's GOP machine had provided a certain number of patronage jobs for blacks, whereas the blacks had nothing but promises from the Democrats.[118] And Philadelphia black leaders like J. C. Asbury and E. W. Rhodes remained loyal Republicans, which must have influenced their followers.

The reasons more black voters did not leave the Republicans in 1932 were various. They found it emotionally difficult to abandon the party of Lincoln; they were hesitant to identify themselves with the southern lynch mobs, who were Democrats; the black leadership, such as professionals and the clergy, were still pro-Republican;[119] and Roosevelt seemed little improvement over Hoover in the eyes of many blacks. Roosevelt's running mate was John Nance Garner of Texas, a hated southern Democrat. And as governor of New York FDR had not appointed blacks to any prominent state positions. The Democratic platform of 1932 made no specific reference to black needs, and fewer than ten blacks attended the convention in an official capacity. Even after Roosevelt's victory, the *Philadelphia Tribune* summed up the view of many blacks: "Mr. Roosevelt makes no definite statement about Negroes. He isn't going to make any of any worth and when he refers to the 'forgotten man,' he might easily mean the Negro during every Democratic administration that good memories recall."[120] However, the showing made by Vann and his black groups in Pennsylvania impressed the Democrats enough that they established full-time black branches of the Democratic national organization in ten other states with large black populations.

And it looked as though Robert Vann would finally receive the major federal appointment to which he had aspired for twelve years; rumors spread that, in addition, he would become an important dispenser of patronage jobs to blacks. Vann was confident enough that the federal position would be an important one that he allowed the *Courier* to report that "Vann is not going to leave his $500,000 business for just any job."[121] But even so, some maneuvering by Joseph Guffey, chief Democrat of Pennsylvania, was still necessary. After a conference with Guffey, J. Max Barber told Vann that he had "some southern friends" who objected to the appointment of a black to a major position.[122] Joseph Guffey visited the president-elect at Hyde Park two days after his victory and asked for a "first-class Federal job" for Vann. He told Roosevelt the position he had in mind was a special assistant to the attorney general. But, Guffey added, "Before you say anything about Bob Vann, I ought to tell you he's colored." The president, mindful that southern Democrats in the Senate might oppose such appointment of a black, asked cautiously "Will I have to get him confirmed by the Senate?" Guffey, grinning, assured him he would not; Roosevelt then said, "The job's yours, Joe." And so it became official; Robert Vann was named special assistant to Attorney General Homer Cummings.[123]

At the same time President Roosevelt was considering and implementing Robert Vann's appointment to the Department of Justice, the *Courier* editor was involved in an important legal case, the Beaver County deportation case, in which Vann acted as the representative of the national office of the NAACP. Walter White chose him for the assignment because he recognized Vann's growing national eminence and power.

In January 1933, Beaver County deported forty blacks. They had all been arrested for disorderly conduct and drunkenness during a large and raucous dance and chitterling supper at a home in Industry, Pennsylvania. During the arrest, the police allegedly beat several of the blacks with their guns. The few who could pay a fee of $2.50 were released; the remaining forty were taken to the Beaver County jail and forced to sleep on the bare concrete floor overnight. The following morning they were all loaded into two open trucks and driven 117 miles to the West Virginia border. There they were put out into the pouring rain, many without coats or hats. According to an NAACP news bulletin, "The armed officers dumped them out of the trucks and told them to 'beat it' out of the state and said if they came back in two years they would have to serve two years in the county workhouse."[124] The local and national press reacted angrily to the inhuman treatment accorded the blacks by the county officials. The *New York Herald Tribune* said, "The method by which the population of Eastern Russian villages have been exiled into Siberia appeared to have an American parallel here,"[125] and the *Pittsburgh Press* called it "AN AMAZING STORY" that "seemed more typical of the race-prejudiced South than of Pennsylvania."[126]

The NAACP immediately began an investigation of the incident, to be followed by a petition presented to Pennsylvania's Governor Pinchot. Homer Brown headed the NAACP delegation from Pennsylvania, and Vann was asked to represent the national office of the association at the meeting with the governor.[127] Vann was now regarded as possibly the most influential black in the state because of his role in the recent presidential election and seemed an appropriate choice. After the visit from Vann and the other NAACP representatives, Pinchot turned the matter over to Attorney General William Schnader. After Schnader completed his investigation, he recommended prosecution of all those involved in the deportation on charges of kidnapping. Governor Pinchot then demanded that the Beaver County district attorney prosecute the county officials on those charges,[128] but he refused to do so, saying he failed to find "sufficient evidence."[129] Governor Pinchot's hands were tied; it was a county case and could be pursued only by the county prosecutor. The governor had no power to overrule the Beaver County district attorney.[130]

After the case had dragged on for some months, Robert Vann acted on his own initiative in the case, separate from the ongoing NAACP efforts. He said he was impatient at the lack of results and felt the state NAACP was not doing enough. Vann told the press he would file charges against the Beaver County commissioners and "such other officials as the evidence may warrant," of "false arrest and imprisonment" in addition to "the kidnapping charge." "We expect no cooperation from the Beaver County District Attorney or from anyone else there," said Vann. "The District Attorney already has indicated that he chooses to ignore the entire affair." Vann added that three of his clients were residents of West Virginia, which placed the case under Federal Court jurisdiction, and "that is where we will take it."[131]

Vann's statement brought a good deal of publicity, but it also greatly provoked Homer Brown, head of the Pittsburgh branch of the NAACP, who felt that Vann was taking over the case and usurping the role of his organization. He wrote Walter White, "I take the position that Vann's article will hurt our position in that it will give Pinchot and Schnader an opportunity 'to get out' on the grounds that if Mr. Vann is going to do so much, then they will turn the matter over to him. Mr. Vann did not consult with me about this article and it certainly gives the people here the idea we are lying down on the job."[132] As in past instances, the charge was renewed that Vann was attempting to control a situation unilaterally for his own gain. Nothing further happened in the Beaver County deportation case, despite Vann's efforts; the state officials could take no action. Nonetheless, Vann's reputation was enhanced.

Robert Vann went off to his post in Washington after a triumphant round of gala farewell banquets. In June, Vann was asked to sit at the speaker's table at a Democratic party banquet held in the William

Time to Turn Lincoln's Picture to the Wall • 201

Penn Hotel in Pittsburgh. Sitting with Vann at the head table were Joseph Guffey; Secretary of the Interior Harold Ickes, a longtime proponent of black causes and former president of the Chicago NAACP branch; Michael Benedum; David Lawrence, head of the Allegheny County Democratic organization; and James Farley. Vann acknowledged that the honor had bittersweet overtones. "I felt that I should have been recognized in such a manner twenty years ago. But during all those years, while a worker in the Republican party, I was not only never asked to sit at a speakers' table but was never invited to a banquet."[133]

Then on July 8 there was a testimonial dinner in Vann's honor at the Pythian Temple in Pittsburgh. After the large meal, first Joe Guffey spoke in praise of Vann's federal appointment, as well as his work as an editor and lawyer. Then David Lawrence, the Democratic chairman of Allegheny County, spoke. After the expected tributes to Vann, he also commended the astuteness of his change of political party:

> He is entitled to another banquet, a loving cup, or a monument-or-something for having had the intelligence to become a Roosevelt-Democrat at a time when Roosevelt-Democrats were as scarce as Hoover-Republicans are today. Robert L. Vann is a living testimonial to the truth of that political proverb said to have originated with Abraham Lincoln that "You can fool all of the people some of the time—you can fool some of the people all of the time—but you can't fool all of the people all of the time."

The testimonial dinner at the Pythian Temple, July 8, 1933. Pictured are Joseph E. Guffey, David L. Lawrence, Mrs. Vann, Robert Vann, and Mrs. Emma Guffey Miller.

> Ever since the Civil War, the Republican Party has been coming around every pay day (and by pay day I mean election day) to collect installments on the debt it insists was created when the Emancipation Proclamation was signed.
>
> It has taken your race about 72 years to begin to realize that physical and political emancipation, while precious and to be highly cherished, without economic emancipation are but hollow and meaningless possessions.[134]

Finally Vann went to the podium. He reiterated his high hopes for the incoming federal administration and the Democrats in general, but concluded with the warning that he was still very committed to the idea of the "liquid vote," that the blacks should go with whichever party at any given time offered them the best treatment with patronage and legislation. He said, "I came to the Democratic party because the Republican party no longer serves the interest of the people. They would not reduce any of their high-sounding phrases to practice, and when this party gets to where they no longer offer my people any service I'll either go back to the Republican party or to some other party."[135]

Vann believed that the Democratic New Dealers would be highly sensitive as to whether he approved of their politics. Once he arrived in Washington, in the midst of a political situation which his background in politics had ill equipped him to understand, he was in for a rude awakening.

· 9 ·

Washington: Confidence and Disillusionment

ROBERT VANN ARRIVED in Washington on a hot July afternoon in 1933. The sunny day seemed full of promise; Vann's personal ambitions were apparently near fulfillment. He would surely enjoy the national prestige to which he had long aspired, he would be able to serve his people by dispensing political patronage, and FDR's New Deal pledges suggested that his fellow blacks were at last on the threshold of fair treatment by a presidential administration.

Even before he departed for Washington, Vann began to be deluged with letters from black office-seekers. As one hopeful wrote, with an eye on a job in the Tax Division, "Now I know you are boss to Negro patronage."[1] The requests went on and on over the months, with writers asking for everything from a minor clerkship in a local post office to a position as special assistant attorney general, the post Vann himself held.[2] Vann's lifelong friend, Eugene Kinckle Jones, executive secretary of the National Urban League, asked that Vann help him get appointed as advisor on Negro affairs in the Department of Commerce.[3] Lawrence A. Oxley, North Carolina's director of Negro relief, requested hopefully that Vann intercede on his behalf to help him obtain the position as commissioner of conciliation in the Department of Labor.[4] When the rumor spread that a black advisor was wanted in the National Relief Administration "to look after the interests of Negro labor," George Schuyler, Vann's top editorial man at the *Courier*, half-seriously joined the crowd of political job seekers. "It is something I believe I can do to perfection," he wrote Vann in his typically jocular manner. "I know quite as much about the Negro labor and economic situation as anybody in 'The Group' [the black intellectual elite]. There are only about a half-dozen Negroes I know of who could creditably fill the job, and most of them are professionals or social workers with the usual limitations."[5] Even W. E. B. DuBois, who had been critical of Vann in the 1920s, appealed to him to use his influence to reinstate in the Boston Post Office one Lovett Groves, "an extraordinary man who supported his widowed mother and two orphan children."[6]

Initially, Vann felt very encouraged about the progress of patronage for blacks. Those he suggested for appointments in the Pittsburgh area received the positions requested: attorneys Theron B. Hamilton and P. J. Clyde Randall in the Title Searching Department; and W. S. Fitts, a realtor, Charles E. Jackson, a real estate agent from East Liberty, and Jacob L. Phillips, banker, all named real estate appraisers in the Home Loan Corporation.[7] Vann's friend Eugene Kinckle Jones received the post he wanted as advisor on Negro affairs in the Department of Commerce. *Opportunity*, the periodical of the Urban League, saw Jones's appointment as a "generous act" by the Democrats which "had done more than any other thing to dispel the doubt which had unquestionably begun to pervade the Negro group as to the ultimate results of the New Deal."[8] And the Democrats appointed many other blacks to positions of some prominence shortly after Roosevelt took office. Lawrence A. Oxley, who had written Vann from North Carolina, received a post as chief of the Division of Negro Labor in the Department of Labor. Robert Weaver became associate advisor on the economic status of Negroes in the Department of the Interior. And at least forty other blacks were named to high federal jobs in FDR's first eighteen months in office.[9] Previous administrations had appointed a few blacks and had made minor attempts to understand black problems. FDR not only appointed more blacks; he placed them in positions that the black population considered important.[10]

However, Robert Vann was quickly disabused of his idea that patronage of real magnitude would be forthcoming for his people. Right from the beginning Julian Rainey, his friend and fellow member of the "Big Four" blacks on the Democratic National Committee, had warned him that a great deal of constant pressure would have to be applied to the leading white Democrats to get significant black patronage. As Rainey advised Vann, "We [must not] sit on the sidelines and wait until everything else has been adjusted before attention is given [our requests]. I am receiving mail from every corner of the country inquiring whether or not our case is being presented. I am sure the same thing is happening to you. Of course, we do not want to appear offensive, but we must be courteously insistent lest we fall into the ways of the old timers, afraid that insistence might hurt our personal ambitions."[11]

Vann persisted in his requests to leading Democrats like James A. Farley and Louis McHenry Howe for more black political jobs than the handful being dispensed. But the replies from Howe and Farley became evasive and noncommittal, implying that many other matters required their attention before the question of black patronage could be dealt with.[12] Vann was placed in the frustrating and humiliating position of having to tell many individuals and local Democratic groups, who believed he was the new repository of political influence for blacks, that they must be patient.[13]

A note of discouragement at the delays was already evident in Vann's correspondence by late July, when he wrote to Floyd Calvin, a journalist who had managed the New York branch office of the *Courier* for him: "I have your letter asking advice about a job. Permit me to state that your letter is one of a thousand asking for the same advice. I do not know what to tell you, therefore I prefer not to advise you at all than to give you faulty and misleading advice. If I can work out anything for you with Mr. Farley I shall certainly do it, but matters are moving slowly in Washington.... I cannot make very much headway in placing deserving Democrats."[14]

But Vann's aggravation over the lack of meaningful patronage available for him to dispense to blacks was minor compared to the total disillusionment and utter frustration he suffered as special assistant attorney general. Vann had gone off to Washington brimming with confidence and not a little proud. He had been a black leader in Pittsburgh politics and a recognized power in the national black press, and now he believed he was going to a position of even greater glory and prominence, one where he would be at the very heart of the exciting "New Deal" that Roosevelt had promised the voters the previous fall.

The reality was shattering. As he painfully recalled later, "It was about six weeks before I got a desk to my liking. I had to put up with what I could find.... It was some time before I could have a stenographer assigned to me. In fact, I was in the department about a month before they knew I was there."[15] Vann got put into a tiny and inconspicuous office. When he did get stenographers assigned to him, they often refused to take dictation because he was black;

he finally asked Joseph Guffey to see if he could improve matters. Guffey's sister said during those days she "never saw such a dejected man in my life."[16]

Nor was it just his inadequate office arrangements that rankled. Vann apparently never received any word of welcome or contact from his new boss, Attorney General Homer Cummings; he could not even get an appointment to see him.[17] He may never have met the man while in Washington—surely a depressing fact. And he was given the most meager, insignificant, routine tasks. Mostly Vann worked in the Lands Division, investigating and verifying titles for the Resettlement Administration and the Reforestation Program, for future post office sites, and for Indian schools.[18] It must have seemed a terrible comedown for the shrewd lawyer who had planned and delivered successful defense pleas at murder trials which had had all Pittsburgh agog. Not once while in the Justice Department did Vann handle any case of importance. His official communiqués consisted mainly of occasional mimeographed instructions from the assistant attorney general, such as the request that on each Wednesday special assistants should submit a weekly report of work done, using the "form of report attached hereto as it is necessary for statistical purposes to have uniform reports for all Special Attorneys."[19] Vann turned out to be just an insignificant cog in the vast bureaucratic machinery, little more than a name on a mimeographed sheet. The huge apparatus that FDR was putting into motion to implement his New Deal had but the smallest of places for him.

To compound Vann's sense of neglect, he was regarded around Washington as an old-line political appointee. In the Department of Justice, Vann was greatly overshadowed by young, aggressive, recent law school graduates. They considered him out-of-date, which indeed he was in some ways. He had not practiced law in some time, but rather had devoted the major part of his life to the practical problems of his newspaper business and local politics. Nor had Vann ever been well versed in the more intricate aspects of complex legal technicalities, such as would have enhanced his value to the Department of Justice.

And the strictly political nature of Vann's appointment separated him from the majority of blacks coming to Washington to work for the New Deal. Vann was, as Ralph Bunche said, strictly a "professional politician,"[20] which made him different from those blacks later referred to as the "Black Cabinet." The Black Cabinet was a group of influential black government advisors, the most prominent of whom were Robert Weaver, Mary McLeod Bethune, and William H. Hastie.[21] They held frequent informal meetings where administration policy toward blacks was discussed at length; rarely was there any formal agenda nor were minutes of their meetings recorded.[22] At the *Courier*, Vann had always been singularly in charge, an imperious loner, and working within a group was not his political style. Robert Vann and friends like Eugene Kinckle Jones and Lawrence Oxley, who were also political appointees, were more important to the Democratic party than to the government as a whole. Vann had no real influence on policy and was in Washington only part-time; he spent half of each week in Pittsburgh trying to nurse the *Courier* through the economic illnesses brought on by the Depression. By contrast, Black Cabinet members like Robert Weaver and William Hastie were not politicians; they were intellectuals (which Vann certainly was not) asked to come to Washington because of their talents and training. They were highly committed to their government positions and politically independent, with little concern for patronage or political "favors." Thus Vann was regarded as an old-style race leader, on the periphery, and was seldom asked to participate in the Black Cabinet meetings at the homes of Weaver or Mrs. Bethune. As the *Chicago Defender* put it, "Things have changed from the old days. No longer is the President surrounded by the elder [black] statesmen whose privilege it is to break the bread and pour the wine... now things are in the hands of the college fraternity, who are said to be running the show."[23]

In some respects, Vann's situation in Washington was full of sad irony. He had started his education late, had been driven by the idea that he had a limited amount of time in which to prove himself, and had worked doubly hard to keep up with the rapidly advancing clock. Now he found himself not too old, as he had feared, but passé among blacks in his outlook and methods. An old-line political race leader like Vann was somewhat anachronistic in FDR's Washington.

A few attempts were made to give Vann small meaningful duties outside the Department of Justice. He was named to two advisory committees, the Negro Advisory Committee of the Advisory and Planning Council for the Department of Commerce, and the Inter-Departmental Group Concerned with the Special Problems of Negroes. The first and more temporary of these comprised ten prominent blacks, including Eugene Kinckle Jones and William Lewis, former assistant attorney general; Vann was named chairman by Secretary of Commerce Daniel Roper.[24] They met for two solid days and evenings in September 1933, discussing nearly every phase of black social, economic, and political activity and its relationship to the general structure of the nation. They heard reports on conditions and recommendations for reform in the NRA program, agriculture, education, labor unions, and the federal government generally as it affected the black man through such agencies as civil service and public works. The committee submitted its findings to Secretary of Commerce Roper, then requested that its recommendations be forwarded to the proper agencies for action.[25] When the conference ended, the group was formally organized on a permanent basis under the Department of Commerce. The Colored News Service touted Vann's committee as "the strongest recognized body of colored men in the history of the country,"[26] but that statement was pure hyperbole, for the committee had power solely to recommend and had no possible way to implement its recommendations.[27]

Just a few days after the Negro Advisory Committee ended its two-day marathon meeting, Robert Vann headed home to Pittsburgh for the weekend in his new black Packard. Near Hagerstown, Maryland, his car slowed up behind a large truck creeping its way up a long hill. Always an impatient driver, Vann rashly decided to pass. As he pulled out from behind the truck, another car appeared over the top of the hill from the opposite direction and smashed head-on into Vann's Packard. No one, fortunately, was killed, but Vann suffered a severe skull fracture and was hospitalized for six weeks.

Vann's spirited concept of the manner in which an automobile should be driven seems to have been unaffected by his nearly fatal 1933 accident. As Wilburt Holloway, the *Courier* cartoonist, was driving Vann back to Pittsburgh after his release from the hospital, Vann became annoyed with him for driving slowly.[28] Yet after that brush with death, the last of a number of increasingly serious accidents Vann had had since he began driving, he was persuaded to drive very little. From then on, either a chauffeur or Wilburt Holloway was behind the wheel.

After Vann was back on his feet, he was named to chair a second committee. This one had the official backing of the president himself. The Inter-Departmental Group Concerned with the Special Problems of Negroes had been the ultimate outgrowth of a discussion between President Roosevelt and Edwin R. Embree of the Julius Rosenwald Fund during the summer of 1933. Embree wanted a government

Washington: Confidence and Disillusionment • 209

agency set up to see that blacks received fair treatment in America, certainly an ambitious concept. Roosevelt was receptive to the idea and suggested that it be under a department head like Secretary of the Interior Harold Ickes. Ickes had been a past president of the Chicago branch of the NAACP and a longtime member of the Urban League and had worked hard to end segregation in the Department of the Interior by employing black architects and engineers in the PWA. Ickes had always befriended all the underprivileged, but particularly the blacks, whom he saw as the most oppressed of minority groups. He told FDR he would take the job and pictured an agency under the aegis of the Department of the Interior to provide him with information and a certain measure of control over all New Deal agencies' relations with blacks. Ickes possibly intended to make the agency a conduit through which blacks could be placed in various government organizations.[29] As head of the projected agency, Ickes selected Dr. Clark Foreman, former director of studies for the Rosenwald Fund.[30]

At first, many blacks objected to the appointment of Clark Foreman. Foreman was a white southerner from Atlanta; they saw his selection as a continuation of the same old white-over-black condescending paternalism. Even Vann's *Courier* joined in the criticism of Ickes's choice. But Ickes stood firm, and the sounds of disapproval died down after Foreman appointed as his assistant Robert C. Weaver, the first black ever to receive a Ph.D. in economics from Harvard.[31] As it turned out, Foreman and Weaver worked well together and within a short time found themselves involved in nearly every New Deal program, though they were primarily concerned with the racial situation in programs under the auspices of the Department of the Interior.[32]

One of their first projects was to form the Inter-Departmental Group, whose purpose would be to see that the various administrative agencies attended to black needs and in particular to arouse the social conscience of the NRA.[33] Ickes asked every cabinet department and major federal agency to send a representative to an organizational meeting to be held on February 7, 1934. Vann chaired meetings of the group, and at the initial meeting all but the Post Office and State Department were represented. In this interracial committee some of the most noted black members were Henry Hunt, assistant to the governor of the Farm Credit Administration, Forrester B. Washington, an Atlanta social worker now of the FERA, and Eugene

Kinckle Jones from the Department of Commerce.[34] White representatives were sent by the Departments of Labor, Navy, War, and Treasury, the Agricultural Adjustment Administration, NRA, and TVA.

The Inter-Departmental Group met regularly for four months with few positive results. A special Sub-committee on Labor reported that widespread violations of NRA codes existed; that thousands of blacks were not receiving regulation wages; and that the wage differential between blacks and whites, particularly in the South, had not decreased. On the contrary, since the NRA's establishment, the differential between the races had actually grown.[35] In President Roosevelt's only recorded statement concerning the special problems of blacks under the NRA, he apparently bowed to the power of southern industrialists. "It is not the purpose of this administration," he declared, "to impair southern industry by refusing to recognize traditional differentials."[36] Other members of the Group complained that the NRA was not living up to its obligation to protect blacks on the TVA and Boulder Dam projects or in the other industries it was supposed to police.

Vann and others charged that organized labor, notably the AFL and the building trade unions, excluded blacks from its ranks. They recommended that the federal government take action to increase black membership in unions. But the Labor Department representative, E. J. Tracy, disagreed, saying he felt the AFL should be left alone "to work out its own problems."[37]

Next the Sub-committee on Agriculture, of which Vann was also a member, reported that blacks were suffering gross inequities in that area. Despite supposed safeguards within the Agricultural Adjustment Administration program, black tenant farmers had been forced off their lands by the cotton reduction program and by hard-pressed landlords. The Farm Credit Administration did not reach as far down as the black man and thus was of little help. Many blacks did not know about the program, and those who did were not allowed to join the southern white loan associations. Propertied black farmers were also at a disadvantage because local southern appraisers often discriminated against them when setting a value on property to be put up as loan security.[38] Despite the report, members of the Agriculture Department, including Secretary Henry A. Wallace, insisted that the criticism was unwarranted, and resisted the recommendation that a black adviser be appointed. Wallace went so far as to claim that

Washington: Confidence and Disillusionment • 211

such an appointment would be "patronizing" or even "discriminatory" and said he felt that "the most progressive among our Negro population... would prefer that the Department of Agriculture render to them the same service through the same organization that is rendered to our entire rural population."[39] Further, Wallace was very unenthusiastic about the Group and viewed it "as another example of Ickes' empire-building."[40]

Charges and countercharges proliferated in the meetings of the Group and frequently led to very heated discussions. Though Ickes, Foreman, and Weaver had hoped to exert pressure for reform through the Inter-Departmental Group, they actually had no jurisdiction over the NRA, the Department of Agriculture or Labor, or any other department or agency. Rather than changing attitudes, the Group actually polarized them among officials who regarded suggestions as intrusions upon their bailiwicks.[41] Thus the Inter-Departmental Group lasted less than six months, without accomplishing to any degree the coordinating function anticipated by Ickes and Foreman. The minutes showed a tone of bureaucratic concern, with each agency man trying to keep the others out of his agency's affairs and to defend the actions of his agency against criticism.[42] The Inter-Departmental Group proved almost useless in aiding the black man, and Vann was little more than an ornament.

In addition to his minor duties in the Department of Justice and sporadic committee work, Vann found the Democrats made limited use of his talents as a speaker along the campaign trail. Occasionally, at the request of James A. Farley or Joseph Guffey, Vann went to Detroit to address the Michigan Association of Colored Brothers at the seventy-second anniversary of the Emancipation Proclamation,[43] or toured the major cities of Indiana by automobile to garner black votes for the Democrats in the 1934 congressional elections,[44] or went to Meadville, Pennsylvania, with Emma Guffey Miller to help form a Roosevelt Club. But that was about all. Contrary to his expectations, Vann had a severely circumscribed role in the Roosevelt administration.[45]

The final thing that destroyed Vann's hopes was the atmosphere of the New Deal and its attitudes toward the black man. Roosevelt had no stated policy about helping the black man on any level. He knew little about blacks and felt no strong commitment to them. He was interested in ameliorating the poverty of all the economically stricken, a group which of course included most blacks. Thus each

New Deal department and agency had its own procedure for handling black problems, and often the fate of the black man depended on the extent to which the dominant personalities in various offices were sensitive to the special needs of blacks. Some economic recovery agencies—the Farm Security Administration, the Public Works Administration, and the Works Progress Administration—did have policies that ensured fair treatment for blacks, but others—like the Agricultural Adjustment Administration and the National Recovery Administration—were not willing to make the necessary efforts to secure racial justice. They took no steps to ensure the distribution of government benefits among blacks, nor did they appoint specialists to keep them posted on black problems.[46] Further, Roosevelt was keenly aware of political forces, and while blacks were weak and poorly organized politically, the reverse was true of white southerners. Hence Roosevelt dared not speak out on any racial issue for fear of alienating the powerful southern bloc in Congress and thus harming much of his New Deal legislation. So Roosevelt stayed at a safe distance from racial controversies like discriminatory practices in the Civilian Conservation Corps or anti-lynching legislation.[47] Not a few blacks were disillusioned by this discovery.

The 1934 Pennsylvania election for senator and governor gave Robert Vann a brief reprieve from his despondency over the way things were going in Washington. That election, in which Democratic candidates were victorious for both offices, represented a dramatic political change in a state where Republicans had held sway for nearly seventy years.

The first evidence of this dramatic change had shown up in the Pittsburgh mayoral election of 1933. Only one Democratic candidate in the twentieth century had been elected mayor of Vann's home city, and that was back in 1906. But Republican control of the city began to disintegrate as the Depression dragged on. The disintegration was furthered by the Republican mayor, Charles H. Kline, who had been forced to resign early in 1933 because of his 1931 conviction and imprisonment for malfeasance in office in connection with irregularities in awarding city contracts for supplies. The acting mayor, John S. Herron, who took over after Kline resigned, could not control the party and make it function effectively.[48] The county organization was equally chaotic. So in November 1933 the Democratic mayoral candidate was able to win. In fact the Democrat, William M. McNair, swamped the Republican by 28,000 votes, 102,658 to 75,304. Under the skillful management of David L. Lawrence, Allegheny County Democratic Chairman, and with strong financial backing from Michael Benedum, the Democrats also made a clean sweep of county offices that year.

Like so many Democrats that year, McNair had run on President Roosevelt's prestige. During the Pittsburgh mayoral campaign, McNair was photographed with FDR, and all of his speeches praised the successes of the New Deal while denouncing Republican economic failures, former Secretary of the Treasury Andrew Mellon, and the utilities.[49] The Democrats had an uphill fight to win the black vote; the odds were still strongly against them. At primary time fewer than twenty-eight hundred Democrats had been registered in the two mostly black wards, and Republicans outnumbered Democrats by four to one in the Third and almost three to one in the Fifth. At Vann's request, Democratic leaders Joseph Guffey and David Lawrence announced the appointment of five blacks to the Pittsburgh office of the Home Owners Loan Corporation. The Democrats publicized these appointments in the Democratic organization's propaganda sheet, *The New Deal Newspaper,* and then published figures on how badly blacks had been treated politically by the Republicans in Pittsburgh; though they numbered 16 percent of the popular vote, blacks had received only slightly more than 3 percent of patronage jobs.[50] The preprimary tactics of the Republicans had been vicious. McNair and Vann charged that in the economically depressed black Fifth Ward, voters who tried to register Democratic were threatened with being cut from the relief rolls. Erasures in the registration books appeared to bear out the claim that police had herded fifty voters of the Fifth Ward who registered as Democrats back to the board and forced them to change their registration to Republican or lose their relief aid.[51]

In the November election, Vann claimed that black votes in the Third, Fifth, Twelfth, and Thirteenth Wards had counted significantly in McNair's margin of victory, but this may have been an overstatement, as the Republican candidate carried all these wards. Nonetheless, even more blacks voted Democratic in Pittsburgh in the 1933 election than in 1932. The black showing was impressive enough that Democrats opened a permanent headquarters in the Third Ward.[52]

The 1934 elections further consolidated Democratic strength in Pennsylvania. George H. Earle III became the new Democratic governor by a plurality of more than 66,000 votes over William A. Schnader, and Joseph Guffey defeated the Republican incumbent David A. Reed for a U. S. Senate seat, 1,494,138 to 1,366,872. Guffey was the first Democratic senator from Pennsylvania in sixty years, and Earle was the state's first Democratic governor in forty-four years. The Democrats even won control over the lower house of the state legislature for the first time since 1877.[53] Five of the new Democratic legislators were black; four came from Philadelphia, and one, Homer S. Brown, was from the First Legislative District in Pittsburgh.

Pittsburgh contributed heavily to the Democratic triumph; Allegheny County showed impressive majorities of 75,000 and 85,000 for Earle and Guffey, respectively.[54] The Third and Fifth Wards of Pittsburgh gave a heavy majority of their votes to the Democrats—a complete reversal in the four short years since 1930. In Philadelphia Earle received slightly less than a majority of the vote (47.97 percent), but his total was 20.46 percent more than the Democrats had received in the 1930 gubernatorial contest. And Earle gained 40.78 percent of the Philadelphia black wards' votes, an increase of 23.52 percent over 1930.[55]

The new governor, George Earle, cheerfully admitted that the popularity of FDR and his New Deal was responsible for the sweeping victories of the Democrats in Pennsylvania that year. Said Earle, "They say we rode in on Roosevelt's coattails. Hell, he carried us in piggyback."[56] And one black summed up the prevailing attitude nicely: "I didn't pay no attention to the political party.... I saw Roosevelt's picture [the Democratic candidates made a point of being photographed often with the chief executive] and I know what he done for me when I was hungry. Anybody that has that picture beside him can get my votes."[57]

Earle was a young Philadelphia millionaire who had previously been a Republican but opposed Hoover's policies in 1932. At the instigation of William C. Bullitt, Earle threw his full support behind FDR and contributed heavily to Roosevelt's 1932 campaign, in return for which Roosevelt appointed him minister to Austria in 1933–34. Earle was still a registered Republican when Guffey, David Stern, publisher of the *Philadelphia Record*, and others turned to him as a gubernatorial candidate for the Democrats in 1934.[58]

George Earle was basically more appealing to black voters than his opponent. Not only did he favor a "Little New Deal" for Pennsylvania, but he made a sincere effort to attract blacks. He emphasized the fact that his grandfather had financed an Underground Railroad station for runaway slaves and had also vigorously opposed exclusion of blacks from suffrage in the Pennsylvania Constitutional Convention in 1834. Just before the November 1934 election, Earle entertained the Negro Citizens' Democratic Committee of One Hundred at his opulent home in exclusive Haverford, a suburb of Philadelphia.[59] On the other hand, Earle's opponent, William Schnader, was thought of with disfavor; as attorney general during the Pinchot administration, he allegedly had urged the governor to veto as "class legislation" an equal rights bill and a measure providing for two Pennsylvania black National Guard units. Schnader also had failed to take any action in the Beaver County deportation case. Earle ran on a platform of social justice; he called for the abolition of child labor, equitable regulation of working hours, a minimum wage law, the right to collective bargaining, a more comprehensive workman's compensation law, the outlawing of sweat shops, more equitable tax laws, and greater economic security through old age pensions and unemployment compensation. Though Earle made no specific mention of the black man's needs, most of these reforms would apply to large numbers of the state's blacks.

All during Vann's campaign speeches that fall, he had emphasized that a vote for Joseph Guffey or George Earle was a vote to maintain the New Deal:

> Support Guffey and Earle and you are supporting the New Deal. . . . March 4, 1933 brought a new Emancipation Proclamation to an enslaved populace. And in eighteen short months we find ourselves headed toward a restoration of our Government to the hands of the people. Fear has been banished from the American fireside, hope is rekindled in the hearts of men, and everywhere the American people are proclaiming a new day and a new deal. For this revival of spirit, of courage and of hope, the full credit belongs to Franklin D. Roosevelt. By his sheer will and courage and his charming personality, our President has shown us the way out. He has wiped out geographical lines; he has abolished sectionalism; he has destroyed strictly partisan affiliations; and he has welded the American people into a democratic whole which gives a new meaning to the United States of America.[60]

Vann was pivotal in the Democratic campaign in Pennsylvania. He left his duties in Washington, such as they were, and spent several weeks stumping around the state. In the contest between Guffey and incumbent Senator Reed, Vann emphasized the fact that back in 1926 Senator Reed had been opposed to the bill sponsored by Congressman

Hamilton Fish of New York, who had been an officer over black troops in World War I, which would have provided $30,000 for a monument to be erected in France in commemoration of black soldiers from the 369th, 371st and 372nd Regiments, attached to the French Fourth Army. "Reed held he had voted against the monument," said the *Courier*, because it had meant segregationist treatment. "Get that, segregation. Did the Senator think it was segregation when he and Hoover sent our Gold Star Mothers to France segregated in a cattle ship? He did not!"[61]

Vann, who had seconded Guffey's nomination at the state Democratic convention, stressed the Democrat's achievements for blacks, especially in the field of patronage. A special *Courier* supplement, "The Voice of the Pennsylvanian," gave a lengthy list of blacks appointed, with the help of Guffey's leadership, to jobs on the national and state levels. The list included, in the Pittsburgh area, a Post Office supervisor and assistant supervisor, a deputy collector of internal revenue, a floor foreman and two special clerks at the Post Office, an attorney to the Home Owners Loan Corporation, and an assistant city solicitor (Wilbur C. Douglass, Vann's junior law partner).[62] When a special newsletter put out by the Republicans attacked Vann in an effort to gain black votes, it instead lost them, for Vann's popularity was at an all-time high in his home state.[63]

The Democratic victory in Pennsylvania in November was instrumental in removing doubts among the national Democratic political leaders about their ability to capture the black vote. Initially the campaign had not been in the national spotlight because attention was focused on Upton Sinclair's campaign for the governorship of California, on Floyd B. Olsen's Farmer-Labor campaign in Minnesota, and on Huey Long in Louisiana. But after the impressive Democratic sweep in Pennsylvania, with Guffey beating Reed by almost one-hundred thousand votes and the party winning twenty-three of the thirty-four House of Representatives seats as well as a majority of the lower house in the state assembly, the *Literary Digest* commented, "The rout of the Republicans in Pennsylvania, their citadel, will serve as a symbol of what occurred in most of the nation."[64] The blacks had played a significant part in that victory. James A. Farley now was motivated to give out 150 jobs each paying more than $3,000 yearly to blacks in the ten cities with large black populations, and the Democratic National Committee added forty-five black professionals, educators, editors, and ministers to its payroll.[65]

Washington: Confidence and Disillusionment • 217

The great significance of the 1934 Democratic victory in Pennsylvania for Robert Vann was that Joseph Guffey, his patron, became the undisputed Democratic leader in the state, with direct access to President Roosevelt and James A. Farley, chairman of the Democratic National Committee.[66] Vann entertained the hope that Guffey might be able to improve his unsatisfactory status in FDR's Washington. At the very least, Guffey would certainly consult him about the dispensation of black patronage jobs in Pennsylvania.[67] Joseph Guffey began the year of 1935 by inviting Vann to be one of just twenty-five special guests to witness Guffey's swearing-in at the Senate. Next, Governor Earle named Vann to a whole series of positions in the new state administration. Vann became a member of no fewer than five committees: the Pennsylvania Committee on Public Assistance, the State Advisory Council on the Federal Writers Project, a committee on constitutional revision, the Governor's Commission for the Celebration of the 150th Anniversary of the Adoption of the State Constitution, and the Governor's Commission to Codify the Laws of Pennsylvania.[68] They were all posts of no major importance but served to take Vann's mind temporarily off the vast dissatisfaction he felt with his work in Washington.

And Vann seemed at last to have significant patronage at his disposal under the Democrats, in contrast to the years in which he had paid fealty to state Republican administrations.[69] One patronage appointment of which Vann was especially proud was that of Paul F. Jones of Pittsburgh, an energetic young state political organizer, as workmen's compensation referee at a salary of $5,000 a year.[70] Another source of satisfaction for Vann and blacks generally was Senator Guffey's control in 1935 of the Works Projects Administration's activities in the state. Though political columnists Alsop and Kintner charged that Guffey used the WPA as a patronage weapon, and that "anyone whose travels take him near the Pennsylvania WPA knows that it stinks as insistently of politics as a ten-day dead whale on a beach stinks of whale,"[71] it provided many badly needed jobs for blacks.

And Vann finally got the long-overdue state equal rights bill for which he had been fighting for twenty years. It was a product of Governor Earle's efforts to live up to his campaign promises to black supporters. He created a "Little New Deal" in Pennsylvania with state versions of the Wagner Act, the NRA, the Brain Trust, and even the fireside chats FDR was instituting. Then on September 1, 1935, Earle signed into law an equal rights bill. Robert Vann had been deeply involved in the effort to pass such a measure since 1915, when his *Courier* was a small but crusading voice in behalf of black rights. He had spent a great deal of time in Harrisburg, the state capital, that year and then again in 1917, 1919, 1921, and 1923, lobbying to have an effective equal rights bill passed. And he had spoken out forcefully from the pages of his newspaper all those years. Some of his most impassioned speeches and editorials were about the need for such a bill. In 1921 he told a House Judiciary Committee, "By the treatment you accord the Negro you are challenging the right of God himself to create people of different colors."[72] Then in 1923, after another equal rights bill (the fifth since 1915) was defeated, Vann vowed to continue his fight. "We are simply asking for the right to enjoy what is ours—ours under the Constitution of the country—under the Laws of Pennsylvania. We are asking—not for the birth right of others, but for *what is ours*."[73]

After so many fruitless attempts over the years, the passage of the 1935 equal rights bill in Pennsylvania seemed almost an anticlimax to Vann. It came about because the legislation had the solid support of Joseph Guffey and David Lawrence, secretary of the Commonwealth and state Democratic leader. Republican members of the state legislature were reluctant to oppose the measure, not only because it might further alienate the black electorate, but because the legislation was sponsored in the House by a black, Hobson Reynolds, Republican of Philadelphia, and in the Senate by Samuel Salus, also a Philadelphia Republican. Vann accused the Republicans of duplicity because they hoped that after passage of the GOP-sponsored legislation, the Democratic governor would veto it.[74] Receiving bipartisan support, Reynolds's measure passed with no dissenting votes in the House; only one member of the Senate voiced an objection. To the surprise of the GOP, on June 11 Governor Earle signed the act into law. But Earle had already notified Vann by telegram, "There was never any doubt in my mind as to the stand I would take on it."[75]

Ten minutes after the bill became law, not realizing that Earle had already signed it, the House attempted to recall the bill as a result of pressure from the Pennsylvania Hotel and Restaurant Association lobby.[76] Apparently the PHRA did not believe the bill would pass and became alarmed when it did. The legislative proceedings had gone almost unnoticed by the white press; only the *Courier* covered them extensively.[77] "Even legislators were unaware of its contents until the representatives of a hotel-men's association saw the

Washington: Confidence and Disillusionment • 219

bill and started the fireworks."[78] The president of the PHRA stated in polite but unequivocal language that hotels would conduct business as they had before the bill's enactment; since the penalty of a $100 to $500 fine or thirty to sixty days in jail for racial discrimination was technically a misdemeanor, hoteliers would contest the act and be willing to face the slight consequences. A manager of one of Pittsburgh's largest amusement parks called the bill "a terrible thing . . . passed purely for political reasons. We will positively not allow Negroes to enter our dance-halls or our swimming pool except when there are Negro picnics. If there is any trouble . . . I don't think there is a jury that will find us guilty."[79]

State Representative Hobson Reynolds declared that there would not be an active campaign by blacks to test the new legislation, but he threatened to prosecute those hoteliers who refused to abide by it. Nevertheless, discrimination against blacks went on almost unabated. An Urban League official was forced to use the freight elevator in the William Penn Hotel,[80] and in the same hotel's beauty salon, two black women were charged five dollars for a "powder test," normally given free to whites.[81] It was obvious the bill was merely "showcase legislation," a political ploy by the Democrats to reinforce their good standing with newly won black supporters. Vann recognized this and told newsmen in Harrisburg that though he favored the law, he knew it would have little effect since its violation was not treated as a serious crime and no court of jurisdiction had been named to impose conviction.[82] The equal rights bill of 1935 was never much enforced.

Vann by now was spending less and less time in Washington. From the beginning it had been his custom to return to Pittsburgh each weekend, but as the time passed and his disappointment with Washington mounted, the weekends became longer and longer. In July 1935, the Roosevelt administration made one last attempt to appease Vann's obvious discontent: Secretary of the Interior Ickes had Vann named to the Virgin Islands Advisory Council.[83] Its purpose was to prepare the Islands for self-government. A series of meetings and hearings on the proposed Virgin Islands Organic Act followed, but Vann by now was little interested in anything centered in Washington. To judge from government records and correspondence, he took little part in the important investigatory phase of the work.[84]

In September 1935 Vann left with his wife for a long and leisurely trip to California. They boarded a cruise ship in New York and followed the coastline south, with a stop in Havana, into the West Indies, then through the Panama Canal and up the Pacific Coast to Los Angeles and Hollywood. While they were at sea, the Vanns became friendly with a number of white passengers, including one couple from the South. These new acquaintances, it became apparent, did

Vann with Bill "Bojangles" Robinson and Shirley Temple, Hollywood, 1935.

not realize the Vanns were American blacks, but thought they were Indians of some sort. Finally someone, with obvious embarrassment, asked the Vanns about their racial origins; when the Vanns answered "Negro," the new friendships died, and relations returned to cool formality on the part of the whites.[85]

While Vann was in Los Angeles, the perfect excuse he needed to resign from the Department of Justice with a minimum of ill feeling arrived in the mail. It was a copy of the *Pittsburgh Courier*—a landmark issue, for it was the one-hundred thousandth copy of that week's run and marked the first time the newspaper had ever reached such a large press run in one week. The entire *Courier* staff had initialled the copy sent to Vann.[86] Vann's newspaper appeared to be on the verge of becoming the nation's leading black weekly, and he should obviously devote much more time to it, which he could not do from Washington. It was the reason Vann had been waiting for. He resigned posthaste from the Department of Justice; his resignation was not effective until January 1936, but Vann was rarely in Washington after September 1935. He found little consolation in the fact that Theron B. Hamilton, a friend of his and also a black attorney from Pittsburgh, was named his successor.[87]

It was a leave-taking tinged with sadness and defeat. After winning blacks over to the Democrats in 1932 and achieving prominence as the head of one of the nation's leading black newspapers, Vann had found himself relegated to a post of negligible importance and accorded almost no recognition in Washington. Indeed, had it not been for the publicity he received from his nearly fatal accident in Maryland in 1933, much of Washington's officialdom might never have heard of him.

When an acquaintance found him clearing papers and personal effects from his Washington office and asked him why he was leaving, Vann remarked grimly, "I'm not doing anything here. It looks like they put me down here in Washington to shut me up."[88] And he later told H. L. Mencken, "The work got a little tedious for me because it developed that such a job as I held was a splendid pastime for old men who are seeking a soft place in their declining years. I did not want to get into the rut of an old man because the only difference between a rut and the grave is that the latter is a little deeper."[89]

· 10 ·

The COURIER
Hits the Jackpot

WITHIN TWO YEARS after Robert Vann gave up his post in Washington, the *Courier* achieved a hitherto unthinkably high circulation of a quarter million, which moved it into the uncontested number-one position among black weeklies in the United States. Vann would live little more than four years after his return to Pittsburgh at the end of 1935; almost as if he knew this, he went about building the paper with a tireless outpouring of energy that belied his age and gradually failing health. The momentum Vann skillfully created was so great that it maintained the *Courier*'s primacy for a good many years after his death.

The 1930s had begun inauspiciously for the *Courier*. The gradually lengthening shadow cast over the country by the Depression fell upon the *Courier* as well, and it would have engulfed the paper totally had it not been for a propitious combination of circumstances, some created by Robert Vann's foresight, some by fate. As it was, the *Courier* merely hovered in a sort of financial penumbra for seven years and escaped the total failure that befell so many of the nation's black newspapers.

One factor that undoubtedly saved the *Courier* from going under was its new printing plant, which had gone into operation at the end of 1929. Though its opening was ill timed, coming less than two months after the stock market crash, and though the debt incurred in the construction was of frightening proportions, the fact that the *Courier* now did its own printing allowed the paper to keep what revenue came in during the lean years, rather than watch it vanish into the coffers of another printing concern. And the new plant could accept job printing orders which provided badly needed additional income to keep the newspaper functioning above the poverty line. Further, the *Courier*'s modern printing equipment made possible an increase in the paper's size from sixteen to twenty pages, which in turn augmented its appeal to the black newspaper-reading public. Before the opening of the new plant, circulation had been about thirty-five thousand; by 1930 it had already grown to an estimated fifty thousand or more. The *Courier* ambitiously printed four editions—local, northern, eastern and southern—and boasted distribution in all forty-eight states, plus Europe, Cuba, Canada, the Philippines, the Virgin Islands, and the British West Indies.[1]

As the Depression continued, Vann instituted another change which aided the *Courier* in its struggle to survive financially. He broke with the William B. Ziff Company, which had been the paper's advertising agent for nearly fourteen years. Though Ziff had been helpful in securing national advertising for the *Courier* in the early 1920s, when the newspaper was beginning its efforts to achieve a nationwide perspective, as the years went on Vann and Ira Lewis became increasingly unhappy with the alliance. One of Vann's objections to Ziff had to do with the illustrated feature magazine that Ziff distributed to all his black newspaper clients. Vann had viewed the magazine as a good business proposition when he began including it in the *Courier* in 1928; he thought it would increase reader interest and circulation and add to the paper's advertising revenues. Vann even intervened with Ziff to get the job of editor for George Schuyler.[2] But as time went on, this rotogravure section began to offend Vann's Victorian sensibilities, for it contained features like "Chocolate Baby," "Struggling Hearts," or "The Confessions of a Black Bootlegger," many of which were illustrated with drawings of seminude women.[3] Vann disliked "Ziff's so-called magazine section . . . filled with salacious and sexual matter, entirely obnoxious to our readers."[4]

Vann's other objections to Ziff were all financial. For one thing, Ziff charged his newspaper customers very high commissions on the advertising he obtained—from 35 to 50 percent. Ziff felt his unusually stiff commission was justified because he eliminated all collection problems for his clients. But the exorbitant rate became more and more painful to Vann as the financial straits of his *Courier* deepened. Also, Vann felt that the *Courier* was not receiving enough money from

Ziff, who was paying the paper on the basis of a net circulation figure ten to twenty thousand less than Vann's estimate. There was no way to settle the circulation dispute, for Vann had never submitted his *Courier* to an official audit; nonetheless, he felt the *Courier* was being grossly shortchanged.

After Vann went to Washington in 1933, the reports from Ira Lewis contained a weekly plea to make the change from Ziff. When Vann planned a trip from Washington to the Ziff New York offices in April 1934, Lewis wrote, "It is becoming almost unbearable to see those birds sitting over there collecting our money and keeping it. . . . Something has to be done. I have every confidence that you are going to New York Saturday with a lot of that 'Ahoskie oxen' in you that will terminate this thing one way or the other."[5]

Vann courageously made the break, though he knew it would instigate a law suit for breach of contract; the litigation lasted for three years. Vann immediately hired the H. B. Crohn Company of New York as his new advertising representative, at terms much more favorable to the *Courier* than Ziff had given. H. B. Crohn had been Ziff's eastern manager, but had only recently set up his own business; his managerial ability was still an unknown quantity. But at least one black newspaper editor commended Vann "for having the courage to revolt and to stay 'revolted.' "[6] Just two other weeklies followed Vann's example, *The Call* of Kansas City and the *Louisiana Weekly* of New Orleans. Most of the other black papers continued to deal with Ziff. Crohn repeated Ziff's warning that unless Vann submitted to an ABC audit, which then turned up a guaranteed circulation of 60,000 or more, valuable advertising accounts like Vicks, Vaseline, and Cheseborough Ponds would be jeopardized.[7] As of 1935, N. W. Ayer had the *Courier* circulation at only 40,920,[8] though the Ayer figures were of doubtful accuracy. Vann should have had the ABC audit, but he stubbornly held out for two more years; the *Pittsburgh Courier* was the last major black weekly newspaper in the country to be audited.[9]

Despite the advantages of having his own printing plant and a more equitable revenue from advertising, Vann found the financial tribulations of his *Courier* during the Depression interminable. At times it must have appeared that the newspaper would forever be plagued by economic woes from which not even the business acumen and hard work of Vann and Lewis could rescue it. Vann had had to begin the new decade by attempting to stave off the *Courier*'s many creditors. His letters of reassurance to them were full of bright, if hollow, optimism. He wrote the International Paper Company that "prospects are considerably brighter for an upturn in business and we are very, very hopeful of being able to take care of the invoice of around seventeen hundred dollars within the next ten days."[10] Vann hired two men, N. Qualey and H. P. Lawless, to sell $45,000 in *Courier* preferred stock to raise money, but to little avail. He was forced to admit to a creditor that "subnormal conditions have made it practically impossible to market any of our preferred stock."[11]

The *Courier*'s difficulties in paying its debts created problems for the institutions that had loaned it money. In 1931, the *Courier* let a ninety-day loan of $1,650 from the Citizens and Southern Bank and Trust Company of Philadelphia go unpaid for more than six months. The bank, a black-run institution, had a meager capitalization and gradually became desperate for payment. The president, R. R. Wright, Sr., wrote an urgent letter explaining the bank's plight. "You must certainly understand that the times are very stringent and oppressive so far as banks are concerned," he pleaded. "We have had as many as fifty banks fail in Philadelphia."[12] The *Courier* president answered with an equally urgent plea for more time to pay off the past-due loan. Vann on occasion had to resort to asking friends for loans to see the paper through, even though he had little to offer in the way of collateral. He wrote a banker friend in Tennessee, hoping flattery might result in the loan of a thousand dollars: "When a fellow gets to the place where he needs a friend, the man to whom he turns is a pretty good indication of what we mean by friends."[13]

As early as September 1930 Vann had to reduce staff salaries drastically. His prize editorial writer, George Schuyler, was given a pay cut of 40 percent, from twenty-five dollars weekly to fifteen, which is a good indication of the straitened circumstances in which the *Courier* found itself. For a time Vann took over the writing of the editorials without compensation; he could afford to pay Schuyler only for his "Views and Reviews" column. Just before he received the cut in pay, Schuyler wrote to Vann inquiring about three weeks' back pay he had not yet received. Vann replied, "Your articles disclose that you know something about the general depression of the country, but your letters to us disclose that [you think] the depression has hit everyone but us."[14]

The *Courier*'s financial troubles continued undiminished during the two years Vann was in Washington. The newspaper operated on a strictly hand-to-mouth basis. Ira Lewis's weekly letters to his chief were preoccupied with finances and always enclosed checks that needed Vann's signature so that the most pressing of the bills could be paid. Excerpts from Lewis's letters of this period reveal the chronic difficulties the paper faced:

> We were able to get through the week okay financially, but I don't care how soon January gets out of the way. It has been a nightmare.
>
> Things have perked up a little bit since I last wrote you, yesterday's collections being very good (over $700.00). This helped me along because it looked as though I would have to defer the pay day until the last of the week, something we have never done before. I paid the girls on Wednesday, and I am trying to make the downstairs today.
>
> Everything is in good shape. The only thing in the world we have any use for or need of is money.[15]

Though the *Courier*'s financial woes were unceasing, Ira Lewis was perennially sanguine that the newspaper would not only survive, but do very well. He constantly reassured Vann to this effect, particularly when it seemed prudent for the *Courier* to take on additional financial burdens that would have obvious long-range benefits, such as the purchase of a lot adjoining *Courier* property in June 1933[16] or the June 1934 expansion of the newspaper to a twenty-four-page format. Lewis supported Vann in these measures and assured him they would "pay handsome returns in the future."[17]

From his office in Washington, Vann tried desperately to get a $50,000 loan from the Reconstruction Finance Corporation to alleviate the *Courier*'s worst financial problems and provide a solid footing for recovery. Vann had good reason to believe he might be granted such a loan. His friend Eugene Kinckle Jones was head of the Negro Division in the Department of Commerce, and one of the duties of Jones's group was to guard the interests of black small businesses. Jones was in a strategic position to plead the *Courier*'s case before the RFC. Moreover, Joseph Guffey, Pennsylvania's leading Democrat and Vann's close ally, processed all loan applications from the state and had written an encouraging recommendation to accompany Vann's loan request.[18] As Vann pointed out, the loan would not only aid the *Courier*, but the Democratic party as well, for "surely the Democrats need [another] national mouthpiece and goodness knows the *Courier* is identified with their cause."[19] Unfortunately, Vann was but one of thousands of supplicants bombarding the RFC with their urgent requests, and his need was evidently not extreme enough. The loan was never granted.

By the time Robert Vann returned from Washington, the newspaper resembled somewhat a lone survivor clinging to a tree in a hurricane. The black-run *Pittsburgh American*, founded in 1919, had gone out of business by 1928. The *Vanguard* was of even shorter duration and failed in 1929 after less than a year in operation. The *Pittsburgh Crier*, established by a young black, P. J. Clyde Randall, in 1933, had trouble from the outset despite the fact that E. Washington Rhodes became its editor in 1934; it went under in 1938. Other black newspapers around the country were also in trouble, suffering from drastic drops in circulation because their readers could no longer afford the ten-cent price. The *Chicago Defender*, which had a circulation of two-hundred thousand in 1925, dipped to one-hundred thousand by 1933 and was down to seventy-three thousand in 1935.[20]

During the years between 1930 and 1935, Robert Vann cast about to find a topic or issue of great interest which could spark the rapid advance of circulation and increase the *Courier*'s national prominence. The *Courier*'s circulation had been helped since 1932 by its backing of Franklin Delano Roosevelt. Moreover, advertising revenue had been added to the weekly's coffers as the Democratic party purchased advertising space. But the New Deal did not provide sufficient excitement to boost the circulation of the *Courier* to the numbers Robert Vann was looking for. Some of the other subjects the paper treated extensively before 1935, when it finally hit upon the two which spelled success, were the "Amos 'n Andy" radio show, the Self-Respect Defense Fund, Marcus Garvey, and the Scottsboro case.

The purpose of the *Courier*'s treatment of "Amos 'n Andy" was to build self-respect and racial pride among the nation's blacks. "Amos 'n Andy" was started in the fall of 1929 by two white former vaudevillians, Freeman Gosden and Charles Correll. Within a few months the two blackface comedians, who broadcast over the NBC network, had taken the country by storm. Many people refused to answer their telephones while the program was on the air. Movie theaters in smaller cities interrupted their shows to turn on the broadcast;

if they did not, they would lose most of their patrons until the program was over. Millions of Americans followed avidly the affairs of the Fresh Air Taxi-cab Company, and Madame Queen and the Kingfish became household words. One man inserted an advertisement in a newspaper to ask his friends not to disturb him while the program was being broadcast.[21]

By early 1931 the *Courier* was reacting angrily to the show and the image it was creating of blacks. It ran an editorial which asked, "What is the damage done? . . . What is the impression made? It is almost everywhere to be met where white people encounter Negroes. . . . On the streets, in the banks, in the business places, Negro help is often referred to as Amos or Andy. Negroes are being put down as being one of two types. We are either Amos or we are Andy."[22] Soon after the paper grumbled about the fact that the theme music which had been added to the silent movie *Birth of a Nation* provided the introduction to "Amos 'n Andy,"[23] and dealt with the question of self-respect being raised by such a show:

> No one will respect us more than we respect ourselves. It was some time before Negroes really caught the real harm we are suffering because of the ridicule heaped upon us. At the "trial" of Andy, Madam Queen was shown to be a Negro woman with three husbands. She was shown to be a bigamist. The Negro lawyers Andy picked out to defend him were shown to be "crooks" and most unfit to practice the profession . . . .
>
> This was a slap at the Negro lawyers, and Madam Queen's bigamy was an insult to all Negro women. There are intelligent lawyers of the Negro race. Why did not the pair select one to represent the profession? The Negro lawyer was presented to the listening world as a crook unfit to go to any court. And yet we sit still and allow this insult to be sent all over the radio world. What sort of stuff are we made of when we can laugh at ourselves outraged?
>
> . . . The air must be free of insult as far as we are concerned. Self respect will do more to stop the insult than anything else. Every home must be a HOME of Self Respect. . . . Out with the insult—and we must wreck the machine of dirty propaganda.[24]

The *Courier* suggested a huge petition to the Radio Commission in an effort to get this "Travesty on Decency off the air."[25] In June the *Courier* began its petition efforts in earnest, with a large front-page copy of the document it proposed:

WANTED! ONE MILLION SIGNERS
A Nation-wide Protest Against "Amos 'n Andy"

WHEREAS, for more than a year, two white men known as "Amos 'n Andy" to the radio world, have been exploiting certain types of American Negro for purely commercial gain for themselves and their employer; and

WHEREAS, the references made to the Negro are of such character as to prove detrimental to the self-respect and general advancement of the Negro in the United States and elsewhere; and

WHEREAS, already Negro womanhood has been broadcast to the world as indulging in bigamy, lawyers as schemers and crooks and Negro Secret Orders as organizations where money is filched from its members by dishonest methods, thereby placing all these activities among Negroes in a most harmful and degrading light; and

WHEREAS, The *Pittsburgh Courier* has inaugurated a nation-wide protest against the further practices of these white men who are commercializing certain types of American Negroes at a reputed salary of Six Thousand Dollars per week;

THEREFORE, We, the undersigned, do most solemnly join the protest of the *Pittsburgh Courier* and ask that the comedians so exploiting our group be driven from the air as a menace to our self respect, our professional, fraternal and economic progress, and to that end do sign our names and addresses hereto. We authorize the *Pittsburgh Courier* and other like agencies to present the protest to whatever authorities may have the power to make this protest most effective and conclusive.[26]

The paper began to run a front-page "thermometer" with the caption, "Self-Respect vs. Amos 'n Andy," to record the weekly total number of signers; the goal was 1,000,000.[27] Petitions swamped the *Courier* offices by the thousands. In July the numbers reached over 100,000; in August, 300,000; in September, 515,000; and by October the thermometer registered 675,000.[28] In August the *Courier* roundly criticized the *Chicago Defender* for hiring Gosden and Correll to entertain at its annual children's "Bud Billiken" picnic in an article, "HAS THE *DEFENDER* TURNED AMOS 'N ANDY?" accompanied by a cartoon which depicted the *Defender* as the *Chicago Surrender*, "World's Greatest Weakly." The piece read, "It was stated by more than one disgusted citizen that the whole thing was a direct slap in the face of the leading ministers who have spoken against the Amos 'n Andy program from their pulpits; the leading white daily papers of the country whose columns have carried sympathetic articles practically encouraging the Negroes of the country to drive Amos 'n Andy from the air."[29]

In October, Vann dealt with the topic of self-respect again, this time in a front-page article under his by-line:

"AMOS 'N ANDY" AND RACIAL SELF RESPECT

> When we started our protest against the Amos 'n Andy type of Negro, we did it solely in the interest of RACIAL SELF RESPECT.
>
> And, pray, what is meant by self respect? ... Do I think of myself in the same terms as I think of the people I admire? Am I as good as other people? Am I as important as other people? Am I part of the great CREATION we read about in the books men have written since RECORDED HISTORY BEGAN?
>
> If I think of myself in these terms, I have self respect, if, on the other hand, I allow myself to think of myself as being black, filthy, dirty of mind and body, ignorant and satisfied; if I allow other men to compare their own progress by pointing to my lack of it; if I allow myself to become the "national joke" for men, women and children of my community, state and nation—and have no desire to change this attitude, then I have absolutely NO SELF RESPECT. I am as good as I make other men admit I am. I must set the conception others have of me by what I do for myself, by what I think of myself. I have in my own group the estimation other men shall place upon me.
>
> My self respect is my very life. If I respect myself others MUST respect me. One follows the other as night the day.[30]

But the *Courier* missed its goal of a million signatures by nearly four-hundred thousand, and the issue died down after 1931.

The second topic Vann treated in his *Courier* in an effort to spark the advance of circulation was Marcus Garvey, whose adventures and misadventures had been much in the news since 1920. The *Courier*'s editorial attitudes had varied over the years, and Vann had even become personally involved in the case at one point.

While the hapless Garvey, head of the Universal Negro Improvement Association, was being heaped with vitriol in the early 1920s by nearly all of the black press and especially the *Chicago Defender* and *The Crisis*, which demanded that "Garvey Must Go," the *Courier* maintained an impartial attitude. There was a UNIA chapter in Pittsburgh, but it was far weaker than those in other major northern cities. When Garvey was indicted in 1923 for using the mails to defraud by selling stock in his ill-fated Black Star Steamship Line, most of the black press reported the fact with glee, including George Schuyler in his "Views and Reviews" column in the *Courier*. The *Courier* editorially said it would wait to see "whether we be friend or foe."[31]

Garvey was tried and convicted of mail fraud in the summer of 1923, and once the verdict was in, Vann wrote a long editorial to the effect that Garvey had brought it upon himself by serving as his own defense counsel during his trial. Vann quoted the old saying, "The man who acts as his own lawyer has a fool for a client," then went on:

> If Garvey conducted his business as he did his trial, there is little wonder that it failed.
> He showed all through the trial that he was simply consumed by his own importance. This native big-headedness spelled the ruin of his gigantic schemes. There was too much Garvey, with little or no respect for the opinions of others. He was the supreme head of all thought, every idea, and every suggestion. It was Garvey's scheme, Garvey's system of operation, Garvey's supreme domination of every phase of his program; it was Garvey's crime, Garvey's case, Garvey's counsel during the trial, and Garvey's conviction.
> Surely Mr. Garvey has no complaint that he and his scheme were embarrassed by the ideas or counsel of any outsider. It was all Garvey at the beginning; and the end has come with Garvey still at the undisputed head of the Garvey Spasm.[32]

From his vantage point as a well-trained criminal lawyer, Vann regarded Garvey's actions as sheer folly, as well as a slight to the legal profession. By the following month, Vann roundly condemned in the *Courier* the former UNIA head for "saying that the light and brown-skinned Negroes are opposed to black-skinned Negroes. If he said this, he ought to be called back to Court and given one hundred years to Atlanta Penitentiary."[33] Such a statement as Garvey allegedly made was utterly unacceptable to the light-skinned Vann; his public hackles were raised by the allegation that there were color castes within the race, though of course many doors had opened to Vann that would have remained closed were he as dark as Marcus Garvey.

When Garvey began serving his sentence in the federal penitentiary at Atlanta early in 1925, Vann and a prominent attorney from Washington, James Cobb, contacted Mrs. Garvey about the possibility of becoming her husband's counsel for a pardon appeal. They planned to charge a substantial fee—ten to fifteen thousand dollars—since Vann was sure they would "sweat [themselves] to death on this case."[34] Mrs. Garvey seemed agreeable to the idea and planned to discuss it with her husband.[35] But Mrs. Garvey never hired them. She said:

> Messrs. Vann and Cobb charged a fee of $15,000 regardless of results, because they thought the U.N.I.A. had that ready cash and was paying Marcus Garvey's expenses. But they were so wrong, I had to travel and speak in order to raise money and pay all his legal expenses and upkeep while in Atlanta Federal Prison. I lobbyed in Washington, D.C. with the assistance of our Congressman and was able to have a Committee see the Attorney General on the matter, and later on President Coolidge. We were instructed to have Marcus Garvey set out his own grounds for a pardon, which he did, and eventually he received the pardon without paying any one or two persons $15,000.[36]

While Garvey was still in prison, Vann got Mrs. Garvey to publish in serial form in the *Courier*, "Who Caused the Imprisonment of Garvey?" But she was not satisfied with the initial installments because some of her original text was deleted and eventually took it to another publication.[37]

Marcus Garvey was released from Atlanta Penitentiary by President Coolidge's executive pardon late in 1927. Because he had committed a felony and was not an American citizen, Garvey was immediately deported as an undesirable alien. Using Kingston, Jamaica, as his base for the next two years, he attempted unsuccessfully to rebuild his UNIA in England, France, and Canada, succeeding to any degree only in his native Jamaica. Since Garvey was unable to return to America and his New York headquarters, he could exercise no control there. He began to quarrel with the New York organization as to

The Courier Hits the Jackpot • 233

where the central location of the UNIA should be, made accusations against New York organization members ranging from mismanagement to dishonesty, and blamed them for his failure. These charges opened a schism between the New York UNIA and Garvey in 1929. Then Garvey again ran into difficulty with the law. While running for election to the Jamaican Legislative Council, he was charged with having made an intemperate campaign speech and cited for contempt for having insulted the integrity of the Jamaican court system. He was sentenced to three months in jail and fined one hundred pounds. Though he was elected while in jail, the prison term hurt his prestige in Jamaica, and Garvey lost a subsequent bid for reelection.[38]

Either from sympathy for Garvey's past misfortunes or knowledge that it would be a good story, Vann invited him in late 1929 to write a weekly serialized account in the *Courier* to set the record straight for both his enemies and friends about the "Garvey idea." Vann suggested the series include a history of the UNIA and a discussion of the philosophy of "Garveyism." Beset by troubles and seeing his power decline, Garvey had few avenues by which to make his ideas known, and he accepted with alacrity. "I do not propose to charge you anything for carrying this release," Vann wrote Garvey, now exiled to Jamaica, "nor do I propose to pay anything for it. I am doing it as a matter of convenience to you and of service to people who want to know, first hand, what Marcus Garvey is doing and what Marcus Garvey is thinking."[39] Garvey agreed to begin installments of his story in 1930 under the title "Negro World" without pay and exclusively for the *Courier*.[40] The paper announced its coup on page one: "GARVEY WRITING EXCLUSIVELY FOR 'AMERICA'S BEST WEEKLY.' "[41]

Garvey chose Vann's paper for several reasons. First, he needed to recapture some of his following in order to make a comeback, and the *Courier* seemed an ideal place to do this, for it had become one of the nation's leading black weeklies. And second, Garvey harbored no resentment against Robert Vann. Vann had chided him for the amateurish manner in which he conducted his own trial and about his statement on color castes, and George Schuyler had passed severe judgment on the UNIA head; but Vann's own attack was not malicious like those of Robert Abbott and W. E. B. DuBois. Garvey's series promised to be one of the *Courier*'s major features for the upcoming year.

The weekly articles began on February 15, 1930. Garvey gave a history of the UNIA and its achievements such as the Black Star Steamship Line, but he used the series mainly as a forum to defend his actions and denounce his enemies. These ranged from the "envy and jealousy" of scheming and unscrupulous black politicians from Harlem like Isaac B. Allen and Samuel Duncan, who Garvey felt attempted to turn his UNIA into a political club,[42] to various associates whom Garvey accused of having swindled him behind his back. His greatest foe of all, W. E. B. DuBois, he charged with hypocrisy and having tried to undermine his movement from the start in an article headlined "GARVEY TAKES RAP AT ATTITUDES OF DUBOIS."[43] Garvey wrote that his greatest difficulties came from "the invisible influences that were operating against me all over the world, caused through the secret propaganda of other Negroes against me in impressing prominent members of the white race and their governments that I was a bad man."[44] Claimed Garvey, "MY OWN RACE BETRAYED ME."[45]

In his final article, Garvey assured the nation's blacks that, despite his many betrayals, the "UNIA IS VERY MUCH ALIVE . . . MARCHING ON TOWARDS ITS GREAT IDEALS." He thanked the *Courier*

> for the opportunity you presented to me to somewhat explain the activities of the Universal Negro Improvement Association and its auxiliary corporations—an opportunity that heretofore was closed to me, because of prejudice. Whilst my enemies have had the right of way to abuse me, I never had the opportunity to reply. Even now, I understand that my enemies are trying to destroy me; but as you know truth cannot die, it shall never perish from the earth; and as you have given me the opportunity to explain the truth, I must thank you, believing with that great American Theodore Roosevelt: "No man is worth his salt who is not ready at all times to risk his body, to risk his well-being, to risk his life in a great cause."[46]

But by 1930, in the depths of the Depression, Garveyism was no longer of much interest to *Courier* readers, and no one raised any objection when the series came to an end.

The next issue the *Courier* attempted to publicize during the early 1930s was the Scottsboro case. Robert Vann and the *Courier* took a stand with regard to the defense in the case quite different from that of most black Americans, and this gained the newspaper a good deal of publicity, if not approval.

The incident known as the Scottsboro case occurred on March 25, 1931. That day some white itinerants "hopped" a freight at Chattanooga; there were already two white women aboard returning from "an overnight hobo escapade." Shortly after, at Stevenson, Alabama, a number of young blacks boarded the train. A fight broke out between the two groups, and seven of the whites were thrown off or jumped from the train. They notified the police and when the freight reached Paint Rock, officers were waiting to arrest the nine young blacks and the remaining three whites, two of them women. What had happened between Stevenson and Paint Rock is not known, but the nine blacks, aged thirteen to twenty, were charged with raping the white women. After a hasty trial, held in an atmosphere of pervasive hostility, the blacks were convicted. All but the youngest were sentenced to the electric chair on the shaky testimony of the two female witnesses, one of whom later repudiated her statements. Though the NAACP had assigned attorneys to defend the boys, suddenly the Communist-led International Labor Defense (ILD) entered the case and tried to wrest control from the NAACP.[47]

Then began the first of a long series of appeals to the higher courts. While the appeals were pending, the ILD sent its representatives to the parents of the condemned boys and persuaded them that the ILD rather than the NAACP should handle the case. This maneuver, perhaps more than any other act of the Communists, showed the disregard they had for moderate black organizations; it showed also the lengths to which the party was willing to go to gain publicity from trials of such obvious propaganda value.[48] To the Communists, Scottsboro was but a steppingstone to organizing the unemployed, recruiting black workers and sharecroppers, and building a massive communist organization among black Americans. The Communists appeared to be more interested in attacking the corrupt system which exploited the Scottsboro boys than in a defense of the nine blacks. The case was widely propagandized in the United States and throughout the world by the party.[49]

Walter White of the NAACP opposed the entrance of the ILD into the case because he knew he needed strong support from white moderate southerners if he was to get a retrial based on anything resembling justice. White believed that if the Communists enflamed the South by the use of propaganda it would only turn the region more against the Scottsboro boys. He thought the ILD did not have the interest of the boys at heart and that they had no real concern whether the boys were martyred or not.

The difficulty was that southern white moderates were also suspicious of the NAACP's motives. One white moderate, who spoke for many, said only white southern liberals should handle the case, because the NAACP and the ILD seemed "engaged in a joint battle to secure the exploiting possibilities of the case rather than to defend the boys themselves."[50] To make things more difficult for the NAACP, the organization's attacks on the ILD and the Communist party were also heavily criticized by the black community, none of whom were very anti-Communist. As *The Crisis* said:

> White had clearly misjudged the temper of the American Negro community. Even during the relatively prosperous twenties, there were few militant anti-Communists. And if America's black masses had not rallied to the red flag as the Communists hoped, they nevertheless remained immune from many of the anti-Communist ideas held by the majority of white Americans.... Frank Davis of the *Atlanta World* believed that the violent opposition by whites to Negro communists in the South might bring trouble to an already overburdened race, but Carl Murphy of the *Afro-American* in Baltimore insisted the Communists were "the only party going our way. They are as radical as the NAACP was twenty years ago." Since the abolitionists had disappeared after the Civil War "no white group of national prominence has openly advocated the economic, political and social equality of black folks."[51]

Robert Vann was one of the few prominent blacks to take a strong stand against the Communists and back the NAACP fully. He was the only vehemently anti-Communist black editor. Vann saw himself as more than an editor; as the owner of large quantities of *Courier* stock and a firm believer in the American economic dream, his self-image was of the successful businessman. As one who had achieved success within the American capitalist system, Vann viewed collectivism as a threat to his own position. His unswerving loyalty to the American system seems perplexing in light of the fact that Vann had been little aided by the vast white segment of the country. Both his legal practice and his newspaper operated solely within the black community; Vann's gains were all from his fellow blacks and owed little to the national system as a whole. Nonetheless he remained loyal to American capitalism and feared the alienation of whites by talk of communism among blacks, as he had clearly spelled out during his break with A. Philip Randolph over the Pullman Porter issue. Vann's sentiments were shared by a number of other anti-Communist blacks, although none were newspaper editors.[52]

More typically, black newspapermen's attitudes were like that of William (Kid) Kelley of Harlem's *Amsterdam News*. Why should the black man not look favorably on communism? asked Kelley. Capitalism had given him little or nothing. "Oppressed on every hand, denied equal educational facilities, Jim-Crowed on street cars and railroad trains . . . even lynched, it would seem that any program [of a group like the Communists] should readily find converts among American Negroes." How was it possible to "go to war with the Communist Party," agreed the *Chicago Defender*, when it was the one organization in white America that practiced complete political, economic, and social equality?[53] Even the cautious P. B. Young, Sr., of the *Norfolk Journal and Guide*, though somewhat pro-NAACP in the case, said that blacks should not view the Communists as a complete evil, but simply as another political group which could aid them in achieving greater economic benefits and legal equality.[54]

From April to October 1931, Vann gave the Scottsboro trial front-page coverage with a strong anti-Communist tint. One editorial treated what occurred when the ILD entered the case: "A little handful of Communists, seeking an opportunity to get cheap publicity, set about with a great hue and cry to give the impression that they were going to release the prisoners here and now." They did many things, "but none capable of doing the boys one iota of good."

> It is our opinion that if the boys convicted ever receive one iota of consideration at the hands of the Courts or at the hands of the Governor of Alabama, it will not be due to anything the Communists have done, want to do, or can do. It is more likely, however, that if mobs break out in Alabama and these eight boys are taken from the jail and lynched, it will probably be due to the nonsensical activities of the Communists, who by their misguided energies will drive the citizens of Alabama to the point of desperation.
>
> The Communists may get some publicity, but if they create a disturbance in Alabama, we shall, some day, ask, "What Price Publicity?"[55]

And in July the subject was again discussed in a front-page article:

The Communists have beclouded the issue to an extent that even intelligent Negroes know not which side to take. Yet, over a period of years, the NAACP has intelligently and consistently fought the legal battles of the race in the courts of the land with uniform success. Negroes should stand firm for the NAACP against the blandishments of the reds. We cannot afford to turn red at this stage of our development in America. Communism extends to us inviting prospects of complete equality but, despite the temptation, we cannot wisely accept. Receiving our sustenance as we do from the hands of the dominant race, it would be folly to anger the hand that bestoweth. The time is far from ripe when we can safely go red—in the meantime, the NAACP, with its conservative program, is our safeguard.[56]

And again in September, the *Courier* warned, "we are more anxious to see the Scottsboro boys escape the electric chair than we are to see them made a sacrifice on the altar of 'revolutionary fanaticism.'"[57]

Vann's readers were mostly critical of the *Courier*'s viewpoint on the Scottsboro case. Many professed to be nonradicals, but disagreed with the paper's stand. "Surely the ILD can't possibly make things any worse than they are," said a young woman from Pittsburgh. "Perhaps there are people who would contribute to one organization and not to the other." A New Yorker praised the activities of the ILD and professed amazement at the NAACP's refusal to associate with the Communists because of their radicalism. "The organization was not so squeamish in having Clarence Darrow, an avowed radical and disbeliever, handle the Sweet case. Why this [sudden] ultra-respectability?"[58]

The *Courier*'s anti-Communist bias was given extra impetus by George Schuyler, Vann's chief editorial writer, who wrote some of the most biting editorials. As he expressed it to a colleague, "I disagree with the so-called Reds in dealing with the Negro and also with the advice they give him. I claim that they make the Negro problem worse instead of better by their insane tactics. They give the murderous Southern Neanderthals the very opportunity and excuse they are looking for to commit additional homicide."[59]

The Scottsboro case never concluded definitively. In the course of numerous appeals and retrials carried on for four years under the auspices of the ILD, the case went twice to the United States

Supreme Court, which ruled in 1932 that due process had been denied by the failure to provide adequate counsel and in 1935 that equal protection of the law had been denied by the systematic exclusion of blacks from Alabama juries. In 1935 direction of the Scottsboro defense passed from the ILD to a coalition committee chaired by Dr. Allen Knight Chalmers of New York. Assisted by an Alabama committee, from 1935 to 1950 this group worked slowly but tenaciously and gradually secured the release of eight of the Scottsboro boys from prison. The ninth escaped in 1948.[60]

After its involvement in the Scottsboro case, the NAACP found its Legal Defense Fund badly depleted, and in 1934 the *Courier* decided to begin a legal defense fund of its own. It started as a self-respect idea and became allied with the NAACP Legal Defense Fund only in the second month. In March 1934 the *Courier* tried to arouse interest in a "Self Respect" program, asking its readers, "Are You Willing to Pay $1.00 to Maintain Your Self-Respect?" It continued, "There should be one million law-abiding, red-blooded, race-loving, self-respecting men and women of the 14,000,000 Negroes in this country willing to put up one dollar for racial defense, and it is defense."[61] The *Courier*'s reasoning was that money for legal redress would give the race self-respect. The black weekly began printing regularly an "I'LL PAY FOR SELF-RESPECT" coupon which was easy for a reader to clip and send with a dollar to the *Courier*. Soon the newspaper reported enthusiastically that a thousand letters had come from 33 states and 378 cities and towns, each enclosing a dollar.[62] The *Courier* headlined, "COURIER NAT'L DEFENSE SELF-RESPECT CRUSADE IS SWEEPING NATION,"[63] and by the end of March had received close to four thousand replies.[64]

Having made what seemed a propitious start, in April the paper proposed to the NAACP that it help the organization raise $1 million for its Legal Defense Fund. The association's board of directors was wary because of the conflicts it had had with the *Courier* over the Garland Fund and the Legal Defense Fund. Also the NAACP and the *Courier* were having a contretemps of another sort that same month. As a result of problems between Walter White, executive secretary of the NAACP, and W. E. B. DuBois, editor of the NAACP publication, *The Crisis*, White and Roy Wilkins, then assistant secretary of the organization, decided to circumvent DuBois and *The Crisis* altogether and approached Robert Vann about having the *Pittsburgh Courier* publish the NAACP's official branch news. Vann agreed, and Wilkins and White began releasing news directly to the *Courier* in an attempt to divert public interest from *The Crisis* and to undermine DuBois. They were angry because DuBois refused to publish branch news in *The Crisis* and told Wilkins "he had never believed in carrying small items from the branches," and turned to the *Courier* because, in Wilkins's opinion, "it is the only so-called national newspaper we have," with a "circulation of between 50,000 and 65,000 weekly" that reached far beyond the "13,000 circulation monthly" of *The Crisis*.[65] This effort came to an abrupt halt when Joel and Arthur Spingarn, the white philanthropists on the NAACP board of directors, discovered what was going on. Arthur Spingarn, remembering the NAACP's battles with Vann in 1926, was very much opposed to the *Courier*'s publication of the association's news because he considered Vann untrustworthy. Spingarn had the board pass a resolution requiring that all NAACP news be submitted to *The Crisis* before its release to other newspapers, so the *Courier*'s brief official journalistic alliance with the NAACP was hastily ended.[66]

Nonetheless, the NAACP board of directors agreed to Vann's offer to assist with the Legal Defense Fund, though it carefully stipulated how the campaign was to be conducted.[67] The paper was to announce that the drive was the *Pittsburgh Courier* Fund and then turn over to the NAACP at least once a month as collected the gross proceeds of the campaign, less expenses not to exceed 25 percent of the amount collected. The NAACP also asked that other leading newspapers simultaneously start similar campaigns, each of which would be known as the fund of the newspaper sponsoring the campaign. "The Board of Directors recommends that all of these newspapers place such safeguards in the collection of these funds as will assure the public that the moneys received shall reach the Defense Fund of the N.A.A.C.P.; and it suggests that an independent audit be made and published by the newspapers at regular intervals."[68] Also each newspaper was to publish weekly the names of contributors.

The *Courier* undertook this expanded project with a certain gusto. The city editor wrote to Walter White, "We're preparing to 'shoot' both barrels in this National Defense Fund Campaign of ours." He told of benefits which would be staged in the largest theaters available, athletic events, including the best black baseball teams of twelve cities, mammoth Defense Fund meetings, speakers, and then a National Defense Fund Ball "all over the country on ONE NIGHT."[69]

The *Courier* gave the Fund constant front-page coverage in April and May, with headlines like "COURIER LAUNCHES DEFENSE FUND DRIVE

The COURIER Hits the Jackpot • 241

AS PRISONER IS SLAIN IN TEXAS COURT," "ENTIRE NATION TO AID IN DEFENSE FUND CAMPAIGN: PROMINENT MEN AND WOMEN WILL HEAD DIVISIONS," "DEFENSE FUND CAMPAIGN SWINGS ALONG: NEW YORK AND CHICAGO POINT WAY," and, on the church pages, "MINISTERS ARE URGED TO AID *Courier*'s NATION-WIDE DRIVE FOR RACIAL SELF-RESPECT."[70] There were of course editorials on the topic of "SELF-RESPECT":

> In launching its gigantic self-respect campaign, the *Pittsburgh Courier* has embarked upon an unprecedented cooperative venture, such as colored America has never before seen.
> It is a drive in which every Negro with red blood coursing through his veins can participate, and should participate. It is an opportunity to once and for all build up an adequate defense fund to protect our rights and privileges as human beings and American citizens.[71]

However, most black weeklies did not respond as avidly as did the Pittsburgh paper. Some newspapers, such as the *Atlanta Daily World* and the *Philadelphia Tribune*, told the NAACP they could not sponsor such a drive at this time,[72] while others, such as the *Norfolk Journal and Guide*, said that since the idea originated with the *Courier*, that paper should see it through alone.[73] Aware of this, Vann told Walter White worriedly, since the *Courier* "seems to be about the only newspaper that has decided to go into this drive and that within itself serves notice on us here that the rest of the newspapers will stand on the sidelines ready to criticize the least little thing that looks shady or questionable ... we have to be very careful about our reports to you and our reports to the public."[74]

The first gala benefit was planned for the end of May. It was a midnight gathering at the Apollo Theater on 125th Street in Harlem. Stepin Fetchit came from Hollywood just to entertain at the affair, and other notables included Ethel Waters, Bill "Bojangles" Robinson, Cab Calloway, W. C. Handy, and Jimmie Lunceford. The *Courier* reported it as a "smash": "CROWDS JAM APOLLO THEATER BENEFIT, *Police Called To Quell Rush: Theater Packed*."[75] Walter White sent effusive thanks:

> "*PITTSBURGH COURIER* BENEFIT AT APOLLO THEATRE SATURDAY NIGHT FOR NAACP DEFENSE FUND ONE OF THE MOST SUCCESSFUL I HAVE EVER SEEN IN NEW YORK STOP

EVERYBODY HAD A GRAND TIME FOR SELDOM HAVE SO MANY DISTINGUISHED STAGE AND SCREEN STARS APPEARED ON ANY BILL STOP OUR PROFOUND CONGRATULATIONS AND APPRECIATION FOR THIS MOST SUCCESSFUL AND AUSPICIOUS OPENING OF THE CAMPAIGN.[76]

After the success of May 26, plans were made for similar benefits in Philadelphia, Pittsburgh, Cleveland, Columbus, Cincinnati, Detroit, Indianapolis, St. Louis, and Chicago.[77] Ethel Waters and Bill "Bojangles" Robinson were scheduled to appear at Pittsburgh's Nixon Theater on June 17, heading "CITY'S BIGGEST CONCERT SHOW."[78] But soon the bubble burst, and disappointment replaced optimism. The St. Louis and Detroit benefits were dismal financial failures, partly because of little advance advertising and poor attendance and also, according to Ira Lewis, because local managers had not allowed the *Courier* staff to go to the cities and personally manage the shows. In Detroit he attributed the failure to "several elements of chiseling and enmity."[79] And Vann charged that the "so-called artists" who had agreed initially to perform free later asked the *Courier* fund for compensation.[80] This happened when Ethel Waters came to Pittsburgh. Daisy Lampkin, regional field secretary of the NAACP, reported to Walter White that Vann had told her, "There isn't a chance of getting Ethel Waters to return any money. She held up the Pittsburgh performance after she saw the crowd, and demanded more that [sic] she had agreed to accept."[81]

What had begun in such a promising manner soon ended in failure, with all the benefits raising just $1,089 for the NAACP, $827.37 of which came from the New York show alone.[82] In Chicago, where it had been hoped that between $1,500 and $2,000 would be earned, a paltry $329 was brought in.

And matters worsened, for as Vann predicted earlier, the *Courier* Fund came under criticism. A controversy arose over the auditing of expenses of the various benefits; there was some question about whether members of the *Courier* staff had padded their expense accounts. Since the fund was specifically the *Courier*'s, complaints sent to NAACP headquarters were all forwarded to Vann. One of the most vocal critics, William H. Davis, president of the New York *Amsterdam News*, complained to Joel Spingarn that neither the NAACP nor the *Courier* had as yet issued any reports on the money taken in or the expenditures to date.[83] Spingarn sent a telegram about the complaint to Vann, who replied hastily that the full reports would be published in the next *Courier* edition.[84] Finally the *Courier* editor decided that because of the controversy over reporting expenses and the internal squabbles, the various benefits would be discontinued; only the Self-Respect Fund would remain.[85]

After the benefits ceased, it was not long before the Self-Respect drive was called off as well. Joel Spingarn wrote Vann that, because of various pressures being applied to the NAACP, it would be best to end the Self-Respect Fund.[86] It had fared poorly: by mid-July only $500 had been collected via the coupons published in the *Courier*. In an editorial headlined "IS IT THE WHITE MAN'S JOB?" the *Courier* remarked dejectedly that in this one effort in which blacks could help themselves they were failing. "Winning the Negro's Freedom is primarily a Negro job. It is not a white folks' job.... [Aren't] you willing to give a dollar for YOUR Self-Respect?"[87] Walter White commented that "this [failure] is not an indictment of our respective organizations so much as it is of the apathy, whatever the reasons for it, on the part of the colored people in fighting for their rights."[88] Vann agreed that "the *Courier* was just a little bit in advance in expecting Negroes to have self-respect.... Walter, we took our chance and have nothing to regret."[89] In fairness to Vann, he certainly must have been exasperated, witnessing still another attempt at racial uplift fail because of black apathy. However, in his severe criticism, Vann, the rags-to-riches success, blocked out the fact that those less fortunate than himself, struggling against a devastating depression, simply could not afford the one-dollar donation to build self-respect.

The various campaigns Vann had conducted in the *Courier* attracted only moderate attention from blacks outside Pittsburgh. But just about the time Robert Vann was packing up his belongings at the Department of Justice, two different and highly significant chains of events were getting underway. Both were inherently of vital interest to nearly every black, and over the next two years Robert Vann used his *Courier* to treat both subjects with such skill and thoroughness that they captured the imagination of all black America. As a result, the newspaper's circulation skyrocketed, and the *Courier* became the country's number-one black weekly.

The two topics which aroused blacks unlike almost anything that had happened since World War I were the invasion of Ethiopia by Italy and the rise of Joe Louis, boxing's Brown Bomber. The two had much in common in the eyes of black Americans. Both represented the black man's fight for survival and self-respect against seemingly insuperable odds, and both were sources of pride for the black man in a dreary, depressed time. The great contribution of the *Courier* was to cover these events better than any other black publication, in a manner noteworthy for the immediacy of its reportage and the quality of its writing.

Italy invaded an apparently helpless Ethiopia in October 1935. The crisis had been predated by conflicts going back to 1890, when Italy became a neighbor of Ethiopia by consolidating the colony of Eritrea. At that time the fierce Melenik was emperor of Ethiopia, and by 1895 the two nations had gone to battle. Ethiopia emerged the victor, and Melenik's reign was thus secured. Haile Selassie, grandson of Melenik, aroused international attention soon after his coronation as emperor in 1930, mostly by his attempts to modernize Ethiopia. But Selassie's rule also reawakened the old hostilities with Italy, and by 1932 it was already evident that armed conflict provoked by Mussolini would soon occur.[90]

By early 1934, the *Courier* began to cover the impending crisis regularly. Vann's newspaper claimed that Mussolini would not rest until he had conquered Ethiopia. The *Courier* published weekly reports on Italy's preparation for the coming war and urgently pleaded for intervention by either the League of Nations or leading neutral nations such as England, the United States, Russia, or Japan. But by July 1935 the *Courier* realized Ethiopia's desperate pleas for help to the League of Nations would go unanswered. "All the civilized nations drew the curtain and Haile Selassie stands alone."[91] Invasion seemed imminent.

Vann's *Courier* began to rally America's blacks to the Ethiopian cause. The paper published two pages of letters to the editor from blacks all over the country who wanted to know how they could contribute money or where they might sign up to fight for Ethiopia. A few offered strategic suggestions on how Ethiopia might defeat Italy. Two hundred young men in Harlem who dubbed themselves "The Harlem Navy" wanted to charter a ship and go to Ethiopia to join the fray. Some blacks crossed into Canada to volunteer for the coming war. Boycotts of Italian products and stores began from Harlem to Birmingham, Alabama. Some blacks wrote to the *Courier* to say that if white Europe went to war with Germany and Italy and the United States offered to help, they would refuse to fight. The *Courier* reported church sermons that expressed concern for the fate of the Ethiopian brothers, and many black churches petitioned the pope to mediate before a war started.[92]

The COURIER Hits the Jackpot • 245

The *Courier* began to act on its own initiative. Vann wired Haile Selassie, "MANY UNITED STATES VOLUNTEERS, WHAT IS ETHIOPIA'S ATTITUDE?" The emperor replied, "Let us know your conditions, we will accept with pleasure."[93] Not under the *Courier*'s auspices, but with the paper's tacit encouragement, enlistment centers sprang up in Pittsburgh, New York, and twenty other American cities. However, recruitment was nipped in the bud when Secretary of State Cordell Hull declared that under United States law, American citizens could not fight against a country which was officially at peace with our nation.[94]

So involved did the *Courier* become in the issue during the summer before Italy actually invaded Ethiopia that Robert Vann soon found himself in an untenable position. The *Courier* attacked the Roosevelt administration for allowing southerners to sell mules and horses to the Italians when there was supposed to be a ban on all sales of war material to both Italy and Ethiopia as a result of the 1935-36 Neutrality Acts;[95] yet Vann was still officially a member of Roosevelt's administration and, implicitly, a supporter of Roosevelt's policies. His own newspaper was embarrassing him. Presumably Vann had some strong words with the *Courier* staff in Pittsburgh after that editorial appeared, for by the following week the newspaper had moderated its position and advised editorially that, in place of a military recruitment program, money should be raised for Haile Selassie.[96] Vann himself later made the trip to the Ethiopian Consulate in New York to donate $400 the *Courier* had raised for medical supplies.[97]

Italy invaded Ethiopia on October 26, 1935. Within less than a month, Vann had made a shrewd journalistic move and capitalized on the growing interest in the battle. The *Courier* portrayed the conflict as a conspiracy on the part of the major European powers to advance their own interests at the expense of Ethiopia and the black man. White imperialism was seen by the *Courier* as the real enemy for presenting a united front against black people.[98]

The topic of Ethiopia appealed intrinsically to American blacks. For many blacks, the name Ethiopia or Abyssinia (one of Haile Selassie's titles was "Lion of Abyssinia") implied a proud and dignified Africanism. As a consequence, "Abyssinian" was used as a descriptive adjective for many black associations and churches; the name was borne by the largest black church in New York City. And in 1932 the name "Ethiopian" was given to a racial movement in Chicago that had inherited Marcus Garvey's "Back to Africa" slogans.[99] The official anthem of Marcus Garvey's UNIA was "Ethiopia, Thou Land of Our Fathers." On a number of occasions Garvey used Ethiopia rhetorically as a synonym for the whole African continent. Black interest in Ethiopia dated from the end of the nineteenth century, when, confronted by a hardening of white racism, some blacks seized upon the idea that their ancestry could be traced to the once-glorious Ethiopian kingdom. This theory had great appeal for a downtrodden people forcibly separated from their cultural heritage.[100]

Robert Vann decided to profit from this interest. Because he had always considered on-the-spot coverage the only means to ensure accuracy and completeness, Vann sent J. A. Rogers to the front to cover the Ethiopian war exclusively for the *Courier*. Rogers was an experienced newspaperman who had spent a good deal of time in Africa in recent years and had reported on the coronation of Haile Selassie.[101] He turned out to be the only war correspondent in Ethiopia sent by a black weekly; other black papers were getting their news secondhand. Vann's decision to send Rogers was unusual for a black publisher of the period. Exclusive foreign reportage was costly, and most black newspapers simply did not have the funds for such ventures. But Vann obviously sensed that in this case his investment would be repaid with interest. Rogers's reporting from Ethiopia was all-inclusive, covering in addition to war news everything from the history and customs of the country to the empress's family life and wardrobe. The *Courier* held back the initial stories from Ethiopia for two weeks before publication so that the weekly could publicize them and so that readers thus would be anxiously awaiting the news. The move was a good one; when the Ethiopia coverage hit the newsstands, circulation rose by approximately twenty-five thousand.

Rogers saved his most dramatic writing for the news from the front. He portrayed the Ethiopian warriors, underequipped and outnumbered, as fighting heroically. "Bravely advancing into the barrels of the Italians' death-dealing machine guns, the fierce Danakilla tribesmen courageously charged upon the Italian advance parties. Undaunted by the withering spray of deadly gunfire which mowed down scores, these border warriors of a nation proud of her independence attacked again and again."[102] Haile Selassie was shown as the leader who fearlessly manned the guns instead of seeking shelter when the Italians dropped their bombs.[103] And Rogers sent pictures of Selassie proudly astride his white horse with an accompanying description of the emperor as "Ethiopia's triumphant God, hurling his thunderbolts from sky-tipped mountain peaks."[104]

The COURIER Hits the Jackpot • 247

It was not what one might call objective reporting. Rogers depicted the Italians melodramatically as cruel brutes—rapists, murderers, and mindless users of poison gas. He wrote from Djibouti, "Italians are having a 'Roman holiday' and the victims of their sex lust are black women."[105]

The primary beneficiary—after the emperor—of Rogers's biased and colorful reportage was Colonel William T. Robinson, an American black and Tuskegee graduate who commanded the Ethiopian Air Force—all five airplanes. Robinson had flown Rogers into Addis Ababa, and perhaps out of gratitude for having arrived safely in the rather rudimentary aircraft, Rogers thereafter described Robinson in his weekly dispatches as a daredevil flying ace, the "Brown Condor of Ethiopia." Rogers gave the pilot constant headline coverage for his heroic feats. "COLONEL ROBINSON STAGED AIR DUEL IN CLOUDS," trumpeted one report. "Seeing an [Italian] bomber [Robinson] attacked it with his machine guns spitting bullets. He was in a position for the 'kill' . . . when the distressed Italian plane was rescued by other ships. Robinson, with his motors roaring escaped into the vain [sic] cloud."[106] When Rogers was not praising Robinson's heroism, he was describing his nonchalance: "Robinson drinks water from plane engine as he returns from the battle front," read one picture caption.[107]

The high point of the Ethiopian coverage came on March 7, 1936, when the *Courier* presented an exclusive interview with the emperor by J. A. Rogers. Rogers was the first newsman to be granted such an interview. He cabled excitedly back from "somewhere in Ethiopia," "I have met the Emperor and I am his." A good part of Haile Selassie's comments were devoted to praise for the aid and friendship American blacks had offered his country. "The devotion of the Afro-Americans to our cause has touched me and my people profoundly," the emperor said. "In the New Ethiopia the colored Americans will find their place."[108] The *Courier* touted the interview as the greatest message since the Emancipation Proclamation,[109] and though the interview did not live up to that grand statement, it was of great interest to American blacks. The circulation of the *Courier* shot up by twenty-five thousand for the single issue that carried the interview.[110]

After the Italians took Addis Ababa on May 5, 1936, and Haile Selassie had fled to England, the *Courier*'s coverage of Ethiopia became less extensive. But by this time J. A. Rogers had become a celebrity in his own right and for a period Vann's newspaper covered the comings and goings of its star reporter. Rogers visited Geneva, gave a speech in London in front of the Lord Mayor's Mansion House, was welcomed in New York by emissaries from the white press, and delivered radio broadcasts. From then on Rogers was much in demand as a traveling lecturer on the subject of Ethiopia.[111]

The Ethiopians had been defeated, but the racial pride generated by the *Courier*'s impassioned coverage of the events in Ethiopia far overshadowed the defeat in the minds of American blacks. Their fellow blacks had lost, but they had fought bravely and proudly, and honor and pride were vindicated. Vann personally, and the *Courier* editorially, viewed the invasion as having revealed the terrible hypocrisy of white Christians, and especially the pope, who "sat idly and watched a Catholic army go into Ethiopia and destroy those people with bombs, bullets and gas, all in the name of Christianity."[112]

Haile Selassie was grateful to the *Courier* for its reporting efforts in behalf of his people. In Bath, England, he presented a member of the *Courier* staff, P. L. Prattis, with a gold ring for Robert Vann in appreciation of what he had done for Ethiopia through his newspaper.[113]

Vann tried to keep his readers' interest in Ethiopia alive. In the summer of 1936, while covering the Olympics in Germany, Vann went to Paris to meet R. W. Merguson, a black American newspaperman who lived there. Vann hired Merguson to do a series of stories on the aftermath of the war in Ethiopia. On September 1, Merguson left for Ethiopia via the "ride of Death," which was what the dangerous plane journey into the country was called by that time. Merguson stayed in Africa for more than a year reporting for Vann, and his dispatches were often featured in the *Courier*.[114] His coverage proved anticlimactic, however; reader interest in Ethiopia was beginning to wane. But Merguson provided first-hand international reportage from Europe for the *Courier* until well into World War II.[115]

Vann's second great journalistic coup of the period was his paper's extensive coverage of a promising young prize fighter from Detroit. The *Courier* "discovered" Joe Louis late in 1934, and as he soared into national prominence over the next few years the *Courier* sports staff recorded his every left jab, right hook, and quotable comment and all but slept in his dressing room. The *Courier* readers devoured every word and asked for more.

Vann, an avid sports fan himself, knew what his readers wanted. Pittsburghers had long been zealous sports enthusiasts. Prior to the advent of Joe Louis, the *Courier*'s most extensive sports coverage was of Pittsburgh's black baseball teams. Pittsburgh's blacks had been relegated by an unwritten rule to all-black teams since 1898;[116] the teams played in inferior facilities, but some of them became legendary. The Homestead Grays, for example, were the offspring of the Blue Ribbon nine which had been organized about 1900 by black steelworkers in Homestead, a grimy industrial town southeast of Pittsburgh. Cum Posey (who later wrote "The Sportive Realm" column in the *Courier*), a former college basketball player, joined the team in 1911 as an outfielder and became the manager in 1916. Within the next decade, the Homestead Grays, as they had been called since 1912, became a top-ranking team in eastern black baseball. The team remained independent of leagues until 1929, when it joined the American Negro League, followed three years later by membership in the East-West League organized by Posey. The Grays ended up in the second Negro National League, where they were the dominant team for many years.[117]

The Pittsburgh Crawfords, a semiprofessional team, were taken over in 1931 by W. A. "Gus" Greenlee, a tavern owner and numbers king in the Hill District, who in 1935 also owned John Henry Lewis, light heavyweight boxing champion of the world. Greenlee had a great deal of money to spend and soon assembled a team that included many of the greatest black baseball players: pitcher Satchel Paige, catcher Josh Gibson, Oscar Charleston, Judy Johnson, Ted Page, and Cool Papa Bell. In 1932, Greenlee built his team a $75,000 stadium on Bedford Avenue in the Hill District, a particular point of pride for Pittsburgh blacks, since almost no other black team had its own ball park. The stadium seated seven thousand for baseball and ten thousand for prize fights; it also became the home field of the Crawfords' archrivals, the Homestead Grays. In that 1932 season, with Satchel Paige pitching his famous blinding fast balls, the Crawfords rolled up a 99–36 record. The Crawfords were so strong that in a postseason series with a team of all-star major leaguers headed by the Chicago Cubs' Hack Wilson, they won five out of seven games.

Catcher Josh Gibson was probably the preeminent power-hitter in baseball history, eclipsing even Babe Ruth. No records were kept for blacks, but Gibson probably surpassed Ruth's record of 714 home runs, and in 1934 Gibson hit a ball over the third tier of Yankee Stadium—the only fair ball in history hit out of the Stadium. Cool Papa Bell was an outfielder so fast that it was said he could flip the light switch and jump into bed before the light went out. Oscar Charleston, the Crawfords' first baseman, had been an outfielder in his younger days with whom, in the judgment of those who remember, Willie Mays suffers by comparison.[118] And the great Satchel Paige, the Crawfords' main drawing card, pitched a 31–4 season in 1934 and then went on to be the winning pitcher in that year's East-West black all-star game.

The East-West game was the most important of all black sports

Vann relaxing at the Schenley Park sandlot, 1936.

events, for it brought together all of the greatest black baseball players, many of whom were better than their white counterparts in the major leagues. Pittsburgh numbers king Gus Greenlee arranged the first East-West match, which was held in 1933 in Chicago's Comiskey Park. The match was undoubtedly engendered by racial competitive spirit, for that same year saw the start of the white American-National League All-Star games, also held in Chicago, at Wrigley Field. Denied entry into white baseball, the blacks created their own sports spectaculars which were equivalent to those of the whites. Players for the East-West teams were selected by popular vote, with the ballots having been printed in the *Courier* and the *Chicago Defender* for readers to clip out, fill in with their choices, and mail in. As a result, the lineups were heavily loaded with players from Pittsburgh and Chicago.[119] Running tabulations of the vote were printed weekly in the *Courier*, which billed the all-star contest as the " 'game of games,' which should go down in diamond history as the greatest achievement ever recorded."[120] The first "Big Chi Dream Game" on September 10 drew between fifteen and twenty thousand baseball fans to Chicago, many of them from Pittsburgh. The game was a huge success, as both a sporting event and a social gala. "WEST TRIUMPHS OVER EAST IN 17–7 THRILLER," roared the *Courier*.[121]

The following year it was all Satchel Paige's game as he pitched the East to a 1–0 victory over the West before a crowd of twenty-five thousand. The audience included many celebrities, city and state officials, countless well-dressed pretty girls, and hordes of reporters. The evening included a musical pageant out on the field, "O Sing a New Song," which depicted the black man's history in America. As *Courier* city editor William Nunn saw it, the pageant "unfolded in a blaze of simple glory . . . as we walked away from the field tonight, we felt that we had been taught an all-important lesson in race pride."[122] During those years Robert Vann's newspaper covered every move the Pittsburgh Crawfords and Homestead Grays made, for the city's blacks were extremely proud of their baseball teams.

When Joe Louis was introduced to two of Vann's best sports writers, William Nunn, Sr., and Ches Washington, late in 1934, there was a temporary lull in newsworthy baseball happenings, and "Louis became 'it' " for the *Courier*.[123] On the basis of Louis's impressive amateur record, Vann's paper began to tout him as a possible heavyweight contender. Then in the first February issue of 1935, the *Courier* began a series written by Ches Washington on the life story of Joe Louis

Barrow. He came from origins with which many *Courier* readers could identify. The Brown Bomber had been born into an impoverished sharecropper family in Alabama. After his father abandoned the family, the farm work was too much for Louis's mother, so she finally took him and her eight other children to Detroit, where they subsisted on relief. When Joe was seventeen he went to work on a Ford assembly line and began to spend all his spare time boxing in a local gymnasium. In 1933, Louis went to Boston to fight for the National AAU lightheavyweight championship. He lost the fight but aroused the interest of John Roxborough, a Detroit lawyer and member of the Urban League who seems also to have had underworld connections. Roxborough took over Louis's management, found a financial supporter in Julian Black, and a competent trainer, Jack Blackburn. The next year the twenty-year-old Louis turned professional and soon had won twelve straight bouts; his earnings increased from $59 a fight to $2,750, a considerable sum for the former welfare recipient. His mother, a proud woman, used part of Joe's winnings to pay back the welfare board for the assistance the family had received.[124]

As Louis's talent led to win after win, the public became increasingly engrossed in his career. Vann and Julian Black were friends, and Black asked Vann if he had a fast typist for secretarial work at Joe Louis's training camp in Pompton Lake, New Jersey. Vann sent Chester Washington, an expert in shorthand, and he quickly became Joe's secretary, answering Louis's seventy-five to one hundred letters a day.[125] Ches was Joe's confidant as well as his secretary, and he was soon doing Louis's biography for the *Courier*. The *Courier* had a virtual monopoly on all the Joe Louis stories. When the NAACP asked Roy Wilkins to do a story on Louis for *The Crisis*, for example, Wilkins responded, "There is nothing left for *The Crisis* to say. The *Pittsburgh Courier* . . . has been running for the past five weeks a serial story of the life history of Joe Louis. . . . As far as I can see, the ground has been covered thoroughly."[126] Soon the *Courier* was calling itself the "Joe Louis paper,"[127] and Ches Washington was touting Louis as the next heavyweight champion of the world. Robert Vann, ever the enthusiastic fight fan, was intensely interested in Louis's career. He assigned all his best sportswriters and an ace photographer to keep Louis closely covered and began to be active personally. Vann went to nearly every Louis fight along with members of his staff. Vann and Ira Lewis usually went by train, because Vann disliked air travel; the others went by plane. So the news could get into the

The COURIER Hits the Jackpot • 253

Courier as quickly as possible, Vann held up the press on Friday night, which was generally fight night. Immediately after the match ended, Vann would send a reporter, usually William Nunn, Sr., back to Pittsburgh by plane with pictures and the story. The reporter would arrive at 2:00 or 3:00 A.M. and get the story onto the presses by 4:30. At 6:00 A.M. the *Courier* issue was ready for the newsstands. Often a large crowd of boxing fans would be milling around the *Courier* plant in the early dawn waiting to grab a paper as it came off the press.[128]

When Louis knocked out ex-heavyweight champion Primo Carnera of Italy in June 1935 in just six rounds, the *Courier* gave the Brown Bomber the biggest headline of the year and devoted nearly the entire issue to stories of Louis's triumph; even Ethiopia was preempted from its front-page position. However, in the light of the Italian-Ethiopian conflict, the fact that a black had beaten an Italian made Louis's victory especially sweet. There was a report from Harlem on how that quarter had reacted to the win with delirious joy and outright pandemonium:

> Harlem had its biggest moment since it became the capital of the Negro world when Joe Louis whipped Primo Carnera Tuesday. Harlem is hilarious with joy. The huge and colorful crowds, reminiscent of Marcus Garvey's best days, caused old-timers to scratch their heads and marvel at the interest aroused through the upward climb and victory of this stolid but handsome youth ... Depression and hard times were forgotten and for once the "good old days" seemed to have turned the corner at last. Seventh and Lenox Avenues and the crosstown streets from 125th to 145th Streets were thronged with gay crowds in carnival spirit. Luxurious motor cars bearing license plates from ... points far and near swept down Seventh Avenue in a triumphant procession, while rousing cheers rent the air. In the many taprooms on the avenue glasses clinked merrily as toasts were offered to the gallant new Prince of Fistiana. ... Their attitude seemed to say, "Everything is hotsy-totsy and the goose is hanging high."[129]

Another *Courier* reporter, William Nunn, Sr., wrote of Louis as "the answer to our prayers, the prayers of a race of people who are struggling to break through dense clouds of prejudice and ... misunderstanding, a race of people who, though bowed by oppression, will never be broken in spirit."[130] Because of the Italian-Ethiopian difficulties, some journalists—for example, Westbrook Pegler—had predicted a riot between the Italians and blacks attending the fight at Yankee Stadium which fortunately never took place. As the *Courier* quoted Damon Runyon, "There is not a ripple of disorder; the whites applaud the amazing performance of the colored boy even more than the blacks."[131] And Ches Washington wrote that the fight was a strike against race prejudice, showing economics were stronger than the color line.[132]

Louis followed up his knockout of Carnera with quick victories over Kingfish Lavinsky in Chicago, and Max Baer in New York. After beating Charlie Retzlaff in January 1936, Louis signed on for the biggest fight yet, against ex-champion Max Schmeling in New York on June 18. By now Louis was the favorite black hero, and the *Courier* reported his every action outside the arena as well as in. One could hardly open the paper without finding some mention of the Brown Bomber. The *Courier* carefully detailed his every appearance at race-uplift rallies and other benefits, which ranged from a gathering in 1935 for A. Philip Randolph's Brotherhood of Sleeping Car Porters to a May 1936 interracial benefit dinner for the disaster-stricken Pittsburgh region after the St. Patrick's Day flood.[133]

Inside the ring, Louis seemed invincible. Since turning professional he had won twenty-seven straight fights. His last four bouts had grossed him close to a million dollars. The black community expected Louis would beat Schmeling handily and then go into a title match with Jimmy Braddock, the reigning champion. Victory over Schmeling would do more than give Louis a shot at the title; it would signify a triumph over a German who represented the oppressive Nazi philosophy of white Aryanism. But on June 18 Schmeling knocked out Louis in the eleventh round.

The black communities of the nation went into mourning. In Pittsburgh's Hill District, Chicago's South Side, Harlem, and Detroit's St. Antoine Street, all was somber and quiet after the fight. As William Nunn, Sr., said, "You could have thrown a stone from 155th Street to Central Park and not hit a soul, Harlem was that quiet."[134] Some blacks cried fraud and said that Louis may have been doped by villains unknown. But Nunn saw it another way, in an article that subsequently received nationwide circulation:

> I confess that I'm still groggy, Joe, but I do want so hard to try and be fair. I know that my people—and

The COURIER Hits the Jackpot • 255

a lot of 'em can't take it—are going to be searching both heaven and hades for an alibi. I know what they're going to say. They're going to talk about dope—about a fix—about "wise money"—about this and about that. But you know, Joe—and so do I—that you were beaten by a man who was your mental superior within that hempen arena tonight. Tonight, Joe, . . . you were beaten by a Better Man.[135]

No gracious winner he, Schmeling gloated a bit. "You should have known better [than to think Louis would win]," he told a Boston newspaperman. "I would not have taken this fight if I did not think I, a white man, could beat a colored man."[136]

Louis, undaunted, immediately began a comeback. In August he knocked out ex-champion Jack Sharkey and by the beginning of 1937 had won three more bouts and was again the top heavyweight contender, along with Schmeling. The German tried to arrange a match with the title-holder, but Louis was awarded the chance to win Jimmy Braddock's crown instead. The fight was held in Chicago in June, and Louis deftly knocked out the aging champion. The *Courier* triumphantly shouted the news from its front page—"JOE FLATTENS BRADDOCK IN EIGHT SAVAGE ROUNDS"—and the hysterically happy demonstrations began in every black quarter from Pittsburgh to Mobile.[137] The Alabama sharecropper's son had become the toast of the black world.

Louis later took his revenge on the arrogant Schmeling. After successfully defending his heavyweight title three times, Louis met Schmeling in June 1938. The *Courier* played up the black-versus-Aryan issue beforehand, as did the German. A prefight issue reported that "charges that Max Schmeling of Germany felt himself called on to carry Hitler's torch of 'Aryan supremacy' were substantiated Thursday when he told reporters, 'the black dynasty of pugilism must come to an end. I am going to stop this black domination by regaining the crown,' he said. 'As for the rest of the divisions that is up to other white fighters to follow my example.' "[138]

Seventy-thousand eager fans crowded into Yankee Stadium for the fight. Some had not even reached their seats before Louis crushed Schmeling with a barrage of powerful blows. The fight was over in two minutes and four seconds of the first round. Ches Washington reported the event at great length under the headline "JOE SMASHES WAY TO QUICKEST VICTORY BY K.O. IN FIGHT HISTORY":

> Schmeling was the one to make a rush from his corner at the opening while Joe proceeded cautiously to the center of the ring. But at the first exchange of punches, when Joe jabbed three lightning lefts at Maxie's midsection, Schmeling halted in his tracks and began to back up.
> One of those paralyzing blows, which caught the Teuton near the kidneys, was the beginning of the end. Then, like a flash came Joe's crushing right. Stunned by the coolness of Joe's attack and dazed from the power of the first left hand punch, Schmeling wobbled....
> Desperate, Schmeling began to back up, with Joe in eager pursuit with the gleam of killer in his eyes. Backing the Teuton onto the ropes, he shot a right into the midsection. Maxie buckled and another blow and a smashing right collided against the sagging Teuton. The last left was so crushing that it left Schmeling hanging on the ropes....
> Sensing the "kill" and determined to end it all, Louis lunged forward for the finishing punch. And then it came—like a bolt of bronzed lightning—it was a right driven by a surge of youthful power and reinforced by a burning desire for revenge. It landed flush on Schmeling's jaw. Maxie dropped like a bull struck with an axe.[139]

Another *Courier* writer saw the Louis win as more than just an athletic triumph:

> It was as if each [black] had been in that ring himself, as if every man, woman and child of them had dealt destruction with his fists upon the Nordic face of Schmeling and the whole Nazi system he symbolized. It was more than the victory of one athlete over another, it was the triumph of a repressed people against the evil forces of racial oppression and discrimination condensed—by chance—into the shape of Max Schmeling.[140]

Joe Louis collected $349,288.40 for his feat, but more important he had defeated the only man to have beaten him as a professional and debunked for many people at least part of the Aryan myth. He did it with a vengeance. As Robert Vann wrote to his wife, who was vacationing in Europe, "Joe was murderous. If the referee had not stepped between him and the German boy, I am sure a death would have resulted in the ring. Schmeling is now in the hospital and this is almost a week after the fight. In two minutes and four seconds, Joe simply slaughtered Schmeling before a two million dollar house, and the American papers have expressed complete satisfaction with the results."[141]

The Joe Louis phenomenon was a marvelous boon, not only to Vann's *Courier* (whose circulation went all the way up to a quarter million in 1938), but for the entire country. Whites along with blacks were hero-hungry during the depression-ridden 1930s, and Louis gave them something to cheer about at a grim time. Louis was probably the most popular heavyweight champion of all time. Hundreds of thousands of Americans listened eagerly to blow-by-blow accounts of every Louis fight on their radios. Blacks especially shared the experience of winning vicariously with Joe. Louis was not only winning, but winning decisively, and with impeccable good sportsmanship. Clean-cut, modest, soft-spoken, and honest, Louis embodied many estimable virtues. His quiet personal life was also admired, especially in contrast to that of the previous black heavyweight champion, the arrogant Jack Johnson. When Louis married a beautiful young black woman, Marva Trotter, his black fans were relieved as well as pleased; they remembered how Johnson's reputation as a roué and pursuer of white women had roused the enmity of white society. As sports writer Grantland Rice said, Joe Louis was "as different a character from Jack Johnson as Lou Gehrig is from Al Capone."[142]

The extensive *Courier* coverage of Joe Louis and Ethiopia paid off handsomely for the newspaper in money as well as prestige. By the end of 1936 the *Courier* paid its shareholders their first common stock dividend in seven years. Vann conceded in the letter that accompanied the dividend that it had been "a long drawn-out pull from the day we began our business until this, the happiest day of [the *Courier*'s] career."[143] In 1937, the year it celebrated its silver anniversary, the *Pittsburgh Courier* was ranked the leading black weekly in the country. Its circulation, according to the official ABC audit to which Vann had finally agreed, peaked briefly at 250,000, and settled into a steady 149,000 over the ensuing years. Of this number, only 20,000 were local Pittsburgh subscribers, so that its national influence was extensive.[144] On the *Courier*'s twenty-fifth anniversary, Vann wrote a local steel executive, "We feel proud of our development, made possible through twenty-five years of hard work and good business judgment. We have an annual payroll of $80,000.00, we employ seventy-two people in the home plant and twenty-three in the field, we have an investment here of $170,000.00 and we pay a federal, state and city tax, mind you, of close to $10,000.00 per year."[145]

Not content with the new circulation levels of the *Courier* created by the coverage of Joe Louis and Ethiopia, Vann was always searching for other topics of intense interest to blacks to sustain the momentum of the newspaper's expansion and further increase its sales. In the middle and late 1930s, therefore, the *Courier* covered the 1936 Olympics in Berlin extensively and featured a column by W. E. B. DuBois.

Shortly after Joe Louis was beaten by the German Max Schmeling in 1936, Vann left for Berlin to cover the Olympic games. It was the first and only time that he reported straight news for the *Courier* under his own by-line. The Olympics were of special interest that year, first because they were held in Berlin, where Hitler was in his third year of power and beginning to fascinate and terrify the entire world, and, second, because several outstanding black American athletes were competing. Vann was so enthusiastic about the latter fact that he contributed $500 to the U. S. Olympic fund. Before leaving Pittsburgh, Vann wrote an editorial predicting victory for the American blacks, which would demonstrate to the world how valuable the race was to America in this field, and, by implication, in many others:

> The victories of these fine young colored men and women in Berlin will be at once a rebuke to both the New Germany and to America, both countries having made a fantastic religion out of skin pigment.
> How ominous the future must seem to the professional Caucasians when 6.5 per cent of the 275 track athletes participating in the Olympic try outs became 22 per cent of the Olympic team![146]

Vann found much to write about in Berlin. The black athletes performed extremely well: Ralph Metcalfe, Cornelius Johnson, and Jesse Owens won a total of eight medals, six of them first-place gold. Owens alone won four gold medals. The Alabama sharecroppers' son was the outstanding phenomenon of the Olympics. Vann wrote enthusiastically:

> It's the greatest thing of its kind I've ever seen. Sunday, I witnessed 110,000 people cheer two Negro athletes, because they were supreme in their field.

> Monday, I saw another vast crowd of 100,000 go "literally crazy" as they saw Jesse Owens, running with the effortlessness of an antelope, completely dominate the field to win "going away" in the 100-meter [race], with Ralph Metcalfe of Marquette University placing second.
> Today . . . under the beaming sun of a typical German afternoon, Johnny Woodruff, the sensational 19-year-old freshman from the University of Pittsburgh, hurdled the barrier from oblivion to the topmost pinnacle of track achievement to win the finals of the 800-meter event.[147]

Of almost equal interest to blacks was Germany's racist attitude. German newspapers reported the results of the meets without including "points scored by the American African auxiliary."[148] Hitler's conduct was, at times, similarly contemptuous toward the black athletes. As Vann reported, "Just at the time when he should have received the winners of the 100-meter race, and everyone knew Jesse Owens was the winner, Hitler found it convenient to leave the stadium. . . . He did not receive the members of the American team except Miss Stephens, and that under peculiar circumstances."[149] And yet Vann was fascinated by Hitler. He sat directly behind the führer during the games and was awed by the powerful effect he had on the German people:

> With Hitler came all Germany . . . the whole breath and spirit of Germany entered that stadium in the person of Adolph Hitler. Packed to the rim, this great stadium with 110,000 people rose as one person and as if coached for weeks in the art of salute, every hand pointed toward Hitler with the methodical precision of a time clock . . .
> I did look down upon him every moment of the time he sat in his seat. Every time he would move his cap, the Germans would yell "Heil Hitler," and all he had to do was move and the salute was almost instantaneous.[150]

A second series of feature stories that Vann added to the *Courier* came from W. E. B. DuBois, the leading black intellectual of his time. DuBois had left the NAACP magazine, *The Crisis*, in 1934 after a falling-out with the organization. He resigned over two issues: disagreement over who was to control *The Crisis* and dissension over a program for black advancement.

The strong-willed DuBois had always believed *The Crisis* to be strictly his province and tolerated little interference from others in the NAACP. He felt he had developed the magazine by himself. By the early 1930s, DuBois had to contend with Walter White, who had replaced James Weldon Johnson as executive secretary. White stipulated that all salaried officers of the NAACP were to come under the executive secretary's direct supervision. This obviously rankled with DuBois, and a feud began. When Roy Wilkins was named to the board of *The Crisis* in 1933, DuBois believed this to be an effort on White's part to undermine his decision-making on the magazine.

The NAACP's official policy was integration of the races. However, after seeing the pervasive effects of the Depression on blacks, DuBois concluded that a segregated economy was the only way to bring about relief for the nation's blacks. He urged blacks to segregate themselves economically and to be self-reliant. DuBois saw integration as unworkable and was disturbed that the NAACP had not modified its program to meet the difficulties posed by the Depression. When the NAACP did not adopt his program calling for the establishment of a black cooperative community, he attacked the organization openly in *The Crisis*.[151] By 1934, DuBois also was urging that the NAACP replace all whites who had anything to do with policy determination.

The *Courier* covered closely the progression of the battle between DuBois and the other NAACP officials. "DUBOIS DEFENDS SEGREGATION.... WHITE ATTACKED,"[152] reported Vann's newspaper in March, saying DuBois "means simply that we must make segregation pay, and at the same time use our many segregated institutions to fight the battle against oppression, discrimination and unjust treatment."[153] George Schuyler, long a critic of DuBois, began to badger him in his weekly column. "DuBois . . . has stepped into the swamp of segregation and flounders helplessly in the muck," he wrote in April. Schuyler disagreed with DuBois's position, saying "the vast Negro masses must live and work among, with and for white people."[154] Finally in June 1934, DuBois gave up the battle. "DR. DUBOIS RESIGNS FROM *Crisis*," noted the *Courier*.[155] He followed this action in July by leaving the NAACP entirely. The *Courier* reported, " 'THERE IS BUT ONE RECOURSE, COMPLETE AND FINAL WITHDRAWAL', DECLARES FORMER *Crisis* EDITOR IN LETTER TO NAACP DIRECTORS—SAYS ASSOCIATION HAS NO SYSTEM."[156] Vann's newspaper editorialized its regret that things had come to this sorry juncture: "We do not believe that the severance of relations which have existed for twenty-five years was necessary. We believe that an intelligent discussion of differences of opinion could have been had, and should have been had; and the organization saved from the embarrassment it must suffer by reason of the resignation of Dr. DuBois."[157] Vann himself agreed with DuBois on economic segregation. The *Courier* as a business enterprise epitomized DuBois's idea, for it functioned solely within the confines of the black community; it was owned, staffed, advertised in, and purchased by blacks.

In January 1936, DuBois wrote to Robert Vann about his desire to do a weekly or monthly open letter to black Americans for the *Courier*.[158] DuBois said his proposed column would have three dimensions. First, it would include the kind of pithy, caustic comments that had characterized his column, "As the Crow Flies," in *The Crisis*. Second, the column would attempt to clarify black thought on "the basic nature of making a living, especially during this time when the whole economic structure of modern society is going to be revolutionized." Finally, the column would, through an analysis of the international affairs of nonwhites, prevent American blacks from considering themselves in isolation. DuBois hoped to build a wide-ranging outlook in blacks and put an end to provincial thinking.[159] Despite the ambitious scope of his planned monthly letter, DuBois could command little money for his efforts; his formidable intellect received small financial reward. He told Vann of his previous experience with the *Amsterdam News*, which had paid him $12.50 per column, which DuBois found too little. "Personally," wrote DuBois to Vann, "I think that $25 a letter would be fair compensation, but I am afraid this is more than a Negro weekly can bear. On the other hand, $15 would not pay me."[160]

With negotiations completed, DuBois left for Europe on June 6 carrying a *Courier* press card Vann had sent him.[161] His destination was "chiefly Germany for the purpose of studying the relation between education and industry. . . . You will realize that the opportunity to be in Europe during this most crucial time perhaps in the world's history will be of tremendous advantage."[162] And he added, "I shall write frankly, except during the time that I am in Germany, and I shall say nothing about the race question until I get out of the country."[163]

In the *Courier* columns entitled "A Forum of Fact and Opinion" which followed his European trip, DuBois wrote of everything that interested him, from Japanese colonialism to a history of black voting patterns to the Kentucky Derby. He discoursed on the Olympics and their meaning for individual countries; he described the importance of Europe as "the center of modern human culture."[164] He wrote of Wagner and the German Museum at Munich.[165] DuBois's column was a potpourri of topics; he often treated several subjects in a single piece. He also used the column to explain at length his philosophy of black separatism. DuBois pictured a "closed economic circle," planned by a black "braintrust." Blacks had suffered degradation for too many centuries, and now was the time to create their own separate nation. DuBois proposed the establishment of cooperatives to enhance blacks' purchasing power; if wholesalers made difficulties for the cooperatives, blacks should then go into manufacturing themselves. They should also found credit unions to "furnish cooperatives with capital."[166] DuBois made clear his credo for America's blacks. It included unity, an end to hateful segregation, the need for a "Talented Tenth" to plan for the race, solution of the employment problem, a cooperative black industrial system, unions, socialism, cessation of lynching, and total black suffrage.[167]

Robert Vann's personal profits from the dramatic growth of the *Courier* included both honors and income. In 1937 he was elected vice-president of the Associated Weekly Publishers of Allegheny County, which included representatives from every weekly newspaper in the region. He was also named general counsel for the organization and was the only black in the entire group. And he bought what could be fairly described as a small estate—a truly expansive gesture for Vann. It was in his nature to live quite modestly, drawing the most minimal salary from his newspaper, though he had earned a good deal of money from his law practice over the years. The house Vann bought from his banker, William K. Gamble of the Potter Trust and Title Company, was known as "Oakmont" from its location in suburban Oakmont, twenty miles outside Pittsburgh. Vann had less trouble convincing Gamble to sell his home in the exclusive all-white residential area to a black than he did persuading his wife, Jesse, to agree to the purchase. She did not want to move twenty miles away from her friends. The home was too big for two people, she felt, and much too expensive. Mrs. Vann also worried about the telephone calls to Pittsburgh, which would now require long-distance charges, but Vann assured her she could call to her heart's content. His mind was made up, and the purchase was completed.[168]

The COURIER Hits the Jackpot • 263

Vann paid $50,000 for the eleven-room Tudor house of stucco and red brick, set on wide lawns and protected by stately poplar trees which Vann came to love. The house, an unusual self-indulgence for Vann, signified that he was at long last going to relax somewhat and spend more time out of the public eye behind Oakmont's tall hedges. Vann thoroughly enjoyed his new home. He added a greenhouse and spent time puttering in the rock garden in the front of the house. He refurbished the servants' quarters and hired a couple named Thomas to help run the household. Proud of his new home, Vann began to entertain a great deal, inviting guests to play billiards in the vast third-floor room and sup in the marble-floored dining room.[169]

Vann spent more and more time in the seclusion of Oakmont. His newspaper had reached the pinnacle of its success and had less need of his shrewd leadership. He was disillusioned with national politics by this time, and his position as unquestioned black leader in Pittsburgh had begun to slip a bit. Vann would make only one more major appearance on the political scene.

"Oakmont," Vann's home in suburban Pittsburgh.

• 11 •

Schism and Decline: 1936-1938

DURING THE LAST YEARS before his death, Robert Vann's political career declined, primarily because he came into conflict with other strong forces within the Democratic party. Though Vann was strong-willed and outspoken, the frictions that caused the gradual eclipse of his political power came about, for the most part, through no fault of his own but through the changing political imperatives within his party. The waning of Vann's influence began during the presidential campaign of 1936 and continued through the 1938 Pennsylvania gubernatorial election.

Though Vann had left Washington at the end of 1935 frustrated and disappointed, he still believed firmly in FDR's New Deal and fully intended to participate in the upcoming presidential campaign. When the Democratic nominating convention opened on June 22, 1936, Vann was on hand as a member of the Pennsylvania delegation, one of thirty black delegates and alternates from twelve states who participated in the convention that year.[1] The Republican party had already met in Cleveland and nominated Alfred Landon of Kansas. The Republicans had written a platform totally devoid of any consideration for the black man and, furthermore, had denied a seat at the press table to a *Courier* reporter because of his color, so Vann was particularly interested in seeing that the Democrats gave equitable treatment to the blacks that year.[2]

There was, of course, no question that FDR would be the Democratic nominee and odds-on favorite to win in November, since his popularity had never been greater. What Vann and other black leaders planned was that the blacks would play a significant role in his reelection.

Schism and Decline: 1936–1938 • 265

Since the beginning of the year, the *Courier* had been running articles to that effect, with such headlines as "RACE HOLDS BALANCE OF POWER IN SEVEN STATES."³ As the Democratic convention opened in Philadelphia, which was heavily populated by blacks and which the party chose because it hoped to take Pennsylvania in 1936, there was every indication that the party would be attentive to black demands. Not only were there thirty black faces on the convention floor, as contrasted with the ten alternate delegates seen in 1932 and the single regular one of 1924, but for the first time in Democratic convention history the opening prayer was delivered by a black minister, Reverend Marshall Shepard of Philadelphia's Olivet Baptist Church and Democratic member of the Pennsylvania state legislature. To be sure, there were the inevitable reactions from southern Democrats, and the *Courier* poked fun at them when Senator "Cotton Ed" Smith of South Carolina and two other southerners showily "walked out until the obnoxious ceremony was over, only to return to find Representative Arthur W. Mitchell speaking."⁴ (Mitchell, a black Democrat from Chicago, had defeated Republican Oscar DePriest in the 1934 congressional elections.) Senator Smith was quoted as saying he would not support "any political organization that looks upon the Negro and caters to him as a political and social equal."⁵ But Smith's words and actions only served to underscore the fact for blacks of how much bona fide attention the Democrats were giving them.⁶ Later the Democratic leaders pointedly chose a black man, Carl Glass of Missouri, to serve on the committee which formally apprised the Texan John Nance Garner of his renomination as vice-president.⁷

On the surface, things seemed to bode well for blacks who supported the Democrats, and in particular for Robert Vann, who now appeared to carry a good deal of weight in the party. He suggested to Democratic National Chairman James Farley that, for purposes of the Democratic campaign directed at blacks, the country be divided into three regions, eastern, midwestern, and western. Vann proposed that his friend Julian Rainey be named to head up the eastern division out of New York City and that "Congressman Arthur W. Mitchell be the pivot man in the Chicago office,"⁸ to lead the midwestern campaign. Farley implemented all these suggestions.⁹

In July, Vann himself assumed the positions of special advisor to the Democratic National Committee for publicity in the black press and manager of the black division of FDR's campaign in Pennsylvania. Pennsylvania was a key state in the 1936 presidential election. There was some hope FDR would carry Pennsylvania in 1936, as he had lost by the slim margin of 157,592 in 1932. Vann was assigned to center all his campaign efforts for FDR on Pennsylvania, which had thirty-six crucial electoral votes.[10] *The Nation* predicted that neither FDR nor Landon would carry Pennsylvania by more than 100,000 votes,[11] but Democratic hopes reached much higher than that. They were still a minority among Pennsylvania's registered voters (out of 4,900,000, 2,750,000 were Republicans, 1,900,000 Democrats and the rest splintered), but their ranks had been swollen by 500,000 since 1934 and 1,000,000 since 1928.[12]

Despite Vann's apparent ascendancy, there were rumblings of discontent among other black Democrats and forces at work which would before long spell a decline in his political power. Some black leaders from cities like New York and Philadelphia resented the Pittsburgher's preeminence and felt that someone from their much larger constituencies should be predominant. Herbert Bruce, Tammany leader from New York's Twenty-first District and head of a "revolt" of New York blacks against Vann's primacy, expressed his displeasure with Vann to James Farley and Senator Robert Wagner of New York, calling Vann a carpetbagger who had "chiselled" his way into the Democratic party in 1932 and had left the Republicans only when a Democratic victory seemed probable.[13] Bruce also felt that Vann was getting a disproportionately large share of the patronage going to blacks, considering the relative smallness of the city from which he came.[14] Dissatisfaction with Vann in another quarter was suggested by *Time*, which said he had alienated "many a black preacher."[15] Vann's anticlericalism was well known, and black ministers were still a potent social and political force in their communities. More important, in Philadelphia, with a potential 146,000 black voters, local black political figures such as the Reverends Marshall Shepard and J. E. Philpot, Mrs. Sommerville Fauntleroy, and Samuel Reading contested Vann for power. They believed themselves, not Vann, to be the spokesmen for the blacks of Philadelphia.[16] Finally, many Democrats believed that Vann's political influence was no longer as formidable as they had thought. In return for his seemingly badly needed support in 1932, Vann had exacted a high payment in patronage, yet the 1934 congressional elections showed that the Democrats got many black votes on the merits of the New Deal and could probably get along without the services of so demanding a supporter as Robert Vann. Moreover, his resignation as special assistant attorney general in 1935 had removed him from the public eye. As his visibility had decreased, so, perhaps, had his influence.

Three major issues were of particular interest to Pennsylvania's blacks in the 1936 campaign: an anti-lynch law, economic recovery, and racial discrimination in the Pennsylvania branches of various federal agencies.

The subject of a federal anti-lynch law had been glossed over at the Democratic convention; mention of it was conspicuously absent from the party platform, though Vann had been one of a group which drafted a resolution calling for such legislation and presented it to the platform committee. Even Landon, the candidate of a "lily-white" nominating convention, was advocating passage of such a law. It turned out that FDR had some politically expedient justification for not coming out strongly in favor of an anti-lynching bill.

The question had first come up not long after Roosevelt entered the White House in 1933. When two white men were lynched in San Jose, California, on November 26, 1933, Governor James Rolph, Jr., called the lynching "the best lesson California had ever given the country." Rolph's callous statement led FDR to denounce lynching in a speech at Washington's Constitution Hall before the Federal Council of Churches of Christ. "We do not excuse those . . . who condone lynch law," said FDR. He spoke out against "that vile form of collective murder" again the following month in his annual address to Congress.[17] Vann's *Courier* praised Roosevelt for being the first president to take such a bold stand.[18] Harding had briefly supported the Dyer anti-lynch bill of 1921–22 but did not pursue the subject when the measure was defeated by a southern filibuster in the Senate. Shortly after Roosevelt's speech, Senators Robert Wagner of New York and Edward P. Costigan of Colorado presented an anti-lynch bill to the Senate, but nothing came of it in 1934. In 1935 Wagner and Costigan reintroduced their bill, and after a favorable report from the Senate Judiciary Committee it reached the Senate floor. But a filibuster led by southerners "Cotton Ed" Smith, Josiah Bailey, Hugo Black, and James F. Byrnes went on for two months. Roosevelt felt a good deal of pressure, particularly from Walter White of the NAACP, to speak out on behalf of the Wagner-Costigan anti-lynch bill. But, as he explained to Walter White in a private conference, FDR knew that if he pushed too forcefully for the measure he would jeopardize all the rest of his legislative program, for southerners were chairmen or in strategic places on most Senate and House committees.

He could not take that risk. Roosevelt did induce Senator Joseph Robinson of Arkansas to permit consideration of the motion to bring up the bill, but after another filibuster, this one five days in length, the Senate adjourned without bringing the measure to a vote.[19]

The Crisis called FDR's inaction the "Great Silence of the Man in the White House."[20] The *Courier* expressed disappointment at the fate of the anti-lynch bill but called it "the best effort yet": "The Anti-Lynching Bill was defeated in Washington last week, but in the face of that defeat a calm review of the history of the struggle for an anti-lynch law reveals that progress is being made. During all the Republican administrations the Anti-Lynch Bill never made the progress that the Costigan-Wagner Bill made in the present Congress."[21]

It would undoubtedly have been an even stronger effort had Roosevelt enthusiastically backed the bill. Aside from FDR's reluctance to alienate needed southern Democratic congressional votes, the president obviously had a basic conservative "leave well enough alone" attitude toward the struggle for black rights, whether it concerned an anti-lynch measure or, more generally, economic and political equality for blacks.[22]

Vann and other Pennsylvania blacks watched the proceedings carefully. The last lynching in the state had occurred back in August 1911 when a hapless black named Zack Walker, who was accused of having killed a policeman, was dragged from his hospital bed in Coatesville and burned alive by an angry mob. But blacks in Pennsylvania talked of the incident for a long time afterward, and the *Courier* carried on a long crusade to have the state legislature revoke the Coatesville charter.[23] When the Ku Klux Klan had a resurgence of power in the 1920s, the blacks in Pennsylvania were aroused to fear and anger. The *Courier* reported each lynching at length, and Vann constantly mentioned the crying need for an anti-lynch law in his editorials. In 1936, the *Courier* cited the Wagner-Costigan bill as a central issue for blacks. Vann understood the dilemma Roosevelt faced with regard to such a measure, but felt that if he defeated Landon that fall with the help of the blacks he would be duty-bound to take up the offensive against lynching. The newspaper said the most important positive result of the 1934–35 troubles of the Wagner-Costigan bill was that the subject of lynching had been brought out into the open and discussed extensively on the floor of the Senate. The conscience of the nation was stirring, and there was hope that the public would demand such a law from FDR's next administration.[24]

Schism and Decline: 1936–1938 • 269

Another important issue of the campaign FDR directed at the blacks in Vann's province was economic recovery. Vann and his newspaper stressed that over $50 million had been allotted to construction of (segregated) housing projects for blacks under the Democrats, and large PWA allotments were going to black universities like Howard and Wilberforce. Not long before election day, on October 29, the *Courier* gave front-page coverage to FDR's dedication of a new $625,000 chemistry building at Howard and reported that FDR had pledged anew his policy "that among American citizens there should be no forgotten man and no forgotten race."[25] As Vann pointed out in his speeches, the WPA, watched over closely by Senator Joseph Guffey, a proven friend to blacks, was providing numerous jobs for blacks in Pennsylvania. The *Courier* ran a much-discussed cartoon by Cornelius Dalton, which showed a black housewife carrying a bag of groceries marked "Emergency Relief" who berates her WPA-employed husband for his ludicrous indecision in choosing FDR or Landon: "Kain't choose, huh? And dere you is wid WPA and me wid releef groceries!"[26] Roosevelt and the Democrats continued to live up to their word regarding the naming of blacks to high-level patronage jobs, including, as specifically requested by Vann, Pittsburgh's Paul Jones as state workmen's compensation referee in the Department of Labor and Industry and Theron Bertram Hamilton, also from Pittsburgh, as Vann's replacement in the Department of Justice.[27]

Moreover, the *Courier* noted, under the "Republican Raw Deal" there had been 5,112 bank failures, but blacks now had nothing to fear, for their deposits were insured through the Federal Deposit Insurance Corporation. Only sixty-one banks had failed since Roosevelt became president.[28] Vann and the *Courier* admitted that of course the economic status of blacks was not yet on a par with that of whites, but said "only those blind to reality expected that."[29]

A third issue much discussed by Pennsylvania blacks during FDR's campaign was the question of racial discrimination in the local branches of federal agencies. There had been many complaints about this from blacks in the state, and it appears that most of them were justified. But it also seems that the discriminatory practices were the fault of state and local officials and were not necessarily attributable to federal policies. The state of affairs in an agency like the Civilian Conservation Corps is revealed in an incident in which Robert Vann became involved. At CCC Camp Vann in Benezette, Pennsylvania, which had been named for the *Courier* editor, five black men wrote to Vann complaining that they were assigned menial labor but were as qualified to be foremen as the whites in those posts. Incensed that this situation could prevail in the camp named to honor him, Vann wrote to Senator Guffey and asked him to rectify matters. Guffey in turn referred the matter to the state officials in the Department of Forests and Waters. They wrote to Vann and assured him that, should any personnel changes occur, blacks would be considered for foremen positions.[30] That seems to have ended the discussion, and it is doubtful that any of the black petitioners were ever promoted. It was a ticklish question for Vann to discuss in his stumping for FDR, but he seems to have rationalized that not only was it more the fault of local officials than FDR himself, but agencies like the CCC were, on the whole, of great benefit to blacks. Vann said wage differentials and other such forms of inequality were but a temporary condition; along with discrimination in federal agencies, they would be dealt with later. The more immediate necessity was to gain jobs for blacks.

Despite the fact that in all three of the issues mentioned FDR had not resolved things entirely to the satisfaction of blacks, as the fall campaign went on, it became obvious that more and more blacks were entering the FDR camp. Such protesting publications as the *Baltimore Afro-American*, which had soundly criticized Roosevelt for not acting forcefully for an anti-lynch bill and not pressing for inclusion of black agricultural workers or domestics under Social Security, reluctantly came out for FDR. Even the NAACP, whose executive secretary, Walter White, regarded himself as the "loyal opposition" and was very vocal against discriminatory practices within the New Deal, agreed that the reelection of Roosevelt was advisable.[31]

As black weeklies continued to come out for Roosevelt, the *Courier* published a scorecard:

For FDR	Circulation
Pittsburgh Courier	174,000
Baltimore Afro-American	70,000
Norfolk Journal and Guide	24,000
Amsterdam News	16,000
Philadelphia Independent	14,000
	298,000

For Landon

Chicago Defender	50,000
St. Louis Argus	15,000
The Call (Kansas City)	16,000
	81,000[32]

Vann claimed that the *Courier*'s readers solidly supported FDR and predicted that between forty thousand and sixty-five thousand blacks in Allegheny County alone would vote for him.[33]

Though the Democrats had cautiously hoped for victory in Pennsylvania, Roosevelt's triumph by a margin of 666,000 votes exceeded their wildest expectations. FDR became the first Democratic presidential candidate to carry the state since James Buchanan in 1856. Philadelphia and Pittsburgh went Democratic by 210,000 and 190,000 votes respectively,[34] and the black wards in both cities were solidly in the Democratic column.[35] In the five Pittsburgh wards where blacks showed political strength, FDR received 76.6 percent of the vote. In the Third and Fifth Wards, the heart of the Hill District, where the *Courier* offices, the black YMCA, and Vann's law offices were located, Roosevelt's victory was particularly striking. He won 5,990 to 645 in the Third Ward and 8,252 to 2,539 in the Fifth.[36]

After the sweeping Democratic victory, Vann perhaps overconfidently remarked that the newly Democratic black vote had provided the balance of power in the key states of Pennsylvania, Indiana, Ohio, Michigan, and Illinois. The truth of the matter is, however, that though the blacks had contributed to FDR's victory, their vote was in no way decisive. If one assumes that in Pennsylvania, where FDR won by 666,000, about 160,000 blacks had voted for him, it is obvious that the black vote would not have been decisive, regardless of which way it went. The significance of this is that it would have boded much better for Robert Vann and Pennsylvania blacks in general if their vote had provided the margin of victory in a very close election. The Democrats would then have had to be much more attentive to the needs of Vann and his race to keep their precariously slim edge in the state. As it was, in 1936 the Democrats did not really need Robert Vann or the votes he influenced in Pennsylvania. Roosevelt's popularity was at an all-time high (Landon had won only eight electoral votes); the Democratic ranks were swollen, and although the blacks contributed to his victory, they were not a major factor.[37] So from that day on Vann was taken somewhat for granted by the party and his sway on a national level with the Democrats decreased even further.

The position of the black electorate in defining Vann's influence in the 1936 presidential race was ironic. In 1932, when Vann made his dramatic switch to the Democratic party, not enough blacks followed to make him a crucial component of FDR's victory. By 1936, when the Democrats realized the enormous potential of the black vote, it was so solidly in the Democratic column that Vann was again not a crucial factor.

Vann was given another push down the ramp of declining political power during the Pennsylvania gubernatorial election in 1938. This time the cause was a tumultuous series of events in the state Democratic party preceding the election which led to a schism in the party and a rearranging of political priorities and personal power. Once again, circumstances were unpropitious for Robert Vann, only this time he was truly backed into a corner. He made a dramatic exit from his corner, but his pride and intransigence sent him out by the wrong door. As a consequence, Vann lost much of his remaining power.

The schism in the Pennsylvania Democratic party which led to Vann's troubles was the product of a rift between Senator Joseph Guffey and David Lawrence of Pittsburgh, the chairman of the Democratic State Committee. Two things implicated Vann deeply in the rift: he was Joe Guffey's political protégé and ally, and he was from the same city as David Lawrence and so his natural competitor. Thus, when the quarrel began, it was not a simple case of Vann's supporting Guffey. Vann had to wage his own personal battle with David Lawrence, and that was a battle for political survival in Lawrence's home territory.

Vann's first falling-out with Lawrence occurred in 1934 with regard to patronage for blacks in Pittsburgh. When William McNair was elected mayor the previous year, he allegedly promised Vann a substantial amount of local black patronage because the black vote in several wards had contributed to his election. The *Courier* reported that Michael Benedum, who gave generously to the McNair war chest, also received the assurance of patronage for blacks from the incoming mayor, as well as from Joseph Guffey and David Lawrence.[38] Initially, Vann believed in McNair's promises, but other black leaders were more apprehensive about possible appointments. Some feared McNair

Schism and Decline: 1936–1938 • 273

would appoint James F. Malone, a white from the predominantly black Fifth Ward, as safety director and that Malone would then award whites, rather than blacks, all subordinate jobs. And though the Democratic leadership could point to 2,290 places to be filled by blacks, by the end of 1933 black politicians were annoyed because many of those positions were federally appointed, and they had not received an equitable share of the higher paying "meaningful" positions on the municipal and county levels.[39]

A committee of three led by Benedum's butler, Joseph Gould, went to McNair in early January 1934 in search of more patronage for blacks. Perhaps because he viewed Gould's action as an incursion upon his own leadership, Vann at first defended Mayor McNair, cautioning blacks that their action was premature. He urged them to be patient, remarking that "until the white people have an opportunity to organize the new administration and settle their own differences, it ill becomes any Negro to start disorganizing and breaking up the work that has been done since 1932, when some of the other Negroes now making the most noise about McNair, were making speeches for Hoover."[40]

At the end of January, with blacks still waiting for their first significant appointment, a second meeting was held in the *Courier* offices, this time attended by all black factions. A patronage committee was established and chaired by Paul F. Jones. Though this appeared to be a challenge to Vann's leadership, Jones assured the *Courier* editor that it was not meant as such. Vann told those gathered in his office that Lawrence had accepted a new plea for black appointments and reacted as though he would act on it positively. The group decided that lists of black office-seekers should be submitted anew to Lawrence, who they hoped would pressure McNair into action.[41] But McNair awarded no position of significance to a black until April, when Wilbur Douglass, Vann's young law partner, was named assistant city solicitor.[42] By then, and in fact ever since Vann himself had held the post in 1918, the assistant city solicitor position was considered a traditional "Negro job." McNair's hesitancy in making the appointment, due probably in part to Lawrence's failure to push for it, was surprising to Vann and a bit suspicious.[43]

During 1934, McNair paid no heed to the requests by Vann and other local black Democrats for city positions for blacks, ranging from city assessor and city magistrate posts down to minor jobs in the Police Department and Department of Public Works. When McNair awarded almost none of these posts to blacks, Vann finally became disgruntled and impatient. He accused the mayor of reneging on his campaign promises and also intimated that much of the responsibility for the omissions rested with David Lawrence, who should have been applying political pressure to McNair. The rumor was bruited about that not only was Lawrence not pushing for black patronage, but he had actually blocked the appointment of a black as city assessor, a post worth $4,500 a year.[44] The fact that there was not a single black in Lawrence's offices also led Vann to advance the idea that Lawrence was not at all amenable to black appointments.[45]

Although McNair may have acceded to Lawrence's wishes about black patronage, he defied him on almost every other matter and in general ignored the Democratic politicos. McNair was particularly slow to put New Deal programs such as the WPA into operation in Pittsburgh. For a time Vann and David Lawrence were allied in wishing McNair out of his mayoral office; Lawrence was in fact actively trying to have McNair "ripped out" of his post by means of a bill in the state legislature.[46] When McNair resigned of his own volition in 1936, Lawrence saw to it that someone over whom he would have more control was appointed mayor—Cornelius Scully. Obviously overjoyed at McNair's resignation, Vann sent him a sarcastic telegram: "MY HEARTY CONGRATULATIONS TO YOU. YOU ARE TWO YEARS LATE DOING THE RIGHT THING."[47] A short time after this, Vann met the former mayor on Grant Street. McNair greeted Vann, "Remember me?" "How in hell shall I ever forget?" answered Vann.[48]

By 1937, Vann was again in conflict with David Lawrence and writing Senator Joe Guffey regularly about his problems with the state Democratic leader. One thing that piqued Vann was the action of one of Lawrence's subordinates, Emmert Kaylor, the white chairman of the predominantly black Fifth Ward. Kaylor had been "shoe-horned" into his job by Paul F. Jones, a workmen's compensation referee who was Lawrence's black protégé in much the same way that Vann was Guffey's. (Jones, just twenty-nine at this time, represented a youthful threat to Vann's power as a black leader. Born in Louisville, Kentucky, in 1909, Jones had graduated from the University of Pittsburgh and Duquesne University Law School. Before Jones became a workmen's compensation referee, he was a clerk in the county treasurer's office for three years.)[49] Now Kaylor was appointing white men rather than blacks "even to the point of neglect-

Schism and Decline: 1936–1938 • 275

ing the very colored committee who voted to make him ward chairman."[50] Vann decided to take his grievance directly to Lawrence in Harrisburg. After several tries, Vann finally managed to meet with Lawrence and James Kirk, the Allegheny County chairman. Vann told them that many blacks in the Fifth Ward were complaining that patronage was going to whites instead of to them, the rightful recipients. In an effort to placate Vann, Lawrence offered two minor appointments to the blacks of the Fifth Ward and assured him that more would follow shortly. Vann then left the room, but having forgotten "to mention to Mr. Lawrence [another] matter, I stuck my head back in the door, only to find the gentlemen laughing at the top of their voices, which laughter suddenly subsided when they saw my head back in." Vann's pride was wounded. But worse, he realized "Mr. Lawrence seemed to be obsessed with the idea of weakening my leadership among my people. I am obsessed with the idea that he is not going to do anything of the kind, and if he cares to have a little scrap about it, I am just as ready to scrap about it as he is, and by the time the matter gets two years older, the scrap ought to develop into a damn nice fight."[51]

Vann had noticed that the Lawrence-dominated Democratic leadership in Pittsburgh no longer felt it needed the black vote. In the 1937 city and county elections, he accused both Lawrence and Mayor Cornelius Scully of "laughing up their sleeve at the Negro vote." Because the black vote was no longer as vital to the Democrats in the county, the Democratic leaders there, in particular Lawrence, began to ignore their pledge that blacks would receive patronage jobs in the proportion of 10 percent of their number of registered voters.[52]

Finally a group of unhappy black leaders led by spokesman Reverend Marshall Shepard, black Democratic member of the Pennsylvania legislature from Philadelphia, went to Governor Earle himself to complain that the positions blacks were receiving from certain members of the executive cabinet were only of the most menial caliber. Governor Earle summoned some of his cabinet members and in the presence of the black delegation told them he would not tolerate such abrogation of a political promise. He turned to Lawrence, who was in the cabinet as secretary of the Commonwealth, and chided him, "Dave, you promised me and told me that the Negroes were being taken care of and now I find that the Negroes are being ignored." Governor Earle then sent for his secretary and told him to inform every cabinet member that "Negroes were to be given jobs in each and every department even if they had to fire some white Democrats to do so."[53]

Though Governor Earle himself made some subsequent black appointments of significance, the pledge of 10 percent black patronage in Pittsburgh continued to be ignored by the Democratic leaders there. Pittsburgh blacks suffered partly from their numbers. In Philadelphia leaders like John Kelly had to keep their "10 percent promise," since the blacks were a sizable force to contend with. The Democrats were much more attentive to black party members in Philadelphia, and once they had the support of the 280,000 (of whom approximately 146,000 were of voting age), they could afford to ignore the 70,000 in Pittsburgh. This of course meant Robert Vann was no longer so important.[54]

Vann continued to be feisty and assertive with the state leaders. He insisted repeatedly that the Democratic "10 percent patronage" pledge be kept, and he refused to pay wholehearted obeisance to the Democratic leaders in return for the merely nominal patronage they gave. Soon the party leaders became a bit wary of Vann; he could not be subdued. But Lawrence and his subordinates could not yet afford to engage in full-scale political battle with Vann, for he still wielded considerable influence among black voters, not only as a political leader but as a newspaper man as well. Blacks still looked to Vann for leadership, seeking him out to redress all their patronage grievances. At this time (1937) Senator Joe Guffey also wished to keep the peace and avoid any overt conflict between Lawrence and Vann; the latter's influence could be crucial in future elections, and Guffey had gubernatorial aspirations. Guffey was also worried about adding intraparty troubles to those the Democrats already had. There was a hint of scandal in the air, with a United States Senate committee investigating charges that the WPA in Pennsylvania was strictly Guffey's political tool. Moreover, the shakily recovering economy was undergoing a recession that year for which Democrats everywhere were being criticized.

Vann's quarrels were primarily with the Democratic state organization, but he also turned to the national leaders to rectify injustices of which he felt they, too, were guilty. Vann began to pay calls on Democratic National Committee Chairman James Farley in Washington and besiege him with letters requesting better political treatment for himself and his "constituents." In this assault, he was goaded on by a friend, Julian Rainey, who told him "you are in a position

Schism and Decline: 1936–1938 • 277

to write a letter different from anybody else. You can express indignity [sic], astonishment and resentment."[55] And Vann's letters to Farley were indeed blunt and resentful, as when he wrote, "I am convinced that Julian [Rainey] and I represent what is known as 'window dressing,' and I do not propose to serve as 'window dressing' because it is embarrassing. . . . I think the Democrats are so drunk with power they have forgotten the fellows who rang the doorbells, and they are headed for defeat unless they can sober up. . . . The party is trying its damnedest to revert to type and when it reverts to type, I want to be away off somewhere fishing."[56]

Vann was particularly dismayed that positions were not found for such men of merit as Ralph Mizelle of New York, who wished a post in the Social Security Bureau, for William L. Houston, who wanted a judgeship, and Julian Rainey, who Vann thought should have been appointed to the attorney general's office, and berated Farley on the matter. "Frankly, Chief, not one of my suggestions so far has been very successful and unless I am able to suggest something that goes over, I ought to resign as special advisor to the Democratic National Committee. Maybe you have some resignation blanks [to send me]."[57] And when an attorney from Missouri asked Vann to help him get a Justice Department position, Vann replied disgustedly, "Under the present set-up, I am not in the mood to write letters to Mr. [Homer] Cummings or to Mr. Farley. I know it would be a waste of time."[58]

It appears, however, that James Farley provided just enough assistance with patronage to mollify Vann occasionally. After Vann prodded and threatened for some time, Farley secured the judgeship for William Houston. Vann was pleased with that result, but annoyed with the procedure apparently required. "The regrettable feature about the whole thing is that we have to threaten to shoot somebody before we can get things done. I think we ought to rate a little higher than that."[59]

Back in Pennsylvania, David Lawrence was making ever greater inroads into the political power of both Vann and Senator Joe Guffey. Much of Vann's authority in Pittsburgh derived from Guffey, who was the leading Democrat in the state and controlled most of the patronage. But with Guffey away in Washington a good deal, Lawrence and his men were gradually usurping much of that control.

Despite the fact that they were serious political rivals, David Lawrence and Joe Guffey had much in common. Both were born in

Pennsylvania of families that had been in politics in a minor way for at least three generations. In 1931, Lawrence was well on his way politically. With Republican support he polled over 120,000 votes for county commissioner. Though he lost the election, his ballot count was impressive, considering that Democrats who had run for that office previously rarely received 10,000 votes.[60] Lawrence's first important political post was Allegheny County Democratic chairman; Guffey had held the same post immediately before him. At the 1932 Democratic Convention, both Guffey and Lawrence switched their support from Al Smith to FDR, and both received political rewards from Roosevelt. In 1934, Lawrence was made Democratic state chairman and became Guffey's political lieutenant in Pennsylvania. Lawrence was smart and a skillful politician, and he had little intention of remaining subordinate to Guffey. He wanted to be the leading Democrat in Pennsylvania, an unofficial title held by Guffey in the early 1930s. Lawrence became a close advisor to Governor Earle after his election in 1934 and may even have run the administration from behind the scenes. He was probably responsible for getting much of the "Little New Deal" legislation through the state assembly.[61] He further strengthened himself by an alliance with three powerful Philadelphians, J. David Stern, publisher of the *Philadelphia Record*, and contractors Matthew McCloskey, Jr. and John B. Kelly.

By 1938, David Lawrence felt ready to challenge Joe Guffey. There was some speculation that Lawrence himself might be the Democratic gubernatorial candidate that year, but he was a Roman Catholic and the consensus was that a Roman Catholic could not win at that time in Pennsylvania, so Lawrence gave up the idea.[62]

The 1938 election in Pennsylvania was crucial for both political parties, and for Robert Vann and the black man generally. For the Republicans it represented a chance to regain the control the party had lost in 1934, and a victory could be a step toward returning the state to GOP ranks in the 1940 presidential election. For the Democrats, it meant a probable showdown between Guffey and Lawrence which could harm the party's chances to win. And the Democrats wanted badly to win; at stake were the governorship, a Senate seat, thirty-four Congressional seats, and state patronage for about thirty thousand employees. The Democratic victor would also control seventy-two delegate votes at the 1940 Democratic National Convention.[63] The blacks were a pivotal factor in the election, for it would show whether they were genuinely in the Democratic column for good, or whether their defection from the Republicans had been only temporary. For Robert Vann, the election meant a struggle for his political survival; if the Lawrence faction won, he would lose the remainder of his influence as black leader in Pittsburgh, for Lawrence's protégé Paul Jones would be ascendant.

Before the Democrats sat down to draw up a slate of candidates in February 1938, victory in November seemed reasonably certain. The general feeling was that Joe Guffey would be the gubernatorial choice and George Earle, who could not by law succeed himself as governor, would receive the nod for the Senate. Allegedly Guffey had reached an agreement with Earle when they ran together in 1934 that they would reverse their positions on the ticket in 1938.[64] Robert Vann wrote with great confidence to a friend that Pennsylvania was safely in the Democratic column and "we are going to elect Senator Guffey as our next governor."[65] Vann probably hoped that Guffey would then be a strong force in the Democratic presidential nominating convention of 1940 and possibly even considered as a vice-presidential candidate. Vann had told Guffey the year before, "I am interested in the election of one Joseph Guffey of Pennsylvania to the Presidency of the United States. . . . If and when this happens, and stranger things have happened . . . put me down for one hundred inaugural seat tickets, payable in advance."[66] Vann's statement was prompted somewhat by flattery, and yet it was not inconceivable that larger things might be in store for Guffey if he continued to be a strong Democratic force in an important state.

But matters began to get complicated for Guffey's gubernatorial aspirations near the end of January when John L. Lewis, forceful head of the CIO with the ability to influence a half-million votes, declared that his choice for governor was Thomas Kennedy, then lieutenant governor of the state and secretary of the United Mine Workers, and also a Guffey cohort. Matters worsened for Guffey when the Democratic State Committee met in February under Lawrence's firm hand and selected neither Guffey nor Kennedy as the gubernatorial nominee, but Charles Alvin Jones, a relatively unknown Allegheny County attorney.[67] Reportedly Guffey stormed out of that meeting in anger, though he publicly denied any rift with Lawrence at that time.[68] Guffey was undoubtedly bypassed because of the antagonism Lawrence felt toward him, and Thomas Kennedy was omitted because he was opposed by the AFL and supported by the CIO's John L. Lewis, who had just been expelled from the AFL. The struggle between the AFL and the CIO for political supremacy over Pennsylvania's organized labor was as much an issue in this Democratic battle royal as was the personal Guffey-Lawrence squabble. The Democrats did not want any fighting between the huge unions and deemed it best for party harmony to have no direct labor representative on the ticket; it was thought that nominating an unknown like Jones would avert such a dispute.[69]

Guffey and Vann, as well as John L. Lewis, were not at all happy about the choice of Jones. Guffey quickly dubbed him "Lawrence's Man Friday" and "Casper Milquetoast Jones" in reference to Jones's conservative leanings. Jones had been a Republican until the New Deal, and Guffey accused him of being a "stop Roosevelt" man at the 1932 convention. Guffey, resentful of Lawrence's role in nominating Jones, considered running for governor on his own antiorganization ticket. But allegedly President Roosevelt called him down to Washington along with the other state Democratic leaders and tried to convince him not to create such a serious split in the state party. FDR wanted Guffey to remain in the Senate, where he was needed more.[70]

The fissure seemed closed, but the new unity lasted only a matter of weeks. Not long after David Lawrence remarked that "the Guffeys and the Lawrences will not part [politically] this side of the grave of either of them,"[71] the State Democratic Committee formalized its choice of Charles Alvin Jones for the gubernatorial nomination and George Earle for the Senate. Almost immediately Guffey, along with John L. Lewis, formed a group to support Thomas Kennedy for governor and Mayor Davis Wilson of Philadelphia for the Senate seat.[72] With Guffey's announcement of his support for Kennedy and Wilson, his breach with David Lawrence became public knowledge. This time it would not be easily closed.

The two factions of the Democratic party squared off for the state primary in May. On the one side there was the Jones-Earle ticket of the regular state organization led by David Lawrence, Matthew McCloskey, and John Kelly, which had control over 27,000 state, county, and local workers, and William Green's AFL, with a membership of about 400,000. On the other side was the Kennedy-Wilson ticket getting support from John L. Lewis's CIO-UMW of about 500,000 workers,[73] from Senator Guffey and the 197,000 WPA employees he essentially controlled, and Robert Vann, who hoped to speak for the majority of the *Courier*'s black readers in Pennsylvania.

Schism and Decline: 1936–1938 • 281

Vann had little doubt that he would follow Guffey's lead from the moment the schism first seemed possible, and had broken away from the regular-organization Allegheny County Democratic Association (then run by Paul Jones) to form the Allegheny County Colored Democratic Organization. And Vann had Guffey's assurance that he would be rewarded with patronage if they were victorious. Guffey wrote to the president of the Negro Security Civic League that "Mr. Vann will see that you and your organization are compensated in the proper manner after the election is over."[74]

Another reason for Vann's (and his newspaper's) allegiance to labor leader Thomas Kennedy was the fact that at this time Vann and the *Courier* were very favorably disposed toward the CIO. Once again,

ATTENTION!
DEMOCRATIC
MASS MEETING
COLORED VOTERS

Come and hear this National Negro Leader, the Principal Speaker on the issue of today.

Hon. Robert L. Vann
OF PITTSBURGH, PA.
Formerly 1st Assistant to U. S. Attorney General

—OTHER SPEAKERS—
Judge Ralph H. Smith, Mrs. Edith Dewitt, Lt. Gov. Thos. Kennedy, other National Leaders and Candidates.

FAYETTE COUNTY COURT HOUSE
UNIONTOWN, PA.

WEDNESDAY, MAY 11, 1938
7:30 P. M.

FREE LUNCH SERVED AFTER MEETING AT HEADQUARTERS
292 1-2 E. MAIN STREET

CAMPAIGN MANAGERS

A flyer announcing one of Vann's political appearances.

Vann had expediently altered his view of labor unions; in this case he had undoubtedly been influenced by Senator Guffey. In 1937, when the CIO was conducting an intensive membership drive all through the major industrial cities of the United States, during which the union threatened or actually began strikes against giant corporations like Chrysler, United States Steel, and Jones and Laughlin, the *Courier* gave close coverage and solid backing to the CIO. George Schuyler took a long tour of all the cities where important labor activity was taking place, which he reported on in long weekly articles for the *Courier*. During that time the paper's editorials applauded the progress of the CIO's drive and endorsed the union's racial policies with statements like "The Committee for Industrial Organization . . . bids fair to become the outstanding labor organization on the continent. . . . [with] a studied policy of NO DISCRIMINATION against Negroes,"[75] or "[The CIO] has done more than any single agency in the history of the country's labor movement to eliminate the biracialism which has so slowed the emancipation of the workers from industrial feudalism. The wisdom of the Negro workers who joined this stand for better working conditions and industrial democracy is to be commended."[76] And Vann personally espoused the CIO's efforts to unionize blacks. He once threatened a group of black steelworkers in Pittsburgh, "I tell you that this effort to organize Negroes in the steel industry is going to be hampered in this district . . . by Negroes who will be paid by this very industry and I serve notice on you now that I shall expose to the reading public the name and address and the mother and father of any Negro I can find who does that."[77]

On April 2, 1938, Vann formally announced in the *Courier* his support of the Kennedy-Wilson ticket and reaffirmed his loyalty to Joe Guffey. "Senator Guffey is the man who brought the Negroes into the Democratic Party and opened the first doors of political economic opportunity to Negroes in the state of Pennsylvania. . . . I came into the party with Senator Guffey and . . . I am going up with him or down with him."[78] Vann followed that up on the evening of April 28 with a radio broadcast over KDKA in Pittsburgh. He told the radio audience how he had been refused entry to the Democratic state convention of February 12 even though he held a legitimate proxy ticket and had been forced to enter as a member of the press. He said the selection of Jones and Earle had been a railroad job, pure and simple. "The candidates . . . were handed to a convention which had been handcuffed and gagged by bosses who arrogated

Schism and Decline: 1936–1938 • 283

to themselves the right to slate their own candidates by force rather than to allow Democrats to speak and choose the ticket by suffrage."[79] Vann went on to denounce Paul Jones, whom Lawrence was trying to appoint to Vann's position as the local black leader.[80] Vann's scathing personal attack on Paul Jones was an effort to discredit him in the eyes of Pittsburgh blacks and thus regather the mantle of leadership about himself. He felt threatened by Paul Jones, who represented the first real challenge to Vann's preeminence among the blacks of the city.

Before the Democratic primary, Vann could not help but feel that his role in the 1938 Pennsylvania election would be of vital importance. His newspaper was nationally prominent and at a circulation of 145,000 weekly was far ahead of its nearest competitor. It completely dominated western Pennsylvania, and its Philadelphia edition had a larger reading public than the other two black Philadelphia weeklies combined. Vann gained additional confidence because of what he called the "nation-wide blow-off," a two-part *Saturday Evening Post* article by political analysts Joseph Alsop and Robert Kintner entitled "The Guffey," which portrayed Vann in great detail as a political power among black Pennsylvanians.[81] On April 26 Vann went with Senator Guffey to see FDR. The ostensible purpose of their visit was to discuss an all-black Army division, but they also talked of Pennsylvania politics, though the exact content of their discussion is not known. Later Vann and Guffey posed for photographers on the steps of the White House.

Vann was also receiving a large amount of publicity as a possible candidate for the Supreme Court, though it was never a serious possibility, because the nation would undoubtedly not have accepted a black justice in that year. The press's attention to Vann arose, paradoxically, from his opposition to FDR on two issues concerning the judiciary. The first was Vann's criticism of Roosevelt's Judiciary Reorganization Act in 1937. The *Courier* received national journalistic acclaim when one of its editorials on this subject was judged "Editorial of the Day" in the May 7, 1937, *Chicago Tribune*. The editorial cautioned that "a high-minded liberal like President Roosevelt" should not allow Democratic party domination of the court, which would prove disastrous. The editorial also lauded the Supreme Court's record since 1915 as one which had forestalled attempts to force black people back into the low status of post-Reconstruction days.[82]

The second topic which put Vann in the news was his opposition

Vann and Joseph E. Guffey leaving the White House, 1938.

Schism and Decline: 1936–1938 • 285

to the appointment of Senator Hugo Black of Alabama to the Supreme Court in 1937 as a replacement for retiring Justice Willis Van Devanter. When FDR nominated Black, Vann's newspaper objected strenuously, at first because of Black's opposition to the Wagner-Costigan anti-lynch bill. Black, however, was hardly a racist demagogue. As a matter of fact, many conservative southern Democrats opposed him as too staunch a liberal and New Dealer and only voted for confirmation out of Senatorial courtesy. At times Black appeared to be more liberal than the FDR administration. Earlier, as an attorney in Alabama, Black had been considered a "poor man's lawyer" who often took on needy blacks as his clients. He also defended the right of R. R. Moton, president of Tuskegee Institute, to vote. Nonetheless, most black leaders opposed his nomination. The opposition was unsuccessful; Black was confirmed by a 63-to-16 vote in August.[83]

Less than a month after Black was sworn in, Ray Sprigle, a reporter for the anti-Roosevelt *Pittsburgh Post-Gazette* broke the story that Black had been a member of the Ku Klux Klan in 1923 and had in fact been given a life membership in the Klan.[84] The *Post-Gazette* stories, for which Sprigle later won a Pulitzer Prize, caused a national sensation. Vann was among the most vociferous of those who demanded Black's immediate resignation. He sent a telegram to FDR, which the *Courier* ran on the front page in bold black type:

> ROOSEVELTIAN COURAGE AS THE AMERICAN PEOPLE KNOW IT DEMANDS YOUR DISAVOWAL OF THE APPOINTMENT OF SENATOR BLACK TO THE SUPREME COURT. THE MORAL ISSUE NOW RAISED FAR TRANSCENDS EVERY POSSIBLE POLITICAL EXPEDIENT.[85]

But FDR remained silent on the matter, and Black gave a speech over nationwide radio in which he stated he had resigned from the Klan in 1925, had not kept his "unsolicited" life membership card, and had every intention of opposing groups like the Ku Klux Klan that interfered with the constitutional rights of others.[86] Eventually the furor died down.

Just two months later, when Justice George Sutherland retired from the Supreme Court, Vann's name came up as a possible successor. Black organizations like the National Bar Association, of which Vann was a past president and, in 1938, the Pennsylvania regional director, the YMCA Serving Colored Men and Boys, the Elks (Black Division), and Urban League chapters, petitioned the president in Vann's behalf.

Among the numerous individuals who endorsed Vann were C. C. Spaulding, president of North Carolina Mutual Life Insurance, one of the country's most important black businessmen.[87] H. L. Mencken tendered an endorsement in the *Baltimore Evening Sun* for which Vann may not have been entirely grateful:

> The *Evening Sun* can see no reason why he shouldn't be appointed. To be sure, his gifts as a jurisconsult do not appear to be staggering, but neither do those of the Hon. Hugo L. Black. If the white Crackers of the South, in return for their votes, deserve to have a reliable agent in the Supreme Court, then why should the colored faithful of both North and South, not to mention East and West, be denied? If a Ku Kluxer is good enough for the ermine, then what is to be said against a respectable colored Elk?
>
> The darker New Dealers have had to put up with a great deal of late and some of them grow uneasy, and even peevish. The White House might have got the anti-lynching bill through very easily, but it preferred to hold aloof. When it inflicted Hugo on the country it amazed and outraged all its colored customers, and even Mr. Vann hollered loudly.[88]

Vann accepted the editorial in good humor, telling Mencken, "I have enjoyed reading the comment. It has provoked no end of laughter among my friends." In the event he was appointed, said Vann, "I shall not ask Mr. Black to move over. Ye gods, no! I shall ask to be seated to the extreme right in order to maintain our traditional distance apart."[89] Humor aside, however, Vann took his legal career seriously and apprised Mencken at some length of his legal background and record of successes since 1910.[90]

Vann knew he had no chance of being named to the Supreme Court. Of the 253 federal judges in the United States, only one, William H. Hastie, was black, and he was down in the Virgin Islands, safely away from the eyes of whites who might object. As the *Courier* carefully pointed out, the highest position ever held by a black man in the Supreme Court was that of messenger.[91] Nevertheless, as Vann himself emphasized, "We will never get anything of this kind until somebody is led to believe we ought to have it, and I am allowing my name to be used solely for the purpose of creating a favorable impression toward the idea."[92]

With all the furor and publicity about the Supreme Court surrounding Vann, it seemed he would contribute a great deal of prestige to the Kennedy-Wilson ticket he was supporting in Pennsylvania. And other things appeared to be going well for the antiorganization slate during April. It was discovered that the Democratic State Committee owed money to Lewis's CIO, which the labor union could demand and then use to finance its campaign against the committee's candidates. Also, a third candidate who had entered the race, Attorney General Charles Joseph Margiotti of Pittsburgh, made accusations against the Earle administration which elated the Kennedy-Wilson supporters. Margiotti charged that the state employees were being "maced," or forced to give back some of their pay for political contributions to the Jones-Earle campaign. He further accused David Lawrence of "selling" protective legislation to the state's brewers for $20,000. Also, Margiotti said Earle had offered to bribe Republican Senator Davis into resigning his seat in Congress and then give it to Margiotti if the latter agreed to withdraw from the gubernatorial race. Earle denied all accusations and demanded that Margiotti produce evidence to substantiate them. Margiotti refused, stating he would do this only before a grand jury. So Earle dismissed him as attorney general, and Margiotti started grand jury action.[93] More charges of malfeasance were brought against Governor Earle. His opponent for the senatorial nomination, S. Davis Wilson, said that Earle had accepted a $30,000 personal loan from Matthew McCloskey, a Philadelphia Democratic leader, and since then McCloskey's construction firm had received nearly $10 million in state contracts.[94]

Vann and Guffey made extensive use of such accusations in their speeches for the Kennedy-Wilson ticket. Senator Guffey denounced "contractor bosses" and asserted that the main issue of the campaign was "whether contractor bosses and race horse gamblers are going to take over the Democratic party and run it or whether it will remain in the hands of the liberals."[95] Vann, in his KDKA speech, warned that the illegal behavior attributed to his foes "must in no way be construed as an indictment of the entire Democratic party. These men . . . will be eliminated from control. . . . Mr. Margiotti's charges will serve to cleanse rather than to destroy the Democratic Party."[96]

The Jones-Earle faction struck back. Guffey was accused of coercing WPA workers and federal officers in Pennsylvania into helping to finance the Kennedy-Wilson campaign, and a federal investigation was demanded. Guffey flatly denied the charge, and a Senate investigating committee went to Pennsylvania where they found no proof that the charges were true. Guffey was cleared, but the incident "added to the bad political odor surrounding the Democratic Party."[97]

Guffey and Vann worked hard to identify their candidates, Kennedy and Wilson, with the magic name of Roosevelt. Guffey told a group of blacks that only by voting for Kennedy and Wilson would they get "a [state] government which will, in all respects, conform to the great liberal program so successfully inaugurated by our President."[98] And Vann stressed that a vote for Kennedy and Wilson was a vote to continue "the same brilliant forward-looking principles which have been so clearly enunciated by our President and which we may consider the birthright and guiding force of every Democratic voter."[99]

But Roosevelt wisely refused to take sides in the Pennsylvania Democratic primary, for both factions were tainted by scandal by the time of the May election. In 1938 Roosevelt was deluged with difficulties of his own and could not face taking on the internal struggle in Pennsylvania.[100] FDR had been heavily criticized in 1937 for attempting to "pack" the Supreme Court; he was held responsible for the recession which continued from 1937 to 1938; he tried, unwisely and unsuccessfully in 1938 to purge his party of anti–New Deal Democrats; and the volatile international situation was requiring a great deal of his time. Even James Farley demurred from making any public comment, until Guffey reminded Farley he had political obligations to himself and John L. Lewis. Not until primary eve did Farley say anything, and then he put a foot in each camp and created great confusion by coming out for Guffey's man Kennedy for governor, but Lawrence's man Earle for senator.[101]

Despite their strenuous efforts, the Kennedy-Wilson ticket and its supporters were at a distinct disadvantage on primary day. To begin with, they were a rebel faction fighting an established group. All the leaders were capable politicians, but they faced a well-organized, long-established machine staffed with experienced ward and precinct workers who reached the voters directly. Second, not only were Kennedy and his supporters dissidents, but they were badly organized. They had been slow to present a full slate to the public, and they failed to do much of the necessary routine spadework at the local level before the primary. Next, John L. Lewis's political control over the CIO was questionable at that time, for he had done two things which disgruntled the union members—taken a substantial increase

Schism and Decline: 1936–1938 • 289

in his salary and assessed the members for political contributions, during a recession year when things were pinched. And last, Vann's estimate that he could get 90 percent of the black vote for his ticket was far-fetched. In Pittsburgh, Lawrence had won over a good many blacks through Paul Jones, and in Philadelphia Lawrence's cohorts Kelly and McCloskey controlled a large share of the black voters.[102]

The Democratic primary was held on May 17. It was a sunny day, and a record number of voters went to the polls. Not too surprisingly, the Jones-Earle slate won with 587,000 votes to Kennedy-Wilson's 522,000, while the third candidate, Margiotti, received 173,000.[103] Of course the real winner that day was the Republican party, who knew that whatever wounds were opened by the bitter primary fight could only work to the advantage of the GOP in November.

The day after the primary the Democrats made a great show of reconciliation at a meeting in Harrisburg at the Penn-Harris Hotel. Guffey was deferred to as the head of the party in Pennsylvania and speechified on the need for party solidarity. But in reality, the power had been realigned. Guffey was dethroned, and Lawrence was the true head of the party.[104] As evidence of that fact, when Robert Vann asked the new gubernatorial candidate, Charles Alvin Jones, in the presence of Lawrence and Guffey, what his attitude was toward fulfilling the earlier agreement that 10 percent of state patronage should go to blacks, Lawrence would not allow Jones to answer the question. Lawrence was unquestionably in command. Seeing that it was hopeless to press his case, Vann left the meeting.[105]

Compared to the Democratic melee, the Republican primary was gentle and friendly. Superior Court Judge Arthur H. James, a conservative, with financial support provided in part by former Senator Joseph Grundy and millionaire Joseph Pew, comfortably defeated former governor Gifford Pinchot. In the Senate race, singularly devoid of interest, incumbent Senator James "Puddler Jim" Davis, slated with James, ran ahead of independent State Senator G. Mason Owlett.

During the early summer months, Vann went off to Europe to join his wife for a vacation and contemplate his next political move. Two things bothered him about the primary victory of Lawrence's faction. For one, it was a personal defeat for Vann as well as the deposition of his mentor Guffey. Vann and Lawrence had always been at odds, and Lawrence was already trying to replace Vann as black leader in Pittsburgh with Paul Jones. Second, Vann was genuinely concerned that Lawrence's ascension to power spelled trouble for all the local blacks, since Lawrence was definitely not giving the blacks their just 10 percent share of patronage and seemed in no way interested in furthering their lot as some white leaders were.

Vann was worried that the black people, who had for the most part blindly followed the lead of the Republicans prior to 1932, would now just as blindly follow the Democrats without giving enough attention to whether the party was adequately serving their interests. Vann's theory of the "liquid vote" was that the blacks should vote for whoever seemed determined to give them the fairest deal and never stay confined in their loyalty to one political party. Vann mentioned the idea of a flexible allegiance to someone who had written that the black vote would never again be Republican. Vann answered, "This is a conclusion not based on any fact, because you do not know, nor do the Republicans know, nor do the Democrats know how long the Negro vote . . . will remain with the Democratic Party."[106]

Vann decided that summer to make a move which would later be deemed either brave or reckless, depending on one's point of view. He decided to throw his support and that of those blacks he could influence to the Republican gubernatorial candidate, Arthur H. James. If he could switch the black vote en masse to an opposition candidate, it would prove to all white political leaders the importance of the "liquid vote" and the error of taking black support for granted. Moreover, if he could demonstrate his ability to force this massive shift in the black vote, it would enhance immeasurably his own stature as a political power to be reckoned with. Events would prove Vann's decision foolhardy, but his reasoning about the liquid vote was not altogether unsound, and the primary results had backed him into a corner. Lawrence was out to undermine Vann's power; if Lawrence's candidate won, Vann would have little hope of maintaining his former authority. But Vann was also a proud and spirited man, and it was unthinkable that he would bow to Lawrence's leadership for the moment and hope to regain his power later.

It was near the end of the summer when Vann first hinted publicly that he could consider a bolt from the Democrats. He sat down with the rebel group, the Allegheny County Colored Democratic Organization, of which he was chairman, and told them that they should be free of political ties and be independent with respect to both candidates and parties. He admonished the members of the ACCDO to "build up our organization as a source of strength and of power. When we have done that, it will not be necessary for us to go out and seek anybody to endorse. Those who need our endorsement will come to us."[107]

Then in September Vann wrote to Senator Guffey to explain the path down which his thoughts were taking him. With somewhat questionable logic he said that he was willing to back the Republican nominee in order to defeat the Lawrence faction, and thus return Guffey to his proper place in Pennsylvania politics:

> When you were undisputed leader, your promises to me were kept and your attitude gave promise of a complete fulfillment of commitments made when Governor Earle, Mr. Lawrence and yourself said publicly that so far as patronage is concerned, my groups were entitled to ten per cent, no more and no less, and the Democratic administration would see to it that we got it.
>
> As long as your leadership was undisputed, this policy was adhered to but after the primaries when your own party opponents developed the idea that they could destroy your leadership, the policy known as the Guffey policy to my group began gradually to wane, and at this writing, we are practically ignored and forgotten. I do not know what your convictions are with respect to party harmony but I am quite certain of my convictions with respect to my group. There is nothing left us but to fight for restoration of the Guffey policy.... If it requires the defeat of the Democratic organization and ticket in order to restore Guffey leadership and the Guffey policy ... then the defeat must be made certain and very definite.[108]

A few days later, Vann wrote to Robert Church of the *Philadelphia Tribune* of his impending defection to James and the Republicans: "I am going to reserve my bolts for a few days later, and when I start bolting, you will probably think I am crazy."[109]

Two weeks before the election, Vann made his move. At a meeting of the ACCDO on October 16, he declared that through Senator Guffey the black man had received all he had, but Guffey had made the mistake of entrusting patronage to men such as David Lawrence, who had misused that trust to wrest control away from the senator. Vann assured his rebel group, "We can pull the feathers out of Dave Lawrence. We can follow the advice of the President, purge the Democratic Party of its undesirable elements, remain Democrat, and vote for Arthur H. James." With that, the ACCDO passed a resolution supporting the Republican candidate for governor, but not the rest of the GOP slate.[110] Vann reasoned it was the only way to end the Lawrence domination and restore Guffey to his proper leadership.[111]

In backing Arthur H. James for governor, Vann was ignoring the fact that James had been an ultraconservative lieutenant governor a decade earlier, and that his present platform called for a retrenchment of Earle's "Little New Deal," part of which would be the termination of the Civil Rights Bureau created by Earle.[112] Vann was so anxious to strike back at David Lawrence that he was willing to accept these aspects of James's attitude toward blacks. And the GOP had condemned the corruption of the New Deal Democrats in Pennsylvania, stressing the Margiotti charges, which had been to the grand jury and were still very much in the news. Vann kept silent on the matter; to Vann the Democratic party was not at fault for the scandal, only those presently in control in the state.[113]

Vann's defection brought an immediate denunciation from Senator Guffey, the very person Vann thought he was attempting to help politically. Guffey disavowed the idea that Vann's action was taken to help the black populace or himself. Guffey claimed that Vann had bolted because the Democrats did not like his attempts to dictate all the dispensation of black patronage. "Mr. Vann's attempt to justify his decision on the ground that it was for my best interest is *deceitful and dishonest*. He knows full well that I am 100 percent behind every Democratic nominee and I am doing everything in my power to bring about their election."[114] Guffey was not about to consider doing anything other than remain loyal to the Democratic machine. The strength of his statement about Vann being "deceitful and dishonest" was motivated by the fact that Lawrence had accused Guffey of having known all along about Vann's intentions to defect without doing a thing to stop him.[115] To show his steadfast allegiance and prove his good faith, Guffey had to strike out at Vann, whom he branded as "a false prophet to his people."[116]

Vann was both hurt and angered by Guffey's statement that he was "deceitful and dishonest." Opportunist he may have been on occasion, attentive to expediency, and arrogant with others, but Robert Vann prided himself on his honesty. He readily altered his viewpoints, but was always forthright and outspoken about his changes of heart. He kept his word until he saw fit to change it, which he did nearly always in an aboveboard manner. Vann was not used to being accused of mendacity.[117] This assault by his friend and mentor stung badly, and Vann was quick to retaliate. He assailed Guffey for being "completely dominated" by Lawrence and said the Democrats had "made a Charlie McCarthy of Senator Guffey and every time Edgar Bergen

Lawrence squeezes Guffey's diaphragm Guffey lets out an attack upon me."[118] Vann insisted that he had early informed Guffey of his intentions during a meeting when Guffey asked him not to press for the patronage promise and to support C. A. Jones for governor, and that on that occasion Vann replied that Jones had acquiesced to Lawrence's refusal to honor the 10 percent agreement and that, moreover, Jones's election meant Lawrence's reappointment as secretary of the Commonwealth and Vann could not support that.[119] Vann emphasized that there had been nothing deceitful about his actions.

Obviously Guffey, being a realist, knew he could not jeopardize his own political career by offering any public encouragement to Vann. Guffey was already on the defensive with the Democratic State Committee. His only recourse was to break with Vann, to prove his loyalty by casting his lot with the politically safe side, with the hope that, if Vann was successful, a reconciliation could be effected after the election. But there was never to be a reconciliation, for Guffey had wounded Vann too deeply.

Guffey undoubtedly also realized Vann could not swing much of the black vote to the GOP. His sister, Emma Guffey Miller, apprised James Farley of this apparent fact. "The defection of Robert L. Vann, the Negro leader, is doing very little harm, and I believe the Negro vote will go generally to the Democrats."[120]

Vann's bolt from the Democrats proved lonely. He and his dissident ACCDO were joined only by the Baptist Convention and one bishop of the AME Church. Nevertheless, the *Courier* claimed the backing of most of the average black voters. He published many letters of encouragement from sympathetic readers: "Congratulations on your wise and courageous policy," "Your courageous action . . . has my personal endorsement," "We are switching with you," and "This move looks like one of intelligent honesty."[121]

Most of the black leadership, however, chastised Vann for his action. The black members of the Central Pennsylvania Democratic State Committee expressed "not only our dismay but our disgust at the stand taken by the Honorable (?) R. L. Vann of Pittsburgh in supporting the candidacy of Judge Arthur James, reactionary Republican candidate."[122] Paul F. Jones, who had recently replaced Vann as the dispenser of patronage to blacks, assured the Democratic leadership that blacks would not be influenced by Vann's actions.[123] The most surprising denunciation of Vann came when Theron B. "Slim" Hamilton, a longtime friend and political ally, criticized Vann's action publicly and declared he would support the Democratic nominee. Vann had been sure he could count on Hamilton's support; Hamilton had been hired by the *Courier* at Vann's recommendation, he then succeeded Vann in Washington as special assistant to the attorney general in 1936, and when he left that post, Vann helped him get a position as assistant city assessor in Pittsburgh. Vann charged that Hamilton had yielded to pressure from Lawrence, who threatened him with the loss of his $4,500-a-year job in the assessor's office.[124]

Some unknown person accused Vann of having been bribed into backing Arthur James for governor. In a long explanatory letter to Judge Stephen Stone, Vann acknowledged that such an attempt at bribery had been made through an intermediary, Robert Church of the *Philadelphia Tribune*, who was acting for Joseph Pew, multimillionaire Republican backer. Pew, who had recently gained control of the state GOP from Joseph Grundy, was said by Vann to be using Church "to trade in the open market for Negro votes." Vann was offered a share of a $100,000 fund, but Vann said he had unconditionally refused the bribe. He added that he had intended to vote for James on principle long before the bribery attempt, and to do so as a Democrat without joining the Republican party.[125] The Republican party leaders also stressed that no political deals whatsoever were being made between the GOP and the *Courier* editor. In fact, the Republicans were somewhat fearful that, if James won with Vann's support, "Vann will demand his *quid pro quo*."[126]

The extensive criticism of Vann's defection began to take its toll of the aging man. For once, he did not seem entirely under control and struck out in every direction with bitter invective. He felt he was being unfairly treated by his own people as well as the whites. He accused Paul Jones of being a betrayer of the race, as subservient to the white man as "Simon Legree's Sambo." He attacked the blacks who had turned against him: "They even stood up in the Watt Street School . . . in the presence of Lawrence and Guffey and some other white leaders, and stuck out their chests and screamed at the top of their voices in abuse of Bob Vann because they thought they were pleasing the white men who were looking on and listening, but not a single white man abused Vann, but oh, how the Negroes did strut their stuff."[127] Vann had never before indulged in this sort of vindictiveness toward members of his own race.

Vann was particularly outraged by a characterization of himself which appeared in a *Time* magazine article as a "sharp-faced, dark-

Schism and Decline: 1936–1938 • 295

skinned personage who occupies a mansion hard by the swank Oakmont Country Club." *Time* called him a political opportunist who as early as 1930 sensed the changing political trend and went over to the Democrats where he made his way "under the wing of Senator Guffey." Vann, said *Time*, "who pictures himself as the guiding mind" behind the black electorate, did not in actuality control the black vote, because half of it was in Philadelphia, and part of the Pittsburgh group was allied solely with Guffey and the WPA, having little allegiance to Vann. The article went on to say that in his early years Vann had "grubbed at the law until he got stock in the *Pittsburgh Courier* for drawing its charter."[128]

Vann sent off an irate letter to *Time* editor Henry Luce:

> Some of your subordinates have seen fit to give me a decided dig. I don't know what I have ever done to offend any of the members of the High Command, but it appears that somebody in your organization is cultivating a very subtle dislike for me, personally, and that somebody, at every opportunity, gives expression to that dislike...
>
> If I have been misled as to the policy of your various publications with respect to members of my racial group, of course, I admit my disillusionment and ask respectfully that my subscriptions, every one of them, be cancelled.... I cannot afford to pay cash to see myself offended.[129]

Vann had forgotten one of the precepts of journalism that, as *Time* pointed out in its answering letter, "requires you to don the same thick skin that our American concepts of freedom of thought and expression force on all men in the public limelight.... Such loss of a certain personal sensitivity [is] a small price for the freedom from the censorship which has strangled so large a portion of the world press today."[130] Something was happening to Vann's equilibrium at this time. A friend said, "He was very unhappy. He was sensitive and did not suffer slights lightly."[131]

Vann's defection in and of itself might not have caused the Democrats undue concern had it not been for the woes already besetting the party. The truce between the Guffey and Lawrence factions was uneasy. Guffey was under fire for blatant political manipulation of the WPA; the Earle administration was under a cloud of scandal stemming from the accusations of Margiotti; and Roosevelt was offering no support in the campaign. Though it was highly unlikely that Vann could control three-quarters of the 275,000 black voters in

Pennsylvania, he did begin to take on the proportions of a key figure who might conceivably divert victory away from the Democrats in a close election.[132] Realizing this, Vann played up his role for all it was worth in the closing days of the campaign. On October 26, he met with President Roosevelt to discuss his proposals for blacks in the armed services. Though he probably did not discuss Pennsylvania politics with the president during the meeting, Vann capitalized on the publicity he received as a result of the encounter. He told newsmen waiting outside the White House, "I don't think you will see Governor Earle coming to Washington. I am not in favor of his coming here."[133] As Kintner and Alsop noted, Vann had played "the best political joke in recent history. . . . The ebullient Vann visited the White House in great pomp—ostensibly to persuade the president to establish a Negro Division in the Army. And on the way out he used the White House steps, hitherto consecrated to the most New Dealish announcements, to endorse the entire Republican ticket in Pennsylvania."[134]

On November 4 Vann spoke to a black audience from his own district, with the speech simultaneously aired over statewide radio. Vann publicly reviewed the events which led to his break with Senator Guffey, in particular Guffey's charge that he had been "deceitful and dishonest," which still rankled badly. He said he had told Guffey of his intentions at an early date and that Guffey had replied, "Now, Bob, as a Democratic Senator, and as the President's Number One Democrat in Pennsylvania I cannot consistently tell you to go ahead, but as your friend and as a friend of the people who followed me, I am not going to tell you not to do it." At the end of the broadcast, Vann made one last public appeal to Guffey: "How could I be deceitful when you knew what I was going to do, and how could I be dishonest when I did exactly what I told you I was going to do?"[135]

As the Democrats had feared, the many troubles which beset the party led to their defeat on November 8. The Republican candidate for governor won 2,035,340 to 1,756,192, and the Senate contender won 2,086,931 to 1,694,367. The Democratic loss in Pennsylvania was also part of a national trend in that year's elections,[136] no doubt in part because the Democrats were being blamed for the 1937–38 recession.

What happened to the black vote was particularly interesting. It might have been expected that a fair number would return to the Republican ranks. Vann had campaigned hard for the Republican contender, and the GOP made a concerted bid for the black vote

Schism and Decline: 1936–1938 • 297

in that election for the first time in some years. The Republicans had attacked discrimination in the New Deal agencies and the failure of the Democrats to pass an anti-lynch bill.[137] They accused Governor Earle of racist tactics because he pressured J. Austin Norris, a black man slated for a federal judgeship, into accepting a position on the Philadelphia Board of the Revision of Taxes instead, allegedly because as a possible presidential aspirant in 1940, Earle feared that the appointment as judge would alienate many of his white supporters.[138] And the Republicans had continuously stressed that for the first time in Pennsylvania a black, Edward Henry, a magistrate from Philadelphia, was nominated for a congressional seat and that it had been the Republicans, and not the Democrats, who had chosen him.[139] But apparently neither Vann nor the GOP had been able to change the black allegiance to the Democrats. In the Third and Fifth Wards of Pittsburgh, for example, the Earle-Jones slate swamped the Republicans, 5,433 to 1,194 and 7,009 to 3,473.[140] In Philadelphia, the Democrats received 53.86 percent of the vote in the city's black wards.[141] As it turned out, the blacks were not about to desert the party that represented relief, job-giving agencies like the WPA and the CCC, significant state and federal appointments, and social legislation. One wry election observer had summed up Vann's chances of changing the black vote: "If I had a penny for every vote Vann can get without Guffey pressure on the WPA, I would go to the movies."[142] The Democratic defeat in Pennsylvania had been in no way connected to desertion by the blacks; on the contrary, they had remained completely loyal to the party. Election figures to the contrary, however, Vann maintained that the black electorate had voted Republican and knocked "the 'Little New Deal' into a cocked hat."[143]

After the election, things settled down in the Democratic party. Charles Alvin Jones, politically unknown before the election, vanished into obscurity. Governor Earle, having lost his bid for the Senate, quietly retired to the ranks of ex-governors. Guffey continued in his Senate seat and regained his number-one position among state Democrats, because Lawrence's faction had been discredited by defeat. But Vann's break with Joe Guffey was final and irrevocable; he vowed he would never ally himself with Guffey again until the senator retracted his "deceitful and dishonest" statement, and Guffey, equally stubborn, refused to do so.[144]

Robert Vann began to plan for a political future unconstricted by party allegiances. He reorganized his Allegheny County Colored Democratic Organization, renamed it the Colored Allegheny Political and Civic League, and set out to make it a strong statewide association. He stated that the CAPCL would not be affiliated with either political party, but would operate on the principle of the "liquid vote."[145] As he explained in very pragmatic terms, "Liquid assets are those that you can turn over and make use of. You can sell them, usually at a profit. Somebody is willing to pay for your assets if they are liquid."[146] He hoped that blacks would consistently vote for the man who offered them the most patronage and favorable legislation; they should "sell" their vote for the greatest consideration, in both senses of the word. It was a good theory in principle, the idea being that both parties would vie to see which could offer the most to the black, so that even the lesser offering would be considerable. But in reality, it could not work very well. The average voter is not flexible enough to weigh all the issues pertinent to himself in an election year and choose rationally the candidate offering the fairest deal. Politics are much more irrational than that and, further, voters tend to stay with one political party over the years.

Initially, Vann believed patronage rewards were in the offing for him from the governor-elect. James conferred with Vann in Pittsburgh on December 28 regarding recognition for his race. After the meeting Vann commented to members of the press that he was "entirely satisfied" with their discussion regarding patronage.[147] But Vann gained nothing from his defection to the Republican candidate in 1938. In fact his losses were considerable. The new governor, Arthur James, invited Vann to his inauguration and thanked him for his help, but that was all. He offered no honors to Vann and no patronage for Vann's black followers.[148] Most of the Republicans regarded Vann as still a Democrat and were little interested in his alliance. With Allegheny blacks so firmly entrenched in the Democratic party, western Pennsylvania Republicans had little use for Vann, and in Philadelphia, the GOP relied instead on "Joe" Black, chairman of the "Negro unit," who was placed on the state GOP payroll as director of Negro work.[149] Since a minority of blacks had voted for him, Governor James had no interest in aiding the race. His retrenchment policies against former Governor Earle's "Little New Deal" included cessation of enforcement of the equal rights program. Within a fortnight after his inauguration, when a newspaperman asked him what would happen to the Civil Rights Bureau, James "replied with finality, 'That's out.'"[150]

· 12 ·

Twilight: 1938–1940

IN 1938, ROBERT VANN ENTERED his sixtieth year. Although that year marked a further decline in his political influence, it nevertheless saw him engrossed in other major undertakings and continuing to work almost without surcease. Second only to his involvement with politics that year was Vann's extensive crusade for racial equality in the armed services.

Vann had been battling in one way or another for black rights in the armed forces since World War I. When that war ended, Vann became one of the strongest supporters of a recommendation that a monument be erected in France to commemorate the black soldiers who had fought and died there in 1917–18. In 1926, at the urging of Vann and other black leaders, Congressman Hamilton Fish of New York, who had been an officer of the all-black 15th New York Colored Volunteers (later known as the 369th Regiment) and a pioneer in advocating equal rights for the black man in the armed services, introduced a bill for the building of such a monument.[1] It was for the soldiers of the 93rd Infantry Division, comprised of four black regiments, the 369th, 370th, 371st, and 372nd, who had landed in France during the winter of 1917. In Vann's words, after "not one single American command would accept them," they were placed under French officers and "fought scattered all through the French army in French uniforms, with French guns, in French divisions." As Vann pointed out,

> These boys were lost to this country except for the fact that they were American citizens and they fought with the French and died with the French, and not a single American officer has ever mentioned these boys in any reports coming from across the pond.... The service they

rendered is so distinct and unparalleled in the war records, that they deserve mention because of the peculiar circumstances under which they fought and died. If they had been white men, several monuments would have been mentioned for them long ago, but somebody wants to forget all about them and I am determined that these boys will not be forgotten.[2]

This particular measure was defeated in the Senate largely by the efforts of the reactionary Senator David Reed of Pennsylvania (whom Vann had supported in the past), a member of the Military Affairs Committee, who opposed it on the grounds that such a monument would imply segregation.[3] The following year, 1927, the measure was reintroduced in the Senate and once again killed by heavy blows from Senator Reed, "and that in spite of the fact that it had been reported by his own committee."[4]

The matter of racial equality in the armed services was dropped for several years while the nation preoccupied itself with the Depression. Then, in 1934, when only 4,000 of the 118,000 soldiers were black, Vann began to stress the need for more black participation in the military. Not only were there few blacks in the services, but those there were were mostly longtime reenlistees, which meant that extremely small numbers of blacks were being exposed to any sort of military training.

Vann sent *Courier* reporter Edgar T. Rouzeau to West Point to survey the duties being assigned blacks in the Tenth Cavalry. Rouzeau found the blacks working only at the degrading tasks of grooming officers' mounts and shoveling manure. The *Courier* further reported that blacks in the Twenty-fourth and Twenty-fifth Infantry at Fort Benning, Georgia, were working just as orderlies or on routine garrison duty. Blacks were excluded from the Artillery, the Coast Guard, the Army Air Corps, the Signal and Tank Corps, the Corps of Engineers, and the Marines. In the Navy, blacks could qualify only for mess duty, as waiters, cooks, or stewards.[5] Three years later, the *Courier* would discover that of the 32,522 men given military training in a given period, only 250 were blacks.[6] As late as 1940, there were just five black officers in the regular Army, three of whom were chaplains; only two were combat-trained. There were 500 black officers in the Army reserves, but most of these had come from the ROTC program at Howard University. Almost none were in ROTC at other colleges.[7]

In 1935, the *Courier* strongly supported a program to aid the black soldier in Pennsylvania. That year Vann's paper crusaded for a state bill to organize and equip two black infantry battalions in the Pennsylvania National Guard. A state legislator, Samuel B. Hart, who had been commanding officer of the last black regiment of the Pennsylvania National Guard prior to the Spanish-American War, succeeded in getting such a bill through the House of Representatives, 192 to 2. The two units were to be established in eastern and western Pennsylvania at an expense of up to $100,000. Hart's bill then went to the State Senate, where it was passed unanimously and signed by Governor Earle.[8] A previous bill for a "colored regiment of infantry," also submitted by Hart, had been vetoed by Governor Pinchot, who reasoned that the measure discriminatorily favored blacks.[9] However, the Hart bill's provisions met a fate of total inaction because the federal government did not fund it. After four years had passed, the black battalions had not been organized, and Vann was still trying to find out why.[10]

By 1938 the issue of blacks in the armed services had become very significant. War clouds were forming on the horizon, and the international situation worsened with each passing day. That year Vann's *Courier* took up in earnest the cudgels for greater military participation by blacks. One of Vann's greatest worries was that war would come to the shores of the United States and that few blacks would be properly trained to fight for their lives. He saw it as a question of prudence and self-preservation.

White military officials had charged that the blacks in the Ninety-second Infantry Division in World War I had fought poorly and used this as a reason for not giving blacks greater military responsibility. But as the *Courier* was quick to point out, the problems of the Ninety-second Infantry would have been avoided through proper training, equal facilities, and a qualified black officer cadre. Many white officers resented being assigned to black units and led them in a lackluster manner. The few black officers available during World War I had received substantially less military training and preparation than their white counterparts. And the *Courier* also noted that, though the blacks of the Ninety-second Infantry may have been charged with cowardice, the Ninety-third Division, which had fought under the French and received fair treatment on the line, had its regimental flag decorated with the Croix de Guerre, the highest military honor awarded by France.[11] Other *Courier* editorials stressed that blacks desired another chance to prove that they were loyal Americans, willing to fight bravely for their nation, and thus put an end to the cowardly image that many whites had formed of them. Blacks could acquit themselves admirably under fire, they could develop skills necessary to serve in the Air Corps, they were not disciplinary problems (as the 1917 Houston riot had led many to believe), and whites—particularly in the South, which housed most of the nation's military installations—need not fear racial turmoil.[12]

Beginning in February 1938, Vann's *Courier* intensified its campaign for better treatment of blacks in the armed services. The ultimate goal of the crusade was integration of the armed services with equal treatment and opportunity for all regardless of color; two more immediate aims were the formation of an all-black Army division and proper training of black officers to lead it.[13] Vann launched his crusade on February 19 with an open letter to President Roosevelt, given top coverage on page one, in which he listed ten reasons why blacks deserved equality in the Army and Navy:

1. **WE DESERVE JOBS IN THE SERVICE**

Of the approximately 165,000 jobs in our regular Army and Navy, the Negro at present had about 5,000 or one thirty-third. The Negroes compose one-tenth of the nation's population. This is a manifest discrimination.

2. **WE PAY FOR JOBS IN THE SERVICE**

We recall that the American nation was born in a glorious protest against "taxation without representation." Time does not alter principles. The Negro helps to pay for the upkeep of the Army and Navy, for the jobs and opportunities each offers. We believe he deserves to receive some return on his contribution.

3. **OUR FIGHTING RECORD SHOULD BE REWARDED**

Crispus Attucks shed the first blood for American independence on Boston Common, March 5, 1775. Negro fighters brought glory to America in the Revolution, in the War of 1812, in the Mexican and Indian wars, . . . in the World War. . . . This fighting record should be rewarded.

4. **WE SEEK THE TEST TO PROVE OUR MERIT**

. . . the nation must be apprised of our record and our contributions to its greatness. . . . Open the doors of the Army and Navy so that the black man can show America his ability to toe the mark.

5. **WE NEED EDUCATION JUST AS THE WHITES**

The Army and Navy are vast educational laboratories.... Black America wants its youth to share the benefits of service.

6. **WE SEEK THE CHANCE TO SHATTER PREJUDICE**

... black soldiers in heroic and exemplary service of their country can help to dissipate this prejudice. Black America seeks this opportunity to help draw all Americans together.

7. **OUR LOYALTY IS AN AMERICAN TRADITION**

... There has never been a black traitor to America's cause, in war or peace.... America cannot, without a sense of shame, continue to ignore these loyal millions. Our defense needs them.

8. **AMERICANISM IS TEST OF OUR FIGHTING MEN**

What, in the final analysis, do we ask? We plead, "Let us die for America if need be!"

9. **WE WANT TO GLORIFY AMERICA BEFORE THE WORLD**

... We are AMERICANS. This is our country which we would glorify before the entire world.

10. **WE WANT TO INSPIRE FUTURE BLACK AMERICA**

The record of black fighting men of the past is a source of inspiration to our race today. We seek the opportunity to make a new record to inspire black Americans of the future to greater and greater contributions to their country.[14]

The following month Vann delegated Percival Prattis, city editor of the *Courier,* who had served in France in 1918 in the 813th Pioneer Infantry Division, to survey congressmen, newspaper editors, college presidents, and religious and civic leaders for their opinions on the armed services controversy. Reportedly Vann chose Prattis because, "God damn it, you're the only soldier here [on the *Courier*]. Go ahead and do it!"[15] The letter Prattis mailed read as follows:

Although colored citizens have participated with honor and distinction in every war the United States has fought and died in the thousands that this grand Republic might live, they are today barred from virtually all service in our army and navy which they help support.

They are not permitted to serve in the air corps, the coastal artillery corps, the tank corps, the engineer corps, the chemical warfare service, the field artillery, the signal or any of the other special services. They serve only in the infantry, cavalry, and to a small extent in the quartermaster and medical corps, and many of these supposedly combat troops are assigned to duty as servants at army service schools. In the navy they are rigidly restricted to service as mess attendants.

Our army and navy are honeycombed with spies of alien extraction and connections who are easily enabled to enlist in our most vital services merely because they are white. No American Negro, soldier or civilian, has ever been suspected or convicted of betraying this country.

We do not believe that the thinking white people of this country are acquainted with this situation or would approve of it if they were. We are trying to have all branches of the army and navy opened to colored youth so that our nation may be certain of a trained reservoir of loyal, intelligent and dependable men. What is your view on this question?

Do you believe that all branches of the army and naval service should be opened to Negroes (they are over 99 per cent native born)? Or do you think there should be an entire Negro division, including all arms of the service and officered, at least in the line, by educated colored men, in the army; and a squadron manned by Negroes in the navy?

We feel that this question is important at this time when the whole matter of national defense is uppermost in our minds and the dangers of fascism, nazism, and communism are more real than ever before.

We shall appreciate a brief reply embodying your candid opinion on this question.

>Yours very truly,
>R. L. Vann, Editor

Vann then published a good deal of the correspondence in the *Courier*. The numerous responses to the question of whether the black man should be given equal opportunity in the military tended to vary according to the regional location of the correspondent. Northerners like Mayor Edward Kelly of Chicago and William A. Shawcross, chairman of the State Democratic Committee of Rhode Island, favored immediate integration of the armed forces with no discrimination whatever.[16] A southerner like Governor Bibb Graves of Alabama declined to answer the question, saying "that this is a matter entirely for Congress and the Federal Government and that my views would be of no interest to anybody."[17] The white editor of the *Harrison* (Ark.) *Daily Times* said the issue should not be pressed. "The colored race has come a long way in the last hundred years. I would like to see them go farther, but they make a mistake if they push themselves on the white race too fast."[18] The general consensus was against full integration. A separate black division should be established in the Army forthwith, but such a unit would be much more difficult to implement in the Navy.[19]

Taking his cue from the correspondence, and also because he believed that the ideal of total integration of the armed services was impossible at that point, Vann began to push for a separate black Army division. He wrote Senator Sherman Minton of Indiana, a member of the Military Affairs Committee, to ask him to sponsor a bill for an all-black division.[20] His canvass had shown that even most southerners would not oppose a separate black division with black officers, though it was unlikely anything could be done in the Navy, "based on social grounds." Vann reassured those who might be reluctant to back his program for a separate black division that "there would be no interracial mixture and no social questions if we had a division of strictly colored Americans. The writer does not expect to see the racial question worked out in his own lifetime."[21]

Vann and Emmett J. Scott of Howard University approached Congressman Hamilton Fish of New York about planning legislation to implement Vann's views. Fish was a logical choice; he had worked with Vann in 1926 on the bill for the World War I monument and was also the ranking Republican on the House Rules Committee.

Vann with Hamilton Fish and Percival L. Prattis, about 1938.

The three men worked closely together on the matter, and on April 5, 1938, Fish introduced three bills in the House. The first called for an end to discrimination by opening all branches of the service to blacks, the second asked for annual appointment by the president of two blacks to the United States Military Academy at West Point,[22] and the third provided for the formation and maintenance of an all-black Army division.[23] Vann conferred with Fish the day after the bills were introduced, after which the congressman dispatched a lengthy telegram to President Roosevelt urging him to support what Vann called "The *Pittsburgh Courier* Army Bills." The essence of Fish's telegram was a request for FDR's approval, which would help in expediting action before the Committee on Military Affairs.[24] Nearly three weeks later, on April 26, Vann himself went to see President Roosevelt about the issue, accompanied by Senator Guffey. The discussion during their conference went unrecorded, but Vann later told reporters that FDR was "very sympathetic" to the *Courier*-Fish bills. According to Vann, "President Roosevelt told Senator Guffey and myself that he felt the formation of a Negro division would be the logical move. He further proposed that the present four Negro regiments be used to serve as the nucleus of a complete Negro division." Vann said Roosevelt was amazed to find out the true status of the American black man in the armed services and at the vast amount of national sentiment favoring equality for the black man militarily.[25]

The NAACP, another leader in the fight for racial equality in the armed services, did not agree with Vann's position. The association was much more militant and advocated total integration of the armed services immediately. The executive secretary, Walter White, was quick to point this out to Vann, thus beginning a dispute which lasted until Vann's death.[26] White, who had always been adamantly pro-integration, chastised assistant executive secretary Roy Wilkins in April for a press release in which Wilkins implied that the NAACP had endorsed H. R. 10166, which provided for a segregated army regiment. "What ever may work out actually, endorsement of segregation is a violation of the Association's fundamental principles. Did you get the approval of the Committee of Administration before sending out this story? I question as well our approval of a plan to establish a Negro quota at West Point but in that case we do not go so diametrically against Association policy and principle. It is less harmful for the *Courier* to agitate for such concessions, but distinctly improper for the NAACP to do this. Did you let Vann's story last week stampede you into doing this?"²⁷ Wilkins replied to White immediately that regarding the NAACP press release, the sentence which read "The N.A.A.C.P. in a memorandum... urges support for the three bills," was an unfortunate error. "It was my feeling—and still is—that the Association could well support the move to hold hearings on these bills, because such hearings will give opportunity to air officially the widespread discrimination against Negroes in the Army. They also will give an opportunity to present the ideal demands of no discrimination and no separate division." Wilkins gave much credit to the *Courier* for bringing the issue before the public and arousing the blacks, thus forcing the NAACP to define its position:

> Although we began the agitation years ago and have an excellent record on the question, the fact remains that the *Courier* at the psychological moment whipped up the enthusiasm of the country into a campaign which has assumed such proportions that this Association could not issue any statement which would seem to be "cold-watering" the *Courier*'s crusade. I think you will realize how unpopular that would make us.
>
> It was for this reason that I said nothing in the release about the Association urging hearings on the bills, *but* condemning the separate division. I simply urged hearings and left off the "but," because that would have been interpreted as an effort to criticize the *Courier*'s campaign.
>
> Nor do I believe we can afford to stay out of the *Courier* campaign and remain silent. The issue is too popular. I would not be surprised if a minimum of seventy-five per cent of our people were in favor of a separate division in the Army. The only evidence we need to support this is the avidity and persistence with which they seek to have separate Negro National Guard units established...
>
> I agree thoroughly that the Committee on Administration and the Board ought to consider this matter, and I do not think that they should omit from their consideration as many estimates as they can get of the possible consequence of our maintaining an inflexible attitude upon this question. I think they should consider also our relations with the Pittsburgh *Courier* and possible consequences of either hostility or non-cooperation in this fight.
>
> P.S.... Vann and Guffey went in to see Roosevelt yesterday or this morning, and F.D.R. said he thought he could accomplish the opening up of the Army by executive order so that the bills would not be necessary. If the executive order is not possible he will put the Administration behind the bills.
>
> The point is that the topic is so popular and is so recognized for what it is by the Democrats that they do not wish the Republicans, with Ham Fish's sponsorship, to get the credit for this move guaranteed to please great numbers of colored people.²⁸

Nevertheless, Walter White held his ideological ground against a segregated division. When a *Courier* editorial appeared on June 11 entitled "THE NEGRO DIVISION IS LOGICAL," White wrote that same day to Vann:

> We do not agree that "The Negro Division is Logical." We are glad, however, that the *Courier* so ably and dispassionately sets forth its specific differences with the position of the N.A.A.C.P. . . . We shall attempt . . . to set forth . . . what seems to us to be dangers in these proposals.
> Our first objection to a Negro division is a practical one—that race prejudice, being the virulent force it is—a Negro division will be ordered to the post of greatest danger where casualties will be heaviest. It will be remembered that that is what was done to the 92nd Division during the World War. . . . Does the *Courier* imagine for a moment that in the next war the same thing will not be done to a Negro division, and that after that division has been wiped out a white division will not come along, capture the objective and go down in history as the heroes?
> But over and above even this ghastly possibility are the principles involved. In the first place, establishment of "quotas" for the Negro would be, in our opinion, unfortunate. Quotas make wards of the beneficiaries of such a system . . .
> The N.A.A.C.P. cannot agree with the *Courier* either in its contention that "The creation of a Negro division will NOT inaugurate segregation in the United States Army because Negroes are already segregated in four regiments, by laws passed in 1867 and 1869." . . . does the fact that there have been segregated units in the Army lessen our obligation to fight the evil of jim-crowism, past, present and future? . . .
> The N.A.A.C.P. commends the *Courier* for its vigorous campaign to end discrimination against the Negro in the armed forces. Our sole difference is an honest disagreement as to method.[29]

Roy Wilkins was not the only NAACP officer who did not share Walter White's hopeful vision of total integration for the armed forces, but instead espoused Robert Vann's commitment to a segregated division as the best the race could hope for at that time. Charles Houston, special counsel for the NAACP, said he backed the *Courier* drive for a separate black division even though that would perpetuate segregation. Houston likened the current situation to that of 1917, when Joel Spingarn fought for a separate training camp for black officers in Fort Des Moines, Iowa. In a letter, a copy of which he sent to Vann, Houston wrote, "Joel Spingarn was the first person to agitate for a separate camp and the hardest plugger for the same before the Negro college men took up the issue themselves. As in 1917, we are faced with a condition and not a theory." He continued, "I frankly do not think that anyone is going to get far at the present time agitating for Negro integration in the Army unless he will accept the principle of segregated units. I believe it absolutely necessary for [the NAACP] to move to get Negroes into all branches of the armed forces, whether we have to accept segregated units or not."[30] Houston shared Vann's more pragmatic view of the situation, that real integration was impossible; both men found themselves in sharp conflict with the more idealistic outlook of Walter White and the majority of the NAACP.[31]

Because little had happened on the question of a separate division for blacks since his April conference with the president, Vann went to see FDR again in October. Once again the president agreed it was time for the inclusion of a black division in the Army. According to Vann, FDR "defined the issue as just and pledged himself to explore the possibilities of improving the situation through executive order."[32] Despite the encouragement Roosevelt was giving personally to Vann, the president was obviously applying little pressure elsewhere on the subject. Even if he had favored the measure, which is doubtful, it is highly unlikely that he would have backed it, since Fish, a Republican, had sponsored it. The Fish bills died in the House Military Affairs Committee, twelve of whose twenty-six members were southerners.[33] Fish, undiscouraged, reported to Vann that shortly after the Christmas holidays he planned to reintroduce his measures.[34] This he did, but omitted the bill which provided for an all-black Army division. One can only conclude that Fish realized, despite the many letters of encouragement Vann had received about a segregated Army unit, that such a bill could not pass without the president's speaking out publicly in its favor or applying pressure to the Military Affairs Committee. That FDR failed to do either was not surprising; he and Fish were antagonistic toward each other, and if such a bill should pass under the aegis of the Republican Fish, it was likely that the GOP and not the Democrats would get credit for it. Another reason that Fish did not back the segregated division bill again may have been Walter White's influence. A series of letters passed between White and Fish late in December, and White arranged a meeting among Fish, White, Arthur Spingarn, and Dr. Louis T. Wright to discuss the subject.[35] Presumably, this meeting altered Fish's viewpoint.

Vann was disappointed that his bill was not included when the Fish measures were reintroduced, and he was also furious at Walter White and the NAACP for interfering and somehow managing to decrease the support for his "*Courier* Bill." He made his displeasure evident, and Walter White soon commented on the fact:

> Vann is so bitter against the NAACP for opposing the legislation for a "Jim-Crow" regiment in the Army that one cannot even talk to him. Daisy [Lampkin] can tell you of the situation last June when Vann had given orders that the NAACP's name was not to be mentioned in the *Courier* if it could possibly be avoided. . . . Several people on the *Courier* told me that Vann had ordered a very bitter attack on the Association and that he cancelled the orders only because some of them had convinced Vann that it wouldn't be a wise or profitable move.[36]

The two measures Fish proposed at the beginning of 1939 called for the presidential appointment of two blacks to West Point annually until a total of eight were appointed and for an end to discrimination against blacks in the appointment and promotion of officers and enlisted men.[37] Thurgood Marshall, then legal counsel to the NAACP, urged Walter White to have the association cooperate with the *Courier* in supporting the two remaining bills. "I would suggest that a letter be written to Bob Vann explaining to him that we have cooperated in the drafting of the two Fish bills introduced this year. . . . It seems to me that the *Courier* and the N.A.A.C.P. should cooperate in bringing pressure for a hearing on the two pending bills rather than to have the two groups fighting at each other."[38] But like those introduced the year before, the two bills proposed by Fish in 1939 never got out of committee.[39] The nation was apparently little interested in the fate of the Fish bills; the *New York Times*, for example, limited its coverage of them during 1938 and 1939 to a single sixty-one-word article on April 27, 1938.

Vann made another effort on this issue. At the end of 1938 and beginning of 1939, the *Courier* organized the Committee for Participation of Negroes in the National Defense. Vann financed the organization, Professor Rayford Logan of Howard University headed it, and P. L. Prattis of the *Courier* did much of the important groundwork, such as publicity. Vann described the reason for the group in a letter to FDR: "I feel, and my people feel, that this is the psychological moment to strike for our rightful place in our National Defense. I need not tell you that we are expecting a more dignified place in our armed forces during the next war than we occupied during the World War."[40] The committee's avowed purpose was to work for racial equality in the military, and, acting as a liaison between extant racial organizations, sent letters, telegrams, and delegations to congressmen and other national political leaders in an effort to achieve some progress.[41] According to historian Ulysses Lee, the campaign was well organized and publicized. Quantities of correspondence poured into the War Department, and when the War Department did not commit itself to any course of action the black press became even more cynical and critical.[42]

Many other black organizations were hard at work on the armed services issue at this time. The NAACP was still pushing for total integration, the National Bar Association created a committee to work for an end to exclusion of blacks from the National Guard in several states, the National Negro Insurance Association adopted a resolution against restriction of Negroes in the Army and Navy, and even a Colored American Legion post in Memphis organized a group to try and establish a black National Guard unit in Tennessee.[43]

Vann, acting on his own for the *Courier,* sent three lobbyists to Washington to work for the inclusion of blacks under the military establishment appropriation bill. The lobbyists Vann chose were attorney Charles Houston, Louis R. Mehlinger, a former captain in the 369th Infantry Regiment during World War I, and newsman Louis Lautier, a Washington-based black correspondent for the *Courier,* the *Baltimore Afro-American,* and the *Chicago Defender.*[44] By August 1940 the lobbyists had achieved some small results; the War Department made provisions for additional black combat troops and agreed to train more black officers.[45] And when one piece of legislation was passed, "An Act to Expedite the Strengthening of the National Defense," Vann's Committee on Participation of Negroes in the National Defense arranged to have Senators Sherman Minton of Indiana and Harry Schwartz of Wyoming, both Democrats, introduce an amendment providing that "no person shall be excluded from any branch of the military establishment on account of race, creed, or color." But the Army objected strenuously to this amendment, being worried that large numbers of blacks might enlist and that racially mixed units would demoralize the white soldiers.[46] In the end an amendment that retained the status quo was substituted: "That no Negro because of race shall be excluded from enlistment in the army for service with colored military units now organized or to be organized for such service."[47]

In September 1940, an amendment to the Burke-Wadsworth selective service bill providing that there be no discrimination in the selection and training of draftees was introduced by Congressman Hamilton Fish and sponsored by Vann's Committee on the Participation of Negroes in the National Defense. When Fish introduced his amendment, he said:

> I am not the originator of my amendment. I am merely sponsoring it in the House for a group of prominent colored leaders who are interested and represent the interests of 12,000,000 Negroes in America.... Dr. Emmett J. Scott, Special Assistant to the Secretary of War, 1917 to 1919, is in favor of the amendment, and is one of its sponsors, and so is Editor Robert L. Vann of Pittsburgh. I think there is every reason to adopt it. I hope there will be no opposition to it, as it is a matter of simple justice and has for its sole purpose doing away with un-American discrimination and giving drafted Negroes a square deal in the Armed Forces of the United States.[48]

Despite the efforts of Congressman Andrew May of Kentucky, the chairman of the House Military Affairs Committee, the amendment passed by a vote of 121 to 99, with most of the nay-sayers being New Deal Democrats. Taking credit for the amendment's passage, the *Courier* ran a headline on its front page,"WE THANK ALL WHO HELPED US":

> The *Courier* takes pardonable pride this week in calling the attention of its readers and many friends to the fact that PARTIAL success has been won in the fight to secure participation of Negroes in national defense.... Those who have followed the fight will recall that the first shot was fired by the *Courier* in an open letter to President Roosevelt on February 19, 1938.[49]

At the same time, Congress also provided for the training of black aviators in the Air Corps Expansion Act.[50]

Many of these concessions to blacks with regard to military equality were forced on the FDR administration by the pressures of the approaching election, in which Roosevelt was anxious to secure the black vote. FDR was very worried about black criticism on this issue. He did too little and acted too late to win Robert Vann's allegiance in 1940, but he did make several announcements designed to reassure blacks in the last two months before the election.[51] The first was made on September 16, when the White House stated that 36,000 out of the first 400,000 men drafted by the military under the new

Selective Service Act would be blacks, and that the Army was beginning to develop black air units. Next, after a meeting with black leaders Walter White, T. Arnold Hill of the National Youth Administration, and A. Philip Randolph, Roosevelt had the War Department issue a policy statement positive to blacks in the military. However, it only angered most blacks because it in fact made no concessions to black demands, but was a reiteration of 1937 policy. Finally, in the last few weeks before the election, Roosevelt made three major appointments of blacks to military-related posts: William Hastie as civilian aide to the secretary of war, Colonel Campbell Johnson as executive assistant to the director of Selective Service, and the nomination of Colonel Benjamin O. Davis as brigadier general.[52] It was not enough for many of the nation's blacks; as one observer noted, "the paucity of [Roosevelt's] response further clarified the disparity between Negro goals and gains—between democratic myths and realities."[53]

The year 1939 began badly for Robert Vann. He had a serious bout with illness in January and spent February and March recuperating at Hot Springs, Virginia. He was so exhausted that he declined an offer to write a syndicated column for the Associated Negro Press.[54] But later in the year he saw two of his lifelong projects come to fruition.

On May 6, after nearly twenty years of watching advertising representatives reap profits by soliciting national advertisements for the *Courier* and collecting a large fee for their services, Vann purchased all the assets of the Howard B. Crohn Company and organized his own firm. The Interstate United Newspaper Company, as Vann called his new organization, would represent black newspapers in obtaining national advertising. The two firms, Ziff and Crohn, which had represented most black newspapers, were run and staffed by whites. This had irritated Vann for many years, for he was a firm believer in racial self-help in economic enterprise. As he told another newspaperman, "Ziff got rich on us [blacks] and is now putting out magazines for white people on the money he made on the *Defender,* you, me and the rest of us. Even Crohn was piling up a nice little fortune in the very same way Ziff made his money."[55] For once, a black group would earn the profits to be had in this lucrative field; the money would stay within the race.

Vann had his Interstate United Newspaper Company prepare special studies on black consumer markets in cities with large black populations. These showed that the purchasing power of the black man had risen from $4 billion in the 1920s to $7 billion in the early 1930s and would probably climb to over $10 billion in the 1940s.[56] Armed with those impressive statistics, Vann began to approach potential advertisers and black weekly newspapers; he needed clients from both sides to make a go of his business. He soon managed to sign up *The Call* of Kansas City, and the *Houston Informer*, but many other newspapers were reluctant to go with Vann, for they had used the Ziff Company for many years. One editor, P. B. Young, Sr., of the *Norfolk Journal and Guide*, wrote Vann that though he found his proposal attractive, he could accept only if Ziff left the black advertising field, as was rumored he would do in July.[57]

The newspaper which it was most crucial that Vann obtain as a client was the *Chicago Defender*, which was second only to the *Courier* in national circulation. If the *Defender* would use the services of Vann's new company, its success would be assured. But the *Defender* proved very difficult to win over, no doubt because Vann's *Courier* had replaced it as the nation's number-one black weekly just a few years before and the administrators of the *Defender* felt resentment and professional jealousy. They were not about to give their business to a company founded by the *Courier* editor and thus further line his pocket. Vann nevertheless reasoned that "the success of the *Defender* was achieved in spite of the *Courier* and [that of] the *Courier* was achieved in spite of the *Defender*. This is a simple fact, and just why we should be at loggerheads because we have both been successful is beyond me to understand."[58] That was a logical enough statement, but Vann was not taking into account the fact that the founder and editor of the *Chicago Defender*, Robert Abbott, was much like himself. Both were strong-willed, individualistic, self-made men who had built their newspapers from nothing over long years. The *Defender* had reigned supreme among the nation's black weeklies for approximately twenty-five years; Abbott could not easily accept being dethroned by Vann's *Courier*. Because of the hostility the *Defender* felt for the *Courier*, one of Vann's friends cautiously suggested they might be better off without the *Defender*'s business: "I'll lay you a dollar to a half that if they come in, we will have more trouble with them than with all the other papers together, so far as trying to serve them is concerned."[59] And Vann's new advertising company never did get the *Defender* as a client, though it eventually became very successful.[60]

Though John H. H. Sengstacke, Robert Abbott's nephew and

successor at the *Defender*, did not join Vann's organization, he did ask Vann to join his newly formed Negro Newspaper Publishers Association. Sengstacke, who was the NNPA president, wrote Vann that at a publisher's conference held in Chicago, which Vann had not attended, in February and March 1940, his organization was formed in hopes of combining all the news-gathering agencies into one body.[61] These agencies were the Associated Negro Press, which was the most important of the news services, Calvin's News Service in New York, Scott Newspaper Syndicate in Atlanta, Crusader News Agency in New York, the Press Service for the NAACP, Hampton Institute Press Service, and Tuskegee Institute Press Service.[62] Sengstacke found establishing the NNPA difficult because major publishers like Vann and Carl Murphy of the *Afro-American* had not cooperated in the past and were not about to now. They distrusted the *Defender* due to the long battles for circulation. Neither Vann nor Murphy wished to join an organization started by a young "upstart" like Sengstacke. So Sengstacke initially was able to enlist only the publishers of smaller black weeklies. Vann merely sent a *Courier* reporter stationed in Chicago to cover the opening meeting on February 29, 1940, coincidentally the same day Robert Abbott died.[63]

One of Robert Vann's major hopes had been to be a member of the Pittsburgh Chamber of Commerce, and in December 1939 he was finally asked to join. Lest that seem of no great significance, it should be noted that the Pittsburgh Chamber of Commerce was regarded as one of the most powerful and influential chambers of commerce in America.[64] In the Smoky City, where industry flourished and industry's overlords were all-powerful, the ultimate honor for which a businessman could hope was an invitation to join the Chamber of Commerce. Vann had tried to join back in 1926, when a "Forward Movement" program was being planned for Pittsburgh. At that time Vann thought his membership, as both a lawyer and journalist, would stimulate progress in the struggle for economic improvement in the city's black community.[65] But his application was turned down that year. When the Chamber of Commerce at last asked Vann to join at the end of 1939, it was in belated recognition of a man who had done an enormous amount for the city and its blacks, politically and journalistically. His *Courier* was nationally acclaimed, and he was a well-known political figure. Robert Vann was the first black man ever to be a member. Unfortunately, the invitation came when his health was beginning to fail seriously and he was never active in the organization.

By early 1940, Robert Vann was very ill. In January he underwent surgery for abdominal cancer. The surgery arrested the cancer for the moment, but Vann remarked in March that, though he was "able to stumble around for a little while, I know that I will not have many more years, and I am going to conserve my strength, regardless of how long or short my time may be."[66] Like many men near the end of life, Vann began in earnest to consider compiling his memoirs and spoke to one of the most talented *Courier* writers about giving him some assistance. He started to put his papers together to "write that book."[67] Vann also thought of doing a work which he planned to call "The Negro in Politics." But there was too little time and energy left; Vann never began the actual writing of either book.

Physically spent though he was, Vann summoned up enough strength that summer for a last sojourn into politics. He managed to attend as an observer both the Republican and Democratic presidential nominating conventions of 1940, for the purpose of getting an end-discrimination-in-the-armed-services plank inserted into both platforms. He went first to Philadelphia, where the Republicans were meeting to nominate their candidate, who turned out to be Wendell Willkie, and saw his resolution added to the platform—that "discrimination in the Civil Service, Army, Navy, and all other branches of the government must cease."[68] Vann then went on to Chicago, where Roosevelt was being nominated for an unprecedented third term. There the Democrats included mention of the black man in their platform for the first time, but neglected to make any resolution about blacks in the armed services; only mention of their past "achievements" was included.[69]

Vann was disappointed by the Democrats' omission, but he had already decided to support Wendell Willkie for the presidency. Vann's reasons for breaking with FDR, the man to whom he had brought a large proportion of the black vote and who in turn had given him a federal appointment in the attorney general's office, were numerous. Some he held in common with other disgruntled blacks and others were strictly personal. The three main reasons were that there had been no real reform in the economic lot of the black man; that FDR had been inactive regarding the blacks and the military; and that he was against a third term for any president.

After Roosevelt was nominated in July, Vann published tally sheets in the *Courier* to show that the Roosevelt administration had not in truth aided the black man to any great extent, but had made only token gestures. Discrimination had not been ended in many of the federal agencies, and projects supported by the Federal Housing Administration, the United States Housing Authority, and the Tennessee Valley Authority remained segregated. Blacks had not been given positions in the higher echelons of the federal civil service. Federal subsidies to vocational education, agricultural research, and scientific study had been awarded disproportionately to white schools and colleges. Agricultural relief for blacks had been sadly lacking. Vann, attempting to offer Mrs. Mary McLeod Bethune, who was director of the Division of Negro Affairs, National Youth Administration, some sage advice about working for the New Deal, commented,

> You cannot afford to travel around the country and talk about the blessings of the New Deal unless there are some real blessings to talk about. The Negro Farmers of the South are not getting the benefits intended for them, and it is the business of the Administration to see to it that they get the full benefit of the Administration's program. If the Administration does not do this, who, in the name of God, is going to do it? The President has a fine attitude, but attitude is not bread and butter. Attitude is not corn and wheat. Attitude is not pork and potatoes.[70]

Social Security did not cover most blacks, a majority of whom were in domestic service or tenant farming. Roosevelt had not ended the Depression as promised, and blacks were still out of work. In 1939, while blacks constituted only 6 percent of the Allegheny County population, they made up 28 percent of its relief recipients, a dramatic increase from 18 percent in 1933.[71] Further, from fear of alienating his southern supporters, FDR had done nothing to effect a federal anti-lynch law despite the fact that there was a Democratic majority in the Congress. Worse, he had appointed Senator Hugo Black of Alabama to the Supreme Court.

The second major issue affecting Vann was that FDR had taken no real steps to achieve racial equality in the armed services, despite the crusade in which Vann had invested so much time and effort, while Willkie was making a concerted appeal to blacks on the subject. The Republican platform, which received hearty *Courier* approval, pledged to end discrimination in all branches of the government, including the military, and to give blacks "a square deal in the economic and political life of the nation."[72] The same *Courier* issue also attacked the Democrats by printing a letter from Roosevelt's secretary to Robert Vann saying the president did not have time to meet and discuss the problem of discrimination in the armed services:

> The President has asked me to acknowledge receipt of your letter of June 13, 1940, addressed to Miss LeHand, wherein you request an appointment for the purpose of discussing your proposal for an increase in the number of colored citizens in the defense forces.
>
> As you know, colored men are now serving in the Army, quite a few units being authorized for colored men exclusively. As rapidly as vacancies occur in these units, new recruits are enlisted to keep up the strength of these units. A large proportion of the men who enlist in the Army make the service a lifelong career. For this reason, there is a comparatively low turnover in colored organizations, and, consequently, a comparatively small number of openings as original enlistments at any one time.
>
> I am informed that the War Department is making definite plans for the creation of new units for colored men, should the proposed increase in the Regular Army now being considered by Congress, be approved.
>
> I regret that the President's schedule will not permit an appointment with you at this time but trust the foregoing information will be of interest to you.[73]

FDR had made only token military appointments of blacks and procrastinated until very late in the fall of 1940 before promoting Colonel Benjamin O. Davis of the Army to general. The *Courier* had been campaigning for the promotion of Davis (whom they called "the American Dreyfus") for months, and he was obviously more qualified than many whites who had been promoted before him. All Roosevelt's efforts in the area of military equality for blacks were last-minute and paltry, obvious concessions to political pressure; thus the topic was a major issue among blacks in the 1940 election.

Vann was also thoroughly opposed to the reelection of any man for a third presidential term. "I am against dictatorship of any type and any man who wants to be elected for a third term is pretty damn close to dictatorship,"[74] he wrote a friend. He thought Roosevelt was hungering after excessive power and was very unhappy with what he regarded as FDR's "skull-duggery in order to secure a nomination by 'draft.' "[75] Other Democrats had also been alienated by FDR's tactics. James A. Farley resigned as Democratic national chairman after the convention, and Vann immediately submitted his resignation as special advisor to the Democratic National Committee. Vann wrote to Farley, "I came into the Democratic party with you and through you and I feel that the most appropriate exit that I could possibly make would be to go out simultaneously with the retirement of my chief."[76]

Robert Vann went over to Willkie for two personal reasons, in addition to his ideological objections to Roosevelt. First, he would have gained little politically by supporting Roosevelt; he had deserted the Pennsylvania Democratic ticket two years previously and was regarded by many in the party as a turncoat and an opportunist. Certainly the Democrats would not receive Vann back into the fold with open arms. He felt his only political future lay with the Republicans. A more important fact that he had suppressed during the years he supported FDR was that the New Deal politics were fundamentally antithetical to his own economic philosophy. Vann was a self-made man who had achieved success against overwhelming odds. He had been born black, a southerner, and probably illegitimate; today he was a wealthy, respected citizen of a major city in the North. If he could accomplish this, surely others could; Vann was not happy about carrying the financial burden of others through heavy taxation on his own wealth. In this sense, he was basically Republican in his outlook.

And Vann admired Wendell Willkie as a fellow self-made man, who had come from humble beginnings and risen to the presidency of the vast Commonwealth and Southern Power Company. In reviewing a speech Willkie made in his hometown of Elwood, Indiana, Vann revealed as much about his own thinking as that of the presidential candidate:

> [Willkie] came up from a poor family who came to this country to escape persecution in Europe. He told how he started with nothing like Henry Ford, Walter Chrysler, Abraham Lincoln . . . and many other men who started from a standstill start and worked their way to the top under our American system. He stood face to face with the American people and said I'm in favor of the kind of America that permits boys to come from nowhere to somewhere. He said he was proud that he was able to succeed in making some money; and the crowd of 100,000 people cheered him to the echo because every man and woman in the country wanted to make $100,000 and they would rather make it than to inherit it. That's the American way.[77]

Vann hoped that Willkie, a man with an outlook much like his own, would lower the income taxes which had skyrocketed since Roosevelt took office. As Vann saw it, "the President has taxed and taxed and taxed with the hope of destroying what he calls the economic royalists," yet it was that same group which was maintaining the nation financially. FDR was draining the hard-earned capital away from honest businessmen to support the dole and the WPA; Vann no longer found this acceptable.

Vann had been admonished on more than one occasion prior to 1940 by the Internal Revenue Service for his delinquency in tax payments. In April 1937, after a series of confrontations with the IRS, he agreed to pay $500 monthly until his 1936 tax debt was liquidated.[78] Then in 1939, when Vann's yearly income ranged between $35,000 and $40,000 by his own estimate, he complained to a friend that "I have a fight on with the Internal Revenue collector as to whether I should pay a $9,000 income tax . . . and this thing has put a lot of iron in my soul."[79] He felt that the *Courier* plant expansion begun in 1937 had been hampered by what he deemed overtaxation, "and by the time I pay the tax out of the fund I have set aside to do that, I won't have enough money to dig the cellar, to say nothing of putting up the building and buying a new press."[80] Vann contended that not enough people were taxpayers. In his own factory, only two persons, he and Ira Lewis, out of seventy-three on the annual payroll of $140,000 paid any federal income tax. Vann thought the tax should be "spread downward" and had apprised Roosevelt of this idea in a letter in 1938. He said there were twenty million untaxed American workers who could pay $5 a year and not suffer by it. He saw this as a means not only to increase revenue, but to instill pride in the citizen who would know he was helping to carry the federal financial burden.[81] It is doubtful, however, whether those workers to whom Vann referred would have been very grateful for that means of gaining "pride." The president thanked Vann for his suggestions but said for the present the nation's tax course was set.[82]

Political observers of 1940 predicted a close presidential election for the first time since 1916, and with approximately 186 of the 266 electoral votes needed for victory coming from states with significant percentages of black voters, Vann's backing of Willkie seemed a reasonable risk.[83] Pennsylvania, for instance, had voted Republican in the 1938 off-year election and might remain in the GOP column

Twilight: 1938–1940 • 321

in this contest. As he had in most previous elections, Vann maintained that the 299,998 blacks eligible to vote in Pennsylvania, approximately 5 percent of the total, would hold the balance of power in a close contest.[84] And Vann was not the only black newspaper editor to oppose Roosevelt. The *Philadelphia Tribune*, which had been strongly Democratic under the editorship of J. Austin Norris, came out for Willkie after Norris's resignation. The *Baltimore Afro-American*, which had backed Democrats since 1924, chose to support the Republican in 1940 over the issue of blacks and the military, because the armed services continued to restrict black enlistment when they were begging for volunteers.[85] "In this regard, President Roosevelt not only forgot us but he neglected us, deserted and abandoned us to our enemies."[86] One poll shortly before the election showed that twenty-seven of the fifty-five major black weeklies favored Willkie; eleven were pro-Roosevelt; and seventeen were undecided.[87]

Robert Vann did not live to see the outcome of the presidential election that year. The cancer for which he had been operated on reappeared, and this time it could not be arrested. He entered Shadyside Hospital in Pittsburgh on October 14. On October 24 he sank into a coma and died.

The November 2 *Courier* carried the sad news under the banner headline, "NATION EULOGIZES VANN."

> Robert L. Vann, who rose from the obscurity of a backwoods from "out from" Ahoskie, N.C., to confer with Presidents on the subject of the Negro, is no more!
>
> Death wrote "Thirty" to the dramatic life saga of America's "Number One Negro Citizen" Thursday at 7:05 P.M., when the internationally-known publisher and editor of *The Pittsburgh Courier* passed away at Shadyside Hospital. Born August 20, 1879, he was 61 years old.
>
> LAWYER . . DIPLOMAT . . CRUSADER . . POLITICAL STATESMAN . . Mr. Vann died as he had lived, fighting to the last.
>
> In a coma since Tuesday, his last words, spoken to his wife, Mrs. Jesse Vann, were, "Don't worry about me. I'll be all right." Only the indomitable courage which had characterized his every public and private action down through the years, had kept him alive until that time.

There was a very large "Memorial Supplement" to the newspaper that week, full of letters and telegrams of condolence to Mrs. Vann. Wendell Willkie wrote, "Please accept my sincere sympathy upon your profound and irreparable loss. All of us know that the passing of your husband takes something vital from our national life. His courageous endeavors through the years to educate public opinion to a high attitude of fairness toward the colored citizens has constituted a great service, not only to the Negroes but equally to every American citizen. You can be sure that Americans everywhere share your sorrow."[88]

Just hours after Robert Vann had died, President Roosevelt announced the nomination for promotion to brigadier general of Colonel Benjamin O. Davis, the first black to be so named. Vann had worked long and hard for Davis's promotion, and it may have been a visit paid FDR by Vann and Walter White of the NAACP which convinced President Roosevelt finally to promote Davis.[89] The *Courier* was cynical about the promotion of Davis and the appointment of two other blacks to high positions. In an editorial which appeared in the same edition as the report of Vann's death, the *Courier* called them political ploys:

> While we are gratified by the elevation of Colonel Benjamin Davis to the rank of Brigadier General, the appointment of Judge William H. Hastie as Civilian Aide to the Secretary of War, and the selection of Major Campbell Johnson as Executive Assistant to the Director of Selective Service, this concession on the eve of election is too little and too late. This last minute desperate maneuver will not swing a single Negro vote, if, as seems likely, it was designed to snare needed support. What the Administration has done is far too little when it has so much power in its hands. The day has passed when colored Americans can be bribed by appointment of two or three Negroes to high positions. Moreover, these appointments have only been made because an aroused Negro electorate seemed about to wreak its vengeance upon those who had denied colored people a square deal in national defense.[90]

It may have been just as well that Vann did not live to see the results of the 1940 presidential election. Vann's efforts in behalf of the Republicans came to even less than they had in 1938. Roosevelt was overwhelmingly supported by the blacks of America. He carried Pennsylvania by 286,187 votes, and for the first time in the state's history a Democratic presidential candidate carried every single ward with a majority of black voters. In Philadelphia, Roosevelt polled 59.4 percent of the vote in the black wards. In Pittsburgh, Roosevelt's majorities among blacks were even more impressive: he tallied 85 percent and 77 percent of the black vote in the Third and Fifth Wards respectively. In the Tenth District of the Third Ward, which was 99 percent black, the vote count was 1,087 for Roosevelt and 80 for Willkie.[91] If indeed the potential black vote of almost 300,000 did provide the balance of power in Pennsylvania as Vann had predicted, it was not for Willkie, but made up a significant part of Roosevelt's 286,187-vote majority.[92] Senator Guffey, whom Vann had not forgiven since 1938, was also successfully reelected, defeating Jay Cooke, Philadelphia Republican chairman. Though Vann had not pressed for Guffey's defeat in the black weekly, it was obviously another setback for the editor of the *Pittsburgh Courier*.

Some months before his death, Robert Vann had ordered a mausoleum which he himself designed constructed in Homewood Cemetery for his final resting place. There he was buried at the end of October, surrounded by stained glass windows which represented the different phases of his life: the Book of Knowledge for his education, the Scales of Justice for his legal career, and the Gutenberg press for his newspaper work.[93] A bronze plaque was placed on the wall in the entrance of the Pittsburgh Courier Publishing Company:

IN LOVING MEMORY OF
ROBERT L. VANN
PUBLISHER   LAWYER   STATESMAN
BRILLIANT EDITOR, LOYAL FRIEND
FEARLESS CHAMPION OF RIGHTS
ERECTED BY HIS ADMIRING EMPLOYEES WHO PROFITED GREATLY
BY HIS PRECEPTS AND EXAMPLE

Vann received a number of posthumous honors. In his childhood town of Ahoskie, a school was named after him, as was one in the Hill District of Pittsburgh. Scholarships were established at Virginia Union University and the University of Pittsburgh in his name, from bequests Vann left to the schools. At Virginia Union University, the Robert L. Vann Memorial Tower was erected. And on October 10, 1943, the Liberty Ship *Robert L. Vann* was launched in Portland, Maine, taking its place alongside two other vessels named after prominent blacks, the *Booker T. Washington* and the *George Washington Carver*.⁹⁴ Because Vann had spent the last years of his life engrossed in the crusade for racial equality in the armed forces, the ship was a particularly fitting tribute.

Epilogue

VANN'S REAL MONUMENT was the *Pittsburgh Courier*. His wife took over the paper after his death because she believed that disposing of her holdings would have constituted a betrayal of the love and trust she and her husband had shared.[1] She retained the majority of *Courier* stock and began learning the newspaper business. Ira Lewis continued to manage the newspaper.

During World War II, a time of prosperity for black newspapers, the *Courier* retained its leading position among black weeklies. It claimed to be the first black weekly to send correspondents around the globe to provide firsthand reports from the front, and a total of ten *Courier* reporters were in the war theater during the conflict.[2] The paper also conducted an effective "Double V" crusade for "Victory Abroad and Victory [Against Discrimination] at Home."

In May 1947 the *Courier* achieved an all-time circulation high of 357,212.[3] By 1948, "the paper was providing the largest news coverage of any of its black contemporaries."[4] *Courier* reporters traveled more than one million miles in America and thirty-one other countries that year. When Ira Lewis died in 1948, Mrs. Vann was named president-treasurer. P. L. Prattis and William Nunn, Sr., executive editor and managing editor, managed the paper, Prattis until May 1965 and Nunn until his death in 1968.[5]

In September 1950 the *Courier*'s circulation had fallen to 280,000. Inspired by the success of the "Double V" campaign of the war years, in 1953 the newspaper undertook a "Double E" crusade for educational equality. This was primarily a fund-raising campaign to support the NAACP's legal fight in the *Brown* v. *Board of Education* case, which culminated in victory for the plaintiff on May 17, 1954.[6]

Without Ira Lewis's financial expertise, the paper declined over the next decade, despite Mrs. Vann's earnest efforts and heavy contributions from her personal funds. Its circulation, at 186,000 in 1954, dropped to just over 100,000 by 1960.[7] Also, during the civil rights crusade of the period, all black weeklies lost circulation because the white dailies gave so much space to black news.[8]

In 1960 the *Courier* was taken over by a board of directors, with S. B. Fuller, a cosmetics manufacturer, as chairman, assisted by Franklin H. Whittaker of Columbus, Ohio. Other board members included Mrs. Vann, Mrs. Daisy Lampkin, William Nunn, and P. L. Prattis. Mrs. Vann retired from the *Courier* board in October 1963. The newspaper struggled along until 1965, when it was bought by John Sengstacke, publisher and owner of the *Courier*'s longtime competitor, the *Chicago Defender*.[9] Mrs. Vann died on June 9, 1967.

Notes

A Bibliographic Note on Unpublished Sources

Index

Notes

Chapter 1. North Carolina and Virginia

1. Much of Vann's early biographical material is in "A Sketch of My Life," written by him for the *Hertford County Herald*, Historical Edition, 1939. The same work appears also in Roy Parker, *The Ahoskie Era of Hertford County* (Ahoskie, N.C., 1939), pp. 268–73. Vann also wrote another brief autobiographical sketch in 1939–40, found in his Papers, Carnegie Library, Pittsburgh. Vann had begun compiling his papers in 1938 for a proposed biography, possibly with assistance from George S. Schuyler, a *Courier* columnist. After Vann's death in 1940, however, Mrs. Jesse Vann commissioned Harry Webber, a former *Courier* employee and also a University of Pittsburgh graduate, to write her husband's story. The unpublished manuscript, "Vann of Pittsburgh, or the Third Emancipation," is on deposit at the Carnegie Library of Pittsburgh. See also James H. Brewer, "Robert Lee Vann and the *Pittsburgh Courier*" (master's thesis, University of Pittsburgh, 1941); and Henry G. LaBrie III, "Robert Lee Vann and the Editorial Page of the *Pittsburgh Courier*" (master's thesis, University of West Virginia, 1970).

2. U.S. Bureau of the Census, *Twelfth Census, 1900*, vol. I, table 92, pp. 992–93. See Parker, *Ahoskie Era*, pp. 243–90, on "Record of the Negro Race in Hertford County and Ahoskie." Other such counties as Hertford included Edgecombe, Bertie, Warren, Franklin, Lenoir, Pasquatank, Jones, and Pitt. See also Frenise A. Logan, *The Negro in North Carolina, 1876–1894* (Chapel Hill, 1964), pp. 75–85; Richard E. Lonsdale, *Atlas of North Carolina* (Chapel Hill, 1967), pp. 9–10.

3. In 1890, 136,467 or 64.6 percent of the total black population in North Carolina were in agriculture, of whom 43.6 percent were hired workers for white farmers (Logan, *Negro in North Carolina*, pp. 76, 82–83).

4. Interviews with Mrs. C. S. Yeates, wife of the principal of Hertford County Training School, Ahoskie, N.C., and Grady Askew, the only surviving child of John O. Askew, May 25, 1971, Harrellsville, N.C.

5. Vann was called "Lee" throughout his childhood, but for the sake of clarity he will be referred to as "Robert," since that is what he was called as an adult.

6. Vann to Miss Jennie L. Vann (no relation), Tyty, Ga., Mar. 31, 1938, Vann Papers. Henry LaBrie, currently of the Charles Warren Center of Harvard University, who is also preparing a biography of Robert Vann, has interviewed many people in the Ahoskie area and substantiates the assertion that Vann was illegitimate.

7. *Hertford County Herald,* 1939; Webber, "Vann," pp. 14–18; and interview with Mrs. C. S. Yeates, May 25, 1971.
8. *Hertford County Herald,* 1939.
9. Roy and Margaret Johnson, "Beautiful Old Harrellsville Issues Welcome," *The Daily News* (Ahoskie, N.C.), July 8, 1959; "Old Houses of Hertford County," *Hertford County Herald,* June 13, 1950.
10. Parker, *Ahoskie Era,* pp. 160–71; interview with Grady Askew, May 25, 1971.
11. *Hertford County Herald,* 1939.
12. Webber, "Vann," p. 18; *Hertford County Herald,* 1939.
13. *Hertford County Herald,* 1939.
14. Webber, "Vann," pp. 10–11; *Hertford County Herald,* 1939.
15. *Hertford County Herald,* 1939; Logan, *Negro in North Carolina,* pp. 76–85.
16. Mrs. R. L. Vann to Brewer, May 21, 1941, in Brewer, "Vann," p. 16.
17. Poem in Vann Papers; also Webber, "Vann," p. 21. Throughout his life Vann enjoyed poetry; he read it avidly and often used poetry to express his ideas. A favorite was the grim "Thanatopsis" by William Cullen Bryant. He also liked Paul Lawrence Dunbar. Dozens of Vann's editorial titles reflected a feeling for poetry, e.g., "They Shall Not Dine," "And There Stood the One Hundred," "Jobs That Once Were Ours," etc. (Webber, "Vann," p. 134).
18. *Hertford County Herald,* 1939.
19. Ibid.
20. Hertford County Economic Development Commission, "Hertford County, North Carolina: An Economic Data Summary," 1966.
21. Roy Johnson, *Tales from Old Carolina* (Murfreesboro, N.C., 1965), pp. 69–70; Parker, *Ahoskie Era,* pp. 26, 136.
22. *Hertford County Herald,* 1939.
23. Such as Vann's 1937 address to the graduating class of Bethune-Cookman College, in which he reminisced about the great patience needed to get an ox to pull a plow and warned the students that if they too wished to reach the top they must learn to conquer such difficulties (*Jacksonville Journal,* June 3, 1937, in Vann Scrapbook, 1935–41).
24. *Hertford County Herald,* 1939; Parker, *Ahoskie Era,* p. 271.
25. Parker, *Ahoskie Era,* p. 271.
26. Interview with Mrs. Vann, April 6, 1967.
27. *Hertford County Herald,* 1939.
28. Parker, *Ahoskie Era,* pp. 44–45.
29. Logan, *Negro in North Carolina,* p. 140, citing *Biennial Report of the Superintendent of Instruction,* 1888, p. xlii; p. 142, citing *Biennial Report,* 1889–1890, pp. xl–xli.
30. Louis Harlan, *Separate and Unequal* (Chapel Hill, 1958), pp. 102–34.
31. Webber, "Vann," p. 32.
32. *Hertford County Herald,* 1939.
33. Parker, *Ahoskie Era,* p. 254.
34. Webber, "Vann," pp. 36–38; interview with Mrs. Vann, Apr. 6, 1967.
35. Interview with Mrs. Vann, Apr. 6, 1967.
36. *Hertford County Herald,* 1939; "Robert L. Vann as I Knew Him," speech delivered by Ira F. Lewis at dedication of R. L. Vann School, Pittsburgh, Dec. 3, 1944, in Vann Papers.
37. Parker, *Ahoskie Era,* p. 270; Lewis, "Vann as I Knew Him."

38. *Courier*, Nov. 2, 1940; Richard Bardolph, *The Negro Vanguard* (New York, 1961), p. 144. The actions of a group of stubborn landowners who refused to sell rights-of-way to the railroad had kept Hertford County isolated until 1885, when the first train ran to Ahoskie, a log train carrying timber trees from local forests to a sawmill at Tunis, two miles east of Winton. Not until 1890, when the line was sold to the Atlantic Coast Line Railroad Company, did passenger trains begin running through Hertford County. Thus the area remained essentially rural and cut off from the rest of the state for many years past the time when other regions were experiencing booms brought about by railway expansion (Parker, *Ahoskie Era*, pp. 492–94).

39. Webber, "Vann," p. 44.

40. Original manuscript in Vann Papers.

41. August Meier, *Negro Thought in America 1880–1915* (Ann Arbor, 1963), passim; June Sochen, ed., *The Black Man and the American Dream: Negro Aspirations in America, 1900–1930* (Chicago, 1971), pp. 3–12.

42. *Virginia Union Bulletin: General Catalog* XXXI (Jan.–Feb. 1931): 92–93, 98–99.

43. Roscoe E. Lewis, *The Negro in Virginia: Compiled by Workers of the WPA in the State of Virginia* (New York, 1940), pp. 266–67; *A Century of Service to Education and Religion: Virginia Union University, 1865–1965* (Virginia Union University Bulletin, Centennial Issue, LXV, June 1965), pp. 5–23; and Miles Mark Fisher, ed., *Virginia Union University and Some of her Achievements* (Twenty-fifth Anniversary Issue, 1899–1924, Virginia Union University, 1924), pp. 23–46.

44. Fisher, *Virginia Union University*, pp. 44–45.

45. W. E. B. DuBois and Augustus Granville Dill, eds., *The College-Bred Negro American*, Atlanta University Publications, No. 15 (Atlanta, 1915); Meier, *Negro Thought*, p. 175.

46. *University Journal*, Jan. 1, 1903, p. 4.

47. Ibid.

48. Lucie Mae Pitts, "New Deal Personalities," *Norfolk Journal and Guide*, Apr. 21, 1934. Nonetheless, Vann retained a lifelong affection for Virginia Union and it for him. He became a trustee and repeatedly contributed to scholarship funds "for a worthy student" (*Courier*, Nov. 2, 1940). In 1926 he delivered the University's commencement address and received an honorary L.L.D. After his death, the tower of the Belgian World's Fair Pavilion, which had been donated by Belgium to Virginia Union University, was dedicated as the Robert L. Vann Memorial Tower (*Richmond News Leader*, June 10, 1941, in Vann Scrapbook, 1940–41).

49. Speech delivered by Mrs. Vann at dedication of Robert L. Vann Memorial Tower, June 7, 1949, Virginia Union University.

50. *Courier*, July 29, 1933; Webber, "Vann," pp. 54–55. Barber was born in Gastonia, N.C., on July 5, 1878. Before receiving a B.A. from Virginia Union in 1903, he was editor of the *Charleston Messenger* (1900–01). After graduation he edited *The Voice of the Negro* from 1903 to 1907. In 1909 he entered Philadelphia Dental School, graduated in 1912, and practiced dentistry in that city. He also continued his work in journalism as editor of the *Philadelphia Independent*, in which he ardently supported Franklin D. Roosevelt during the New Deal.

51. Webber, "Vann," p. 60.

52. Webber, "Vann," pp. 54–55. Eugene Kinckle Jones's papers, in Flushing, N.Y.,

Notes to Pages 16–20 • 331

might provide additional data on this era of Vann's life, but they are currently unavailable. Guichard Parris and Lester Brooks note that Vann is mentioned in Jones's papers (*Blacks in the City: A History of the National Urban League* [Boston, 1971], p. 272). Vann was godfather to Jones's son, and in 1937 Jones succeeded in getting Vann appointed to the executive board of the Urban League (Jones to Vann, Feb. 15, 1937).

53. Parker, *Ahoskie Era*, pp. 162–63.
54. Benjamin B. Winborne, *The Colonial and State History of Hertford County, North Carolina* (Murfreesboro, N.C., 1906), p. 285.
55. Parker, *Ahoskie Era*, p. 143.
56. Richard R. Wright, Jr., commented that perhaps the Wilmington riot and the fear of more mob violence by whites against blacks had a greater effect upon North Carolina blacks in convincing them to migrate northward than any other incident (*The Negro in Pennsylvania: A Study in Economic History* [Philadelphia, 1912], p. 60). See also Meier, *Negro Thought*, p. 38; C. Vann Woodward, *Origins of the New South, 1877–1913*, vol. 9 of A History of the South, ed. Wendell Holmes Stephenson and E. Merton Coulter (Baton Rouge, 1951), p. 350; and Helen G. Edmonds, *The Negro and Fusion Politics in North Carolina, 1894–1901* (Chapel Hill, 1951), pp. 198–217.
57. Edmonds, *Fusion Politics*, p. 174.
58. Ibid., citing Henry Hayden, *The Story of the Wilmington Rebellion* (Wilmington, N.C., 1936), p. 26.
59. Edmonds, *Fusion Politics*, p. 209, citing "Comparison Table of Negro Vote in 1896 and 1900," *North Carolina Manual, 1913*, R. D. W. Connor, comp. and ed., (Raleigh, N.C., 1913).
60. Parker, *Ahoskie Era*, p. 143.
61. Edmonds, *Fusion Politics*, pp. 209–10.
62. Woodward, *Origins of the New South*, pp. 235–90, 321–68; Edmonds, *Fusion Politics*, pp. 212–14.
63. August Meier and Elliott Rudwick, "The Boycott Against Jim Crow Street Cars in the South," *The Journal of American History* LV (Mar. 1969): 767–68. See also Charles E. Wynes, *Race Relations in Virginia* (Charlottesville, Va., 1961), pp. 67–83; James H. Brewer, "The Futile Trumpet: The Wars of the *Richmond Planet* Against Disfranchisement and Jim Crow, 1900–1904" (author's manuscript, Virginia State College, 1959); and Andrew Buni, *The Negro in Virginia Politics, 1902–1965* (Charlottesville, Va., 1967), pp. 36–38.
64. Speech delivered by Mrs. Vann at Virginia Union, June 7, 1949.
65. Logan, *Negro in North Carolina*, p. 169. According to the U.S. Census of 1890, 1,940 of the 2,036 black professionals in North Carolina worked either as clergymen or as teachers.
66. Henry Allen Bullock, *A History of Negro Education in the South from 1619 to the Present* (Cambridge, Mass., 1967), pp. 147–66.
67. Rollin L. Hartt, "When the Negro Comes North," *World's Work* (May 1924): 85.
68. *New York Globe*, Feb. 16, 1884, cited in Gilbert Osofsky, *Harlem: The Making of a Ghetto* (New York, 1966), p. 20.
69. *Courier*, Nov. 2, 1940; interview with Mrs. Vann, Apr. 6, 1967.
70. Interview with Mrs. Vann, Apr. 6, 1967.

Chapter 2. North Toward Home

1. Sarah H. Killikelly, *The History of Pittsburgh: Its Rise and Progress* (Pittsburgh, 1906), pp. 244–88; *The Story of Pittsburgh and Vicinity*, edited by *The Pittsburgh Gazette Times* (Pittsburgh, 1908); Chamber of Commerce of Pittsburgh, *Pittsburgh and the Pittsburgh Spirit* (Pittsburgh, 1927–28), passim; Stefan Lorant, ed., *Pittsburgh: The Study of an American City* (New York, 1964), pp. 177, 364; and Leland D. Baldwin, *Pittsburgh: The Story of a City* (Pittsburgh, 1938), p. 341.

2. The Pittsburgh district includes, besides the city itself, all of Allegheny County and four adjoining counties—Armstrong, Butler, Washington, and Westmoreland (Lorant, *Pittsburgh*, p. 178). Also in Lorant, see chap. v, Sylvester, "The Hearth of the Nation," pp. 177–208, and chap. vii, Blum, "The Entrepreneurs," pp. 219–60.

3. John R. Commons, "Wage Earners of Pittsburgh," *Charities and the Commons* (Jan. 2, 1909): 1052–53; Lorant, *Pittsburgh*, pp. 272–75. For other accounts of the growth of the major Pittsburgh industries, see *Pittsburgh and the Pittsburgh Spirit*, passim.

4. Samuel Harden Church, *A Short History of Pittsburgh, 1758–1908* (New York, 1908), pp. 85–86.

5. Peter Roberts, "The New Pittsburghers: Slavs and Kindred Immigrants in Pittsburgh," *Charities and the Commons* (Jan. 2, 1909): 533–47; Philip Klein, *A Social History of Pittsburgh* (New York, 1938), table 27, "Country of Birth of Foreign Born White Population in Allegheny County, 1850–1930," p. 288; and Bertram J. Black and Aubrey Mallack, *Population Trends in Allegheny County, 1840–1943* (Bureau of Social Research, Federation of Social Agencies of Pittsburgh and Allegheny County, no. 1, Apr. 1944), pp. 1–7. For a general discussion of the impact on the city of immigration by foreign-born and blacks between 1870 and 1920, see Sam Bass Warner, Jr., *The Urban Wilderness: A History of the American City* (New York, 1972), pp. 166–79.

6. Roy Lubove, *Twentieth Century Pittsburgh: Government, Business and Environmental Change* (New York, 1969), p. 4.

7. *Pittsburgh Gazette*, Jan. 23, 1901, cited in Charles Dahlinger, *Pittsburgh: A Sketch of its Early Social Life* (New York, 1916), pp. 38–39. For pre–Civil War history of the black in Pennsylvania, see Edward Raymond Turner, *The Negro in Pennsylvania: Slavery–Servitude–Freedom, 1639–1861* (Washington, D.C., 1911); and Ira V. Brown, *The Negro in Pennsylvania History* (Gettysburg, 1970). Recently a lengthy manuscript by J. Ernest Wright, "The Negro in Pittsburgh," dated 1940 and prepared for the WPA Writers Project, has been discovered in the State Library, Harrisburg. Professor Rollo Turner, of the Department of Black Studies of the University of Pittsburgh, is editing the work for publication.

8. Carter G. Woodson, *Free Negro Heads of Families in the United States* (Washington, D.C., 1925), p. 25.

9. Louis V. Kennedy, *The Negro Peasant Turns Cityward* (New York, 1930), p. 29; Abraham Epstein, *The Negro Migrant in Pittsburgh* (Pittsburgh, 1918), pp. 24–25.

10. Turner, *Negro in Pennsylvania*, pp. 241–42; Erasmus Wilson, ed., *Standard History of Pittsburgh* (Chicago, 1898), pp. 810–35; and Victor Ullman, *Martin R. Delany: The Beginnings of Black Nationalism* (Boston, 1971), pp. 1–183.

11. Baldwin, *Pittsburgh*, p. 237; Turner, *Negro in Pennsylvania*, pp. 241–42.

12. Dahlinger, *Pittsburgh*, pp. 38–39.

13. Helen A. Tucker, "The Negroes of Pittsburgh," *Charities and the Commons* (Jan. 2, 1909): 600.

14. Joseph A. Hill, "Recent Northward Migration of the Negro," *Monthly Labor Review* XVIII (Mar. 1924): 475–79; John Nicely Rathmell, "Status of Negroes in Regard to Origin, Length of Residence and Economic Aspects of Their Life" (master's thesis, University of Pittsburgh, 1935), table III, p. 26; Tucker, "Negroes of Pittsburgh," p. 599; and Kennedy, *Negro Peasant Turns Cityward*, p. 29.

15. Leslie Fishel, "The Negro in the North, 1865–1900: A Study in Race Discrimination" (doctoral dissertation, Harvard University, 2 vols., 1953), Appendix I-A, table 3. Philadelphia had 62,613 blacks; New York, 60,666; Chicago, 30,150; and Brooklyn, 18,367.

16. A. G. Moron, "Distribution of the Negro Population in Pittsburgh, 1910–1930" (master's thesis, University of Pittsburgh, 1933), pp. 37–39; Tucker, "Negroes of Pittsburgh," pp. 599–600. Because so many of the young unmarried males lived as lodgers, often changing their addresses, it was difficult for census takers to make an accurate count of the number of blacks (John G. Van Deusen, *The Black Man in White America* [Washington, D.C., 1944], p. 31).

17. Tucker, "Negroes of Pittsburgh," p. 600.

18. Richard R. Wright, Jr., *The Negro in Pennsylvania: A Study in Economic History* (Philadelphia, 1912), pp. 211–12.

Cities in Pennsylvania with Negro Population over 500 in 1900

City	Population
Allegheny	3,315
Braddock Borough	558
Carlisle	1,148
Chambersburg	769
Chester City	4,405
Columbia	521
Harrisburg	4,107
Homestead Borough	640
Lancaster	777
McKeesport	748
Norristown Borough	728
Philadelphia	62,613
Pittsburgh	17,040
Reading	534
Scranton	521
Steelton Borough	1,508
Uniontown Borough	803
Washington Borough	984
West Chester Borough	1,777
Wilkes-Barre	680
Williamsport	1,142
York	776

19. *Pittsburgh Dispatch*, Mar. 2, 1904.

20. Rathmell, "Status of Negroes," p. 26; Wright, *Negro in Pennsylvania*, pp. 61–63; and Kennedy, *Negro Peasant Turns Cityward*, p. 29.

21. Tucker, "Negroes of Pittsburgh," pp. 600–01; Alexander Z. Pittler, "The Hill District of Pittsburgh: A Study in Succession" (master's thesis, University of Pittsburgh, 1930), pp. 10–26.

22. Tucker, "Negroes of Pittsburgh," pp. 600–01.
23. Wright, *Negro in Pennsylvania*, p. 67.
24. Ibid., p. 228; Pittler, "Hill District," pp. 31, 42. In 1928, based on the biennial census of Jewish children in Pittsburgh, Professor Israel Abrams of the Hebrew Institute showed that the exodus was almost complete and that remaining Jewish families were leaving the Hill area at a rate of 350 per year.
25. Tucker, "Negroes of Pittsburgh," p. 603; *Old Organizations in Pittsburgh* (prepared by H. W. Correll for the Chamber of Commerce, 1929). See p. 38 of this work for Mrs. Vann's attempt to pass as a white clerk at Solomon and Bibrow, and p. 70 for the *Courier*'s efforts to have Kaufmann's employ blacks.
26. Commons, "Wage Earners of Pittsburgh," p. 1056.
27. Tucker, "Negroes of Pittsburgh," pp. 602–04; Sterling D. Spero and Abraham L. Harris, *The Black Worker: The Negro and the Labor Movement* (New York, 1931), pp. 53–86.
28. Spero and Harris, *Black Worker*, pp. 128–46.
29. Ibid., p. 16.
30. Gerald E. Allen, "The Negro Miner in Western Pennsylvania" (master's thesis, University of Pittsburgh, 1927), p. 20; Spero and Harris, *Black Worker*, p. 210.
31. Moron, "Distribution of the Negro Population," p. 18; Tucker, "Negroes of Pittsburgh," pp. 602–03. See Henry David, "Problems of Labor," in Lorant, *Pittsburgh*, pp. 207–18, for labor disputes, especially 1892.
32. Commons, "Wage Earners of Pittsburgh," p. 1063; John A. Fitch, "The Steel Industry and the Labor Problem," *Charities and the Commons* (Mar. 6, 1909): 1079–92.
33. Spero and Harris, *Black Worker*, p. 153.
34. Thomas Augustine, "The Negro Steel Worker of Pittsburgh and the Unions" (master's thesis, University of Pittsburgh, 1947), pp. 1–7; Wright, *Negro in Pennsylvania*, pp. 96–97.
35. Tucker, "Negroes of Pittsburgh," p. 603.
36. Ibid.
37. Ibid., p. 602.
38. Ibid., p. 605.
39. Ibid., p. 606.
40. Lincoln Steffens, *The Autobiography of Lincoln Steffens* (New York, 1931), p. 401.
41. F. Elizabeth Crowell, "Housing Situation in Pittsburgh," *Charities and the Commons* (Feb. 6, 1909): 871.
42. Florence L. Lattimore, "Skunk Hollow," *Charities and the Commons* (Feb. 6, 1909): 899.
43. Fitch, "Steel Industry and the Labor Problem," p. 1065.
44. Lubove, *Twentieth Century Pittsburgh*, pp. 39–40, 42–43; Samuel Hopkins Adams, "Tomfoolery with Public Health," *Survey* XXV (Dec. 17, 1910): 43; and Frank E. Wing, "Thirty-Five Years of Typhoid: The Fever's Economic Cost to Pittsburgh and the Long Fight for Pure Water," *Charities and the Commons* (Feb. 6, 1909): 923–39.
45. Anna Reel, "The Jewish Immigrants of Two Pittsburgh Blocks," *Charities and the Commons* (Jan. 2, 1909): 609.
46. Tucker, "Negroes of Pittsburgh," pp. 600–01.
47. Ibid., pp. 606–07.
48. Tucker, "Negroes of Pittsburgh," p. 607.
49. M. R. Goldman, "The Hill District of Pittsburgh as I Knew It," *Western Penn-*

sylvania Historical Magazine LI (July 1968): 285.

50. Tucker, "Negroes of Pittsburgh," p. 608.

51. Agnes Lynch Starrett, *Through One Hundred and Fifty Years: The University of Pittsburgh* (Pittsburgh, 1937), p. 209.

52. Ibid., pp. 233–34.

53. Ibid., p. 213.

54. Ibid., p. 217.

55. *The Western University Courant*, May 1906; Thomas Baker, "Higher Education in Pittsburgh," in *Pittsburgh and the Pittsburgh Spirit*, p. 326; and Lorant, *Pittsburgh*, p. 362.

56. Church, *A Short History of Pittsburgh*, pp. 98–99.

57. Wright, *Negro in Pennsylvania*, pp. 129–32; Fishel, "The Negro and the North," vol. II, pp. 296–97.

58. Wright, *Negro in Pennsylvania*, pp. 136–38; Tucker, "Negroes of Pittsburgh," pp. 606–07.

59. Interview with Mrs. Vann, Apr. 16, 1967. Vann's undergraduate academic record at WUP was either lost or discarded by the university, perhaps during the time when the school was enlarging and moving to the Schenley Farms area.

60. Webber, "Vann," p. 53. According to the 1914 Virginia Union University catalogue, Rooks, a 1903 graduate of Wayland Academy, was a dentist in Detroit in 1914.

61. Ernest Rice McKinney, "These Colored United States, Pennsylvania: A Tale of Two Cities," *The Messenger* V (May 1932): 692; *Courier*, Aug. 25, 1925; and Webber, "Vann," pp. 99–100.

62. Wright, "Negro in Pittsburgh," pp. 9–12.

63. Interview with Ernest Rice McKinney, New York City, Jan. 25 and 26, 1973. McKinney was born in Malden, West Virginia, on December 7, 1886, and moved to Pittsburgh in 1912. In 1915 he became work secretary of the Centre Avenue branch of the YMCA. Active in the organization of the Pittsburgh NAACP, he was its executive secretary in the early 1920s. Between 1920 and 1928 McKinney was twice editor of the *Pittsburgh American*. After that weekly folded, he wrote a column and special features for the *Courier*. He was on friendly terms with Ira Lewis, who consulted him on a number of matters crucial to the *Courier* during those years, including the decision to raise the price of the newspaper from five to ten cents and the feasibility of building a *Courier* printing plant. •

64. Webber, "Vann," pp. 67–73.

65. Interview with Mrs. Vann, Apr. 6, 1967; P. L. Prattis, biography of Mrs. Vann written for television program, "This Is Your Life," Oct. 14, 1953, in Prattis Papers, Pittsburgh; Mrs. Vann to Brewer, May 21, 1941, cited in Brewer, "Vann," p. 49; and *Courier*, May 1, 1915.

66. Visit to Red Hill, N.C.; Webber, "Vann," pp. 174–75.

67. *Boston Advertiser*, Aug. 20, 1904; *Lewiston* (Me.) *Journal*, Aug. 3, 1904; *Bar Harbor Record*, Aug. (undated), 1904 (all newspapers found in Scrapbook-1904, Box 1036, Booker T. Washington Papers, Library of Congress); Samuel R. Spencer, *Booker T. Washington and the Negro's Place in American Life* (Boston, 1955), p. 39; and Webber, "Vann," pp. 67, 73.

68. Interview with Mrs. Vann, Apr. 6, 1967.

69. Ibid.

70. Webber, "Vann," p. 69.

71. *The Western University Courant* XXI (May 1906): 11.
72. Ibid.
73. Undated letter from Arthur Calhoun (dean of Sterling College, Sterling, Kans., from 1937 to 1955), cited in Webber, "Vann," p. 68. Calhoun told the author by telephone, November 17, 1970, that the letter was written in about 1950, when Mrs. Vann was gathering material for Webber's biography of her husband.
74. MS in Vann Papers.
75. W. E. B. DuBois and Augustus Granville Dill, eds., *The College-Bred Negro American*, Atlanta University Publications, No. 15 (Atlanta, 1915), pp. 45–46.
76. DuBois and Dill, *College-Bred Negro American*, p. 83. One had graduated from 1890 to 1894, two more during the years from 1895 to 1899, two from 1902 to 1904, and five between 1905 and 1909. In Vann's class there were three other blacks: his friend Charles Carroll, in the Medical School; F. L. Dougherty, in the School of Engineering; and James Fowler, in the School of Pharmacy (Webber, "Vann," p. 83).
77. Webber, "Vann," p. 57.
78. Vann to Mencken, Mar. 14, 1938, Vann Papers.
79. Webber, "Vann," p. 84; telephone interview with Calhoun, Nov. 17, 1970.
80. Webber, "Vann," p. 85; interview with Mrs. Vann, Feb. 15, 1967.
81. Telephone interview with Thomas O. White, associate dean of the University of Pittsburgh Law School, May 31, 1973; Frederick A. Hetzel to Buni, May 25, 1973.
82. Webber, "Vann," p. 85; interview with Ernest Rice McKinney, Jan. 25 and 26, 1973. In the 1908 Pittsburgh Directory, Vann listed his occupation as "notary," with an office at 424 Fifth Avenue.
83. Tucker, "Negroes of Pittsburgh," pp. 606–07.
84. The following biographical background came from three interviews by the author with Mrs. Vann. Also helpful was the biography written for "This Is Your Life," Prattis Papers.
85. Interview with Mrs. Vann, Feb. 15, 1967.
86. Ibid.; interview with Mabel V. Johnson (daughter of Mr. and Mrs. William N. Page), Apr. 23, 1973.
87. Frederick A. Hetzel to Buni, May 25, 1973; *Announcements of the Pittsburgh Law School, 1897–1910* (Pittsburgh, 1911), p. 23 in the 1909–1910 Announcement.
88. Interview with Mrs. Vann, Jan. 18, 1967.
89. *Courier*, Dec. 16, 1922; Kennedy, *Negro Peasant Turns Cityward*, p. 86.
90. W. E. B. DuBois, *The Philadelphia Negro* (New York, 1899), p. 115. Much of this information came from Homer S. Brown, judge of the Court of Common Pleas in Pittsburgh. Brown also graduated from Virginia Union and then matriculated at the University of Pittsburgh. His acquaintance with Vann began in 1919. After graduating from the University of Pittsburgh Law School, Brown founded a law firm with Richard F. Jones, one of his classmates (telephone interview with Brown, Oct. 6, 1967; "In the News Column: Homer S. Brown," *Opportunity* XVII [Jan. 1939]: 16–17; biographical folder, "Pittsburgh—Negroes," Pennsylvania Division, Carnegie Library).
91. Webber, "Vann," p. 85.
92. Telephone interview with Calhoun, Nov. 17, 1970.
93. Carter G. Woodson, *The Negro Professional Man and the Community, with Special Emphasis on the Physician and the Lawyer* (Washington, D.C., 1934), pp. 190–96.
94. Such as William H. Stanton, for whom Vann clerked, who earned extra money by making small mortgage loans of $500 to $1,500 and collecting interest.
95. Woodson, *Negro Professional Man*, p. 222.

Notes to Pages 42–45 • 337
Chapter 3. Birth of the COURIER

1. Richard Bardolph, *The Negro Vanguard* (New York, 1961), p. 146. Vann's recollections of the *Courier*'s beginnings are found in a letter from him to Elizabeth Amelia Pinckney, a Fisk University graduate student, Apr. 2, 1936, in Pinckney's master's thesis, "The Editorial Page of the *Pittsburgh Courier*," pp. iii–iv.
2. Webber, "Vann," p. 97; Brewer, "Vann," p. 17.
3. Vann to Pinckney, Apr. 2, 1936, in Pinckney, "Editorial Page," pp. iii–iv.
4. Lewis to Brewer, May 6, 1941, cited in Brewer, "Vann," p. 17.
5. Except for a few copies in the possession of P. L. Prattis and in the Virginia Union University Library, and a microfilm roll (Mar. 25, 1911 to Dec. 27, 1912), no issues of the *Courier* for the years 1910 to 1923 have survived. Robert Vann's scrapbooks for those years are available, however; they contain primarily a large collection of editorials, most of them written by Vann.
6. Interview with Mrs. Vann, Apr. 6, 1967.
7. George Swetnam, *The Bicentennial History of Pittsburgh* (Pittsburgh, 1955), vol. II, p. 357; Webber, "Vann," p. 99; Vann to Pinckney, Apr. 2, 1936, in Pinckney, "Editorial Page," pp. iii–iv; Thomas J. Johnson to Emmett J. Scott, Feb. 12, 1914, Box 841, Booker T. Washington Papers, Library of Congress; *Courier*, Dec. 9, 1911; William G. Nunn, Sr., "The *Pittsburgh Courier* Story, 50th Anniversary, 1910–1960"; and interview with Mabel V. Johnson (daughter of William N. Page), Apr. 23, 1973.
8. Vann to Pinckney, Apr. 2, 1936, in Pinckney, "Editorial Page," pp. iii–iv.
9. Bayless to Brewer, May 27, 1941, in Brewer, "Vann," p. 20.
10. Frederick G. Detweiler, *The Negro Press in America* (Chicago, 1922), pp. 6, 11; John H. Burma, "An Analysis of the Present Negro Press," *Social Forces* XXVI (Dec. 1947): 172; and Gunnar Myrdal, *An American Dilemma* (New York, 1944), p. 909.
11. According to Emma Lou Thornbrough, nine of the black weeklies begun in the 1880s were still operating in 1914 (*Washington Bee, New York Age, Philadelphia Tribune, Cleveland Gazette, Richmond Planet, Savannah Tribune, Indianapolis Freeman*, and *Appeal*, published simultaneously in Chicago and St. Paul); nineteen begun in the 1890s were still printing, the more noted being the *Baltimore Afro-American, Indianapolis Recorder, Dallas Express*, and *Charleston Messenger;* of those begun after 1900, most prominent were the *Chicago Defender,* the New York *Amsterdam News,* and the *Pittsburgh Courier* ("American Negro Newspapers, 1880–1914," *Business History Review* XL [Winter 1966]: 467–90). See also Vishnu V. Oak, *The Negro Newspapers* (Yellow Springs, Ohio, 1948), pp. 122–32; Irvine Garland Penn, *The Afro-American Press and its Editors* (Springfield, Mass., 1891), passim.
12. P. L. Prattis, "The Negro Press in Action," manuscript, Prattis Papers; Eugene Gordon, "The Negro Press," *American Mercury* VIII (June 1926): 208.
13. Thornbrough, "American Negro Newspapers," pp. 102–03; idem., *T. Thomas Fortune: Militant Journalist* (Chicago, 1972), passim.
14. Peter Bergman, *The Chronological History of the Negro in America* (New York, 1969), pp. 130, 140; Ira V. Brown, *The Negro in Pennsylvania History* (Pennsylvania Historical Association, Gettysburg, 1970), p. 39.
15. Victor Ullman, *Martin R. Delany: The Beginnings of Black Nationalism* (Boston, 1971), pp. 45–76; Warren Brown, *Checklist of Newspapers in the United States, 1827–1946* (Jefferson City, Mo., 1946), pp. 3–37; Ruth Salisbury, ed., *Pennsylvania Newspapers: A Bibliography* (Pittsburgh, 1969); Helen A. Tucker, "The Negroes of Pittsburgh," *Charities and the Commons* (Jan. 2, 1909): 81; and Richard R. Wright, Jr., *The Negro in*

Pennsylvania: A Study in Economic History (Philadelphia, 1912), p. 81.

16. Wright, *Negro in Pennsylvania*, pp. 81–82.

17. Milton Anderson Lawson, "The Influence of the Migration upon Negro Newspapers" (master's thesis, Fisk University, June 1941), pp. 6–7.

18. Webber, "Vann," p. 86; Lewis to Brewer, May 6, 1941, in Brewer, "Vann," p. 20. For brief histories of the *Dispatch, Post, Telegraph, Leader, Press,* and *Sun*, see Leland D. Baldwin, *Pittsburgh: The Story of a City* (Pittsburgh, 1938), pp. 351–53; Sarah H. Killikelly, *The History of Pittsburgh: Its Rise and Progress* (Pittsburgh, 1906), pp. 483–502.

19. Ruth Lucretia Stevenson, "The Pittsburgh Urban League" (master's thesis, University of Pittsburgh, 1936), p. 27. There was little communication between whites and blacks; not until 1924 was the Urban League successful, through a series of newspaper articles, in bringing facts about the city's blacks before the white public.

20. Webber, "Vann," pp. 100–01.

21. Lewis to Brewer, May 6, 1941, in Brewer, "Vann," p. 22; minutes of special meeting, board of directors, June 7, 1922, Prattis Papers.

22. *Courier*, Mar. 16, 1911.

23. Webber, "Vann," p. 94.

24. *Courier*, Nov. 4, 1911.

25. Ibid., Oct. 15, 1911.

26. Ibid., Dec. 13, 1912.

27. Ibid., May 11, 1911; "YMCA Dedicated," ibid., Feb. 17, 1912. Thanks largely to contributions from the Rosenwald Fund, the YMCA building was finally completed in 1923. It filled a basic need within the black community. Politically, it became the meeting hall for blacks during election campaigns. The gymnasium was converted into an auditorium for larger meetings. The "Y" on Centre Avenue, across the street from the *Courier* building in the black neighborhood, became a *de facto* segregated branch. In a 1928 brochure listing fourteen branches, only the Centre Avenue YMCA had the word "Colored" in parentheses beside its name (Prattis to Buni, Dec. 18, 1967; Ira DeA. Reid, *Social Conditions of the Negro in the Hill District of Pittsburgh* [General Committee on the Hill Survey, 1930], p. 107; and YMCA, *Annual Concerted Operating Budget Canvas*, Oct. 15, 1928, Prattis Papers).

28. Beatrice Posey Bayless to Brewer, May 27, 1941, in Brewer, "Vann," p. 19.

29. Ibid.

30. Gordon, "Negro Press," p. 208.

31. *Courier*, Aug. 5, 1911.

32. Ibid., Mar. 9, 1912.

33. Ibid., Mar. 25, 1911.

34. Ibid., 1911–12, passim. See also Detweiler, *Negro Press*, pp. 113–15; Samuel Auerbach, "Quackery," *Opportunity* V (Dec. 1929): 373–75, reprinted in Gilbert Osofsky, ed., *The Burden of Race: A Documentary History of Negro-White Relations in America* (New York, 1967), pp. 277–84; and Guy B. Johnson, "Negro Advertisements and Negro Culture," *The Journal of Social Forces* IV (May 1925): 706–09.

35. *Courier*, Jan. 14, 1916; Reid, *Social Conditions of the Negro*, p. 115; and Rhode Gooden-Irving, "Advertising in Negro Newspapers" (master's thesis, Ohio State University, 1935), chap. v.

36. *Courier*, June 7, 1912.

37. Ibid., Mar. 25, 1911.

38. Interview with Ernest Rice McKinney, Jan. 25 and 26, 1973.

39. Webber, "Vann," pp. 109, 141; *Courier*, Dec. 14, 1929. See also *Courier*, Mar. 20, 1965; *Pittsburgh Post-Gazette*, Mar. 11, 1965; biographical folder, "Pittsburgh—Negroes," Pennsylvania Division, Carnegie Library. Born in Reading, she came to Pittsburgh in 1909 and married William Lampkin, a restaurateur, in 1912. She began her public career by organizing black housewives into consumer groups. Mrs. Lampkin was active in the suffrage movement as a member and president of the Lucy Stone League. During the 1920s, she was instrumental in revitalizing the Pittsburgh branch of the NAACP. An excellent fund raiser, she became national field secretary for the association during the 1930s.

40. *Courier*, Jan. 13, 1912.

41. Program of "Proceedings of the National Negro Press Association," Muskogee, Okla., Aug. 17–21, 1914, in National Negro Business League Correspondence, 1914, Box 854, Booker T. Washington Papers, Library of Congress. This National Negro Press Association had no relationship to the one established by John Sengstacke in 1940.

42. *Courier*, July 14, 1916.

43. Ibid., Nov. 7, 1925; Gordon, "Negro Press," p. 213; Horace David Murdock, "Some Business Aspects of Leading Negro Newspapers" (master's thesis, University of Kansas, 1936), p. 19; Chicago Commission on Race Riots, *The Negro in Chicago: A Study of Race Relations and a Race Riot* (Chicago, 1923), pp. 567–68; and Cyril E. Zoerner II, "Associated Negro Press: Its Founding, Ascendancy and Demise," *Journalism Quarterly* XLVI (Spring 1969): 47–48.

44. *Courier*, Feb. 27, 1912.

45. Biographical sketches in *The Dispatch*, Lexington, N.C., May 2, 1946, and *The Ohio State News*, Sept. 4, 1948, both in Vann Papers; Lewis to Brewer, May 6, 1941, in Brewer, "Vann," p. 23; and Webber, "Vann," pp. 107–14. Lewis left no manuscript collection.

46. Lewis to Brewer, May 6, 1941, in Brewer, "Vann," p. 23. After Vann's death, Lewis became president of the *Pittsburgh Courier*. He served in that capacity and as general manager until his death on August 29, 1948. He was also president of the Interstate United Newspapers, Inc. and regional vice-president of the Negro Publishers Association. Two years before his death, he commented on the success of the *Courier*, with its circulation of over 300,000: "This company does a million and a half dollars' worth of business a year. The newspaper is published in fourteen editions and has branch offices in twelve cities in the country. I won't say exactly right here how much salary and income I am getting but I will say that I paid over $18,000 in federal taxes last year" (*The Dispatch*, Lexington, N.C., May 2, 1946; *The Ohio State News*, Sept. 4, 1948, Vann Papers).

47. Webber, "Vann," p. 116; interview with Ernest Rice McKinney, Jan. 25 and 26, 1973.

48. Interview with William G. Nunn, Sr., Mar. 13, 1969; Webber, "Vann," p. 116.

Chapter 4. The COURIER as a Social Force

1. August Meier, *Negro Thought in America 1880–1915* (Ann Arbor, 1963), pp. 130–31.

2. Helen A. Tucker, "The Negroes of Pittsburgh," *Charities and the Commons* (Jan. 2, 1909): 605; Richard R. Wright, Jr., *The Negro in Pennsylvania: A Study in Economic*

History (Philadelphia, 1912), p. 220. At least thirty Baptist churches held services in Pittsburgh. There were also ten Methodist churches, one Presbyterian, one Protestant Episcopalian, one Congregational, and one Roman Catholic. Moron was more conservative in his 1910 estimate, listing twenty-seven black churches (not including store-front churches), of which fourteen were Baptist (A. G. Moron, "Distribution of the Negro Population in Pittsburgh, 1910–1930" [master's thesis, University of Pittsburgh, 1933]).

3. W. E. B. DuBois, *The Philadelphia Negro* (New York, 1899), pp. 206, 197–221.

4. Tucker, "Negroes of Pittsburgh," p. 605; interview with Ernest Rice McKinney, Jan. 25 and 26, 1973. For the same complaints against Pittsburgh churches in the 1920s, see Abraham L. Harris, Jr., "The New Negro Worker in Pittsburgh" (master's thesis, University of Pittsburgh, 1924), pp. 77–78; and Pennsylvania Department of Welfare, *Negro Survey of Pennsylvania* (Harrisburg, 1925), pp. 62–67.

5. Meier, *Negro Thought*, p. 133.

6. Tucker, "Negroes of Pittsburgh," pp. 605–06. In a similar study done twenty years later, the situation had not changed appreciably. In 1928–29, of the forty-five churches investigated in the Hill District, eighteen were store-front and seventeen were Baptist (Ira DeA. Reid, *Social Conditions of the Negro in the Hill District of Pittsburgh* [General Committee on the Hill Survey, 1930], pp. 99–106). In 1929 there was a central church organization seeking reform, the Department of Work Among Negroes, Pittsburgh Council of Churches of Christ (ibid., pp. 104–05).

7. "Please, Please, Please," *Courier*, July 7, 1923. Vann To Rev. Glenn T. Settle, Cleveland, Ohio, Aug. 2, 1937, Vann Papers.

8. Tucker, "Negroes of Pittsburgh," p. 606; *Negro Survey of Pennsylvania*, p. 78; Vishnu V. Oak, *The Negro Newspapers* (Yellow Springs, Ohio, 1948), p. 26; and Maxwell R. Brooks, *The Negro Press Reexamined: Political Content of Leading Negro Newspapers* (Boston, 1959), p. 13.

9. Interviews taped by Henry LaBrie with C. A. Scott, publisher, *Atlanta Daily World*, July 14, 1971, and with William O. Walker, publisher, *Cleveland Call and Post*, June 11, 1971. Both Scott and Walker stated that the NAACP would never have succeeded without the help of the black press.

10. *Courier*, Jan. 15, 1915. For an account of the recruiting effort, see Charles Flint Kellogg, *NAACP: A History of the National Association for the Advancement of Colored People, 1909–1920* (Baltimore, 1967), vol. I, chap. vi; *Negro Survey of Pennsylvania*, p. 77; Henry Arthur Schooley, "A Case Study of the Pittsburgh Branch of the National Association for the Advancement of Colored People" (master's thesis, University of Pittsburgh, 1952), p. 8, appendix IV, p. 44; and telephone interview with Judge Homer Brown, Pittsburgh, Oct. 6, 1967. Unfortunately, the Pittsburgh branch of the NAACP did not save its records prior to 1941; those after that date are deposited in the University of Pittsburgh Library.

11. Rabbi Rudolph I. Coffee to Miss May Childs Nerney (New York City NAACP secretary), Jan. 12, 1915, Branch Files, Box G-190, NAACP Papers, Library of Congress.

12. Morsell to Nerney, Feb. 1, 1915, Nerney to William M. Randolph, Feb. 27, 1915, both in Box G-190, NAACP Papers.

13. *Courier*, Feb. 12, 1915.

14. Ernest Rice McKinney to Mary White Ovington, Aug. 2, 1920, Box G-190, NAACP Papers.

15. Rev. J. C. Austin to Ovington, Feb. 11, 1921, Box G-190, NAACP Papers.

16. R. W. Bagrall (director of branches, NAACP) to Dr. R. W. Taylor, Apr. 6,

1922, Box G-190, NAACP Papers. See Box G-190 also for the immense improvement made by Homer Brown on the Pittsburgh branch.

17. "No Excuse Now," *Courier*, Jan. 22, 1915.

18. Ibid., Jan. 28, 1916, Dec. 17, 1917.

19. Epstein's study was the result of questionnaires sent to over five hundred individuals who had migrated from the South in July and August 1917. Questions dealt with the kinds of labor in which migrants were engaged, wages paid them, housing, rents, health, and other social conditions. An effort was made to visit and study every area of Pittsburgh, but most of the information came from the Hill District and Upper Wylie and Bedford Avenues; the Lawrenceville District about Penn Avenue between Twenty-Eighth and Thirty-Fourth Streets; the North Side black quarter around Beaver Avenue and Fulton Street; the East Liberty section in the vicinity of Mignonette and Shakespeare Streets; and the new downtown black section on Second Avenue, Ross, and Water Streets (Abraham Epstein, *The Negro Migrant in Pittsburgh* [Pittsburgh, 1918], pp. 9, 69–70).

20. Manuscript on Pittsburgh Branch of Urban League, Prattis Papers; P. L. Prattis, *The Pittsburgh Urban League: The 50th Year* (Pittsburgh Urban League Magazine); and Ruth L. Stevenson, "The Pittsburgh Urban League" (master's thesis, University of Pittsburgh, 1936), pp. 4–15. Officers included Walter A. May, president; Rev. G. B. Howard, first vice-president; Rev. C. Y. Trigg, second vice-president; S. R. Morsell, secretary; and J. D. Fraser, treasurer. For background of the Urban League, see Guichard Parris and Lester Brooks, *Blacks in the City: A History of the National Urban League* (Boston, 1971), pp. 3–65; Arvarh E. Strickland, *History of the Chicago Urban League* (Urbana, Ill., 1966), chap. I.

21. Stevenson, "Pittsburgh Urban League," pp. 4–15; Wendell F. Grigsby, "Pittsburgh Plans for Its Future," *Opportunity* XVII (Dec. 1939): 362–64; and Antoinette Hutchings Westmoreland, "A Study of the Requests for Specialized Services Directed to the Urban League of Pittsburgh" (master's thesis, University of Pittsburgh, 1938).

22. Stevenson, "Pittsburgh Urban League," pp. 16–24; The author would especially like to thank Percival L. Prattis for allowing him to use research findings from the Pittsburgh Urban League records. Among the sources used by Prattis in preparing *The Pittsburgh Urban League: The 50th Year* are minutes of the executive board in the Urban League files, annual reports to the executive secretary, and the monthly bulletin of the Pittsburgh branch, *The Informer*.

Percival L. Prattis was born in Philadelphia in 1895. After service in World War I, he began his newspaper work with the foundling *Michigan State News* (Grand Rapids) in 1919. In 1921, he took a job as a reporter for the *Chicago Defender*. After one month he was promoted to city editor, a position he held until 1923. He was news editor of the Associated Negro Press from 1923 to 1935, when he also became city editor of the *Amsterdam News*. In 1936 he moved on to the *Pittsburgh Courier* as city editor. From 1940 to 1956 he was its executive editor, and its editor from 1956 to 1962 (interview taped by Henry LaBrie with Prattis, June 15, 1972). Prattis is now writing his autobiography.

23. Meier, *Negro Thought*, p. 137.

24. Interview with Ernest Rice McKinney, Jan. 25 and 26, 1973.

25. Edward David Cronon, *Black Moses: The Story of Marcus Garvey and the Universal Negro Improvement Association* (Madison, Wis., 1955), p. 37; Schooley, "Pittsburgh Branch of the NAACP," p. 38.

26. *Courier*, Dec. 18, 1916.
27. Ibid., Mar. 5, 1915.
28. A. G. Moron, "Distribution of the Negro Population," p. 29. For thorough coverage of the housing problem from 1907 to 1930 see Emily W. Dinwiddie and F. E. Crowell, "The Housing of Pittsburgh's Workers," in Paul U. Kellogg, ed., *The Pittsburgh Survey* (New York, 1909–14), vol. 5, pp. 87–123; Epstein, *Negro Migrant in Pittsburgh*, passim; Harris, "New Negro Worker," pp. 14–23; *Negro Survey of Pennsylvania*, pp. 31–36; Wiley A. Hall, "Negro Housing and Rents in the Hill District of Pittsburgh" (master's thesis, University of Pittsburgh, 1929); and Verne Colson Wright, "The Social Aspects of Housing" (master's thesis, University of Pittsburgh, 1927), passim. In 1910 there were 25,623 blacks in Pittsburgh, 4.8 percent of the total 533,905 population. Blacks were still scattered throughout the city's twenty-seven wards, but almost half (10,354 or 22.6 percent of the total 46,376 in the Third and Fifth Wards) lived in the Hill District. There was also a fair-sized group in East Liberty—4,345 blacks, representing 16.9 percent of that area's total population of 60,613. In the Thirteenth Ward (East End), one of the older settlements of blacks, there were 973 black residents.
29. *Negro Survey of Pennsylvania*, p. 32.
30. Epstein, *Negro Migrant in Pittsburgh*, pp. 8, 12, 38; Elsie Witchen, *Tuberculosis and the Negro in Pittsburgh* (Pittsburgh, 1934); Minnie H. Bachrach, "The Immigrant on the Hill" (master's thesis, Carnegie Institute of Technology, 1921), pp. 6–7; and Louis V. Kennedy, *The Negro Peasant Turns Cityward* (New York, 1930), p. 152.
31. Telephone interview with Mrs. Howard Rickmond, Jr., Apr. 2, 1973.
32. Webber, "Vann," p. 105; interview with Mrs. Vann, Apr. 6, 1967.
33. Webber, "Vann," p. 125; interview with Mrs. Vann, Apr. 6, 1967.
34. Moron, "Distribution of the Negro Population in Pittsburgh," p. 32; telephone interview with Mrs. Howard Rickmond, Jr., Apr. 2, 1973.
35. *Courier*, May 18, 1917.
36. Ibid., Feb. 26, 1915.
37. *Negro Survey of Pennsylvania*, p. 27.
38. United States Bureau of the Census, *Negro Population in the United States, 1790–1915* (Arno Press and *New York Times* edition, 1968), p. 335; idem., *Negroes in the United States, 1920–1932* (Arno Press and *New York Times* edition, 1969), pp. 240–41, 455; and Epstein, *Negro Migrant in Pittsburgh*, pp. 56–60. By 1928 the black rate was down to 19.5, but the white rate was lower at 12.0. In that year the infant mortality rate per 1,000 births for whites was 78, but for blacks it was 113.1. Excess of births over deaths for whites was 4,044 but for blacks only 274. In 1928, using the Third and Fifth Wards as examples, while blacks comprised 8.9 percent of the total city population, in those wards they had 9.8 percent of the city's total deaths, 13.9 percent of the deaths from tuberculosis, 14.0 percent of deaths from pneumonia, 19.9 percent of deaths from syphilis and gonorrhea, and 9.2 percent of the infant deaths (Reid, *Social Conditions of the Negro*, pp. 39–41; *Negro Survey of Pennsylvania*, pp. 33–34, 44–45).
39. "White Plague Scare," *Courier*, Feb. 16, 1917; ibid., Feb. 3, 1923; Kellogg, *NAACP*, pp. 197–98. The Urban League noted that not until 1920 was the first black patient admitted to the Tuberculosis Hospital Sanitorium on Bedford Street (Stevenson, "Pittsburgh Urban League," p. 17; Reid, *Social Conditions of the Negro*, p. 47).
40. *Courier*, June 22, 1935; Philip Klein, *A Social History of Pittsburgh* (New York,

1938), p. 278. In 1925 there were only 29 black physicians in the city—a very low figure, considering that the black population was 45,106 (Reid, *Social Conditions of the Negro*, pp. 51, 93, 115).

41. *Courier*, Mar. 24, 1916.
42. Ibid., Feb. 16, 1917; *Negro Survey of Pennsylvania*, p. 47.
43. *Courier*, Dec. 18, 1916.
44. See DuBois, *Philadelphia Negro*, p. 230, for the fight which had to be waged for a black hospital, despite cries from some blacks and whites that it would only deepen segregation and race prejudice. See also Allan H. Spear, *Black Chicago: The Making of a Negro Ghetto, 1890–1920* (Chicago, 1967), pp. 97–100.
45. *Courier*, Apr. 22, 1922; Reid, *Social Conditions of the Negro*, p. 51.
46. Reid, *Social Conditions of the Negro*, pp. 12–13, 111–13.
47. *Courier*, Feb. 20, 1930, July 12, 1930; and Vann to Governor Earle, Mar. 22, 1937, Vann to H. Ford Mercer, Mar. 22, 1937, Vann Papers.
48. *Courier*, Jan. 29, 1915.
49. Ibid., Mar. 5, 1915.
50. In 1915 blacks numbered 4,083 of the total student body of 102,572. In the Hill District's eleven schools there were 1,415 blacks in January 1917; this figure increased to 1,973 by October 1917, and by 1924 there were 3,167 black students, about 39 percent of the total, in the Hill District schools (*Courier*, July 10, 1915; Epstein, *Negro Migrant in Pittsburgh*, pp. 71–72; Harris, "New Negro Worker," pp. 64–70; *Courier*, Feb. 11, Aug. 11, 1916; miscellaneous materials, Urban League files, 1925–29; and Reid, *Social Conditions of the Negro*, pp. 82–84, 88–89).
51. *Courier*, Feb. 5, 1915.
52. Ibid., Aug. 20, 1915.
53. Ibid., July 9, 1915.
54. Ibid., Feb. 4, May 1, 1916.
55. Ibid., Feb. 11, 1916.
56. Ibid., Apr. 7, 1916.
57. Speech made by Vann to Literary Society of Brown Chapel, 1906 (undated), Vann Papers; "Our School Needs," *Courier*, Sept. 11, 1914.
58. *Courier*, Aug. 11, 1916.
59. Statement made by board member Dr. A. W. Lewin, May 1924, Urban League notes, Prattis Papers; Stevenson, "Pittsburgh Urban League," p. 21; Daisy E. Lampkin (Negro Women's League of Allegheny County) to Vann, Aug. 5, 1927, Vann Papers; and *Negro Survey of Pennsylvania*, pp. 58–59.
60. *Pittsburgh Dispatch*, June 16, 1914.
61. Ira DeA. Reid, "The Negro in the Major Industries and Building Trades of Pittsburgh" (master's thesis, University of Pittsburgh, 1925), pp. 33–44; Sterling D. Spero and Abraham L. Harris, *The Black Worker: The Negro and the Labor Movement* (New York, 1931), pp. 158–61; Reid, *Social Conditions of the Negro*, pp. 53–54; and *Negro Survey of Pennsylvania*, pp. 14–17, 22. For example, by 1925 there were only 18 blacks of a total of 1,200 members in the Brick Layers' Local Union; 15 blacks in the 25 Carpenters' Local Unions, with a total membership of 5,200; and only 518 blacks affiliated with the AFL in Pittsburgh.
62. *Courier*, Jan. 14, 1916.
63. Ibid., Jan. 22, 1915.
64. "Let Negroes Take Notice," ibid., Nov. 29, 1912.

65. "Demand and Supply," ibid., Aug. 30, 1912.
66. "Negro Waiters Dismissed," ibid., Dec. 9, 1911.
67. Ibid., June 7, 1912.
68. Interview with Ernest Rice McKinney, Jan. 25 and 26, 1973; interview with Walter C. Rainey, Apr. 21, 1973.
69. *Courier*, Dec. 15, 1916, Jan. 16, 1917.
70. Ibid., Jan. 16, 1917.
71. "Set Back Twenty Years," ibid., June 22, 1917.
72. Ibid., June 29, 1917; Epstein, *Negro Migrant in Pittsburgh*, p. 43. Epstein writes: "Appeals to union people based on race issues were then carried to the patrons of that store until the department store was forced to discharge all of its colored drivers and re-instate the white ones. This was done in spite of the fact that the Union was not recognized, and was broken up, and although the manager of the store is said to have admitted that almost half of the colored drivers had proved one hundred per cent efficient." Not until January 1947 did the five major department stores of Pittsburgh agree that there would be no further discrimination against blacks in hiring, salaries, firing, and promotions. These results came after a concerted drive led by the Urban League in Pittsburgh (manuscript on Urban League, Prattis Papers; Stevenson, "Pittsburgh Urban League," p. 37).
73. *Courier*, Dec. 15, 1916.
74. Ibid., Jan. 15, 1915.
75. Ibid., Dec. 28, 1917.
76. "A Bad Start, Boys," ibid., Sept. 29, 1916. See also Spero and Harris, *The Black Worker*, pp. 164, 167–68; Reid, "The Negro in the Major Industries," p. 17.
77. *Courier*, Sept. 18, Oct. 12, 1918. This material was based on Joseph A. Hill, "Recent Northward Migration of the Negro," *Monthly Labor Review* XVIII (Mar. 1924): 475–76; Henderson H. Donald, *The Negro Migration of 1916–1918* (Washington, D.C., 1921), pp. 23–24; F. D. Tyson, *Negro Migration in 1916–1917* (Washington, D.C., 1918), p. 157; Kennedy, *Negro Peasant Turns Cityward*, pp. 74–76; Emmett J. Scott, *Negro Migration During the War* (New York, 1920), pp. 30–37; Epstein, *Negro Migrant in Pittsburgh*, pp. 7–31; and John Nicely Rathmell, "Status of Negroes in Regard to Origin, Length of Residence and Economic Aspects of Their Life" (master's thesis, University of Pittsburgh, 1935), pp. 23, 26.
78. *Courier*, Mar. 22, 1918.
79. "Pittsburgh Jews Different," ibid., Dec. 25, 1914; "The Example of the Jew," ibid., Oct. 6, 1917. See also DuBois, *Philadelphia Negro*, p. 178; Lenora E. Berson, *Case Study of a Riot: The Philadelphia Story* (New York, 1966), p. 46.
80. A study of prisoners entering the Eastern Penitentiary of Pennsylvania indicates that the number of crimes by blacks increased more rapidly than the black population increased. More than half the crimes were disorderly conduct, breach of the peace, drunkenness, and shooting craps (Wright, *Negro in Pennsylvania*, pp. 144, 148; Alexander Z. Pittler, "The Hill District of Pittsburgh: A Study in Succession" [master's thesis, University of Pittsburgh, 1930], pp. 46–59; Tucker, "Negroes of Pittsburgh," pp. 607–08; Epstein, *Negro Migrant in Pittsburgh*, p. 48).

Much the same was true of arrests in Pittsburgh during the 1920s (Reid, *Social Conditions of the Negro*, pp. 58–63; Harris, "New Negro Worker," pp. 29–39). In 1920, while blacks constituted only 6.4 percent of the Pittsburgh population, in 1923 they accounted for more than twice that percentage of arrests (13.8 percent). Most of the crimes were petty, mainly drunkenness, disorderly conduct, gambling, and being "of suspicious character." The greatest number of arrests occurred among males between the ages of 20 and 25. Over 22 percent of the total commitments to the Western State Penitentiary during the 1913–23 decade were blacks, and 28 percent of the total numbers committed to the Work House from 1914 to 1922 were blacks.

81. *Courier*, Sept. 17, 1918; Reid, *Social Conditions of the Negro*, p. 70. See also Harris, "New Negro Worker," pp. 28–44, 72. Especially helpful in preparing this crime section was my interview with Walter C. Rainey of Pittsburgh, April 21, 1973. Rainey was with the Allegheny County Detective Bureau for twelve years and a longtime political associate of Vann, particularly from 1920–38. Rainey helped organize the Third Ward Voters' League in 1927, was chairman of the County Campaign Committee in the Democratic State Committee (Negro Section) in the 1936 presidential election, and bolted with Vann to the GOP in 1938.

82. *Courier*, Sept. 17, 1918; Epstein, *Negro Migrant in Pittsburgh*, pp. 19, 50–51.

83. Epstein, *Negro Migrant In Pittsburgh*, p. 51; Harris, "New Negro Worker," pp. 35–36.

84. "Save Our Community," *Courier*, Dec. 1, 1916; "Police Hysteria," ibid., Mar. 6, 1920; "If We Don't Stop It," ibid., Feb. 19, 1919; and "Are They Mad?" ibid., Oct. 28, 1922. See also, Epstein, *Negro Migrant in Pittsburgh*, pp. 46–47, 51; Reid, *Social Conditions of the Negro*, p. 63; and Harris, "New Negro Worker," p. 35.

85. *Courier*, June 14, 1923.

86. *Pittsburgh Dispatch*, Jan. 23 and 24, 1920; "Squibbs," *Courier*, July 14, 1923; "Give Us More Colored Policemen," ibid., Mar. 22, 1924.

87. The Committee on Resolutions included Vann, Dr. C. Y. Trigg, Stewart Holmes, William H. Stanton, G. W. Murray, George H. Newman, and E. C. Alexander.

88. Webber, "Vann," p. 95.

89. "The Raid," *Courier*, Dec. 3 and 16, 1916. See also "Police Hysteria," ibid., Mar. 6, 1920.

90. Ibid., Mar. 6, 1920.

91. Elizabeth Jones to Henry A. Boyd (corresponding secretary of the National Negro Press Association), Aug. 14, 1914, National Negro Business League Correspondence, Box 854, Booker T. Washington Papers, Library of Congress.

92. See Martin E. Dann, ed., *The Negro Press, 1827–1890: the Quest for National Identity* (New York, 1971), pp. 12–14; George Eaton Simpson, *The Negro in the Philadelphia Press* (Philadelphia, 1936), pp. 38–76.

93. "Truth Will Out," *Courier*, Jan. 4, 1918. See also "Ask Only the Truth," ibid., Mar. 5, 1915; Epstein, *Negro Migrant in Pittsburgh*, p. 47; and Reid, *Social Conditions of the Negro*, p. 64.

94. Samuel R. Spencer, *Booker T. Washington and the Negro's Place in American Life* (Boston, 1955), p. 176.

95. *Courier*, Mar. 25, 1911. On Oliver, see J. Cutler Andrews, *Pittsburgh's Post Gazette: The First Newspaper West of the Alleghenies* (Boston, 1936), pp. 262–65.

96. *Pittsburgh Dispatch*, Aug. 4, 1917.

97. Ibid.

98. Ibid., Aug. 6, 1917.

99. Ibid., Aug. 10, 1917.

100. Ibid., Oct. 19, 1919.

101. "What They Call Us," *Courier*, Jan. 20, 1912.

102. "Silent Contempt," ibid., Aug. 5, 1911.
103. Ibid., Aug. 26, 1911.
104. Ibid., Sept. 23, 1911.
105. "Our Policy," ibid., Jan. 21, 1916.
106. Ibid., Mar. 16, 1912.
107. Ibid., Sept. 20, 1912.
108. Ibid., Jan. 6, 1912. See also Spear, *Black Chicago*, pp. 56–57.
109. *Courier*, Sept. 20, 1912.
110. Ibid., Nov. 11, 1911.
111. Ibid., Mar. 12, 1912.
112. Ibid., Jan. 6, 1912.
113. Ibid., Jan. 27, 1912.
114. Ibid., Sept. 6, 1912.
115. Ibid., Mar. 6, 1912.
116. Ibid., May 4, 1912.
117. Ibid., Mar. 9, 1912.
118. Ibid.
119. Ibid., Mar. 25, 1911.
120. Ibid.
121. Ibid., Jan. 6, 1912.
122. Frederick G. Detweiler, *The Negro Press in America* (Chicago, 1922), pp. 130–65.
123. Leslie Fishel, "The Negro in the North, 1865–1900: A Study in Race Discrimination" (doctoral dissertation, Harvard University, 2 vols., 1953), vol. II, pp. 394–95, 433, 500–01; Milton R. Konvitz, *A Century of Civil Rights* (New York, 1961), p. 157.
124. Wright, *Negro in Pennsylvania*, pp. 172, 186–87.
125. "The Hippodrome Jim Crow," *Courier*, July 19, 1912.
126. "And Yet We Go," ibid., Jan. 13, 1912.
127. Ibid., Feb. 4, 1916.
128. Schooley, "Pittsburgh Branch of the NAACP," pp. 8–9.
129. Interview with Randolph, Nov. 26, 1969; interview with Mrs. Vann, Apr. 6, 1967.
130. *Courier*, Apr. 13, 1912; *Legislative Journal for the Session of 1911* (Harrisburg, 1912), vol. I, p. 591.
131. *Legislative Journal for the Session of 1915* (Harrisburg, 1915), vol. I, p. 388, House Bill 662.
132. *Courier*, Mar. 5, 1918.
133. Ibid., Apr. 9, 1915; Kellogg, *NAACP*, p. 201.
134. *House Bills, 1915 Session*, p. 1630.
135. *Courier*, Apr. 23, 1915.
136. Kellogg, *NAACP*, p. 201.
137. *Vetoes by the Governor of Bills and Resolutions Passed by the Legislative Session of 1915* (Harrisburg, 1915); Kellogg, *NAACP*, p. 201.
138. "Newspaper Silence," *Courier*, Nov. 15, 1915; *Harrisburg Patriot*, Sept.–Nov. 1915, passim; Wayland Fuller Dunaway, *A History of Pennsylvania* (New York, 1935), pp. 577-78.
139. *Courier*, July (undated), 1915.
140. Ibid., Sept. 3, 1915.
141. Ibid., Sept. 17, 1915.

Notes to Pages 85-90 • 347

142. Ibid., Dec. 31, 1915.
143. Ibid., Mar. 15, 1917.
144. Ibid., Mar. 30, 1917.
145. *Legislative Journal for the Session of 1917* (Harrisburg, 1917), vol. I, p. 511, House Bill 849.
146. *History of House Bills*, 1921 Session, p. 51; 1923 Session, p. 102.
147. *Courier*, Apr. 19, 1921. See also file of the Pennsylvania House of Representatives Session of 1921, Bill No. 269, introduced by Mr. Asbury, Jan. 31, 1921, File Folio 1057.
148. *Courier*, Dec. 28, 1917.

Chapter 5. Politics and Patriotism

1. "All Voters Ought to Get Registered," *Courier*, Feb. 10, 17, and 24, 1912.
2. "Lessons from the Italian," ibid., Sept. 27, 1912.
3. "Negro as a Politician," ibid., Sept. 23, 1911.
4. "The Political Muddle," ibid., Sept. 16, 1911.
5. Bruce M. Stave, *The New Deal and the Last Hurrah: Pittsburgh Machine Politics* (Pittsburgh, 1970), pp. 24-26; Richard C. Keller, "Pennsylvania's Little New Deal" (doctoral dissertation, Columbia University, 1960), p. 101.
6. James E. Miller, "The Negro in Pennsylvania Politics, with Special Reference to Philadelphia Since 1932" (doctoral dissertation, University of Pennsylvania, 1945), p. 101.
7. Magee was born in Pittsburgh on April 14, 1848, was educated in the city's schools, and for a time attended WUP as a special student. His father died when Magee was fifteen, leaving his mother with four children to support. In 1864 Christopher secured a clerkship in the city controller's office, helping to support the family. From then on his rise in municipal government was sure and steady. In 1869 he was made cashier of the City Treasury and in 1871 was elected city treasurer, receiving 2,600 more votes than the candidate for mayor on the same ticket. He was reelected in 1874, and during his eight-year tenure he reduced Pittsburgh's debt from $15 million to $8 million.

His reputation also made him influential in county and state circles. With two exceptions he attended every state convention from 1872 until his death in 1901, was twice secretary to the state committee, and twice elected to the state senate. Prominent in Pittsburgh business circles, Magee invested wisely and was president of the Duquesne Traction Company, which controlled thirty-two miles of street railway. He owned considerable stock in over fifty enterprises and served as a director of fifteen banks, insurance companies, and traction companies. In 1884 he purchased the *Pittsburgh Times* and made it one of the strongest newspapers in western Pennsylvania (Harold Zink, *City Bosses in the United States* [Durham, N.C., 1930], p. 232; Eugene C. Thrasher, "The Magee-Flinn Political Machine, 1895-1903" [master's thesis, University of Pittsburgh, 1951], pp. 2-3; Lincoln Steffens, *Shame of the Cities* [New York, 1904], pp. 118-19; George Swetnam, *The Bicentennial History of Pittsburgh* [Pittsburgh, 1955], vol. I, pp. 209-10; and Stave, *New Deal and Last Hurrah*, p. 27).

8. Flinn was born in Manchester, England, on May 26, 1851, but migrated to America with his parents in the same year and settled in Pittsburgh. A self-made man, he

attended school only until he was nine years old, worked in the brick yards, and was apprenticed to the trade of brass finishing and gas and steam fitting. He became a contractor and in 1877 formed a partnership with James J. Booth. The most notable project of Booth and Flinn, Ltd. was the Mt. Washington Tunnel (Liberty Tubes), which opened a new residential area to thousands of workers. Like Magee, he had a keen business sense. He became president and director of the Duquesne Lumber Company and of the Pittsburgh Silver Peak Gold Mining Company, the Gulf Oil Corporation, the Manufacturers Light Company, and the Pittsburgh Coal Company. Flinn was elected to the Pittsburgh Board of Fire Commissioners in 1877. For twenty years he was chairman of the Republican City Executive Committee, and from 1881 to 1901 he chaired the Republican Committee in Allegheny County. In 1879 and 1881 he was elected to the Pennsylvania House of Representatives, and from 1890 until he resigned in 1902 he served in the state senate (Steffens, *Shame of the Cities*, pp. 118–19; William Flinn Scrapbooks, Dec. 1898–1921, Special Collections Department, Archives of Industrial Society, Hillman Library, University of Pittsburgh).

9. Stave, *New Deal and Last Hurrah*, p. 27.

10. Ibid., pp. 27–28; Steffens, *Shame of the Cities*, pp. 118–58, passim; and Thrasher, "Magee-Flinn Political Machine," pp. 8–22, passim. Graft and corruption were part of the Ring's means of maintaining control of Pittsburgh. On the lower levels it ranged from police protection for houses of prostitution and ignoring vice and special commissions paid to city officials for beer and liquor licenses, to giving patronage to corrupt voters and padding registry and title assessments. On the higher levels, it meant stifling public competition on contracts and awarding them instead to Booth and Flinn, Ltd. Though the law provided that contracts were to be awarded to the lowest responsible bidder, and though Flinn's contracting company asked much more for paving than any other bidder, it received all of the $3,551,131 worth of paving for nine years.

11. Leland D. Baldwin, *Pittsburgh: The Story of a City* (Pittsburgh, 1938), pp. 353–54.

12. Ibid., p. 354; Steffens, *Shame of the Cities*, p. 108; and Keller, "Pennsylvania's Little New Deal," pp. 105–09.

13. Thrasher, "Magee-Flinn Political Machine," pp. 8–15; Steffens, *Shame of the Cities*, p. 127. Guthrie's father, John Brandon, a prominent attorney, served twice as mayor of Pittsburgh. The son graduated from WUP in 1866, received his master's degree in 1868, and a law degree from Columbian University (now George Washington University) in 1869. He practiced law in Pennsylvania and was recognized as a leader in his profession. He took an active part in Democratic politics and was one of the secretaries to the Democratic National Convention in 1884 (John H. Frederick, "George Wilkins Guthrie," in *Dictionary of American Biography* [Allen Johnson and Dumas Malone, eds., 1931], vol. iv, p. 127).

14. *Pittsburgh Dispatch*, Feb. 12, 1898, cited in Thrasher, "Magee-Flinn Political Machine," p. 22.

15. *Pittsburgh Post*, Feb. 3 and 18, 1906. There is a need for a political history of Pittsburgh covering the years from 1903 to 1930. Except for Thrasher's dissertation and Bruce Stave's *The New Deal and the Last Hurrah*, no major study has been done. Undoubtedly, this is due in part to the lack of manuscript collections available. Efforts by the author, by Mr. Frank Zabrosky, curator of the University of Pittsburgh Library Archives, and by members of the Western Pennsylvania Historical Society staff failed to uncover significant papers of political figures for that time period, except for William Flinn's scrapbooks.

16. Webber, "Vann," p. 85.
17. Helen A. Tucker, "The Negroes of Pittsburgh," *Charities and the Commons* (Jan. 2, 1909): 603; A. G. Moron, "Distribution of the Negro Population in Pittsburgh, 1910-1930" (master's thesis, University of Pittsburgh, 1933), p. 18; and "Robert L. Vann as I Knew Him," speech delivered by Ira F. Lewis at dedication of Robert L. Vann School, Pittsburgh, Dec. 3, 1944.
18. Stave, *New Deal and Last Hurrah*, p. 28; Swetnam, *Bicentennial History of Pittsburgh*, vol. I, pp. 211-12. On Mayor Guthrie's attempted reforms, see Robert A. Woods, "A City Coming to Itself," *Charities and the Commons* (Feb. 6, 1909): 785-800; Clinton Rogers Woodruff, "Guthrie of Pittsburgh," *The World Today* XVII.(Nov. 1909): 1171-73.
19. On the nature of reform efforts in Pittsburgh, see Samuel P. Hays, "The Shame of the Cities Revisited: The Case of Pittsburgh," in Herbert Shapiro, ed., *The Muckraker and American Society* (Boston, 1968), pp. 75-81.
20. Roy Lubove, *Twentieth Century Pittsburgh: Government, Business and Environmental Change* (New York, 1969), p. 22, citing "Civic Grit and Pittsburgh Churches," *Survey* XXVIII (June 22, 1912): 463-65; "The Trial of the Pittsburgh Directors," *Survey* XXIX (Nov. 9, 1912): 169-70.
21. *Courier*, Apr. 8, Dec. 3, 1911; Miller, "Negro in Pennsylvania Politics," p. 101.
22. Stefan Lorant, ed., *Pittsburgh: The Study of an American City* (New York, 1964), pp. 308-09.
23. "Negroes Moving Hump," *Courier*, Apr. 27, 1912.
24. "Mayor Magee Makes Record," ibid., Dec. 27, 1912.
25. "The Voters' League," ibid., June 7, 1912.
26. Ibid., Dec. 27, 1912.
27. W. E. B. DuBois, "The Black Vote in Philadelphia," *Charities and the Commons* XV (Oct. 7, 1905): 33-34.
28. Ibid., p. 34; see also James Q. Wilson, *Negro Politics: The Search for Leadership* (New York, 1960), pp. 71-72.
29. "Flinn-Roosevelt Politics," *Courier*, Jan. 27, 1912; "Choosing a President," ibid., Nov. 1, 1912.
30. "Poor Politics," ibid., Sept. 6, 1912; "Woodrow Wilson," ibid., Aug. 30, 1912.
31. Webber, "Vann," p. 121.
32. Alfred D. Keator, ed., *Encyclopedia of Pennsylvania Biography* (New York, 1950), vol. XXVII, pp. 237-42.
33. Interviews with William Nunn, Sr., Mar. 13, 1969, Ernest Rice McKinney, Jan. 25 and 26, 1973, and Walter C. Rainey, Apr. 21, 1973.
34. Samuel Hopkins Adams, "Tomfoolery with Public Health," *Survey* XXV (Dec. 17, 1910): 453; Lubove, *Twentieth Century Pittsburgh*, p. 43.
35. *Courier*, Jan. 19, 1917; see also Miller, "Negro in Pennsylvania Politics," p. 105.
36. Interviews with William Nunn, Sr., Mar. 13, 1969, Ernest Rice McKinney, Jan. 25 and 26, 1973, and Walter C. Rainey, Apr. 21, 1973. All agreed that such an offer was made by Babcock and that it was accepted as fact at the time in the black community.
37. Abraham Epstein, *The Negro Migrant in Pittsburgh* (Pittsburgh, 1918), p. 7; Henderson H. Donald, "The Negro Migration of 1916-1918," *Journal of Negro History* VI (Oct. 1921): 23-24; and F. D. Tyson, *Negro Migration in 1916-1917* (Washington, D.C., 1918), p. 157.
38. *Courier*, Nov. 8, 1917.
39. Ibid., Aug. 12, 1917. In the Sept. 21, 1921, issue, Vann charged that blacks

were taking money from William Magee's opponent, even though they knew he could not beat Magee. At a meeting of the *Courier*'s board of directors on October 18, 1923, various members said they had been approached by "certain politicians and city officials" of the Magee faction to get them to repudiate Vann's editorial stand in recent primaries. None of the members did so, however.

40. *Pittsburgh Dispatch*, Sept. 20, 1917.
41. Ibid., Sept. 21, Nov. 5, 1917.
42. *Courier*, Oct. 28, 1917; interview with Austin J. Norris, Nov. 27, 1971, Philadelphia. Norris, one of the protesters, was a recent graduate of Yale University.
43. *Courier*, Nov. 2, 1917, and "The Most Dangerous Traitor," ibid., Feb. 22, 1918.
44. Ibid., Nov. 5, 1915.
45. *Courier*, Nov. 1, 1917; interview with Austin J. Norris, Nov. 27, 1971. Eventually the men were transferred to the 351st Artillery Unit at Fort Meade, Md.
46. *Courier*, Nov. 1, 1917.
47. Miller, "Negro in Pennsylvania Politics," pp. 184–85. See also Pennsylvania Department of Welfare, *Negro Survey of Pennsylvania* (Harrisburg, 1927), p. 77; Harold F. Gosnell, *Negro Politicians: The Rise of Negro Politics in Chicago* (Chicago, 1935), pp. x–xi, 370–71; Wilson, *Negro Politics*, pp. 57, 71–72; and Gunnar Myrdal, *An American Dilemma* (New York, 1944), pp. 720–35.
48. Epstein, *Negro Migrant in Pittsburgh*, p. 30. According to Miller, what was true of black political leadership in Pittsburgh was true throughout the state. Except for a select few in Philadelphia, Pennsylvania was devoid of effective black leaders. Men like Harry W. Bass, J. C. Asbury, Amos Scott, B. Frank Potts, Harry Pinckney, "Jimmy" Stevens, and Moses Johnson were spokesmen in that city, but their major role was to answer questions about blacks asked by whites. Most of the men were "safe" Vare men such as Bass, who had been elected to the state assembly from the First Legislative District in 1911 and 1914, the only black to hold a statewide elective position of any note ("Negro in Pennsylvania Politics," pp. 105–08).
49. Webber, "Vann," p. 117.
50. *Pittsburgh Dispatch*, Nov. 7 and 8, 1917.
51. Babcock to Vann, Dec. 14, 1917; City Solicitor Stephen Stone to Vann, Mar. 18, 1918; and City Solicitor Charles B. Prichard to Vann, Feb. 10, 1921; all in Vann Papers.
52. Miller, "Negro in Pennsylvania Politics," pp. 101–02; *Negro Survey of Pennsylvania*, p. 79; and Ira DeA. Reid, *Social Conditions of the Negro in the Hill District of Pittsburgh* (General Committee on the Hill Survey, 1930), pp. 55–57.
53. Vann Scrapbook, undated.
54. Ira Lewis to Brewer, May 4, 1921; in Brewer, "Vann," p. 79; *Courier*, Jan. 1, 1918.
55. Interview with Mrs. Vann, Apr. 6, 1967.
56. Webber, "Vann," p. 18.
57. Miller, "Negro in Pennsylvania Politics," pp. 101, 184–85. Philadelphia, under the control of William S. Vare, had similar positions, such as inspector of customs, city physician, and probation officer. See also W. E. B. DuBois, *The Philadelphia Negro* (New York, 1899), pp. 378–80; Leslie Fishel, "The Negro in the North, 1865–1900: A Study in Race Discrimination" (doctoral dissertation, Harvard University, 2 vols., 1953), vol. II, pp. 511–12.
58. Autobiographical sketch in Vann Scrapbook; Vann to Stephen Stone, Oct. 12,

1938; Clyde S. Edeburn, chief of city detectives, to City Solicitor Stephen Stone, Dec. 11, 1918; all in Vann Papers.

59. Vann to Mencken, Mar. 14, 1938, Vann Papers.

60. *Courier*, Sept. 11, 1914.

61. "The Aristocracy of Bullets," ibid., June 30, 1916.

62. "Why not Pennsylvania?" ibid., Nov. 16, 1917. In 1912 a black delegation which included Vann lobbied for a bill in the state legislature for a colored company, but Governor Tener stated there was no need for one. See also P. J. Drotning, *Black Heroes in Our Nation's History* (New York, 1969), ch. 9; H. G. Proctor, *The Iron Division, National Guard of Pennsylvania in the World War: The Authentic and Comprehensive Narrative of the Gallant Deeds and Glorious Achievements of the 28th Division in the World's Greatest War* (Philadelphia, 1919), passim.

63. "Our Heroes," *Courier*, Oct. 26, 1917.

64. "Establishing a Precedent," ibid., Oct. 12, 1917; "Our Boys Commissioned," ibid., Oct. 19, 1917. For more general examples of black willingness to "do their part," see Constance McLaughlin Green, *Secret City*, pp. 184–85; Charles Flint Kellogg, *NAACP: A History of the National Association for the Advancement of Colored People, 1909–1920* (Baltimore, 1967), pp. 247–75; L. M. Jones, "The Editorial Policy of Negro Newspapers of 1917–1918 as Compared with that of 1941–1942," *Journal of Negro History* XXIX (Jan. 1944): 24–31; *Courier*, Oct. 26, 1918; and "The Whole Regiment Honored," ibid., Dec. 7, 1918. For the story of the 369th Regiment, see Emmett J. Scott, *Scott's Official History of the American Negro in the World War* (New York, 1919), pp. 197–213; Charles H. Williams, *Sidelights on Negro Soldiers* (Boston, 1923), 193–208; and Arthur W. Little, *From Harlem to the Rhine: The Story of New York's Colored Volunteers* (New York, 1936).

65. "After First World War," typewritten manuscript, Vann Papers.

66. "Over a Million Subscribed," *Courier*, Oct. 26, 1918; see also issues of Jan. 11, Sept. 28, and Oct. 5, 1918.

67. Vann to Babcock, Jan. 3, 1919, Vann Papers. It should be noted that Vann's name did not appear with the fifty-nine others listed on the Mayor's Committee of Welcome to Home-Coming Troops; Vann was a member of a "special" committee (Babcock to Vann, May 1, 1919, Vann Papers).

68. *Courier*, March 1 and 9, 1919, and Vann to Babcock, Apr. 29, 1919, Vann Papers.

69. *Courier*, Mar. 12, 1919.

70. Ibid.

71. Richard M. Dalfiume, *Fighting on Two Fronts: Desegregation of the Armed Forces, 1939–1953* (Columbia, Mo., 1969), p. 11; Scott to Vann, Apr. 18, 1918, Vann Papers.

72. "Establishing a Precedent," *Courier*, Oct. 12, 1917; Scott to Vann, July 6, 1918, Vann Papers.

73. Vann to Scott, July 20, 1918, and Scott to Wilson, July 26, 1918, Vann Papers.

74. R. R. Moton to Wilson, June 15, 1918, and Scott to Wilson, July 17, 1918 (copies of both letters forwarded to Vann), Vann Papers.

75. "Room at the Front," *Courier*, July 6, 1917; Elliott Rudwick, *Race Riot at East St. Louis, July 2, 1917* (Carbondale, Ill., 1964).

76. "Let Pittsburgh Awake," *Courier*, Aug. 3, 1917.

77. "So Far So Good," ibid., Aug. 24, 1917.

78. "Report of East St. Louis Riot," ibid., July 20, 1918.

79. *Pittsburgh Dispatch*, July 26–30, Aug. 24, 1917; *Courier*, Aug. 4 and 28, 1917; and August Meier and Elliott M. Rudwick, *From Plantation to Ghetto: An Interpretive History of American Negroes* (New York, 1966), p. 217.
80. Edgar A. Schuler, "The Houston Race Riot, 1917," *Journal of Negro History* XLIX (July 1964): 300.
81. "Thirteen Hanged," *Courier*, Dec. 14, 1917.
82. William M. Tuttle, Jr., *Race Riot: Chicago in the Red Summer of 1919* (New York, 1970); Allan H. Spear, *Black Chicago: The Making of a Negro Ghetto, 1890–1920* (Chicago, 1967), pp. 214–22.
83. John Hope Franklin, *From Slavery to Freedom: A History of Negro Americans* (New York, 1947), pp. 482–83.
84. "The Reward of Riots," *Courier*, Aug. 9, 1919. For a similar reaction, see Robert R. Moton, *What the Negro Thinks* (New York, 1929), pp. 66–67, 140–41.
85. Zecharaiah Chafee, Jr., *Free Speech in the United States* (Cambridge, Mass., 1942), pp. 147–49; "Radicalism and Sedition Among Negroes as Reflected in their Publications," in *Investigation Activities of the Department of Justice*, 66th Congress, 1st sess., United States Senate Document No. 153, XII (1919), pp. 161–87.
86. Kellogg, *NAACP*, pp. 287–89.
87. *Courier*, Mar. 12, 1920; *Eleventh Annual Report of the NAACP for the Year 1920* (New York, Jan. 1921).
88. Robert H. Brisbane, "The Rise of the Protest Movement Among Negroes Since 1900" (doctoral dissertation, Harvard University, 1949), p. 81; Roi Ottley and William Weatherby, eds., *The Negro in New York* (New York, 1967), pp. 223–28; and Kellogg, *NAACP*, p. 290.
89. "We Are Americans," *Courier*, May 31, 1916.
90. *Courier*, undated, 1924, Vann Papers.
91. "When the Country Gets Ready," *Courier*, Dec. 27, 1919.
92. "Deport Berger," ibid., Jan. 18, 1919.
93. Ibid., Aug. 19, 1919.
94. "When the Negro is a Bolshevist," ibid., Oct. 25, 1919; see also Moton, *What the Negro Thinks*, p. 164.
95. *Courier*, Sept. 27, 1919.
96. Ira DeA. Reid, "The Negro in the Major Industries and Building Trades of Pittsburgh" (master's thesis, University of Pittsburgh, 1925), pp. 11–12; William Z. Foster, *The Great Steel Strike and Its Lessons* (New York, 1920), pp. 206–08; Sterling D. Spero and Abraham L. Harris, *The Black Worker: The Negro and the Labor Movement* (New York, 1931), pp. 257–59; and David Brody, *Labor in Crisis: The Steel Strike of 1919* (Philadelphia, 1965), pp. 162–63 and passim.
97. John Nicely Rathmell, "Status of Negroes in Regard to Origin, Length of Residence and Economic Aspects of Their Life" (master's thesis, University of Pittsburgh, 1935), p. 17; Louis V. Kennedy, *The Negro Peasant Turns Cityward* (New York, 1930), p. 108.
98. *Courier*, Oct. 25, 1925.
99. Cited in Louis R. Harlan, *Booker T. Washington* (New York, 1972), p. 90.
100. Ibid., p. 75.
101. Ibid., p. 90.
102. Ibid.

103. *Courier*, Sept. 27, 1919; *Pittsburgh Dispatch*, Oct. 3, 1919, The *Dispatch* wrote, "This is no ordinary strike. Rather must it be looked upon as a diabolical attempt of a small group of radicals to disorganize labor and plant revolution in America."
104. *Courier*, Apr. 17, 1920.
105. Ibid., May 1, 1920.
106. Ibid., Apr. 8, 1922.

Chapter 6. Vann as Entrepreneur: The 1920s

1. June Sachem, ed., *The Black Man and the American Dream: Negro Aspirations in America 1900–1930* (Chicago, 1971), p. 3. In the same volume, see Eugene Kinckle Jones, "The Negro's Opportunity Today," pp. 196–203, reprinted from *Opportunity* VI (Jan. 1928): 10–12. See also Robert R. Moton, *What the Negro Thinks* (New York, 1929), pp. 29–46; and E. Franklin Frazier, "Durham: Capital of the Black Middle Class," in Alain Locke, ed., *The New Negro* (New York, 1925), pp. 333–40.
2. *Courier*, Sept. 20, 1912.
3. Ibid.
4. Ibid.
5. Ibid., Sept. 23, 1911.
6. Ibid., Aug. 11, 1911.
7. Ibid., Mar. 25, 1911.
8. Ibid., Feb. 10, 1912.
9. Ibid., Apr. 13, 1912.
10. August Meier, *Negro Thought in America 1880–1915* (Ann Arbor, 1963), pp. 246–47; Leslie Fishel, "The Negro in the North, 1865–1900: A Study in Race Discrimination (doctoral dissertation, Harvard University, 2 vols., 1953), vol. 2, pp. 491–92.
11. *National Negro Business League* XXV (1924), quoted in Ronald G. Walters, "The Negro Press and the Image of Success: 1920–1939," *Midcontinental American Studies Journal* (Fall 1970): 44.
12. "Negro Capital in Negro Business," address to members of the National Negro Business Insurance Association, Cleveland, June 2, 1938, manuscript in Vann Papers. See also Vann to B. T. Bradshaw, Virginia Mutual Life Insurance Company, Apr. 18, 1938, Vann Papers; *York (Pa.) Dispatch*, Feb. 12, 1936.
13. Vann, "Negro Capital in Negro Business." See also Meier, *Negro Thought*, chap. 9, passim.
14. Vann to Binder–McNelis Cadillac Co., Altoona, Pa., Apr. 26, 1926, Vann Papers.
15. Interviews with Mrs. Vann, Apr. 6, 1967, and William G. Nunn, Mar. 13, 1969.
16. Jesse Moorland, "Why Work?" *The Competitor* I (Feb. 1920): 43–45. See also "Do You Know?", a one-page collection of short paragraphs demonstrating black achievement. Typical were "That a $20,000 corporation known as the League Realty Company has been launched at Bryn Mawr, Pennsylvania," "That two colored banks of Norfolk and Portsmouth, Virginia, distributed $180,000 on December 10 to their eight thousand members of the Christmas Savings Club," and "That Mrs. R. C. Ransom has been elected a member of the Metropolitan Board of Directors of the YMCA in New York City. Mrs. Ransom is the first colored woman to be elected on this board" (ibid., p. 59).

17. For an approbatory account of *The Competitor*'s contents, see Charles W. Dahlinger, "The Rising Tide of Color," *Western Pennsylvania Historical Magazine* IV (Apr. 1921): 72–73.
18. Interviews with Mrs. Vann, Apr. 6, 1967, and William G. Nunn, Mar. 17, 1969; W. E. B. DuBois, *Dusk of Dawn* (New York, 1968), p. 270; Gilbert Osofsky, *Harlem: The Making of a Ghetto* (New York, 1966), p. 187.
19. Charles S. Johnson, "The Rise of the Negro Magazine," *Journal of Negro History* XIII (Jan. 1928): 7–21.
20. Ibid., p. 16.
21. *The Crisis* VIII (Sept. 1919): 235, cited in Frederick G. Detweiler, *The Negro Press in America* (Chicago, 1922), p. 63.
22. Webber, "Vann," p. 130. Robert Abbott of the *Chicago Defender* also tried magazine publishing with *Abbott's Monthly* in October 1929. It initially prospered and boasted a circulation of 100,000, but the Depression forced its suspension (Roi Ottley, *The Lonely Warrior: The Life and Times of Robert S. Abbott* [Chicago, 1955], pp. 293–94).
23. Minutes of the 1919 report of business, Feb. 11, 1920, and minutes of the eleventh annual meeting of stockholders, Jan. 12, 1920, Prattis Papers. Except for the financial reports mentioned, there appear to be no records available for 1923 to 1940. It is also difficult to relate an accurate financial record of the *Courier* because it did not have a cost accounting system even as late as 1935 (interview with Mrs. Vann, Apr. 6, 1967).
24. Minutes of the meeting of the board of directors, Feb. 11, 1920, Mar. 10, 1920, Prattis Papers.
25. Lewis to Brewer, June 6, 1941, cited in Brewer, "Vann," p. 26. See *Chicago Defender*, Dec. 27, 1919, and Aug. 7, 1920.
26. Minutes of meeting of board of directors, July 28, 1920, Prattis Papers; Lewis to Brewer, June 6, 1941, cited in Brewer, "Vann," p. 26. Ayer's Directory had the *Courier*'s circulation at 15,870 in 1919 (N. W. Ayer and Sons, *American Newspaper Annual and Directory* [Philadelphia, 1919], p. 1261).
27. Dahlinger, "The Rising Tide of Color," pp. 70–71; Webber, "Vann," p. 138; Monroe Work, ed., *Negro Year Book, 1921–1922* (Tuskegee, Ala., 1922), p. 425; and Lewis to Brewer, May 6, 1941, cited in Brewer, "Vann," p. 26. Lewis maintained that at the end of 1920 circulation was 14,000, while Ayer listed it as 11,459.
28. Vann to Arthur, Oct. 16, 1925, Vann Papers.
29. Arthur to Vann, Oct. 19, 1925, Vann Papers.
30. J. E. E. Clements, (Vann's African agent), Gold Coast Products Co., Sekondi, Gold Coast, to Vann, Apr. 7 and June 2, 1928; Vann to Clements, Jan. 26, 1928, Vann Papers.
31. Robert H. Kinzer and Edward Sagarin, *The Negro in American Business* (New York, 1950), pp. 68–69.
32. "One Cure For It," *Courier*, May 18, 1917.
33. Minutes of the eleventh annual meeting of stockholders, Jan. 12, 1921, Prattis Papers. See also Joseph N. LaCour, "The Negro Press as a Business," *The Crisis* XLVIII (Apr. 1941): 108, 141.
34. Minutes of the thirteenth annual meeting of the stockholders of the *Pittsburgh Courier* Publishing Company, Jan. 17, 1923, and of the special meeting of the board of directors, Mar. 5, 1923, Prattis Papers. Ninety days after the $500 loan was made, Lewis stated that the *Courier* could not meet the principal but could continue paying the 6 percent interest. However, if any of the investors desired, they could have their

principal through an issuance of stock valued at $5 per share. Vann agreed to settle all his past notes for 63 shares through such a settlement (minutes of the special meeting of the board of directors, June 4, 1923).

35. "An Example of Service," *Courier*, Feb. 11, 1924; "Our Own Bank," ibid., Jan. 25, 1919; "Where Is Pittsburgh?" ibid., Mar. 14, 1921; Kinzer and Sagarin, *Negro in American Business*, pp. 68–69; and Ira DeA. Reid, *Social Conditions of the Negro in the Hill District of Pittsburgh* (General Committee on the Hill Survey, 1930), p. 115. Most of the 874 black businesses in Pittsburgh in 1925 were of the barber shop–shoe shine parlor variety.

36. Vann to Austin, Aug. 21, 1925; Vann to E. W. Schallman, Board of Directors, Master Street Bank, Philadelphia, Aug. 13, 1925; Schallman to Vann, Nov. 20, 1925; Vann to Harry C. Pace, president of Northeastern Life Insurance Company, Newark, N.J., Aug. 6, 1925; all in Vann Papers; Pennsylvania Department of Welfare, *Negro Survey of Pennsylvania* (Harrisburg, 1927), pp. 26, 76.

37. See Reid, *Social Conditions of the Negro*, p. 98; W. E. B. DuBois, *The Philadelphia Negro* (New York, 1899), pp. 184, 191; and Meier, *Negro Thought*, pp. 142–46, for early banking history. Only Philadelphia and New York had black-owned banks before World War I.

38. *Courier*, Jan. 16, 1926; Abraham L. Harris, *The Negroes as Capitalists: A Study of Banking and Business Among American Negroes* (Philadelphia, 1936), p. 124.

39. Kinzer and Sagarin, *Negro in American Business*, pp. 68–71; Harris, *Negroes as Capitalists*, p. 142.

40. *Courier*, Aug. 18, 1928.

41. Vann to A. L. Humphrey, Pittsburgh Chamber of Commerce, Jan. 29, 1926, Vann Papers.

42. Interviews with Mrs. Vann, Feb. 15, 1967, William G. Nunn, Mar. 13, 1969, and Ernest Rice McKinney, Jan. 25 and 26, 1973, bear out this reasoning.

43. Detweiler, *Negro Press*, p. 222.

44. U. S. Bureau of the Census, *Fourteenth Census of the United States, 1920*, (Washington, D.C., 1922), vol. II, pp. 302–68, passim; Abraham L. Harris, Jr., "The New Negro Worker in Pittsburgh" (master's thesis, University of Pittsburgh, 1924), p. 7; James E. Miller, "The Negro in Pennsylvania Politics, with Special Reference to Philadelphia Since 1932" (doctoral dissertation, University of Pennsylvania, 1945), table 8, p. 388; and Joseph A. Hill, "Recent Northward Migration of the Negro," *Monthly Labor Review* XVIII (Mar. 1924): 480.

45. "Our Efforts at the Polls," *Courier*, Sept. 24, 1921.

46. Vann to Secretary of Fifth Ward Protective Organization, Aug. 5, 1921, Vann Papers.

47. Two other blacks ran unsuccessfully for office in the same election: George G. Stinson for jury commissioner, and J. M. McLellan for City Council (*Courier*, Sept. 24, 1921; Webber, "Vann," p. 131).

48. *Negro Survey of Pennsylvania*, p. 76; interviews with Ernest Rice McKinney, Jan. 25 and 26, 1973, and Walter C. Rainey, Apr. 21, 1973.

49. *Courier*, Nov. 18, 1911.

50. "The Primary Election," ibid., Sept. 20, 1919.

51. Reid, *Social Conditions of the Negro*, p. 98.

52. Ernest Rice McKinney, "These Colored United States, Pennsylvania: A Tale of Two Cities," *The Messenger* V (May 1932): 694.

53. *Courier*, May 18 and 25, 1918; interview with Walter C. Rainey, Apr. 21, 1973;

and Harold F. Gosnell, *Negro Politicians: The Rise of Negro Politics in Chicago* (Chicago, 1935), p. 64.

54. Interview with Walter C. Rainey, Apr. 21, 1973; Miller, "Negro in Pennsylvania Politics," pp. 101–02; Robert Hughes Brisbane, "The Rise of Protest Movements Among Negroes Since 1900" (doctoral dissertation, Harvard University, 1953), pp. 112–42; and Ira DeA. Reid, *The Negro Immigrant: His Background, Characteristics and Social Adjustment, 1899–1937* (New York, 1939), pp. 233–49.

55. *Courier*, Sept. 24, 1923.
56. Ibid., Feb. 13, 1926.
57. Bruce M. Stave, *The New Deal and the Last Hurrah: Pittsburgh Machine Politics* (Pittsburgh, 1970), p. 28.
58. *Courier*, July 18, Oct. 10, 1925; interviews with Ernest Rice McKinney, Jan. 25 and 26, 1973, and Walter C. Rainey, Apr. 21, 1973.
59. *Courier*, Mar. 18, July 18, 1925.
60. Ibid., Sept. 5 and 12, 1925.
61. Ibid., Sept. 19, 1925.
62. Ibid., Oct. 31, 1925.
63. Ibid., Sept. 24, 1927; *Pittsburgh Post-Gazette*, Sept. 12, 1927. The lowest winners polled about 120,000 votes.
64. *Courier*, Nov. 26, 1927.
65. *Negroes in the United States, 1920–1932* (Washington, D.C., 1935), pp. 6, 14, 24–25, 799. After World War I, migration of blacks to the North generally and to Pittsburgh in particular increased the black population markedly. By 1930, there were 83,326 blacks in Allegheny County (54,982 in Pittsburgh), of whom 53,632 were of voting age. Among Northern cities, Pittsburgh ranked behind New York (327,706), Chicago (233,903), and Philadelphia (219,599). Pennsylvania had more blacks (431,257) than any other northern state, followed by New York (412,814), Illinois (328,972), Ohio (309,304), New Jersey (208,828), Michigan (116,453), and Indiana (111,982). Vann must have realized the voter potential represented by the increases during the 1920s.
66. Interview with Walter C. Rainey, Aug. 21, 1973.
67. *Courier*, Feb. 28, 1927.
68. Ibid.
69. Vann to Kline, May 19, 1927, Vann Papers.
70. Edward G. Lang, Deputy Director of Public Works, to Vann, May 24, 1927, Vann Papers.
71. *Courier*, Sept. 14, 1929.
72. Ibid., June 7, 1930.
73. Ibid., Aug. 29, Sept. 5, 1931, July 5, 1930.
74. Interview with Walter C. Rainey, Aug. 21, 1973.
75. In 1930, black leaders from the First, Third, and Fifth Wards, which comprised the First Legislative District, endorsed black attorney Theron B. Hamilton as a candidate for one of the two seats from the district. Mayor Kline supported another black, Walter Tucker. Both remained in the primary race, and both lost. Vann blamed local black leadership for weakness and disunity: "The outcome serves notice in a decisive fashion that the old political regime with its cowering Negro leadership must go, and a new emancipated Negro willing to play the game in true political fashion must take the reins if a Negro will ever sit in the Pennsylvania Legislature for the First Legislative

District" (*Courier*, May 24, 1930). Vann also saw the outcome as the result of a political trick played on the race by white leadership; his headline was "RACE TRICKED AGAIN: WHITE CANDIDATES WIN" (ibid.). Later, however, Mayor Kline appointed Tucker to run in the November election when one of the white candidates died unexpectedly, and the *Courier* hailed this action (Nov. 1 and 8, 1930). Tucker won the election and became the first black legislator from the district.

By 1931 Vann was asking for aggressive, unified black leadership. In a front-page editorial he requested an intensive election campaign in Wards Three and Five. In Ward Five Robert Logan was again running for alderman and Earl Sams for constable; with *Courier* support, both were elected in close races (*Courier*, Aug. 29, Sept. 12 and 19, Oct. 3, 1931). In the Third Ward, run by boss John Verona and a suborganization of racketeers tacitly supported by Mayor Kline, blacks had more trouble gaining a political foothold (Ruth L. Simmons, "The Negro in Recent Pittsburgh Politics" [master's thesis, University of Pittsburgh, 1945], p. 7). Roy Anderson ran for constable, backed by the black Third Ward Voters' League and Vann, who worried aloud that the Third Ward's black voters might not go to the polls to support Anderson. "If such should be true by any paradoxical twist, then all promise of the past hundred years is wasted" (*Courier*, Aug. 29, Sept. 12, 1931). Vann envisioned Anderson in office: "The racial complex of the entire city will be changed. More opportunities will be available. We can demand a number of things for which we now beg. The entire atmosphere will be healthier, the children will be more respected, and the man who earns by the sweat of his brow can have more comfort and face the world without being ashamed if we put Anderson over" (ibid., Sept. 12, 1931). Vann brought in Congressman Oscar DePriest and other dignitaries from Chicago in behalf of Anderson's campaign, and the Third Ward Voters' League worked hard to register black voters. But Verona was equally determined that Anderson lose and resorted to beatings, arrests, jailings, and intimidation to keep black voters from casting their ballots for Anderson. In a series of bitter articles the *Courier* catalogued these abuses (Sept. 12 and 19, 1931). Vann and other lawyers went to court to end the strong-arm tactics, but Verona persisted, and Anderson lost decisively in the primary (*Courier*, Oct. 17 and 24, 1931).

When the 1932 elections for state representative came around, Walter Tucker announced that he would run for reelection, and Homer Brown also entered the race (ibid., Jan. 3, Feb. 20, Mar. 26, 1932). Brown, son of a minister and brother of a physician, was a lawyer best known for his work with the NAACP in the 1920s. He was an appealing candidate, and Tucker was in an unenviable position because his support came from Mayor Kline, who had recently been indicted for corruption (ibid., Apr. 2, 16, and 23, 1932). Tucker was asked to drop out of the race but refused. The black vote was split, and both were eliminated in the primary. Vann erupted in anger, blaming blacks for their lack of political astuteness and their leaders for inept management of the campaign. "The Pittsburgh Negro is still dumb on the subject of politics. He holds the unique position of being the most backward of Negroes to be found in any large city, North or South. He either will not listen to the truth or he is too ignorant to understand the truth when he hears it. The Pittsburgh Negro is absolutely in a class by himself when it comes to the question of civic and political advancement. . . . It is a thankless task to try to tell Negroes in Pittsburgh what is best to do or even how to do it. They are too dumb to see the picture after it has been painted. This thing has been going on for years and years. It is sickening" (ibid., Apr. 30, 1932).

76. *Pittsburgh Press*, Nov. 22, 1922.
77. Ibid.
78. Undated newspaper clipping, Vann Scrapbook, 1921–24, Vann Papers.
79. *Courier*, Dec. 16, 1922.
80. Minutes of special meeting of the board of directors, Mar. 14, 1922, Prattis Papers; see also Prattis, "The Negro Press in Action," manuscript in Prattis Papers, p. 282, and Vann Scrapbook, 1921–24.
81. Minutes of special meeting, Mar. 14, 1922, Prattis Papers. As one black journalist put it, black newspapers were on "short rations" and if they could not receive sufficient revenue from advertising, the news editor was almost forced to resort to sensational news to build up circulation and increase revenue (Floyd J. Calvin, "The Negro Press in the United States," *Inter-Racial Review* [Aug. 1939]: 119–20; Eugene Gordon, "A Survey of the Negro Press," *Opportunity* V [Jan. 1927]: 7). These tactics had been successfully initiated by the white Hearst newspapers. Also, the black weekly, being strictly for a black audience, through its "sensational" reports was presenting news of interest to its readers. As Roy Wilkins said, "The Negro newspaper is of necessity a class newspaper. It came into being and has lived because it serves a particular class of readers not completely served through general newspapers. Therefore the importance or trivial nature of the news it publishes must be judged within the sphere it serves, not by standards applicable to other class publications, or to metropolitan papers" ("The Negro Press," *Opportunity* VI [Dec., 1928]: 363–65; see also V. V. Oak, "What About the Negro Press?" *The Saturday Review of Literature* XXVI [Mar. 6, 1943]: 4-5, in reply to an earlier article by Warren H. Brown criticizing the black press for its immaturity and sensationalism, "A Negro Looks at the Negro Press," *Saturday Review of Literature* XXV [Dec. 19, 1942]: 5–6).

Chapter 7. The Primacy of the COURIER

1. *Courier*, Apr. 27, 1927; "Founder's Day Impressively Observed," *The Southern Letter* (Tuskegee Institute) XLIII: I. See also *Courier*, Aug. 6, 1927.
2. *Courier*, Dec. 20, 1920; Maxwell R. Brooks, *The Negro Press Reexamined: Political Content of Leading Negro Newspapers* (Boston, 1959), p. 86; Roi Ottley, *The Lonely Warrior: The Life and Times of Robert S. Abbott* (Chicago, 1955), pp. 302–03; Vishnu V. Oak, *The Negro Newspapers* (Yellow Springs, Ohio, 1948), pp. 113–14; Frederick G. Detweiler, *The Negro Press in America* (Chicago, 1922), pp. 124–26; and George S. Schuyler, *Black and Conservative* (New Rochelle, N.Y., 1966), p. 165.
3. John H. Burma, "An Analysis of the Present Negro Press," *Social Forces* XXVI (Dec. 1947): 178–79; John Syrjamaki, "The Negro Press in 1939," *Sociology and Social Research* XXII (Sept.–Oct. 1939): 51; and Brooks, *Negro Press Reexamined*, pp. 84–85.
4. Interviews taped by Henry LaBrie with Chester Washington, Aug. 20, 1971, and with John Sengstacke, June 23–24, 1972.
5. Ziff to Vann, Aug. 14, 1923, Sept. 28, 1926, July 12, 1927, Vann Papers.
6. Interviews with P. L. Prattis, May 18, 1970, and with Henry LaBrie, May 15, 1973; Detweiler, *Negro Press*, p. 6.
7. Vann to Harvey S. Firestone, Feb. 8, 1928, Vann Papers.
8. Vann to N. W. Ayer and Sons, Feb. 8, 1928, Vann Papers.

9. Much of the information about the *Courier* staff from 1925 to 1931 was furnished by Mrs. Mabel Page Johnson, who worked in the circulation department from 1923 to 1931. See also Eugene Gordon, "The Negro Press," *The Annals of the American Academy of Political and Social Sciences* CXL (Nov. 1928): 252; Detweiler, *Negro Press*, p. 61; Horace David Murdock, "Some Business Aspects of Leading Negro Newspapers" (master's thesis, University of Kansas, 1936), pp. 36–40; and interview with Prattis, May 18, 1970.

10. P. L. Prattis, "The Negro Press in Action," manuscript in Prattis Papers; interview with Prattis, May 18, 1970.

11. *Courier*, Apr. 13, 1929. He was P. B. Young, Jr., son of the editor of the *Norfolk Journal and Guide*, at Ohio State University.

12. See Schuyler's autobiography, *Black and Conservative*, passim; Jervis Anderson, *A. Philip Randolph: A Biographical Portrait* (New York, 1972), pp. 144–46; and "The Reminiscences of George S. Schuyler," interviews by William Ingersoll with Schuyler, 1960, in the Oral History Collection, Columbia University. These recollections, along with those in the interview taped by Henry LaBrie, are essentially what is found in his written autobiography.

13. Interview with Schuyler, May 23, 1967; Schuyler, *Black and Conservative*, p. 147.

14. Letter from Lewis to board of directors, Feb. 18, 1920, Prattis Papers. Lewis had another reason for keeping his position in the sheriff's office. He wrote, "It is seriously doubted whether the Sheriff would assure us my place for another colored man, and if I resign from the position and cannot place another colored man on it, we will bring down the censure of the people for having plugged up an opening which belonged to the race. I assume that I am giving the race creditable representation in the Sheriff's office in a new opening, and I think we owe it to the people to at least keep this opening through the term"; Ottley, *Lonely Warrior*, pp. 102, 117.

15. Vann to Schuyler, undated, 1927, Vann Papers.

16. "The Lynching League," *Courier*, Jan. 7, 1927.

17. Ibid., Jan. 30, 1926.

18. Ibid., Feb. 20, Mar. 13, 1926; see also Schuyler, *Black and Conservative*, pp. 153–57.

19. Vann biographical sketch, Vann Papers; interview with Schuyler, May 23, 1967.

20. The reporter was Harry B. Webber, who in 1927 became editor of the short-lived *Pittsburgh Guard* (minutes of special meeting of board of directors of the *Pittsburgh Courier* Publishing Company, Mar. 5, 1923, Prattis Papers).

21. Eugene Gordon, "A Survey of the Negro Press," *Opportunity* V (Jan. 1927): 8–9, 11.

22. *Courier*, Oct. 3, 1925.

23. "Housing," ibid., May 25, 1929.

24. *The Nation* CXXII (June 16, 1926): 662–63.

25. Schuyler, *Black and Conservative*, pp. 120, 122–24.

26. *Courier*, Dec. 4, 1926.

27. Ibid., Nov. 26, 1926.

28. "Letters to the Editor," ibid., Nov. 16, 1929.

29. "Poston Names Preacher to Convert Schuyler, His Gospel is 'Turn Other Cheek', and also 'Throw Brick-Bat' if Necessary," ibid., Nov. 12, 1927.

30. Schuyler, *Black and Conservative*, p. 221; see also pp. 187–205, 218–24.
31. Ibid., pp. 253–54; interview with Schuyler, May 23, 1967.
32. "The Afro-American Today," *The Messenger* X (Mar. 1928): 58.
33. *Courier*, Nov. 19, Dec. 3, 1927.
34. Schuyler, *Black and Conservative*, p. 234. At a time when few blacks were being accepted as writers in the nation's white magazines, Mencken encouraged them and published more of their work than did any others. Schuyler contends that Mencken often used excerpts from Schuyler's columns (interview with Schuyler, May 23, 1967).
35. *Courier*, Feb. 12, 1926.
36. Ibid., Mar. 27, 1926.
37. Richard Bardolph, *The Negro Vanguard* (New York, 1961), p. 179.
38. *Courier*, Apr. 30, May 23, 1927.
39. White to Sinclair Lewis, May 17, 1926, Box C-94, NAACP Papers, Library of Congress.
40. White to Editor, Doubleday, Page and Co., Mar. 11, 1926, Box C-94, NAACP Papers.
41. White to Lewis, Box C-94, NAACP Papers.
42. White to Editor, Doubleday, Page and Co., Mar. 11, 1926, and White to Kahn, June 16, 1926, Box C-94, NAACP Papers.
43. "The Camera," *Courier*, Feb. 12, 1927; interview with Henry LaBrie, May 15, 1973.
44. "The Camera," *Courier*, Feb. 12, 1927.
45. Ibid., Feb. 5, 1927.
46. Eugene Gordon, "The Negro Press," *American Mercury* VII (June 1926): 212; P. Bernard Young, Jr., "News Content of Negro Newspapers," *Opportunity* VII (Dec. 1929): 370–72.
47. Eugene Gordon, "Negro Press," *American Mercury*, p. 212.
48. *Courier*, Dec. 21, 1929, Dec. 10, 1927, and Dec. 29, 1928; telephone interview with Chester Washington, Mar. 23, 1973.
49. Interview with Nunn, Mar. 13, 1969; Nunn biographical folder in "Pittsburgh—Negroes," Pennsylvania Division, Carnegie Library.
50. *Courier*, Oct. 15, 1927.
51. Ibid., Oct. 20, 1928.
52. Ibid., Jan. 30, 1926.
53. Ibid., Jan. 2, 1926.
54. Ibid., Jan. 16, 1923.
55. Ibid., Jan. 20, 1923.
56. W. H. Hollins, "The Negro Press in America: Content Analysis of Five Newspapers" (master's thesis, University of Minnesota, 1945), p. 39.
57. *Courier*, Feb. 11, 1928; Gordon, "Negro Press," *The Annals*, p. 256; and Ira DeA. Reid, *Social Conditions of the Negro in the Hill District of Pittsburgh* (General Committee on the Hill Survey, 1930), p. 98.
58. *Courier*, Dec. 20, 1930.
59. Ibid., Feb. 16, 1924; Stephen R. Fox, *The Guardian of Boston: William Monroe Trotter* (New York, 1970), p. 248; and J. W. Johnson to Vann, Jan. 29, 1924, Box C-379, NAACP Papers. For full details see Administration Files, "24th Infantry Division," Boxes C-379 and C-380, NAACP Papers. William Monroe Trotter and three others represented the National Equal Rights League, which presented its own delega-

tion but did endorse the petition of the NAACP.

60. "SPECIAL EXTRA—WAR DEPARTMENT REPORTS TO NAACP ALL HOUSTON MARTYRS GET REDUCED SENTENCES—18 LONG-TERM MEN TO BE RELEASED AT ONCE—10 LIFERS ELIGIBLE FOR RELEASE WITHIN A YEAR," Press Service of the NAACP, May 16, 1924, Box C-379, NAACP Papers.

61. *Courier*, May 3 and 24, 1924.

62. Ibid., Dec. 14, 1917.

63. Johnson to Vann, May 20, 1924, Box C-379, NAACP Papers.

64. *Courier*, Nov. 7, 1925.

65. Ibid., Oct. 9, Jan. 26, 1926.

66. For example, the *Atlanta Independent*, Nov. 18, 1926, editorialized: "James Weldon Johnson and Charles S. Johnson [editor of *Opportunity*] are in accord in praising that dirty and insulting book of Carl Van Vechten's entitled *Nigger Heaven*. These Johnson boys can have little fundamental pride in their race and very little appreciation for real literature if they can see virtue in this wicked novel. It is a hard thing to insult some of these New York [Negro] high-brows. They feel flattered when some white writer 'takes tea' with them and they are constrained to be impervious to the shafts and darts of insidious writings falling from the pens of these writers. This is the same Weldon Johnson who is seeking to immortalize the shameful songs of slavery.... How these men can praise *Nigger Heaven* can be explained only by the fact that their batteries have been silenced through associating with Gene Tunney and the rest of the lights of Greenwich Village" (cited from Administration Files, "*Pittsburgh Courier* Controversy, News Clippings, 1926," Box C-202, NAACP Papers).

67. Telegram, White to Vann, Aug. 15, 1926, personal correspondence of White, Box C-94, NAACP Papers. For in-depth pro and con coverage of the impact of *Nigger Heaven*, see Nathan I. Huggins, *Harlem Renaissance* (New York 1971), pp. 84–118.

68. Vann to White, Aug. 16, 1926, personal correspondence of White, Box C-94, NAACP Papers.

69. Eugene Levy, "James Weldon Johnson" (manuscript to be published by University of Chicago Press), pp. 285–86, citing J. W. Johnson to E. Franklin Frazier, Nov. 9, 1936; Johnson to Storey, Oct. 14, 1926, NAACP Papers.

70. "Press Service of the NAACP, Oct. 15, 1926, James Weldon Johnson Issues Statement on 'Slush Fund' Attack on NAACP Papers," NAACP Papers.

71. Ibid. Johnson's statement was strongly substantiated when *The Crisis* shortly thereafter published two of its reports, "The Negro Common School in Georgia," and "The Negro Public School in Mississippi." (*The Crisis* XXXII [Dec. 1926]: 60, 62–63).

72. Eugene Levy to Buni, Sept. 11, 1972. The Johnson Papers, Beinecke Rare Book Room and Manuscript Library, Yale University, New Haven, have very little material covering the years 1925 through 1929. There is no record of any correspondence with Vann. Perhaps either Johnson or his wife removed any correspondence from this period which might have depicted Johnson in a disparaging manner. Levy does not believe this to be true, but he does note that Johnson "was capable of glossing over or ignoring events in his own past which did not, at least in his view, fit his public image. Johnson, for example, in his autobiography did not mention his friendship with Booker T. Washington, a friendship which by 1933 was not something to brag about. Nevertheless, whatever public image he wished to convey, he did not cull his private papers re BTW or several other aspects of his life which he ignored in *Along*

This Way" (Levy to Buni, Sept. 11, 1972).
73. *Courier*, Oct. 23 and 30, 1926.
74. Vann had heartily endorsed the Sanhedrin idea, attended the meeting called by Miller in Chicago, and was appointed to standing committees (*Courier*, Feb. 16, 1924).
75. *Norfolk Journal and Guide*, Nov. 14, 1926. Reprinted by permission of the publisher.
76. W. E. B. DuBois, "Opinion," *The Crisis* CXXVII (Jan. 27, 1927). The DuBois papers were unavailable for research. According to Professor Herbert Aptheker, editor of the collection being published by the University of Massachusetts Press (Fall 1973), correspondence between Vann and DuBois will be included in volume 1 (Aptheker to Buni, Apr. 2, 1973).
77. *Courier*, Jan. 19, 1927.
78. *The Crisis* XVIII (May 1919): 9.
79. Ibid., p. 10.
80. "Dr. DuBois on Moton and Scott," *Courier*, May 17, 1919.
81. Scott to Vann, May 23 and May 27, 1919, Box 108, Folder S, Scott Papers, Soper Library, Morgan State College, Baltimore, Md.
82. *The Crisis* XXXI (Feb. 1926): 166.
83. White to Vann, Oct. 13, 1926, Administration Files, Box C-95, NAACP Papers.
84. Vann to White, Oct. 14, 1926, Administration Files, Box C-95, NAACP Papers.
85. White to H. S. Murphy, Atlanta, Oct. 21, 1926, Box C-95, NAACP Papers.
86. White to Vann, Oct. 16, 1926, Box C-95, NAACP Papers.
87. B. Joyce Ross, *J. E. Spingarn and the Rise of the NAACP 1911–1939* (New York, 1972), p. 191.
88. *St. Paul* (Minn.) *Echo*, Oct. 23, 1926, in Administration Files, "*Pittsburgh Courier* Controversy, News Clippings, 1926," Box C-202, NAACP Papers.
89. *Arizona Times*, Oct. 15, 1926, in Administration Files, "*Pittsburgh Courier* Controversy, News Clippings, 1926," Box C-202, NAACP Papers.
90. Ross, *J. E. Spingarn*, p. 122.
91. *Charleston Messenger*, Oct. 30, 1926; *Philadelphia Tribune*, Oct. 23, 1926. See also *Baltimore Afro-American*, Oct. 26, 1926; *Palmetto Leader* (Columbia, S.C.), Oct. 23, 1926; *Chicago Bee*, Oct. 23, 1926; all in Box C-202, NAACP Papers.
92. *Philadelphia Tribune*, Oct. 23, 1926.
93. Ross, *J. E. Spingarn*, p. 122.
94. *St. Luke Herald* (Richmond, Va.), Nov. 6, 1926, and *Richmond Planet*, Oct. 23, 1926, in Box C-202, NAACP Papers.
95. Eugene Levy to Buni, Sept. 11, 1972.
96. *Courier*, Sept. 14, 1929, and "The Pittsburgh Courier," *The Crisis* XXXVI (Nov. 1929): 387.
97. *Courier*, Sept. 14, 1929; see also DuBois to Vann, Aug. 27, 1929, Administration Files, Box C-202, NAACP Papers.
98. Vann's conversation with White and five other NAACP officers, recorded by George Murphy, July 5, 1938, Administration Files, Box C-109, NAACP Papers.
99. Ibid.
100. See E. Franklin Frazier, *Black Bourgeoisie* (Glencoe, Ill., 1957), p. 83. The Boule, the first black Greek letter society, was organized in 1904, partly because white societies had refused to admit blacks. It had been organized when there were relatively few

black college graduates and professionals in America. According to Frazier, however, "I thought the original aim of this society was to bring together the 'aristocracy of talent', instead it has become one of the main expressions of social snobbishness on the part of the black bourgeoisie."

101. Memorandum to Mr. White from Mr. Murphy, July 5, 1938, Administration Files, Box C-109, NAACP Papers.

102. Eugene Levy to Buni, Sept. 11, 1972.

103. A. Philip Randolph, "The Truth About the Brotherhood of Sleeping Car Porters," *The Messenger* VIII (Feb. 1926): 37–38, 61–62; Anderson, *Randolph*, pp.153–69; and Sterling D. Spero and Abraham L. Harris, *The Black Worker: The Negro and the Labor Movement* (New York, 1931), pp. 430–35. In 1929, when a Senate subcommittee subpoenaed Howard's bank records, it was found that he had received $4,000 from the Pullman Company. However, no direct link between the money and Howard's opposition to the union could be ascertained (*Hearings Before Senate Subcommittee Investigating the Influencing of Appointments of Postmasterships*, 70th Cong., 2nd sess., vol. CCCXVII, no. 2, p. 363).

104. Anderson, *Randolph*, pp. 171–73; Spero and Harris, *The Black Worker*, pp. 438–39; and Arvarh E. Strickland, *History of the Chicago Urban League* (Urbana, Ill., 1966), pp. 72–73.

105. B. R. Brazael, *The Brotherhood of Sleeping Car Porters* (New York, 1946), pp. 51–52.

106. "The Neglected Truth," *The Messenger* VIII (Feb. 1926): 48–49.

107. "The Negro Press in the Hands of the White Folks' Niggers," *The Messenger* VIII (Mar. 1926): 83–85; Anderson, *Randolph*, pp. 171–72; and Ottley, *Lonely Warrior*, p. 264.

108. Vann to Robert Mayes (Confidential), Nov. 7, 1925, Vann Papers.

109. *Courier*, Feb. 13 and 20, 1926.

110. Ibid., Mar. 13, 1926.

111. Ibid., Apr. 10, 1926; "Give the Porters Adequate Pay," ibid., Aug. 28, 1924.

112. Vann to Robert Mayes, Nov. 7, 1925, Vann Papers.

113. *The Messenger* III (Jan. 1921): 217; Arna Bontemps, *One Hundred Years of Negro Freedom* (New York, 1961), p. 242. Unfortunately, Randolph's papers for these years were destroyed in a fire in 1930.

114. "Negro Republican Leaders," *The Messenger* III (Jan. 1921): 216–17.

115. Interview with A. Philip Randolph, Nov. 26, 1969.

116. Telegram, Randolph to Vann, Jan. 10, 1927, Vann Papers.

117. *The Messenger*, Feb. 4, 1927.

118. *Courier*, Feb. 26, 1927.

119. Vann to Randolph, Apr. 21, 1927, Vann Papers.

120. Telephone interview with C. L. Dellums, May 24, 1973. Dellums, one of the Brotherhood vice-presidents at that time, is now international president of the B.S.P.U.

121. Spero and Harris, *The Black Worker*, pp. 454–56.

122. Vann to Randolph, Jan. 30, 1928, Vann Papers.

123. Interview with Randolph, Nov. 26, 1969.

124. Vann to Randolph, Apr. 7, 1928, Vann Papers.

125. Vann to Alice Martin, Apr. 9, 1928, Vann Papers.

126. "Randolph Replies to Vann," *The Messenger* X (May–June 1928): 114.

127. *Courier*, Apr. 28, 1928.

128. Interview with Randolph, Nov. 26, 1969.
129. Vann to Pickens, reply to an open letter from Pickens, Apr. 17, 1928, in *Courier*, Apr. 28, 1928.
130. Interview with Ernest Rice McKinney, Jan. 25 and 26, 1973.
131. Telephone interview with C. L. Dellums, May 24, 1973.
132. Interview with Randolph, Nov. 26, 1969.
133. Telephone interview with Bennie Smith, Nov. 29, 1970; interview with Randolph, Nov. 26, 1969.
134. Telephone interviews with Jervis Anderson, May 1 and 19, 1973; Anderson, *Randolph*, p. 195; and telephone interview with Dellums, May 24, 1973. Another source, who prefers to be unidentified, said Vann received $50,000. However, none of this is borne out by the Brotherhood of Sleeping Car Porters Union Papers, Chicago Historical Society. The Pullman Company Papers in Chicago's Newberry Library are at present in disarray, being catalogued, and must await the future research of other historians.
135. Webster to Randolph, Apr. 7, Mar. 31, 1928, Brotherhood Papers, Chicago Historical Society.
136. Interview with Raymond Pace Alexander, Nov. 27, 1971; Eugene Davidson, "The Black Cabinet in the New Deal: The Inside of the Outer Circle," undated Associated Negro Press Feature Release, Vann Papers. Davidson wrote, "He is a 'fixer' and he likes to fix things for political friends and for Vann. . . . He is shrewd and calculating. He is not well liked. Those who know him best call him an 'opportunist'. He has illusions that he is the greatest race politician that ever came along, but likes to play a lone hand of influence."
137. After a decade of nonrecognition by Pullman and several jurisdictional conflicts with various AFL unions, along with a struggle through the Depression, repressive tactics by the Pullman Company, and a severe drop in membership, the Brotherhood was finally chartered as a national union by the AFL in 1936. The Brotherhood received its charter despite the bitter protests of several national unions, and the black labor organization's case was strengthened in 1935 when it won a National Mediation Board election and acquired sole bargaining rights for the porters (Anderson, *Randolph*, pp. 187–240, passim; Edward Peeks, *The Long Struggle for Black Power* [New York, 1971], pp. 274, 281–84).
138. *A Supplement to the 1926 Edition of The American Newspaper Annual Ad Directory*, p. 1380.
139. Vann to Eve Lynn Crawford, Philadelphia, Dec. 8, 1925, Vann to Floyd J. Calvin, New York, and Vann to Henry H. Pace, Mar. 23, 1927, Vann Papers.
140. Vann to Calvin, Feb. 13, 1926, Calvin to Vann, June 1, 1927, and Vann to Calvin, Sept. 20, 1927, Vann Papers.
141. George Swetnam, *The Bicentennial History of Pittsburgh* (Pittsburgh, 1955), vol. II, p. 273.
142. Minutes of *Courier* board of directors meeting, Dec. 14, 1923, Prattis Papers.
143. "An Opportunity to Become a Stockholder in the *Pittsburgh Courier*," brochure dated 1929, Vann Papers; *Courier*, Special Edition, Dec. 14, 1929; Lewis to Brewer, May 6, 1941, in Brewer, "Vann," p. 29; and Webber, "Vann," pp. 141–42.
144. "An Opportunity to Become a Stockholder"; Vann to Bessie Page Posey, New Bedford, Mass., Oct. 2, 1926, Vann to Mrs. E. A. Alexander, Pittsburgh, Nov. 15, 1937, Vann Papers; and Webber, "Vann," p. 135.

145. *Courier*, Dec. 3, 1927; Vann to Moton, May 26, 1928, Vann Papers; and Webber, "Vann," pp. 141–42.
146. Interview with Nunn, Mar. 3, 1969; Webber, "Vann," p. 141.
147. Interview with Mrs. Vann, Apr. 6, 1967; interview with Nunn, Mar. 3, 1969; interview with Prattis, May 18, 1970; Webber, "Vann," p. 160; and Sam Thomas Mallison, *The Great Wildcatter: Michael Benedum* (Charleston, W.Va., 1953), p. 165.
148. Benedum to Vann, Nov. 28, 1930; see also Eugene Kinckle Jones to Vann, Apr. 2, 1936, asking Vann to approach Benedum for funds; Herbert T. Miller, executive secretary of Centre Avenue YMCA, to Benedum, Oct. 18, 1932; Miller to Vann, Oct. 24, 1932; and "Report of 1932," all in Vann Papers.
149. Interview with reliable source who preferred to remain anonymous. See pp. 190–91 of this work.
150. Interview with Nunn, Mar. 3, 1969; interview with Prattis, May 18, 1970.
151. Vann to Col. Arthur W. Little, International Paper Company, New York, Dec. 19, 1921, Vann Papers; Webber, "Vann," pp. 141–42.
152. Syrjamaki, "The Negro Press in 1939," p. 47; Oak, *Negro Newspapers*, pp. 23, 72–75. Even the *Chicago Defender*, the *Courier*'s major rival, had not opened its own plant until 1921 (interview taped by LaBrie with John Sengstacke, June 23 and 24, 1972).
153. Murdock, "Some Business Aspects of the Leading Negro Newspapers," pp. 61–63; Joseph N. LaCour, "The Negro Press as a Business," *The Crisis* XLVIII (Apr. 1941): 108, 141.
154. Vann to Ward Lather, New York, Sept. 28, 1921, Vann to Col. Arthur W. Little, Dec. 9, 1929, Vann Papers.
155. Spero and Harris, *The Black Worker*, pp. 228–29, 230–45; Gerald E. Allen, "The Negro Miner in Western Pennsylvania" (master's thesis, University of Pittsburgh, 1927), p. 31; Bertram J. Black and Aubrey Mallach, *Population Trends in Allegheny County 1840–1843* (Bureau of Social Research, Federation of Social Agencies of Allegheny County, I, Apr. 1944), p. 21; and U.S. Bureau of the Census, *Negroes in the United States 1900–1932* (Washington, D.C., 1935), pp. 6, 14, 24–25, 799.

Chapter 8. Time to Turn Lincoln's Picture to the Wall

1. Perry Howard to Vann, July 30, 1920, and William C. Matthews, eastern division director of National Division of Colored Voters, to Vann, Oct. 29, 1920, Vann Papers.
2. *Courier*, Jan. 3, 1920.
3. Ibid., July 2, 1921.
4. Vann to Congressman Steven B. Porter of Pennsylvania, Feb. 15, 1922, Vann Papers; see also Richard B. Sherman, "The Harding Administration and the Negro: An Opportunity Lost," *Journal of Negro History* XLIX (July 1964): 151–69. For thorough and comprehensive coverage of the black man's politics during the 1920s, see Richard B. Sherman, *The Republican Party and Black America from McKinley to Hoover, 1896–1933* (Charlottesville, Va., 1973).

After a decade of supporting the Republican party, Vann considered himself a likely candidate for a federal position in the Harding and then in the Coolidge administrations. However, the lack of material relating to Vann in both the Warren G. Harding Papers (Ohio Historical Society, Columbus) and the Calvin Coolidge Papers

(Library of Congress, Washington, D.C.) indicates that Vann was not seriously considered for patronage in either 1921 or 1925. New to national politics, Vann had overrated his own importance. Neither he nor the *Courier* had yet achieved national status. A telephone interview with Professor Richard B. Sherman, the College of William and Mary, November 1, 1973, supports this conclusion.

5. Sherman, "Harding Administration," pp. 164–65.

6. Monroe Work, ed., *Negro Year Book, 1931–1932* (Tuskegee, Ala., 1932), p. 91.

7. Sherman, "Harding Administration," pp. 164–65; idem, *Republican Party and Black America*, pp. 174–99.

8. Elbert Lee Tatum, *The Changed Political Thought of the Negro, 1915–1940* (New York, 1951), p. 95.

9. The Klan organ, *The Searchlight*, sold regularly in Pittsburgh's newsstands (Kenneth T. Jackson, *The Ku Klux Klan in the City, 1915–1930* [New York, 1967], pp. 170–73, 237, 239; Emerson H. Loucks, *The Ku Klux Klan in Pennsylvania* [Harrisburg, 1936], pp. 52–55). There had also been incidents of intimidation and terror. A cross was burned in the Borough of Elizabeth, a few miles from the city line ("The Ku Klux Klan in Pittsburgh," *Courier*, Apr. 29, 1922; also June 3 and Dec. 2, 1922, and June 29, 1924). On another occasion Klan members dressed in full regalia entered a black church in Oil City, marched to the front of the congregation, then in mockery made a $25.00 donation and stalked out of the building ("KKK in Church," *Courier*, June 24, 1922). The most publicized action of the Pittsburgh Ku Klux Klan occurred in Carnegie. On August 25, 1923, ten thousand members gathered for initiation ceremonies and a parade through the town. When the mayor of the town, fearful of violence, refused them a permit, Imperial Wizard Hiram W. Evans defied the order and made the march anyway. A fight began between Klansmen and white Catholics, shots were fired, killing one Klan member, and the meeting quickly came to an end (Jackson, *KKK in the City*, pp. 172–73).

10. "The Tuskegee Tangle," *Courier*, June 10, 1923; "The Whole Truth About the Tuskegee Hospital," ibid., June 30, 1923; Pete Daniels, "Black Power in the 1920s: The Case of Tuskegee Veterans Hospital," *Journal of Southern History* 26 (August 1970): 368–88.

11. *Courier*, Aug. 6, 1921.

12. Ibid., Jan. 5, June 2, July 21, 1923.

13. Eugene Gordon, "The Negro Press," *American Mercury* VII (June 1926).

14. *Courier*, June 14, 1924.

15. Vann To Republican National Committee, New York City, Oct. 31, 1924, Vann Papers.

16. *Chicago Defender*, Nov. 2, 1924.

17. This was indicated in letters Vann received from white Republican leaders, including those from William M. Butler, the chairman of the Republican National Committee (Oct. 4, 1924, Vann Papers), Guy Emerson, chairman of the National Contributors Committee, and Charles D. Hillers, vice-chairman of the Republican National Committee, declining Vann's invitation to attend the formal opening of the Harlem party headquarters. See also Gilbert Osofsky, *Harlem: the Making of a Ghetto* (New York, 1966), p. 169. For the 1924 campaign and the black man, see Sherman, *Republican Party and Black America*, pp. 203–13.

18. Vann to F. C. Hicks, director of the Republican National Committee, Sept. 29, 1924, Vann Papers.

19. Johnson to Senator David A. Reed of Pennsylvania, Dec. 6, 1924, Vann Papers, asking Reed to use his influence in getting Vann the position. See also Emmett J. Scott, secretary-treasurer of Howard University, to Vann, July 12, 1924, Vann Papers; Eugene Gordon, "The Negro Press," p. 211; and David M. Tucker, *Lieutenant Lee of Beale Street* (Nashville, 1971), p. 84. On Coolidge's administration and blacks, see Sherman, *Republican Party and Black America*, pp. 214-23.

20. Interviews with Judge Raymond Pace Alexander and J. Austin Norris, Philadelphia, Nov. 27, 1971; Floyd J. Calvin, "Negro Editors of Prominence," *Courier*, Oct. 20, 1928.

21. *Courier*, Jan. 7, 1928.

22. Ibid., Aug. 25, 1928.

23. Ibid., Oct. 20, 1928. Rainey, the son of a South Carolina Reconstructionist who served five terms in the United States Congress, was an attorney for the Boston Elevated Railroad. He had been a Republican until 1922, "when I could not consider myself a man if I would swallow the things the Republican party has been feeding the colored voters and supporters." He said the GOP had treated blacks badly because "the Republicans knew it was not necessary to make political recognition because they were assured of the bulk of the Negro votes and on the other hand the Democrats would not give the Negro anything because they knew he supported the Republicans." In 1928, Rainey became chairman of the Smith for President Colored League in the New York City National Democratic Headquarters. He was by then a strong force among black Democrats (J. Joseph Huthmacher, *Massachusetts People and Politics, 1919-1933* [Cambridge, Mass., 1959], pp. 121–22, 142, 205, 246).

24. Farley to Vann, Aug. 17 and 22, 1928, Vann Papers. Farley stated to the author in a letter (May 23, 1967) and a telephone interview (Jan. 18, 1968) that the arrangement was definitely political, with a reward intended, but he could not recall what the specific provisions were. Vann's later correspondence to Farley (Apr. 27, 1939 and July 20, 1940, Vann Papers) also recounts the meetings.

25. Interview with James A. Farley, May 23, 1967.

26. McIntosh to FDR, Jan. 20, 1929, Box 33, Howe Papers, FDRL, cited in Charles E. Halt, "Joseph F. Guffey: New Deal Politician from Pennsylvania" (doctoral dissertation, Syracuse University, 1965), p. 119.

27. *Courier*, Sept. 1, 1928.

28. See Vann correspondence, Vann Papers: Frank A. Parkinson, Republican state chairman of Oklahoma State Committee, to Vann, Aug. 16, 1928; T. J. Johnson, editor, *Memphis Triangle*, to Vann, Aug. 4, 1928; H. H. Starks, editor, *The Milwaukee Defender*, to Vann, Oct. 6, 1928; N. B. Dodson, president of Dodson News Service, New York, "Agency for all Weekly Papers," to Vann, Aug. 8, 1928; Willis Cole, editor, *The Louisville Leader*, to Vann, Aug. 3, 1928; Joseph B. Brown, editor, *The Postal Alliance*, "Organ of the National Alliance of Postal Employees," to Vann, Aug. 13, 1928.

29. Vann, "The Negro in Politics," speech distributed by the Eastern Speakers' Bureau, Oct. 1928, Vann Papers; Harold F. Gosnell, *Negro Politicians: The Rise of Negro Politics in Chicago* (Chicago, 1935), p. 32.

30. *Courier*, Oct. 20, 1928.

31. Tatum, *Changed Political Thought*, p. 131; V. O. Key, Jr., *Southern Politics in State and Nation* (New York, 1948), pp. 286–88; Sherman, *Republican Party and Black America*, pp. 230–31.

32. *Courier*, July 21, 1928.

33. Ibid., July 28, 1928.

34. Ibid., July 21, 1928.

35. Smith's showing was strong, however, in the Third and Fifth Wards, where he won 46 and 38 percent of the votes, respectively (Bruce Stave, "Pittsburgh and the New Deal," [unpublished manuscript], table 2, p. 15a; James E. Miller, "The Negro in Pennsylvania Politics, with Special Reference to Philadelphia Since 1932" [doctoral dissertation, University of Pennsylvania, 1945], pp. 193–94, based on figures in *Annual Report, Registration Commission for Philadelphia, 1928*).

36. See Bruce Stave, *The New Deal and the Last Hurrah: Pittsburgh Machine Politics* (Pittsburgh, 1970), pp. 35–40, on inroads into Republican power in the state beginning with the 1924 presidential election. Jerome M. Clubb and Howard W. Allen statistically examine Smith's inroads into urban areas ("The Cities in the Election of 1928: Partisan Realignment?" *American Historical Review* LXXIV [Apr. 1969]: 1205–20). In Pittsburgh and Philadelphia he received 42.4 and 39.5 percent, respectively, of the vote. These percentages were a sharp increase over the 8.7 and 12.1 percent cast for the Democratic candidate in 1924.

37. *Courier*, Nov. 17, 1928.

38. Walter F. Brown, postmaster general of the United States, to Vann, Mar. 18, 1929, acknowledging that Vann's name was under consideration at the Department of Justice, Vann Papers; *Washington Post*, July 6, 1928; *Baltimore Afro-American*, May 25, 1929; *Courier*, May 25, 1929; and DePriest to Vann, May 15, 1929, DePriest to Brown, May 28, 1929, Emmett J. Scott to Attorney General William D. Mitchell, May 1, 1929, Senator Reed to Vann, May 13, 1929, Vann Papers.

39. Stave, *New Deal and Last Hurrah*, pp. 33–34; Samuel John Astorino, "The Decline of the Republican Dynasty in Pennsylvania, 1929–1934" (doctoral dissertation, University of Pittsburgh, 1962), p. 177.

With the steady rise to national prominence of the *Courier* during the mid-1920s, Vann was able to make serious attempts for a federal position in the aftermath of Hoover's 1928 victory. References to activities in his behalf directed to Hoover himself are to be found in the Hoover Papers, Herbert Hoover Presidential Library, West Branch, Iowa: Seth Richardson, assistant attorney general, to Hoover about a recommendation by R. R. Church for Vann, June 10, 1929; T. A. Huntley, secretary to Senator Reed, to Hoover, urging Vann's appointment, June 1, 1929; and Emmett J. Scott to Hoover, arguing for Vann's placement, July 9, 1929. Since Hoover was relying most heavily on Robert Russa Moton, a longtime friend of Vann, for advice on black patronage, it appeared that the Pittsburgh editor had an excellent chance for placement. Vann's disappointment when no offer was forthcoming, therefore, was all the keener (Sherman, *Republican Party and Black America*, pp. 233–34).

40. See G. James Fleming, "A Philadelphia Lawyer," *The Crisis* XLVI (Nov. 1939): 329–31, 347–48.

41. Interview with Alexander, Nov. 27, 1971.

42. See pp. 194–97 of this work.

43. Allen Francis Kifer, "The Negro Under the New Deal" (doctoral dissertation, University of Wisconsin, 1961), vii; Jane R. Motz, "The Black Cabinet: Negroes in the Administration of Franklin Delano Roosevelt" (master's thesis, University of Delaware, 1964), p. 29.

44. *Courier*, Feb. 8, 1930.

45. Webber, "Vann," p. 140.

46. *Courier*, Oct. 26, 1929.
47. Ibid., Nov. 16, 1929. Vann also declined to serve on the President's Conference on Home Building and Home Ownership (Vann to Hoover, Dec. 22, 1931, Hoover Papers).
48. Ibid., Nov. 11, 1928.
49. Ibid., Apr. 13 and 20, May 4, June 11, 1929; and "Atta Boy, DePriest," June 22, 1929.
50. Ibid., Dec. 28, 1929.
51. Ibid.
52. J. T. Salter, "The End of Vare," *Political Science Quarterly* L (June 1935): 214–35; M. Nelson McGreary, *Gifford Pinchot: Forester-Politician* (Princeton, 1960), pp. 318–20, 326; Sam Bass Warner, Jr., *The Private City: Philadelphia in Three Periods of Its Growth* (Philadelphia, 1968), pp. 215–19; and William S. Vare, *My Forty Years in Politics* (Philadelphia, 1933), passim.
53. Interview with Judge Alexander and J. Austin Norris, Nov. 27, 1971.
54. *Courier*, May 10, 1930.
55. Ibid., May 17, 1930.
56. McGreary, *Pinchot*, pp. 349–50.
57. *Pittsburgh Post-Gazette*, Sept. 4, 1930; Campaign Correspondence, Spring 1930, T-V Box 750, Pinchot Papers, Library of Congress; Vann to Pinchot, Sept. 4, 1930, Vann Papers.
58. Vann to Stahlnecker, Oct. 1, 1930, Vann Papers.
59. Interview with Alexander, Nov. 27, 1971.
60. Vann to Wilson, Sept. 20, 1930, Vann Papers.
61. *Philadelphia Tribune*, Oct. 23, 1930.
62. *Courier*, Oct. 18, 1930.
63. Ibid., May 12, 1930; Richard C. Keller, "Pennsylvania's Little New Deal," (doctoral dissertation, Columbia University, 1960), pp. 19–20.
64. Stave, *New Deal and Last Hurrah*, p. 25; Astorino, "Decline of the Republican Dynasty," p. 129; Miller, "Negro in Pennsylvania Politics," p. 199; and Alexander Kendrick, "The End of Boss Vare," *The Nation* CXXXVII (Nov. 29, 1933): 21–22.
65. *Courier*, Nov. 8, 1930.
66. Telegram, Pinchot to Vann, June 11, 1930; Pinchot to Vann, Nov. 12, 1930, Vann Papers.
67. Vann to R. R. Moton, Apr. 2, 1931, Vann Papers.
68. Vann to Pinchot, Nov. 16, 1931, Administration Correspondence, 1931, Box 936, Pinchot Papers.
69. Vann to Dr. S. A. Furniss, Republican Headquarters, Colored Division, Indianapolis, Ind., Oct. 2, 1930, Vann Papers.
70. Stave, *New Deal and Last Hurrah*, p. 33.
71. *Courier*, Nov. 15, 1930.
72. Ibid., Nov. 29, 1930.
73. Ibid., Dec. 6, 1930.
74. Ibid., Dec. 20, 1930.
75. In Philadelphia, 34.4 percent of blacks were on relief, compared to 8.2 percent of whites. Statewide, according to the 1930 census, 151,726 of the total 431,828 blacks (35.2 percent) were on relief (Keller, "Pennsylvania's Little New Deal," pp. 67–77; Miller, "Negro in Pennsylvania Politics," p. 265; Joseph H. Willits, "Some Impacts

of the Depression Upon the Negro in Philadelphia," *Opportunity* XI [July 1933]: 200–04, 219; and Bonnie Fox Schwartz, "Unemployment Relief in Philadelphia, 1930–1932: A Study of the Depression's Impact on Voluntarism," *Pennsylvania Magazine of History and Biography* XCII [Jan. 1969]: 86–108).

76. Arthur Dunham, "Pennsylvania and Unemployed Relief, 1929–1934," *Social Service Review* VII (June 1934): 249. See also Wayland Fuller Dunaway, *A History of Pennsylvania* (New York, 1935), pp. 590–94; Keller, "Pennsylvania's Little New Deal," pp. 66–101, passim; McGeary, *Gifford Pinchot*, pp. 358–86.

77. Dunham, "Pennsylvania and Unemployed Relief," pp. 253–54.

78. Keller, "Pennsylvania's Little New Deal," pp. 25–26; Astorino, "Decline of the Republican Dynasty," p. 27.

79. Thomas E. Williams, "Will Pennsylvania Go Democratic?" *The Nation* CXXXV (Nov. 9, 1932): 451; Astorino, "Decline of the Republican Dynasty," p. 188.

80. Halt, "Guffey," p. 89, citing Guffey's diary, April 7, 8, and 9, 1932, and interview with Lawrence, June 6, 1964; Sam Thomas Mallison, *The Great Wildcatter: Michael Benedum* (Charleston, W. Va., 1953), pp. 403–04; Frank C. Harper, *Pittsburgh: Forge of the Universe* (New York, 1957), pp. 206–09.

81. Miller, "Negro in Pennsylvania Politics," pp. 11, 182, 380; U.S. Bureau of the Census, *Sixteenth Census of the United States, Population*, VI, pp. 22–23.

82. "Races: Elks and Equality," *Time* XXVI (Aug. 12, 1935): 9–10.

83. Mallison, *Great Wildcatter*, p. 403.

84. Interview with Mrs. Emma Guffey Miller, Aug. 18, 1967; autobiographical sketch, Emma Guffey Miller Papers, Slippery Rock, Pa. Mrs. Miller, who died in February 1970 at the age of ninety-five, had been an activist, championing women's rights since she first became involved in Democratic politics at the turn of the century. A graduate of Bryn Mawr College, she fought hard for women's suffrage, equal rights for women, and the repeal of prohibition. She served as precinct committeewoman in Allegheny County, county committeewoman, member of the Democratic State Executive Board, and in 1932 became a Democratic national committeewoman from Pennsylvania. She was a delegate to five national conventions, and at the 1924 convention she received a vote for the presidency, the first woman so honored. She delivered seconding speeches for Al Smith in 1924 and Franklin D. Roosevelt in 1932 and 1936 and was as strong a New Dealer as her brother. A favorite among Democrats, Mrs. Miller was toasted to the playing of "The Old Gray Mare."

85. Joseph Alsop and Robert Kintner, "The Guffey, Biography of a Boss New Style," *Saturday Evening Post* CCX (Mar. 26 and Apr. 16, 1938), Mar. 26, p. 103. For biographical material on Guffey, see Halt, "Guffey"; Joseph F. Guffey, *Seventy Years on the Red Fire Wagon* (Lebanon, Pa., 1952); and Alsop and Kintner, "The Guffey" (Mar. 26), pp. 5–7, 98–99, 101, and Apr. 16, pp. 16–17, 98, 100–01, 103.

86. Stave, *New Deal and Last Hurrah*, p. 32.

87. Guffey, *Seventy Years on the Red Fire Wagon*, p. 170; Alsop and Kintner, "The Guffey," Mar. 26, p. 103; Halt, "Guffey," pp. 5–6; and interview with Mrs. Miller, Aug. 18, 1967.

88. Alsop and Kintner, "The Guffey," Mar. 26, pp. 5–6; Guffey, *Seventy Years on the Red Fire Wagon*, p. 117.

89. Guffey to Howe, Jan. 26, 1932, Box 645, Franklin D. Roosevelt Papers, Hyde Park, N.Y.; interview with Farley, May 23, 1967; and Vann to Farley, June 22, 1940, Vann Papers.

90. Ruth L. Simmons, "The Negro in Recent Pittsburgh Politics" (master's thesis, University of Pittsburgh, 1945), pp. 4–5.

91. The fact that Farley as Democratic National Committee chairman made no mention of blacks in the 1932 campaign either in his writings or in a personal interview with the writer, along with his recollection of the establishment of the Negro Division, gave the impression that though he went along with the effort, he did not consider the blacks a potential political force to be won over from the Republicans (interview with Farley, May 23, 1967; James A. Farley, *Behind the Ballots: The Personal History of a Politician* [New York, 1948], ch. 2).

92. "The Colored Advisory Committee Report to the National Democratic Committee," financial statement, Dec. 1, 1932 to Dec. 21, 1933, and Rainey to Vann, Nov. 16, 1932, Vann Papers; Joseph L. Johnson to Louis McHenry Howe, July 6, 1933, Official File 93, FDRL; Miller, "Negro in Pennsylvania Politics," pp. 291–92; Guffey, *Seventy Years on the Red Fire Wagon*, p. 171; and interview with Farley, May 23, 1967.

93. Interview with Norris, Nov. 27, 1971; Alsop and Kintner, "The Guffey," Mar. 26, p. 6; and Tatum, *Changed Political Thought*, p. 147.

94. Philadelphia, with a population of 219,599 blacks, was exceeded only by Harlem and Chicago in the number of blacks (Miller, "Negro in Pennsylvania Politics," p. 12).

95. Astorino, "Decline of the Republican Dynasty," p. 177; Miller, "Negro in Pennsylvania Politics," p. 292; *Courier*, Oct. 1, 1932; and "Report of Robert L. Vann, Member: Executive Committee, Democratic National Campaign, 1932," Vann Papers. These clubs became the nucleus of a permanent black Democratic organization in Pennsylvania after the 1932 election.

96. *Courier*, Oct. 8, 1932; manuscript in Vann Papers.

97. "Report of Robert L. Vann," Vann Papers; Halt, "Guffey," p. 120; and *Courier*, Oct. 1, 1932.

98. H. E. C. Bryant, "Reminiscences," *Charlotte* (N.C.) *Observer*, Mar. 4, 1941, Vann Papers.

99. According to Lewster A. Walton, when Hoover posed with the One Hundred, it was the first time he had posed with blacks since entering the White House ("Vote for Roosevelt," *The Crisis* XXIX [Nov. 1932]: 343).

100. *Courier*, Oct. 8, 1932. Similar coverage is in the *Norfolk Journal and Guide*, Oct. 8, 1932. See also Vann to Mrs. Rose E. Upton Bascom, Framingham, Mass., June 17, 1938, Vann Papers.

101. *Courier*, Oct. 22, 1932. Other important black weeklies supporting FDR were the *Norfolk Journal and Guide*, the *Baltimore Afro-American*, the *Washington Tribune*, and the *Indianapolis Recorder*. The *New York Age* remarked that while it was not supporting FDR, neither could it back Hoover.

102. *Courier*, July 16 and 23, Oct. 1, 1932. On Hoover and the Depression see Tatum, *Changed Political Thought*, pp. 99–138; Henry L. Moon, *Balance of Power: The Negro Vote* (New York, 1948), pp. 105, 114.

103. *Courier*, Aug. 14, 1932.
104. Ibid.
105. Ibid., May 22 and 29, 1932.
106. Ibid., Sept. 17, 1932.
107. Ibid., July 19, 1930.
108. Ibid., July 26, 1930.

109. Ibid., Aug. 2, 1930; see also issues of Apr. 5 and May 10, 1930.
110. Walter White, *A Man Called White: the Autobiography of Walter White* (New York, 1948), pp. 102–11.
111. *Courier*, Apr. 26, 1930.
112. Ibid., Sept. 26, 1930.
113. Ibid., Oct. 15, 1932.
114. Astorino, "Decline of the Republican Dynasty," p. 189; Brewer, "Vann," p. 88; and *Pennsylvania Manual, 1933* (Harrisburg, 1933), pp. 432–39.
115. Stave, *New Deal and Last Hurrah*, pp. 33–34; Miller, "Negro in Pennsylvania Politics," p. 221; and Robert H. Brisbane, "The Rise of the Protest Movement Among Negroes Since 1900" (doctoral dissertation, Harvard University, 1949), p. 142. Before the election Third-Ward Republicans had a registration majority over the Democrats, 2,004 to 493. It was 4,801 to 632 in the Fifth Ward (Simmons, "Negro in Recent Pittsburgh Politics," pp. 15–16; *Courier*, Nov. 12, 1932).
116. *Courier*, Nov. 19, 1932; Stave, *New Deal and Last Hurrah*, p. 34; Astorino, "Decline of the Republican Dynasty," p. 120; and James E. Allen, "The Negro in the 1940 Presidential Election" (master's thesis, Howard University, 1955), table 12.
117. Ernest M. Collins, "Cincinnati's Negroes and Presidential Politics," *Journal of Negro History* XLI (Apr. 1956): 131–37; John M. Allswang, "The Chicago Negro Voter and the Democratic Consensus: A Case Study, 1918–1936," *Journal of Illinois State Historical Society* LX (Summer 1967): 145–75; Rita Werner Gordon, "The Change of the Political Alignment of Chicago's Negroes During the New Deal," *Journal of American History* LVI (Dec. 1969): 584–603; Astorino, "Decline of the Republican Dynasty," pp. 174–75, 189, 192–93; Miller, "Negro in Pennsylvania Politics," pp. 209, 221; William Leuchtenburg, *FDR and the New Deal* (New York, 1963), p. 185; Tatum, *Changed Political Thought*, pp. 135–41; Brisbane, "Rise of Protest Movements," table I, p. 142; John M. Allswang, *A House for All Peoples: Ethnic Politics in Chicago, 1890–1936* (Lexington, Ky., 1971), pp. 42, 187; and David Burner, *The Politics of Provincialism: The Democratic Party in Transition, 1918–1932* (New York, 1968), p. 241.
118. Astorino, "Decline of the Republican Dynasty," pp. 174–75, 189, 192–93; Keller, "Pennsylvania's Little New Deal," pp. 103–04; Paul W. Ward, "Wooing the Negro Vote," *The Nation* CXLIII (Aug. 1, 1936): 119–20; Miller, "Negro in Pennsylvania Politics," p. 209; and *Courier*, Nov. 12, 1932. See also J. T. Salter, "The End of Vare," *Political Science Quarterly* L (June 1935): 214–35.
119. Gosnell, *Negro Politicians*, p. 32.
120. *Philadelphia Tribune*, Sept. 29, 1932; Moon, *Balance of Power*, pp. 17–19; John G. Van Deusen, "The Negro in Politics," *Journal of Negro History* XXI (July 1936): 256–75; Leuchtenburg, *FDR and the New Deal*, pp. 185–86; and Arthur M. Schlesinger, Jr., *The Age of Roosevelt: The Politics of Upheaval* (Boston, 1960), p. 431.
121. *Courier*, Apr. 1, 1933; Farley to Vann, Apr. 17 and 29, 1933, Vann Papers, assuring Vann he would be properly placed.
122. Barber to Vann, Apr. 14, 1933, Vann Papers.
123. Alsop and Kintner, "The Guffey," p. 6; James T. Patterson, *Congressional Conservatism and the New Deal: The Growth of the Conservative Coalition, 1933–1939* (Lexington, Ky., 1967), pp. 97–98; and Guffey, *Seventy Years on the Red Fire Wagon*, p. 171.
124. Press Service of the NAACP, Feb. 1, 1933, Administration Files, Box G-190, NAACP Papers, Library of Congress; *Courier*, Jan. 28, 1933.
125. *New York Herald Tribune*, Feb. 3, 1933, in Box G-190, NAACP Papers.

Notes to Pages 199–203 • 373

126. *Pittsburgh Press*, Aug. 27, 1933; *Courier*, Apr. 22, 1933.
127. Walter White to Vann, Jan. 25, 1933, Administration Files, Box G-190, NAACP Papers. Others present were W. Justin Carter, the Rev. W. L. Campbell, John P. Scott, and Mrs. Maud Coleman, all representing the Harrisburg Branch; Dr. Harry Jones and Max Martin of the Philadelphia Branch; W. T. Poole of the Pittsburgh Branch; and Congressmen Hart and Harris of the state legislature.
128. *Pittsburgh Press*, Aug. 31, 1933.
129. Ibid.
130. Ibid., Sept. 20, 1933.
131. Ibid., Sept. 1, 1933.
132. Brown to White, Sept. 6, 1933, Box G-191, NAACP Papers. There was little love lost between Brown and Vann thereafter. In 1934, when Brown ran for the state legislature and was endorsed by both political parties, Vann opposed him. According to Earl Brown, of the New York *Amsterdam News*, the victorious Brown mocked Vann's slight, recalling, "I received more Democratic votes in Pittsburgh when I was elected to the Legislature, because Vann opposed me than I would have if he had favored my endorsement" (*New York Herald Tribune*, July 16, 1936).
133. *Courier*, June 10, 1933.
134. Vann Scrapbook, "1933 Guests and Letters Incidental to July 8, 1933 Testimonial at Pythian Temple, Pittsburgh," Vann Papers. The scrapbook contains many congratulatory letters and telegrams to Vann and the names of guests from nineteen states who attended the testimonial. There was even a small delegation from a Robert L. Vann Club in Arizona.
135. *Courier*, July 28, 1933, Nov. 12, 1932. Vann was briefly a member of the Non-Partisan League founded by Congressman DePriest in December 1931. DePriest, its first president, attempted to bring together without regard to political affiliation prominent blacks from the religious, political, civic, fraternal, and educational fields "for the purpose of formulating certain definite measures [opposing lynching, discrimination in the civil service, disfranchisement, and unfair distribution of educational funds] to be urged upon the President and the Congress of the United States and all political parties." Vann broke with the movement, accusing DePriest of turning the League into a political arm of the GOP during the 1932 presidential campaign (DePriest to Vann, July 27, 1931, Vann to DePriest, Feb. 9, 1933, and DePriest to Vann, Feb. 11, 1933, Vann Papers; *Courier*, Nov. 19, 1932).

Chapter 9. Washington: Confidence and Disillusionment

1. O. C. Hall to Vann from 727 St. Anthony Avenue, St. Paul, Minn., Feb. 17, 1933, Vann Papers. Also J. Max Barber to Vann, Apr. 14, 1933, and Guffey to Vann, Oct. 15, 1933, assuring Vann that he was in charge of Philadelphia patronage. Dr. George W. Graham, president of the Citizen's Civic League of Philadelphia, wrote Vann seeking advice from him as "the acknowledged leader of Negro Democrats in Pennsylvania."
2. Attorney Joseph L. McLemore, director of the Negro Division of the Democratic State Committee, St. Louis, Mo., to Vann, Feb. 28, 1933, Vann Papers.
3. Jones to Vann, Apr. 20, 1933, Vann Papers.
4. Oxley to Vann, Nov. 28, 1932, Apr. 10, 1933, Vann Papers.

5. Schuyler to Vann, Aug. 5, 1933, Vann Papers. Vann's reply (Aug. 7, 1933) assured Schuyler that the position existed only in rumor. See also Roi Ottley, *New World A-Coming: Inside Black America* (Boston, 1943), pp. 255–56.
6. DuBois to Vann, Sept. 14, 1933, Vann Papers.
7. Webber, "Vann," pp. 160–61.
8. *Opportunity* XL (Nov. 1933): 327.
9. For a complete list of officeholders see "summary of Services Rendered Negroes by the Federal Government in Connection with the Recovery Program," Oct. 1, 1934, four-page carbon copy of U.S. Government report in Vann Papers; Henry L. Moon, *Balance of Power: The Negro Vote* (New York, 1948), pp. 28–29. According to Monroe Work, there were fifty-four major black appointments in 1933 and 1934 (*Negro Year Book, 1937–1938* [Tuskegee, Ala., 1938], pp. 112–14).
10. Samuel Krislov, *The Negro in Federal Employment: The Quest for Equal Opportunity* (Minneapolis, 1967), pp. 22–27.
11. Rainey to Vann, Mar. 20 and Apr. 14, 1933, Vann Papers.
12. M. H. McIntyre, assistant secretary to the president, to Vann, Sept. 12, 1933, White House Alphabetical File (1937–1940), Folder 3534, Box 276, FDRL; Vann to Howe, Mar. 10 and 23, 1933; Howe to Vann, Mar. 17, 1933; Rainey to Howe, Mar. 7, 1933; Howe to Rainey, Mar. 20, 1933; all in Official File 93, FDRL.
13. E. L. Powell, secretary of the Negro Democratic State Executive Committee in West Virginia, to Vann, Apr. 11, 1933, voicing his organization's dismay over the lack of patronage given to "the Big Four" for dispensation to blacks, Vann Papers.
14. Vann to Calvin, July 24, 1933, Vann Papers.
15. Vann to J. Twing Brooks, Dec. 17, 1935, Vann to William H. Lewis, Oct. 10, 1935, and Vann to William L. Houston, Sept. 8, 1937, Vann Papers.
16. Interview with Mrs. Emma Guffey Miller, Aug. 8, 1967.
17. *The East Tennessee News* (Knoxville), undated, Vann Papers.
18. Vann to Rainey, Aug. 7, 1933, and Vann to Mencken, Mar. 14, 1938, Vann Papers.
19. Harry W. Blair, assistant attorney general, "To All Special Assistants: Department of Justice, August 20, 1935," Vann Papers.
20. Ralph Bunche, "The Negro Office Holders in the Federal Court," xvii, book vi, pp. 1442–43 of "The Political Status of the Negro," Schomburg Collection, New York Public Library; telephone interview with Robert Weaver, June 16, 1970; Charles R. Lawrence, "Negro Organizations in Crisis: Depression, New Deal, World War II" (doctoral dissertation, Columbia University, 1953), pp. 216–17; and Jane R. Motz, "The Black Cabinet: Negroes in the Administration of Franklin Delano Roosevelt" (master's thesis, University of Delaware, 1964), pp. 23–25.
21. Motz, "Black Cabinet," pp. 23–24; telephone interview with Weaver, June 16, 1970; and Raymond Wolters, *Negroes and the Great Depression: The Problem of Economic Recovery* (Westport, Conn., 1970), pp. 165–66.
22. Allen F. Kifer, "The Negro Under the New Deal" (doctoral dissertation, University of Wisconsin, 1963), p. 273; Motz, "Black Cabinet," pp. 10–11; and Arthur M. Schlesinger, *The Age of Roosevelt: The Politics of Upheaval* (Boston, 1960), p. 432.
23. *Chicago Defender*, May 27, 1933.
24. Other members included Harry H. Pace, president of the Supreme Liberty Life Insurance Company, Chicago; G. David Houston, principal of the Armstrong High School, Washington, D.C.; Rev. Marshall A. Talley of Indianapolis; Benjamin

F. Hubert, Savannah, Ga.; Mrs. Helen W. Crossley, State College, Denver, Del.; Eugene K. Jones, adviser on Negro Affairs in the Department of Commerce; William H. Lewis, Boston attorney and former assistant attorney general of the United States; Garnet C. Wilkinson, first assistant superintendent of public schools, Washington, D.C.; and Mary F. Waring, M.D., president of the National Federation of Colored Women's Clubs, Chicago.

25. U.S. Department of Commerce, "Summary of Report of the Negro Advisory Committee of the Advisory and Planning Council for the Department of Commerce," for release not earlier than the afternoon of Dec. 29, 1933; "The Newly Appointed Negro Advisory Committee," Negro Advisory Committee Special from Colored News Service, Sept. 11, 1933, Vann Papers; and *Pittsburgh Press*, Sept. 10, 1933.

26. "Newly Appointed Negro Advisory Committee."

27. Telephone interview with Weaver, June 16, 1970.

28. Webber, "Vann," p. 157. Vann was sued but settled the matter out of court on March 9, 1934 (interview by Henry LaBrie with attorney Omer T. Kaylor, Hagerstown, Md., Nov. 12, 1969, in LaBrie, "Vann," p. 34).

29. Kifer, "Negro Under New Deal," p. 220; W. M. Kiplinger, *Washington is Like That* (New York 1942), pp. 148–49; Montgomery J. Harmon, "Harold Ickes: A Case Study in New Deal Thought" (doctoral dissertation, University of Wisconsin, 1953), pp. 339–45; and *Courier*, Sept. 2, 1933.

30. See Wolters, *Negroes and the Great Depression*, pp. 142–46, for a thorough explanation.

31. *Courier*, Sept. 9, 1933; Vann to Howe, Dec. 15, 1933, enclosing copy of *Baltimore Afro-American*, Dec. 15, 1933, headlined "Expose Secret NRA Document in Washington," in GSA, NRA, 93, FDRL; and Kifer, "Negro Under New Deal," pp. 218–19.

32. Wolters, *Negroes and the Great Depression*, p. 143.

33. Ibid.

34. Minutes of the Inter-Departmental Group Concerned with the Special Problems of Negroes, Feb. 7, 1934, RG 48, National Archives, Washington, D.C.; Wolters, *Negroes and the Great Depression*, p. 143, and Kifer, "Negro Under New Deal," pp. 220–21.

35. Inter-Departmental minutes, Mar. 2, 1934, 3-7, in file "Negroes," Office of the Secretary of the Interior, NA, RG 48, National Archives; Wolters, *Negroes and the Great Depression*, p. 144.

36. Wolters, *Negroes and the Great Depression*, p. 145.

37. Ibid.

38. Kifer, "Negro Under New Deal," p. 225, citing Report of the Agricultural Committee, pp. 6–11, file 1-280, Central Files, Department of the Interior.

39. Wolters, *Negroes and the Great Depression*, pp. 42–43.

40. Kifer, "Negro Under New Deal," p. 224, citing Inter-Departmental minutes, June 1, 1934, file 1-280, Central Files, Department of the Interior; "Report of the Agricultural Committee of the Inter-Departmental Group Concerned with the Special Problems of Negroes," Department of the Interior; Inter-Departmental minutes, passim, file 1-280, Central Files, Department of the Interior.

41. Kifer, "Negro Under New Deal," pp. 229–30.

42. Motz, "Black Cabinet," pp. 13–19.

43. J. L. Cowling, president of the Michigan Association of Colored Brothers, to Farley, Nov. 30, 1935, and Vann to Farley, Dec. 6, 1935, Vann Papers.

44. "Memorandum for Mr. Howe: Statement of Expenses of Robert L. Vann,"

Oct. 23–Nov. 5, 1934, and "Memorandum for L. M. Howe, Subject: State of Indiana," Nov. 23, 1934, Vann Papers.

45. Mrs. Emma Guffey Miller to Vann, Sept. 25, 1933, Vann Papers; interview with Mrs. Miller, Aug. 18, 1967.

46. Wolters, *Negroes and the Great Depression,* pp. x–xi.

47. Harmon, "Harold Ickes," p. 385; Frank B. Freidel, *FDR and the South* (Baton Rouge, 1965), pp. 72–83; and Schlesinger, *Politics of Upheaval,* p. 434.

48. Bruce M. Stave, *The New Deal and the Last Hurrah: Pittsburgh Machine Politics* (Pittsburgh, 1970), pp. 29–31.

49. Samuel John Astorino, "The Decline of the Republican Dynasty in Pennsylvania, 1929–1934" (doctoral dissertation, University of Pittsburgh, 1962), pp. 199–200; *Courier,* Nov. 11, 1933; Ruth L. Simmons, "The Negro in Recent Pittsburgh Politics" (master's thesis, University of Pittsburgh, 1945), pp. 14–15; and Vann to McNair, Jan. 26, 1934, Vann Papers.

50. Stave, *New Deal and Last Hurrah,* pp. 59–61, 78.

51. Ibid., p. 65.

52. *Courier,* Nov. 18, 1933. According to Bruce M. Stave's unpublished manuscript, "Pittsburgh and the New Deal," p. 15a, table 2, McNair won 37 percent of the vote in the Third Ward and 48 percent in the Fifth. Though he did not get a majority in either ward, he did far better than the Democratic candidate in 1929, who had gotten 6 and 12 percent, respectively. In 1937 the totals for the Democrats were 86 percent in the Third and 66 percent in the Fifth.

53. The previous Assembly had 140 Republicans and 65 Democrats in the House. In 1934 the Democrats won control, 116 to 90. In Allegheny County the entire Democratic slate to the House was elected (*Pittsburgh Press,* May 24, 1934).

54. For excellent coverage of the 1934 campaign, see Edwin B. Bronner, "The New Deal Comes to Pennsylvania: The Gubernatorial Election of 1934," *Pennsylvania Magazine of History and Biography* XXVII (Jan. 1960): 44–68; Richard C. Keller, "Pennsylvania's Little New Deal" (doctoral dissertation, Columbia University, 1960), pp. 121–55; and Charles E. Halt, "Joseph F. Guffey: New Deal Politician from Pennsylvania" (doctoral dissertation, Syracuse University, 1965), pp. 141–67.

55. *Pennsylvania Manual, 1935–1936* (Harrisburg, 1936), pp. 422–65; *Pennsylvania Manual, 1931* (Harrisburg, 1931), p. 540; H. F. Alderfer and F. H. Luhrs, *Gubernatorial Elections in Pennsylvania, 1922–1945* (State College, Pa., 1946), p. 15; and Simmons, "Negro in Recent Pittsburgh Politics," p. 18. In Pittsburgh's Third Ward, Guffey and Earle polled 2,800 and 2,754 to Reed's 1,245 and Schnader's 1,366. In the Fifth, the winners received 4,070 and 3,881 to the losers' 3,267 and 3,513.

56. Bronner, "New Deal Comes to Pennsylvania," p. 67; Joseph Alsop and Robert Kintner, "The Guffey, Biography of a Boss New Style," *Saturday Evening Post* CCX (Apr. 16, 1938): 16.

57. James E. Miller, "The Negro in Pennsylvania Politics, with Special Reference to Philadelphia Since 1932" (doctoral dissertation, University of Pennsylvania, 1945), p. 227; Bronner, "New Deal Comes to Pennsylvania," pp. 62–64.

58. Bronner, "New Deal Comes to Pennsylvania," pp. 49–50.

59. Astorino, "Decline of the Republican Dynasty," pp. 207–09.

60. Manuscript, undated, 1934, Vann Papers.

61. "The Voice of the Pennsylvanian," *Courier,* Oct. 20, 1934; see also *Courier* editorial, "The Battles Monument Commission," June 10, 1923.

62. "The Voice of the Pennsylvanian," *Courier*, Oct. 20, 1934; see also *Courier*, Apr. 14, 21 and 28, May 12, 1934.
63. Astorino, "Decline of the Republican Dynasty," p. 213; Simmons, "Negroes in Recent Pittsburgh Politics," p. 17.
64. *Literary Digest* CXVIII (Nov. 17, 1934): 5–6; *Newsweek* IV (Nov. 7, 1934): 13.
65. Miller, "Negro in Pennsylvania Politics," p. 124; Halt, "Guffey," p. 122; and Joseph F. Guffey, *Seventy Years on the Red Fire Wagon* (Lebanon, Pa., 1952), p. 171.
66. Halt, "Guffey," pp. 52–54, 123–37; Astorino, "Decline of the Republican Dynasty," p. 194, citing correspondence to and from Attorney General Homer Cummings (Box 400, FDRL) refusing to make Pennsylvania appointments without Guffey's consent; and Alsop and Kintner, "The Guffey," p. 103.
67. *Courier*, Jan. 12, 1935.
68. Earle to Vann, Mar. 20, 1935, and Herbert F. Goodrich, dean of the Law School, University of Pennsylvania, and chairman of Constitutional Revision Committee, to Vann, Mar. 14, 1936, Vann Papers; *Pittsburgh Post-Gazette,* Mar. 21, 1935, Jan. 2, 1936; and Keller, "Pennsylvania's Little New Deal," pp. 246–55 passim.
69. *Courier*, Nov. 2, 1935.
70. Ibid., Apr. 27, 1935.
71. Alsop and Kintner, "The Guffey," p. 103; Roy Sprigle, "Lord Guffey of Pennsylvania," *American Mercury* XXXIX (Nov. 1936): 273–84.
72. *Courier*, Apr. 19, 1921.
73. "Fight On," ibid., Mar. 10, 1923.
74. Ibid., June 15, 1935; Maximillian Martin, "The Pennsylvania Civil Rights Act," *The Crisis* XLII (Nov. 1935): 341, 350; "Races: Elks and Equality," *Time* XXVI (Aug. 12, 1935): 9–10; and Keller, "Pennsylvania's Little New Deal," pp. 201–02. The act prohibited under penalty discrimination because of race or color in any place of public accommodation such as hotels, restaurants, hospitals, barrooms, theaters, bathhouses, music halls, gymnasiums, libraries, schools, colleges, trains, and resorts. The penalties were fines of $100 to $500 and imprisonment from thirty to sixty days.
75. Earle to Vann, June 10, 1935, and Vann to Earle, June 15, 1935, Vann Papers.
76. Keller, "Pennsylvania's Little New Deal," pp. 201–02, citing *Lancaster* (Pa.) *Intelligencer Journal*, June 12, 1935; "Races: Elks and Equality," *Time*, p. 10.
77. *Courier*, June 8, 1935.
78. "Race Equality: Raising the Jim Crow Issue," *Literary Digest* CCX (Sept. 7, 1935): 18.
79. Ibid.
80. Ibid., pp. 18–20. See also "Pittsburgh—Negro Discrimination, 1935–37: Operation of Pennsylvania Equal Rights Legislation, 1935," in "Pittsburgh—Negro" file, Pennsylvania Division, Carnegie Library, Pittsburgh.
81. Moss to McQuaide, Apr. 9, 1938, cited by Prattis in manuscript on Urban League and discrimination; also introductory by E. Digby Baltzell in W. E. B. DuBois, *The Philadelphia Negro: A Social Study* (New York, Schocken edition, 1967), xxxviii–xxxix.
82. Alsop and Kintner, "The Guffey," p. 6; *Courier*, July 17, 1935.
83. FDR to Vann, July 19, 1935, Vann Papers. Other members included Harold Ickes, Secretary of Agriculture Wallace, Alfred K. Stern, George Foster Peabody, Mrs. Joanna C. Colcorn, Charles W. Taussig, and Mordecai Johnson. For background reading, see Luther H. Evans, *The Virgin Islands: From Naval Base to New Deal* (Ann Arbor,

1945); John H. Franklin, *From Slavery to Freedom: A History of Negro Americans* (New York, 1947), p. 428.

84. Lawrence W. Cramer, governor of the Virgin Islands, kept Vann abreast of what was happening in the Islands, particularly economic rehabilitation, growth of tourism, PWA projects such as the $275,000 air facility at St. Thomas for the Marines, housing problems at St. Croix and St. Thomas, and sugar and rum developments (Cramer to Vann, Mar. 13 and 21, 1936, Vann Papers).

85. Interview with Mrs. Vann, Apr. 6, 1967.

86. Ibid., and interview with Nunn, Mar. 17, 1969.

87. *New York Herald Tribune*, July 16, 1936, Vann Papers; interview with Mrs. Vann, Apr. 6, 1967.

88. Webber, "Vann," p. 178.

89. Vann to Mencken, Mar. 14, 1938, Vann Papers. Evidently Vann's experience was typical for many blacks in Washington during that period. Robert Weaver said that advisory committees such as those on which Vann served were "a dime a dozen" (telephone interview with Weaver, June 16, 1970). Blacks like Forrester B. Washington "worked doggedly against repeated frustrations, often without authority, usually relying on persuasion," and "after spending six weary months answering thousands of complaints at the FERA, quit in disgust" (Kifer, "Negro Under New Deal," p. 233). Louis Lautier, the Associated Negro Press's representative and the only full-time black correspondent in Washington, considered all racial advisors in the New Deal as little more than apologists (Motz, "Black Cabinet," pp. 54–55).

Chapter 10. The COURIER Hits the Jackpot

1. N. W. Ayer and Sons, *Directory of Newspapers and Periodicals, 1930* (Philadelphia, 1930), p. 880, estimated *Courier* circulation at 38,760. "An Opportunity to Become a Stockholder in the *Pittsburgh Courier*," brochure dated 1929, Vann Papers; Ira Lewis, "The *Pittsburgh Courier*," undated typewritten manuscript on *Courier* history, Vann Papers.

2. George S. Schuyler, *Black and Conservative* (New Rochelle, N.Y., 1966), pp. 165–66.

3. Feature section, *Courier*, Nov. 3, Dec. 15, 1928.

4. Vann to Ziff, Dec. 5, 1928. P. B. Young, Sr., of the *Norfolk Journal and Guide*, and Benjamin J. Davis, of the *Atlanta Independent*, also expressed concern (Young to Vann, Oct. 25, 1929, Davis to Vann, Oct. 22, 1929, Vann Papers). Vann was always rather straight-laced. When he became president of Pittsburgh's prestigious Loendi Club in 1938, he insisted that a rule forbidding women at the club's bar be rigorously enforced. But most of the members opposed Vann's strict stand, and he was eventually forced to back down on the issue.

5. Lewis to Vann, Apr. 3 and 11, 1934, Vann Papers.

6. P. B. Young, Sr., to Vann, July 20, 1935, Vann Papers; *New York Age*, Nov. 2, 1940, Vann Papers; and interview with Prattis, Mar. 13, 1969. When John Sengstacke gained control of the *Chicago Defender*, one of his first moves was to get rid of Ziff (interview taped by Henry LaBrie with Sengstacke, June 23 and 24, 1972).

7. H. B. Crohn, Publisher's Representative, 545 Fifth Avenue, New York, to Vann, Mar. 20, 1935, Vann Papers. This was a common problem for other newspapers as well; see C. A. Franklin, editor of *The Call* (Kansas City), to Vann, Nov. 20, 1936,

Vann Papers, cautioning Vann that the ABC audit was the only way advertisers would believe their potential; Horace David Murdock, "Some Business Aspects of Leading Negro Newspapers" (master's thesis, University of Kansas, 1936), p. 75.

8. N. W. Ayer and Sons, *Directory of Newspapers and Periodicals, 1930*, p. 1257.

9. Vann to H. B. Crohn, June 25, 1937, Vann Papers. The Ayer *Directory* recorded circulation of 149,019 (p. 1202). Those before the *Courier* were *The Call* (Kansas City), the *Amsterdam News*, the *Baltimore Afro-American*, the *Norfolk Journal and Guide*, the *Dallas Express*, the *Philadelphia Tribune*, the *Houston Informer*, and the *St. Louis Argus*.

10. Vann to Mrs. Helen A. Maycrink, assistant treasurer of International Paper Company, Oct. 22, 1930, May 20, June 15 and 27, 1932, Vann Papers.

11. Vann to Qualey and Lawless, Mar. 4, 1930; Vann to Maycrink, Oct. 22, 1930, Vann Papers.

12. Wright to Vann, Apr. 29, July 23, 1931, and Lewis to Wright, May 7, 1931, Vann Papers.

13. Vann to James Boyd, Feb. 4, 1930, Vann Papers.

14. Schuyler to Vann, Sept. 11, 1930, and Vann to Schuyler, Sept. 13, Oct. 1, 1930, Vann Papers.

15. Lewis to Vann, Apr. 10, Apr. 5, Jan. 19, 1934, Vann Papers.

16. Lewis to Brewer, May 6, 1941, in Brewer, "Vann," p. 33.

17. Lewis to Vann, June 6, 1934, Vann Papers.

18. Lewis to Vann, Apr. 10, 1934, Vann Papers.

19. Vann to Lewis, Jan. 18, 1934, Vann Papers.

20. Roi Ottley, *The Lonely Warrior: The Life and Times of Robert S. Abbott* (Chicago, 1955), p. 298. There were other reasons for the decline of the *Defender*, including Abbott's poor health, his recent divorce, and serious in-fighting for control of the paper (interview taped by Henry LaBrie with John Sengstacke, June 23 and 24, 1972).

21. William E. Leuchtenburg, *The Perils of Prosperity, 1914–1932* (Chicago, 1958), pp. 197–98.

22. *Courier*, Apr. 15, 1931.

23. Ibid., May 16, 1931.

24. Ibid.

25. Ibid., May 9, 1931.

26. Ibid., June 13, 1931.

27. Ibid.

28. Ibid., July 11, Aug. 8, Aug. 15, Sept. 21, Oct. 10, 1931.

29. Ibid., Aug. 22, 1931. Nor could *Courier-Defender* relations have been helped when the Pittsburgh weekly headlined Abbott's divorce proceedings from his wife, Helen, in June and July 1933 with such front-page coverage as "SOCIETY WIFE FILES NEW CHARGES, *Nurse is Named as Abbott's 'Friend'* " and " 'WHY NOT A MILLION?' ASKS MRS. ABBOTT WHEN INFORMED NURSE HAS SUED HER FOR $100,000" (*Courier*, June 10 and 24, 1933). The divorce controversy continued for nearly a year, during which time, according to Mrs. Abbott, the *Pittsburgh Courier* unsuccessfully attempted to interview her. She refused, stating, "I should hate to have reports of our affairs circulated which would embarrass him or me or injure his influence with the public" (Ottley, *Lonely Warrior*, pp. 321–22).

30. *Courier*, Oct. 10, 1931.

31. "Garvey's Day in Court," ibid., Feb. 10, 1923.

32. Ibid., June 23, 1923.

33. Ibid., July 21, 1923.
34. Vann to Cobb, July 8, 1925; also Vann to Cobb, June 10 and 24, 1928; Cobb to Vann, July 11, 1925; and Vann to Mrs. Garvey, July 15, 1925; all in Vann Papers.
35. Mrs. Garvey to Cobb, July 8, 1925, Vann Papers.
36. Mrs. Garvey to Buni, Aug. 9, 1972; telephone interview with Mrs. Garvey, May 15, 1972.
37. *Courier*, Aug. 6, 20, and 27, 1927; Amy Jacques Garvey, *Garvey and Garveyism* (New York, 1963), p. 175.
38. Edward David Cronon, *Black Moses: The Story of Marcus Garvey and the Universal Negro Improvement Association* (Madison, Wis., 1955), pp. 154–57.
39. Vann to Garvey, in Kingston, Jamaica, Oct. 23, 1929, Vann Papers.
40. Garvey to Vann, Dec. 9, 1929, Vann Papers.
41. *Courier*, Dec. 21, 1929.
42. Ibid., Feb. 22, 1930.
43. Ibid., Mar. 22, 1930.
44. Ibid.
45. Ibid., Mar. 29, 1930.
46. Ibid., May 31, 1930.
47. Dan T. Carter, *Scottsboro: A Tragedy of the American South* (Baton Rouge, 1969), p. 57; George B. Tindall, *The Emergence of the New South, 1913–1945* (Baton Rouge, 1967), pp. 380–81.
48. Wilson Record, *The Negro and the Communist Party* (Chapel Hill, 1951), pp. 86–87.
49. Record, *Negro and the Communist Party*, pp. 70–80, passim.
50. Carter, *Scottsboro*, p. 87.
51. "Negro Editors on Communism: A Symposium of the American Negro Press," *The Crisis* XXXIX (Apr.–May 1932): 117.
52. Record, *Negro and the Communist Party*, pp. 312–15.
53. Ottley, *Lonely Warrior*, p. 350.
54. "Negro Editors on Communism," pp. 117–19, 154–56; Carter, *Scottsboro*, p. 419.
55. "What Price Publicity?" *Courier*, May 15, 1931.
56. Ibid., July 4, 1931.
57. Ibid., Sept. 26, 1931.
58. Ibid., May 16, 23, and 30, 1931, cited in Carter, *Scottsboro*, p. 88.
59. Schuyler, *Black and Conservative*, p. 193.
60. Carter, *Scottsboro*, passim; Tindall, *Emergence of New South*, pp. 381–82.
61. *Courier*, Mar. 3, 1934.
62. Ibid., Mar. 10, 1934.
63. Ibid., Mar. 24, 1934.
64. Ibid., Mar. 17, 1934.
65. Roy Wilkins to Arthur Spingarn, Apr. 10, 1934, Box 7, Spingarn Papers, Library of Congress.
66. B. Joyce Ross, *J. E. Spingarn and the Rise of the NAACP* (New York, 1972), pp. 204–05.
67. City Editor William G. Nunn, Sr., to Walter White, Apr. 9, 1934, and Nunn to Roy Wilkins, Apr. 10, 1934, Administration Files, *Pittsburgh Courier*, Sept. 15, 1933–May 22, 1934, Box C-388, NAACP Papers, Library of Congress.
68. Telegram, Walter White to the *Pittsburgh Courier*, Apr. 23, 1934, Vann Papers.

69. Nunn to White, May 2, 1934, Box C-388, NAACP Papers.
70. *Courier*, Apr. 28, May 5 and 12, 1934.
71. "Self Respect," ibid., May 19, 1934.
72. E. Washington Rhodes to Wilkins, May 1, 1934, and Frank Marshall Davis to Wilkins, May 7, 1934, Box C-388, NAACP Papers.
73. Young to Wilkins, Apr. 26, 1934, Box C-388, NAACP Papers.
74. Vann to White, May 31, 1934, Box C-388, NAACP Papers.
75. *Courier*, June 2, 1934.
76. Telegram, White to Nunn, May 28, 1934, Box C-388, NAACP Papers.
77. Vann to White, June 8, 1934, Box C-388, NAACP Papers.
78. *Courier*, June 9, 1934.
79. Lewis to White, July 6, 1934, Box C-388, NAACP Papers.
80. Vann to White, Aug. 11, 1934, Box C-388, NAACP Papers.
81. Lampkin to White, Aug. 13, 1934, Box C-388, NAACP Papers.
82. "Extracts from Minutes of the NAACP Board of Directors, September 10, 1934," and "Report on Midnight Benefit Held at 125th Street, Apollo Theatre, New York, Saturday, May 26, 1934," Box C-388, NAACP Papers.
83. Davis to Spingarn, Sept. 15, 1934, Box C-388, NAACP Papers.
84. Spingarn to Vann, Sept. 18, 1934, and Vann to Spingarn, Sept. 19, 1934, Box C-388, NAACP Papers; Arthur Spingarn to Vann, Sept. 24, 1934, Box 7, Arthur B. Spingarn Papers, Library of Congress.
85. Vann to White, Sept. 15, 1934, Box C-388, NAACP Papers.
86. Spingarn to Vann, Oct. 7, 1934, Box C-388, NAACP Papers.
87. *Courier*, July 21, 1934.
88. White to Romeo Dougherty, Sept. 22, 1934, Box C-388, NAACP Papers.
89. Vann to White, Oct. 8, 1934; Vann to Arthur B. Spingarn, Sept. 30, 1934, Box 7, Arthur B. Spingarn Papers.
90. *Courier*, Nov. 26, 1932.
91. Ibid., July 13, 1935.
92. Ibid., July 20, 1935.
93. Ibid., July 13, 1935.
94. Ibid., July 20, 1935. See also Brice Harris, Jr., *The United States and the Italo-Ethiopian Crisis* (Stanford, Calif., 1964), pp. 29–39.
95. *Courier*, July 13, 1935.
96. Ibid., July 20, 1935.
97. Ibid., Dec. 14, 1935.
98. Ibid., Oct. 12, Nov. 2, 1935, from Robert G. Weisbord, "Black America and the Italian-Ethiopian Crisis: An Episode in Pan-Negroism," *The Historian* XXXIV (Feb. 1972): 237–38.
99. "It is the duty of every black man and woman to render the maximum moral and material support to the Ethiopian struggle against Italian Fascism and a not-too-friendly world," and "The rape of Ethiopia is the rape of the Negro race" (Harold Isaacs, *The New World of Negro Americans* [New York, 1963], pp. 61, 149–50). See also *Courier*, Aug. 6, 1932; John H. Franklin, *From Slavery to Freedom: A History of Negro Americans* (New York, 1947), p. 600; and *The Crisis* (May, Sept., Oct. 1935): passim.
100. Weisbord, "Black America and the Italian-Ethiopian Crisis," pp. 230–32.
101. Born in Jamaica in 1887, Rogers came to the United States in 1906, worked as a Pullman Car Porter, and wrote in his spare time. The work that eventually got

him his first newspaper job was "From Superman to Man," conversations between an educated porter and a United States Senator in which they try to solve the race problem. In 1921 Rogers worked for the *Chicago Enterprise*. In 1925 he made the first of many trips to Europe, and the *Courier* was one of the newspapers that purchased his articles, most of which dealt with the life of blacks in European cities. In 1930 he covered the coronation of Emperor Haile Selassie in Addis Ababa. The *Courier* bought this story and others from Somaliland, Anglo-Egyptian Sudan, and other African countries (H. Pluski and R. Brown, eds., *The Negro Almanac* [New York, 1967], p. 840).

102. *Courier*, Dec. 14, 1935.
103. Ibid.
104. Ibid., Jan. 4, 1936.
105. Ibid., Nov. 23, 1935.
106. Ibid., Dec. 14, 1935.
107. Ibid., Jan. 11, 1936.
108. Ibid., Mar. 7, 1936.
109. Ibid.
110. Interviews with Prattis, Apr. 6, 1967, Mar. 13, 1969.
111. *Courier*, May 2, 1936.
112. Vann to Eli Tartle, May 14, 1938, Vann Papers.
113. Interview with Prattis, Mar. 13, 1969.
114. Webber, "Vann," pp. 189–90.
115. Ibid.; Brewer, "Vann," pp. 40–42. From then on, Vann searched for material on blacks overseas to which his readers would respond as they had to Ethiopia. In 1938 he thought of doing a series on England's mistreatment of her black colonies in the West Indies. There had been stirrings of revolt in Jamaica, serious labor unrest, riots, and walkouts by employees of the Jamaica Public Service Company (*New York Times*, June 9, 15, and 17, 1938). Vann sensed a possible story for the *Courier*. After being thoroughly briefed by George Schuyler on the West Indian situation, Vann went to England to speak to U.S. Ambassador Joseph Kennedy and the British secretary of state for the colonies, Sir William Ormsby-Gore, about the problem of British policy toward its colonies. "[VANN] WILL SEEK TO GET 'LOW-DOWN' ON WEST INDIES SITUATION," promised the *Courier* (July 30, 1938). Vann sincerely hoped that he was going to "break something really worthwhile" (Vann to Schuyler, July 16, 1938, Vann Papers; see also Guffey to Joseph P. Kennedy, July 16, 1938, Vann Papers, introducing Vann to Kennedy). But his expectations came to naught. Both Ambassador Kennedy and Secretary Ormsby-Gore gave Vann a cool reception and granted him only brief interviews. Ormsby-Gore apparently evaded Vann's more pointed questions, and Vann learned nothing for his hoped-for newspaper series.

After Vann returned, the *Courier* made little mention of the West Indian situation again, except for one open letter on the front page signed by Vann in which he urged justice for all black people in the West Indies and asked his readers to give financial support to W. Algernon Crawford, editor of the *Barbados Observer*, which he deemed the "only mouthpiece with a vestige of independence left" (*Courier*, Sept. 10, 1938).

116. Robert W. Peterson, *Only the Ball Was White* (Englewood Cliffs, N.J., 1970), p. vi.
117. Ibid., pp. 91–92.

118. Robert W. Peterson, "Josh Gibson was the Equal of Babe Ruth, but . . . ," *New York Times* (Apr. 11, 1971): IV, 12–13.
119. Peterson, *Only the Ball Was White,* pp. 100–01.
120. *Courier,* Aug. 5, 1933.
121. Ibid., Sept. 16, 1933.
122. Ibid., Sept. 1, 1934. When Wendell E. Smith joined the *Courier* staff in 1937, the weekly began a longtime crusade for integrated baseball in the major leagues.
123. Interview with Nunn, Mar. 13, 1969; telephone interview with Chester Washington, Mar. 23, 1973.
124. *Courier,* Feb. 2–Mar. 30, 1935, passim.
125. Telephone interview with Washington, Mar. 23, 1973.
126. Special correspondence, Wilkins to William Pickens, Mar. 29, 1935, Administration File, Box C-80, NAACP Papers; telephone interview with Chester Washington, Mar. 23, 1973.
127. Interview with Nunn, Mar. 13, 1969; Prattis, "Negro Press in Action," manuscript in Prattis Papers.
128. Ibid.
129. *Courier,* June 29, 1935; see also Roi Ottley, *New World A-Coming: Inside Black America* (Boston, 1943), ch. 14, "Joe Louis and His People."
130. *Courier,* June 29, 1935.
131. Ibid.; see also Harris, *United States and the Italo-Ethiopian Crisis,* p. 41.
132. *Courier,* June 29, 1935.
133. Ibid., Apr. 11, 1936; see also Saunders Redding, *The Lonesome Road* (New York, 1958), p. 292.
134. Interview with Nunn, Mar. 13, 1969.
135. *Courier,* June 27, 1936.
136. Redding, *Lonesome Road,* p. 296; George Spandou, "Schmeling's A Cultural Victory," *Der Weltkampf* (Aug. 1936), reprinted in *The Crisis* XLIII (Oct. 1936): 301, 309. See also Sterling A. Brown, "The Negro in American Culture," sec. 1, Sports, 1940, in Ralph Bunche manuscript, Schomburg Collection, New York Public Library, p. 82.
137. *Courier,* June 5, 12, and 19, 1937.
138. Ibid., June 11, 1938.
139. Ibid., June 25, 1938.
140. Ibid.
141. Vann to Mrs. Vann, June 27, 1938, Vann Papers.
142. Richard Vidmar of the *New York Herald Tribune,* quoted in Lester Bromber, *Boxing's Unforgettable Fights* (New York, 1962), p. 63. See also Grantland Rice, *The Tumult and the Shouting* (New York, 1954), p. 176; Roi Ottley and William Weatherby, eds., *The Negro in New York* (New York, 1967), p. 291.
143. Vann to "Dear Stockholder," Dec. 16, 1936, Vann Papers.
144. N. W. Ayer and Sons, *Directory of Newspapers and Periodicals,* lists the 1938 circulation as 145,022; for 1939, 138,299; and for 1940, 126,962. In a letter to Brewer (May 6, 1941), Ira Lewis asserted that it fluctuated between 150,000 and 180,000 (Brewer, "Vann," p. 38). The Vann biographical sketch said that in 1938 it was up to 175,000. According to P. L. Prattis, the figure of 20,000 local subscribers was constant, with the remainder distributed throughout the nation (telephone interview, June 18, 1973).

145. Vann to William Voight, Carnegie-Illinois Steel Company, Pittsburgh, Feb. 15, 1937, Vann Papers.
146. "The Rising Tide of Color in Sports," *Courier*, July 25, 1936.
147. Ibid., Aug. 8, 1936.
148. Webber, "Vann," pp. 188–89; Richard Bardolph, *The Negro Vanguard* (New York, 1961), p. 272.
149. *Courier*, Sept. 5, 1936; see also Richard D. Mandell, *The Nazi Olympics* (New York, 1971), p. 236, for Hitler's reaction to the black victories.
150. *Courier*, Sept. 5, 1936; Webber, "Vann," pp. 188–89.
151. W. E. B. DuBois, "Segregation," *The Crisis* XLI (Jan. 1934): 20; Walter White, "Segregation: A Symposium," *The Crisis* XLI (Mar. 1934): 80–81; Raymond Wolters, *Negroes and the Great Depression* (Westport, Conn., 1970), pp. 230–58; Francis L. Broderick, *W. E. B. DuBois, Negro Leader in a Time of Crisis* (Palo Alto, Calif., 1959), pp. 172–74; and Elliott Rudwick, *W. E. B. DuBois: Propagandist of the Negro Protest* (New York, 1960), pp. 266–82, passim.
152. *Courier*, Mar. 31, 1934.
153. "Cash—Not Criticism," ibid.
154. "To Build or Not to Build," ibid., Apr. 7, 1934.
155. Ibid., June 16, 1934.
156. Ibid., July 7, 1934.
157. Ibid., July 21, 1934.
158. DuBois to Vann, Jan. 4, 1936, Vann Papers.
159. DuBois to Vann, Jan. 4 and 23, 1936, Vann Papers; see also Broderick, *DuBois*, pp. 151–79.
160. DuBois to Vann, Jan. 6, 1936, Vann Papers.
161. DuBois to Vann, May 25 and 27, 1936, Vann Papers. Upon his return to California in January 1937, he planned to arrange five lectures on "The World in 1937," preferably in Los Angeles, St. Louis, Chicago, Pittsburgh, and New York.
162. DuBois to Vann, Jan. 6, 1936, Vann Papers.
163. DuBois to Vann, Apr. 9, May 4, 1936, Vann Papers.
164. *Courier*, Sept. 19, 1936.
165. Ibid., Oct. 3, 1936.
166. Ibid., May 2, 1936.
167. Ibid., June 20, 1936.
168. Interview with Mrs. Vann, Apr. 6, 1967; interview with Nunn, Mar. 13, 1969; and Webber, "Vann," pp. 178–79.
169. Interviews with Nunn and Prattis, Mar. 13, 1969; Webber, "Vann," p. 180.

Chapter 11. Schism and Decline: 1936–1938

1. Monroe Work, ed., *Negro Year Book, 1937–1938* (Tuskegee, Ala., 1938), p. 102.
2. *Courier*, June 13, 1936; Robert L. Vann, "Our Obligation to Reelect President Roosevelt," *Philadelphia Independent*, Nov. 2, 1936; and James E. Miller, "The Negro in Pennsylvania Politics, with Special Reference to Philadelphia Since 1932" (doctoral dissertation, University of Pennsylvania, 1945), pp. 299–300.
3. *Courier*, Jan. 28 and Oct. 8, 1936. The states with 147 electoral votes, including Pennsylvania, Illinois, Ohio, Michigan, Missouri, Indiana, and West Virginia, contained

approximately 1,020,000 black voters.

4. *Courier*, July 4, 1936; *New York Times*, June 25 and 26, 1936; Herbert B. Alexander, "The Political Progress of the Northern Negro, 1932-1936," *Negro History Bulletin* IV (May 1941): 185-86; and Miller, "Negro in Pennsylvania Politics," pp. 371-74.

5. Work, *Negro Year Book 1937-1938*, pp. 102-03; George B. Tindall, *The Emergence of the New South, 1913-1945* (Baton Rouge, 1967), p. 556; and *Courier*, July 4, 1936.

6. Arthur M. Schlesinger, *The Age of Roosevelt: The Politics of Upheaval* (Boston, 1960), p. 598.

7. *Courier*, July 4, 1936.

8. Memorandum, Vann to Farley, July 20, 1936, Vann Papers.

9. Press Release #93, Sept. 4, 1936, Democratic National Committee International News Service, Vann Papers; interview with Farley, May 23, 1967; and Vann to Farley, July 22, 1940, Vann Papers.

10. *Pittsburgh Press*, Aug. 1, 1936; *New York Times*, Aug. 1, 1936.

11. Paul L. Ward, "Wooing the Negro Vote," *The Nation* CXLIII (Aug. 1, 1936): 119-20.

12. "Political Trends...." Democratic National Committee Special Correspondence (Farley), 1936, Official File 300, Box 102, FDRL. Farley cautiously predicted in this correspondence that FDR would carry Pennsylvania; see also Jesse Laventhal, "Pennsylvania Hits the Roosevelt Trail," *The Nation* CXLIII (Oct. 31, 1936): 513-15; and Harold F. Gosnell and William G. Coleman, "Political Trends in Industrial America: Pennsylvania," *Public Opinion Quarterly* IV (Sept. 1940): 473-86.

13. *New York Herald Tribune*, July 16, 1936; see also "Black Purge," *Time* XXXII (Oct. 31, 1936): 14.

14. *New York Herald Tribune*, July 16, 1936. For a similarly critical view of Vann as a political opportunist, see Eugene Davidson, "The Black Cabinet in the New Deal: The Inside of the Outer Circle," undated Associated Negro Press Feature Release, Vann Papers.

15. *Time* XXVII (Aug. 17, 1936): 11.

16. Interviews with J. Austin Norris, Nov. 27, 1971, and William G. Nunn, Mar. 13, 1969.

17. Schlesinger, *Politics of Upheaval*, pp. 346-47.

18. "The President Speaks Out," *Courier*, Dec. 9 and 16, 1933; Schlesinger, *Politics of Upheaval*, pp. 436-37; and Robert Lewis Zangrando, "The NAACP and a Federal Anti-Lynching Bill, 1934-1940," *Journal of Negro History* L (Apr. 1965): 106-17.

19. "NAACP, 1933-1945, Anti-Lynch, 1934-1937," Official File, 2538, FDRL; Administration Files, Boxes 234-243, NAACP Papers, Library of Congress; Schlesinger, *Politics of Upheaval*, pp. 437-38; Frank Freidel, *FDR and the South* (Baton Rouge, 1965), pp. 83, 87, 89; and Walter White, *A Man Called White: The Autobiography of Walter White* (New York, 1948), pp. 167-70.

20. "The Best of the Anti-Lynching Fights," *The Crisis* XLII (June 1935); White, *A Man Called White*, pp. 166-70.

21. *Courier*, May 11, 1935.

22. Allan Morrison, "The Secret Papers of FDR," *Negro Digest* IX (Jan. 1951): 3-13; Schlesinger, *Politics of Upheaval*, p. 431; and Freidel, *FDR and the South*, pp. 73, 81, 97. According to Richard Dalfiume, it may have been because of his conservatism that Roosevelt privately disclosed his dislike for the NAACP, the principal organization leading the fight for an anti-lynch bill. Dalfiume writes, "In 1943, Arthur B. Spingarn,

president of the NAACP, asked him to write a letter praising the twenty-five years service by White to that organization. On one version of the proposed letter there is an attached note which reads: 'Miss Tully brought this in. Says the President doesn't think too much of this organization—not to be to[o] fullsome—tone it down a bit' " (Roosevelt to Spingarn, Oct. 1, 1943, PPF 1226, Roosevelt Papers, in "The 'Forgotten Years' of the Negro Revolution," *Journal of American History* LV (June 1968): 104–05, n. 69). See also pp. 318–19, 322 of this work for a similar reaction by Roosevelt toward blacks seeking equality in the armed forces in 1938–1940.

23. *Courier*, Jan. 15, 1915; Charles Flint Kellogg, *NAACP: A History of the National Association for the Advancement of Colored People, 1909–1920* (Baltimore, 1967), pp. 212–14.

24. *Courier*, May 4 and 11, 1935, July 13 and 20, 1936.

25. Ibid., Oct. 10 and 17, 1936; Work, *Negro Year Book 1937–1938*, p. 22.

26. *Courier*, Oct. 10, 1936.

27. Ibid., Oct. 24, 1936; *New York Herald Tribune*, July 16, 1936.

28. *Courier*, Oct. 16, 1936; Bruce M. Stave, *The New Deal and the Last Hurrah: Pittsburgh Machine Politics* (Pittsburgh, 1970), p. 26, citing speeches by Guffey, Oct. 31, 1935 and 1936 from Guffey Papers, Washington and Jefferson College, Washington, Pa.

29. *Courier*, Oct. 16, 1936.

30. Vann to Guffey, Mar. 7, 1935; Ralph M. Bashore, secretary of the Department of Forests and Waters of Pennsylvania, to Vann, Mar. 23, 1935; Odell Edwards (black CCC worker) to Vann, Mar. 23, 1935; all in Vann Papers. See also Woodrow Avery, 336 Forestry Company, CCC, Kane, Pennsylvania, to Walter White, July 17, 1934, Box G-191, NAACP Papers. For detailed accounts of the CCC and the black man, illustrating that the agency "made all the mistakes it was possible to make in its relation to the Negro," see Allen Francis Kifer, "The Negro Under the New Deal" (doctoral dissertation, University of Wisconsin, 1961); John A. Salmond, "The Civilian Conservation Corps and the Negro," *Journal of American History* LII (June 1965): 75.

31. For a further explanation of how a segment of the black leadership could abide by discriminatory practices and back FDR, hoping for the best in the future, see James A. Harrell, "Negro Leadership in the Election Year 1936," *Journal of American History* XXXIV (Nov. 1968): 558–59.

32. Typewritten manuscript speech, Vann Papers. See also *Pittsburgh Post-Gazette*, Oct. 22, 1936; Frederick G. Detweiler, "The Negro Press Today," *American Journal of Sociology* XLIV (Nov. 1938): 391–93.

33. *Courier*, Oct. 31, 1936.

34. *The Pennsylvania Manual, 1937* (Harrisburg, 1937), pp. 176, 185; Miller, "Negro in Pennsylvania Politics," pp. 240–42; and Richard C. Keller, "Pennsylvania's Little New Deal" (doctoral dissertation, Columbia University, 1960), p. 237. The Democrats also strengthened their hold on the lower house of the state legislature (154 to 54) and for the first time since 1871 controlled the senate with 34 seats.

35. *Philadelphia Independent*, Nov. 22, 1936, cited in Miller, "Negro in Pennsylvania Politics," p. 294. For changes in other major cities such as St. Louis, Chicago, Cleveland, and Detroit, see William J. Bryant, "Negro Politics," ch. XV, pp. 1242–1356, in "Negro Politics in the North," Bunche manuscript, Myrdal study, Schomburg Collection, New York Public Library; John M. Allswang, "The Chicago Negro Voter and the Democratic Consensus: A Case Study, 1918–1936," *Journal of Illinois State Historical Society* (Summer 1967): 145–75.

36. Ruth L. Simmons, "The Negro in Recent Pittsburgh Politics" (master's thesis,

University of Pittsburgh, 1945), p. 21; Miller, "Negro in Pennsylvania Politics," p. 264. According to Bruce M. Stave, FDR's percentages in the Third and Fifth Wards were 90 and 76 percent, respectively ("Pittsburgh and the New Deal" [unpublished manuscript], p. 15a).

37. Lawrence Sullivan, "The Negro Vote," *Atlantic Monthly* CLXVI (Oct. 1940): 477–84.

38. *Courier*, Nov. 11, 1933; Stave, *New Deal and Last Hurrah*, p. 88; Simmons, "Negro in Recent Pittsburgh Politics," pp. 14–15; Vann to McNair, Jan. 26, 1934, Vann Papers.

39. Interview with Professor Bruce M. Stave, May 16, 1973. Stave observed that the change-over from Republicans to Democrats in the city government was largely nominal. Many of the same people who had been in control on the ward level prior to the New Deal maintained their authority after 1933. The only way blacks could get political patronage, therefore, was to build a vote base broad enough that whites would pay attention to it *(New Deal and Last Hurrah,* p. 174).

40. *Courier*, Jan. 6 and 13, Feb. 10, 1934, cited in Stave, *New Deal and Last Hurrah*, pp. 88–89. Mr. Gould has been ill for some time and was unavailable for comment.

41. *Courier*, Feb. 3, 1934.

42. Ibid., Apr. 21 and 28, 1934.

43. Webber, "Vann," p. 186; interview with Walter C. Rainey, Apr. 21, 1973.

44. Stave, *New Deal and Last Hurrah*, p. 88.

45. *Courier*, Jan. 6 and 13, Oct. 4, 1934; Webber, "Vann," pp. 176, 186; and interview with Walter C. Rainey, Apr. 21, 1973.

46. Stave, *New Deal and Last Hurrah*, pp. 84–138, passim.

47. Vann to McNair, undated, 1936, Vann Papers; Webber, "Vann," p. 192.

48. Webber, "Vann," p. 176; interview with Mrs. Vann, Apr. 6, 1967.

49. George Swetnam, *The Bicentennial History of Pittsburgh* (Pittsburgh, 1955), pp. 587–88.

50. Vann to Guffey, Feb. 15 and 19, Mar. 2, 1937, Vann Papers; *Courier*, Apr. 2, 1938.

51. Vann to Guffey, Mar. 2, 1937, and Vann to Thomas H. Cosby, Oct. 18, 1938, Vann Papers; Webber, "Vann," pp. 200, 212.

52. Editorial, *Courier*, undated, Vann Papers; interview with Walter C. Rainey, Apr. 21, 1973.

53. Miller, "Negro in Pennsylvania Politics," pp. 311–12, from Miller's interview with Shepard, Oct. 14, 1944; *Philadelphia Independent,* May 17 and 27, 1936; Talmadge Jackson, "Earle Called Fairest Governor to Negroes in Pennsylvania History," *Courier,* Aug. 12, 1944.

54. Miller, "Negro in Pennsylvania Politics," pp. 12, 312–13. Only Harlem and Chicago's South Side had more potential black voters.

55. Julian Rainey to Vann, Mar. 25, Apr. 29, 1937, Apr. 27, 1938, Vann Papers.

56. Vann to Farley, July 27, 1937, Vann Papers.

57. Vann to Farley, June 10, 1937, Vann Papers.

58. Vann to Einbinder, Mar. 29, 1937, Vann Papers.

59. Farley to Vann, Aug. 3, 1937, May 4, 1938; Vann to Rainey, Sept. 8, 1937, Vann Papers.

60. Stave, "Pittsburgh and the New Deal," p. 14. For biographical material on Lawrence see Sally O. Shames, "David L. Lawrence, Mayor of Pittsburgh: Development of a Political Leader" (doctoral dissertation, University of Pittsburgh, 1958), pp. 11–30;

Charles E. Halt, "Joseph F. Guffey: New Deal Politician from Pennsylvania" (doctoral dissertation, Syracuse University, 1965), pp. 167–74; Keller, "Pennsylvania's Little New Deal," pp. 112, 190–99; and Frank Hawkins, "Lawrence of Pittsburgh: Boss of the Mellon Patch," *Harper's* CCXIII (Aug. 1956): 55–61. The Lawrence Papers, in the possession of his daughter, Mrs. T. K. Donahoe, were not examined by the author. According to Mrs. Donahoe, her father's papers contain little of political value. She described them as personal, stating that her father preferred the spoken word, particularly using the telephone, to the written letter, memo, or briefing (telephone interview with Mrs. Donahoe, Apr. 19, 1973). The Allegheny County Democratic Headquarters files for 1933 to 1940, housed in Pittsburgh, were also unavailable. Professor Stave, who did have access to the records, graciously allowed me to read and cite from his unpublished manuscript his findings for the New Deal years.

61. Joseph F. Guffey, *Seventy Years on the Red Fire Wagon* (Lebanon, Pa., 1952), p. 103.

62. Ibid.; interview with Farley, May 23, 1967.

63. Guy V. Miller, "Pennsylvania's Scrambled Politics," *The Nation* CXLVI (May 14, 1938): 555.

64. Halt, "Guffey," p. 171; Guffey, *Seventy Years on the Red Fire Wagon*, p. 103; and Stave, *New Deal and Last Hurrah*, p. 155.

65. Vann to William E. Sweet, Denver, Colo., Jan. 8, 1938, Vann Papers.

66. Vann to Guffey, Feb. 15, 1937, Vann Papers.

67. *New York Times*, Jan. 21, Feb. 1 and 18, 1938; *Pittsburgh Post-Gazette*, Feb. 1, 1938.

68. Stave, *New Deal and Last Hurrah*, p. 155.

69. *New York Times*, Feb. 20, 1938.

70. Ibid., Feb. 24, 1938; Halt, "Guffey," pp. 175–76; and Guffey, *Seventy Years on the Red Fire Wagon*, pp. 106–07.

71. *Courier*, Apr. 2, 1938; Vann speech on KDKA radio, Pittsburgh, Apr. 28, 1938, manuscript in Vann Papers.

72. *New York Times*, Mar. 12, 1938; Halt, "Guffey," p. 178. For thorough coverage of the Democratic primary, see Halt, "Guffey," pp. 167–84.

73. Miller, "Pennsylvania's Scrambled Politics," p. 555.

74. Mrs. Cookman to Guffey Apr. 19, 1938, and Guffey to Mrs. Cookman, Apr. 22, 1938, Vann Papers.

75. "Industrial Unionism Marches On," *Courier*, Mar. 13, 1937.

76. "The Year of the CIO," ibid., Sept. 18, 1937.

77. Undated speech, 1937, cited in Horace Cayton and George Mitchell, *Black Workers and the New Union* (Chapel Hill, 1939), p. 397.

78. *Courier*, Apr. 2, 1938.

79. Ibid.; KDKA speech, Apr. 28, 1938, manuscript in Vann Papers.

80. KDKA speech, Apr. 28, 1938. According to both William Nunn, Sr., and Walter C. Rainey, it was Vann who had recommended Jones to Guffey initially for his position as workmen's compensation referee.

81. Alsop and Kintner, "The Guffey," Mar. 26, pp. 5–7, 98–99, 101–02, and Apr. 16, 1938, pp. 16–17, 98, 100–01, 103.

82. *Chicago Tribune*, May 7, 1937.

83. John P. Frank, *Mr. Justice Black: The Man and His Opinions* (New York, 1949), p. 59; Charlotte Williams, *Hugo L. Black: A Study of the Judicial Process* (Baltimore,

1950), pp. 1–67, passim; Irving Dillard, *One Man's Stand for Freedom* (New York, 1963), pp. 1–27; and *New York Times*, Aug. 13, 1937.

84. *Pittsburgh Post-Gazette*, Sept. 13–18, 1937; Frank, *Mr. Justice Black*, pp. 102–03.

85. Vann to FDR, Sept. 16, 1937, Vann Papers; *Pittsburgh Press*, Sept. 21, 1937; "Hugo Black, Justice of the Supreme Court," *Opportunity* XV (Sept. 1937): 293; Williams, *Hugo L. Black*, p. 25; and "The Case of Mr. Justice Black," *New Republic* LXXXXII (Sept. 29, 1937): 200–01. Walter White was heavily criticized for supporting Black as an appointee (White, *A Man Called White*, pp. 177–79).

86. "FDR Takes a Run-Out Powder," *New Republic* LXXXXII (Sept. 29, 1937): 213; Williams, *Hugo L. Black*, pp. 27–30. For the full text of Black's speech, see *New York Times*, Oct. 2, 1937.

87. Alphabetical File (File 1937–1940), Vann–Vas, Folder 3534, Box 276, FDRL. For a sampling of endorsements see C. C. Spaulding, president of North Carolina Mutual Life Insurance Company, Durham, to Vann, July 22, 1938, Vann Papers.

88. *Baltimore Evening Sun*, Mar. 1, 1938.

89. Vann to Mencken, Mar. 4, 1938, and Mencken to Vann, Mar. 7, 1938, Vann Papers.

90. Vann to Mencken, Mar. 14, 1938; Vann Papers.

91. *Courier*, July 16, 1938. It had also been traditional for one of the ten judges in the Municipal Court of Washington, D.C., to be black. Judge Armond W. Scott held that position in 1938 (*Courier*, Feb. 17, 1938).

92. Vann to Attorney Harry H. Pace, Chicago, Feb. 8, 1938, and Vann to Thomas W. Young, Sr., Norfolk, Apr. 4, 1938, Vann Papers. See also Schuyler to Mencken, Mar. 15, 1938, explaining that blacks realized Vann could not receive the nomination but that Vann was the choice of "a group of prominent Negroes eager to hammer home the idea of Negroes being in every branch of the government, holding offices high and low."

93. For full coverage of the Margiotti charges, which continued long after the primary, see Keller, "Pennsylvania's Little New Deal," pp. 326–52; Miller, "Pennsylvania's Scrambled Politics," p. 556; and *New York Times*, Apr. 19, 1938.

With his Republican support in Harrisburg, Margiotti got District Attorney Carl B. Shelley to start a grand jury investigation of the Earle regime after the Earle-Jones primary victory. The Pennsylvania Supreme Court refused to halt the move. Governor Earle then called a special session of the Democrat-dominated general assembly, to which the GOP would certainly object because of the cost ($300,000 to $750,000) and because Earle was trying to whitewash the corruption charges. Clearly Earle called it to stave off the grand jury investigation, but the reason he gave was that the state constitution designated the legislature, not a grand jury, as the agency to investigate members of the executive branch. The Democratic legislature quickly pushed through four bills giving it the power to supersede grand juries and to suspend all other investigations "retroactively and prospectively" until legislative committees had conducted their own inquiries. Nevertheless, on August 8, Judge Paul N. Schaeffer impounded all the records at issue and declared that the grand jury would convene. As a result it was rumored that Earle might call out troops or state police to uphold executive power ("Earle's Court Feud Threatens to Cost Democrats His State," *Newsweek* XII [Aug. 8, 1938]: 7–8; "Pennsylvania: Earle's Brawl," *Time* XXXII [Aug. 8, 1938]: 11).

94. Miller, "Pennsylvania's Scrambled Politics," p. 556; *New York Times*, Apr. 19, 1938.

95. *Pittsburgh Post-Gazette*, May 3, 1938.
96. KDKA speech, Apr. 28, 1938, Vann Papers; *Pittsburgh Post-Gazette*, Apr. 29, 1938.
97. Halt, "Guffey," p. 181; Keller, "Pennsylvania's Little New Deal," p. 348; and *New York Times*, Aug. 11, 1938. See also Stave, *New Deal and Last Hurrah*, pp. 142–50. Alsop and Kintner were thoroughly convinced of Guffey's unscrupulous tactics, charging that he distributed approximately forty thousand jobs in the WPA, other agencies such as the CCC, and the Social Security Board. "Joe said who got what, and he distributed his largesse so intelligently that he changed the face of Pennsylvania politics in a year and a half" ("The Guffey," pp. 98–99).
98. *Pittsburgh Post-Gazette*, May 3, 1938.
99. KDKA speech, Apr. 28, 1938, Vann Papers.
100. See Personal File, Box 300, and Official File 300, Pennsylvania, Box 106, FDRL.
101. *Newsweek* XII (May 30, 1938): 8.
102. *Courier*, Apr. 30, 1938.
103. *Newsweek* XII (May 30, 1938): 8.
104. Keller, "Pennsylvania's Little New Deal," pp. 343–44; Shames, "Lawrence of Pittsburgh," pp. 28–29.
105. Vann to Guffey, Sept. 12, 1938, Vann Papers; Brewer, "Vann," p. 95.
106. Frank Kent, undated article, *Baltimore Sun*, Vann Papers.
107. *Pittsburgh Post-Gazette*, July 16, Aug. 27, 1938; Webber, "Vann," p. 209.
108. Vann to Guffey, Sept. 12, 1938, Vann Papers.
109. Vann to Church, Sept. 17, 1938, Vann Papers.
110. Vann did urge, however, that Philadelphia blacks support the Republican candidacy of Magistrate Edward W. Henry for the United States House of Representatives.
111. Resolution of the CCDO, Oct. 16, 1938, Vann Papers; *Pittsburgh Sun-Telegraph*, Oct. 17, 1938; and interview with Walter C. Rainey, Apr. 21, 1973.
112. Burt Evans and Samuel Botsford, "Pennsylvania After the New Deal," *New Republic* CII (May 6, 1940): 600.
113. Keller, "Pennsylvania's Little New Deal," pp. 347–49, citing *Philadelphia Inquirer*, Oct. 8, 1938.
114. *Pittsburgh Post-Gazette*, Oct. 18, 1938, italics added.
115. According to Mrs. Vann, the Senator had known as early as September 12, because of a letter Vann had written him. Guffey had replied, "I cannot consistently tell you to go ahead, but as your friend and as a friend of the people who have followed me, I am not going to tell you not to do it" (interview with Mrs. Vann, Apr. 6, 1967; Guffey to Vann, Sept. 15, 1938, Vann Papers; and Webber, "Vann," p. 213). Vann repeated the statement on a statewide radio broadcast on November 4, 1938 (*Pittsburgh Post-Gazette*, Nov. 5, 1938).
116. *Pittsburgh Post-Gazette*, Oct. 27, 1938.
117. Although several persons who were interviewed by the author were critical of Robert Vann for various other reasons, no one questioned his honesty. See also Daisy Lampkin to Walter White, Nov. 28, 1938, Personal Correspondence, Box C-109, NAACP Papers.
118. *Pittsburgh Sun-Telegraph*, Oct. 18, 1938.
119. Ibid.; Keller, "Pennsylvania's Little New Deal," p. 360, from Keller's interview

with Edward Noel Jones, Jan. 30, 1959; interview with Mrs. Vann, Apr. 6, 1967; and *Philadelphia Inquirer,* Nov. 5, 1938.

120. Mrs. Miller to Farley, Oct. 28, 1938, "Election Trends . . . Pennsylvania," Official File, Box 106, FDRL.

121. *Courier,* Oct. 22, 1938; telegram, David Henry Simms to Vann, undated, Vann Papers.

122. *Pittsburgh Post-Gazette,* Oct. 27, 1938.

123. Keller, "Pennsylvania's Little New Deal," p. 360, citing the *Washington* (Pa.) *Observer; Pittsburgh Post-Gazette,* Oct. 29, 1938.

124. "So Long Slim," *Courier,* Oct. 29, 1938; interview with Mrs. Vann, Apr. 6, 1967; and interview with Walter C. Rainey, Apr. 21, 1973.

125. Vann to Stone, Oct. 12, 1938, Prattis Papers.

126. Raymond F. Brandt, "How 'Loose-Leaf' Negro Democrat Plays Politics," *St. Louis Post-Dispatch,* Nov. 1, 1938, Vann Papers.

127. *Courier,* Nov. 5, 1938; Keller, "Pennsylvania's Little New Deal," pp. 359–60; and Webber, "Vann," p. 212.

128. "Black Purge," *Time* XXXII (Oct. 31, 1938): 13–14.

129. Vann to Luce, Nov. 3, 1938, Vann Papers.

130. James West to Vann, Nov. 7, 1938, Vann Papers.

131. Webber, "Vann," p. 189, citing undated letter written by Professor Francis Tyson of the University of Pittsburgh after Vann's death.

132. "Black Purge," *Time* XXXII (Oct. 31, 1938): 14; Brandt, "How 'Loose-Leaf' Negro Democrat Plays Politics."

133. *Pittsburgh Press,* Oct. 28, 1938; Webber, "Vann," p. 211.

134. *Pittsburgh Press,* Oct. 28, 1938.

135. *Pittsburgh Post-Gazette,* Nov. 5, 1938.

136. *New York Times,* Nov. 10, 1938. The Republicans jumped from 89 to 170 seats in the House and picked up 8 seats in the Senate; 15 of the sixteen states electing governors went Republican. Only California prevented it from being a clean sweep ("Election Trends and Analysis of Results, Pennsylvania," Official File 300, Box 106, FDRL; Keller, "Pennsylvania's Little New Deal," pp. 362–68; and *Pennsylvania Manual, 1939* [Harrisburg, 1939], pp. 143, 145).

137. Miller, "Negro in Pennsylvania Politics," p. 299; Hobson R. Reynolds to Vann, Nov. 18, 1937, Vann Papers; and Sullivan, "The Negro Vote," p. 477.

138. Miller, "Negro in Pennsylvania Politics," citing Miller's interview with Norris, Feb. 9, 1963. Yet Norris told me that he was just as happy to get the second position because the pay was the same and it was a powerful position. Norris said he preferred security to honors (interview, Nov. 27, 1971).

139. Telegram, David Henry Simms to Vann, Nov. 4, 1938, urging Vann to endorse the entire GOP slate, Vann Papers.

140. *Pennsylvania Manual, 1939,* pp. 153–56, 175; Simmons, "Negro in Recent Pittsburgh Politics," p. 23; and Keller, "Pennsylvania's Little New Deal," p. 363.

141. See Miller, "Negro in Pennsylvania Politics," table XXXVIII, p. 252, pp. 254–65, for ward vote count.

142. "Black Purge," *Time* XXXII (Oct. 31, 1938): 14; G. William McKinney, "The Negro in Pennsylvania Politics," *Opportunity* XVII (Feb. 1939): 50–51.

143. Vann to Raymond P. Brandt, *St. Louis Post-Dispatch* reporter, Nov. 12, 1938, Vann Papers.

144. Interview with Mrs. Vann, Apr. 6, 1967.
145. Typewritten manuscript, Dec. 12, 1938, Vann to C. H. Galloway, Kansas City, Nov. 14, 1938, both in Vann Papers.
146. *Courier*, Dec. 17, 1938.
147. *Pittsburgh Sun-Telegraph*, Dec. 29, 1938.
148. Vann to Rainey, Feb. 6, 1939; Hobson Reynolds to Vann, Jan. 12, 1939; Vann to Emmett J. Scott, Jan. 1, 1940; *Beaver Falls* (Pa.) *Tribune*, Dec. 20, 1938; all in Vann Papers.
149. Miller, "Negro in Pennsylvania Politics," p. 290.
150. Evans and Botsford, "Pennsylvania After the New Deal," p. 600.

Chapter 12. Twilight: 1938–1940

1. *The Evening News* (Newburgh, N.Y.), Oct. 21, 1969, Hamilton Fish Papers, in Fish's possession, New York City; Maxine Block, ed., *Current Biography, 1941* (New York, 1942), pp. 278–80; and Clifford P. Reynolds, comp., *Biographical Directory of the American Congress, 1774–1961* (Washington, D.C., 1961), p. 889.
2. Vann to Benjamin J. Davis, May 26, 1926, Vann Papers; Richard J. Stillman III, *Integration of the Negro in the United States Armed Forces* (New York, 1968), p. 14; and Emmett J. Scott, *Scott's Official History of The American Negro in the World War* (New York, 1919), pp. 75–82.
3. See pp. 215–16 of this work.
4. Vann to Fish, Mar. 3, 1927, Vann Papers; *Congressional Record, Senate*, Feb. 28, 1927, p. 5050. See p. 216 of this work for Vann's revenge on Reed in the 1934 senatorial election.
5. *Courier*, May 12, June 9, Aug. 25, 1934; "Organization of Colored Troops (National Defense, January 1, 1935)," memorandum in Vann Papers. For definitive background on the black man's military status between the wars, see Ulysses Lee, *The Employment of Negro Troops: United States Army in World War II, Special Studies* (Washington, D.C., 1966), passim; Richard Dalfiume, "The 'Forgotten Years' of the Negro Revolution," *Journal of American History* LV (June 1968): 90–106; and Lee Nichols, *Breakthrough on the Color Front* (New York, 1959), pp. 26–29.
6. *Courier*, July 16, 1938; John Hope Franklin, *From Slavery to Freedom: A History of Negro Americans* (New York, 1947), p. 576.
7. *Courier*, Oct. 5 and 12, 1940; Walter White, "It's Our Country Too," *Saturday Evening Post* CCXIII (Dec. 14, 1940): 27.
8. *Courier*, Mar. 30, Apr. 13, June 8, 1935; *History of House Bills and Resolutions, Session of 1935* (Harrisburg, 1936), Jan. 15–May 29, 1935, House Bill #88.
9. *History of House Bills, 1931 Session,* (Harrisburg, 1932) June 26, 1931; *Legislative Journal, 1931,* (Harrisburg, 1932) p. 107.
10. Vann to Rep. Charles I. Faddis, Mar. 7, 1939, Vann to Colonel A. W. Little, Feb. 23, 1938, Vann Papers.
11. The all-black 92nd Division fought under American command, and elements of one regiment, the 368th, became demoralized and fled from the Germans during five days in the Meuse-Argonne offensive beginning September 26, 1918 (Nichols, *Breakthrough on the Color Front*, p. 32; Eli Ginzberg, *The Negro Potential* [New York,

1956], p. 63; and David G. Mandelbaum, *Soldier Groups and Negro Soldiers* [Berkeley, 1952], p. 97).

12. *Courier*, Apr. 23, 1938; Roi Ottley, *New World A-Coming: Inside Black America* (Boston, 1943), p. 268; Walter Wilson, "Old Jim Crow in Uniform," *The Crisis* XL (Mar. 1939): 71–73; and Stillman, *Integration of the Negro in the United States Armed Forces*, p. 5.

13. *Courier*, Feb. 19, 1938.

14. Ibid.; see also issue of Mar. 26, 1938; Lee, *Employment of Negro Troops*, pp. 52–53.

15. Interview with P. L. Prattis, Aug. 16, 1967.

16. See *Courier*, Mar. 19, 1938, for full text of letter; ibid., Mar.–Apr. 1938, passim. See also Mayor Edward Kelly, Chicago, to Vann, Mar. 21, 1938; A. D. Anderson, president of Antioch College, to Vann, Mar. 9, 1938; William A. Shawcross, chairman of the State Democratic Committee of Rhode Island, to Vann, Mar. 15, 1938; all in Vann Papers.

17. Graves to Vann, Mar. 7, 1938, Vann Papers.

18. John Fremmar to Vann, Mar. 18, 1938, Vann Papers.

19. M. J. Rubin, editor of Charleston, S.C., *Evening Post*, to Vann, undated; John G. Green, managing editor of the *Portsmouth* (Ohio) *Times*, to Vann, Mar. 7, 1938; William Green, president, AFL, to Vann, Mar. 12, 1938; all in Vann Papers.

20. Vann to U.S. Senator Sherman Minton of Indiana, a member of the Military Affairs Committee, Mar. 14, 1938, Vann Papers. Vann hoped to get him to sponsor a bill for a Negro division.

21. Vann to Dr. L. L. Crawford, president of the University of Hawaii, Apr. 4, 1938, Vann Papers.

22. Vann had always wanted very much to see blacks accepted to the military academies, and when Congressman Oscar DePriest of Chicago's First District was successful in getting Alonzo S. Parham of Chicago appointed to West Point in 1929, Vann viewed it as a triumph. Then Parham failed math the following year and was forced to leave. Vann had some acid comment to make in his weekly column, "The Camera":

> Get this one. The other day our daily papers carried the report that the only colored boy at West Point had failed to pass one of his subjects—mathematics. The NEWS was heralded the world over. A Negro has failed. What a glorious piece of news was that! But if you read the whole story, you found that several white boys had also failed—some 50 of them. Their failure was not NEWS. They had a right to fail, we imagine. At least, white boys are supposed to fail at West Point. But the lone colored boy, subjected to every conceivable disadvantage known to the Nordic customs [sic], he had no business failing. His failure was NEWS for the world. We are wondering what kind of democracy this country had in mind when its press deliberately emphasizes the failure of a boy because he is colored, and accepts the failure of 50 white men as a matter of doubt. Great stuff, this. We venture the suggestion that if that colored boy had passed with an average of 99 per cent the world would never have heard about it. The names of the white boys were not mentioned. Shame on those Nordics! (*Courier*, Jan. 1, 1930).

And a *Courier* editorial some weeks later was also devoted to the subject. "Now that the young man [Parham] is out, all is cordial and contented on the Hudson. Nothing is said about Parham having failed in mathematics because he was kept 'walking the line' during his study period, but there have been rumors to that effect. He will, it is said, along with 45 other cadets, have an opportunity in March to take a reexamination" (Jan. 25, 1930).

23. Interview with Fish, Nov. 3, 1971; *Congressional Record: Appendix of the Third Session of the Seventy-Fifth Congress, April 5, 1938*, p. 1870; *Congressional Record: . . . June 21, 1939*, p. 7649; *Courier*, Apr. 16, 1938; and Vann to Schuyler, Mar. 30, 1938, Vann Papers.

24. *Courier*, Apr. 16, 1938.

25. Ibid., Apr. 30, 1938; Prattis, "Negro Press in Action," manuscript, Prattis Papers.

26. White to Vann, Jan. 16, 1939, and Louis Lautier to Vann, Jan. 18, 1939, Vann Papers.

27. White to Wilkins, Apr. 25, 1938, Administration Files, "Military, Fish Army Bill, 1938–1939," Box C-376, NAACP Papers, Library of Congress.

28. Wilkins to White, Apr. 26, 1938, Box C-376, NAACP Papers.

29. White to "The Editor," June 11, 1938, Box C-376, NAACP Papers.

30. Houston to Marshall, Apr. 24, 1940, which Houston forwarded to reporter Lautier to send on to Vann as encouragement for his cause; Lautier to Vann, Apr. 25, 1940. On 1917 segregated camp see Box C-376, NAACP Papers; Walter White, *A Man Called White: The Autobiography of Walter White* (New York, 1948), pp. 186–90.

31. At this time Vann and White were having a similar conflict over procedure in pressing for an anti-lynch bill. In January 1937, though Vann regarded an anti-lynch law as high priority in Roosevelt's second administration, he cautioned blacks not to expect much favorable legislation from the Seventy-Fifth Congress (Robert L. Vann, "What Should We Expect of the National Administration," *Opportunity* XV [Jan. 1937]: 14–16; "Chronology of Anti-Lynch Fight, 75th Congress, 1937–1938," typewritten manuscript, Vann Papers). One was proposed, which became the Gavagan–Wagner–Van Nuys bill. The battle for it had dragged on for almost a year and a half before it went down to defeat. White was very committed to his crusade for such a bill, and in the spring of 1938 he asked Vann to serve on a committee which would attempt to pressure FDR on the matter. Vann refused, saying White was being unrealistic in making such an attempt at that time. "If you consider how much trouble the President is having with his own bills, and if you will take the time to analyze the reason, you will know that the present session is in no temperament to handle any legislation which may in the least jeopardize the election of any or all of the Senators and Congressmen who must go before the electorate this year. Now you are not a child, so what's the use of making yourself ridiculous?" (Vann to White, Apr. 4, 1938, Vann Papers).

32. *Courier*, Oct. 6, Nov. 5, 1938.

33. Ibid., Dec. 10, 1938. According to Richard Dalfiume, Roosevelt's general reluctance to press the issue of racial justice was evident again during World War II. When asked by Edwin R. Embree of the Julius Rosenwald Fund to form a commission of experts on race relations to advise him on steps to improve conditions, the president replied that race relations was one of the reform areas which had to be sacrificed for the present in order to prosecute the war. FDR reasoned that "there is a danger of such long-range planning becoming projects of wide influence in escape from the realities of the war. I am not convinced that we can be realists about the war and planners for the future at this critical time" ("The 'Forgotten Years' of the Negro

Revolution," pp. 104–05, citing Roosevelt to Embree, Mar. 16, 1942, in answer to Embree, Feb. 3, 1942, OF 93, Roosevelt Papers).

34. Interview with Fish, Nov. 3, 1971; Fish to Vann, Dec. 23, 1938, Vann Papers; and *Courier*, Feb. 4, 1939.

35. Interview with Fish, Nov. 3, 1971. See also White to Dr. Louis T. Wright, Dec. 22, 1938; White to Fish, Dec. 22, 1938; Fish to White, Dec. 20 and 24, 1938; all in Box C-377, NAACP Papers.

36. White to Houston, Dec. 16, 1938, Box C-516, NAACP Papers.

37. White to Vann, Feb. 5, 1939, Vann Papers.

38. Memorandum, Marshall to White, Feb. 2, 1939, Administration Files, Box C-377, NAACP Papers.

39. *Congressional Record Index: History of Bills and Resolutions, 1938–1939* shows they did not make the House floor. *Courier*, Feb. 4, 1939; Vann to Congressman Charles I. Faddis, Mar. 7, 1939; and Wilson, "Old Jim Crow in Uniform," p. 43.

40. Vann to FDR, Jan. 19, 1939, Vann Papers; Richard M. Dalfiume, *Fighting on Two Fronts: Desegregation of the Armed Forces, 1939–1953* (Columbia, Mo., 1969), p. 26.

41. Dalfiume, "The 'Forgotten Years' of the Negro Revolution," p. 93, citing *Courier*, Sept. 9, 1939; telephone interview with Rayford Logan, Oct. 29, 1969; interview with P. L. Prattis, Aug. 16, 1967; Herbert Garfinkel, *When Negroes March: The March on Washington Movement in the Organizational Politics for FEPC* (Glencoe, Ill., 1959), p. 33; Wilson, "Old Jim Crow in Uniform," pp. 71–73; and White, "It's Our Country Too," pp. 27, 61, 63, 66, 68.

42. Lee, *Employment of Negro Troops*, pp. 52–53.

43. Dalfiume, "The 'Forgotten Years' of the Negro Revolution," p. 28; Harvard Sitkoff, "Racial Military and Interracial Violence in the Second World War," *Journal of American History* LVIII (Dec. 1971): 664.

44. Vann to Senator Elmer Thomas, May 6, 1940, and all others on Military Appropriations Committee; Houston to Vann, June 11, 1940; Mehlinger to Vann, June 15, 1940; and Lautier to Vann, June 15, 1940, Vann Papers.

45. *Courier*, Aug. 3 and 26, 1940.

46. Dalfiume, *Fighting on Two Fronts*, pp. 30–31.

47. Ibid., p. 31; *Courier*, June 22 and 29, 1940; and Lee, *Employment of Negro Troops*, pp. 68–69.

48. "Democrats and New Dealers Vote Against First Amendment Preventing Discrimination Against Negro Draftees," extension of remarks by Hon. Hamilton Fish of New York in House of Representatives, Sept. 24, 1940, Fish Papers.

49. *Courier*, Sept. 28, 1940.

50. Ibid., Nov. 2, 1940; Percival Prattis, "Negro Press in Action," manuscript, Prattis Papers. Unfortunately, the first major breakthrough for blacks in the military did not come until 1948, with President Truman's Executive Order 9981, which required equal opportunity in the armed forces regardless of race. Actual full-scale integration took place during the Korean conflict. One historian called the 1930s, when Vann was crusading for racial military equality, "the forgotten years." During that time, however, there was an awakening of racial consciousness and a desire to destroy the old military practices. Then the war crisis provided American Negroes with the opportunity to point out for all to see the difference between the American creed and practice (Dalfiume, "The 'Forgotten Years' of the Negro Revolution," pp. 90–106).

51. Dalfiume, *Fighting on Two Fronts*, p. 36.
52. Ibid., pp. 37–42; Sitkoff, "Racial Military and Interracial Violence," p. 664.
53. Sitkoff, "Racial Military and Interracial Violence," p. 664; *Courier*, Nov. 2, 1940.
54. Vann to Charles A. Barnett, Apr. 6, 1939, Vann Papers.
55. Vann to C. A. Franklin; Carter W. Wesley, general manager of the *Houston Informer*, to Vann, May 11, 1939; both in Vann Papers.
56. Vishnu V. Oak, *The Negro Newspapers* (Yellow Springs, Ohio, 1948), pp. 114–15.
57. Young to Vann, June 16, 1939, Vann Papers.
58. Vann to Franklin, May 29, June 3, 1939, Vann Papers.
59. Interview with Prattis, May 20, 1968; Carter W. Wesley to Vann, May 24, 1939, Vann Papers.
60. By 1948 the Interstate United Newspaper Company, begun by Vann in 1939 and managed by his colleague, Ira Lewis, after his death, had become the largest representative of black publishers in the advertising field, with 135 periodicals as clients. These included, besides the *Courier*, the New York *Amsterdam News*, *The Call* (Kansas City), and the Scott Newspaper Syndicate. Its major advertisers were Coca Cola, Royal Crown Cola, General Motors, Ford, Chrysler, General Baking, American Sugar Refineries, Safeway Stores, Atlantic and Pacific Tea Company, and Pabst Brewing Company (Oak, *Negro Newspapers*, pp. 115–16).
61. Sengstacke to Vann, May 7, 1940, Vann Papers. See also Maxwell R. Brooks, *The Negro Press Reexamined: Political Content of Leading Negro Newspapers* (Boston, 1959), p. 83; Oak, *Negro Newspapers*, p. 107.
62. John Syrjamaki, "The Negro Press in 1939," *Sociology and Social Research* (Sept.–Oct. 1939): 48. Unlike the other services, Calvin's was individually owned. It was founded in 1935 by Floyd Calvin, who had been a feature writer and editor of the *Courier*. Upon his death in 1939, his widow, Mrs. Willa Lee Calvin, took over the business, which included theatricals, sports, general news, editorials, labor news, photographs, and several syndicated columns (W. H. Hollins, "The Negro Press in America: A Content Analysis of Five Newspapers" [master's thesis, University of Minnesota, 1945], pp. 32–33).
63. Interview taped by Henry LaBrie with Sengstacke, June 23 and 24, 1972.
64. James H. Greene, executive vice president of the Pittsburgh Chamber of Commerce, to Vann, Dec. 20, 1939, Vann Papers; *Norfolk Journal and Guide*, Jan. 20, 1940. For congratulatory correspondence to Vann from the black community, see 1935–1940 Vann Scrapbook.
65. Vann to A. L. Humphrey, Chamber of Commerce, Jan. 29, 1926, Vann Papers.
66. *Courier*, Nov. 2, 1940; Vann to Emmett J. Scott, Mar. 10, 1940, Vann Papers.
67. Vann to Schuyler, Mar. 31, 1938, Vann Papers; *Columbus* (Ohio) *Advocate*, Nov. 2, 1940, in 1940 Scrapbook: Clippings on Death, Vann Papers.
68. Vann to E. Louis Moore, an Indianapolis attorney who was Sergeant-at-Arms at the Democratic National Convention in Chicago, July 8, 1940, Vann Papers.
69. The full section regarding blacks read, "Our Negro citizens have participated actively in the economic and social advances by this administration, including fair labor standards, social security benefits, health protection, work relief projects, decent housing, aid to education, and the rehabilitation of low-income-farm families. We have aided more than a half of a million Negro youth in vocational training, education and employment. We shall strive for complete legislative safeguards against discrimination in government service and benefits in the national defense forces. We pledge

to uphold due process and equal protection of the laws for every citizen, regardless of race, creed or color." See also Henry L. Moon, *Balance of Power: The Negro Vote* (New York, 1948), p. 31.

70. Vann to Mrs. Bethune, Jan. 11, 1939, Vann Papers. Judging from Vann's correspondence with Mrs. Bethune, they were good friends. Both were of the "old school," and had made their way up from poverty. Vann, who became a trustee of Bethune-Cookman College in 1937, generously donated money to the school, gifts such as $500 in cash and $165 for the purchase of a mule to do farm work at the college. He also sent $10 a week to Mrs. Bethune in Washington for personal spending money. Mrs. Bethune replied gratefully, "I do feel so rich every week. I have my own $10 to get what I want. I have been getting new dresses and having my hats fixed. I have new shoes and I feel that I can have what I want. I have $10 every week of my own and do not have to share it with anybody. You have made me so independent that I can at least have $10 I can call my very own. This independence came at a very strategic time—not a minute too early. Blessings on you, my friend" (Mrs. Bethune to Vann, Apr. 23, 1937; see also Mrs. Bethune to Vann, June 11, Oct. 13, 1937, Vann Papers).

71. *Courier*, July–Nov. 1940, passim; see also Lawrence Sullivan, "The Negro Vote," *Atlantic Monthly* CLXVI (Oct. 1940): 477–84; James E. Allen, "The Negro in the 1940 Presidential Election" (master's thesis, Howard University, 1955), pp. 97–122; Allan Morrison, "The Secret Papers of FDR," *Negro Digest* IX (Jan. 1951): 74–75; Moon, *Balance of Power*, p. 239; Ralph Bunche, "Report on the Needs of the Negro for the Republican Program Committee," unpublished manuscript, July 1, 1939, Schomburg Collection, New York Public Library; and Samuel Krislov, *The Negro in Federal Employment: The Quest for Equal Opportunity* (Minneapolis, 1967), pp. 24–25.

72. *Courier*, July 6, 1940; *New York Times*, June 27, 1940.

73. *Courier*, July 6, 1940; Dalfiume, *Fighting on Two Fronts*, p. 34.

74. Vann to Carter W. Wesley, Houston, July 8, 1940, Vann Papers.

75. Ibid.

76. Vann to Farley, July 22, 1940, Vann Papers.

77. Thirty-page typewritten manuscript endorsing Willkie, Aug. 24, 1940, Vann Papers. Apparently either Mrs. Vann or Ira Lewis entitled it "Last Public Utterance" after Vann's death. See also Webber, "Vann," p. 225. While Vann praised Willkie's speech, black Democrats charged that the Republican candidate was a racist. They argued that Willkie, a public utilities magnate who opposed the TVA, never hired blacks, but they centered their attack around the history of Elwood, Willkie's home town. His father was one of its leading citizens and helped to shape its policies, which included the exclusion of blacks from residence. In carrying out this policy, signs were conspicuously displayed reading, "Nigger, don't let the sun go down on you" (*New York Times*, Oct. 12, 1940; *Norfolk Journal and Guide*, Oct. 19 and 26, 1940).

78. Vann to William P. O'Malley, deputy collector, Internal Revenue Service, Pittsburgh, Apr. 30, May 12, June 15, 1937, Vann Papers.

79. Vann to Julian Rainey, Feb. 6, 1939, Vann Papers.

80. Vann to Guffey, Mar. 11, 1937, Vann to Judge Stephen Stone, 1938, for salary figures, Charles F. Miller, secretary-engineer of Board of Adjustment, to Vann, Oct. 23, 1939, all in Vann Papers; interview with Prattis, May 20, 1968.

81. Vann to FDR, Jan. 11, 1938, and Vann to Guffey, Nov. 15, 1937, Vann Papers.

82. FDR to Vann, Jan. 27, 1938, and Herbert E. Gaston, assistant to the secretary

of the treasury, to Vann, Feb. 11, 1938, Vann Papers.

83. The states included were Illinois, Indiana, Michigan, Missouri, New York, Ohio, and Pennsylvania (Allen, "Negro in 1940 Presidential Election," appendix, table VI; Moon, *Balance of Power*, p. 239; and Sullivan, "Negro Vote," p. 478).

84. U.S. Bureau of the Census, *Sixteenth Census of the United States*, 1940 series, 10, no. 1; Allen, "Negro in 1940 Presidential Election," p. 21.

85. Dalfiume, "The 'Forgotten Years' of the Negro Revolution," p. 35.

86. Ibid., citing *Baltimore Afro-American*, Aug. 31, 1940.

87. *Baltimore Afro-American*, Oct. 19, 1940; "Negro Editors Line Up," *Time* XXXVI (Oct. 21, 1940): 48.

88. *Courier*, Nov. 2, 1940. Vann's death did not receive as much coverage as might have been expected throughout the rest of the black press due to the death that same week of the Reverend L. K. Williams, pastor of the huge Olivet Church in Chicago and president of the National Negro Baptist Convention, who was killed in an airplane crash on October 29. Williams was one of the nation's leading black churchmen. He also headed an insurance company and was a prominent figure in the Republican party (*Chicago Defender*, Nov. 9, 1940; Richard Bardolph, *The Negro Vanguard* [New York, 1961], pp. 141–43).

89. *Courier*, Nov. 2, 1940.

90. Ibid.

91. Bruce M. Stave, "Pittsburgh and the New Deal" (unpublished manuscript), p. 15a; Miller, "The Negro in Pennsylvania Politics, with Special Reference to Philadelphia Since 1932" (doctoral dissertation, University of Pennsylvania, 1945), pp. 240, 261–62, 264; and Allen, "Negro in 1940 Presidential Election," pp. 20–22, pp. 17–27 for similar examples of black majorities in Chicago, St. Louis, and New York.

92. Allen, "Negro in 1940 Presidential Election," p. 22.

93. Mrs. Mabel V. Johnson to Buni, Feb. 3, 1969.

94. Ira Lewis to Mark O'Dea, director of public relations, United States Maritime Commission, Washington, D.C., Mar. 21, 1943, courtesy of Mrs. Mabel V. Johnson. Lewis successfully petitioned the Maritime Commission to name the merchant vessel after Vann.

Epilogue

1. P. L. Prattis, biography of Mrs. Vann for "This Is Your Life"; William Nunn, Sr., "The Pittsburgh Courier Story. 50th Anniversary, 1910–1960," Vann Papers; Mrs. Mabel Page Johnson to Buni, Feb. 3, 1968.

2. Henry LaBrie, "Robert Lee Vann and the Editorial Page of the *Pittsburgh Courier*" (master's thesis, University of West Virginia, 1970), p. 37, citing *Courier*, Oct. 15, 1940. See also Frank Mott, *American Journalism* (New York, 1962), p. 794.

3. LaBrie, "Vann," p. 37, citing *Courier*, Jan. 23, 1960.

4. LaBrie, "Vann," p. 42, citing interview with Prattis, Oct. 8, 1969.

5. LaBrie, "Vann," p.42.

6. LaBrie, "Vann," p. 44, citing *Courier*, Jan. 23, 1960.

7. LaBrie, "Vann," pp. 42,45.

8. Ibid., pp. 45–46, citing "Victim of Negro Progress," *Newsweek* (Aug. 26, 1963), p. 50.

9. LaBrie, "Vann," p. 47; interview taped by LaBrie with Sengstacke, June 23 and 24, 1972.

A Bibliographic Note on Unpublished Sources

ALL SOURCES USED in writing this book are cited fully in the notes, often accompanied by evaluative and explanatory material. However, for the convenience of the reader, the unpublished sources that the author found most useful are listed below:

Robert Vann's papers, assembled by Vann and his wife, were made available to the author by Mrs. Vann. Upon the completion of this biography, they were placed in the Carnegie Library, Pittsburgh, Pennsylvania. When Mrs. Vann died, her papers, including all of her husband's letters to her, were destroyed.

The papers of Percival L. Prattis, in Mr. Prattis's ownership in Pittsburgh, are also a valuable source, especially on the Urban League of Pittsburgh. The papers of that group, located at its offices in Pittsburgh, are also useful.

Several collections of papers at the Library of Congress are of great value. The NAACP Papers are useful for the years 1925 to 1940, especially regarding the Houston affair, the Garland affair, the Self-Respect Program, the anti-lynching movement, and the armed services controversy. The Booker T. Washington Papers are of some use for material concerning the period from 1900 to 1910. Information concerning the Pennsylvania gubernatorial election of 1930 is contained in the Gifford Pinchot Papers. Also helpful are the Arthur B. Spingarn Papers.

Vann's role in the Roosevelt administration is documented by material from the "Minutes of the Inter-Departmental Group Concerned with the Special Problem of Negroes," located in the National Archives, RG 48, Washington, D.C. The Franklin D. Roosevelt Papers, at the Presidential Library in Hyde Park, New York, are particularly valuable for the folders of election information filed by year and state. The Joseph F. Guffey Papers, at Washington and Jefferson College, Washington, Pennsylvania, proved disappointing, as the forty diaries contained mainly appointment notes and little else of substance. Similarly, his correspondence was disappointing. Other

A Bibliographic Note on Unpublished Sources

paper collections used were the Hamilton Fish Papers, in Mr. Fish's possession in New York City; the papers of Mrs. Emma Guffey Miller, in her possession at Slippery Rock, Pennsylvania; and the Emmett J. Scott Papers, at Soper Library, Morgan State College, Baltimore, Maryland.

A great number of unpublished master's theses and doctoral dissertations were used in writing this book. Many of them were written at the University of Pittsburgh, which during the mid-1920s and 1930s was especially strong in research on blacks in Pittsburgh. The following are of special interest:

Astorino, Samuel John, "The Decline of the Republican Dynasty in Pennsylvania, 1929–1934" (doctoral dissertation, University of Pittsburgh, 1962).

Brewer, James H., "Robert Lee Vann and the *Pittsburgh Courier*" (master's thesis, University of Pittsburgh, 1941).

Halt, Charles Eugene, "Joseph F. Guffey, New Deal Politician from Pennsylvania" (doctoral dissertation, Syracuse University, 1965).

Keller, Richard C., "Pennsylvania's Little New Deal" (doctoral dissertation, Columbia University, 1960).

Kifer, Allen Francis, "The Negro Under the New Deal" (doctoral dissertation, University of Wisconsin, 1961).

LaBrie, Henry G., III, "Robert Lee Vann and the Editorial Page of the *Pittsburgh Courier*" (master's thesis, University of West Virginia, 1970).

Miller, James E., "The Negro in Pennsylvania Politics, with Special Reference to Philadelphia Since 1932" (doctoral dissertation, University of Pennsylvania, 1945).

Motz, Jane R., "The Black Cabinet: Negroes in the Administration of Franklin Delano Roosevelt" (master's thesis, University of Delaware, 1964).

Shames, Sally O., "David L. Lawrence, Mayor of Pittsburgh: Development of a Political Leader" (doctoral dissertation, University of Pittsburgh, 1958).

Simmons, Ruth L., "The Negro in Recent Pittsburgh Politics" (master's thesis, University of Pittsburgh, 1945).

Thrasher, Eugene C., "The Magee-Flinn Political Machine, 1895–1903" (master's thesis, University of Pittsburgh, 1951).

Finally, two useful unpublished manuscripts are available for study:

Webber, Harry, "Vann of Pittsburgh, or the Third Emancipation," Pennsylvania Division, Carnegie Library, Pittsburgh, Pennsylvania.

Wright, J. Ernest, "The Negro in Pittsburgh," 1940, Pennsylvania State Library, Harrisburg.

Index

Abbott, Robert, 314, 315; divorce, 379n29
Abyssinia. *See* Ethiopia
Advertising, 49–51, 53, 118; *Courier* firm in, 313–14; H. B. Crohn Company and, 224; national, 134–35; paucity of, in black press, 44; of Van Vechten's book, 150; William B. Ziff Company and, 134, 223, 313, 314
African Methodist Episcopal Church: Brown Chapel, 32
Agriculture: discriminatory practices in, 210–11
Ahoskie, North Carolina, 3
Ahoskie Colored School, 9
Alexander, Elliot C., 117
Allegheny County Colored Democratic Organization, 297; support of James's gubernatorial candidacy, 290–91, 293
Allegheny County Colored Protective League, 95
Allen, Clarence D., 131
Amalgamated Association of Iron, Steel and Tin Workers: blacks in, 25
American Dream, 12–13, 113, 114
American Federation of Labor (AFL), 210; influence on Pennsylvania Democratic party, 279; 1919–20 strike against steel industry, 109; opposition to Parker, 197
"Amos 'n Andy" radio show, 227–28; *Courier*'s treatment of, 228–30
Anderson, Roy, 356n75
Anti-lynch legislation, 267–68; Vann's crusade for, 104; White's crusade for, 394n31
Armed forces: treatment of blacks in, 156–57, 395n50; Vann's fight for black rights in, 299, 300, 302–13, 316, 317–18
Askew, "Captain" David, 8
Askew, John O., 4, 5
Askew, Mary, 6
Associated Negro Press, 52, 145, 315
Associated Weekly Publishers of Allegheny County, 262
Attorneys: black, in Pittsburgh, 40
Audit Bureau of Circulation, 134
Austin, J. C., 121
Avery College Trade School, 28

Babcock, Edward Vose, 123; in Kirker murder case, 130, 131; mayoral candidacy of, 95–99
Barber, J. Max, 15, 330n50; influence on Vann, 36; support of Roosevelt, 193
Bar Harbor, Maine, 33
Barrow, Joe Louis. *See* Louis, Joe
Baseball: discriminatory practices in, 249, 251
Beaver County deportation case, 199–200; Schnader's lack of action in, 215
Benedum, Michael L., 201, 272; financial support of *Courier* from, 172–73; Vann's defection to Democratic party and, 190–91
Bethune, Mary McLeod, 207, 317, 397n70
Black, Hugo, 285
Black, Julian, 252
Black business, 25–26; banks, 120–22; DuBois's views on, 262; Vann's views on, 63, 114–16
Black Cabinet, 206–07
Black crime: legal defense and, 40–41; newspaper coverage of, 45; in Pennsylvania, 344n80; in Pittsburgh, 62, 73–74,

• 401 •

344n80; police treatment and, 74–75; white attitudes toward, 48
Black education: college-level, 30, 31, 36; inadequacy of, 9–10; in Pittsburgh, 28, 67; in South, 10; Vann's views on, 67
Black employment: on Boulder Dam construction, 195, 210; among educated, 19; effect of World War I on, 71–72; in journalism, 135; in public office, 125–28; in PWA, 209; as strikebreakers, 25, 69, 70–71, 109, 173; in U.S. Army, 102; in WPA, 217, 269. *See also* Black patronage
—in Pittsburgh, 24–26, 68–73, 344n72; on city payroll, 92–93; during Depression, 188; in teaching, 67–68
Black housing: black banks and, 121; in Pittsburgh, 23, 27–28, 61–63
Black patronage, 94, 203, 204–05, 216; Guffey's promise of, 281; Guffey-Vann conflict and, 292, 293; from James, 298; Lawrence and, 289–90; in Pennsylvania, 216, 217, 278; in Pittsburgh, 93, 99, 216; resentment of Vann's control of, 266; under Roosevelt, 203, 204–05, 269, 313; for Vann under Hoover, 368n39
Black press: advertising representatives for, 313–14; defection to Democratic party, 179; early failures of, 44–45; effect of Depression on, 227; in Garland Fund controversy, 159–60; growth of, 135; news agencies and, 51–52; in Pennsylvania, 45; position on communism, 237; position on 1919–20 steel strike, 109; position on Roosevelt, 270, 321; reluctance to submit to circulation audit, 134; response to Defense Fund drive, 241; responsibility for race riots, 106–07; sensationalism in, 52–53, 146, 358n81; support of Coolidge, 177; support of Landon, 271; unionization of porters and, 162–63; wages in, 137; war correspondents of, 103–04, 246. *See also* specific newspapers
Blacks: in Fusionist alliance, 16; population in Pennsylvania cities, 333n18; Southern position of, in 1903, 16–18
—in Pittsburgh, 22–23; efforts toward political unity, 128–29; middle-class, 32; political powerlessness of, 125, 126–27; population, 22, 23, 62, 97, 124, 128, 173, 342n28, 356n65; racial organizations and, 60

Black Star Steamship Line, 231, 234
Black vote: *Courier*'s readers urged to use, 84–85, 87–88; flexibility of, 290, 298; importance of, 278–79; in Pittsburgh, 92, 275; selling of, 88; Vann's influence over, 97, 98–99, 177, 192, 193–94. *See also* Disfranchisement
Boothe, A. C., 9
Boston, Massachusetts, 11–12
Boulder Dam: black employment on, 195, 210
Boule. *See* Sigma Pi Phi
Boycott: as method to end discrimination, 82, 83
Braddock, Jimmy, 254; defeat by Louis, 255
Brotherhood of Sleeping Car Porters, 364n137; attempt to organize, 161–71
Brown, Calvin S., 10, 13, 117
Brown, Homer S., 200, 214, 336n90, 356n75
Brown, Samuel, 193
Brown Bomber. *See* Louis, Joe
Brown Chapel AME Church, 56
Bruce, Herbert, 266
Brumbaugh, Martin G., 84
Bryce, Tileston T., 110
Buchanan, Walter S., 33–34; financial help for Vann from, 118–19
Building trades: black employment in, 68–69
Business: *Courier*'s coverage of, 114–15, 142–43. *See also* Black business

Calvin, Floyd J., 140, 205
Camp Vann: discriminatory practices at, 269–70
Car: as success symbol, 117
Carnegie, Andrew, 21, 27
Carnegie Technical Schools, 30
Carter, Hepburn, 43
Cartoons: in *Courier*, 140
Cash, Thomas: Vann's defense of, 47–48
Cass, Thomas. *See* Cash, Thomas
Chavis, Mattie, 11, 19–20
Chicago Defender: circulation during Depression, 227; in controversy over unionization of porters, 162, 163, 165, 169–70; during Coolidge campaign, 177; Interstate United Newspaper Company and, 314; price increase for, 119

Child labor, 27
Church, Robert, 294
Churches, 26; as instruments of social reform, 55–56; in Pittsburgh, 339n2, 340n6; Schuyler's criticism of, 139
Citizen's Municipal League, 91, 92
Civilian Conservation Corps (CCC): discriminatory practices in, 270
Clark, John C., 141
Coal industry: black employment in, 25, 69
Cocaine: black crime and, 28, 29
Coke: influence on Pittsburgh's industrialization, 21
College: black enrollment in, 30. *See also* Black education
Color castes, 232
Colored Allegheny Political and Civic League, 297–98
Colored Orphans' Home, 26
Colored Protective League of Allegheny County, 125
Committee for Industrial Organization (CIO): *Courier*'s position on, 282; influence on Pennsylvania Democratic party, 279–80
Committee for Participation of Negroes in the National Defense, 310–11
Committee of One Hundred, 103
Communism: influence on black press, 107, Schuyler's criticism of, 139; Scottsboro case and, 235–36; Vann's opinion of, 108, 236–37
Competitor, The, 34; establishment of, 117; failure of, 118–19
Coolidge, Calvin: failure to appoint Vann to federal office, 178; Vann's support of, 176–78
Courant, The: Vann's editorship of, 34
Crime. *See* Black crime
Crisis, The, 107, 118; DuBois's resignation from, 259–60; NAACP branch news in, 239–40
Cummings, Homer, 206

Davis, Benjamin O., 181; promotion to general, 318, 322
Death rate: black, in Pittsburgh, 64–65, 342n38
Debating: Vann's interest in, 34
Democratic party: attitude toward blacks, 179; black delegates to convention of 1936, 264–65; blacks' attitudes toward,
95, 197–98, 297; Colored Advisory Committee in, 192–93; Fusionist defeat by, 16; rejection of Vann, 178–79; Vann's defection to, 174, 187–88, 190–94, 202; Vann's power in, 265–67, 271–72, 275, 276, 279, 295–96
—in Pennsylvania, 90, 266, 271; gain of control in, 212–17; Guffey-Lawrence conflict and, 278–81, 295
—in Pittsburgh, 91–92, 192, 197
Dennis, Thomas, 125–26
Depression, 187; *Courier* and, 207, 222–28, 257; Democratic party and, 192; effect on DuBois's views on integration, 260; effect on Pittsburgh, 188
DePriest, Oscar: *Courier's* coverage of, 183–84; support of Pinchot, 185–86
Dickinson, Blanche Taylor, 141
Disease: in Pittsburgh's black community, 61, 64–65; respiratory, in Pittsburgh, 27
Disfranchisement, 17–18; in Pittsburgh, 213; Republican National Convention resolution concerning, 176–77
DuBois, W. E. B., 204; break with NAACP, 259–61; column in *Courier*, 261–62; conflict with White, 239–40; in Garland Fund controversy, 146–60; Garvey's attack on, 234

Earle, George H., III, 214; election as governor, 213, 214–15, 217; equal rights bill passed under, 217–18, 219; in Guffey-Lawrence conflict, 279, 282; Margiotti's accusations against, 287, 292, 295, 389n93; senatorial candidacy, 279, 280, 282, 289, 297; support of black patronage, 275–76
Economic recovery: under Roosevelt, 269
Education. *See* Black education
Embree, Edwin R., 208–09
Employment. *See* Black employment
Equal rights legislation: passage under Earle, 217–18, 219; Schnader's opposition to, 215; Vann's fight for, 83–85
Ethiopia: *Courier*'s coverage of invasion of, 244–48

Farley, James A., 265, 319; in patronage conflict, 276–77
Fish, Hamilton, 299; bills for equal rights in armed forces and, 305–06, 309–10, 312

Flinn, William, 347n8; employment of blacks by, 93; in Pittsburgh Republican machine, 90–91, 93
Foreman, Clark, 209, 211
Frick, Henry Clay, 21, 25
Frog Week, 141
Fusionists: Democratic defeat of, 16

Garland Fund controversy, 149–61
Garvey, Marcus, 232–33; contribution to *Courier*, 233–34; Ethiopian invasion and, 245; position of *Courier* on, 231–32
Garvey, Mrs. Marcus, 232
Germany: DuBois's trip to, 261; Vann's trip to, 258–59
Ghetto: development in Pittsburgh, 62
Gibson, Josh, 249
Gold Coast: Vann's investment in, 120
Gold Star Mothers: segregation of, 196, 215
Gompers, Samuel, 109
Gordon, Eugene, 146
Great Crash, 173
Greenlee, W. A. "Gus," 129; sports interests of, 249–51
Guffey, Joseph, 191–92, 201, 213, 269, 270, 277–78; conflict with Lawrence, 272, 276, 277–81, 295; control over WPA jobs, 217, 390n97; election to U.S. Senate, 214, 215–16, 217, 323; Reconstruction Finance Corporation and, 226; role in passage of equal rights bill, 218; Vann's appointment as special assistant attorney general and, 198–99; Vann's break with, 297; Vann's defection to Democratic party and, 192; Vann's defection to Republican party and, 292–93
Guthrie, George Wilkins, 91–92, 348n13

Hall, Joseph, 4
Hamilton, Theron B., 269; criticism of Vann, 293–94
Hance, William N., 43
Harding, Warren G.: position on black issues, 175–76, 267; Vann's campaign for, 175
Harleston, Edwin Nathaniel, 42, 45; resignation as editor of *Courier*, 45–46
Harrellsville, North Carolina, 4–6, 9, 11, 330n38
Hart, Samuel B., 301
Hastie, William H., 207

Henry, Edward W., 186, 187
Herbick and Held Company, 171
Herring: importance to Hertford County, 8
Hill District, 23–24; *Courier* column on, 141; crime in, 73–74; housing in, 28, 61–62; Roosevelt's victory in, 271; schools in, 67
Hitler, Adolf: Vann's impressions of, 259
Holloway, Wilburt, 140, 195, 208
Home for Aged and Infirm Colored Women, 26
Homestead Grays, 249, 251
Hoover, Herbert, 178; attempt to win black vote, 195; denial of federal appointment for Vann, 181–82; lack of support in Pennsylvania, 190; treatment of blacks, 195–96; Vann's support of, 179–81
Hospital: attempt to build for blacks, 65–66
Housing: of laborers, 27–28. *See also* Black housing
Houston, Charles, 308–09, 311
Houston, William L., 277
Howard B. Crohn Company: as *Courier*'s advertising representative, 224; *Courier*'s purchase of, 313
Howard, Perry, 162, 181

Ickes, Harold, 209, 211
Illiteracy: as problem of black journalism, 44, 45
Immigrants: Vann's opposition to, 107–08, 109
—in Pittsburgh, 22, 29; employment of, 25; resentment by "OPs," 32; voter registration among, 87
Industrialization of Pittsburgh, 21–22; environmental effects of, 26; labor sources for, 23, 24–25
Infant mortality, 27
Integration: in armed forces, 302, 305; as NAACP's official policy, 260
Inter-Departmental Group Concerned with the Special Problems of Negroes, 208–11
International Labor Defense (ILD): in Scottsboro case, 235–39
Interstate United Newspaper Company, 313–14, 396n60
Italians: Ethiopian invasion by, 244; voter registration among in Pittsburgh, 87

Index • 405

James, Arthur H., 298; gubernatorial candidacy of, 289, 290–94
Jenkinson, A. M., 92
Jews: in clothing business, 143; in Hill District, 24, 28, 334n24
Jim Crowism: influence on Vann's move to North, 16, 18
Johnson, Henry Lincoln, 178
Johnson, James Weldon, 260, 361n66; attempt to remove Vann from Sigma Pi Phi, 161; in Garland Fund controversy, 160–61; Vann's attack on, 146–55
Jones, Charles Alvin, 279–80, 282, 289, 297
Jones, Eugene Kinckle, 15, 207, 209–10; as advisor on Negro affairs in Department of Commerce, 203, 204, 226; as contributor to *Competitor*, 117
Jones, Julia Bumbrey, 141
Jones, Paul F., 274, 281; black patronage and, 217, 269, 273, 274
Journalism: Vann's interest in, 36. See also Black press; White press
Judgeship: Vann's candidacy for, 123–25, 127
Judiciary Reorganization Act, 283

Kaufmann's Department Store: black employment at, 70–71
Kaylor, Emmert, 274
Kennedy, Thomas, 279, 280; Vann's support of, 280–82, 287–89
Kirker, Anna: murder of, 129–30
Kline, Charles H., 127; recognition of blacks by, 128–29; resignation as mayor, 212; Vann's support of, 128–29
Ku Klux Klan: Hugo Black's membership in, 285; in Pennsylvania, 176, 268; in Pittsburgh, 176, 366n9; Smith's position on, 178

Labor unions: blacks in, 24–25, 69, 109–10, 210; in Pennsylvania gubernatorial election, 280–82; suppression of, 27; Vann's stand against, 109–12; Vann's support of, 112. See also American Federation of Labor; Committee for Industrial Organization
Lampkin, Daisy, 51, 147, 242, 339n39; on *Courier* board, 326; financial support of *Courier* from, 172; in NAACP, 59; support of Vann's judgeship candidacy, 125; treatment of, at William Penn Hotel, 83
Lautier, Louis, 145
Lawrence, David, 213, 277–78; conflict with Guffey, 272, 276, 277–81, 295; Margiotti's accusations against, 287; role in passage of equal rights bill, 218; tribute to Vann, 201–02; Vann's conflict with, 273–76, 289–90
Lewis, Ira, 53–54, 325, 326, 339n46; appointment as clerk to sheriff, 99; *Courier* price increase and, 119; *Courier* wages of, 137; criticism of Defense Fund drive, 242; dissatisfaction with Ziff, 223, 224; optimism regarding *Courier*, 226; photographs in *Courier* and, 145; printing plant construction and, 172; as secretary of *Competitor*, 117; as Vann's campaign publicity manager, 124; views on sensationalism, 132
Lewis, John L.: influence on Pennsylvania Democratic party, 279, 280, 288–89
Liberty Loan drives: black support of, 103
Lincoln, Abraham, 193, 194
"Little Hayti," 23
Livingstone Hospital, 65–66
Loendi Club, 32
Logan, Robert, 125, 127
Louis, Joe, 252, 253–55, 257; *Courier*'s coverage of, 248, 251, 254–56
Lynching, 104; in Pennsylvania, 268; in South, 138. See also Anti-lynch legislation

McCormick, Samuel Black, 30
McKinney, Ernest Rice, 335n63
McNair, William M.: black patronage and, 273–74; mayoral victory of, 212–13; resignation as mayor, 274
Magazines: acceptance by blacks, 118
Magee, Christopher Lyman, 90–91, 347n7
Magee, William A., 92–93; mayoral candidacy of, 95–96, 97–99, 123, 126, 127
Malone, James F., 96; black patronage and, 273; defeat by Kline, 128–29; political power of, 127, 128
Margiotti, Charles Joseph: accusations against Earle and Lawrence, 287, 292, 295, 389n93
Marshall, Thurgood, 310
Matthews, Jessie Ellen. See Vann, Jessie Ellen
Medical care: for Pittsburgh's black community, 64–67

406 • Index

Mellon, Andrew, 182
Mencken, H. L., 286
Merguson, R. W., 248
Messenger, The, 118; in controversy over unionization of porters, 162–63, 164, 170; editorial position on *Courier*, 164
Migration: reasons for, 16–19, 173
—to Pittsburgh: effect on crime, 73; employment and, 72; housing shortage caused by, 62; reasons for, 173; Urban League services and, 59–60
Miller, Emma Guffey, 191, 370*n*84
Miller, Kelly, 153–55
Ministers: black, 55–56; dislike of Vann, 266
Mitchell, Arthur W., 265
Moore, T. Mason, 31–32
Moton, Robert R., 157

NAACP (National Association for the Advancement of Colored People), 56; attempt to obtain pardon for Houston rioters, 147; Beaver County deportation case and, 199–200; black rights in armed forces and, 306–11; branch news publication for, 239–40; *Courier*'s aid with Legal Defense Fund of, 239, 240–43; DuBois's resignation from, 260–61; in Garland Fund controversy, 149–60; official policy of integration, 260; opposition to Parker, 197; in Pittsburgh, 56–59; Roosevelt's opinion of, 385*n*22; in Scottsboro case, 235–39; segregation of Gold Star Mothers and, 196; support of Roosevelt, 270; Vann's support of, 57
National Association of Afro-American Steam and Gas Engineers and Skilled Workers, 24
National Equal Rights League, 59
National Negro Business League, 115, 116
National Negro Press Association, 51–52
National Recovery Administration (NRA): attention to black needs, 209–10, 212
Negro Newspaper Publishers Association, 315
New Deal: Vann's support of, 215
Newspapers. *See* Black press; White press; specific newspapers
Norris, J. Austin, 297
North Carolina: Fusionist defeat in, 16–17
Nunn, William, Sr., 145; on *Courier* board,
326; as *Courier* manager, 325; coverage of Joe Louis, 251, 253–55

"Oakmont," 262–63
"Old Pittsburghers," 32
Olympic games: *Courier*'s coverage of, 258
"OPs," 32
Oratory; Vann's collegiate achievements in, 34
Owen, Chandler, 161, 163

Page, Mabel, 38
Page, William N., 38, 40, 43
Paige, Satchel, 250, 251
"Painter's Row," 27
Palmer, A. Mitchell, 106–07, 108
Parker, John J., 196–97
Passing, 6; by Jessie Vann, 38; Vann's attitude toward, 31
Patronage. *See* Black patronage
Penman, Edward, 43
Pennsylvania, Western University of, 29; growth of, 30–31; Vann's attendance at, 19, 29, 34–35, 36–37, 40
Pennsylvania Hotel and Restaurant Association: attempt to recall equal rights bill, 218–19
Pennsylvania National Guard: crusade for black unit in, 300–01
Peoples, Lucy. *See* Simon, Lucy
Pew, Joseph, 294
Philipot, Goff and Company, 122
Photographs: on *Courier* front page, 145
Physicians: black, lack of in Pittsburgh, 65
Pinchot, Gifford: Beaver County deportation case and, 199–200; Democratic leanings of, 190; failure to reward Vann for his support, 186–87; gubernatorial defeat of, 289; position on welfare, 189; Vann's support of, 184–86
Pittsburgh: black population of, 22, 23, 62, 97, 124, 128, 173, 342*n*28, 356*n*65; effect of Depression on, 188; Vann's move to, 19–20. *See also* Hill District
—industrialization of, 21–22; environmental effects of, 26; labor sources for, 23, 24–25
Pittsburgh, University of, 30; black medical students at, 65. *See also* Pennsylvania, Western University of
Pittsburgh American, 120, 126
Pittsburgh Chamber of Commerce: Vann's application to, 122; Vann's in-

Index • 407

vitation to join, 315
Pittsburgh Council of Social Services Among Negroes, 59
Pittsburgh Courier: advertising firm of, 313–14; branch offices of, 171; dedication of, 54; early beginnings of, 42–46; financial struggles of, 49–51, 225–28, 257; price of, 119–20; printing plant built by, 171–73, 222–23; publication of NAACP branch news in, 239–40; quality of, 146; staff of, 43, 45–47, 51, 53–54, 135–46, 326; Vann's concentration on, 133–35, 222; after Vann's death, 325–26; Vann's selection as editor of, 46–47
—circulation of, 138, 142, 147, 171, 221, 240, 326; all-time high in, 325; attempts to increase during Depression, 228–57; *Competitor*'s failure and, 119; controversy over unionization of porters and, 163, 165, 169–70; editorial position and, 89, 112; effect of new printing plant on, 223; Ethiopian coverage and, 246, 247; largest in U.S., 222, 243, 257, 283; price increase and, 119–20; sensationalism and, 132; Vann's refusal of audit of, 134, 224
—status of: in 1914, 54; in 1926, 171; in 1937, 257–58
"*Pittsburgh Courier* Hour," 140
Pittsburgh Crawfords, 249–50, 251
Pittsburgh Press: Beaver County deportation case and, 199; black news in, 45, 75–76
Poetry: of Harleston, 42; Vann's interest in, 42, 329n17; written by Vann, 7
Police: method of dealing with blacks, 74–75
Political organization: Vann's plea for, 87–88
Political reform: blacks' attitudes toward, 94
Politics: influence on Vann's move to North, 16–18; powerlessness of blacks in, 85, 125, 126–27; Vann's interest in, 35; Vann's views on, 126–27
Populists: in Fusionist alliance, 16, 17
Porter, Stephen G., 95
Porters: attempt to organize, 161–71
Posey, Cumberland, Jr., 145, 249
Posey, Cumberland, Sr., 43
Poston, U.S., 139
Prattis, Percival L., 310, 341n22; armed forces controversy and, 303; on *Courier* board, 326; as *Courier* manager, 325
Prejudice: of blacks toward black attorneys, 40–41. *See also* Social discrimination
Press. *See* Black press, White press
Pullman Company: alleged payoff of Vann, 170; resistance of organization of porters, 162

Quay, Matthew S., 90, 91–92

Race riots: of Chicago, 105–06; of East St. Louis, 104; of Houston, 105; reasons for, 106; Vann's reaction to, 104–06, 108; of Wilmington, North Carolina, 17, 331n56
Rainey, Julian D., 265, 367n23; black patronage and, 204–05, 276–77
Rainey, Walter C., 128, 129, 345n81
Randolph, A. Philip: attempt to organize porters, 161–71; Vann's relationship with, 163–71
Red Hill, 11; Vann's life at, 7–8, 11
Reed, David A.: defeat by Guffey, 214, 215–16; monument to black soldiers and, 300
Religion: Vann's attitude toward, 13
Republican party: attitude toward blacks, 193–94; black support of, 17–18, 95, 198; in Fusionist alliance, 16; reluctance to endorse black candidates, 125–26; Vann as delegate to national conventions of, 174, 176–77; Vann as state chairman of blacks in, 123; Vann's allegiance to, 89–90, 92–95; Vann's defection from, 174, 187–88, 190–94, 201–02; Vann's return to, 290–98
—in Pennsylvania, 90, 266, 296–97; lack of unity in, 190; loss of power in, 212–17
—in Pittsburgh, 35, 90, 127; blacks' relationship to machine, 92–93, 94
Reynolds, Hobson, 218, 219
Robinson, William T., 247
Rogers, Joel A., 141, 381n101; as *Courier* correspondent in Ethiopia, 246–48
Roosevelt, Franklin Delano, 208–09, 288; Benedum's support of, 190–91; black support of, 197, 270–71, 323; *Courier*'s criticism of policy toward Ethiopia, 245; effort to maintain party unity, 280; Guffey's support of, 192; local Democratic victories and, 213, 214; opinion of

NAACP, 385n22; policy toward blacks, 211–12, 269, 394n33; position on antilynch legislation, 267–68; position on black rights in armed forces, 306, 309, 312–13, 317–18; Vann's break with, 316–19; Vann's criticism of, 283–85; Vann's support of, 193–98, 265–67
Rosemond, Samuel, 43
ROTC (Reserve Officers' Training Corps): blacks in, 300
Rouzeau, Edgar T., 300
Roxborough, John, 252
Russell, Sylvester, 141

Sams, Earl, 127
Sanhedrin, 153, 154
Sanitation: in Hill District, 61–62, 67
Schmeling, Max, 254–57
Schnader, William A., 200, 213, 215
Schuyler, George, 136, 203, 223; attack on DuBois, 260; on *Courier* staff, 136–40; coverage of labor unions, 282; position on Garvey, 231, 233; salary during Depression, 225; views on communism, 238
Scott, Emmett J., 157
Scottsboro case, 235–36; *Courier*'s position on, 234, 236–39
Scully, Cornelius, 274, 275
Segregation: in armed forces, 306–09; *de facto*, in Hill District, 67; DuBois's views on, 260, 262; of Gold Star Mothers, 196, 215; Vann's views on, 261
Selassie, Haile, 244, 245; *Courier*'s coverage of, 246, 247; gratitude to *Courier*, 244, 248
Self-respect: "Amos 'n Andy" radio show and, 228–30; *Courier* defense fund and, 239, 243
Sengstacke, John H. H., 314–15; purchase of *Courier* by, 326
Sensationalism: in black press, 52–53, 358n81; in *Courier*, 131, 132, 145–46; in white press, 75–77
Sigma Pi Phi, 161, 362n100
Simon, John, 7, 9, 11; Vann's feelings toward, 8
Simon, Lucy (née Peoples), 3–6, 7, 11, 32–33
Simpson, Joshua: influence on Vann, 14–15
Smith, Alfred E., 178, 179, 180, 182
Smith, Bennie, 170

Smith, "Cotton Ed," 265
Smith, Wendell, 145
Social clubs: in Pittsburgh, 26, 32; role in social reform, 60
Social discrimination: in armed forces, 102, 300–02, 306; in baseball, 249, 251; boycott as method to end, 82, 83; effect on clergy, 56; in federal agencies, 269–70; Hoover and, 195–96; legislation against, 83–85; in Pennsylvania hotels and restaurants, 83, 219; suffered by Vanns on cruise, 220–21; against Vann as special assistant attorney general, 205–07. *See also* Segregation
—in Pittsburgh: in housing, 62–64; in medical care, 64–67; by police, 74–75; in public places, 81–83
Socialism: of Randolph, 169
Social reform
—*Courier* crusade for: beginnings, 61; in education, 67–68; in employment, 67–72; in medical care, 65, 66; in newspaper reporting, 76–81; in police treatment, 74–75; in social discrimination, 81–86
—in Pittsburgh: churches as instruments of, 55–56; political and fraternal organizations in, 60; racial organizations in, 56–60
Social welfare agencies: black, 26
Spingarn, Arthur, 240
Spingarn, Joel, 57, 240, 308; Defense Fund drive and, 242–43; in Garland Fund controversy, 159
Spingarn Medal, 147
Sports coverage of *Courier*, 79–80, 143–45; of baseball, 249, 251; of Louis's fights, 248, 251, 254–56; of Olympic games, 258–59
Sprigle, Ray, 285
Springfield Colored School, 6–7
Steel City Bank, 121; failure of, 122
Steel industry: black employment in, 25, 69; 1919–20 strike against, 109
Stein, A. C., 83; equal rights bill of, 83–84, 85
Stewart, Frank, 125–26
Strike: in 1919–20 against steel industry, 109; threatened by porters, 165
Strikebreakers: blacks employed as, 25, 69, 70–71, 109, 173
Supreme Court: possible appointment of Vann to, 283, 285–86

Sweet, Ossian, 148; Garland Fund support for defense of, 149, 151
Syndication: need for, 51–52

Talbot Act, 189–90
Tanner, Harvey, 43
Taxes: Vann's delinquency on, 320
Teachers: black, in Pittsburgh, 9, 67–68
Third Ward Voters' League, 128, 129
Thomas, James C., 115
Thomas, Joe: murder trial of, 130–32
Travelers Aid Program, 59–60
Tucker, Walter, 356n75
Tuskegee Institute: founding of, 133; Vann's impression of, 133
Typhoid fever: in Pittsburgh, 27

Underground Railroad, 22–23
Unemployment during Depression: in Pennsylvania, 189; in Pittsburgh, 188
United Mine Workers: blacks in, 25; influence on Pennsylvania Democratic party, 280
U.S. Department of Commerce: Negro Advisory Committee of Advisory and Planning Council for, 207–08
Universal Negro Improvement Association, 231, 232–33, 234, 245
Urban League, 56; in Pittsburgh, 56–57, 59–60, 338n19

Vann, Jessie Ellen (née Matthews), 39–40, 321; appearance, 37, 38; childhood, 37, 38
Vann, Lucy. *See* Simon, Lucy
Vann, Robert Lee: on advisory committees in Washington, 207–11; appearance, 6, 12, 31, 48, 124–25; as assistant city solicitor, 99, 100, 123; birthplace, 3; burial place, 323; business acumen, 113, 120; career as attorney, 40–41, 74–75, 124, 129–32, 133; contribution to war effort, 103; *Courier's* influence on, 47–48; death, 321; devotion to social reform, 61; driving ability, 100, 208; early employment, 7–9; education, 6–7, 9–11, 12, 13–14, 29, 34–35, 36–37, 40; first political appointment, 92; health, 8, 33, 114, 208, 313, 315–16; homes, 3–8, 62–63, 262–63; leisure activities, 263; marriage, 40; name, 3–4, 328n5; parents, 3–6, 7, 33; personality, 32, 54, 207, 292; political moderation of, 104–05, 108; political power of, 103, 264, 265–67, 271–72, 275, 276, 279, 290, 293, 295–96, 298; posthumous honors, 323–24; reasons for move to North, 16–19; recognition of achievements, 262; valedictory address at Waters Training School, 12–13
—*Courier* and: acceptance of editorship of, 46–47; concentration of energies on, 133–35, 222; earliest association with, 42–44; as major stockholder, 172
—as special assistant attorney general, 205–07; appointment, 199, 201; resignation, 221
Van Vechten, Carl, 150
Vare, William Scott, 190, 198; Vann's position on, 184–86
Velar, M. T., 37
Virginia Union University, 13, 330n48; friendships formed by Vann at, 14–15; Vann's education at, 13–14
Virgin Islands Advisory Council, 219
Voters Civic League: attitude toward blacks, 93–94; exposure of political corruption by, 92

Wages: of black journalists, 137; of *Courier* staff, 136–37, 225, 261, 320; of laborers, 27; under NRA, 210; of porters, 162
Wagner-Costigan bill, 267–68
Washington, Booker T.: *Courier's* coverage of, 115–16; founding of Tuskegee Institute, 133; influence on Vann, 18, 33; Vann's attitude toward, 15; views on labor unions, 110; in white press, 76
Washington, Chester, 143, 144–45; association with Louis, 252; coverage of Louis, 251, 254, 255–56
Waters Training School, 10; Vann's education at, 10–11, 12
Wayland Academy, 13
Weapons: availability in Hill District, 73–74
Weaver, Robert C., 207, 209, 211
Webster, Milton P., 170
Welfare: dependence on voter registration, 213; during Depression, 188, 189
Westinghouse Electric Company: employment of blacks by, 72
Whip, The: unionization of porters and, 162–63
White, Walter, 141–42, 199; conflict with DuBois, 239–40, 260; crusade for anti-

lynch legislation, 267, 394*n*31; Defense Fund drive and, 240, 241–42, 243; in Garland Fund controversy, 158–59; Johnson-Vann conflict and, 161; opposition to ILD in Scottsboro case, 235–36; position on black rights in armed forces, 306–07, 308, 309–11; support of Roosevelt, 270
White press: coverage of black news in, 45, 60, 75–78, 84, 98, 104, 131
Wilkins, Roy, 239, 252; armed forces controversy and, 306–07, 308; on board of *The Crisis*, 260
William B. Ziff Company, 313, 314; *Courier*'s advertising and, 134, 223
Willkie, Wendell, 397*n*77; letter of condolence to Jessie Vann, 322; Vann's support of, 316, 319–21
Wilson, Davis, 280

Wilson, Woodrow, 191; anti-lynch legislation and, 104; segregation under, 95
Wilson, W. Rollo, 143–44
Wood, Scott, Jr., 43
Woodward Act, 189
Work: value placed on by Vann, 8–9, 12, 18
Working conditions: in Pittsburgh mills, 27
Working Girls' Home, 26
Works Projects Administration (WPA), 269; Guffey's control over jobs in, 217, 390*n*97
Work week, 27
World War I: *Courier*'s coverage of, 100–03; effect on black employment, 71–72

YMCA (Young Men's Christian Association): in Hill District, 49, 338*n*27

PN 4874 .V35 B8 1974

DATE DUE

PN 4874 .V35 B8 1974

Buni, Andrew

AUTHOR
Robert L. Vann of the

TITLE
Pittsburgh Courier

DATE DUE	BORROWER'S NAME
	Yacuarino, Anna Maria 839-4950
JUN 07 1993	